Cybersecurity 5.0

IEEE Press
445 Hoes Lane
Piscataway, NJ 08854

Cybersecurity 5.0

AI-Driven Strategies for Proactive Threat Defense

Hewa Majeed Zangana
Duhok Polytechnic University
Iraq

IEEE Press
WILEY

Published by John Wiley & Sons, Inc., Hoboken, New Jersey.

For general information on our other products and services or for technical support, please contact our Customer Care Department within the United States at (800) 762-2974, outside the United States at (317) 572-3993 or fax (317) 572-4002.

Wiley also publishes its books in a variety of electronic formats. Some content that appears in print may not be available in electronic formats. For more information about Wiley products, visit our web site at www.wiley.com.

Library of Congress Cataloging-in-Publication Data applied for

Hardback ISBN: 9781394426232

Cover Design: Wiley
Cover Image: wacomka/stock.adobe.com

Set in 9.5/12.5pt STIXTwoText by Straive, Pondicherry, India

This book is dedicated to the memory of my father, whom I never had the chance to meet but whose presence has lived in my heart through the stories, values, and legacy he left behind. To my dear mother, for her endless sacrifices, prayers, and unwavering strength in guiding our family. To my beloved brothers and sister, for their constant encouragement and support. To my wonderful wife, for her patience, understanding, and steadfast belief in me. And to my precious sons, Majeed and Meer, who are the light of my life and my greatest inspiration to keep striving for a better future.

Contents

About the Author

Hewa Majeed Zangana is an Assistant Professor currently affiliated with Duhok Polytechnic University (DPU) in Iraq. He has a PhD in IT Management from DPU. He has over 15 years of academic and administrative experience, serving in key leadership roles such as Acting Dean of the College of Computer and IT at Nawroz University, Head of the Computer Science Department, Director of the Curriculum Division at DPU, and Manager of the Information Unit at DPU's Research Center.

His research expertise includes network systems, cybersecurity, computer vision, intelligent systems, and information technology, with a strong emphasis on integrating classical methodologies with advanced AI-driven approaches. Dr. Zangana has authored and co-authored numerous peer-reviewed journal articles, conference papers, and more than 10 academic books published by IGI Global and Wiley, indexed in Scopus and Web of Science (Clarivate). His work has appeared in reputable venues such as IEEE, EAI Endorsed Transactions on AI and Robotics, Sistemasi, BAMJ, and others.

In addition to his research contributions, he actively serves the academic community as a reviewer, editorial board member, and scientific committee member. He is currently on the Editorial Board of *EAI Endorsed Transactions on AI and Robotics* (Scopus Q2) and collaborates with several international journals and organizations. He is also a member of professional associations including the European Alliance for Innovation (EAI), the International Association of Engineers (IAENG), and the Computer Science Teachers Association (CSTA).

Fluent in Kurdish, Arabic, and English, Dr. Zangana is committed to advancing research and education in AI, cybersecurity, and IT management while mentoring future generations of scholars and professionals.

Preface

The world today has advanced digitally in so many ways, and with that came the opportunity of a lifetime; unprecedented risks were unfortunately part of that opportunity. The development of artificial intelligence (AI), machine learning, quantum computing, and the Internet of Things (IoT) reshapes the cybersecurity environment, creating a new domain for technological changes. These transformations solidify the need for changes in defense mechanisms to proactive systems rather than the outdated traditional methods termed defensive passive responses. *Cybersecurity 5.0: AI-Driven Strategies for Proactive Threat Defense* would translate into gift-wrapping the need for such a paradigm shift, taking readers through the change in thinking in the development of cybersecurity into a proactive, intelligent, and self-defending ecosystem.

Indeed, at the core of Cybersecurity 5.0 lies its premise that the future of security is not about responding to threats once they materialize but about prediction, prevention, and real-time dynamic adaptation to threats with AI-led intelligence. The sweeping gains made by the book value the study of how products and processes in the AI, machine learning, deep learning, and related spaces redefine the field from static protection into interactive resilience.

The opening chapter constitutes the historical trajectory of cybersecurity—from primitive firewalls and signature-based detection systems existing in the first days of computerized security to today's intelligent, adaptive defenses—which sets the basis for understanding this transformation.

Chapter 2 gives a modern picture of the threat surface—the forms in which modern attackers use AI and automation to go past traditional defenses.

Chapter 3 covers the mathematical and analytical foundations of machine learning and data analytics required for applications in cybersecurity; Chapters 4 and 5, on the other hand, present the implementation of these mechanisms in intrusion detection and the analysis of malware and ransomware defense.

Emerging are the fields of adversarial AI and the countermeasures to protect from it for Chapter 6. Chapter 7 presents blockchain as a complementary framework for ensuring data integrity, transparency, and trust. The remaining chapters, 8–10, present urgent topics of IoT, edge, and cloud security; quantum-safe cryptography; and the ever-important human component of insider threats and behavioral vulnerabilities.

Later sections of the book, starting with Chapter 11, are dedicated to exploring ethical, legal, and governance issues around AI for cyber defense, emphasizing the balance needed in the fast tailoring of such technologies against their responsible deployment. Chapters 12 and 13 envision cybersecurity systems that are resilient, self-healing, and autonomous, capable of self-optimization and adaptive learning. Chapter 14 brings theory into practice through several case studies from finance, health care, and government, demonstrating real-world applicability. The last chapter is Chapter 15, giving a forward-looking roadmap toward Cybersecurity 5.0—full of visions of intelligent, anticipatory, and integrated defense ecosystems meant to be able to thrive in the face of future digital uncertainties.

This is the work of cybersecurity professionals and researchers as well as students who seek to capture how AI in cyber defense converges. It would also serve as a guideline for policymakers, system architects, and industry leaders in charge of building the next generation of secure digital infrastructures. Keeping theory and practice together, it equips the readers with conceptual clarity sidelined by the actionable strategies to tackle current modern cyber warfare complexities.

Cybersecurity 5.0 is a total rethink of the perception, as well as the design and implementation, of security in an era when the lines between the physical and digital worlds continue to blur. It will cover the journey from reaction to prediction, from vulnerability to resilience, and from human-dependent defense to AI-empowered autonomy.

Hewa Majeed Zangana
Duhok Polytechnic University – Iraq

Part I

Foundations of Cybersecurity 5.0

1

The Evolution of Cybersecurity: From Firewalls to AI

1.1 Introduction

Cybersecurity is no longer a niche issue of the IT departments but an important pillar of the global digital infrastructure. The growing pace of digital transformation in every industry, government, and healthcare, as well as finance and education, has contributed to the unprecedented growth of the cyber threat environment [1, 2]. The initial defense measures included firewalls and antivirus software that offered only basic perimeter protection, and the increasing sophistication of any cyberattack has made old methods insufficient. As Alvarez-Teleña and Díez-Fernández [3] claim, cybersecurity has taken a new dimension that requires adaptive, intelligent, and context-aware systems that can defend proactively. Such a paradigm shift highlights the development of what scholars and professionals now refer to as Cybersecurity 5.0; an integrated method of predicting and preventing the emergence of contemporary digital threats through the use of artificial intelligence (AI), automation, big data analytics, and human expertise [4, 5].

The chronological development of cybersecurity, with the emphasis on major technological advances, is presented in Figure 1.1, such as the period of unchanging firewalls and antivirus systems to the development of AI-based predictive protection systems. This visualization aids in putting the concept of cybersecurity into perspective in terms of its development being more reactive rather than autonomous and adaptive.

The theoretical parameters of cybersecurity are based on the ultimate objective of confidentiality, integrity, and availability—CIA triad [6, 7]. These principles are still applicable; however, the ways of how to apply them have changed tremendously. The reality of contemporary threats, according to Ekanayake et al.[8], goes beyond typical data breaches and malware attacks and includes advanced persistent threats (APTs), ransomware, intrusion into the physical system, and

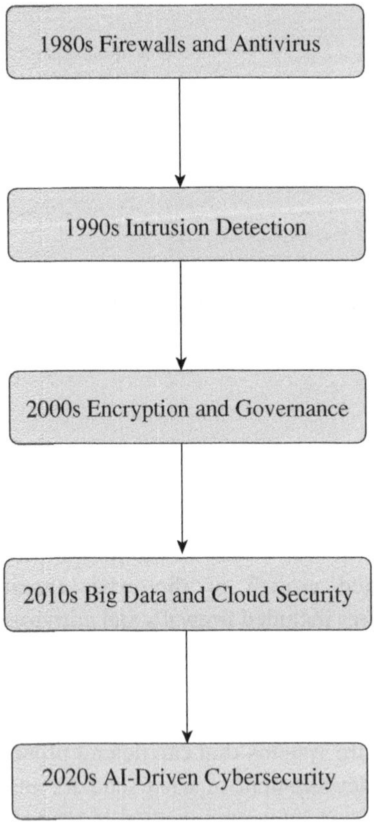

Figure 1.1 Evolution of Cybersecurity from Firewalls to AI-Driven Systems. "*Source:* Hewa Majeed Zangana"

disinformation campaigns. The requirement to deal with this increasing complexity has led to the evolution of a move away from isolated and reactive defenses to interconnected and predictive systems. Kumar et al. [9] grasp cybersecurity as an ecosystem, which is dynamic, not as one that mostly remains unchanged, but as one that innovates in response to adversarial innovation and technological change.

The development of the cybersecurity strategy has been heavily conditioned by the development of network security, cryptography, and data protection. Bock [10] asserts that contemporary cryptography is the foundation of digital trust, which facilitates the provision of a safe communication framework and ensures the protection of the vital assets within distributed networks. On the same note, França et al. [11] note the growing importance of big data in cybersecurity, in which intelligent analytics can detect anomalies and correlate threats at a scale never before seen. Along with this evolution, however, comes the issue of cybersecurity preparedness assessment and measurement. As Aboelfotoh et al. [12] note, even though many assessment models have been developed, organizations have yet to effectively measure security maturity. This raises a chronic disparity of technical capacity and strategic management.

Modern cybersecurity is interdisciplinary in nature. Sharp [13] refers to it as a multidisciplinary challenge, which is a combination of computer science, psychology, policy, and ethics. Manjikian [14] adds to this opinion with the focus on ethical aspects of cybersecurity, especially when it comes to surveillance, privacy, and AI-inspired decision-making. Cybersecurity governance in an ethical manner has become more urgent with the advent of intelligent systems that take the place of a human analyst. Both Hasib [15] and Ozkaya [16] embrace the role of leadership in resilience development in an organization, saying that cybersecurity today is a human issue as much as a technical one.

The use of digital technologies in the system of modern industries is growing (both in agriculture [17] and automotive systems [18]). Indicatively, the emergence of smart grids has opened up novel targets of cyber-physical attacks, which require specific protection systems [19]. The management of cybersecurity in the financial and fintech industries is associated with the problem of regulatory compliance and real-time monitoring of transactions [20]. In every field, the integration of operational technology (OT) and information technology (IT) has led to the need to have hybrid defense methods that combine traditional controls with AI-enhanced predictive software.

Human awareness and training are also very important in this transformation. Hatzivasilis et al. [21] and Varbanov [22] emphasize that cybersecurity training programs have to keep up with the threat and include cognitive modeling [23] and learning based on scenarios to equip professionals with more adaptive, real-world problems. In the absence of this correspondence between human competence and advancement in technology, organizations will have the risk of generating a gap in security even in highly automated systems.

AI and machine learning (ML) have taken center stage in restructuring the model of operation of cybersecurity. As Rohatgi et al. [24] and Diogenes and Ozkaya [25] point out, the AI-based systems facilitate real-time threat intelligence, detection of anomalies, and automatic response, which is a significant shift in the defense paradigm, where previously it was not possible to move to an active defense paradigm. Such developments, though, also present novel threats like adversarial AI attacks and algorithmic bias that have to be mitigated by ethical and transparent frameworks [26].

The contemporary problems of cybersecurity also overlap with the issues of governance and socio-politics. Holovkin et al. [27] emphasize that corruption and poor governance can be considered an indirect source of cybersecurity as they weaken the resiliency of institutions and public confidence. Likewise, Ajayi et al. [28] hold that the increasing complexity of cybercriminals' activities implies that multi-layered and globally organized responses are needed to counter them, combining technical novelties and cross-border cooperation.

To conclude, the release of Cybersecurity 5.0 is a step in the continuation of digital defense development. It expands on the decades of advances in network security [29], encryption, and behavioral analytics and incorporates AI, automation, and human-oriented leadership. The fusion of these forces contributes to the future of cybersecurity, a field in which proactive protection, cognitive intelligence, and ethical control are the cornerstones of robust digital ecosystems [4, 30]. This chapter explores these developments in depth, mapping the journey from traditional firewalls to AI-driven systems and analyzing how the next generation of cybersecurity strategies will shape global digital resilience.

1.2 Foundations of Early Cybersecurity

The history of cybersecurity dates back to the early 20th century of computer networking in the 1960s and 1970s when information security was mainly referred to as data protection of mainframe systems and the confidentiality of data. Security at this time was more of a technical than a strategic field since it mainly focused on avoiding unauthorized access to physical computer systems [6]. With the creation of ARPANET, as the predecessor of the modern Internet, networks came into contact, and the principle of cybersecurity as a professional sector that deals with the security of digital information and communication systems developed [29]. These formative years were centered on developing defensive systems like passwords, access control listing, and authentication systems that restrict user access and avoid intrusion.

The principle of perimeter defense was one of the factors that shaped early cybersecurity, as systems were defended at their edges in order to prevent an infiltration [7]. The firewalls turned into the feature of such an approach and the initial stage of defense against unauthorized access to the network. This strategy worked at the time, but it also made an assumption that the threats would come solely outside of the network. According to Dutta et al. [1], this fortress mentality prevailed in the cybersecurity thinking at the beginning of digital development—constructing digital walls around important systems instead of adopting the comprehensive, multi-layered protection frameworks. These defenses were further advanced in the 1980s and 1990s with the advent of intrusion detection systems (IDSs) and antivirus software, but they continued to be reactionary in nature and only detected threats once they had happened [25].

Another foundation for cryptography development in the history of early cybersecurity was the advancement of cryptography. The methods of encryption developed from simple ciphers to complicated mathematical systems, which are capable of protecting sensitive information both upon transit and at rest. According to Bock [10], cryptography resulted in providing not only a better level of confidentiality but also new authentication, integrity testing, and non-repudiation mechanisms, which are key components of trust in online communication. These foundations of cryptography formed the technical basis on which future-oriented cybersecurity would base its systems, which were flexible and based on AI.

Besides technical processes, the ethical and conceptual foundations of cybersecurity were also developed in the course of the early period. According to Manjikian [14], ethical issues related to privacy, surveillance, and responsible use of data started to emerge as the digital systems were growing. Early cybersecurity experts had to strike a balance between the need to protect and the necessity to be free and transparent. Such dilemmas provided the foundations of the contemporary discussion about cybersecurity ethics, data regulation, and human rights in the digital realm.

The early 2000s, especially the 1990s, were a turning point in which cybersecurity started as a reactive field to a strategic enterprise issue. The aftermath of cyber incidents became more harmful as organizations became more reliant on interconnected systems [20]. Firms started to consider cybersecurity a part of the risk management process, and policies, audits, and compliance models became a part of their routine [12]. Nonetheless, as Ajayi et al. [28] note, initial mitigation processes were not very automated or intelligent like the current cybersecurity systems.

Network security protocols were another important step in early cybersecurity. Gohel [6] and Thakur and Pathan [26] record the creation of safe communication protocols, including the SSL/TLS and IPSec, that made the transfer of encrypted data across public networks possible. These inventions not only secured Internet transactions but also led to secure e-commerce and cloud computing development. In the same manner, as Kim et al. [18] state, the increasing sophistication of automotive and industrial control systems at this time facilitated the realization of the necessity of cybersecurity in cyber-physical systems (CPS), which would become the challenge of Industry 4.0.

Early cybersecurity measures were efficient in countering threats that were familiar but were incapable of countering the swift diversification of the attack vectors. Ekanayake et al. [8] note that cyber threats moved more quickly than defensive technologies, which created a cycle of innovations and exploits. This dynamic of the game of cat and mouse highlighted the shortage of reactive measures and showed the necessity of proactive and adaptive mechanisms, as well as intelligence-based systems, which would later become the hallmark of Cybersecurity 4.0 and 5.0 [3, 4].

Simultaneously, cybersecurity as a subject of education and training started to take shape. Hatzivasilis et al. [21] and Varbanov [22] note that with an increase in the complexity of cybersecurity, training programs had to change to no longer be the learning of static and procedural education but to evolve to dynamic and scenario-based learning. Initial steps in cybersecurity education were too focused on technical, which, however, did not pay enough attention to cognitive and behavioral facets of the subject—a shortcoming that modern models aim to address [23].

The initial 21st century has also seen the integration of cybersecurity within the industrial and wider societal systems. Angyalos et al. [17] explain the manner in which the agricultural sector initiated the use of cybersecurity to safeguard newer smart farming technologies. Likewise, França et al. [11] reveal the beginning of the involvement of big data analytics in threat detection and risk assessment that preconditions the emergence of predictive security models. Holovkin et al. [27] further explain that the vulnerability to cybersecurity of certain areas was increased by corruption and the lack of sound governance structures, confirming that the technical solutions were not able to guarantee resilience without effective institutional control.

Thought leadership and governance also affected the establishment of fundamental cybersecurity frameworks. According to Hasib [15] and Ozkaya [16], leadership was one of the most important elements that influenced the formation of the early cybersecurity culture, where focus was on communication, trust, and organizational alignment. These pioneers have understood that cybersecurity is not only a field of technology but also a socio-technical field that needs to be seen as strategic and needs human cooperation.

Overall, early cybersecurity was based on three pillars, including technical defense mechanisms, ethical and policy frameworks, and organizational awareness. Firewalls and encryption, governance and education—all these factors were a part of the infancy of cybersecurity as a science and a strategic need. Even with this narrow focus and reactive character, these innovations led to the foundation of the intelligent, automated, and integrated security designs of the modern era [5, 24, 30].

1.3 The Rise of Intrusion Detection and Prevention Systems (IDPSs)

As cyber threats advanced in terms of complexity and frequency in the early 21st century and late 20th century, the defense mechanisms that were common in the earlier years like firewalls and antivirus software were not adequate to counter the increasing sophistication of attacks. It is the time when the intrusion detection and prevention systems (IDPSs) emerged and developed—technologies that are capable not only of detecting the potential security breach but also of preventing it in real time [25, 29]. These systems saw a change of paradigm in the reactive security models to the more adaptive, intelligence-driven defense models that were a milestone in the development of the cybersecurity infrastructure.

The first IDS came out in the 1980s as a result of academic and government research, and it is based on the principle of anomaly detection and pattern recognition algorithms. These initial systems were based on tracking network traffic and comparing behavior to a standardized baseline to identify any form of anomaly that can be indicative of intrusion [6]. Nevertheless, the primitive models tended to achieve high false-positive rates because of the absence of contextual awareness and the ability to provide real-time analytics. Integrated IDPS started to emerge in the late 1990s, having automated response systems that were able to block malicious traffic as it happened [20].

Ekanayake et al. [1] assert that the development of IDPS technologies was in tandem with the rapid growth of cyberattacks to enterprise networks. Attackers were no longer operating on the scale of individual exploits, but large-scale, automated, and coordinated attacks, which required correspondingly intelligent countermeasures. According to Aboelfotoh and Hikal [12], the introduction of IDPS proved critical in providing quantifiable cybersecurity performance metrics because organizations needed more accurate systems to assess their defense stance. Such systems have allowed the enterprises to gather, analyze, and correlate large amounts of security data, which further enhances situational awareness and responds to incidents.

Another of the major innovations that contributed to the effectiveness of the IDPS was signature-based detection, as well as the detection based on anomalies. Signature-based systems determined well-known attack patterns via the pre-existing databases, and anomaly-based systems used ML and statistical models to identify an abnormality in behavior [26, 30]. França et al. [11] note that the increased speed and accuracy of intrusion detection was dramatic after the possibility of analyzing the large-scale network data using big data analytics. This feature turned out to be even more essential when it came to the realms of modern businesses, which depended on cloud-based systems and architectures.

Another revolution in cyber defense strategies was the implementation of IDPS in any industry. As an example, in critical fields such as agriculture and manufacturing, the adoption of IDPS technologies ensured that cyber-physical infrastructures were not affected by cyber and operational attacks [17, 18]. Likewise, data integrity and availability are the primary concerns in the financial and healthcare sectors, where IDPS has become a critical part of compliance and governance policies [15]. These systems not only strengthened technical defenses but also promoted the organizational culture of constant monitoring and proactive security management [16].

The emergence of IDPS was also associated with the increased awareness of cybersecurity leadership and training as part of resiliency. According to Hatzivasilis et al. [21] and Varbanov [22], the practical application of IDPS demanded trained specialists who could interpret the alerts, examine the patterns, and adjust the detection level. The initial applications proved to be unsuccessful because of the human factor of a lack of proper training and overdependence on auto tools. To overcome these issues, the simulation-based and cognitive training methods were introduced into the concept of cybersecurity education [23] to guarantee that human analysts would be able to work with intelligent systems.

Further, cryptographic security and intrusion prevention were to be incorporated to make network communications safe. As explained by Bock [10], the encryption technologies were used to facilitate the process of authenticated user, data protection in transit, and man-in-the-middle attack prevention in combination with IDPS. This combination of cryptography and active detection was a significant breakthrough in the direction of the defense-in-depth architectures [5], in which several layers of defense acted in unison to reduce various types of threats.

Adaptive and cognitive intrusion prevention started to form its idea once AI and ML technologies were applied to IDPS. Alvarez-Teleña and Díez-Fernández [3] and Rohatgi et al. [24] point out that the transition to adaptive intelligence, with the necessity to learn past attack history and constantly update detection models, resulted in systems acquiring the ability to respond to new threats on their own. Such flexibility became a necessity in complex systems, like smart grids [19] and industries, where milliseconds might be the only distinction between stability and collapse.

Ethically and strategically, the introduction of IDPS brought up new issues concerning data privacy, governance, and accountability. According to Manjikian [14], when the network activity is constantly monitored, it can be easy to confuse between what is an acceptable practice in terms of security and what amounts to a breach of privacy. To achieve transparency and adherence to the data protection standards, organizations were to strike the proper balance between the security demands and ethical considerations [13]. Secondly, Holovkin et al. [27] caution that any vulnerabilities in governance and systemic corruption in particular areas would make the use of IDPS less effective because of insider attacks and failure to enforce audit controls.

The IDPS implementation in the enterprise context shortly became a symbol of well-developed cybersecurity governance systems. As cyberattack vectors became more diverse (such as phishing and ransomware but also more complex and more APT), Ajayi et al. [28] note that IDPS became multi-layered platforms with behavior analytics and threat intelligence feeds as well as automated response orchestrations. According to Omar and Zangana [4], such an evolution can be defined as the origin of the so-called cyber AI age, where the ML algorithms are able to anticipate and block threats on the fly.

Moreover, the IDPS helped to facilitate industry-specific resilience, especially for those industries where automation and data analytics have played an essential role. As an example, in smart agriculture, IDPS helped protect IoT-based systems against sensor manipulation [17], whereas in industrial automation, it helped defend connected machines against denial-of-service (DDoS) and ransomware attacks [9]. The technologies, as Ekanayake et al. [8] highlight, were applicable in terms of connecting the traditional network defense with the new necessity of autonomous, adaptive cyber protection.

The maturity of IDPS was also associated with the development of data mining and pattern recognition methods used in relation to cybersecurity. Salem et al. [30] show that the use of data-driven approaches has greatly contributed to the possibility of detecting hidden attack patterns, maximizing detection accuracy, and false alarms. These developments matched França et al. [11] as they emphasized that big data analytics and ML are now unavoidable in increasing the power of IDPS in high-volume network settings.

Lastly, the popularization of IDPS marked the shift in security posture from reactivity to proactive defense ecosystems. The modern organizations started to understand IDPS not as independent systems but as a part of an overall cybersecurity framework with predictive analytics and automated response and cognitive decision-making [2, 15]. Omar and Zangana [4] state that the adoption of AI-based intrusion systems is the cornerstone of Cybersecurity 5.0, which is a paradigm where the security systems do not just detect and prevent threats but also predict and respond to changes in threats.

To sum up, the emergence of IDPSs advanced cybersecurity beyond a passive, monitoring-oriented model and turned it into a dynamic, ecosystem-oriented learning model. Encryption combined with big data, ML, and ethical governance provides a foundation for the intelligent, adaptive, and self-defending networks that define the contemporary landscape of cybersecurity [1, 5, 25].

1.4 The Emergence of Cloud and IoT Security Challenges

The development of cloud computing technology and the Internet of Things (IoT) has essentially transformed the sphere of cybersecurity and created new opportunities and threats requiring flexible and intelligent defense solutions. Since organizations shifted their infrastructures to distributed and virtualized conditions, the security perimeter has become more blurred, rendering it difficult to manage risks, detect threats, and govern data using the usual methods [1, 9]. These paradigm changes became a breakthrough as individual enterprise systems evolved into the interconnected ecosystems of data, devices, and applications that engage in continuous cross-boundary interaction.

1.4.1 Cloud Security: From Centralized Control to Shared Responsibility

Cloud computing has transformed the way IT is done since it provides scalable, cost-effective, and flexible resources. Nevertheless, the change also created some vulnerabilities related to the models of multi-tenancy, data localization, and shared responsibility [6, 12]. Traditional infrastructures constituted systems whereby organizations had full control of the system. Conversely, cloud environments split duties between the service providers and the clients, which creates the possibility of unclarity in the responsibility for data breaches or misconfigurations [13]. The huge volumes of data in the cloud environments, as França et al. [11] stressed, must be subject to advanced encryption, constant surveillance, and automated compliance models to retain data integrity and confidentiality.

Homomorphic encryption and zero-trust architecture are considered to be modern cryptographic techniques that have become central to cloud-based operations [3, 10]. These inventions will be used to secure sensitive information during transmission, processing, and storage, even on untrusted systems. Nevertheless, account hijacking, insider threats, and insecure APIs are some of the significant threats posed by cloud attacks [25]. Hasib [15] has maintained that the management of cloud security is a task that necessitates both technical skills and the culture of responsibility and constant evaluation. This opinion is in line with the architecture suggested by Omar and Zangana [4], who point to the idea of the integration of cyber-AI as an opportunity to anticipate and address the threats of the cloud at the proactive level.

1.4.2 IoT Ecosystems: Security at the Edge

The advent of new IoT devices, such as smart homes and industrial sensors and self-driving cars, brought with them a new level of connectivity and efficiency and multiplied security threats [18]. Any device, which is in many cases limited in its computational capability and insufficient in encryption, is a possible attack point [8]. Goutam [7] and Gupta and Goyal [29] suggest that the security of IoT requires a trade-off between lightweight cryptography, edge-based anomaly detection, and secure communication protocol. Otherwise, there is a high probability of cascading failures and huge distributed DDoS attacks.

IoT vulnerabilities have impacted, especially the agriculture, healthcare, and automotive industries [17, 19]. As an example, tampered agricultural sensors might alter the production information, and the security holes on the vehicles connected might result in physical security risks. Hatzivasilis et al. [21] emphasized the necessity of flexible cybersecurity education programs as a way to consider the challenges of IoT and teach professionals to work on dynamic data-intensive systems.

1.4.3 The Convergence of Cloud and IoT: A Complex Security Fabric

The combination of IoT systems and cloud infrastructure that became known as the Cloud-IoT paradigm served to establish a hybrid environment with massive data generation and remote control. This integration makes the analytics, automation, and decision-making possible and, at the same time, increases the attack surface [24]. Salem et al. [30] indicated that attackers are increasingly using ML

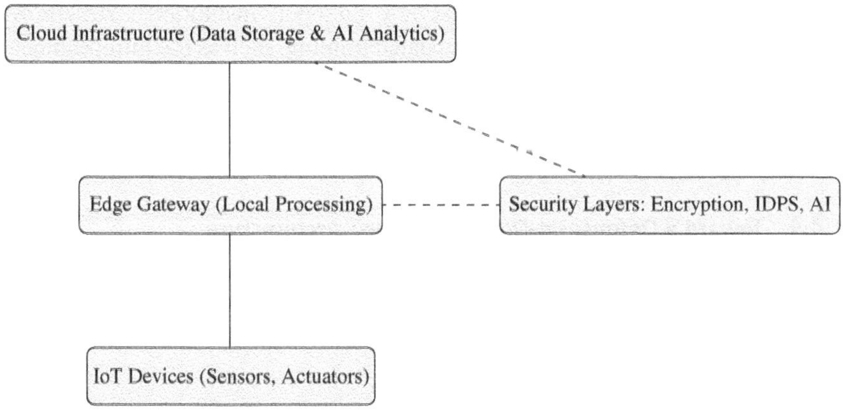

Figure 1.2 Interaction Between Cloud and IoT Security Layers. "*Source:* Hewa Majeed Zangana"

and data mining to take advantage of vulnerabilities in interconnected devices and supplant traditional models of security management in reactive mode.

As Kaur et al. [20] noted, FinTech and healthcare industries are among the sectors that face this twofold problem in general because sensitive financial and personal information is passed through IoT sensors and cloud servers. The issue of ensuring compliance across jurisdictions also creates additional complexity. The application of such cognitive modeling methods to forecast and model security behavior in both cloud and IoT networks is currently being implemented, as Lapshina and Kravets [23] argued, and serves as the basis of intelligent defense mechanisms.

As shown in Figure 1.2, cloud and IoT security layers intersect, and all three layers are working together to provide end-to-end security in distributed settings by using encryption and anomaly detection in conjunction with AI-based analytics.

1.4.4 Leadership and Policy Dimensions in Cloud-IoT Security

The transition toward cloud and IoT ecosystems has forced cybersecurity executives to implement progressive policies that are both technical, ethical, and organizational in nature. The role of leadership that would provide the technical knowledge and strategic governance was emphasized by Hasib [15] and Ozkaya [16], who assert that operational resilience is equally important as data privacy. Ethics are essential in this aspect because, as described by Manjikian [14], the ethical obligation of organizations to protect the data of the users is vital.

In addition, Holovkin et al. [27] associated systemic corruption and bad governance with cybersecurity vulnerabilities because they consider that effective cloud and IoT threat management systems rely on open institutional structures. Varbanov [22] recommended a more updated training, such as the European network of Cybersecurity centres and competence Hub for innovation and Operations (ECHO) approach, meant to certify personnel in areas of cybersecurity to effectively meet the changing technological landscapes.

1.4.5 Toward a Defense-in-Depth Cloud-IoT Architecture

Defense in depth is still the mainstay of contemporary cybersecurity policies, as highlighted by Zangana [5]. This is a multi-layered solution that incorporates encryption, intrusion detection, AI-based analytics, and behavioral observation in both cloud and IoT systems. Ajayi [28] reported that the current mitigation measures have to integrate predictions, trust management via blockchain, and decentralized identity. Diogenes and Ozkaya [16] also supported the idea that organizations should stop responding to all kinds of attacks and implement proactive measures that can be sustained through the use of continuous threat intelligence.

To sum up, the advent of cloud and IoT security threats has been a paradigm shift in the philosophy of cybersecurity, both in terms of perimeter protection and adaptive, intelligent, and integrated ecosystems. The future of this sphere is the convergence of AI, automation, and ethical regulation toward having a robust digital infrastructure that can withstand the intricacies of hyperconnected structures [3, 4].

1.5 Machine Learning and Automation in Cyber Defense

ML and automation have turned cybersecurity into a proactive and not a reactive field. Conventional security systems like signature-based detection and the rule-driven systems could not keep pace with the changing threats. On the contrary, frameworks and automation pipelines based on ML constantly process extensive data volumes, detect abnormalities, and forecast new attack vectors. It is a significant transition from manual monitoring to intelligent and self-adaptive cyber defense ecosystems [4, 5, 24].

1.5.1 The Rise of Data-Driven Security Intelligence

Digitization of contemporary business nations has created more data with security implications than was previously witnessed. This data is processed by ML algorithms, specifically, supervised and unsupervised learning models, to identify the latent correlations and provide indications of possible security incidents in advance [30]. To illustrate, novel malware families may be revealed through clustering algorithms, and zero-day attacks may be identified through deep neural networks with a minimum of human supervision [1].

França et al. [11] also note that big data analytics and ML are synergistic in the context of cybersecurity, as they allow making decisions in real time and running an adaptive policy. This is a critical integration in critical infrastructures where mitigation strategies can be made or lost based on the responsiveness of the infrastructures. Equally, Lapshina and Kravets [23] stated that cognitive modeling applied to cybersecurity improves situational awareness and assists in simulating the behavior of the threat within different system configurations.

1.5.2 Automation and Intelligent Orchestration

The essence of the current Security Orchestration, Automation, and Response (SOAR) platforms is automation that integrates ML models and automated processes to drive incident response effectively. These systems have the ability to triage alerts, use preset remediation measures, and continuously learn based on the results of their operation [25]. Using automation, organizations reduce the importance of human error and create uniformity in security operations [28].

Bock [10] observes that cryptographic management systems that are automated utilize ML to boost key rotation, encryption strength, and real-time anomaly detection in cryptographic operations. In the meantime, Gupta and Goyal [29] argue that the high-risk behavior of weak access control settings or insider threats is becoming easier to uncover with the help of predictive algorithms that can be implemented at an early stage. Automation not only makes the work of analysts less significant but also provides a base of autonomous cyber defense systems that could repair themselves and dynamically reconfigure [22].

1.5.3 Predictive and Adaptive Threat Modeling

ML allows systems to move away from predictive and context-aware models of defense. Cyber defense agents might be trained to adopt the best strategies through reinforcement learning when they are interacting with the changing adaptive attack environments [15]. This feedback loop has helped increase the detection and prevention.

Mashima et al. [19] show how AI-based methods of defense are crucial in protecting the smart grids, with adaptive models being observed and reactive toward variations in parameters of the system. Equally, Kim et al. [18] address the discussion of how automotive cybersecurity relies increasingly on adaptive AI algorithms to detect anomalies within automotive networks. Angyalos et al. [17] propose this paradigm also to the sphere of agriculture, where automated cybersecurity systems ensure that sensor networks and precision agriculture systems are not subjected to the threat of data modification and disruption.

1.5.4 The Role of Automation in Reducing Human Dependency

One of the most important benefits of automation is the decrease in the number of human analysts who perform routine and repetitive tasks [8]. Although human knowledge is still indispensable in strategic decision-making, automation performs log analysis, patch management, and vulnerability scanning at machine speed [6]. As Aboelfotoh et al. [12] emphasize, automated assessment procedures help to measure the level of cybersecurity preparedness in businesses and provide a continuous opportunity to estimate the resilience level.

Nevertheless, Holovkin et al. [27] note that automation should be followed by effective governance to avoid abuse or corruption of the system operation, particularly in politically unstable conditions. On the same note, Alvarez-Teleña and Díez-Fernández [3] emphasize that automation must be aligned with the current cybersecurity strategies that integrate the ethical and regulatory frameworks, making the decision-making processes by AI-driven to be transparent.

1.5.5 AI-Augmented Training and Human–Machine Collaboration

Automation simplifies the process of defense, but human analysts cannot be replaced in their ability to analyze complex threat situations. Simulation environments based on AI are also starting to be integrated into modern cybersecurity training initiatives, which modify to changes in the learner behavior and skill development [21]. These dynamic systems use ML analytics to dynamically customize training modules, creating continuous professional development in fast-changing cyber landscapes.

According to Sharp [2] and Varbanov [22], human–AI cooperation must become the main secret of the new era of cybersecurity training because, in this way, the specialists will be able to be competent in the interpretation of automated results and confirmation of algorithmic judgments. Manjikian [14] further notes that such ethical aspects as algorithmic bias and the transparency of decisions should be in focus during the implementation of ML-based security systems.

1.5.6 Applications Across Industry Domains

Cybersecurity in various fields is being transformed by ML and automation. AI-based threat analytics are a part of industrial automation and Industry 4.0, where anomalies in industrial control systems are detected [24]. Financial Products Automated Systems in the financial sector recognize suspicious patterns in real-time transactions using automated fraud detectors that are enabled by deep learning [20]. Kumar et al. [9] and Thakur and Pathan [26] note that automated IDSs combined with ML are especially useful in detecting polymorphic attacks within a CPS.

As Hasib [15] and Ozkaya [16] emphasize, the AI age of cyber defense needs a powerful leadership that can streamline automation technologies to organizational missions. Omar and Zangana [4] also note that Cyber AI is the next stage of the evolution of digital defenses with deep learning, natural language processing, and cognitive reasoning being integrated to create self-defending ecosystems.

1.5.7 Challenges and Future Directions

ML and automation have issues with cybersecurity implementation, in spite of their potential. The obstacles are still false positives, adversarial ML attacks, and the interpretability of their model [31]. Moreover, continuous learning is complicated by data imbalance and the changing threats. To be more resilient, Dutta et al. [1] encourage the use of hybrid models, which are a combination of supervised, unsupervised, and reinforcement learning.

According to Goutam [7] and Sharp [13], successful implementation of ML requires interdisciplinary collaboration between computer science, behavioral analytics, and ethics. The new frameworks should include quantum-resistant cryptography [10] and AI-based reasoning [23] to withstand the new post-quantum and AI-generated threats.

To sum up, automation and ML are the pillars of cybersecurity in the next generation. Their real-time flexibility, anticipatory intelligence, and responsiveness create a new meaning of how organizations protect digital assets in a constantly changing threat environment. According to Zangana [5], AI and automation combination brings in the age of defense in depth, where human intelligence and artificial cognition collaborate to provide resilient and adaptive security environments.

1.6 AI-Driven Cybersecurity: The Modern Era (Cybersecurity 5.0)

The digitalization of the world has entered the period of convergence of AI, automation, data intelligence, and cognitive computing, which nowadays has become known as Cybersecurity 5.0 among specialists. The new model of defense architecture is the combination of human skills with intelligent systems that can anticipate threats in advance, make decisions independently, and be adaptable to resilient. Cybersecurity 5.0 is no longer a paradigm of rule-based firewalls and static IDSs but the self-evolution ecosystem based on ML, predictive analytics, and contextual intelligence [3, 4].

1.6.1 Conceptualizing Cybersecurity 5.0

The concept of Cybersecurity 5.0 indicates the fifth phase of the evolutionary model of digital defense: a phase characterized by autonomous, intelligent, and connected protection systems seamlessly functioning across the hybrid cloud, IoT, and cyber-physical layers [5]. Most previous phases were based on securing the network boundaries, encryption, and reactive defense, whereas Cybersecurity 5.0 is based on AI-driven situational awareness and self-learning that can anticipate, identify, and suppress threats on the fly (as explained by Dutta et al. [1] and Sharp [2]).

The paradigm is based on the incorporation of ML, natural language processing (NLP), cognitive modeling, and autonomous orchestration to establish cyber ecosystems, which can think and adapt to changing attack surfaces [23]. França et al. [11] emphasize that these changes not only the technological aspect but also the organizational culture in which data-driven intelligence becomes the keystone of the security operations and decision-making process.

Figure 1.3 shows the architecture of Cybersecurity 5.0, which uses AI, ML, automation, and human supervision. It stresses the interconnected circles between the data collection, AI analytics, automated defense, and strategic governance.

1.6.2 From Reactive Defense to Predictive Intelligence

The characteristic of Cybersecurity 5.0 is predictive intelligence, which is the capacity to predict possible attack vectors even before they become real. The AI algorithms examine terabytes of unstructured data: network logs, user actions, and threat intelligence feeds and extract weak signals and early signs of compromise [24]. Through a combination of deep learning and reinforcement learning, these systems keep improving their accuracy to detect objects, thereby vastly lowering false positives that had been very common with previous detection systems [28].

Diogenes and Ozkaya [25] point to the fact that this type of adaptive system makes cybersecurity not an inactive but an active participant in combating the current adversaries with the lowest number of latency issues. This paradigm is the cornerstone of preventive defense systems, in which smart systems give responses

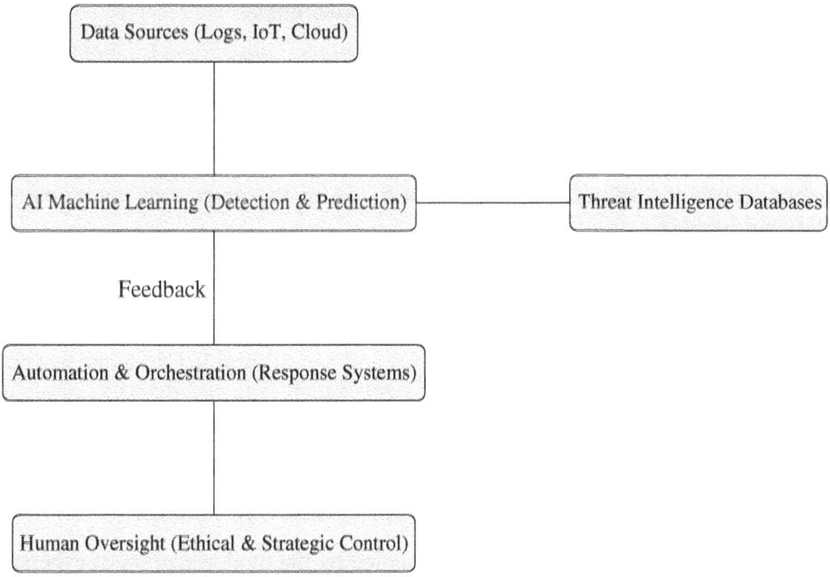

Figure 1.3 Architecture of Cybersecurity 5.0 Integrating AI, Automation, and Human Oversight. "*Source:* Hewa Majeed Zangana"

to threats proactively. Bock [10] further contends that AI is also being used to supplement cryptographic processes with dynamically optimizing encryption algorithms and enhancing quantum-resistant communication channels.

1.6.3 The Rise of Autonomous Security Ecosystems

Cybersecurity based on AI in the new age works in autonomous ecosystems, whereby Security Operations Centers (SOCs), threat intelligence platforms, and cloud coordination tools are integrated [15]. These integrated systems use AI-driven reasoning engines with the ability to correlate millions of security incidents in real time and enable the containment of advanced attacks on the spot [7, 29].

According to Ekanayake et al. [8], automation and self-correction are systems that guarantee continuity of operations even when there is a massive attack. The AI-based cybersecurity is also applied to behavioral biometrics, AI-based authentication, and predictive anomaly detection that dynamically changes with user and system behavior [26, 31]. The appearance of such self-defending systems is a symptom of the transition to computing resilience, a state of ability to survive, as well as learn and recover on their own, automatically in response to threats.

1.6.4 Cognitive Modeling and Situational Awareness

The concept of cognitive modeling is one of the main pillars of Cybersecurity 5.0. Through the modeling of human thought processes, AI-powered systems read the situation, elevate priority warnings, and dynamically change strategies [23]. This merging creates some kind of cyber cognition, in which intelligent agents combine various sources of data to aid in the process of autonomous decision-making.

As shown by Mashima et al. [19], AI-based situational awareness can be useful in securing smart grids, and adaptive models forecast cascading failures and cyber-physical disruptions. Equally, Angyalos et al. [17] and Kim et al. [18] demonstrate the defense of connected vehicles and agricultural IoT systems, respectively, by AI-based cybersecurity frameworks, which indicates the cross-domain applicability of cognitive intelligence in contemporary defense.

1.6.5 Ethical and Leadership Dimensions of AI-Driven Defense

Ethical and leadership demands are presented by the modernization of cybersecurity by AI. Manjikian [14] emphasizes the ethical obligation of deploying autonomous systems capable of autonomously making security decisions that have an effect on privacy and autonomy. Within the context of algorithms having increasingly greater influence on defensive and offensive behavior, ethical transparency, explainability, and human control are critical protection measures.

In its governance aspect, Hasib [15] and Ozkaya [16] believe that a combination of technical expertise and strategic perspective is an essential part of leadership in Cybersecurity 5.0, and that AI implementation should be aligned with organizational values and compliance systems. Holovkin et al. [27] also caution that institutional integrity may be at risk due to corruption, manipulation of data, and unethical use of AI without policy and accountability.

1.6.6 Cross-Sectoral Implementations of Cybersecurity 5.0

The power of AI-based cybersecurity is experienced in various industries and fields. The development of AI models is used in industrial and manufacturing systems to identify anomalies in CPS early enough to avoid downtime and sabotage [9]. Financial applications and FinTechs use deep ML systems to stop fraud by identifying minor variations in the pattern of transactions [20]. AI strengthens precision farming as it shields sensor networks against interference in agriculture [17].

Salem et al. [30] describe that data mining and pattern recognition continue to be the major supports of such sectoral implementations, providing scalable, automated risk and vulnerability distribution insights. Additionally, Dutta et al. [1] and Gohel [6] add that such systems should be constantly trained and educate users in terms of their correct setup and use as they become more interconnected.

1.6.7 Training, Education, and Human-AI Collaboration

Cybersecurity 5.0 transition also changes the human aspect of cyber defense. Adaptive learning systems based on AI are gradually supplementing the traditional training programs by adjusting the curriculum according to the personal performance and the immediate development of threats [21]. According to Varbanov [22], the current architecture of cybersecurity courses is focused on simulation environments, where trainees will be exposed to autonomous systems that can help them acquire interpretive and supervisory capabilities.

Collaboration between humans and AI is not a replacement measure but rather an augmentation of the decision-making ability of analysts. According to Sharp [13], AI needs to supplement human intuition, enabling analysts to emphasize high-level strategy, with automation doing repetitive detection. Aboelfotoh and Hikal [12] also claim that the quantitative assessment framework contributes to organizations assessing AI preparedness regarding the ratio between automation, human control, and performance results.

1.6.8 Challenges and the Road Ahead

Although Cybersecurity 5.0 remains a spectacular development, there are still issues. Categories of problems like adversarial ML, data privacy, interpretability of AI models, and bias need to be resisted and governed [31]. According to Alvarez-Teleña and Díez-Fernández [3], cybersecurity in the future has to be taken in a holistic approach that incorporates technological advancement with moral governance, whereby AI-driven defenses are transparent and fair.

The next stage in cybersecurity, as envisioned by Zangana [5], will be the establishment of completely autonomous and quantum-resistant ecosystems that operate using Cyber AI, which is able to reason, learn, and act both in the digital and physical realms in real time. The introduction of Cybersecurity 5.0 is not an incremental change, but a paradigm revolution. Omar and Zangana [4] conclude that the emergence of intelligent, self-governing defense infrastructures redefines the concept of digital security in the 21st century.

1.7 Comparative Analysis: Traditional Versus AI-Based Cyber Defense

Cybersecurity has dramatically changed its look since the earlier days of reactive defenses that had rules to follow and the present-day paradigm of proactive systems supported by AI. This section provides the comparative evaluation of conventional cybersecurity systems and the AI-based defense systems, focusing on their functionality concepts, advantages, and disadvantages and the changing role of human skills in cybersecurity.

1.7.1 Traditional Cyber Defense: Reactive and Perimeter-Oriented

The conventional model of cybersecurity mostly depended on the defense mechanisms that were based on perimeter like firewalls, antivirus software, intrusion detector systems (IDS), and signature-based threat recognition. These were tools that worked in a set of predefined rules and recognized databases of threats and became the initial point of defense against unauthorized access or malicious activity [1, 6]. Firewalls were used to filter traffic based on preset policies, whereas IDS technologies were used to identify anomalies based on pattern matching or heuristic analysis.

Despite these systems, which were the foundation of early digital security, having important shortcomings, they had severe weaknesses. They were mostly reactive, that is, they reacted only when an attack had happened or a signature was detected [26]. Besides, the growing sophistication of networks and the spread of sophisticated persistent threats (APTs) made fixed defense systems ineffective. With the polymorphic malware and zero-day exploits, traditional tools could not match the dynamism of the modern cyber threats [12, 28].

1.7.2 AI-Based Cyber Defense: Predictive, Adaptive, and Autonomous

The emergence of AI provided a new approach to cybersecurity. AI-driven systems can use ML, deep learning, and cognitive analytics to identify, forecast, and prevent threats independently [4]. In contrast to the rule-based systems, the AI-based defense mechanisms are constantly updated on the new attack vectors, learning by default to adapt to them. This is a paradigm shift in behavioral analysis as compared to signature-based recognition in terms of ability and speed.

As Alvarez-Teleña and Díez-Fernández [3] observe that today, AI-based predictive analytics is becoming part of modern cybersecurity frameworks to detect anomalies in large volumes of evidence-based data—the ability to identify more advanced intrusions. These systems monitor and assess user and network traffic, identify abnormalities, and activate automated responses before a breach is escalated. According to Rohatgi et al. [24], predictive modeling operated by AI yields a high response time and false-positive rates, lower than those achieved by traditional IDS tools.

Moreover, ML systems have been used to augment endpoint detection and response (EDR) systems, security information and event management (SIEM) tools, and threat intelligence platforms [30]. The concept of AI in cybersecurity architectures facilitates the notion of continuous learning, self-healing networks, and context-sensitive decisions, hence the nature of Cybersecurity 5.0.

1.7.3 Comparative Advantages and Limitations

Adaptability and autonomy are the main differences between conventional and AI-driven cybersecurity. The old approaches, including those presented by Diogenes and Ozkaya [25], rely on fixed settings and updating them manually, which may cause weaknesses in the face of rapidly changing threats. The way AI-based models such as those outlined by Lapshina and Kravets [23] are developed, in their turn, displays cognitive adaptability in the way that they develop novel vectors of attack by use of unsupervised or reinforcement learning.

The AI-applied systems have their difficulties, though. The quality and availability of data are always a critical issue; inadequate data labeling or biased data sets will affect the quality of threat detection [19]. Also, there are new risks to adversarial ML, in which attackers can manipulate input data to fool algorithms [11]. Therefore, according to the writing of Manjikian [15], successful implementation of AI should be associated with strong leadership, human supervision, and ethical governance.

This comparison may be represented in Table 1.1 and may be characterized by such parameters as detection method, response time, adaptability, automation, and accuracy.

Figure 1.4 compares traditional and AI-based cyber defense mechanisms and lists the transition to predictive and adaptive security mechanisms and their perimeter-based counterparts. This graphical comparison is a supplement to the discussion in Table 1.1.

1.7.4 Human and Organizational Roles in Both Paradigms

The human factor is also central to both standard and AI-based defense despite the presence of automation. Conventional cybersecurity required human administration and setups, and firewalls, patches, and intrusion notifications were managed by administrators [29]. Conversely, AI-driven systems decrease the amount

Table 1.1 Comparison Between Traditional and AI-Based Cyber Defense Systems

Parameter	Traditional Cyber Defense	AI-Based Cyber Defense
Detection Method	Signature-based or rule-driven; identifies known attack patterns.	Behavior-based and predictive; learns from data to detect known and unknown threats.
Response Time	Reactive; requires manual analysis and updates after incidents.	Real time and autonomous; automatically responds and mitigates threats instantly.
Adaptability	Static configurations; limited adaptability to new or zero-day attacks.	Highly adaptive; continuously refines detection models through machine learning.
Automation Level	Low; manual monitoring, patching, and response workflows.	High; incorporates automated orchestration and self-healing mechanisms.
Detection Accuracy	Moderate accuracy; prone to false positives and missed detections.	High accuracy; context-aware analysis with reduced false alarms.

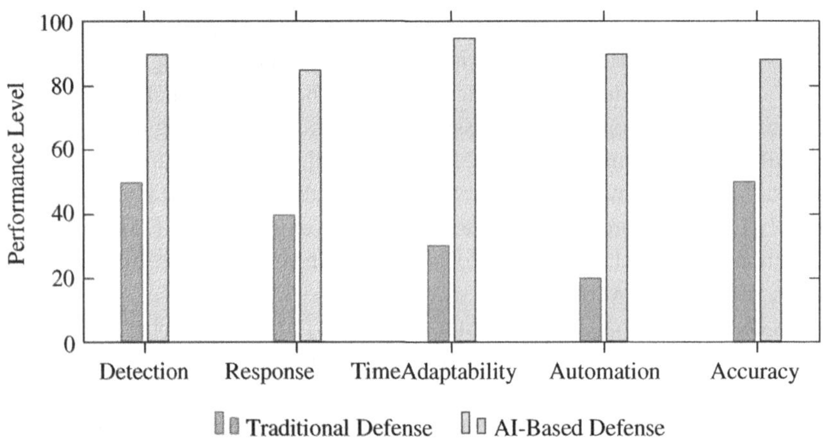

Figure 1.4 Performance Comparison Between Traditional and AI-Based Cyber Defense. "*Source:* Hewa Majeed Zangana"

of human labor, automate the process of correlating data, and suggest the most effective countermeasures [16].

However, the emergence of AI requires advanced AI training courses, as Hatzivasilis et al. [21] and Varbanov [22] mention, which keep up with the changing technologies. Cognitive modeling, which is considered by Lapshina and Kravets [23], improves decision-making and builds human-machine cooperation.

So, although AI enhances the effectiveness of the defense, it replaces the requirements of the skills of the workforce, underlining analytical thinking, AI proficiency, and operational planning.

1.7.5 Contextual Applications and Sectoral Implications

According to various industries, the shift toward AI-enhanced cyber defense is evident. In the field of automotive cybersecurity, AI allows monitoring the vehicle's network in real time and identifying the anomalies of autonomous systems [18]. Angyalos et al. [17] also claim that the concept of agricultural cybersecurity positively uses AI-based IoT protection to reduce threats to smart farming systems. Likewise, the AI is used more often in industrial control systems and smart grids to predict and prevent cyber-physical distortions [19].

Cryptography-based fraud detection with AI-enhanced cryptographic algorithms and behavioral profiling is applied to financial institutions and FinTech settings [20]. Besides, transparency and anti-corruption efforts contributed by AI-driven systems include integrity in digital transactions, as noted by Holovkin et al. [27].

1.7.6 Ethical, Strategic, and Structural Considerations

Although AI-based cybersecurity is used to provide efficiency and foresight, it brings ethical and strategic challenges as well. Manjikian [14] emphasizes that AI-based decision-making in cyber defense will create issues of accountability, in particular, in connection with automated retaliation or privacy concerns. On the same note, Sharp [2] and Kumar et al. [9] state that cybersecurity cannot be considered a technical field anymore but a multidisciplinary issue that is to be balanced between automation and humanism.

Technically, to ensure the security, which is anticipatory and resilient, as Omar and Zangana [4] and Zangana [32] argue, the current-day model of defense-in-depth must incorporate AI at all levels, including endpoint protection, cloud orchestration, etc. Hasib [15] and Ozkaya [16] propose the vision of leadership as a main factor in the development of AI-enhanced security ecosystems with a technical and ethical long-term sustainability.

1.7.7 Synthesis: From Defense to Anticipation

The relative development of conventional to AI-driven cyber defense is characterized by a radical change in the process of detection and response to prediction and prevention. Conventional systems are aimed at the protection of established boundaries, whereas AI-based systems protect dynamic and boundaryless spaces with predictive analytics, automation, and adaptive intelligence. The collaboration of human skills and AI, as Alvarez-Teleña and Díez-Fernández [3] put it, characterizes the next stage of the development of cybersecurity. The ability of digital defense to stop cyberattacks is not a reactive barrier but an active, intelligent protector.

1.8 Challenges and Ethical Implications of AI in Cybersecurity

AI has become a revolutionary aspect of cybersecurity, allowing it to be automated, predictive, and adaptive to defendants, which are much more effective than conventional systems. Nevertheless, together with these positive aspects, the adoption of AI brings new technical, ethical, and administrative issues that are to be handled with utmost care to avoid unintentional dangers and abuses. This section addresses the complex issues and ethical concerns that surround AI-based cybersecurity systems and the necessity to strike the right balance between innovation, responsibility, and human regulation.

1.8.1 Technical and Operational Challenges

Although AI can be used to improve the detection accuracy and speed of cyber defense, it also introduces new weaknesses. Among the greatest obstacles is the dependency of the data; the data needs to be of high quality and in large amounts to learn how to behave in the most optimal way using AI models. False positive and misclassification due to inaccurate or biased datasets are capable of decreasing the quality of automated defense systems [11, 30]. Besides, such vulnerabilities can be exploited by attackers by means of adversarial ML, where malicious entities are manipulating the training data or input features so that AI systems are misled to perceive a threat [24].

According to Diogenes and Ozkaya [25], AI-based cybersecurity systems can only be as robust as the integrity of the data and underlying models. Aboelfotoh and Hikal [12] also stress the significance of regular assessment and metrics of validation in the measurements of cybersecurity performance with regard to AI-based enterprises. Nevertheless, the existing assessment systems tend to be unsophisticated than the adaptive learning systems, which leave gaps in resilience measurement.

There are also issues of scalability and interoperability. AI solutions should be harmonized with old infrastructures, which can be constructed based on rigid defense systems [1]. Hybrid systems may also create a fragmented security architecture, which exposes systems to zero-day attacks [28]. Moreover, the dependency on the power of computers and the cloud presents the trade-off of energy consumption and privacy concerns in relation to AI, especially when processing encrypted or sensitive data [7, 10].

1.8.2 The Ethical Dimension: Bias, Transparency, and Accountability

The use of AI in cybersecurity raises significant ethical concerns on the autonomy of choices, equity, and responsibility of human beings. According to Manjikian [14], cybersecurity ethics should change to respond to the ethical implications of outsourcing threat detection and response to computers. The responsibility issue arises and becomes ethically complicated when an AI system misses an important identification of malicious activity in a benign situation or takes automatic countermeasures.

Training dataset bias may also lead to increased inequality in digital protection. As an example, biased AI models can be used to target or overlook certain activities on the network, creating a disproportional defense in various systems or industries [23]. The ability of AI algorithms to make decisions independently and transparently is therefore an important element to develop trust and compliance with new governance norms [2].

According to Alvarez-Teleña and Díez-Fernández [3], to prevent strengthening the existing vulnerabilities of the system, it is important that ethical AI frameworks are implemented alongside technical innovation. Equally, Omar and Zangana [4] highlight that AI-based cybersecurity must work within definite limits of ethics guided by the principles of explainable AI (XAI), which enables human auditors to interpret, justify, and challenge automated security judgments.

1.8.3 AI Weaponization and Dual-Use Dilemmas

The other urgent issue is the cyber weaponization of AI. On the one hand, AI can be used to conduct defensive automation, but on the other hand, it may fall into the hands of attackers and be used for malicious purposes, including intelligent phishing, deception based on deepfakes, and autonomous malware development [8, 9]. AI can be reverse-engineered or adapted to detect vulnerabilities in the target defenses, i.e., the so-called dual-use dilemma, where a single technology could be used both to protect and to attack [6].

According to Hasib [15], in the absence of proper governance, the spread of AI features can lead to an increase in cyber confrontations, allowing nation-states and organized groups to engage in massive and automated attacks. Ozkaya [16] and Zangana [32] also support the idea of leadership-based cybersecurity ethics to address such threats, with transparency, accountability, and international cooperation being the key to controlling the use of AI in warfare, including digital ones.

1.8.4 Privacy, Surveillance, and Human Rights Considerations

AI-enabled cybersecurity systems tend to be based on huge data gathering, such as user behavior analytics, network logs, and personal identifiers. Although this kind of information can increase the detection rate, it poses significant privacy and human rights issues. According to Thakur and Pathan [26], constant monitoring based on AI-driven monitoring tools may act as a barrier between security and invasion, which can potentially harm user consent and other data protection regulations.

Against this background, in industries such as smart agriculture [17] and automotive cybersecurity [18], AI-driven systems constantly survey the operations to detect anomalies and with this, are collecting personal or proprietary information either without intent or not. In conjunction with these developments, ethical governance must address the inherent conflict between enhanced surveillance capabilities and the fundamental right to privacy [20]. The necessity to balance the interests of proactive threat detection with the interests of individual protection is one of the trickiest ethical issues in the new-day cybersecurity.

Holovkin et al. [27] move the discussion further to list the risks of corruption and misuse and how AI technologies may be used against insiders or the state to make surveillance or manipulate politics. As Sharp [13] and Hasib [15] argue, ethical cybersecurity leadership should ensure that it has robust governance structures that guard against such types of abuse without losing the effectiveness of the system.

1.8.5 Governance, Regulation, and Workforce Adaptation

The concept of AI in cybersecurity requires dynamic governance and human expertise. According to Hatzivasilis et al. [21] and Varbanov [22], it is important to approach AI-driven tools in a responsible manner, and it is impossible without continuous training and professional development of cybersecurity practitioners. The training based on cognitive modeling and simulation can serve to make security experts familiar with intricate AI systems and predict possible biases or failure modes [23].

Regulatory authorities have a problem with developing international guidelines of AI accountability and transparency. According to França et al. [11], the governance frameworks of big data remain disjointed, as there are variabilities in the regions and the industry. Similarly, Alvarez-Teleña and Díez-Fernández [3] support international collaboration to provide ethical consistency and adherence to the AI-driven security activities.

Organizationally, Hasib [15] and Ozkaya [16] believe that the culture of ethical innovation that should be fostered by leadership is that of responsible integration of AI and ensuring that decisions are made by humans-in-the-loop. Good governance can make AI an instrument of empowerment and not control to maintain institutional integrity and public confidence.

1.8.6 The Path Forward: Balancing Innovation and Responsibility

The cybersecurity issue of AI has an ethical aspect, highlighting the inherent conflict between innovation and control. Although AI offers previously unheard-of abilities in identifying and addressing risks, there is the issue of who determines reasonable risk, who oversees algorithmic fairness, and who is held accountable for the nonfunctioning of automation. Omar and Zangana [4] also wrote that the future of Cybersecurity 5.0 relies on integrating the ethical intelligence—convergence of technical correctness with moral decision-making at all levels of digital security.

To do that, Diogenes and Ozkaya [25] recommend a "human-centric" approach to AI, based on transparency, inclusiveness, and accountability. Similar views and opinions are expressed by Goutam [7] and Gupta and Goyal [29], who state that education, awareness, and ethical literacy are essential to maintain secure and fair cyber ecosystems. To sum up, as the field of AI is constantly reshaping the boundaries of the concept of cybersecurity, providing that the creation of this technology does not contradict societal values and human dignity is the most urgent issue of the digital era.

1.9 Future Trends and Directions

The convergence of AI, automation, cloud computing, and the IoT is redefining the future of cybersecurity, and new opportunities and challenges are being offered (including quantum computing and cognitive modeling). The emphasis on predictive analytics, intelligent automation, and adaptive defenses, and the stance in both articles of Dutta et al. [1] and Jadey et al. [31] illustrate that cybersecurity will cease to be a reactive discipline but a proactive ecosystem. This transformation is the shift where old methods of perimeter-based systems are changed to contextual, self-mending, and autonomous cybersecurity frameworks.

1.9.1 AI-Driven Adaptive Cyber Defense

The next decade of cybersecurity strategy will be controlled by AI and ML. According to Rohatgi et al. [24], AI-based systems have the ability to predict emerging attack patterns before they occur to offer dynamic risk assessment and continuous adaptation. This predictive capability is core to what Alvarez-Teleña and Díez-Fernández [3] refer to as "Cybersecurity 5.0," in which intelligent systems are driven with minimal human effort. On the same note, Omar and Zangana [4] contend that the implementation of Cyber AI in enterprise defense frameworks turns the concept of security into cognitive security, and real-time threat detection and automated attack mitigation can be realized.

This evolution will be further advanced with the help of cognitive modeling analyzed by Lapshina and Kravets [23] that will simulate adversarial behavior and will create anticipatory defenses. These algorithms, which are driven by deep learning, have the capability to adjust to the dynamics of the network automatically, bridging the detection and reaction time. Nonetheless, this change brings up the ethical considerations, which Manjikian [14] emphasizes, as moral accountability and transparency are required when assigning security judgments to smart systems.

1.9.2 Quantum-Resistant Cryptography and Zero-Trust Architectures

A major shake in all the shambles that will be created by the inevitable advance of quantum computing will be on the current encryption standards. The authors of [10] and [11] have noted that quantum algorithms are capable of breaking classical cryptographic schemes. Attendant to this is that researchers need to create quantum-resistant alternatives that can be applied to contours such as lattice-based, hash-based, and multivariate cryptographic algorithms to secure data integrity in the post-quantum era.

Meanwhile, Zero-Trust Architectures (ZTAs) are growing to be the backbone of next-generation cybersecurity strategies [2, 6]. It has the principles of "never trust, always verify" through continuous authentication and micro-segmentation of all systems. According to Hasib [15] and Ozkaya [16], strong leadership together with a cybersecurity culture is rooted in accountability and adaptability in today's world, dubbed the Human Algorithm: how leading-edge enterprises will define the category of safe enterprise ecosystems.

1.9.3 Cybersecurity in Cyber-Physical and IoT Systems

A type of intensive digitization across many industries will be the fact that CPS and IoT networks have grown into a major area of concern regarding digital security. Actually, there is a reference to a single publication by Goutam [7] and Kim et al. [18] that states that increasing connections build complex multi-vector attacks across critical infrastructures due to the following examples: industrial control systems, autonomous vehicles, and smart devices. So, future defense mechanisms will build on lightweight encryption, AI-based anomaly detection, and decentralized authentication.

As stated by Mashima et al. [19], smart grids and industrial IoT systems will have to incorporate predictive maintenance, blockchain-based security, and distributed ledgers toward ensuring data authenticity and fungibility. Angyalos et al. [17] point out that cybersecurity is taking up a small but steadily emerging space in agriculture, where IoT-driven precision systems are to be kept in check permanently to shield sensors from data manipulation or sabotage.

To make it resilient, Ekanayake et al. [8] advocate cross-layer defense mechanisms covering IoT nodes, communication channels, and cloud backends. This defense-in-depth principle, as reiterated by Zangana [5], will therefore continue to underpin such frameworks with encryption, AI, and multi-factor authentication underlying all levels of infrastructure.

1.9.4 Data-Centric Security and Big Data Analytics

The increasing shares of data across sectors have builders sparking the construction of a different type of security called data-centric security, which will now prove the old ideologies of network-centricity obsolete. According to França et al. [11] and Salem et al. [30], sophisticated data mining and big data analytics can be the cutting edge in spotting anomalies, involving predictive modeling for insider-threat detection, and automating compliance verification. The explainability of AI (XAI) in securing data will increase accountability and understanding, as this attends to one of the major ethical contentions raised by Manjikian [14].

Include AI in data analytics, and organizations will have the power to detect what is hidden in those massive data sets, as Kumar et al. [9] point out. Future research will likely be geared toward federated learning models, creating an avenue for collaborative cybersecurity analytics among enterprises without revealing sensitive information. Such a pan-intelligence approach synchronizes with the proactive models envisioned by Alvarez-Teleña and Díez-Fernández [3].

1.9.5 Human-Centric Leadership and Ethical Governance

Cybersecurity evolution rests, despite all advancements in technology, on human input. Hasib [15] and Ozkaya [16] note that the future cybersecurity leader will be one who mingles ethical governance with technical competence, transparency, and strategic foresight. Those in strategic leadership positions will also have to deal with AI ethics, privacy laws, and global regulations, while championing diversity, continuous learning, and adaptive training for their workforce.

Hatzivasilis et al. [21] and Varbanov [22] underscore continuous cybersecurity education through adaptive and personalized learning frameworks as essential. These frameworks will draw from simulation and gamification to educate professionals on adapting to the dynamic threat landscape. That said, Holovkin et al. [27] warn against the risk of corruption and poor governance undermining national cybersecurity resilience, calling for an urgent need for institutional reforms and integrity-driven leadership.

1.9.6 Integration of Cognitive, AI, and Ethical Models in Cyber Defense

It will also be seen that the future of cybersecurity will also involve self-aware, context-sensitive defense mechanisms integrating cognitive computing together with ethical AI frameworks [4]. According to Dutta et al. [1] and Jadey et al. [31], we expect that these systems of the future will generally understand and be able to predict not just the possibility of attacks but also socio-technical attacks. By 2035, fully autonomous "digital immune systems" learning, reasoning, and enforcing policy without human supervision are expected to emerge [24].

Sharp [2] and Manjikian [14] provide the fact that this autonomy has further ethical and regulatory implications. Thus, future frameworks will need to be carefully balanced between automation and accountability in ensuring that AI-driven decisions remain transparent, fair, and aligned to human values.

1.9.7 A Vision for Cybersecurity 5.0

From now on, we go in the direction of Cybersecurity 5.0—the holistic and AI-driven model of the future characterized by marketing automation, cognitive awareness, and ethical government. As will be described by Omar and Zangana [4] and Zangana [32], this era will incorporate defense in depth, predictive AI, and adaptive intelligence, making ecosystems capable of defending against evolving digital threats.

Figure 1.5 presents the futuristic vision of Cyber Security 5.0, showing a self-healing ecosystem where AI, quantum resistance, automated governance, and ethics are networked under one architecture for resilient digital defense.

In sum, intelligent automation, quantum-resistant cryptography, IoT protection, ethical governance, and continuous learning will shape the next generation in cybersecurity. The fusion of these dimensions will create a self-sustained cybersecurity environment—one that detects and neutralizes threats while advancing the greater goals of trust, transparency, and digital sustainability [12, 26, 28].

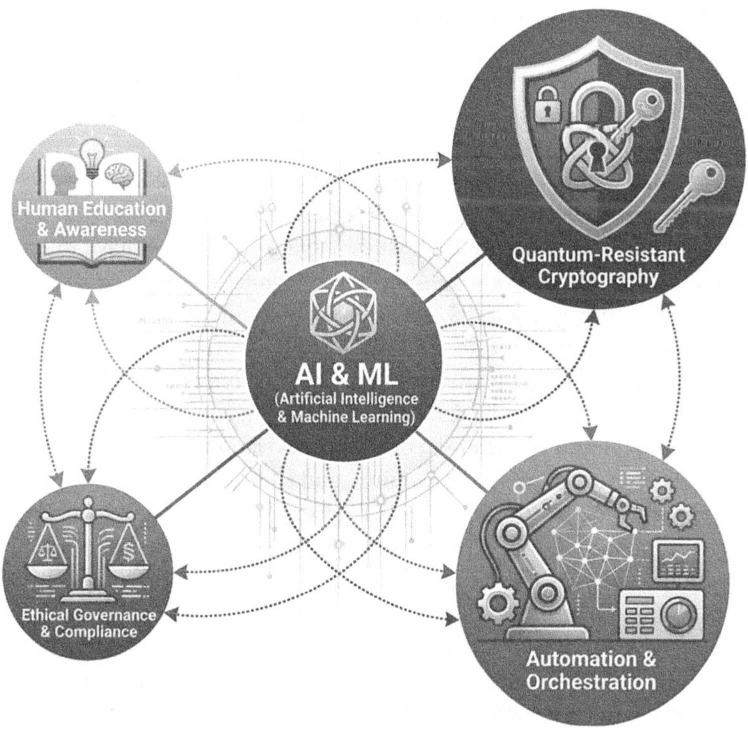

Figure 1.5 Vision of the Future Cybersecurity 5.0 Ecosystem. "*Source:* Hewa Majeed Zangana"

1.10 Conclusion

Cybersecurity has undergone dramatic transformations from historical, negative reaction mechanisms to proactive, AI-based strategies. These threats are increasingly turning sophisticated and intelligent, going beyond targeting infrastructures and enterprises. Modern-day attacks target individuals also, requiring detection, prediction, and mitigation based on intelligent, adaptive solutions using real-time behavior. The advent of AI to cybersecurity systems transformed the way organizations manage risks as they brought improved threat intelligence, anomaly detection, and automated response across complex digital environments.

Indeed, the comparisons between traditional and AI approaches in cyber defenses reveal the insufficient nature of traditional methods, such as reliance on static signatures and delayed detection, which are clearly no longer effective against rapidly changing threats. By contrast, AI-enabled architectures provide dynamic defense against large-scale data analysis, predictive modeling, and adaptive learning coupled with context-aware security measures. This context-awareness is especially critical in the new emerging domains such as smart grids, the IoT, and cyber-physical systems, where scale and connectedness are magnifying vulnerabilities.

However, some challenges still come with the full introduction of AI into cybersecurity, such as ethical dilemmas and possible biases inherent in algorithms, as well as transparency and accountability issues. Organizations now have to trade the efficiency of solutions driven by AI for responsible governance, one that equally upholds user privacy, fairness, and regulatory compliance. Thus, continuous improvement and upscaling of leaders in cybersecurity to manage more sophisticated and integrated AI-enabled systems become imperative.

Of course, in the future, it can be defined by intelligent, autonomous, and resilient mechanisms deployed on defense concepts. Innovations such as quantum-resistant cryptography, zero-trust architectures, and adaptive threat management are expected to provide a central role in this landscape. With the combination of cutting-edge technology by foresight and governance, organizations can erect a sustainable framework for cybersecurity, which can mitigate threats of today and tomorrow.

Indeed, as far as AI speaks for cybersecurity, it is more than just a feature of the computer. It does comprise a wider transition concerning risk management, operational resilience, and trust within organizations. Intelligent systems coexisting with ethical articulation and continuous adaptation will thus ensure that the digital infrastructure in the future is never made insecure as the world becomes ever more interconnected.

References

1. Dutta, N., Jadav, N., Tanwar, S. et al. (2022). *Cyber security: Issues and current trends*. Springer.
2. Sharp, R. (2023). Introduction: Why cybersecurity? In: *Introduction to Cybersecurity: A Multidisciplinary Challenge*, 1–16. Springer.
3. Alvarez-Teleña S, Díez-Fernández M. Modern cybersecurity: New era, new strategies. *New Strategies.* 16 September 2024.
4. Omar, M. and Zangana, H.M. (2024). *Redefining security with cyber AI*. IGI Global.
5. Zangana HM. Introduction to modern cybersecurity. In: Defense in Depth [Internet]. Wiley; 2025. p. 1–21. Available from: https://doi.org/10.1002/9781394340750.ch1.
6. Gohel, H.A. (2015). *Introduction to Network & Cybersecurity*. Hardik Gohel.

7 Goutam, R.K. (2021). *Cybersecurity fundamentals: understand the role of cybersecurity, its importance and modern techniques used by cybersecurity professionals*, Englishe. BPB Publications.

8 Ekanayake N, Karunarathna H, Miyuranga R. What is cybersecurity: The reality of modern threats. 2020.

9 Kumar, M., Darshan, S.L.S., and Yarlagadda, V. (2023). Introduction to the cyber-security landscape. In: *Malware Analysis and Intrusion Detection in Cyber-Physical Systems*, 1–21. IGI Global.

10 Bock, L. (2021). *Modern cryptography for cybersecurity professionals: Learn how you can leverage encryption to better secure your organization's data*. Packt Publishing Ltd.

11 França, R.P., Monteiro, A.C.B., Arthur, R., and Iano, Y. (2021). The fundamentals and potential for cybersecurity of big data in the modern world. In: *Machine Intelligence and Big Data Analytics for Cybersecurity Applications*, 51–73. Springer.

12 Aboelfotoh, S.F. and Hikal, N.A. (2019). A review of cyber-security measuring and assessment methods for modern enterprises. *JOIV: International Journal on Informatics Visualization.* 3 (2): 157–176.

13 Sharp, R. (2023). *Introduction to cybersecurity: a multidisciplinary challenge*. Springer Nature.

14 Manjikian, M. (2017). *Cybersecurity ethics: An introduction*. Routledge.

15 Hasib, M. (2022). *Cybersecurity leadership: Powering the modern organization*, vol. 1. Tomorrow's Strategy Today.

16 Ozkaya, E. (2022). *Cybersecurity Leadership Demystified: A comprehensive guide to becoming a world-class modern cybersecurity leader and global CISO*. Packt Publishing Ltd.

17 Angyalos, Z., Botos, S., and Szilágyi, R. (2021). The importance of cybersecurity in modern agriculture. *Agrárinformatika/Journal of Agricultural Informatics.* 12 (2): 1–8.

18 Kim, S., Shrestha, R., Kim, S., and Shrestha, R. (2020). Introduction to automotive cybersecurity. In: *Automotive Cyber Security: Introduction, Challenges, and Standardization*, 1–13. Springer.

19 Mashima D, Chen Y, Roomi MM, Lakshminarayana S, Chen D. Cybersecurity for modern smart grid against emerging threats. arXiv preprint arXiv:240404466. 2024.

20 Kaur, G., Habibi Lashkari, Z., Habibi Lashkari, A. et al. (2021). Introduction to cybersecurity. In: *Understanding Cybersecurity Management in FinTech: Challenges, Strategies, and Trends*, 17–34. Springer.

21 Hatzivasilis, G., Ioannidis, S., Smyrlis, M. et al. (2020). Modern aspects of cyber-security training and continuous adaptation of programmes to trainees. *Applied Sciences.* 10 (16): 5702.

22 Varbanov, P. (2022). Perspectives in the design of a modern cybersecurity training programme: The ECHO approach. *Information & Security.* 53 (2): 177–190.

23 Lapshina, I.V. and Kravets, A.V. (2023). Modern cybersecurity from the perspective of cognitive modeling. *Инженерный вестник Дона.* 1 (97): 80–95.

24 Rohatgi, S., Abinash, B., Joshi, S. et al. (2023). Introduction to artificial intelligence and cybersecurity for industry. In: *Artificial Intelligence and Cyber Security in Industry 40*, 1–22. Springer.

25 Diogenes, Y. and Ozkaya, E. (2019). *Cybersecurity–Attack and defense strategies: Counter modern threats and employ state-of-the-art tools and techniques to protect your organization against cybercriminals.* Packt Publishing Ltd.

26 Thakur, K. and Pathan, A.S.K. (2020). *Cybersecurity fundamentals: A real-world perspective.* CRC Press.

27 Holovkin, B.M., Tavolzhanskyi, O.V., and Lysodyed, O.V. (2021). Corruption as a cybersecurity threat in conditions of the new world's order. *Linguistics and Culture Review.* 5 (S3): 499–512.

28 Ajayi, W., Ibeto, O., Olomola, T., and Madewa, M. (2022). Analysis of modern cybersecurity threat techniques andavailable mitigating methods. *International Journal of Advanced Research in Computer Science.* 13 (2).

29 Gupta, C.P. and Goyal, K.K. (2020). *Cybersecurity: a self-teaching introduction.* Mercury Learning and Information.

30 Salem, I.E., Mijwil, M.M., Abdulqader, A.W. et al. (2022). Introduction to the data mining techniques in cybersecurity. *Mesopotamian Journal of Cybersecurity.* 2022: 28–37.

31 Jadey, S., Girish, S.C., Raghavendra, K. et al. (2022). Introduction to cyber security. In: *Methods, Implementation, and Application of Cyber Security Intelligence and Analytics*, 1–24. IGI Global.

32 Zangana, H.M. (2025). Conclusion: Building a resilient cyber defense framework. In: *Defense in Depth [Internet]*, 237–263. Wiley Available from: https://doi.org/10.1002/9781394340750.ch10.

2

The Cyber Threat Landscape in the AI Era

2.1 Introduction

The current cyber threat environment is also witnessing a radical change with the aftermath of the Fourth Industrial Revolution and the introduction of artificial intelligence (AI) technologies. The combination of AI, automation, and digital networks has radically changed both offensive and defensive tactics in cyberspace, providing new avenues through which state and non-state actors could use vulnerabilities in critical infrastructure, armed forces, and civilian digital resources [1, 2]. With the transition of warfare toward nonconventional needs based on hybrid and multi-domain interactions, the emerging cyber threat environment has become priority number one for policymakers, security specialists, and corporate executives [3, 4].

Traditionally, cyber threats were rather reactive, which meant targeting the individual cases of data breaches, malware infections, or distributed denial-of-service (DDoS) attacks [5, 6]. Nevertheless, a paradigm shift has also been brought by the AI era that allows complex attack schemes that incorporate machine learning, automation, and predictive analytics. The increased complexity and adaptability of cyber threats in recent years can be seen through the examples of AI-controlled cyber threats like autonomous malware, social engineering campaigns with the involvement of deepfakes, and attacks on machine learning models [7, 8].

The AI usage in cyber war has very deep strategic implications. AI algorithms can now be used to augment intelligence gathering, threat analysis, and operational planning with the abilities to quickly discover vulnerabilities and preemptive attack approaches [9, 10]. On the other hand, attackers take advantage of AI to develop offensive forces, where they make predictions based on what is expected to occur on the defensive side and automate attack procedures [11, 12]. Such a two-use character of AI leads to the re-examination of conventional defense models and indicates the increased significance of active and responsive cybersecurity approaches [13, 14].

Simultaneously, there has been a complication of the cyber threat environment due to the geopolitical landscape. The actors in the nation-state environment are starting to incorporate cyber operations into their overall military and strategic plans, and the boundary between conventional warfare and military engagement, hybrid wars, and cyber conflicts is becoming blurred [15–17]. States have to start thinking about AI-strengthened cyber capabilities when developing defense postures, military doctrines, or international security arrangements [18, 19].

Another aspect of AI age concerns ethical, legal, and societal aspects of cyber war. The introduction of autonomy and AI-controlled offensive solutions casts the question of accountability, proportionality, and international humanitarian law (IHL) [20–22]. To ensure the responsible use of AI technologies in cyber defense strategies, it is essential to include interdisciplinary approaches to the problem, with a combination of technical skills, development of policies, legal frameworks, and futuristic visions [23–25].

In addition, the development of multi-domain operations has made the battlefield broader to include not only terrestrial and air domains but also cyber, space, and electromagnetic spectrums [26–28]. AI technologies have become essential in the process of monitoring, analyzing, and protecting all these interconnected domains, as adversaries are becoming more and more adept at using AI-related vulnerabilities to benefit through the asymmetric approach [29].

To conclude, the adoption of AI in cyberspace has radically changed the character of threats and approaches needed to overcome them. This chapter focuses on the dynamic nature of cyber threats in the age of AI with a focus on the overlap of technology, strategy, and policy. Through awareness of emerging threats, including AI-driven malware, self-directed cyber campaigns, and deepfake-facilitated attacks, the stakeholders will be able to create resilient, dynamic, and proactive defenses to protect digital ecosystems in an ever-competitive and complicated cyberspace.

2.2 Evolution of Cyber Threats: From Traditional to AI-Empowered Attacks

The history of cyber threats is a manifestation of the ongoing technical revolution and countermeasures. Initial cyber threats were comparatively unsophisticated and usually random with their main aim of stealing data, disrupting services, and spreading simple malwares. They were mostly directed to individual systems, networks, and small organizational resources [5, 6]. As the digital infrastructures were increasingly integrated, the nature of the cyberattacks has transformed, and

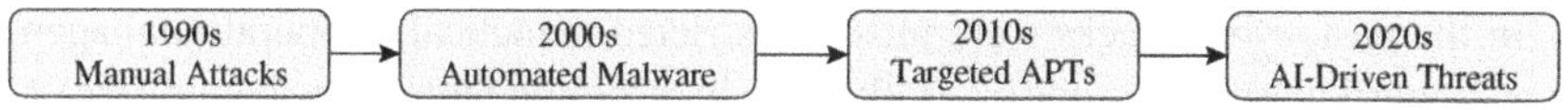

Figure 2.1 Evolution of Cyber Threats from Traditional to AI-Empowered Attacks. "*Source:* Hewa Majeed Zangana"

the focus also includes coordinated campaigns against critical infrastructure, military systems, and massive industrial production [1, 2].

Figure 2.1 follows the historical development of cyber threats, in which the traditional and manual attacks have evolved into fully automated attacks, AI-powered. The timeline highlights the way machine learning, automation, and deepfakes have transformed the magnitude and complexity of cyber warfare.

The post-appearance of the Fourth Industrial Revolution era was characterized by adopting new computing technologies and AI, as well as networked devices, which had a tremendous impact on the threat landscape. Phishing, malware, and denial-of-service remain classical approaches to attacking the network, but automated and adaptive methods were increasingly added to them, making threat actors attempt to use vulnerabilities at an unprecedented rate and scale [12, 14]. This change also allowed attackers to execute multi-stage attacks comprising reconnaissance, intrusion, and exploitation that use precision targeting, which in many cases relies on the AI algorithms to seek vulnerable points and anticipate defensive actions [9, 13].

The most recent wave in the development of cyber threats is the utilization of AI in attacks. These are adversarial machine learning, in which AI models are trained to generate incorrect results, and AI-powered malware that has the capability to independently evolve to countermeasures [7, 8]. Deepfake technologies also contribute to the extent of social engineering attacks, as it allows actors to defraud individuals and organizations with the help of state-of-the-art synthetic media [21, 25]. The emergence of autonomous cyber operations has shifted the dichotomy between the reactive and the preemptive threats and requires new defensive mechanisms, which would combine predictive analytics, real-time monitoring, and an automated response mechanism [23, 26].

The use of AI in cyber warfare is strategic in nature with implications in its offensive and defensive use. The collection of intelligence and operational planning is being progressively AI-controlled, as it is possible to quickly process large flows of data and have greater awareness of the situation [10, 11]. On the other hand, attackers use AI to improve offensive operations, launching multi-vector attacks, which evolve network defense in real time [15, 16]. The environment of threat is further complicated by the multi-domain nature of the contemporary conflicts, which include land, air, sea, space, and cyberspace, necessitating integrated approaches to defend critical assets that may be reinforced by AI [4, 19].

In the past, cyberattacks were mostly restricted to tactical or operational agendas. Nevertheless, in the age of AI, they are incorporated into more general strategic and geopolitical agendas. AI-based cyber campaigns are used by nation-state actors to gain asymmetric benefits, interfere with the decision-making process of adversaries, and affect the way people perceive things [17]. On a similar note, non-state actors are using AI to drive the effect of an attack to the maximum and reduce exposure to operations, which makes them a complex and rapidly changing threat environment [1, 27].

The change in the nature of traditional attacks to AI-empowered attacks also has serious ethical and legal issues. The speed and scale of autonomous cyber systems are beyond the control of humans, which is a matter of accountability, proportionality, and the applicability of international law [20, 22]. Defense mechanisms should, therefore, combine tech-based solutions with the inclusion of legal, regulatory, and policy frameworks that would help to create responsible and effective responses to AI-based threats [18, 28].

Lastly, the introduction of AI to the threat environment of cyber has triggered a fresh new arms race in cyberspace. The machinery of state and non-state actors is constantly creating AI-powered devices and countermeasures, and the environment is dynamic, with innovation directly affecting the results of security [3, 12, 29]. The nature of cyber threat development is not only a technological phenomenon but also a strategic necessity, which requires continuous attention, flexible defense systems, and a progressive attitude toward cybersecurity in the era of AI [9, 21].

2.3 AI as a Double-Edged Sword in Cybersecurity

The concept of AI has become a technological revolution in the field of cybersecurity and has provided unparalleled opportunities to improve defensive systems, automate the process of detecting threats, and provide a predictive forecast of threats. Simultaneously, the emergence of AI has brought about new vulnerabilities and increased the complexity of attacks, which have resulted in a dual-use dilemma where the same technology can be used by both attackers and defenders [1, 2]. Because of this duality of AI, a sensitive perception of its advantages and dangers in the contemporary cyberspace is required.

On the defensive side, AIs are used in cybersecurity systems to identify abnormalities on the network, predictive analytics, and machine learning algorithms to monitor network activity, which helps anticipate potential threats even before they happen [9, 10]. It is estimated that automated incident response, smart threat hunting, and adaptive intrusion detection have become very important tools in the sustainability of critical infrastructure, government networks, and corporate digital ecosystems [5, 8]. Multi-domain situational awareness (interacting information over cyber, physical, and operational domains) is also supported by AI-enabled tools to assist in making strategic decisions [4, 15].

But it should not be forgotten that AI has offensive possibilities. The threat actors are automating their attacks, developing more successful social engineering campaigns, or leveraging vulnerabilities at scale with the help of AI [12, 13]. As an example, adversarial AI may be used to overcome security measures by training machine learning models, and deepfake technologies can be used to create highly persuasive phishing and fake misinformation campaigns [21, 25]. The malware that can adapt itself in real time to any countermeasures is also an indicator of the increased complexity and uncertainty surrounding AI-enhanced cyber threats [23, 26].

The AI strategic implications on cybersecurity are not limited to technical capabilities. The AI enhances the speed of a cyber war, allowing it to have multivectoral attacks that can rapidly affect the geopolitical outcomes and alter the balance of power in the context of conflict [3, 16, 17]. The nation-state actors use AI-driven capabilities to generate strategic benefits, including disrupting the command and control systems of their adversaries, influencing the masses, and undertaking operations covertly in the disputed digital space [1]. On the other hand, the defenders are forced to keep up with the competition and apply AI to the proactive defense models as well as threat intelligence systems [14, 18].

The AI dual-use problem revolves around ethical, legal, and operational issues. The introduction of autonomous systems that can perform cyber operations with machine speed brings up the issue of accountability because human control might fall behind the execution of the operations [20, 22]. To guarantee compliance with the IHL, especially in the case of multi-domain or hybrid warfare, it is necessary to exercise strict control over the use of AI both in offensive and defensive scenarios [19, 28].

Additionally, AI transforms the cyber deterrence dynamics. On the one hand, AI increases defensive power, but at the same time, it reduces the threshold to advanced attacks and forms part of the environment where strategic uncertainty and rapid escalation are major threats [8, 11]. The aspect of an invisible front enabled by AI-powered tools makes attributing threats and responding even more difficult, as it disrupts the conventional theories of warfare and requires adapting intelligence-driven security approaches [13, 29].

Figure 2.2 explains the two-way issue of AI in cybersecurity. Although AI enhances defensive functions by automating and predicting analytics, there is a threat to it, providing attackers with adaptive and self-learning offensive means.

To sum up, AI is a two-sided sword when it comes to cybersecurity. On the one hand, it gives defenders the ability to be automated, predictive, and multi-domain in situational awareness, but it is also exposing adversaries to safer, more advanced, and undetectable attacks. Successful implementation of AI in cybersecurity will

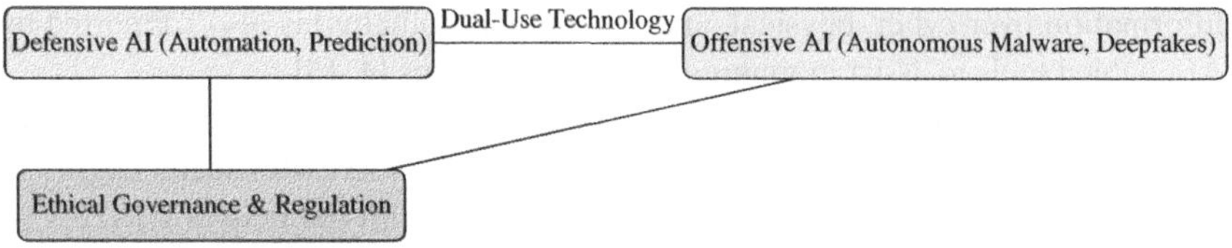

Figure 2.2 AI as a Double-Edged Sword: Balancing Defensive and Offensive Uses. "*Source:* Hewa Majeed Zangana"

need a complex strategy that will incorporate technical innovation and strategic vision, legal regulation, and ethical control. It is only through recognizing and dealing with this dual-use aspect that organizations and states will be able to tap into the power of AI and, at the same time, reduce the risks to which it can expose them [6, 20, 24, 27, 28].

2.4 Emerging Categories of AI-Era Cyber Threats

The high speed of AI adoption in the digital ecosystems has radically changed the landscape of cyber threats. The threat of AI-powered threats is becoming more advanced, dynamic, and able to process its tasks much faster than human control, which is why the conventional understanding of cybersecurity is being contested [1, 2]. These threats may be grouped broadly in a few emerging classifications that indicate technological innovation and changing adversarial strategies.

2.4.1 AI-Powered Malware

Conventional malware has become an AI-powered version that can independently adjust to detection systems and become dynamically adaptable to its behavior to target the vulnerability in real time [12, 26]. Such malwares use machine learning to create vulnerabilities in network defenses and plot propagation plans. These are polymorphic ransomware, AI-driven spyware, and self-learning worms that have the ability to modify their payloads to suit the target environment [5, 14]. Such advances are a major increase in the threat environment, with automated flexibility decreasing the time responders have to respond.

2.4.2 Adversarial Attacks on AI Systems

Even AI machines are targets. The concepts of adversarial machine learning attacks are based on manipulation to deceive AI models and lead to a misclassification, inaccurate prediction, or malfunction of automated systems [9, 13]. The critical infrastructure, military activities, and autonomous systems dependent on AI in decision-making are the most worrying of these attacks. These attacks define an invisible digital front, which also points to the possibility of strategic disruption without the engagement of kinetic means [3, 4].

2.4.3 Deepfakes and Synthetic Media Exploitation

AI and deepfake technology have presented novel social engineering, disinformation, and psychological operations vectors. The threat actors can manipulate the perception of the population, commit numerous fraudulent actions, or influence the political and military results by creating the most persuasive audio, video, or text messages [21, 25]. The fact that these kinds of technologies have increased highlights the indistinct nature of the line separating cybercrime, cyber warfare, and information operations [20, 29].

2.4.4 Autonomous Cyber Campaigns

The autonomous cyber operations are a paradigm shift in the view that attacks can be carried out without human control. According to these campaigns, AI is used as a reconnaissance, targeting, and payload delivery tool, which in most cases involves a multi-domain approach to the land, air, sea, space, and cyberspace [16]. The pace and scope of this type of campaign pose a threat to traditional defense, which necessitates defenders to embrace AI-supported monitoring systems, predictive analytics, and frameworks of automated responses [15, 19].

2.4.5 Advanced Persistent Threats (APTs) Enhanced by AI

The power of Advanced Persistent Threats (APTs) has been enhanced by AI, with long-term, hidden actions penetrating and staying in the target networks [11, 26]. These AI-powered APTs can foresee the defensive strategies, change their strategies during the course of time, and focus on vital industries such as defense, finance, healthcare, and energy [7, 23]. With this type of operation, the strategic aspect of AI becomes highlighted in both offensive and defensive cybersecurity planning [6, 24].

2.4.6 AI-Enabled Multi-Domain and Hybrid Attacks

The new forms of cyber conflicts are more and more associated with AI in a variety of spheres, integrating traditional cyberattacks with e-warfare, information operations, and kinetic activity [12, 28]. Such hybrid methods capitalize on the system interdependence and enhance the strategic effects of attack, as can be seen in the geopolitical cyber battles of the recent past [1, 17]. The interplay of AI, big data analytics, and interconnected networks has expedited multi-domain attacks and made them more accurate and difficult to trace.

2.4.7 Threats to Networked Autonomous Systems

The development of the Internet of Things (IoT), the Internet of Battlefield Things (IoBT), and autonomous systems has attained a greater attack surface of AI-based threats [28, 29]. Attackers can use the vulnerabilities between networked devices to cause disruption, steal confidential information, or alter system activities [3, 14]. The adoption of AI increases these dangers by making it possible to target them predictively and exploit them in large quantities.

Figure 2.3 groups the major threats of AI-era cyberspace as illustrating their interdependence with one another and the convergence of automation, autonomy, and deception to become the main tool in digital warfare. The visualization structures the threats based on data-driven control to autonomous system exploitation.

To recap it all, AI has created smarter, more adaptable, and more strategically decisive cyber threats than ever. Such new types indicate that a cohesive system of cybersecurity needs to be implemented, which incorporates AI-based defenses, proactive threat intelligence, ethical control, and policy-based governance [9, 21, 22]. Since AI is still being exploited by its opponents, the cybersecurity community should expect the development of new strategies and invest in multi-layered and dynamic defense capabilities to ensure that these threats do not succeed [4, 18, 20].

2.5 Threat Actors and Motivations in the AI Era

The AI era has transformed the landscape of cyber threats and added new categories of threat actors, as well as increasing the complexity of their motives. Although conventional cyber threats could be aimed at opportunistic targets or monetary goals, AI-driven capabilities have expanded the target audience and the scope of the targeted strategic goals [1, 2]. It is essential to learn about the actors and their motives to devise specific defense measures and improve the resilience to cybersecurity.

2.5.1 State-Sponsored Actors

Nation-states are still one of the most advanced and proficient cyber enemies. With the help of AI, such players can engage in massive contingency operations, cyber spying, and targeted cyberattacks against critical infrastructure, defensive systems, and government networks [3, 4]. Geopolitical benefit, national security, and strategic deterrence are the motivations of the state-sponsored actors [15, 18].

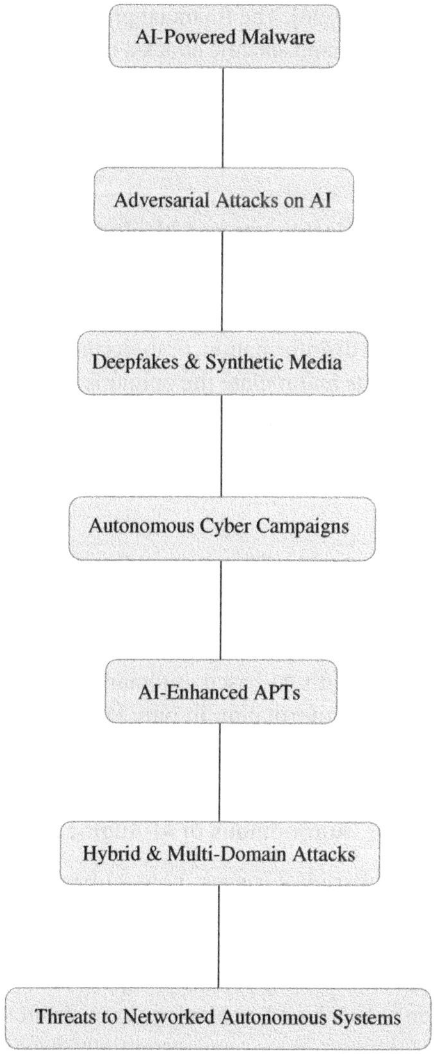

Figure 2.3 Hierarchical Categories of AI-Era Cyber Threats. "*Source:* Hewa Majeed Zangana"

According to recent research, states are beginning to use AI in the cyber arsenal to automate reconnaissance efforts, identify weaknesses, and coordinate multi-domain operations [12, 13].

2.5.2 Cybercriminal Organizations

Sophisticated criminal syndicates have also embraced AI-based approaches to increase effectiveness, magnitude, and avoidance. They use AI to automate phishing campaigns and serve adaptive ransomware, as well as optimize attack vectors [9, 26]. The financial profit is still the main incentive, but AI allows more advanced and specific attacks, making the differences more influential to companies and individuals [7, 23]. It is also now possible to use predictive models when analyzing the high-value targets as well as predicting the countermeasures, which complicates mitigation [6, 10].

2.5.3 Hacktivists and Ideologically Driven Actors

Politically driven or hacktivist groups leverage AI to increase their own campaigns of civil disobedience, social interference, or ideology. By creating deepfakes, automating disinformation, or undermining communication infrastructure, these participants manipulate the opinions of the population and the political process [21, 25]. With the help of AI, the range of their activity is increased, and it is possible to spread the news significantly faster and organize decentralized campaigns without the involvement of large human resources [20, 29].

2.5.4 Insider Threats and Opportunistic Actors

The AI era has further enhanced the dangers of insiders or opportunistic attackers who use AI systems to personal gain, sabotage, or to spy. Insider risks may also tamper with AI-based automation, attack machine learning algorithms, or steal valuable information in bulk [16, 17]. These reasons can be money, professional disdain, political beliefs, or pressure by outside parties [5, 14].

2.5.5 Autonomous or AI-Augmented Threat Agents

Recent studies suggest how AI-based autonomous actors can become actors of cyber threats on their own. These systems are capable of detecting vulnerabilities, executing attacks, and changing strategies without requiring any human input directly, causing new challenges to attribution and response [11, 15]. These agents do not act based on ideology or on profit but increase the scope and sophistication of human actors and essentially expand the powers of states, criminals, or hacktivists [28].

2.5.6 Hybrid and Multi-Domain Adversaries

Having merged AI and other emerging technologies, hybrid threat actors have been able to combine cyber activity with electronic warfare, misinformation, and kinetic activity [2, 19]. The motives of these actors are strategic, political, and economic in nature, and their motives are difficult to distinguish as cybercrime, espionage, and warfare [1, 4]. Multi-domain attacks may use AI to provide real-time coordination and decision-making that can build asymmetric advantages over normal defense solutions [22, 27].

2.5.7 Motivational Frameworks in the AI Era

Motivations of cyber threat actors in the AI age can be divided into strategic, financial, ideological, and opportunistic. By increasing the efficiency of the work of these actors and enabling them to develop multi-objective campaigns of greater accuracy and less risk of being spotted [9, 21], AI will enable them to be more effective in their work and decrease their exposure to consequences, thus making the operations of such actors more difficult to detect. Both actor profiles and their behavioral patterns require more profound comprehension to create relevant threat intelligence and proactive defense approaches [20, 29].

To sum up, the AI age has increased the range of cyber threat actors and broadened their capacity. These actors are more rapid, massive, and sophisticated than ever cars and trucks, or even nation-states. It is essential to know their motivations within the context of a strategic, financial, ideological, or opportunistic attack to predict attacks and create robust cybersecurity architectures capable of combating AI-empowered attacks [16, 24, 28].

2.6 AI-Driven Attack Vectors and Techniques

The advent of AI has dramatically changed the face of cyberattacks by introducing new vectors and methods that go beyond traditional methods. The AI-based attacks take advantage of machine learning, natural language processing, and automation to enhance the efficiency, scalability, and flexibility of the cyber activities [1, 2]. Such evolution not only increases the effectiveness of the old types of attacks but also creates completely new types of digital threats that pose a challenge to the current security architecture [5, 6].

2.6.1 AI-Enhanced Phishing and Social Engineering

AI tools allow threat actors to design highly customized and adaptive phishing attacks (investigating social media profiles, communication behavior, and behavioral data). In contrast to traditional phishing, AI-optimized attacks are capable of dynamically altering the content to evade security filters and have a higher chance of the user interacting with it [9, 23]. With the help of generative AI, attackers can now produce persuasive emails, messages, and even deepfaked audio or video content to make social engineering attacks much more powerful [21, 25].

2.6.2 Automated Vulnerability Exploitation

AI algorithms are capable of scanning and detecting vulnerabilities in networks, applications, and devices quickly, which was done manually in large volumes before [12, 13]. Intrusion attempts become quicker and smarter as machine learning models are able to predict the flaws in the system, create exploit codes, and generate new attack strategies in real time [15, 16]. This feature enables the attackers to scale and attack several systems at a time, enhancing the magnitude and productivity.

2.6.3 Intelligent Malware and Ransomware

Malware that is artificially intelligent is capable of self-optimizing to suit various categories of operating systems, impersonating itself, and improving its distribution tactics. These encompass self-modifying code, polymorphic ransomware, and intelligent trojans that have the ability to learn because of defense systems [9, 26]. AI is also useful to predictively target valuable systems or data in order to get the most financial or strategic benefit out of ransomware campaigns [6, 7].

2.6.4 AI-Powered Denial-of-Service (DoS) Attacks

AI has been used to complement traditional denial-of-service attacks to make them more effective. Machine learning is able to optimize traffic flows, detect the bottlenecks in the target systems, and update attack vectors dynamically to flood the infrastructure with minimal exposure to the attacker [3, 4]. This type of intelligent DoS attack is capable of disrupting vital services and cascading failures in interdependent digital ecosystems [14, 20].

2.6.5 AI-Assisted Reconnaissance and Espionage

AI enables the use of tools that are very efficient for collecting reconnaissance and intelligence. Pattern recognition, automated data mining, and predictive analytics enable attackers to map organizational networks, determine vulnerabilities, and predict response [10, 17]. They are commonly used by state-backed agents in espionage, attacks on infrastructure, military, and government systems [1, 15].

2.6.6 Adversarial Attacks on AI Systems

One distinct type of attack during the AI era entails the manipulation of AI models in an adversarial manner. Hackers use machine learning algorithms like input perturbation, model inversion, or data poisoning to disrupt decision-making or to evade security [11, 29]. These are of specific concern to the autonomous systems, AI-based surveillance, and critical infrastructure dependent on AI-driven analytics [28].

2.6.7 Multi-Domain and Hybrid AI-Driven Operations

AI allows the coordination of attacks in various systems, combining cyber, electronic warfare, and information action. Hybrid AI-based approaches enable outlawed acts to coordinate digital interruption with physical or psychological ones and produce multidimensional efforts that are hard to notice or counter [2, 19]. These multi-domain capabilities are especially useful in the case of military and strategic actors that seek to attain asymmetric benefits in the context of conflict [22, 27].

2.6.8 Implications for Cyber Defense

The multiplication of the AI-based attack vectors is the reason that adaptive and AI-based defense strategies are necessary. The conventional system of cybersecurity needs to be updated to adopt predictive analytics, real-time threat intelligence, and autonomous response tools to combat AI-powered threats [16, 24]. To realize a robust security architecture that can withstand human and machine-level attackers, it is crucial to understand the scope of AI-driven technologies, such as automated reconnaissance or attacks on adversarial models [12, 28].

The visualization of the major AI-based attack vectors in this section, as illustrated in Figure 2.4, represents a graph of the correlation between attack methods and the purposes thereof. It emphasizes the way AI improves conventional cyber strategies in each phase of operations, including reconnaissance and execution.

To conclude, attack vectors supported by AI have significantly increased the magnitude, complexity, and intensity of cyber threats. Using intelligent malware and adaptive phishing, as well as semi-domain and multi-domain hybrid attacks, AI gives threat actors unprecedented capabilities. To reduce mitigation, highly

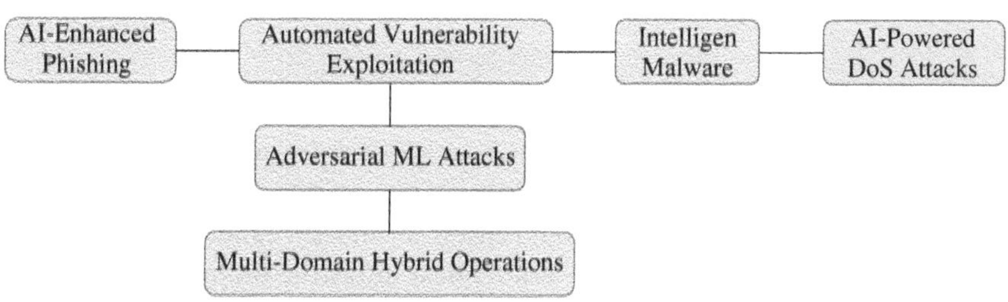

Figure 2.4 AI-Driven Attack Vectors and Techniques Across the Cyber Kill Chain. "*Source:* Hewa Majeed Zangana"

developed defensive capabilities need to be considered, which use AI to predict, identify, and react to these dynamic and changing risks [9, 20, 23].

2.7 Defensive Strategies Against AI-Empowered Threats

The conventional strategies to cybersecurity are regularly inadequate, particularly due to the advanced forms of cyberattack and the use of AI-based systems. Anti-AI approaches would have to adapt to AI-powered attacks, which would involve technological advancement, human factors, and organizational readiness [1, 2]. Such strategies include proactive threat exposure, adaptive countermeasures, as well as all-embracive security systems that can be used to counter both automated and human-sponsored cyber activities.

2.7.1 AI-Enhanced Threat Detection and Monitoring

Application of AI in defense also enables the constant tracking of network operations and identification of threats in real time. Machine learning models have the ability to detect uncharacteristic behaviors, forecast upcoming attack vectors, and categorize threats according to their risk, providing better and quicker responses to the incident [9, 23]. The use of AI-enhanced intrusion detection systems (IDS) is capable of keeping pace with the changing attack patterns, decreasing the success rate of AI-driven phishing attacks, malware attacks, and denial-of-service attacks [21, 25].

2.7.2 Predictive Vulnerability Management

Making a proactive vulnerability identification and elimination is essential in the fight against automated exploits. Based on past attack history, software configuration, and network topology, AI systems can identify possible weak points, allowing organizations to focus their patching and risk reduction efforts [12, 13]. These predictive strategies limit the opportunity of attackers to use AI-enabled exploit tools [15, 16].

2.7.3 Defensive AI Against Adversarial Attacks

Attacks on AI models themselves involve the use of defensive strategies that are specific to adversarial attacks. Adversarial training, model hardening, and anomaly detection are the methods that could ensure an attacker cannot use AI systems for their malicious intentions [11, 29]. Critical infrastructure and autonomous systems, and cybersecurity applications that are based on AI analytics, must incorporate the integrity and reliability of AI-driven systems [28].

2.7.4 Multi-Layered Cybersecurity Frameworks

The AI-driven threats can only be defended by means of a multi-layered strategy, including endpoint protection, network security, data encryption, and identity management [5, 6]. Multiplexing ensures that the attack is more complex and requires the adversaries to go through several obstacles, which makes automated AI-based attacks less effective [14, 20].

2.7.5 Cyber Threat Intelligence and Collaboration

The exchange of threat intelligence across organizations, governments, and international alliances improves joint protective measures against cyber threats that can be controlled by AI. There is early detection of novel attack methodologies that is made possible through open-source intelligence (OSINT) and collaborative platforms, which allow quick defensive modification [3, 4]. Intelligence-based defense systems are implemented to make sure that the government and nongovernmental organizations can predict the trends of attacks and organize the mitigation program [10, 17].

2.7.6 Human-AI Synergy in Cyber Defense

Although AI is a very powerful tool that enhances defensive abilities, human experience is still crucial. AI-derived insights require skilled experts in cybersecurity to analyze, build strategic responses, and operate complicated working environments [1, 18]. Social engineering and phishing attacks that are enhanced by AI are also less susceptible when it comes to training and awareness [9, 21].

2.7.7 Strategic Deterrence and Policy Measures

In addition to technical protection, deterrence, and policy are also important to contain AI-based cyber threats. The use of AI in cyber operations may be curtailed through cyber norms, international agreements, and military strategies regarding the deterrence of the misuse of AI (in the context of multi-domain and hybrid warfare), in particular [8, 28]. The presence of policy-based defense makes the domain accountable and sets the boundaries in the digital realm [22, 27].

2.7.8 Continuous Evolution and Adaptive Defense

Since the threats posed by AI are adaptive, defensive approaches should also be continuously changed. The organizations are advised to follow flexible security architectures, dynamic risk assessment tools, and self-learning and threat predictive autonomous response systems [12, 24]. Adaptive defense is based on integrating real-time operational intelligence with AI-based predictive modeling to face the cyber threats as they happen or emerge [9, 15].

Figure 2.5 shows a layered defense model that can be used to deal with AI-enhanced cyber threats. The model brings together AI-based detection, predictive analytics, human control, as well as policy-based governance as a single defense architecture.

To sum up, combating AI-enhanced cyber threats must be an integrated solution consisting of sophisticated AI technologies, human knowledge and skill, and strategic policies. Preemptive threat detection, preemptive vulnerability risk

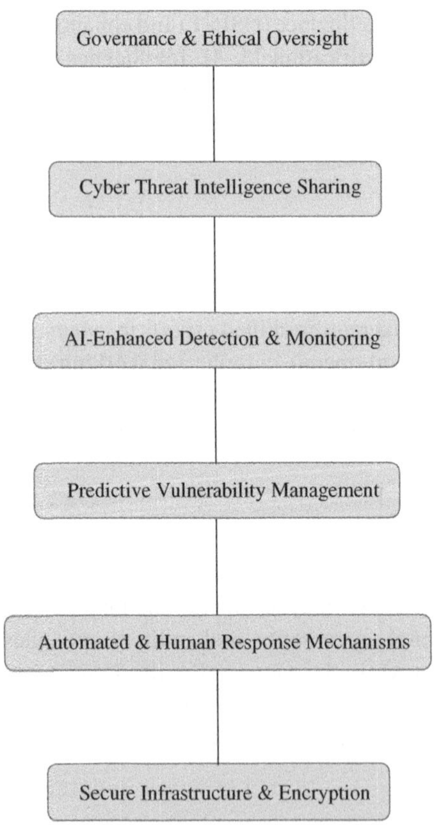

Figure 2.5 Multi-Layered Defensive Framework Against AI-Empowered Cyber Threats. "*Source:* Hewa Majeed Zangana"

management, multi-layered security model, and global cooperation are the pillars of an efficient defense posture in the AI era. Organizations and states can reduce the threat that AI-advanced cyber adversaries present to the world in unprecedented severity by adopting adaptive and intelligence-driven approaches [6, 20, 23].

2.8 Regulatory and Ethical Implications

The emergence of AI-powered cyber threats has put the aspect of regulation and ethical considerations at the center of cybersecurity discussions. With the broadening of the digital battlefield outside the conventional military sphere, countries, organizations, and foreign institutions have to adjust their regulation systems to regulate the use and response to AI-supported cyberattacks [1, 2]. This change is necessary to ensure accountability, safeguard civil liberties, and curb the rising conflicts in cyberspace.

2.8.1 Legal Frameworks and International Regulation

Cyber warfare based on AI is expected to challenge traditional norms of legal discourse, such as the IHL and armed conflict laws. Researchers point out that cyber activities should be considered in the framework of the available agreements, but the specificity of autonomous AI attacks should be taken into account [11, 22]. It is becoming more urgent to establish global contracts that would establish allowable actions, duties, and red lines of state and non-state actors in cyberspace [4, 27].

Practically, such frameworks have to deal with the attribution issue of AI-driven cyberattacks, where attackers can obstruct their identity, automate the progression of attacks, and use international infrastructures [13, 29]. It is hence essential to come up with clear standards and mechanisms of enforcing them in order to discourage evil practices and instill responsibility.

2.8.2 National Cybersecurity Policies

Nations are also writing AI-focused cybersecurity policies to enhance offensive and defensive forces. Such policies include national AI regulations, threat intelligence exchange, and proactive defense actions that will help in countering APTs [15, 26]. As an example, the regulatory framework of network security and digital infrastructure is essential to the strategic advantage of countries with well-developed technology, including the United States [21, 28]. The introduction of AI into the crucial industries such as energy, finance, and healthcare is also covered by national regulations to minimize vulnerability to automated cyberattacks [7, 9].

2.8.3 Ethical Considerations in AI-Driven Cyber Operations

The ethics have been at the forefront of defining the application of AI in offensive and defensive cyber operations. Autonomous decision-making systems have to be created to reduce collateral damage, ensure that no civilians get hurt, and that they meet the requirements of human rights [16, 18]. With AI being used to control information, destabilize critical infrastructure, and/or perform surveillance, there are deep ethical issues of accountability, fairness, and transparency [6, 25].

Researchers believe that every stage of AI governance, including designing algorithms and placing them into operation, should include ethical principles to make sure that autonomous systems do not conflict with the social values [12, 20]. Furthermore, the ethical aspect involves how the bias of the AI systems is managed, sensitive information is kept safe, and how it is not abused by malicious users [9, 10].

2.8.4 Compliance and Organizational Responsibilities

Companies that work in the digital sphere are not only obliged to the regulatory bodies but also to the stakeholders and people as well. Good compliance systems and procedures involve technical protection and human education as well as ongoing oversight to reduce the risks of AI-enhanced cybercriminals [5, 23]. Encryption, intrusion detection, and threat intelligence sharing are some of the multi-layered strategies that are needed to remain compliant without violating the ethical landscape of AI in cybersecurity [14, 17].

2.8.5 Balancing Security and Privacy

The implementation of AI in cybersecurity tends to create stress between security and privacy. The regulatory frameworks should find a balance to ensure that they can successfully detect and defend against threats and still not violate the rights of individuals [3, 4]. Unregulated use of AI-based surveillance and monitoring can be a breach of the laws and regulations of data protection and confidence of the population. They are thus urged to put in place governance mechanisms that would give precedence to the national security as well as the ethical responsibility [28].

2.8.6 Future Directions in Regulation and Ethics

Regulatory and ethical provisions should be dynamic and progressive as AI is set to improve. Such emerging trends as the creation of autonomous regulation tools based on the application of AI to monitor compliance, adaptive policies in the environment of hybrid warfare, and harmonization of the law across borders are noted [8, 19]. These measures provide the solution that AI-controlled cyber activity is performed according to the legally enforceable and ethically acceptable limits [2, 24].

In short, AI's regulatory and ethical aspects of cyber warfare are manifold and complicated. The responsible AI use in cybersecurity is based on legal frameworks, national policies, ethical rules, organizational compliance, and privacy issues. These frameworks must be constantly adjusted so that AI-driven capabilities can be more effective at improving security without violating legal and ethical norms [1, 22].

2.9 Future Outlook of the Cyber Threat Landscape

The cyber threat environment today is changing faster than ever, due to the acceleration of technology, geopolitical changes, and the growing use of AI and autonomous systems both in the civil and military spheres. It is important to understand the direction of cyber threats to develop effective defense measures, regulatory, and international security policies [1, 2].

2.9.1 Emerging Technologies and Their Implications

The development of AI, machine learning, and the IoT is altering the cyber battlefield. More complex AI-helped attack vectors, such as automated malware, intelligent phishing, and adaptive persistent threats, are likely to get more advanced [26, 29]. NATO and other international entities acknowledge the fact that these novel technologies can dramatically change the detection and response capabilities related to threats and that, thus, the security strategies have to be dynamically changed [3, 4].

Moreover, the fusion of cyber-physical systems, e.g., industrial control systems and smart city infrastructure, exposes vulnerabilities that adversaries may use remotely and create a large-scale disruption without face-to-face contact [7, 25]. A good example is the IoBT and how interconnected platforms can become an asset of strategic value in warfare and also present a new risk vector at the same time [13, 29].

2.9.2 Hybrid and Multi-Domain Threats

The cyber threats in the future would be mostly multi-domain and hybrid in character, whereby they involve both traditional kinetic missions and advanced digital attacks. Such hybrid operations erase the boundary between traditional and cyber warfare, exposing the current legal and ethical standards to the challenge [14, 21]. Multi-domain operations utilize information warfare, cyber spies, and autonomous systems to affect the events on the battlefield and political results without necessarily initiating a direct armed conflict [20].

The emergence of the invisible digital fronts where state and non-state actors use cyber tools to meet their strategic goals underscores the necessity to have a strong intelligence and cyber situational awareness [10, 13]. Defense mechanisms should then be prepared to handle attacks that are fast, dynamic, and very decentralized, which require constant monitoring and predictive analytics [9, 15].

2.9.3 Evolving Cyber Warfare Strategies

Cyber warfare is also changing its reactive approach to proactive. Countries are investing in cyber deterrence, red-teamings, and AI-assisted threat simulations to predict and counter the possible attacks even before they can grow [8, 16]. It is emphasized in research studies that AI must be incorporated into defensive and offensive actions and that the strategic benefit needs to be weighed against ethical and legal standards [11, 12].

Additionally, the cooperation on the international level is becoming more and more important. The sharing of information, exercises together, and standard procedures are the crucial steps to mitigate the threats of the cross-border that utilize the global digital infrastructure [6, 17]. The inability to form collaborative models can also result in the ability of opponents to use regulatory loopholes and increase the effect of AI-enabled cyber activities [18, 27].

2.9.4 Regulatory, Ethical, and Policy Considerations

Along with the development of cyber capabilities, the regulatory and ethical factors should be provided. Attributing, using proportionality, and adherence to the IHL are complicated by autonomous systems and AI-stimulated attacks [2, 22]. The national and international policies are being revised to balance the two demands of accountability and security, with a focus on being transparent, protecting privacy, and using AI responsibly [23, 28].

The growing sophistication of the cyber threat environment also suggests the need to have adaptive laws, such as regulations of new technologies, guidelines of autonomous operations, and standards of cross-border cooperation [1, 19]. The risks linked to the AI-driven threats will be reduced with the help of ethical governance, workforce training, and compliance monitoring [9, 26].

2.9.5 Strategic Outlook and Recommendations

In the future, we may expect a cyber threat environment that is both highly innovative and multi-domain in nature with more and more applications of AI and autonomous technologies [15, 24]. The strategic imperatives are:

- Investing in AI defense systems and predictive analytics that identify and respond to adaptive threats.
- Improving global cooperation and setting norms, distributing intelligence, and implementing cyber deterrents.
- Modifying regulatory and ethical policies to control autonomous functions and safeguard civil liberties.
- Ensuring that the required critical infrastructure is resilient to both traditional and cyberattacks [3, 4].

Finally, the future cyber threat landscape requires that it is a multi-layered approach that is both proactive and incorporates technology, policy, ethics, and international inter-agency collaboration. The constant innovation based on the historical trends and new findings will be critical in ensuring strategic advantage and assuring global digital security [9–11].

2.10 Conclusion

The changing cyber threat situation is one of the most challenging and unresolved issues of the present world. Since the digital technologies are striving to evolve, the character of cyber threats has gained a more advanced, versatile, and global character, influencing not only the national security but also the stability of the critical infrastructure, the economic environment, and societal stability. Similar to the incorporation of AI, autonomous systems, and network connectivity, both the abilities of attackers and the vulnerabilities of potential targets have risen, which has put the traditional approaches of defense strategies in an inadequate setting.

The solution to these challenges is multidimensional, which involves technological innovation, strategic planning, and good governance. Companies and governments need to invest in superior systems of detection, predictive analytics, and self-adjusting defense systems to be ahead of more intelligent and increasingly automated threats. Meanwhile, there should be simultaneous developments of ethical and regulatory frameworks to ensure the responsible use of emerging technologies without compromising privacy, accountability, and meeting the requirements of international standards.

The future of cybersecurity and cyber warfare will be based on dynamic and multi-domain operations, exercising intersections of physical, digital, and cognitive domains. The very success of this environment will rest on the ability to convene governments, private sectors, and international institutions in a proactive manner. Building resilience, knowledge sharing, and a culture of preparedness are vital to risk mitigation and strategic advantage.

The cyberspace battle integrates the technological canvas as well as the sociopolitical fabric. In what already amounts to a tangled web of actors and interests, actors may cleverly distinguish themselves by carving out niches for integrating innovation, policy, and ethical considerations into comprehensive defense strategies; in this way, it may be possible to traverse the complexity of the digital battlefield, predict emerging threats, and protect critical systems on which life in the modern world depends. The lessons learned today will inform the ability to muster timely and effective responses to the escalating sophistication of tomorrow's challenges.

References

1 Ahmad, S. and Jahangir, J. (2023). Cyber warfare: Emerging non-traditional threat to Pakistan's security. *Pakistan Horizon.* 76 (2): 39–58.

2 Bardin, J.S. (2025). Cyber warfare. In: *Computer and Information Security Handbook*, 1345–1380. Elsevier.

3 Bellasio J, Silfversten E. The impact of new and emerging technologies on the cyber threat landscape and their implications for NATO. Cyber Threats and NATO 2030: *Horizon Scanning and Analysis.* 2020;88.

4 Black J, Lynch A. Cyber threats to NATO from a multi-domain perspective. Cyber Threats and NATO 2030: *Horizon Scanning and Analysis.* 2020;126–150.

5 Ciepiela, P. and Venkateshwaran, B.V. (2017). Evolution of cyber threats and the development of new security architecture. In: *World Petroleum Congress*, D023S017R003. WPC.

6 Cunningham, C. (2020). *Cyber warfare–truth, tactics, and strategies: Strategic concepts and truths to help you and your organization survive on the battleground of cyber warfare.* Packt Publishing Ltd.

7 Efe, M.N. (2023). The effect of technological transformation on the management of security strategies. *İstanbul Kent Üniversitesi İnsan ve Toplum Bilimleri Dergisi.* 4 (2): 65–82.

8 Digmelashvili, T. and Lagvilava, L. (2023). Cyber deterrence strategies in the 21st century. *Future Human Image* 20: 6–17.

9 Faizan, A. (2024). Guardians of the digital realm: Navigating the frontiers of cybersecurity. *Integrated Journal of Science and Technology.* 1 (2).

10 Gioe, D.V., Goodman, M.S., and Stevens, T. (2020). Intelligence in the cyber era: Evolution or revolution? *Political Science Quarterly.* 135 (2): 191–224.

11 Goldman, E.O. (2024). Postscript: reflections and future directions for research and practice on cyber in competition, crisis and armed conflict. In: *Research Handbook on Cyberwarfare*, 390–400. Edward Elgar Publishing.

12 Kim, S.K., Cheon, S.P., and Eom, J.H. (2019). A leading cyber warfare strategy according to the evolution of cyber technology after the fourth industrial revolution. *International Journal of Advanced Computer Research.* 9 (40): 72–80.

13 Kostyuk, N. and Zhukov, Y.M. (2019). Invisible digital front: Can cyber attacks shape battlefield events? *Journal of Conflict Resolution.* 63 (2): 317–347.

14 Lehto, M. (2018). The modern strategies in the cyber warfare. In: *Cyber Security: Power and Technology*, 3–20. Springer.

15 Lewis, J.A., Lonergan, E.D., Voo, J. et al. (2023). *Evolving cyber operations and capabilities.* Center for Strategic and International Studies.

16 Nguyen, M. (2024). Cyber warfare and international security: Analyzing threats and defense strategies. *International Journal of Research and Review Techniques.* 3 (2): 10–18.

17 Noel, G.E. and Reith, M.G. (2021). Cyber warfare evolution and role in modern conflict. *Journal of Information Warfare.* 20 (4): 30–44.

18 O'hanlon ME. Military innovation and technological change: Preparing for the next generation of cyber threats. 2022.

19 Pruteanu, I.M., Fechete, L.A., and Gheţău, V.A. (2023). Navigating the complexities of air domain operations: Adapting to evolving environments. In: *International Scientific Conference "Strategies XXI". "Carol I"*, 479–492. National Defence University.

20 Sanders, C.M. (2018). The battlefield of tomorrow, today: Can a cyberattack ever rise to an act of war. *Utah Law Review.* 2018: 503.

21 Shahzad, A. (2024). Metamorphosis of warfare: War without warriors or battlefields. *Policy Perspectives.* 21 (1): 1–21.

22 Zakir, M.H., Allaudin, H., Khan, S.H., and Sultan, M. (2024). Adapting international humanitarian law for the digital battlefield: Navigating cyber warfare and technological advancements. *Pakistan Journal of Law, Analysis and Wisdom.* 3 (3): 54–66.

23 Sharma, P. and Gupta, H. (2024). Emerging cyber security threats and security applications in digital era. In: *2024 11th International Conference on Reliability, Infocom Technologies and Optimization (Trends and Future Directions) (ICRITO)*, 1–6. IEEE.

24 Smith, R. (2023). The evolution of cyber warfare strategies: A comparative analysis. *International Journal of Defence and Strategic Studies.* 1 (1): 1–11.

25 Song, U., Hur, G., Lee, S., and Park, J. (2024). Unraveling the dynamics of the cyber threat landscape: Major shifts examined through the recent societal events. *Sustainable Cities and Society* 103: 105265.

26 Sfetcu, N. (2024). *Advanced persistent threats in cybersecurity–cyber warfare.* MultiMedia Publishing.

27 Whyte, C. and Mazanec, B. (2023). *Understanding cyber-warfare: Politics, policy and strategy*. Routledge.

28 Ziauddin, F. (2024). Network security in modern warfare: The strategic advantage of the US in the digital battlefield. *Law, Policy and Society*. 1 (7): 69–92.

29 Zhu, L., Majumdar, S., and Ekenna, C. (2021). An invisible warfare with the internet of battlefield things: A literature review. *Human Behavior and Emerging Technologies* 3 (2): 255–260.

3

Fundamentals of Machine Learning and Data Analytics for Security

3.1 Introduction

The contemporary cybersecurity environment has become a dynamic and high-context ecosystem due to the sense of rapid digital transformation, the spread of devices with interconnected networks, and the increase in the sophistication of cyberattacks. The use of machine learning (ML) and data analytics has become a fundamental accelerator of developing intelligent, responsive, and active defense mechanisms in organizations in the age of Cybersecurity 5.0. Defense-in-depth (DiD), a multi-layer approach to security, which was initially applied in the military and industrial sphere, has recently become one of the primary digital protection paradigms [1, 2]. It combines the layered security models, artificial intelligence (AI), and predictive analytics to strengthen the systems against an ever-changing threat environment [3, 4].

In the past, DiD was theorized as a principle of safety in nuclear and industrial systems [5, 6]. Nonetheless, its inclusion in cybersecurity is a paradigm change to multi-layered, comprehensive protection that guarantees confidentiality, integrity, and availability of information in a wide range of industries, including healthcare, finance, transportation, and defense [7, 8]. According to the studies of Crossler et al. [9] and Naagas et al. [10], one security control cannot be used in the present-day digital environment, and instead, various layers of defense, including access control and encryption, behavioral analytics, and AI-based anomaly detection, should be combined and used in unison to decrease vulnerabilities.

The combination of machine learning and DiD has introduced a level of cybersecurity resilience. The ML algorithms have the ability to identify and forecast threats automatically through the analysis of extensive amounts of network traffic, user behavior, and system logs [11, 12]. Such data-driven systems are good at discovering sophisticated attack vectors, such as ransomware, phishing, and advanced persistent threats (APTs) [13, 14]. As an example, Mofidi et al. [15]

introduced a multi-layered intrusion detection system (L-IDS) to the Internet of Things (IoT) networks that implements the use of ML-based analytics in order to identify ransomware in an exceptionally accurate manner. Equally, Das [16] has shown that embedded defense modules are effective in protecting SCADA controllers by monitoring them adaptively and regulating them by learning.

DiD has also been found especially useful in the industrial setting, and autonomous vehicles and manufacturing plants are part of smart grids, autonomous vehicles, and manufacturing plants that are classified under cyber-physical systems [8, 17]. These systems rely on real-time data analytics and layered defenses so that the integrity of operations is guaranteed. Kurkute et al. [18] also highlighted the importance of the multi-layered defense concept in autonomous vehicles, noting that the ML algorithms play an important role in real-time intrusion prevention. In a similar vein, Matsuoka [19] also emphasized a data-centric DiD model, in which the central security asset is data, which is secured by encryption, access control, and ongoing behavioral analytics.

A layered defense has turned out to be a source of resilience in critical infrastructures. Netkachov et al. [20] quantitatively assessed the effectiveness of DiD in reducing systemic risks in cyber-physical infrastructures, but Hitefield [21] and Rahman et al. [22] discussed its use in software-defined and hardware security using logic locking and modular architecture. The combination of AI-based analytics into these layers allows for a response with speed to the decisions and taking automated actions to countermeasures that transform stationary defenses into adaptable ecosystems [11, 23].

New studies also focus on the idea that successful defense should be enforced not only by the traditional scope of protection but also by new ideas like Zero Trust architecture (ZTA) and Bayesian reasoning. Singh et al. [24] developed the DiD and Zero Trust model of 5G network security, and Alexander [4] used Bayesian networks to prioritize and optimize security investments in the context of layered controls. This paper points to the increased need for probabilistic, information-based security designs that can learn and respond to new attack patterns based on previous experience.

To protect the neobank technologies against the dynamically emerging cyber threats, AI and ML are becoming more prominent in the financial sector [11]. Data analytics is used in the detection of anomalous transactions, insider fraud, and regulatory violations in real time. Similarly, Saranya et al. [25] have shown that to achieve privacy and compliance, cloud environments need to be provided with effective multi-layered encryption and monitoring performed with analytics. Goldbarsht [26] additionally explained the role of multi-layered global structures and multi-layered soft law processes in reducing risks related to cyberterrorism and financial crimes.

In addition to businesses, DiD concepts have been applied to national security and national defense. Iman et al. [27] examined the concept of multi-layered weapon systems as an air defense of cities, whereas Thawani et al. [28] used the idea of layered protection in military scenarios with the help of advanced numerical computations. The importance of DiD in cybersecurity efforts of the military and the government was highlighted by Mughal [23] and Naseer [29], who noted the essential role of incorporating AI-driven analytics into situational awareness.

Although it has its benefits, DiD has tremendous problems in the age of AI and big data. These are the problems with data quality, the inability of different layers of defense to interact, and the growing complexity of adversarial attacks that seek to take advantage of the weaknesses of machine learning. Both Godakanda [30] and Patyal et al. [31] in their articles stressed the necessity of defense-conscious threat modeling and multi-layered ransomware protection, paying attention to the quality of resilient architectures. With organizations still moving toward Cybersecurity 5.0, machine learning, data analytics, and layered defense mechanism integration are groundbreaking solutions to sustainable, adaptive, and intelligent security systems.

Overall, the chapter provides the theoretical and practical basis of comprehending the synergies between machine learning and data analytics and the DiD principles to develop a proactive cybersecurity dynamic. It provides an extensive summary of the essentials underpinning Cybersecurity 5.0, an ecosystem characterized by resilience and automation along with smart threat anticipation [15, 17] by drawing upon classical notions of security [1] and providing a more modern-day approach (AI-driven methodology).

3.2 Foundations of Machine Learning in Cybersecurity

ML has become a revolutionary technology in the history of developing modern cybersecurity systems, as systems are able to automatically identify, process, and react to the emergence of threats in real time. ML models generate predictive data and dynamic defense features that are not directly fulfilled by traditional security protocols by analyzing data and extracting latent patterns. The combination of ML and DiD principles has resulted in a multi-layered design of smart, self-adaptive security, one that never stops changing to adapt to increasingly advanced cyber threats [2, 3].

3.2.1 Conceptual Overview of Machine Learning in Cyber Defense

In its most basic use, ML helps systems detect abnormal behavior, recognize unfamiliar attack vectors, and respond to those in an automated manner to reduce the exposure of risk. The majority of ML-based cybersecurity solutions are based on the foundational learning paradigms, namely, supervised, unsupervised, and reinforcement learning [11]. Decision trees, support vector machines, and neural

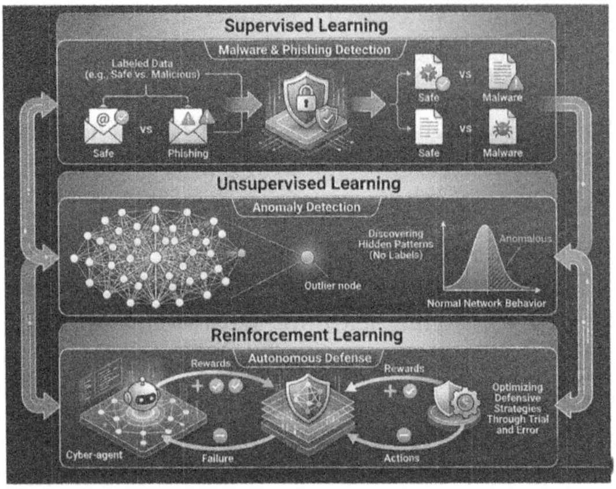

Figure 3.1 Machine Learning Paradigms in Cybersecurity Applications. "*Source:* Hewa Majeed Zangana"

networks are some of the most common supervised learning models used in malware classification and intrusion detection. The unsupervised learning methods, including clustering and principal component analysis (PCA), allow finding anomalies in large, unlabeled datasets, and it is essential to recognize the previously unknown threats [16]. The reinforcement learning provides an additional level of flexibility where security systems can learn the best response by taking trials and feedback, especially in a dynamic network setup [8].

Figure 3.1 outlines the basic machine learning paradigms, such as supervised, unsupervised, and reinforcement learning, and illustrates how these were applied in cybersecurity, including intrusion detection and autonomous network defense.

3.2.2 Defense-in-Depth and Machine Learning Integration

DiD is a military and nuclear safety concept, which was developed as a military and nuclear concept [1, 5] and has become the key to cybersecurity. It is based on the combination of several overlapping security layers, which ensure systems fail or get compromised. ML adds intelligence, flexibility, and automation to every level of defense provided by DiD. As an example, probabilistic ML models in the form of Bayesian networks can be used to prioritize and combine layers of defenses according to the probability of certain threat events [4].

Figure 3.2 demonstrates that machine learning is used to supplement the classic structure of Defense-in-Depth (DiD). Both security layers enjoy intelligent automation, data analytics, and adaptive learning, turning inactive protective measures into dynamic and predictive defense ecosystems.

ML-based DiD models have been very useful in critical systems like industrial control systems (ICS) and SCADA. Gubbi et al. [12] introduced an automated and optimized design flow to secure IC, which can use ML to detect threats and mitigate

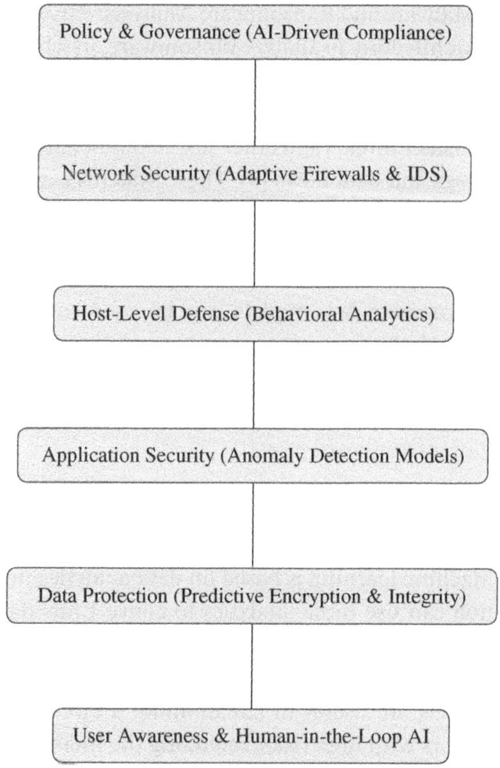

Figure 3.2 Integration of Machine Learning in the Defense-in-Depth Architecture. "*Source:* Hewa Majeed Zangana"

risks on hardware levels. Equally, Wai and Lee [17] implemented ML-enhanced DiD in SCADA networks for Industry 4.0, which guarantees real-time security control and predictive abnormalities. These systems take advantage of data-focused security designs that focus on lifelong learning and situational awareness [19, 22].

3.2.3 Machine Learning Applications in Cyber Threat Detection

Machine learning is beneficial to a number of functions in cybersecurity:

- Intrusion Detection Systems (IDS): ML algorithms have the ability to categorize the networks as malicious or benign. Mofidi et al. [15] proposed L-IDS, which is an IoT ransomware IDS based on the ML approach and optimizes features to improve detection accuracy.
- Phishing Detection: Rendall et al. [14] designed a multi-layered phishing detection that applies ensemble learning to detect deceptive URLs and email messaging with a high level of accuracy.

- Malware and Ransomware Analysis: Patyal et al. [31] developed a multi-layered architecture to analyze ransomware, in which ML models are constantly trained on new ransomware signatures to enhance the protection of endpoints.
- Anomaly and Insider Threat Detection: ML algorithms can be used to identify insider threats and other suspicious behavioral patterns of users based on access logs and data flows [9]. These systems can leverage defense-through deception [10], whereby ML models detect deceptive actions that are aimed at deceiving the attackers.

Moreover, ML models can be used to provide real-time threat intelligence through data aggregation and correlation across many layers of defense, and this feature is necessary to perform in a highly complex system like autonomous vehicles [18] and power transmission [8].

3.2.4 Data Analytics and Bayesian Reasoning in Predictive Security

Machine learning is based on data analytics in cybersecurity, where an organization can use these analytics to convert raw data into actionable intelligence. As explained by Alexander [4], Bayesian reasoning offers probabilistic models to analyze the security measures and prioritize mitigation strategies. Such analytical models are useful in streamlining a layered security architecture, especially in sectors with high risks, including the finance and defense sectors.

As an example, George [11] highlighted the revolutions of AI, blockchain, and ML analytics in the financial cybersecurity of neobanking systems to secure effective protection against fraud and unauthorized access. In like manner, Goldbarsht [26] pointed to the significance of multi-layered, data-enhanced frameworks in international counter-terrorist financing, in which ML models help identify suspicious money transactions.

3.2.5 Machine Learning for Critical Infrastructure Protection

Nuclear facilities, defense systems, and transportation networks are the most vulnerable to cyberattacks since they are critical infrastructure. The fraught of ML in DiD infrastructures improves the robustness of these infrastructures by means of predictive maintenance, anomaly detection, and autonomous response states. Ghidu et al. [6] also revealed the effectiveness of the DiD principles implementation in using intelligent analytics to enhance the security of nuclear power plants in their operations. On the same note, Das [16] developed ML-based embedded DiD modules on SCADA controllers to identify cyber intrusion early in the industrial processes.

ML-based layered security can also be applied in the military and defense sectors. Iman et al. [27] considered the topic of multi-layered weapon systems in contemporary warfare, pointing out the similarity of physical and cyber defense mechanisms. Thawani et al. [28] also presented multi-layered protection against guided mortar attacks, which resembles the defense in digital systems by applying layering. The significance of ML in defense operations was also highlighted in works by Mughal [23] and Naseer [29], with the importance of situational awareness models being adaptive and threat mitigation models being dynamic.

3.2.6 Challenges and Considerations in ML-Based Security

Although the potential of ML in cybersecurity is enormous, there are various challenges related to integrating it. The credibility of the ML systems can be undermined by data imbalance, adversarial attacks, and a lack of explanations. To reduce these threats, Godakanda [30] has suggested defense-aware threat modeling of IoT systems to prevent these threats by contextual defense mapping. Another theme emphasized by Ajayi [3] and Cherenko and Williams [7] is that to protect data confidentiality, data integrity, and data availability, it is necessary to align the capabilities of the ML with the human controls and policy-driven controls.

Furthermore, the emergence of ZTA frameworks has also had an impact on the implementation of ML models in security ecosystems. A DiD with a Zero Trust model of 5G networks was proposed by Singh et al. [24], in which the model assumes that the trust relationships between interconnected entities are constantly validated by ML.

3.2.7 Quantitative and Analytical Evaluation of Defense Models

The quantitative study is still essential in measuring the effectiveness of the ML-based defense systems. A detailed evaluation of DiD models in critical infrastructure conducted by Netkachov et al. [20] demonstrated that multi-layered and ML-enhanced systems significantly improve the resiliency to cyber-physical threats. Another author [1, 13] also made some groundwork in defense against APTs and stated that ML-based analytics should work in concert with layered controls to ensure long-term system resilience.

3.2.8 Toward Adaptive and Resilient Machine Learning Systems

The integration of ML, big data analytics, and DiD frameworks is being unveiled as the support system of digital resilience as organizations move to Cybersecurity

5.0. Hitefield [21] showed the integration of ML in software-defined systems to make real-time decisions, and Rahman et al. [22] investigated logic locking, a DiD-based ML system to implement hardware designs. The next generation of ML systems should thus be able to balance between automation and explainability and provide transparency without the loss of security performance [25].

Overall, machine learning in cybersecurity is based on three principles, namely, data-driven learning, layered defense, and adaptive intelligence. Nuclear and ICS, financial and IoT ecosystems, and more—ML has turned into the foundation of proactive defense, and it is defined by the age of intelligent systems that not only react against cyber threats but also foresee them [17]. The further entrapment of ML and data analytics in the DiD architectures is a paradigm shift—turning cybersecurity into a reactive field into a predictive science [2, 3, 11].

3.3 Essential Algorithms and Models for Security Applications

ML and data analytics are now the foundations of the modern strategies of cybersecurity because they allow organizations to construct adaptive and proactive structures of defense. Some of the largest to make their contribution to security applications are the algorithms and models that are created to enforce DiD and multi-layered protection—the methods that encompass redundancy, diversity, and smart automation to withstand advanced cyberattacks [1, 2]. In this section, the authors discuss the important algorithms and models, which are the foundations of these strategies, and their application in anomaly detection, threat intelligence, secure network design, and automated defense mechanisms.

3.3.1 Defense-in-Depth and Multi-Layered Security Architectures

The DiD approach is a paradigm that is still central to cybersecurity, where the approach has been focusing on a number of layers of security to counter vulnerabilities of hardware, software, and human interfaces. The concept goes beyond the scope of the traditional perimeter protection to encompass behavioral monitoring, intrusion prevention, and AI-assisted anomaly detection [19]. Chengcheng [5] notes that in contemporary adoption of DiD, physical, procedural, and digital security safeguards are used to respond to traditional and non-traditional attack vectors.

The empirical studies conducted by Crossler et al. [9] have proven that multi-layered user protection can play an important role in minimizing exposure to phishing and malware attacks. On the same note, Cherenko and Williams [7] also noted that layered defense models play a crucial role in safeguarding healthcare information in the context of HIPAA rules, ensuring the confidentiality and availability of information. Mughal [23] further claimed that implementing layered security on wireless networks would increase their ability to withstand data interception and denial of service (DoS) attacks.

The DiD model has been developed to include redundancy and smart automation in critical infrastructures. As an example, Ghidu et al. [6] have shown that the implementation of the principles of DiD in the work of nuclear power plants reduces the risks of cascade failures in the system to a minimum. A combination of intrusion detection algorithms and adaptive response models was suggested by Khanna et al. [8] as a multi-layered defense framework to protect the power transmission systems against cyber-induced outages.

3.3.2 Machine Learning Algorithms for Security Intelligence

Machine learning offers the analytical support of the layered defensive framework by automating the recognition and ranking of threats. Alexander [4] showed that Bayesian networks have the power to jointly perform depth-based defense mechanisms, which allow probabilistic threat analysis and the optimal use of resources to be conducted. These strategies make it easier to make smart decisions in which threats are prioritized in terms of threat and probability.

Decision trees, random forests, and support vector machines are supervised learning models that are commonly used to identify and classify malware [11]. On the contrary, unsupervised algorithms like clustering and PCA can boost the process of anomaly detection because of their capacity to detect abnormal network functioning [10]. Rahman et al. [22] combined DiD with logic locking in order to develop hardware-level protection features that are not susceptible to reverse-engineering attacks.

CNNs and deep learning models, in particular, convolutional and recurrent neural networks, have been utilized more often to detect phishing and classify ransomware in real time [14, 15]. These algorithms are used to detect complex patterns of temporal and spatial data and enhance detection and false positive rates.

3.3.3 Defense Models for Critical and Emerging Technologies

The new technologies, e.g., autonomous vehicles, IoT systems, and industrial control environments, require specific defense algorithms to address domain-specific threats. Kurkute et al. [18] also identified the importance of multi-layered cybersecurity systems to secure an autonomous vehicle network, with policies that denote the safe communication format and real-time intrusion detection. On the same note, Godakanda [30] streamlined IoT threat modeling through defense-conscious diagrams, hence improving situational awareness and system robustness.

In factories, Wai and Lee [17] created an AI-based multi-layer defense framework of SCADA systems within Industry 4.0, which incorporates predictive analytics to identify anomalies in the streams of operational data. Das [16] built upon this model by including the defense modules directly into the SCADA controllers, which would allow identifying the cyberattack on interdependent systems earlier.

The DiD concept spreads to government and military cybersecurity activities as well. Both Iman et al. [27] and Naseer [29] pointed to multi-layered weapon and network defense concepts, which can withstand redundancy and flexibility when used in critical mission settings. The use of such layered modeling strategies, even applied to physical defense systems against guided threats, has been shown to apply to physical defense systems as well and has been shown to be cross-domain useful when simulated numerically [28].

3.3.4 Integrating AI and Blockchain for Layered Security

The integration of AI and blockchain provides a revolutionary solution to digital ecosystem security. George [11] addressed the application of AI and blockchain technologies together within the financial sector to establish security in the neobank infrastructure through transparency and traceability of the data transactions. To improve the 5G network security, Singh et al. [24] integrated these technologies into a DiD and ZTA to overcome insider threats and authentication vulnerabilities.

Goldbarsht [26] also highlighted the idea that multi-layered solutions can reinforce global counter-terrorist funding efforts when used together with regulatory soft law frameworks, as it shows the flexibility of DiD strategies outside of conventional IT domains.

3.3.5 Optimized and Automated Security Design

The second stage of the evolution of DiD is automation of security engineering. Gubbi et al. [12] offered a perfectized strategy of secure IC design flow, consisting of multi-layered verification and encryption measures, which are resistant to the hardware level of attack. Likewise, an architecture of software-defined radio systems that use automated defense mechanisms to combine AI-based intrusion detection and signal integrity checks was introduced by Hitefield [21].

Both Mughal [2] and Ajayi [3] underlined that, besides deterring the stealing of intellectual property, a layered security defense is also able to reduce the harm done to information systems due to redundancy and adaptive protection. The effectiveness of such methods in the resilience of critical infrastructure was quantitatively confirmed by Netkachov et al. [20], who revealed the quantitative positive change in threat reduction.

Saranya et al. [25] also proved that the empirical implementation of the multi-layered security frameworks within the cloud systems can improve data privacy and regulatory compliance dramatically, and Mui et al. [31] were the first to introduce the ransomware defense systems that feature both reactive and proactive ML layers to ensure data integrity.

3.3.6 Summary of Algorithmic Defense Paradigms

The collective knowledge of the recent studies confirms that successful cybersecurity is based on layered, adaptive, and intelligent systems that are able to combine ML algorithms with DiD architectures. Such systems should never stop changing to accommodate the new vectors of attacks, using Bayesian reasoning [4], automation under AI control [12], and knowledge-specific modeling [8, 17]. These two strategies together will be a paradigmatic shift to Cybersecurity 5.0—a phase where machine intelligence and layered analytics become the foundation of active, resilient, and self-defending networked systems.

3.4 Data Analytics in Cybersecurity

Data analytics is the brain force of modern cybersecurity, and it enables systems to convert raw security data into actionable intelligence. Data analytics seals the divide between machine learning, automation, and DiD approaches in the context of Cybersecurity 5.0, as it allows adaptive threat detection, situational awareness, and prediction mechanisms of defense. The combination of sophisticated analytics and multifaceted security frameworks has transformed the way companies identify, process, and react to cyber threats in sophisticated digital contexts [1, 2].

3.4.1 The Role of Data Analytics in Layered Security Defense

The cornerstone of modern cybersecurity architecture, the principle of DiD, depends greatly upon the aggregation and analysis of multidimensional points of view of the different layers of the system. By using data-driven monitoring, security analysts will be able to detect abnormal trends that can indicate insider threats, malware propagation, or coordinated attacks [5, 19]. Ajayi [3] highlighted that the partnership between layered security and analytical insights is the determinant of preventing intellectual property theft and reducing the harm when it comes to information systems.

Cherenko and Williams [7] showed the same in the medical field, where the ongoing data analytics assist with HIPAA compliance by safeguarding patient information and system availability. Similarly, Crossler et al. [9] presented empirical results that multi-layered analytic systems enhance user safety against phishing and ransomware by correlating various behavioral and system-level signals.

3.4.2 Data Sources and Analytical Pipelines

In today's cybersecurity world, substantial amounts of data are produced, both in the form of endpoint sensors, IDS, and log servers and also in the form of cloud workloads. Analytical pipelines are therefore developed to aggregate, normalize, and correlate information between several levels of defense [23]. Das [16] suggested the implementation of analytics-based DiD modules into the SCADA controllers, which would identify and react to uncharacteristic system interactions in power and industrial systems. On the same note, Ghidu et al. [6] depicted that real-time analytics implemented via the DiD framework are useful in nuclear plant safety operations.

To measure the risk in such critical infrastructure, Netkachov et al. [20] created statistical models to assess the effectiveness of layered defenses, providing the number of measurements of the efficacy of resilience and vulnerability propagation. Such information-based methods allow the decision-makers to distribute defensive resources in a better way, which is the Bayesian model of prioritizing and combining multi-layered defense provided by Alexander [4].

Figure 3.3 is a common example of a cybersecurity data analytics pipeline, which shows how raw data can be converted to actionable threat intelligence in terms of preprocessing, feature engineering, model training, and feedback integration.

3.4.3 Analytical Models for Threat Detection

One of the core elements of cybersecurity analytics is the use of machine learning models in the identification of patterns and the detection of anomalies. Alexander [4] defines Bayesian inference as forming probabilistic reasoning, which is applicable in threat assessment by synthesizing uncertain evidence across several layers of security. It improves predictability when it comes to the detection of zero-day vulnerabilities and insider assaults.

Classification of malicious behaviors in IoT networks and enterprise networks is done through supervised learning algorithms, including decision trees, random forests, and neural networks [11]. In systems of early anomaly detection, where there is limited labeled data, unsupervised analytics is used, such as clustering and dimensionality reduction [10]. Mofidi et al. [15] extended this by a

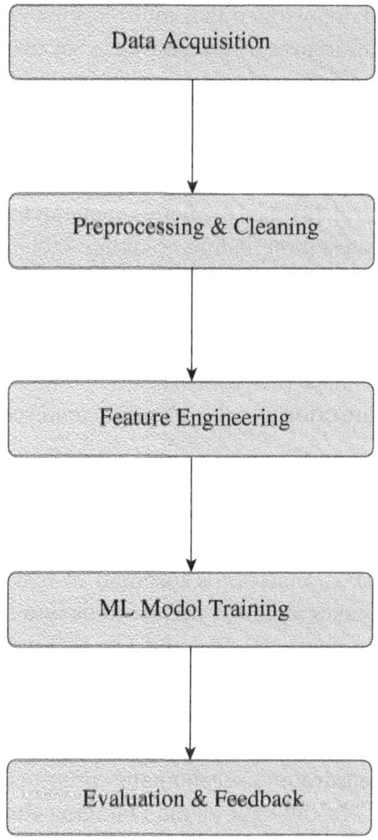

Figure 3.3 Data Analytics Pipeline for Machine Learning-Based Cybersecurity. "*Source:* Hewa Majeed Zangana"

multi-layered ransomware detector model of IoT systems (L-IDS) with the help of correlation analysis between the anomalous encryption patterns.

Moreover, Rendall et al. [14] have shown that the use of advanced phishing detection systems, which are based on statistical and semantic analytics, is more effective than the use of traditional rule-based detection. These systems are dynamically adjusted to the changing behavior of threats using natural language processing and feature engineering.

3.4.4 Predictive and Behavioral Analytics

Predictive analytics is a game-changer based on cybersecurity as a discipline, turning it into a proactive one. Through time-series modeling and deep learning, organizations may predict new trends in attacks and strengthen defenses before attacks happen [18]. Military studies by Iman et al. [27] and Naseer [29] demonstrated that multi-layered analytic frameworks are superior to situational awareness by forecasting cyber maneuvers by the enemy and also improving the resilience of command systems.

These two contributions were made by Godakanda [30], who provided defense-conscious threat modeling diagrams based on the integration of analytical data streams of the IoT network to optimize the detection efficiency. Equally, Khanna et al. [8] used predictive analytics to protect the power transmission system against substation failure, making their DiD model integrate the use of ML-based predictions.

Using cloud environments, Saranya et al. [25] were able to empirically prove that predictive analytics can contribute to increased privacy and regulatory compliance because it detects anomalies in access and prevents breaches early. These are critical to the adaptive cloud security and multi-tenant data governance.

3.4.5 Data Analytics for Critical Infrastructure and Emerging Technologies

Data analytics is essential in real-time surveillance and management in high-stakes sectors of autonomous systems, critical infrastructure, and 5G networks. In Industry 4.0, Wai and Lee [17] used a multi-layered analytic defense system on SCADA infrastructures that combined behavioral analytics, fault tolerance, and anomaly detection. Their methodology is similar to that of Gubbi et al. [12], who gave automated secure IC design flows based on analytic optimization to find hardware-level anomalies prior to deployment.

In the case of the emerging financial technologies, George [11] emphasized how the combination of AI, machine learning, and blockchain analytics ensures neobank ecosystems resist fraudulent and adversarial actions. Similarly, Singh et al. [24] implemented zero-trust analytics in the 5G networks to dynamically evaluate the performance of users and devices so that adaptive trust checks can be performed at each access point.

Physical systems are also covered by defensive analytics. Thawani et al. [28] used numerical modeling analytics to model the protection of a guided mortar threat through the use of layers, which shows the cross-domain capabilities of the data-driven model of defense. Kurkute et al. [18] applied the multi-modal analytics to protect the vehicular networks in the context of autonomous systems, where the telemetry, sensor, and network streams are combined.

3.4.6 Quantitative and Governance-Oriented Analytics

Not only does data analytics provide technical defenses, but it is also used to inform cybersecurity governance and compliance. In its proposal, Goldbarsht [26] suggested the application of the layered analytic frameworks in the global counter-terrorist financing systems to enhance cross-border cyber resilience through the mechanism of soft law. Likewise, Holmberg [1] and Matsuoka [19] have pointed to the fact that the principles of data-centric DiD are the foundation of safety assurances and risk-based governance.

The article by Patyal et al. [31] was a first-of-its-kind multi-layered ransomware defense model that employed quantitative analytics to determine vulnerabilities in the system. Their style uses data visualization dashboards to give real-time information about network health. This was augmented by Hitefield [21] with analytics-based architectures of software-defined radio systems, where dynamic security configurations are provided according to ongoing signal evaluation.

According to Ajayi [3] and Mughal [23], data analytics is the only means to maintain the continuity of layered defenses that allow timely warning systems and real-time forensic analysis and related countermeasures in both civilian and defense environments.

3.4.7 Integrated Analytical Frameworks for Cyber Resilience

With the increasing volume of data and the sophistication of attacks, it is now necessary to incorporate analytics into all layers of cybersecurity architecture. Mughal [2] and Rahman et al. [22] emphasized that data-driven DiD policies increase logic locking, hardware certificates, and encryption hardiness. Ghidu et al. [6] and Das [16] highlighted that continuous analytics in the defense and industrial space offers feedback loops that enhance the operational safety and security performance.

The approach of multi-layered frameworks, defined by Chengcheng [5] and Wai and Lee [17], is now due to the combination of statistical analysis, AI-driven modeling, and context-aware correlation engines to produce dynamic defense ecosystems. These systems are developed through continual analytics, and therefore, Cybersecurity 5.0 becomes one of predictive flexibility, self-recovering structures, and automated reaction.

3.4.8 Summary

Cybersecurity data analytics do not represent the past monitoring of an event; rather, they are a strategic facilitator of flexible defense. With a combination of machine learning, predictive model, and multi-layered defense structures in place, organizations can now recognize, foresee, and intercept threats at a level that has never been seen before. A combination of Bayesian reasoning [4], automation [12], and governance analytics [26] forms the basis of cybersecurity 5.0 of resilient, intelligent, and proactive digital defense systems.

3.5 Feature Engineering and Data Preprocessing for Cybersecurity

In the changing field of cybersecurity, the use of feature engineering and preprocessing of data is the basis of creating accurate, reliable, and intelligent ML models. The superiority of any ML-based security system is highly determined by the quality, relevance, and representation of the features of data generated by different digital ecosystems. In DiD, feature engineering is closely aligned with multilayered defense design, which is aimed at detecting, preventing, and addressing cyber threats on a variety of levels within the framework of the system [1, 3].

The initial defense mechanism is data preprocessing, where raw, messy, or unfinished cybersecurity data (typically obtained through logs, sensors, firewalls, IDS, etc.) are cleaned, normalized, and transformed [2, 9]. These measures are necessary to ensure consistency and accuracy, particularly in processing heterogeneous data streams of networks, the IoT, and vital infrastructures. Chengcheng [5] and Ghidu et al. [6] point out that the contemporary understanding of the DiD principle transcends more than merely conventional barriers and focuses on the integrity of data and awareness of the situation, which makes preprocessing an essential part of proactive cyber protection.

3.5.1 Data Acquisition and Cleaning

Cybersecurity data is generally of a high-dimensional nature, and it is usually represented as IP addresses, timestamps, protocols, and metrics of behavior. Data cleaning must be done before any ML model can be trained to learn meaningful patterns and remove redundant, inconsistent, and erroneous entries. Cherenko and Williams [7] emphasized that the healthcare systems depend on careful preprocessing in order to maintain the confidentiality of patient data and still ensure the availability of the systems. Likewise, Das [16] stressed that preprocessing steps, including the removal of noise through interdependent sensor log elimination, are necessary in order to protect SCADA controllers, as they can lead to a significant improvement of model reliability in identifying cyberattacks.

To support a network environment on a large scale, the data deduplication and imputation methods are essential. Structured data cleaning is efficient in avoiding false positives in detecting DoS/DDoS attacks, which, as Naagas et al. [10] showed in a campus network defense model, is effective in avoiding false positives. Moreover, in financial and cloud environments, George [11] and Saranya et al. [25] showed that robust preprocessing enhances fraud detection and data privacy through normalization and outlier management.

3.5.2 Feature Extraction and Transformation

The feature extraction converts uninformed network and system data to informative features that indicate the underlying security state. As suggested by Gubbi et al. [12] and Mughal [23], automated pipelines are proposed based on embedded analytics to extract context-sensitive security properties based on encrypted communications and circuit design. On the same note, Khanna et al. [8] adopted a layered defense framework that removed temporal and spatial associations among power system events to identify cyber-induced outages.

Widely used feature transformation methods are:

- Traffic pattern analysis: statistical encoding (mean, variance, and entropy).
- Dimensionality reduction (e.g., PCA or autoencoders) to eliminate unnecessary correlations [14].
- Frequency-domain and logarithmic maps that enable the signals in a SCADA and IoT system to be more interpretable [17].

Such transformations contribute to the alleviation of the imbalance in the data and skewness as a result of the effective discrimination of benign and malicious behavior by the ML classifiers, including random forests, SVMs, or deep neural networks [15, 22].

The feature engineering process in cybersecurity analytics is represented in Figure 3.4; it demonstrates how the raw network and system data can be turned into meaningful representations that enhance the quality and effectiveness of ML models.

3.5.3 Feature Selection and Dimensionality Optimization

Since the amount of network data is enormous, the features should be filtered to improve the computational efficiency and prevent overfitting. Alexander [4] showed how Bayesian networks could be used to rank features that provided the highest levels of detection at each level of defense. On the same note, Godakanda [30] suggested defense-conscious threat modeling, which distinguishes security attributes, including vulnerability exposure or frequency of privilege escalation, as the most applicable to the IoT setting.

There are broadly known feature selection methods:

- Filter-based (e.g., Chi-square, information gain)
- Wrapper-based (e.g., recursive feature elimination)
- Embedded techniques (e.g., LASSO, random forest importance)

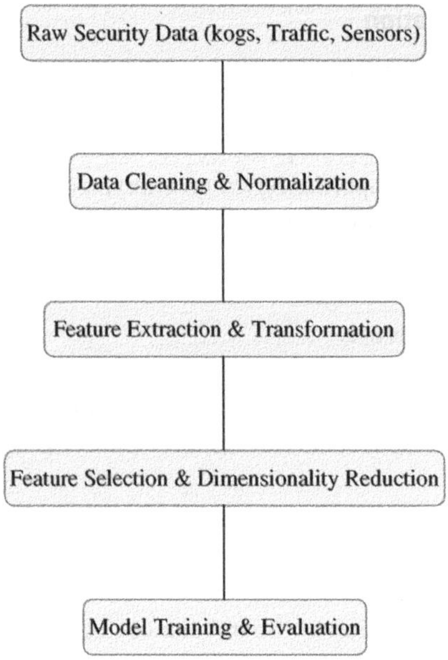

Figure 3.4 Feature Engineering Workflow for Machine Learning in Cyber Defense. "*Source:* Hewa Majeed Zangana"

The study by Kurkute et al. [18] used a hybrid system that optimized the features to protect autonomous vehicles and make sure that each detection pipeline layer provided distinct knowledge without duplication. On the same note, Matsuoka [19] placed special focus on data-centric defense, where the critical attributes are given priority by encryption strength, frequency of access, and authentication pattern, to represent the risk profile of the system.

3.5.4 Data Normalization, Encoding, and Balancing

It should be trained with normalized and coded data. Min-max scaling or z-score normalization are some methods that make sure that the model is not biased by features of varying magnitudes. One-hot encoding or label encoding is used to encode qualitative data into a numeric format when knowing the protocol types or user access level (categorical attributes).

In their works, Iman et al. [27] and Thawani et al. [28] emphasized the significance of data standardization in layered defense simulation, demonstrating that the inconstancy of the input scales may undermine the quality of defense models. Besides, class imbalance is solved with data balancing, including synthetic oversampling of SMOTE or adaptive reweighting, which is a common issue in cybersecurity data, where attacks and normal operations are far more common [31].

3.5.5 Advanced Feature Engineering Using AI and Analytics

Recent innovations use AI to engage in feature engineering to automate the process of finding more complex relations in cybersecurity data. An example of how the principles of ZTA were combined with an ML pipeline to create access control features on the fly on the basis of behavioral analytics was presented by Singh et al. [24]. Similar research conducted by Netkachov et al. [20] and Naseer [29] demonstrated the quantitative advantages of automated feature learning to critical infrastructure and military systems to increase resilience due to adaptive pattern recognition.

Autoencoders, graph neural networks (GNNs), or transformers are increasingly being applied to learn hierarchical feature representations with deep learning models. Gubbi et al. [12] and Rahman et al. [22] found that logic locking and circuit defense systems could be made more resilient with the inclusion of AI-driven optimization, whereas Ajayi [3] asserted that the adaptive analytics framework could enhance the intellectual property protection by providing the context of threat intelligence.

The importance of multi-layered analytical frameworks to compliance and transparency is also mentioned by Holmberg [1] and Goldbarsht [26], where the characteristics based on transaction monitoring and behavior modeling feed into soft law mechanisms of cyber governance.

3.5.6 Integration with Multi-Layered Defense Systems

The process of feature engineering is not a standalone process aspect of the multi-layered security architecture, as it provides contextual knowledge to every level of defense. The architecture proposed by Hitefield [21] is a layered security architecture of software-defined radio systems: In this case, preprocessed data streams can be used to detect anomalies in real time. On the same note, Mui et al. [32] showed that the richness of features enables a DiD system to identify a zero-day threat with the help of ensemble analytics.

According to Wai and Lee [17] and Mughal [23], the incorporation of engineered features into SCADA, IoT, and industrial systems will guarantee coordinated threat detection on both the physical and digital levels. These AIs enable predictive surveillance, measurement of risks, and proactive control and move the paradigm to Cybersecurity 5.0, where ML and analytics are used to provide sustained situational awareness.

To conclude, intelligent cybersecurity systems are developed on the basis of feature engineering and data preprocessing as the analytical foundation. They convert raw and heterogeneous data into high-quality and structured data that can be used by AI to make decisions. All these processes can be used to achieve adaptive and layered protection in both networks and industrial architectures and in national infrastructures by incorporating statistical rigor, machine learning, and DiD principles [6, 8, 24]. Since the digital threat environment continues to evolve into more skilled, the capacity to design pertinent features and preprocess information efficiently will still be a determinant in the success of proactive and hardy cyber defense systems.

3.6 Applications of ML and Data Analytics in Cybersecurity

ML and data analytics have transformed the sphere of cybersecurity as they allow detecting, preventing, and responding to threats in an intelligent, automated, and adaptive manner. These technologies are an analytical foundation of DiD architectures, which make sure that cybersecurity systems keep up with more sophisticated attacks. ML and analytics can be combined to persistently track, define the behavior, and proactively defend against attacks, which would yield resilience in various sectors such as industrial systems, finance, healthcare, IoT, and critical infrastructure [3, 5].

3.6.1 Intrusion Detection and Anomaly Detection Systems

Intrusion detection is one of the most developed and significant applications of ML in cybersecurity. ML models are trained with the help of algorithms, such as decision trees, random forests, support vector machines (SVMs), and neural networks, to differentiate between normal and malicious activities. A study by Das [16] applied an embedded DiD module in identifying cyberattacks in interdependent SCADA controllers, showing how a supervised learning model can be used to minimize false positives and enhance situational awareness of ICS. On the same note, Wai and Lee [17] introduced an ML-based, multi-layered SCADA protection system in Industry 4.0 settings that took into account the use of real-time analytics to identify anomalies at the operational layers.

Mofidi et al. [15] have proposed L-IDS as a layered IDS that is fueled by ML to detect the presence of ransomware attacks based on network patterns and device actions within the IoT ecosystem. Godakanda [30] further developed it with an idea of defense-conscious threat modeling, which allows maximizing the protection of the IoT devices by incorporating the principles of DiD and incorporating them into intelligent analytics. These adaptive systems illustrate how ML can be used to provide dynamic pattern recognition to facilitate the evolution of defenses to address system changes in type and strength.

3.6.2 Malware and Ransomware Detection

Machine learning has taken center stage in the classification of malware and ransomware detection through automation of feature extraction and classification. Patyal et al. [31] proposed a multi-layered defense architecture with ML models to identify ransomware behavior prior to the start of encryption processes to significantly enhance response time. Rahman et al. [22] also highlighted the significance of the DiD logic locking system, which incorporates ML with circuit-level security to ensure intellectual property is safeguarded in hardware systems.

The latest developments also include deep learning when convolutional networks and recurrent networks process binary files and logs of the system and detect anomalous sequences that may indicate malware activity [2, 4]. Mughal [23] further applied it to wireless network security, whereby the classifier of ML was used to detect suspicious communication channels. This multi-layered ML application throughout the network stack prevents data exfiltration and stealing intellectual property, as Ajayi [3] noted, which makes this a multi-dimensional threat resilience objective.

3.6.3 Phishing, Fraud, and Social Engineering Detection

Phishing has been among the most widespread forms of cybersecurity risks, and ML has been a successful solution. In their study, Rendall et al. [14] created a multi-layered phishing detection model that utilizes the supervised learning algorithm to classify malicious URLs, emails, and domains depending on linguistic, structural, and behavioral characteristics. The research by Cherenko and Williams [7] also indicated that layered ML-based methods defend the HIPAA data in medical systems because phishing content is filtered, and the service remains available.

George [11] demonstrated the application of AI and data analytics in the financial industry, revealing how these technologies ensure the security of the new neobank technologies by detecting fraud cases with the help of transaction analysis, user behavioral profiling, and anomaly scoring. Likewise, Goldbarsht [26] has emphasized applying multi-layered analytical models to trace and disrupt terrorist funding chains, which indicates that ML-facilitated forensics is no longer limited to corporate security but can be used in global anti-terror operations.

3.6.4 Cyber Defense for Critical Infrastructure and Industrial Systems

The use of machine learning in critical infrastructure security is critical in terms of sustaining operational stability within the energy, nuclear, and transportation sectors. Ghidu et al. [6] used a DiD approach to improve the safety of nuclear power plants by applying predictive analytics using ML to identify failure modes and faults caused by cyberattacks. Khanna et al. [8] created an ML-based power transmission defense system in which a regression and reinforcement learning algorithm identifies abnormalities in the substation due to a cyberattack.

Netkachov et al. [20] presented a quantitative analysis of the DiD systems based on the ML implementation in cyberspace infrastructure, showing significant resilience enhancements by the introduction of the ML-driven layers of decision-making. Both Chengcheng [5] and Hitefield [21] pointed out that ML can be used to enhance the scalability and adaptability of defense layers through learning the data flows in real time, which is critical to industrial automation systems that exist in the environment of a constant threat.

3.6.5 Data Analytics for Threat Intelligence and Predictive Security

Data analytics transforms unrefined security logs and network traces into thwartable threat information. More sophisticated tools like clustering, association rule mining, and graph analytics enable companies to find relationships between attack indicators and predictive threat modeling. Matsuoka [19] talked about the data-centric DiD paradigm according to which analytics is the basis of real-time decision-making in cyberspace operations.

According to Alexander [4], Bayesian networks are instrumental in quantifying and prioritizing risks on an inter-layer of defense. These probabilistic models involve analytics to predict the likelihood of threats and suggest the best means of allocation of defenses. Likewise, as Iman et al. [27] have shown, ML-optimized analytical models can streamline city air defense with prioritization of threats in real time—a concept also relevant to the operations centers of cybersecurity (CSOCs).

Naseer [29] highlighted the value of ML-based analytics in strategic cyber defense in the military and governmental scenario, where real-time monitoring of data enhances response speed and minimizes the risk of a massive data breach. The deception-based analytics that emulate decoy systems to deceive the attackers were proposed by Naagas et al. [10] and Mughal [23] as useful in strengthening data-driven countermeasures.

3.6.6 Cloud Security and Privacy-Preserving Analytics

Data privacy, compliance, and resilience are the most important requirements that organizations face as they move to cloud infrastructure. Saranya et al. [25] conducted an empirical study on best practices in cloud data protection, and in that study, the authors emphasize that ML contributes to improving the encryption management system and intrusion detection with the help of continuous data analytics. Singh et al. [24] suggested combining the ZTA with DiD solutions under the CRM of ML verification of user and device behavior in a dynamic manner more so in 5G networks.

Gubbi et al. [12] suggested an automated secure IC design flow, which uses ML analytics in the optimization of circuit integrity and the detection of hardware-level intrusions in attributes of IoT and cloud-enabled settings. These inventions highlight the expansion of the conventional security perimeter by AI-based analytics to instill intelligence into all layers of the system [17].

3.6.7 Multi-Domain and Layered Security Architectures

ML combined with analytics enhances the multi-layered defense architectures on which Cybersecurity 5.0 is based. Holmberg [1] theorized the DiD model as the hierarchical framework of protection processes, including policy-based controls and technical protection. John [13] further discussed this by demonstrating how the ML can be used to identify APTs in network and application layers with anomaly-based classifiers.

Kurkute et al. [18] used a comparable structure within the framework of autonomous vehicles, whereby the analysis of the ML was used to implement end-to-end cybersecurity, including sensor fusion and network traffic analysis. Iman et al. [27] and Thawani et al. [28] have shown that the multi-layered predictive modeling that is originally developed to serve a physical defense system can be effectively transferred to cyber defense using cross-domain analytics.

Both Mughal [2] and Ajayi [3] point out that genuine resilience in cybersecurity can be attained when the three principles of ML, analytics, and DiD intersect and create adaptive ecosystems that can learn from each attempted breach. This integration not only reduces the vulnerability but also encourages continuous self-improvement of the digital infrastructures.

The convergence of machine learning and analytics with DiD is shown in Figure 3.5. Every layer is also empowered with intelligent automation and adaptive analytics, which make it possible to have proactive and predictive defense capabilities across domains.

3.6.8 Summary

Data analytics and machine learning have changed the nature of cybersecurity from reactive protection to proactive intelligence. They are also used in intrusion detection, malware prevention, phishing defense, and critical infrastructure

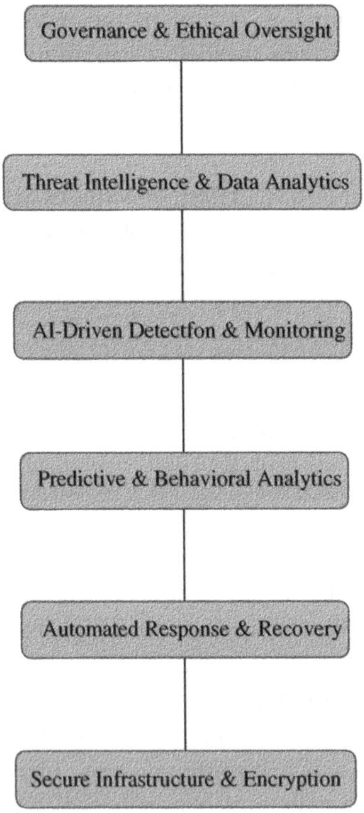

Figure 3.5 Machine Learning-Enhanced Multi-Layered Defense-in-Depth Framework. "*Source:* Hewa Majeed Zangana"

protection and reflect the spirit of layered and adaptive security [9, 22]. Through predictive modeling, automation, and data-driven decision-making, organizations can transform the vision of Cybersecurity 5.0, in which the combination of ML algorithms and analytical insights will ensure networks, systems, and data are defended in the constantly changing digital environment.

3.7 Evaluation Metrics and Model Validation

ML model evaluation and validation are a foundation toward building trust, reliability, and practicality in DiD models. Performance metrics are vital in the field of cyber defense, where it is necessary to measure the accuracy, strength, and generalization of the algorithm used to identify, foretell, and counter threats. It expounds on performance indices, model validation techniques, and domain-specific assessment frameworks through which the requirements of current, multi-layered protection architectures (that demand high standards) are met by the ML-driven cybersecurity systems.

3.7.1 Importance of Evaluation in Cyber Defense Systems

The testability of the ML models in the context of cybersecurity environments will mean that the detection systems can be effectively used in the changing and unstable environment of threats. The DiD principle, according to Holmberg [1], is that every level of protection has to be evaluated separately on its ability to cover up failures at the next level. Correspondingly, Crossler et al. [9] focused on the empirical validation of the mechanisms of protection in layers that can be used as the basis of both user confidence and resilience of operations. Assessment procedures should therefore not be restricted to the induction of technical performance but should determine flexibility in the presence of adversarial and zero-day attacks [13].

3.7.2 Common Evaluation Metrics in Cybersecurity ML Models

Most machine learning models that are applied in cybersecurity are assessed by a mix of general statistical measures along with domain-specific ones. Some of the most commonly employed ones are:

- Accuracy, Precision, Recall, and F1-score: These measures give a basic understanding of the forming ability of a model. Precision and recall especially play a pivotal role in ransomware or phishing detection because false positives may overload an analyst, whereas false negatives may lead to undetected intrusions [14, 31].
- Receiver Operating Characteristic (ROC) Curve and AUC: According to Alexander [4], Bayesian-based defense prioritization, ROC–AUC is used to visualize trade-offs between true positive and false positive rates at different thresholds, which is important in tuning real-time IDS.
- Confusion Matrix: Confusion matrices are used to specify the performance of the classification based on several threat categories, which provide an opportunity to analyze individual types of attacks in detail, the most difficult to identify [16].
- Mean Time to Detect (MTTD) and Mean Time to Respond (MTTR): In industrial control networks and other operation systems in particular, time measures are a necessity to evaluate the efficiency of automated mitigating measures [6, 17].
- False Alarm Rate (FAR) and Detection Rate (DR): This is a common metric in IDS and ransomware detection systems [15] to strike a balance between the sensitivity of the system and its reliability.

3.7.3 Model Validation Techniques

Model validation guarantees the extension of the ML algorithms beyond their training sets. Conventional methods, such as k-fold cross-validation and hold-out validation, continue to be popular; however, domain-specific structures have adopted layered testing environments. As an example, Chengcheng [5] and Khanna et al. [8] suggested the hierarchical validation of the multi-layered cyber defense model in power and energy systems, allowing the model to remain stable in different threat conditions.

- Cross-Validation of Defense Models: Multi-stage cross-validation can be used to measure the resilience of models to detect coordinated or cascading cyber-physical attacks [20].
- Monte Carlo Simulations: Alexander [4] proposed using Bayesian inference and simulation-based validation to measure uncertainty in security prioritization models.
- Scenario-Based Validation: Kurkute et al. [18] used scenario-based validation for the operation of autonomous vehicle defense systems that showed the usefulness of ML algorithms in the case of simulated multi-vector cyber intrusions.

3.7.4 Defense-in-Depth Validation Frameworks

The validation of layered security systems needs a technical and architectural assessment to be defined. Mughal [2], Hitefield [21], and Mughal [23] emphasized the need to validate interdependencies across levels of security within the system, including physical access controls and network encryption up to behavioral anomaly detection. Godakanda [30] built upon this concept and proposed a defense-aware IoT threat modeling framework with predictive analytics based on a machine learning framework and authenticated using attack simulations. In a similar fashion, Gubbi et al. [12] pointed at the automation of secure integrated circuit (IC) design flows, where the ML models were quantitatively tested to be used in a zero-trust fashion by the DiD validation.

Resilience testing is also part of holistic validation, as Ghidu et al. [6] show in nuclear infrastructure security and redundancy evaluation, as implemented by Iman et al. [27] and Naseer [29] in the context of a military network. They also make sure that every layer of defense is used to counter the potential weaknesses of other layers, which is in line with the concept of multi-tier principles proposed by Holmberg [1] and Matsuoka [19].

3.7.5 Quantitative and Qualitative Performance Evaluation

Although quantitative measures give performance metrics that can be measured, qualitative appraisal is essential when it comes to determining interpretability, transparency, and flexibility. Goldbarsht [26] emphasized that security assessment should be based on the aspects of governance and compliance, particularly in soft-law systems, such as international counter-terrorist financing strategies. This opinion was supported by Saranya et al. [25] when it comes to cloud security assessment, since privacy-saving solutions should strike a balance between lawfulness and AI performance.

George [11] and Singh et al. [24] also addressed the topic of hybrid validation of emerging financial and 5G systems, which involved explainable ML evaluation and ZTA evaluations. By combining these approaches, cybersecurity systems can be better predictable, and the integration of AI can be ethical.

3.7.6 Benchmarking and Continuous Model Assessment

Continuous validation pipelines and benchmark datasets play an important role in the preservation of model efficacy. To achieve adaptive learning, Ajayi [3] and Thawani et al. [28] stressed the importance of iterative benchmarking based on multi-domain datasets. Periodic retraining on new threat signature countermeasures makes models resilient to dynamically changing environments.

In continuous validation, e.g., as proposed by Naagas et al. [10] and Mui et al. [32], the networks of deception and multi-layered traps are used to challenge the adaptability of models to adversarial pressure. Rahman et al. [22] showed that logic locking (DiD validation) can also prevent the reverse-engineering attack on the model integrity, which is becoming an urgent issue in hardware-based security.

3.7.7 Summary of Evaluation Practices

Extensive testing and model validation systems can allow ML-based security systems to work in the DiD paradigm. Such practices not only guarantee great accuracy in threat detection but also guarantee operational resilience, interpretability, and compliance of finance, IoT, industrial control, and critical infrastructure domains. The combination of ML and data analytics in cybersecurity has been continually developing and is currently advancing toward complete adaptability, explainability, and proactive defense models through quantitative and qualitative evaluation and simulation-based testing.

To conclude, the intersection between statistical rigor, domain-specific validation, and layered testing models, which have been demonstrated in works by Mughal [2] and Wai and Lee [17] and others, will lead to the implementation of reliable AI-driven cybersecurity systems in the age of Cybersecurity 5.0.

3.8 Challenges and Limitations

Although ML and DiD have demonstrated impressive advancements in the field of cybersecurity, it is important to note that there are still a number of issues and constraints that hinder the exploitation of these techniques. These shortcomings are the technological, architectural, operational, and human factors leading to the creation of resilience of contemporary defense frameworks. Knowledge about these limitations is critical to improve future cybersecurity systems and make sure that the AI-based, layered-defense architectures work well in dynamic threat spaces.

3.8.1 Complexity of Multi-Layered Defense Architectures

DiDmodels are based on the integration of various security levels; however, this comes at the cost of management and scaling as well as performance. Holmberg [1] stressed that DiD can strengthen resilience, but complex relationships between layers of the concept might build unpredictable vulnerabilities. As an illustration, a conflict in the area of detection could lead to overlaps and resource wastefulness, especially in such critical infrastructures as power systems [8] and nuclear operations [6]. Likewise, Chengcheng [5] observed that with the development of defense strategies, interoperability between technological layers is becoming more challenging, and it needs to be highly synchronized and aligned in policies across systems.

3.8.2 Data Quality, Availability, and Bias

The quality and representativeness of the data are important to machine learning models applied to security analytics. Das [16] emphasized that SCADA systems data are highly likely to include noise, inconsistencies, and incomplete data, which influence the accuracy of models. Moreover, biased or unbalanced datasets may cause biased threat detection results, which raise false positives or false negatives. The author of the study [30] asserted that IoT environments have an extra limitation on data labeling and contextual interpretation, and it is hard to obtain strong, defense-conscientious threat modeling systems. Moreover, according to Matsuoka [19], data-centric DiD also demands constant data validation and normalization, which is still a resource-intensive and error-prone activity.

3.8.3 Integration Challenges and System Interoperability

The existing DiD architectures and AI and ML solutions are almost always faced with compatibility and operation challenges. Gubbi et al. [12] talked about the interoperability between heterogeneous hardware and software elements required by automated secure IC design processes, but integration vulnerabilities can occur because of gaps. Iman et al. [27] observed that multi-layered systems of weaponry develop challenges in synchronization between various layers of operation, and such challenges may slow or skew real-time processes of responding to them in an organization. Equally, Ajayi [3] has highlighted that to seamlessly implement layered security defenses across the business systems, strong alignment is needed among organizational policy, network settings, and AI-supported monitoring systems.

3.8.4 Resource Constraints and Performance Overheads

Implementation of multi-layered defense systems in networks, IoT, and industrial systems is very costly in terms of calculation and money. According to Mughal [2, 23], the preservation of defense layers in multiple wireless networks creates bandwidth and latency trade-offs, especially in the high-frequency communication system. Similarly, Wai and Lee [17] noted that the implementation of layered AI-based monitoring in the SCADA system of Industry 4.0 requires a significant amount of computational power that small organizations might not have. Rahman et al. [22] also cautioned that logic locking in hardware security can be taught with DiD mechanisms that impose limitations on the escalation of system complexity and power consumption.

3.8.5 Adversarial Attacks and Model Robustness

Machine learning models are also prone to adversarial manipulation, whereby attackers tamper with the data fed into them to fool classification algorithms. Indeed, as shown by Rendall et al. [14], adaptive adversarial methods can be used to evade phishing detection systems due to the vulnerability of the MLs. Likewise, Mofidi et al. [15] found out that IoT ransomware detection systems have lower reprogramming resistance to adversarial reprogramming. Alexander [4] suggested a possible countermeasure of uncertainty estimation, Bayesian networks, but probabilistic models do not defend against dynamic zero-day exploits.

3.8.6 Human Factors and Behavioral Limitations

One of the poorest areas of cybersecurity is human behavior. Crossler et al. [9] discovered that despite having well-thought-out multi-layered defense strategies, users must be negligent, have poor password habits, and not follow security procedures in order to discredit the strategies. Cherenko and Williams [7] cited these problems in healthcare systems, whereby, in spite of strong HIPAA-compliant protection, human error still led to the repeat of phishing attacks. According to John [13], to fight APTs, one needs continuous training, situational awareness, and behavioral adaptation, which is challenging to maintain in a large organization.

3.8.7 Lack of Standardization and Regulatory Alignment

The fact that there are no international regulations regarding multi-layered defense and AI-oriented cybersecurity systems is one of the significant shortcomings. According to Goldbarsht [26], the enforcement of unified counter-cyberterrorism strategies is restricted by the soft law and fragmented models of governance. George [11] also noted that new FinTech ecosystems, including neobanks, frequently have no standardized levels of cybersecurity compliance, which generates regulatory imbalance. Similar outcomes were identified by Saranya et al. [25], who found that cloud-based security services lack alignment (in terms of policies related to privacy and data protection) that would ease the cross-border compliance process and auditing.

3.8.8 Validation Difficulties and Performance Measurement Gaps

The research on DiD architectures and AI-based detection systems is intrinsically complicated to validate their performance. Netkachov et al. [20] emphasized that the effectiveness of layered defenses in critical infrastructures is hard to quantify, as there are too many interdependencies that hinder direct cause–effect relationships. Holmberg [1] and Das [16] both noted that the existing evaluation frameworks were not very successful at capturing the dynamic interaction of defense mechanisms in real-world conditions. Moreover, as noted by Mughal [2] and Hitefield [21] simulation-based validations are not scalable and cannot be completely used to simulate the unpredictability of large-scale cyberattacks.

3.8.9 Rapidly Evolving Threat Landscape

The rate at which cyber threats are developed is quicker than the defense system developed to counter them. Both Chengcheng [5] and Khanna et al. [8] wrote that digital infrastructures have an increasing number of attack surfaces that appear and are outpaced by defensive measures, which cannot be updated more quickly. Singh et al. [24] also stressed that the ZTA of 5G networks should be constantly adjusted to the latest changes in the threat vectors, which is a significant scalability challenge. In the cloud environment and industrial system, Thawani et al. [28] and Naseer [29] cautioned that permanent retraining and fine-tuning of ML models are required because of continuous innovation of attack tools, a resource-intensive activity.

3.8.10 Ethical and Operational Risks of AI-Driven Defense

The increased reliance on AI poses ethical and operational problems. George [11] argues that the use of opaque ML models in financial cybersecurity poses problems with explainability, resulting in the inability to hold anyone responsible.

Equally, Kurkute et al. [18] expressed worries regarding autonomous defensive machine systems that could misinterpret benign messages and incorrectly conceive them as dangerous, which could cause operational risks. Moreover, Ajayi [3] proposed that the excessive dependence on automation would weaken human control, which also raises the risk of a system failure in case the AI develops mal functions or is hacked.

3.8.11 Limitations in Defense Coordination and Response Automation

The challenge of effective coordination between the layered defenses is still there. Naagas et al. [10] managed to show that defensive-by-deception networks on campus grounds are not always aligned with outside response networks, which diminishes the effect of automated mitigation. Mui et al. [32] identified the same problems with DiD detection models: they do not allow integration between the detection and response mechanisms, which constrains the speed of reaction. Similar ideas were also expressed by Ghidu et al. [6] and Wai and Lee [17] regarding the necessity of real-time cooperation between physical and digital defense tiers, particularly in infrastructures of critical importance, such as power grids and industrial plants.

3.8.12 Scalability and Adaptability Constraints

Scalability is a significant challenge when more and more cyber threats arise every day and with greater velocity. Gubbi et al. [12] and Rahman et al. [22] have observed that the defense mechanisms based on hardware are very secure but can be highly inflexible to address new attacks. As highlighted by Ajayi [3] and Patyal et al. [31], the cost and complexity of multi-layered architecture merit a reduction in the adoption of small and medium-sized enterprises. In addition, Holmberg [1] noted that to strike the right balance between the depth of protection and operational efficiency, there should be a constant trade-off between security and usability.

3.8.13 Summary

The complexity of contemporary digital ecosystems is closely connected to the challenges and constraints of the DiD and AI-based approaches to cybersecurity. There are data bias, difficulty in integration, resource-intensive, human error, and regulatory fragmentation issues that remain severe bottlenecks. To surmount these difficulties, as George [11], Wai and Lee [17], and Singh [24] observed, it is necessary to be holistic, that is, introduce explainable AI, continuous learning, global standardization, and human-centric design principles to make the Cybersecurity 5.0 systems more resilient and transparent.

3.9 Emerging Trends and Future Directions

The convergence of ML, data analytics, and DiD is defining the future of cybersecurity, and the combination of these concepts is transforming the approaches systems use to predict, prevent, and respond to cyber threats. With organizations moving to Cybersecurity 5.0, they are shifting to focus less on reactive security frameworks and moving toward adaptive and intelligence-driven security frameworks. The emergence of AI automation, ZTA, quantum-resilient encryption, and multi-layered defense systems based on cross-domain are factors behind this change [3, 24].

The collaboration of AI and ML in layered defense mechanisms is among the key new trends that enable the real-time learning of threats based on changing data. George [11] points out that AI-driven analytics is useful in financial systems in detecting abnormalities, reducing insider threats, and enhancing fraud detection. Likewise, Mofidi et al. [15] design a multi-layered ransomware detection model for the IoT, which proves that ML-based anomaly detection is highly scalable and effective in a distributed network. These developments are one step toward self-adaptive cyber defense, in which algorithms are continuously updated to new patterns of attacks, and as a result, human intervention and response time are greatly minimized.

The industrial and critical infrastructure sectors are the ones that lead the pack in this evolution as well. According to Ghidu et al. [6] and Khanna et al. [8], the growing significance of DiD frameworks of power and nuclear infrastructures is presented, and multi-level security guarantees continuous operation and the ability to withstand cascading cyber-induced outages. Wai and Lee [17] apply the same strategy to SCADA systems under Industry 4.0 and how intelligent monitoring and data-based predictive analytics enhance the integrity and reliability of the system. Due to the appearance of cyber-physical defense integration, a more visible environment and coordination across layers can be achieved, especially in situations where cyberattacks may also have physical effects.

It will also be developed in the future in the area of Bayesian intelligence and probabilistic reasoning, which covers risks in cybersecurity. Alexander [4] provides an example of the use of Bayesian networks to maximize the order of priorities of DiD security measures, which enable the prioritization in response to the changing likelihood of threats. This probabilistic process allows the organization to model different attack scenarios, predict vulnerabilities, assign defensive resources, and use them efficiently. Combined with AI, Bayesian models will probably form the basis of autonomous cyber risk management systems that learn and adapt without being explicit.

This latest model of Zero Trust has been largely regarded as another paradigm shift in today's contemporary cybersecurity models. As Singh et al. suggest, DiD with ZTA for 5G networks will help minimize cross-domain intrusions and lateral movement of threats. This model relies on its premise that there is no implicit trust, as ZTA follows the dynamic checking for every transaction rather than the traditional perimeter-oriented model. When fused with data analytics based on machine learning, this contributes to more competent visibility granularity, especially in decentralized and hybrid network ecosystems.

On the other hand, the demand for expanding DiD into nontraditional domains is also accelerating very fast. DiD principles are extended as well to very complex systems such as nuclear operations and smart grids [5, 6]. The abstraction of DiD into OT frameworks thus stands even outside pure IT. Multi-layered defense applications in modern warfare have also been surveyed, where algorithmic defense strategies have been shown capable of deterring guided weapon systems and urban air threats [27, 28]. Such findings amply reveal that cybersecurity in the future will be inherently multi-domain and interdisciplinary in physical, cyber, and cognitive dimensions.

Research and application foci of the future in cybersecurity will also be data-centric defense architecture. Matsuoka [19] sets up a data-centric DiD framework such that the data itself is treated as the primary security object, not either the system or the network. This position conforms to developments within a broader industry trend toward data sovereignty, safe edge computing, and federated analytics by letting organizations secure and analyze sensitive information without having to centralize it. The same observation is shared by Mughal [23], not forgetting that having a well-architected wireless network security will take data protection through cloud systems to edge devices through adaptive encryption and anomaly access control.

Quantum-safe adaptive hardware security, and further integrated with AI will continue to inspire the advancement of in-depth models in the years to come. An automated secure IC design flow using multi-layered defense against an emerging threat on hardware circuits is proposed by [12]. Rahman et al. [22] added that their works on logic locking will be further counseled as it comprises very fundamental techniques against reverse engineering of hardware and theft of intellectual property. These are symbolic manifestations of convergence involving security, design, and machine intelligence, aimed at establishing trust from end-to-end.

The future of cloud security and distributed security will mainly rely on adaptive defense mechanism developments and advanced encryption. As Saranya et al. [25] describe best practices to ensure data privacy in cloud ecosystems, encryption, multi-factor authentication, and continuous threat monitoring would be some of the many defense layers. Empirical evidence supporting this will be provided with examples of how deception-based and detection-by-depth action strategies are technically applied to protect distributed university and enterprise networks from denial-of-service and phishing attacks [10, 32]. Likewise, Rendall et al. [14] foresee an even brighter future for highly developed multi-layered anti-phishing detection systems that study in real time the contextual and behavioral indicators.

Emerging trends also include virtualization and multi-layered cyber-secure governance as soft laws and global policy frameworks. Goldbarsht [26] supports a call for concerted effort in international coordination through multi-layered frameworks against terrorist financing while emphasizing the defense layers of regulatory and policy-driven measures in addition to technical safeguards. Further backing on the layered defense approach toward protecting healthcare data is Cherenko and Williams [7]; that is, how organizational and procedural layers improve the confidentiality of patients' data under frameworks such as HIPAA.

AI-driven defense strategies will continue into the next phase of Cybersecurity 5.0 in military and public government jurisdictions. As Mughal [2] and Naseer [29] suggest, DiD should be attached to national and institutional strategies in cyber defense to protect mission-critical data. Likewise, Netkachov et al. [20] and Godakanda [30] cite defense-aware threat modeling and complete quantitative evaluation of DiD systems as groundwork for predictive, simulation-based approaches toward real-time cyber resilience assessment.

It will eventually integrate machine learning with probabilistic reasoning and data-centric DiD architectures. This is what will finally lead to autonomous cybersecurity ecosystems that will always analyze, adapt, and respond to rapidly emerging threats from both the cyber and physical domains. According to Holmberg [1], however, the base of DiD will always remain fundamentally in safety and redundancy—principles that will keep changing but never disappear with the evolution of defense paradigms through automation and intelligence. Future studies should focus rather on sustainable AI-driven defense ecosystems capable of, among other characteristics, ethical reasoning, interoperability, and self-healing.

The next generation of cybersecurity will have convergence, autonomy, and adaptivity characteristics. From Zero Trust integration and AI-augmented learning to quantum-resilient and data-centric defense architectures, the field moves to a very near future of a unified, intelligent, and multi-layered security posture. Cybersecurity 5.0 will need an all-inclusive, layered, and intelligent defense ecosystem that can construct a learning and anticipatory environment, one which can evolve faster than the threats it is intending to counter [3].

3.10 Conclusion

Through the entire history of its development, it has become clear that no single countermeasure can actually protect such complicated digital ecosystems. Information, systems, and critical infrastructure continue to be best protected with layered and multifaceted approaches that integrate technical and organizational measures. After this has been said, it is wise to add that the increasing growth of the sophistication of cyber threats makes it all the more important for organizations to adopt adaptive strategies combining prevention, detection, and rapid response capabilities to ensure resilience.

Emerging technologies such as AI, machine learning, and blockchain are changing the cybersecurity paradigm by providing better intelligent protection mechanisms, which are proactive and automated. Such technologies allow systems to anticipate possible attacks and conduct real-time responses while constantly adapting to the shifting threat environments. Also, the need for an integration of physical and cyber defenses is becoming more critical, particularly in industrial and critical infrastructure, where cyberattacks could effectively lead to real-world consequences.

Despite drastic advancements, challenges still stand in the way of the implementation of comprehensive, cost-effective, and sustainable cybersecurity strategies. Ongoing dilemmas include balancing security with usability, managing complex networks, and ensuring interoperability across different systems. The prospect of cybersecurity would rely on how organizations would embrace technology, create situational awareness, and nurture a culture of continuous improvement and vigilance.

Ultimately, it requires a holistic and futuristic approach to curb the evolving threat landscape. With multi-layered defense frameworks, newer technologies, and proactive risk management, organizations can earn some measure of resilience, protect their critical assets, and earn trust in the digital age. Cybersecurity is about ongoing transformation, constant learning, and continuous innovation. It measures success less by an organization's actual ability to prevent attacks and more by its ability to successfully respond to and recover from them.

References

1 Holmberg J. Defense-in-depth. In: Handbook of Safety Principles. John Wiley & Sons; 2017. p. 42–62.

2 Mughal, A.A. (2018). The art of cybersecurity: Defense in depth strategy for robust protection. *International Journal of Intelligent Automation and Computing.* 1 (1): 1–20.

3 Ajayi, O.O. (2023). Layered security defense, a panacea to loss of intellectual properties and damages to information system. *International Journal of Scientific Research & Engineering Trends* 9 (4).

4 Alexander, R. (2020). Reducing threats by using Bayesian networks to prioritize and combine defense in depth security measures. *Journal of Information Security.* 11 (3): 121–137.

5 Chengcheng, W. (2020). New requirements of defence in depth and extension of its application. In: *International Conference on Nuclear Engineering*, V001T02A001. American Society of Mechanical Engineers.
6 Ghidu, M.A., Ilisescu, I., and Nemes, C. (2023). Improving security in the operation of nuclear power plants using defence in depth principle. In: *In: 2023 10th International Conference on Modern Power Systems (MPS)*, 1–6. IEEE.
7 Cherenko I, Williams G. Reducing the Incidents of Phishing, Protecting the Confidentiality of HIPAA Data and, Ensuring the Availability of Critical Systems Vital to the Success of the Healthcare System Using a Layered-Defense Approach. Metropolitan State University of Denver-Department of Computer Sciences, Denver; 2021.
8 Khanna K, Ravikumar G, Govindarasu M. Defense-in-depth framework for power transmission system against cyber-induced substation outages. In: 2023 IEEE Texas Power and Energy Conference (TPEC). *IEEE*; 2023. p. 1–6.
9 Crossler, R.E., Bélanger, F., and Ormond, D. (2019). The quest for complete security: An empirical analysis of users' multi-layered protection from security threats. *Information Systems Frontiers.* 21: 343–357.
10 Naagas, M.A., Mique, E.L. Jr., Palaoag, T.D., and Dela, C.J.S. (2018). Defense-through-deception network security model: Securing university campus network from DOS/DDOS attack. *Bulletin of Electrical Engineering and Informatics.* 7 (4): 593–600.
11 George, A.S. (2023). Securing the future of finance: how AI, Blockchain, and machine learning safeguard emerging Neobank technology against evolving cyber threats. *Partners Universal Innovative Research Publication.* 1 (1): 54–66.
12 Gubbi, K.I., Latibari, B.S., Chowdhury, M.A. et al. (2024). Optimized and automated secure ic design flow: A defense-in-depth approach. *IEEE Transactions on Circuits and Systems I: Regular Papers* .
13 John, J.T. (2017). State of the art analysis of defense techniques against advanced persistent threats. *Future Internet (FI) and Innovative Internet Technologies and Mobile Communication (IITM) Focal Topic: Advanced Persistent Threats* 63.
14 Rendall K, Nisioti A, Mylonas A. Towards a multi-layered phishing detection. *Sensors.* 2020;20(16):4540.
15 Mofidi, F., Hounsinou, S.G., and Bloom, G. L-IDS: A multi-layered approach to ransomware detection in IoT. In: *2024 IEEE 14th Annual Computing and Communication Workshop and Conference (CCWC)*, vol. 2024, 387–396. IEEE.
16 Das R. An Embedded Defense-in-Depth Module for Detecting Cyberattacks on Interdependent SCADA Controllers. PhD diss., The University of Alabama in Huntsville; 2020.
17 Wai E, Lee CKM. *Depth in defense: A multi-layered approach to cybersecurity for SCADA systems in Industry 4.0.* In: Science and Technology – Recent Updates and Future Prospects Vol. 2. B P International; 2024. p. 124–144.

18 Kurkute, M.V., Selvaraj, A., and Selvaraj, A. (2023). End-to-end cybersecurity strategies for autonomous vehicles: Leveraging multi-layered defence mechanisms to safeguard automotive ecosystems. *Cybersecurity and Network Defense Research* 3 (2): 134–177.

19 Matsuoka, H. (2019). The data-centric defense-in-depth approach in the cyberspace operations. In: *Cyber Defense–Policies, Operations and Capacity Building*, 39–45. IOS Press.

20 Netkachov, O., Popov, P., and Salako, K. (2019). Quantitative evaluation of the efficacy of defence-in-depth in critical infrastructures. In: *Resilience of Cyber-Physical Systems: From Risk Modelling to Threat Counteraction*, 89–121. Springer.

21 Hitefield SD. A Defense-In-Depth Security Architecture for Software Defined Radio Systems. Doctor of Philosophy, Faculty of the Virginia Polytechnic Institute and State University; 2020.

22 Rahman, M.T., Rahman, M.S., Wang, H. et al. (2020). Defense-in-depth: A recipe for logic locking to prevail. *Integration.* 72: 39–57.

23 Mughal, A.A. (2022). Well-architected wireless network security. *Journal of Humanities and Applied Science Research.* 5 (1): 32–42.

24 Singh, K., Kumar, B., Saxena, R., and Lohani, V. A defense in depth with zero trust architecture for securing 5G networks. In: *31st Telecommunications Forum (TELFOR)*, vol. 2023, 1–4. IEEE.

25 Saranya, N., Sakthivadivel, M., Karthikeyan, G., and Rajkumar, R. (2023). Securing the cloud: an empirical study on best practices for ensuring data privacy and protection. *International Journal of Engineering and Management Research.* 13 (2): 46–49.

26 Goldbarsht, D. (2020). *Global counter-terrorist financing and soft law: Multi-layered approaches.* Edward Elgar Publishing.

27 Iman, K.F., Triharjanto, R.H., Wibowo, H.B., and Ruyat, Y. (2023). Comparative analysis of a multi-layered weapon system for city air defense in the modern warfare. *International Journal Of Humanities Education and Social Sciences.* 3 (3).

28 Thawani, B., Lim, S.K., Brown, L. et al. (2023). Design of multi-layered protection against guided mortar threats through numerical modeling. *Defence Technology.* 29: 55–65.

29 Naseer, I. (2020). Cyber defense for data protection and enhancing cyber security networks for military and government organizations. *MZ Computing Journal.* 1 (1).

30 Godakanda ML. Optimising a Defence-Aware Threat Modelling Diagram Incorporating a Defence-In-Depth Approach for the Internet-of-Things. Thesis, Edith Cowan University; 2023.

31 Patyal, M., Sampalli, S., Ye, Q., and Rahman, M. (2017). Multi-layered defense architecture against ransomware. *International Journal of Business and Cyber Security* 1 (2).

32 Mui, S., Askin, A., and Banal, R. (2018). *Detection by defense in depth.* Lawrence Livermore National Lab. (LLNL).

Part II

AI-Driven Cyber Defense

4

Intrusion Detection with Machine Learning

4.1 Introduction

Cyber threats in the growing information age have become ever more complex and quickly overwhelm traditional signature-based systems of intrusion detection (IDS). In view of the stark innovations in malware sophistication, zero-day exploits, and advanced persistent threats, conventional means can hardly carry threat detection in time and with the required level of accuracy [1, 2]. To combat this dilemma, the more dynamic and rapidly evolving machine learning (ML) technology provides the cornerstone of novel approaches in cybersecurity for adaptive, predictive, and automated defense against known and unknown threats [3, 4].

Machine-learning-based IDS attempts to distinguish patterns of malicious behavior [5] by employing computational models previously trained on historical data from networks and systems. Supervised learning methods comprising decision trees, SVM, and neural networks work through labeled datasets, which classify events as normal or malicious [6, 7]. In contrast, unsupervised learning methods such as clustering and anomaly detection algorithms detect new attacks through deviations from expected behavior [8, 9]. A hybrid implementation that can incorporate both supervised and unsupervised techniques has managed to achieve higher accuracy and robustness in real-world deployment [10, 11].

The vast datasets generated by Industry 4.0 technologies, IoT, and cloud computing ago, required for intelligent analysis, further accelerated the adoption of ML in IDS [12, 13]. The superior handling of high-dimensional data, capturing the time-following context, and attack pattern recognition by the deep learning methods, convolution neural networks, and recurrent neural networks (RNNs), was substantiated in [14, 15]. Moreover, ensemble methods that combine predictions from multiple models, thereby partially alleviating high false positives commonly associated with IDS, showed effectiveness [16, 17].

Despite the promising features of ML-based IDSs, the real-world deployment of these systems faces various challenges, among them being the quality of input data, selection of relevant features, interpretability of the trained model for cybersecurity experts, and efficiency [18, 19]. Explainable AI (XAI) had indeed been proposed to enable heightened transparency and trust in the machines' automated decisions so that cybersecurity experts can understand and validate the alerts triggered by the ML mechanisms [20, 21]. There exist different ethical implications, including data privacy, bias in the training datasets, and the defenses targeting ML models, which will need to be discussed to ensure the secure and responsible deployment of ML tools [22, 23].

ML-based IDS, when integrated into organizational cybersecurity frameworks, will present numerous advantages. With these systems, there is proactive detection of threats, fast response to emerging attacks, and less human workload in monitoring complex networks [24, 25]. Advances in federated learning and continuous learning systems will improve the adaptability of IDS solutions while protecting sensitive data [26, 27]. AI will integrate with emergent technologies such as metaverse and smart cyber-physical systems, thereby creating the necessary opportunities for holistic, AI-driven cybersecurity solutions [6, 18].

The overall workflow of an IDS is outlined in Figure 4.1. It captures how network data goes through stages of collection, preprocessing, feature extraction, model training, and detection, culminating in either alert generation or mitigation response.

ML can be viewed as the backbone of contemporary intrusion detection, providing powerful means of identifying, classifying, and responding to cyber threats in real time. If challenges that are both technical and ethical are tackled, the future of ML-driven IDS would therefore see handy solutions that could be seen as resilient, transparent, and adaptive security mechanisms over varied and changing digital environments [3, 28]. The chapter discusses the concepts, approaches, applications, and future directions of intrusion detection based on ML and its transformative power over proactive cybersecurity.

4.2 Fundamentals of Intrusion Detection Systems (IDS)

In modern cybersecurity frameworks, IDS are precious in the sense that they watch, detect, and respond to unauthorized or malicious activities inside the networks, systems, and applications [1, 2]. The prime objective of an IDS is to allow identification of some form of threat so that it can trigger any counteraction before actual damage occurs, thereby providing a proactive defense of systems in a rather complex digital environment [3, 4].

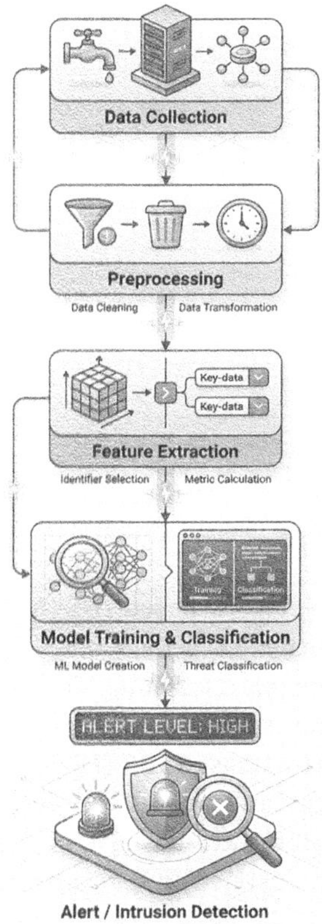

Figure 4.1 General Workflow of an Intrusion Detection System (IDS). "*Source:* Hewa Majeed Zangana"

4.2.1 Definition and Purpose of IDS

IDS are software or hardware systems that constantly inspect the activities in systems and networks to identify anomalies, intrusions, and attacks [10, 24]. They are used in several functions, such as early threat detection, maintenance of the audit trail, adherence to the regulatory requirements, and supporting forensic investigations [28, 29]. Intelligent detection mechanisms allow IDS to advance situational awareness, decrease the responsiveness, and augment the overall situational resilience of organizations [6, 7].

4.2.2 Types of Intrusion Detection Systems

IDS may be divided by their monitoring strategy, methods of data analysis, and the strategy of deployment:

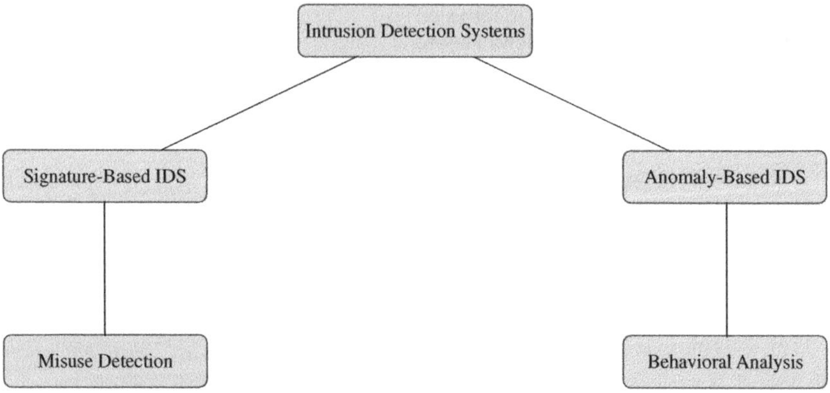

Figure 4.2 Classification of Intrusion Detection Systems (IDS). "*Source:* Hewa Majeed Zangana"

a) **Network-based IDS (NIDS):** The systems track network traffic to detect any malicious activity. They process the packet data and detect suspicious behavior, e.g., scanning, denial-of-service attacks, and suspicious communication flows [12, 13].
b) **Host-based IDS (HIDS):** HIDS are systems-driven, looking at logs, file integrity, and process activity to identify unauthorized access or modification [1, 8].
c) **Signature-based IDS:** The systems match the incoming data with a list of predefined attack signatures. Although they can never be completely accurate on the known threats, they are also ineffective in detecting novel or polymorphic attacks [30, 31].
d) **Anomaly-based IDS:** The anomaly detection systems establish the profile of normal conduct and indicate abnormalities as a possible threat. They are useful in identifying zero-day attacks and unknown malware [9, 15].
e) **Hybrid IDS:** The hybrid IDS is an improvement of the signature-based and anomaly-based methods, which, by combining the advantages of both methods, improve detection accuracy and reduce false positives [5, 14].

Figure 4.2 presents the key types of intrusion detection systems (IDSs) in comparison with signature and anomaly detectors. The former is based on some default patterns of known attacks, whereas the latter identifies new or unknown threats through deviations from normal behavior.

4.2.3 Components of IDS

A good IDS has a number of essential components that work together to offer overall protection:

a) **Data Collection:** Data collection will first involve the collection of data on network devices, logs, and system processes. Data quality and granularity are important in the context of successful threat detection [4, 18].
b) **Feature Extraction:** IDS needs pertinent features so as to distinguish between evil and normal behavior. This step entails the choice of critical network traffic properties, system measurements, and user behavioral patterns [17, 19].
c) **Detection Engine:** This is the principal element that targets suspicious activity with the help of algorithms. ML models, rule-based methods, or a mixture of both may be deployed to detection engines to increase their detection functionality [16, 26].
d) **Alert and Response Module:** When a potential threat is detected, the IDS can produce alerts and can automatically issue the responses (blocking traffic, isolating systems, or notifying security personnel, etc.) [6, 25].

4.2.4 Challenges in IDS Deployment

Although very vital, IDS has a number of limitations in modern cybersecurity settings. They have the ability to manage high network traffic, low rates of false positives, real-time detection, and scalability [32, 33]. Moreover, the opponents are also using AI and automated attackers to avoid detection, which requires continuous updates to the IDS algorithms [22, 23].

The data privacy and compliance issues also become of paramount importance, whether it is the activity of users in enterprise networks or cloud computing [2, 18]. Moreover, IDS decisions should be explainable and transparent in order to establish trust among cybersecurity professionals and enforce a regulatory balance [20, 21].

4.2.5 Evolution of IDS with Artificial Intelligence

New developments in AI and ML have unlocked the capabilities of IDS to a great extent. The AI-based IDS will be able to study the existing attack patterns, adapt to new threats, and automate complex detection methods [1, 3, 24]. To offer interpretable insights and allow security departments to confirm the alerts and enhance incident response efforts, XAI techniques are becoming more and more widely implemented [17, 19].

Additionally, due to the integration of AI into the IDS, systems are more resistant to advanced attacks because they can detect anomalies in real time in IoT networks, cloud infrastructures, and new cyber-physical systems [12, 13, 18]. The combination of AI and IDS makes it possible to create a proactive protection system that can engage in constant learning, predicting threats, and self-protecting [11, 15].

4.2.6 Summary

IDSs are, in other words, the foundation of the proactive approach to cybersecurity. Conventional IDS offers the essential functions of monitoring and alerting, whereas AI-based IDS offers improved detection features, the minimization of the human workload, and adaptive and real-time defense. Knowledge of the underlying principles, architectures, and issues of IDS is key to successful use in the current cybersecurity processes [5, 14, 26].

4.3 Role of Machine Learning in Intrusion Detection

ML has become a foundation of up-to-date IDSs that allow proactive, dynamic, and intelligent responses to cybersecurity issues. In contrast to conventional rule-based IDS, the ideas based on ML will use knowledge-driven patterns in order to identify known and unknown threats, decreasing the use of predefined attack signatures [1, 2]. ML-based intrusion detection is more accurate and allows responding to threats in real time, predicting them, and learning constantly in dynamic network environments [3, 4].

4.3.1 Supervised Learning in Intrusion Detection

Supervised learning is where the models are trained using labeled data so that they can identify network events as either normal or malicious. The popular algorithms are Decision Trees, Support Vector Machines (SVM), Random Forests, and Neural Networks [25]. These techniques are very useful in identifying known attacks, and they can also give accurate detection accuracy when trained on sample data [7, 29]. Nevertheless, supervised methods demand large amounts of labeled data, which may be difficult to access in the case of changing threats [4, 8].

4.3.2 Unsupervised Learning for Anomaly Detection

Unsupervised ML methods can recognize the abnormalities of behavior without labeling. Clustering (k-means, DBSCAN), Autoencoders, and Principal Component Analysis (PCA) are some of the methods that are used to detect anomalies that are indicative of possible intrusions [5, 30]. This is especially useful in determining zero-day attacks, insider threats, and previously unknown malware [9, 28]. Unsupervised learning can result in more false positives, which might be harmful even though it has more benefits, so it requires close feature selection and model optimization [14, 32].

Figure 4.3 demonstrates that machine learning improves the process of intrusion detection by being trained on the normal and abnormal behavior patterns.

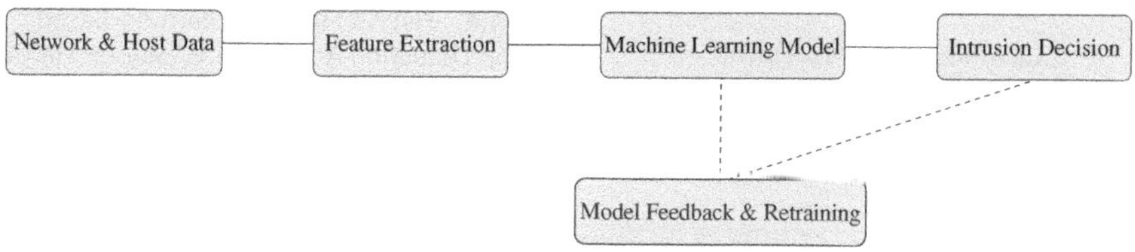

Figure 4.3 Integration of Machine Learning in Intrusion Detection."*Source:* Hewa Majeed Zangana"

It highlights the feedback loop that is two-way and allows improvement of the model continuously and real-time adaptability in detection.

4.3.3 Semi-Supervised and Hybrid Approaches

In semi-supervised learning, both the labeled and the unlabeled data are combined, offering an intermediate approach to intrusion detection in the setting where a limited number of labeled data exist [6, 31]. The hybrid models, which combine unsupervised and supervised approaches, boost detection rates and make them less prone to false alarms by complementing each other [12, 13]. As an example, the initial stage of clustering to identify possible anomalies can be followed by classification models to confirm malicious behavior [3, 11].

Figure 4.4 demonstrates a hybrid intrusion detection structure, which is a combination of signature-based and anomaly-based modules. This architecture combines the multiple classifiers and the various layers of analysis to harness the advantages of each tool to find more and reduce false positives.

4.3.4 Deep Learning for Advanced Intrusion Detection

Deep Learning (DL) represents an extension of traditional ML, which utilizes multi-layered neural networks to automatically extract complex features on large-scale data [1, 6]. CNNs and RNNs (such as Long Short-Term Memory [LSTM] networks) are also very useful in the analysis of time and space patterns in network traffic [2, 7]. DL-based IDS is also very well suited to high-dimensional and heterogeneous data in the cyberspace of IoT networks, cloud infrastructures, and cyber-physical systems [13, 18].

4.3.5 Explainable AI in ML-Driven IDS

Although ML can improve intrusion detection, the lack of interpretability and lack of trust are problems with many models, in particular deep learning, due to its opacity [17, 20]. XAI methods can also give meaningful insights into the

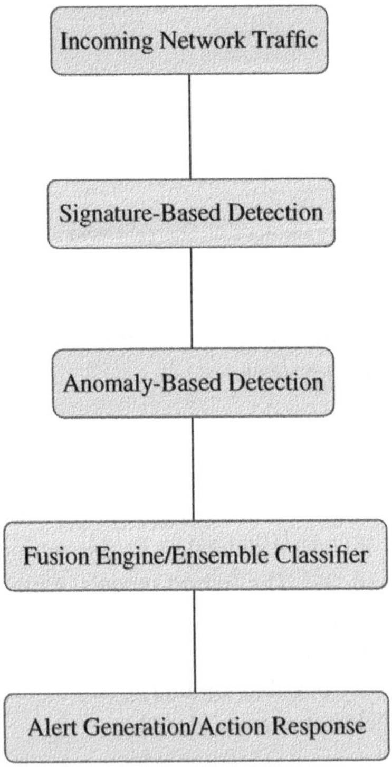

Figure 4.4 Hybrid Machine Learning-Based Intrusion Detection Architecture. "*Source:* Hewa Majeed Zangana"

decisions made by a model, allowing cybersecurity professionals to confirm alertness on the received alerts, how the attack occurred, and the decision made to respond [19, 21]. The application of XAI is becoming increasingly important in the fields where the level of compliance is significant, including finance, healthcare, and critical infrastructure [16, 26].

4.3.6 Benefits of ML-Based Intrusion Detection

ML-based IDS has a wide range of benefits:

- Proactive Threat Detection: Anticipates and avoids attacks before they are damaging [3, 24].
- Adaptive Learning: It is a continuous improvement based on new data and improves the detection of evolving threats [1, 14].
- Scalability: Able to work with large-scale and heterogeneous data of a network [12, 27].
- Less Human Intervention: Automates the analysis, alerting, and incident response systems [15, 29].

4.3.7 Challenges and Limitations

Despite their efficiency, ML-based IDS has the following challenges:

- Data Quality and Availability: Quality-labeled data is usually limited [4, 8].
- Evasion Techniques: Fraudsters use adversarial AI to avoid detection by ML [10, 33].
- Computational Complexity: Sophisticated models, such as deep learning, are highly computationally expensive [6, 7].
- Explainability and Trust: It is the ability to interpret the rationale behind the decisions made by MLs that can make it legitimate to be deployed to critical settings [22, 23].

4.3.8 Future Directions

The applications of ML in intrusion detection will likely grow and include reinforcement learning, federated learning, and hybrid AI methods to enhance adaptive threat detection in distributed systems [11, 15, 18]. It will also be fortified with blockchain and IoT security systems, which will help to improve the level of resilience, transparency, and resistance to high-tech cyber attacks [12, 13, 28].

4.3.9 Summary

ML has revolutionized intrusion detection to be more proactive and smart instead of reactive monitoring in cybersecurity. ML-based IDS can identify intricate and dynamic attackers effectively by exploiting supervised, unsupervised, hybrid, and deep learning strategies. Although there are obstacles to data, computation, and explainability, the continuous development of AI and ML can introduce more robust, dynamic, and reliable IDSs [3, 14, 24].

4.4 Datasets for Training and Evaluation

ML-based IDS is based on datasets that present information required to effectively train, validate, and assess models. High-quality datasets guarantee that the models have the ability to identify known threats, extrapolate to new attacks, and reduce false positives and false negatives [1, 3]. When it comes to cybersecurity, the diversity and dynamism of network traffic, malware-based actions, and the development of attack plans make the choice and preparation of datasets a critical issue [4, 24].

4.4.1 Publicly Available IDS Datasets

Various popular benchmark datasets include labeled network traffic or system activity data, which are used in intrusion detection studies. These datasets enable the researchers to create, test, and compare the models of ML in standard conditions.

- **KDD Cup 1999 (KDD'99)**: It is one of the first and most popular datasets of IDS, which is based on the DARPA 1998 dataset. It stores network connection logs, which are marked as regular or as a particular type of attack, including DoS, probe, and R2L [2, 8]. Although KDD'99 is significant in history, it is too big, and its attack patterns are old, which might not allow the model to be generalized on current threats [29, 33].
- **NSL-KDD**: A better version of KDD-99, which solves several problems, such as duplicate records, and gives a more balanced dataset [31, 34]. It is still a conventional standard of testing supervised and semi-supervised ML models.
- **UNSW-NB15**: A current dataset of real-life traffic measured through the IXIA traffic generator and containing normal and malicious events [4, 14]. UNSW-NB15 has a greater number of more modern types of attacks, like worms, backdoors, and exploits, which are more suitable when evaluating the ML in real-world conditions [5].
- **CIC-IDS2017**: The dataset is created to reflect the latest attack trends, such as brute force, DDoS, botnet traffic, and others. It can be applied to assess deep learning and anomaly detection models since it has high-dimensional feature representations and realistic traffic patterns [10, 25].
- **Bot-IoT and TON-IoT**: These datasets are concerned with the IoT settings and industrial control repositories, which are often reflected by the growing significance of IoT security in the Industry 4.0 settings [12, 13, 18]. They are able to receive traffic data on sensors, smart devices, and industrial controllers, and allow ML models to detect botnet attacks and other threats that are unique to the IoT [6].

4.4.2 Dataset Characteristics and Preprocessing

In the case of ML-based IDS, the quality of the data set and preprocessing become very important. Other significant features are:

- Feature Representation: It contains features of the network (packet size, flow lifetime), features of the system (metrics), and features of the protocol [1, 3]. Embedding, statistical aggregation, or PCA are feature extraction methods that improve the performance of the models [17, 20].

- Data Labeling: To classify traffic as malicious or benign, either manual annotation, simulation-assisted labeling, or hybrid methods are used [29, 35].
- Data Balancing: Cybersecurity data sets tend to be imbalanced with the normal traffic significantly exceeding the events of attacks. The use of Synthetic Minority Over-sampling Technique (SMOTE), oversampling, or cost sensitive learning methods helps to address this problem to avoid bias in the ML models [2, 4].
- Data Normalization and Cleaning: The elimination of noise, duplications, and inconsistencies enhances the generalizing capacity of the model, as well as lowers the false alarm rates [1, 9].

4.4.3 Synthetic and Simulated Datasets

Synthetic datasets are frequently produced to overcome the lack of labeled data, which is done through network simulation software (NS-3, Mininet) or traffic generators. These data sets are especially tested when rare attacks are to be tested or even futuristic threat models [6, 11]. Synthetic data is also able to test IDS in a controlled, repeatable setting without putting real-world systems at risk [27, 34].

4.4.4 Evaluation Metrics

IDS training data are directly linked to evaluation measures. Key metrics include:

- Accuracy, Precision, Recall, F1-score: Evaluate the classification of performance and false positive and false negative [7, 29].
- Receiver Operating Characteristic (ROC) and Area Under Curve (AUC): Evaluates the model discrimination ability [19, 21].
- Detection Rate and False Alarm Rate: Necessary to measure the IDS in the operational setting, where false positives are not as significant as the detection rates [10, 28].

4.4.5 Challenges in Dataset Usage

Although there are publicly available datasets, a number of challenges still exist:

- Obsolescence: Old datasets can be an inaccurate depiction of the current attack patterns and network characteristics [2, 33].
- Heterogeneity: The datasets in modern ones, such as IoT and cloud systems, have to reflect the variety of devices and protocols [13, 18].
- Privacy Concerns: The information in real-world networks is often sensitive, and it should not be made publicly available but needs to be anonymized [22, 23].
- Scalability: Data with a high volume of traffic requires a lot of storage and computation resources to train complex ML models [12, 28].

4.4.6 Summary

The success of the ML-based IDSs relies on the selection and preparation of datasets. Similar datasets that are publicly available, including KDD99, NSL-KDD, UNSW-NB15, CIC-IDS2017, and IoT-specific datasets, are valuable training and testing material. The appropriate preprocessing, feature engineering, and evaluation metrics will guarantee that ML models will be able to adjust to the dynamic situation of threats, minimize false alarms, and become resolute in their detecting abilities [1, 3, 14]. Synthetic datasets also offer additional opportunities for research, whereby it is possible to test the rare or emerging threats under controlled conditions.

4.5 Machine Learning Algorithms for Intrusion Detection

ML has become one of the pillars of the design and implementation effort of the modern IDS to allow automated, adaptive, and scalable security infrastructure. Conventional signature-based IDS are less effective at identifying zero-day attacks and other advanced adversarial behaviors, whereas ML-based ones use previous data and real-time data to identify an anomaly and a pattern that may signal malicious activity [1].

4.5.1 Supervised Learning Algorithms

The most common methods of IDS are supervised learning methods since they have the capability of learning using labeled data. They need a training set that has normal and malicious data and is targeted at mapping input features to predetermined types of attacks [5, 29].

- **Decision Trees (DT) and Random Forests (RF)**: These tree-based algorithms are useful in classification applications, and they offer interpretable decision boundaries and work with high-dimensional network features. Random Forests are used to increase the generalization to multiple decision trees to average their results [7, 10].
- **Support Vector Machines (SVM)**: SVMs help to determine the best hyperplanes that can be used to differentiate between benign and malicious data points. They are especially efficient in high-dimensional spaces, yet not always computationally efficient with large datasets [2, 6].
- **k-Nearest Neighbors (k-NN)**: The algorithm is used to classify cases by the majority of nearby cases. Though easy to use and understand, k-NN may have difficulty with unbalanced data that is typical of cybersecurity [1, 31].

Supervised learning models are also used in benchmark, each of which attains high accuracy on known types of attacks with challenges in detecting unknown types of attacks [14, 25].

4.5.2 Unsupervised Learning Algorithms

Unsupervised learning does not consider labeled data and is applicable in identifying unknown or emerging threats through the identification of patterns that are not normal [9, 30].

- **Clustering Techniques**: Recurring pattern Algorithms like k-means, DBSCAN, and hierarchical clustering are used to cluster similar network flows. These clusters are also marked with outliers that might be labeled as possible attacks [8, 36].
- **Autoencoders and Deep Anomaly Detection**: Autoencoders are neural networks that are trained to discover small representations of normal traffic and detect anomalies that are indicative of intrusions. Such techniques are being implemented more in IoT and cloud systems because of their flexibility [13, 18].

The use of unsupervised learning is also effective in dynamic or zero-day attack scenarios, which supplements the capabilities of supervised methods and adds more functionality to detect anomalies [27, 34].

4.5.3 Semi-Supervised Learning

The semi-supervised approach, which is based on very few labeled sets and tremendous amounts of unlabeled sets, balances between supervised and unsupervised approaches [6, 16]. Self-training, co-training, and graph-based methods are some of the techniques that enable IDS to learn the attack data when there is a limited number of labeled attack data [28, 29].

4.5.4 Ensemble Learning Methods

Ensemble methods are used to combine several models to enhance the accuracy of detection, decrease variance, and enhance strong resistance to noisy data [10, 17]. Fashionable ensemble methods in IDS are:

- **Bagging and Boosting**: Bagging (e.g., Random Forest) is used to reduce overfitting by training many models on bootstrapped datasets. Gradually, boosting (e.g., AdaBoost, XGBoost) is an ML technique that targets the instances that are misclassified to improve the performance of the model [7, 19].

- **Hybrid Models**: Hybridizations between the various learning algorithms, including SVM + decision trees or neural networks + ensemble classifiers, have been applied to help improve the detection of known and unknown attacks [3, 11].

4.5.5 Deep Learning Approaches

The use of deep learning models has become a prominent trend because it can automatically find hierarchical features in bare network traffic to increase their capacity to detect complex attack patterns [14, 25].

- **Convolutional Neural Networks (CNNs)**: CNNs are efficient to work with traffic data in the form of image-like matrices, where spatial correlations of features are used to capture the information [5, 24].
- **Recurrent Neural Networks (RNNs) and LSTMs**: These models are appropriate with sequential data and can be used to detect multi-stage attacks and intrusions across time, as they capture time-dependent aspects of network traffic [2, 6].
- **Generative Adversarial Networks (GANs)**: GANs are applied in order to generate attack traffic that can be used to augment data and test IDS models [10, 18].

4.5.6 Explainable AI in Intrusion Detection

According to recent studies, XAI is prioritized with a view to interpret ML decisions, especially in high-stakes security solutions where it is necessary to know why an intrusion has been detected [17, 21]. The approaches to XAI increase trust, allow compliance, and human-in-the-loop verification of ML-based IDS [19, 20].

4.5.7 Challenges and Future Directions

Although there has been great advancement, ML-based IDS are faced with several drawbacks:

- **Evolving Threat Landscape**: The patterns of attacks constantly change, and the adaptive and incremental learning methods are necessary [4, 15].
- **Data Scarcity and Quality**: Quality-labeled datasets are not available, especially in the case of the IoT and industrial setting [12, 13].
- **Computational Complexity**: Deep learning models need a significant number of resources to be trained and inferred in real time [7, 14].
- **Adversarial Attacks**: ML models themselves are also vulnerable and require stable and hardy algorithms [22, 23].

The new solutions are hybrid learning supervised, unsupervised, and reinforcement, combining XAI to ensure transparency, and using transfer learning to generalize models to new environments [11, 26].

4.5.8 Summary

The intrusion detection ML algorithms have a wide range of possibilities, including both low-tech supervised classifiers and more advanced deep learning and ensemble models. Every type of algorithm has its own advantages in identifying both known and unknown attacks and issues, including the changing threats, the constraints of the data, and the manipulation by the adversaries, which are some of the key directions in research. The future generation of intelligent, robust, and explainable IDS will be determined by the combination of XAI, hybrid solutions, and adaptive learning [3, 14, 18].

4.6 Feature Engineering and Selection

The rules of feature engineering and selection are important to the creation of an efficient ML-based cybersecurity system. The quality, relevance, and interpretability of features have a great influence on the model performance, cost-effectiveness, and resistance to changing attacks in intrusion detection and threat analysis [1, 3].

4.6.1 Importance of Feature Engineering in Cybersecurity

The feature engineering technique implies the development of informative input features to reflect the trends of normal and malicious actions in network traffic, system logs, or IoT devices [24, 25]. Good feature engineering may enhance detection, cause fewer false positives, and allow the models to generalize to new environments [5, 29].

Features that are often engineered in cybersecurity are:

- **Network traffic statistics**: Flow length, source/destination IPs, protocol, and packet size [2, 28].
- **Temporal features**: The frequency of login attempts, time-related features, and the duration of sessions, which will be critical in identifying brute-force attacks and distributed attacks [6, 13].
- **Behavioral features**: User activity profiling, command sequences, and API call patterns to detect insider threats or abnormal behavior [16, 18].
- **Statistical and derived features**: Entropy, correlation measures, and measures based on aggregation in order to describe deviations of the normal network behavior [17, 21].

4.6.2 Feature Selection Methods

The feature selection is done with the purpose of dimensionality reduction, increased model interpretability, and avoiding overfitting, selecting the most appropriate features to be used in intrusion detection [4, 30].

One can distinguish three types of feature selection methods:

- **Filter Methods**: This is a type of feature evaluation that is not based on the learning algorithm but is measured statistically as mutual information, chi-square, or correlation coefficient. Filter methods are efficient and fast with large-scale data, but can have feature interaction overlooked [8, 9].
- **Wrapper Methods**: Wrapper methods are many-to-many feature evaluation methods that are based on training and evaluating a model in a repeated, iterative manner. Recursive feature elimination (RFE) and forward/backward selection are also very accurate yet computationally demanding techniques [1, 14].
- **Embedded Methods**: These are the ones that combine feature selection in the model training process. Among them are the Lasso regression, tree-based scores of importance, and neural network regularization methods [2, 25, 37]. Embedded techniques strike a balance between performance and computation efficiency and make sure that the chosen features have a direct contribution to the quality of prediction.

4.6.3 Feature Representation Techniques

Besides selection, the encoding of features also has a great influence on model learning. Common approaches include the following:

- **Normalization and Scaling**: Standardization of features provides proper contributions and eliminates bias against features with large ranges of numbers [24, 28].
- **Dimensionality Reduction**: Principal Component Analysis (PCA), t-SNE, and autoencoders are the techniques that decrease the complexity of the feature space and, at the same time, retain the most important information [5, 27].
- **Encoding Categorical Features**: Categorical features can be utilized with one-hot encoding, label encoding, or embeddings, which are effective at processing ML models with nonnumerical inputs [7].

4.6.4 Challenges in Feature Engineering and Selection

The significance notwithstanding, feature engineering in cybersecurity is fraught with a number of problems:

- **Dynamic and Evolving Threats**: The attack pattern and malware behaviors are continuously evolving, and they need dynamic feature updates and constant monitoring [4, 18].
- **High-Dimensional Data**: IoT and Industry 4.0 systems generate huge and heterogeneous data, and it is particularly important that feature selection and computational efficiency are important [12, 13].
- **Class Imbalance**: The number of malicious cases is usually small in comparison to the normal data, which may bias the model selection and performance [1, 30].
- **Interpretability vs. Accuracy**: Minutely complicated features or embeddings can enhance detection and decrease elucidation, which is a fundamental necessity in compliance and trust in security activities [17, 19].

4.6.5 Emerging Trends

Recent developments in feature engineering are concerned with automation, flexibility, and explainability:

- **Automated Feature Engineering (AutoFE)**: The tools that automatically generate and select features via deep learning or reinforcement learning are less labor-intensive and faster toward the deployment of IDS [3, 11].
- **Graph-Based Features**: Graphs allow identifying attacks that are organized and movement between systems in a lateral manner [10, 28].
- **Explainable Features**: Incorporation of XAI methods can guarantee that the chosen features are contributing to the process of making interpretable and transparent decisions [20, 21].
- **Cross-Domain Transferability**: Feature selection models that are trained within an IoT setting and trained in a cloud and enterprise setting become retrained less frequently when applied to changing cybersecurity infrastructures [26, 27].

4.6.6 Summary

ML-based cybersecurity is still based on feature engineering and selection. Well-designed and chosen features enhance the accuracy of detection, the efficiency of computation, as well as the interpretability, and deal with the issue of high-dimensional, dynamic, and heterogeneous data. The future of smart IDSs in a variety of cyber spaces is assured by the further development of automated and explainable feature engineering [3, 14, 18].

4.7 System Architecture of ML-Based IDS

The ML-based Intrusion Detection Systems (ML-IDS) system architecture is a plan of action to implement intelligent cybersecurity frameworks that can be used to identify, categorize, and counteract cyber threats. Architectures based on ML-driven IDS are also built on the principles of several layers of data processing and feature analysis, as well as decision-making modules, which are optimized to achieve accuracy in detection, flexibility, and robustness in complex networked systems [1, 3].

4.7.1 Core Components of ML-Based IDS

A typical ML-IDS contains multiple layers (connected to each other), each with a specific purpose:

1) Data Acquisition Layer: This layer gathers raw data from different sources such as network traffic, system logs, cloud services, and IoT devices. The quality and correct data input for a model are of utmost importance to form sound ML models, where noise or partial data can have dire consequences [2, 12, 28].
2) Preprocessing and Feature Engineering Layer: Raw data is processed to manage missing data, duplicate data, and normalize the numerical data. The feature engineering derives significant patterns about the normal or abnormal state of the system [17, 21, 29]. In many cases, this layer has dimensionality reduction methods, coding of discrete variables, and temporal statistics aggregation in order to train the model efficiently [5, 6].
3) Training and Learning Layer Model: It is a layer that contains ML algorithms that are trained to differentiate between malicious and benign activities. Common ML models include:
   - Learning Models Supervised (e.g., Random Forests, SVM, Neural Networks) that were trained on a dataset with labels [8, 30].
   - Unsupervised Learning Models (e.g., clustering, autoencoders) capable of detection of novel attacks without an instance of any attack [1, 7].
   - Adaptive IDS with Reinforcement Learning to enhance its capacity to detect based on the response of the surrounding environment [18, 28].
4) Decision-Making Layer and Detection Layer: The layer includes the analysis of the outputs of the ML models to detect network activities as normal or malicious. To make the decisions more reliable and transparent, advanced IDS systems may use probabilistic reasoning, ensemble techniques, and XAI functionality [17, 19, 20].
5) Response Layer: Mitigation Layer: After the detection, the IDS may launch automated reactions like the creation of alerts, blockages, quarantine of

impacted nodes, or rearrangement of network policies. It is integrated with tools of security information and event management (SIEM) to guarantee the prompt mitigation of threats [3, 10, 16].

6) Feedback and Model Update Layer: Lifelong learning plays a crucial role in terms of dynamic threat settings. Feedback loops enable retraining and optimization of models after new threat patterns, so that they make sure the system is effective against zero-day attacks and emerging malware [18, 27].

4.7.2 Architectural Variants

The IDS models of today can be divided into the following types according to the deployment models and operational environment:

- Host-Based IDS (HIDS): It is a system that monitors single systems with abnormal activities, based on behaviors and logs [6].
- Network-Based IDS (NIDS): Surveys the traffic on the network to identify attacks like DDoS, man-in-the-middle, and reconnaissance [24, 31].
- Hybrid IDS: This is a type of IDS that is based on both host and network data sources to enhance detection accuracy and minimize false positives [1, 15].
- IoT and Cloud-Oriented IDS: Designed to the scalability and heterogeneity of the IoT-based devices and cloud platforms, often working with the help of edge computing and federated learning approaches [12, 13].

4.7.3 Integration with Explainable AI

To offer interpretable outputs, XAI is becoming common in ML-IDS architectures, particularly when used in decision-critical applications [17, 19, 20]. XAI enables cybersecurity experts to have confidence in automated decisions, meet regulatory requirements, and conduct root cause analysis successfully because it shows the role played by features and decision paths [16, 21].

4.7.4 Challenges and Considerations

Nevertheless, ML-IDS architectures have a number of challenges:

- Data Quality and Diversity: In real-life settings, quality and diversity of data are usually scarce to enable accurate detection [4, 8].
- Latency and Real-Time Processing: Ultralatency Detection: Fast networks require the extraction of features and lightweight models that are optimized [6, 18].
- Adversarial Attacks on ML Models: Model weaknesses can be used by attackers with the help of adversarial examples, which require resilient and strong ML models [10, 14].

- Scalability: Large-scale enterprise, cloud, and IoT applications need to have a design capable of scaling effectively without loss of accuracy [12, 13].

4.7.5 Emerging Trends

New architectural tendencies are supposed to make it more flexible, automated, and transparent:

- Federated and Distributed ML-IDS: Allows the collaborative threat detection between multiple nodes and maintains the privacy of the data [11, 18].
- Integration with Metaverse Security: ML-IDS will be expanded to the virtual environment to identify malfunctions in the immersive environment and digital twins [18].
- Adaptive and Self-Learning Architectures: This implies the use of reinforcement learning and online learning models that will enable continuous adaptation to the changing threats [3, 27].

4.7.6 Summary

The architecture of the system of ML-based IDS offers a rather detailed framework that includes data acquisition, preprocessing, model learning, decision-making, and automated response. The contemporary architectures place a lot of value on flexibility, elucidation, and scalability to deal with the heterogeneous and evolving threat world of cyber. XAI, federated learning, and metaverse-focused solutions integration have become the future of smart intrusion detection and mitigation [14, 17, 18].

4.8 Evaluation Metrics and Performance Assessment

Analyzing the functioning of ML-based cybersecurity systems, specifically IDS, is an important measure to provide reliability, accuracy, and efficiency. When assessments are conducted appropriately, the researchers and practitioners can compare various algorithms, optimize settings, and find out possible vulnerabilities in detection of threats [1, 3]. The importance of performance assessment is especially evident in dynamic and complex structures, e.g. cloud environments, IoT, and the upcoming metaverse [12, 18].

4.8.1 Key Evaluation Metrics

The metric of evaluation of ML-based IDS can be broadly classified into statistical metrics, cost-sensitive metrics, and domain-specific performance metrics.

1) Statistical Metrics: The accuracy of detecting and the nature of errors of the IDS models are often measured using statistical measures. These include:
   - Accuracy: is the ratio of classification correctly done instances (both normal and anomalous) to the overall data. Good accuracy shows the strength of the model in general, but is not that helpful to detect attacks that are uncommon in an unbalanced dataset [2, 14].
   - Precision: This is defined as the ratio of the true positives (correctly identified attacks) to all the predicted positives. Accuracy is very important to reduce false alarms in the areas of operation [5, 17].
   - Recall (Detection Rate): This is the proportion of real attacks that the system has detected. The recall is necessary to determine the sensitivity of an IDS to threats [10, 29].
   - F1-Score: The harmonic mean of the precision and recall, where one has a balanced measurement that includes the presence of false positives and false negatives [16, 19].
2) Error Metrics: Error measures assess the nature of the misclassification that may be made:
   - False Positive Rate (FPR): Percent of the benign cases that are mistaken for attacks, which is crucial to the trust of operations [1, 37].
   - False Negative Rate (FNR): Percent of attacks that the IDS misses. In critical infrastructure with undetected attacks, FNR minimization is essential, as even small damages might be disastrous [6, 7].
3) Cost-Sensitive and Compounds Metrics: Some of the evaluation measures consider several areas of performance or incorporate the operation costs:
   - Receiver Operating Characteristic (ROC) Curve and Area Under Curve (AUC): The metrics of trade-off between true positive and false positive rates at different levels, which give an idea about model strength [24, 34].
   - Matthews Correlation Coefficient (MCC): This is a balanced measure that is adequate in cases of imbalanced data, and it indicates the quality of binary classifications [8, 31].
4) Time-Based Metrics: The real-time IDS systems should be examined in terms of latency and computation efficiency:
   - Detection Time: This is a measure of the interval between when the attack happens and when it is detected. The importance of low latency is in preventing damage [18, 27].
   - Throughput and Scalability: Measures how well the system can increase network traffic or IoT deployment volumes without compromising the performance [12, 13].

The essential evaluation values in IDSs, such as accuracy, precision, recall, and F1-score, and false positive rate, have been visualized in Figure 4.5. All these metrics are used to provide an overall measure of the effectiveness and reliability of IDS models.

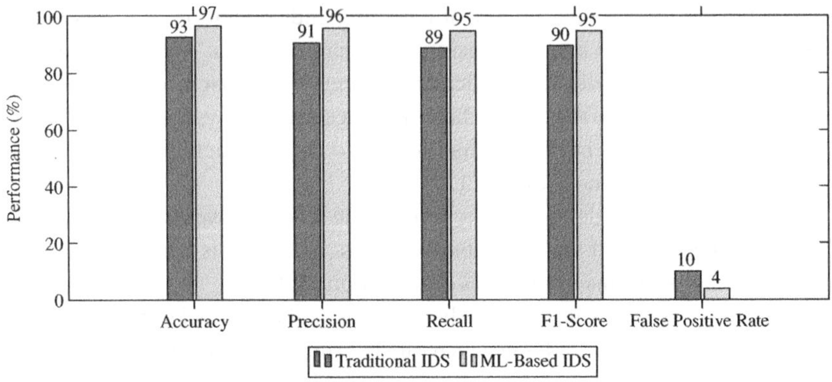

Figure 4.5 Performance Comparison Between Traditional and ML-Based Intrusion Detection Systems. "*Source:* Hewa Majeed Zangana"

4.8.2 Benchmark Datasets and Standardized Evaluation

The quality of databases assessed in performance evaluation relies on the quality of the datasets used. NSL-KDD, CICIDS2017, UNSW-NB15, and dataset-specific to the IoT traffic are some of the common benchmark data sets [1, 6]. Correct division of training, validation, and test subsets will make sure that models are tested in a fair manner and can be applied to unknown threats 3, 28].

4.8.3 Explainable AI and Performance Transparency

XAI is now an important element of performance measurement. XAI methods enable cybersecurity analysts to understand the decisions made by the model, evaluate its trustworthiness, and detect possible biases in the results of detection [17, 20, 21]. Organizations may use automated security decisions as a way of justification by connecting the metrics of evaluation with model interpretability and meeting regulatory standards [16, 19].

4.8.4 Challenges in Performance Assessment

Although it has a strong set of metrics, there are many issues in the context of ML-based IDS evaluation:

- **Imbalanced Data**: The samples of cybersecurity data are usually not balanced between benign and malicious, which distorts accuracy indicators [4, 30].
- **Adversarial Threats**: ML models can be evaded by attackers, and such testing, to determine robustness, should be performed together with traditional evaluation [10, 14].

- **Dynamic Environments**: Applications in the cloud, IoT, and metaverse have introduced fast-changing patterns of traffic that require the constant reassessment of the model [12, 18].
- **Scalability and Resource Constraints**: Tests should take into account performance and consumption of computing, especially in the edge and IoT scenarios [3, 13].

4.8.5 Emerging Evaluation Strategies

New trends are on holistic, adaptive, and automated assessment systems:

- **Continuous Performance Monitoring**: Monitoring of IDS metrics every minute to identify the drift in detection power [11, 27].
- **Federated and Collaborative Evaluation**: Large-scale benchmarking of a model by utilizing distributed assessment of the model at many nodes maintains privacy [18].
- **Integration with Threat Intelligence Feeds**: The connection between IDS performance and the external threat data can be relevant to newly developed attack vectors [6, 15].

4.8.6 Summary

The implementation of ML-based IDS is based on evaluation metrics and performance assessment. A set of statistical, cost-sensitive, time-based, and explainability-oriented metrics was used to give a holistic view of how well the system works. New approaches focus on ongoing, joint, and dynamic assessment in order to make sure that IDS can be used to react to dynamic, large-scale, and complex cyber threats [3, 14, 17, 18].

4.9 Adversarial Attacks and Model Robustness

Cybersecurity systems, especially IDSs and anomaly detection frameworks, are now implemented with ML to detect threats in complicated digital environments. Nevertheless, such systems are susceptible to adversarial attacks, a malicious attempt to prevent misclassification or evasion by manipulation of input data [3, 4]. Familiarizing with adversarial attacks and model robustness is a critical concept to the integrity, availability, and reliability of AI-based cybersecurity solutions.

4.9.1 Overview of Adversarial Attacks

Adversarial attacks take advantage of the weaknesses in ML models by placing minimal damaging perturbations or changes to input data. These kinds of attacks can be generally divided into a few classes:

- **Evasion Attacks**: The attackers will use inputs to avoid being detected without changing the underlying malicious action. This poses a very serious danger to IDS in networks and IoT systems [1, 10].
- **Poisoning Attacks**: The presence of malicious actors introduces corrupt (or misleading) data into the training process, resulting in the model learning wrong patterns and decreasing the overall accuracy [4, 11].
- **Model Extraction and Inference Attacks**: Attackers seek to get confidential information regarding the model, such as parameters, training data, or decision boundaries, which could be used to perform additional attacks [24, 28].
- **Adversarial Perturbations**: In the case of deep learning-based IDS, Fast Gradient Sign Method (FGSM), Projected Gradient Descent (PGD), as well as Carlini-Wagner attacks subtly modify the features to cause misinterpretation, which is also known as adversarial attacks [17, 21].

4.9.2 Implications of Adversarial Attacks

Adversarial attacks have more than mere misclassification. The attackers are able to circumvent security controls, steal confidential information, and disrupt critical infrastructure [6, 7]. The effect of successful attacks in novel settings such as the metaverse and the cloud-integrated IoT networks can be multiplied quickly by a high interconnection rate and real-time interaction of data [12, 18]. Additionally, such attacks damage the trust toward AI systems, which highlights the importance of explainable and transparent ML models [19, 20].

4.9.3 Assessing Model Robustness

Model robustness denotes the quality of models to sustain functionality in adversarial conditions and environmental change. The testing of robustness needs to be done in a systematic manner and on a variety of attack conditions:

- **Robustness Testing Frameworks**: The researchers can simulate adversarial tasks on benchmark data with the help of resilience against evasion, poisoning, and perturbation attacks [8, 28].
- **Adversarial Training**: Adversarial examples help to improve the ability of the model to resist manipulation [15, 34].
- **Ensemble Approaches**: The robustness of a combination of several models or a hybrid architecture may be improved by diversification of decision paths and a general inability of attackers to break all the models at the same time [5, 6].
- **Explainable AI (XAI)**: Techniques to give transparency in model decisions are used to detect weaknesses and indicative suspicious patterns that could show signs of adversarial manipulation [17, 19, 21].

4.9.4 Challenges in Maintaining Robustness

Nevertheless, a number of problems remain in the defense of ML-based cybersecurity systems against adversarial attacks:

- **Dynamic and Evolving Threats**: Attack vectors are in a dynamic state and constantly changing, which needs models to be quickly updated without the need to be retrained extensively [3, 18].
- **Resource Constraints**: The implementation of powerful ML models on edge devices or the Internet of Things (IoT) is incompatible with the constraints of computation and memory [12, 13].
- **Trade-off Between Robustness and Accuracy**: Excessive focus on adversarial resilience can cause a decrease in the overall predictive performance in favor of standard conditions [4, 10].
- **Ethical and Trust Considerations**: There are also the risks of creating blind spots when humans do not interpret or audit the decisions in case of overreliance on AI-based defense mechanisms [22, 23].

4.9.5 Emerging Approaches to Enhance Robustness

Current studies focus on multi-layered and adaptive approaches to strong cybersecurity:

- Hybrid AI Architectures: Deep learning is combined with rule-based or traditional statistical models to increase the resistance to unknown or zero-day attacks [26, 37].
- Federated and Collaborative Learning: The sharing of adversarial knowledge between distributed nodes enhances their robustness without compromising privacy [18, 27].
- Continuous Monitoring and Self-Healing Models: Adaptive architectures that provide the capability of updating models in real time, retraining, and correcting anomalies are crucial in dynamic cyber ecosystems [11, 28].
- Threat Intelligence Integration: It is possible to mitigate the attacks that are yet to be identified with the help of global threat feeds and the use of ML predictions [14, 16].

4.9.6 Summary

Adversarial attacks are a significant threat to an ML-based IDS, as they cause issues with the reliability, accuracy, and trustworthiness of cybersecurity systems. To achieve robustness, it is necessary to undertake thorough assessment, adversarial training, a hybrid structure, XAI, and adaptive strategies. The future trends focus on proactive, cooperative, and self-curative systems that have the potential to protect against more and more advanced attacks in dynamic digital ecosystems, such as IoT, cloud, and metaverse applications [3, 14, 17, 18].

4.10 Deployment and Real-World Applications

Artificial intelligence (AI) has been moving beyond theoretical studies and is now becoming increasingly widespread within cybersecurity infrastructures, thus allowing organizations to get ahead of cyber threats, preventing and responding to them. AI applications in practice cut across a variety of fields such as enterprise networks, critical infrastructure, cloud environments, IoT, and new digital ecosystems such as the metaverse [3, 18].

4.10.1 Enterprise and Network Security

IDSs and SIEM platforms based on AI are widely applied in the enterprise setting to track network traffic, spot anomalies, and indicate possible security breaches [1, 24]. The ML algorithms, especially the supervised and unsupervised learning models, are used to extract patterns used to identify malware, ransomware, or phishing attacks in a large amount of network data [4, 10]. As an example, AI-based anomaly detection has been effectively adopted in corporate network structures to positively impact the early detection of threats and the decreased number of false positives [6, 16].

4.10.2 Cloud and Industrial IoT Security

As cloud computing and Industry 4.0 have become increasingly popular, AI has played a key role in ensuring the security of highly distributed and heterogeneous systems [12, 13]. The AI-based monitoring systems can be used in industrial control systems to detect the abnormal behavior of devices, identify misconfigurations, and predict the risk of cyberattack of critical infrastructure [27, 37]. Federated learning has been used as well to facilitate joint cybersecurity among several IoT gadgets without loss of data confidentiality [18, 26].

4.10.3 Cybersecurity in the Metaverse and Emerging Digital Ecosystems

In the ever-expanding virtual and augmented reality platforms, AI is a crucial factor in ensuring that immersive environments are not targeted by advanced cyber threats [18]. Defenses that are based on AI in the metaverse include behavior analysis, content moderation, and fraud detection systems, as well as identity verification systems. ML algorithms are trained using historical and simulated attacks to prevent unauthorized access, phishing, and social engineering attacks in the virtual setting before they happen [17, 19].

4.10.4 Explainable AI for Security Decision-Making

XAI approaches are frequently paired with AI deployment in practical cybersecurity systems to ensure the established automated decisions are transparent and understandable [20, 21]. XAI is more useful where stakes are high, like in financial systems and healthcare networks, where it is essential to understand the rationale behind the threat detection and mitigation strategies to comply and manage risk [15, 17]. XAI enhances trust and helps to respond quickly to incidents by allowing human operators to interpret AI-driven alerts [16, 19].

4.10.5 AI in Cyber Threat Intelligence and Incident Response

In addition to threat detection, AI can be used in predictive threat intelligence, automated incident response, and risk assessment [28, 29]. Threat reports, dark web forums, and system logs could also be processed by natural language processing (NLP) and graph-based AI models to detect new patterns in attacks. Mitigation measures or recommendations can then be suggested or activated by automated decision support systems, which makes operations more resilient [6, 7].

4.10.6 Challenges in Real-World Deployment

There are a number of challenges to the implementation of AI in the operational cybersecurity setting, even though its applications are promising:

- Scalability and Computational Constraints: Large-scale networks and IoT ecosystems will produce large data streams that will require huge amounts of computational resources to analyze in real time using AI [12, 13].
- Quality and Bias of Data: The quality of training data is extremely important to AI models. Bias or incomplete data sets may decrease the accuracy of detection and cause blind spots [4, 24].
- Adversarial Vulnerabilities: Adversarial attacks may be applied to AI models and need to be defended, with the need to continuously train them [3, 10].
- Interaction with Legacy Systems: Implementation of AI in firms having an established cybersecurity framework should be planned to maintain its interoperability [2, 30].

- Ethical and Privacy Issues: In the real world, it is necessary to consider the issue of privacy and comply with the regulations on the use of data, especially when using sensitive personal or organizational data [22, 23].

4.10.7 Case Studies of AI Deployment

There are a number of real-life applications proving the efficacy of AI in increasing cybersecurity:

- Financial Sector: Banks will use AI-based anomaly detection to stop fraud and phishing attacks in real time, eliminating the loss of money [14, 31].
- Healthcare Networks: AI can be deployed to observe network traffic and identify ransomware targeting electronic health records, and XAI can give understandable alerts to human operators [17, 29].
- Smart Cities and Critical Infrastructure AI-based surveillance systems can identify abnormalities in traffic, energy grids, and water supply systems and preclude possible outages brought about by cyberattacks [1, 27].
- Automotive Cybersecurity: AI-driven infrastructure is used to protect connected and autonomous cars against cybercrime, such as sensor spoofing and vehicle-to-everything (V2X) opposing [37].

4.10.8 Summary

Implementation of AI in cybersecurity has proven to provide quantifiable threat detection, incident response, and operational resilience in various sectors. The key to success in implementation is the ability to combine explicable and strong AI models, use real-time threat intelligence, and overcome such aspects as adversarial attacks, data bias, and system scalability. With the further evolution of AI, its use in securing new digital environments, such as IoT networks, industrial environments, and the metaverse, will probably increase, with its options providing dynamic, adaptive, and proactive cybersecurity solutions [3, 7, 18, 28].

4.11 Challenges and Future Trends

The advent of AI in cybersecurity has provided wider threat detection, prevention, and mitigation capabilities than ever before. Nevertheless, in the real world, the implementation is surrounded by major issues and dynamic trends that must be attentively addressed in order to successfully implement and ensure sustainable development in cybersecurity environments [3, 4].

4.11.1 Technical Challenges

Cybersecurity systems developed by AI experience various technical challenges. Scalability concerns in real-time processing of large-scale network and IoT data streams are due to high computation requirements, in particular, deep-learning models [12, 13]. Good datasets are crucial in model accuracy, but incomplete data, noisy data, and biased data can undermine the detection and prediction possibilities [4, 24]. Besides, AI models are also vulnerable to adversarial attacks, through which bad actors can attempt to harm input data to circumvent detectors [3, 10].

The other technical challenge is integration with legacy systems. Most companies have outdated security systems that cannot be retrofitted with AI solutions with ease without causing operational risks [2, 30]. The diversity of devices and devices, in particular, in the industrial field of the IOT and smart cities, makes real-time monitoring and anomaly detection difficult [1, 27].

4.11.2 Explainability and Trust

AI models, especially those based on deep learning, can be considered black boxes, which offer a limited level of interpretability when it comes to the decision-making process [17, 20]. XAI systems are also becoming more popular to make them more transparent and allow human operators to trust automated warning systems and suggestions [19, 21]. Although XAI has been improved, striking a balance between interpretability, model performance, and model complexity is a dilemma [15, 16].

4.11.3 Ethical, Legal, and Privacy Concerns

Deployment of AI in cybersecurity poses an ethical issue, such as possible abuse of AI in conducting offensive cyber activities and breach of privacy in information-intensive systems [22, 23]. The swift development of AI technologies is also shifting far ahead of the legal regulations, leading to uncertainties in the regulation of AI-based surveillance, automated threat reduction, and data processing [33, 38]. These issues are compounded in metaverse use and digital ecosystems because the environment is highly immersive and interactive, and it is capable of gathering much personal and behavioral data [18].

4.11.4 AI and Cyber Threat Evolution

Cyber threats are ever-changing, and thus there is a need for these AI systems to adapt with continuous learning and updating capabilities [6, 14]. The attackers are now using AI themselves, that is, an arms race, whereby AI offensive tools lay down innately intelligent malware, deepfakes, and phishing strategies [8, 10]. So, the cybersecurity AI should evolve toward resilience through adversarial training, reliable learning, and multi-tiered defense systems [3, 7].

4.11.5 Future Trends

There are several things that will define the future of AI applied to cybersecurity:

- Integration With Industry 4.0 and IoT: AI is expected to provide autonomous security-management solutions for industrial environments, smart grids, and IoT networks, predictive maintenance, and anomaly detection [12, 13].
- Metaverse and Immersive Security: Monitoring of behavior, validation of identity, and real-time threat mitigation would be handled by the AI to provide security in virtual places, augmented reality platforms, and digital twins [18].
- Explainable and Responsible AI: More emphasis will be placed on ethically correct, interpretable, and accountable AI so that transparent automated decision-making is achieved while still being operationally efficient [17, 19].
- AI-Driven Cyber Threat Intelligence: NLP, graph analysis, and predictive modeling will increasingly be employed to collect and analyze threat intelligence from a variety of sources to underpin proactive defense activities [28, 29].
- Hybrid Human-AI Cybersecurity: In the future, systems will likely combine human intelligence with AI automation, allowing human operators to concentrate on strategic choices while AI will oversee large-scale monitoring and real-time reactions [16, 26].

4.11.6 Research Directions

Future research should put a greater emphasis on enhancing AI robustness in defense against adversarial attacks, improving computational efficiency in developing solutions for large-scale deployments, and establishment of universal frameworks for ethical AI governance [5, 15]. Interdisciplinary approaches whereby cybersecurity, ML, and legal/ethical areas intersect are essential to ensure a sustainable adoption of AI in the complex and interlinked cyber world [2, 14, 34].

4.11.7 Summary

Even if AI has immensely transformed cybersecurity in intelligent, adaptive, and proactive threat management, there are still surrounding issues with regard to its technical, ethical, and operational grounding. Industry 4.0 integrations, metaverse security, XAI, and hybrid human AI systems: these are several trends that define the future direction of research and practice. Adversarial vulnerabilities and the enhancement of interpretability and responsible AI governance are central to pursuing the benefits AI can bring to the field of cybersecurity [3, 5, 14, 18].

4.12 Conclusion

From its inception, AI instantly became revolutionary in the realm of cybersecurity. It provided exceptionally high-performance visibility through threat detection, risk assessment, and automated response. It establishes a very important processing speed, allowing organizations to identify and sort out threats in real time. Thus, creating a proactive, rather than a reactive, approach to cyber defense. With proven evidence, AI systems are well established and effective in handling comprehensive complexities and the large scale of modern cyber environments, such as IoT networks, industrial infrastructures, and modern digital ecosystems, such as the metaverse.

This holds much promise, and yet it is not without its own difficulties. It poses real technical challenges based on model interpretability, data quality, and computational demands, as there is room to be made for extracting solid reliability within implementation. Where AI will be integrated with data-sensitive and automated decision-making capabilities, ethics, law, and privacy will face different problems. Then there is the dynamic nature of the current cyber threat set and their misuse of AI, thus bringing about the need for continuous innovations and adaptations in cybersecurity strategies.

Brightly looking ahead, AI promises to be more resilient, explainable, and ethically governed. The AI-hybrid model is likely to dominate in most situations but will leave critical strategic decisions to human operators while integrating AI for large-scale monitoring and fast intervention. Indeed, the full advantage of what AI can do toward risk will depend on continued research and collaboration across technical, regulatory, and ethical domains. In any case, an integration of AI into cybersecurity should open doors toward the future, with a more intelligent, adaptable, proactive defense landscape that can counter the evolving threats of the digital age.

References

1 Bhatele, K.R., Shrivastava, H., and Kumari, N. (2019). The role of artificial intelligence in cyber security. In: *Countering cyber attacks and preserving the integrity and availability of critical systems*, 170–192. IGI Global.

2 Li, J. and hua. (2018). Cyber security meets artificial intelligence: A survey. *Frontiers of Information Technology & Electronic Engineering* 19 (12): 1462–1474.

3 Ali, A., Khan, M.A., Farid, K. et al. (2023). The effect of artificial intelligence on cybersecurity. In: *2023 International Conference on Business Analytics for Technology and Security (ICBATS)*, 1–7. IEEE.

4 Ansari, M.F., Dash, B., Sharma, P., and Yathiraju, N. (2022). The impact and limitations of artificial intelligence in cybersecurity: A literature review. *International Journal of Advanced Research in Computer and Communication Engineering.* 11 (Issue 5): 595–601.

5 Kaur, R., Gabrijelčič, D., and Klobučar, T. (2023). Artificial intelligence for cybersecurity: Literature review and future research directions. *Information Fusion* 97: 101804.

6 Jun, Y., Craig, A., Shafik, W., and Sharif, L. (2021). Artificial intelligence application in cybersecurity and cyberdefense. *Wireless Communications and Mobile Computing* 2021 (1): 3329581.

7 Kumar, S., Gupta, U., Singh, A.K., and Singh, A.K. (2023). Artificial intelligence: Revolutionizing cyber security in the digital era. *Journal of Computers, Mechanical and Management.* 2 (3): 31–42.

8 Mohammed, I.A. (2020). Artificial intelligence for cybersecurity: A systematic mapping of literature. *Artificial Intelligence* 7 (9): 1–5.

9 Wiafe, I., Koranteng, F.N., Obeng, E.N. et al. (2020). Artificial intelligence for cybersecurity: A systematic mapping of literature. *IEEE Access* 8: 146598–146612.

10 Chakraborty, A., Biswas, A., and Khan, A.K. (2023). Artificial intelligence for cybersecurity: Threats, attacks and mitigation. In: *Artificial Intelligence for Societal Issues*, 3–25. Springer.

11 Mijwil, M. and Aljanabi, M. (2023). Towards artificial intelligence-based cybersecurity: The practices and ChatGPT generated ways to combat cybercrime. *Iraqi Journal for Computer Science and Mathematics* 4 (1): 65–70.

12 De Azambuja, A.J.G., Plesker, C., Schützer, K. et al. (2023). Artificial intelligence-based cyber security in the context of industry 4.0—A survey. *Electronics (Basel)* 12 (8): 1920.

13 Kuzlu, M., Fair, C., and Guler, O. (2021). Role of artificial intelligence in the Internet of Things (IoT) cybersecurity. *Discover Internet of things* 1 (1): 7.

14 Zhang, Z., Ning, H., Shi, F. et al. (2022). Artificial intelligence in cyber security: Research advances, challenges, and opportunities. *Artificial Intelligence Review* 55: 1029–1053.

15 Tao, F., Akhtar, M.S., and Jiayuan, Z. (2021). The future of artificial intelligence in cybersecurity: A comprehensive survey. *EAI Endorsed Transactions on Creative Technologies* 8 (28): e3–e3.

16 Jonas, D., Yusuf, N.A., and Zahra, A.R.A. (2023). Enhancing security frameworks with artificial intelligence in cybersecurity. *International Transactions on Education Technology* 2 (1): 83–91.

17 Capuano, N., Fenza, G., Loia, V., and Stanzione, C. (2022). Explainable artificial intelligence in cybersecurity: A survey. *IEEE Access* 10: 93575–93600.

18 Awadallah, A., Eledlebi, K., Zemerly, J. et al. (2024). Artificial intelligence-based cybersecurity for the metaverse: Research challenges and opportunities. *IEEE Communications Surveys & Tutorials.* 26 (Issue 1): 301–339.

19 Hariharan, S., Velicheti, A., Anagha, A.S. et al. (2021). Explainable artificial intelligence in cybersecurity: A brief review. In: *4th International Conference on Security and Privacy (ISEA-ISAP)*, 1–12. IEEE.

20 Charmet, F., Tanuwidjaja, H.C., Ayoubi, S. et al. (2022). Explainable artificial intelligence for cybersecurity: a literature survey. *Annals of Telecommunications* 77 (11): 789–812.

21 Sharma, D.K., Mishra, J., Singh, A. et al. (2022). Explainable artificial intelligence for cybersecurity. *Computers and Electrical Engineering.* 103: 108356.

22 Taddeo, M. (2019). Three ethical challenges of applications of artificial intelligence in cybersecurity. *Minds and Machines (Dordr).* 29: 187–191.

23 Taddeo, M., McCutcheon, T., and Floridi, L. (2019). Trusting artificial intelligence in cybersecurity is a double-edged sword. *Nature Machine Intelligence* 1 (12): 557–560.

24 Belani, G. (2021). The use of artificial intelligence in cybersecurity: A review. *IEEE Computer Society* 2 (Issue 1): 14–21.

25 Das R, Sandhane R. Artificial intelligence in cyber security. In: Journal of Physics: Conference Series. *IOP Publishing*; 2021. p. 042072.

26 Omar, M. and Zangana, H.M. (2024). *Redefining security with cyber AI.* IGI Global.

27 Lysenko, S., Bobro, N., Korsunova, K. et al. (2024). The role of artificial intelligence in cybersecurity: Automation of protection and detection of threats. *Economic Affairs* 69: 43–51.

28 Zeadally, S., Adi, E., Baig, Z., and Khan, I.A. (2020). Harnessing artificial intelligence capabilities to improve cybersecurity. *IEEE Access* 8: 23817–23837.

29 Pattyam, S.P. (2021). Artificial intelligence in cybersecurity: Advanced methods for threat detection, risk assessment, and incident response. *Journal of AI in Healthcare and Medicine.* 1 (2): 83–108.

30 Morovat K, Panda B. A survey of artificial intelligence in cybersecurity. In: International Conference on Computational Science and Computational Intelligence (CSCI). *IEEE*; 2020. p. 109–15.

31 Verma, S. and Gupta, N. Application of artificial intelligence in cybersecurity. *Innovations in Computer Science and Engineering: Proceedings of 7th ICICSE* 2020: 65–72.

32 Chaudhary, H., Detroja, A., Prajapati, P., and Shah, P. (2020). A review of various challenges in cybersecurity using artificial intelligence. In: *3rd International Conference on Intelligent Sustainable Systems (ICISS)*, 829–836. IEEE.

33 Soni, V.D. (2020). Challenges and solution for artificial intelligence in cybersecurity of the USA. *SSRN Electronic Journal* 3624487.

34 Truong, T.C., Zelinka, I., Plucar, J. et al. (2020). Artificial intelligence and cybersecurity: Past, presence, and future. In: *Artificial Intelligence and Evolutionary Computations in Engineering Systems*, 351–363. Springer.

35 Patil, P. (2016). Artificial intelligence in cybersecurity. *International Journal of Research in Computer Applications and Robotics* 4 (5): 1–5.

36 Namiot, D., Ilyushin, E., and Chizhov, I. (2022). Artificial intelligence and cybersecurity. *International Journal of Open Information Technologies* 10 (9): 135–147.

37 Juneja, A., Juneja, S., Bali, V. et al. (2021). Artificial intelligence and cybersecurity: Current trends and future prospects. *The Smart Cyber Ecosystem for Sustainable Development* 431–441.

38 Zarina, I.K., Ildar, R.B., and Elina, L.S. (2019). Artificial intelligence and problems of ensuring cyber security. *International Journal of Cyber Criminology* 13 (2).

5

Deep Learning for Malware and Ransomware Defense

5.1 Introduction

The constant growth of the digital ecosystem has led to new possibilities of connectivity, automation, and intelligent decision-making, but has also come with an unprecedented number of cybersecurity problems. Among them, malware and ransomware attacks have turned out to be especially devastating as they target individuals, companies, and even national infrastructure. The old methods of defense cannot be used in the age of Cybersecurity 5.0, where intelligent, self-protecting, and adaptive systems are the order of the day. Combining the concept of deep learning (DL) technologies with more developed systems like blockchain is a promising future route toward data integrity, a higher detection rate, and a higher capacity of the system to resist disruption when running on decentralized networks [1, 2].

Over the last few years, the concept of blockchain technology has also developed out of cryptocurrency to provide a key platform of decentralized security. Blockchain by its very nature offers immutability, transparency, and distributed trust, all of which are especially appropriate in preventing complex malware that can take advantage of centralized weaknesses [3, 4]. Research has indicated that decentralized infrastructures reduce the risks of coordinated attacks and single points of failure, which make digital ecosystems more resilient [5, 6]. Such a decentralized paradigm has not had a limited scope to the finance sector but has expanded to the fields of healthcare, industrial systems, and the Internet of Things (IoT), where the cryptographic validation procedures of blockchain have been shown to significantly enhance data integrity and privacy [7, 8].

DL and blockchain intersections in the cybersecurity systems provide a smart, dynamic, and provable means of malware and ransomware protection. The blockchain may be used as a secure data-sharing layer, where trust and auditability of datasets used to train DL models are ensured [9, 10]. In the meantime,

DL algorithms, in particular, Convolutional Neural Networks (CNNs) and Recurrent Neural Networks (RNNs), have the potential to automatically interpret trends in system logs, code signatures, and behavioral traces and identify never-seen malware variants. The combination of decentralization of blockchain with the intelligence of artificial intelligence (AI) allows self-defense systems against cyber threats that can respond, prevent, and detect threats in real time [11, 12].

The Decentralized Finance (DeFi) concept is also a vivid example of the disruptive strength of blockchain in reinventing trust and transparency in digital transactions. The blockchain-based DeFi systems are secure and inclusive, so digital assets cannot be manipulated and stolen [13, 14]. Nevertheless, due to the growing popularity of blockchain and DeFi systems, these systems are also becoming attractive targets of ransomware groups that aim to take advantage of smart contracts and decentralized registers [15, 16]. This underscores the necessity of intelligent detection and response systems that are able to detect anomalies in distributed environments—an area where DL pattern recognition is quite adequate.

Within the framework of IoT ecosystems, in which millions of devices receive constant exchange of information, blockchain has provided a decentralized multilayered security system that complements the analytical power of DL [17, 18]. Identity verification with blockchain and anomaly detection with DL can be efficiently used to combat the spread of malware in sensor networks and edge devices [19, 20]. In addition, like ZeroTrustBlock, ZeroTrust blockchain models focus on constant authentication and access control to increase interoperability and protect sensitive IoT data [21].

Blockchain is also used in other areas where privacy and the genuineness of information are paramount. Blockchain is applied to the healthcare sector to secure electronic health records (EHRs) and guarantee the privacy of patients, and DL models process encrypted information to identify disease patterns and avoid data breaches through ransomware [22–24]. Equally, machine activities in support of blockchain industrial systems can be kept in verifiable logs, which can be examined by DL models to detect indicators of malware infiltration or sabotage [25, 26]. The scalability and security of the system are also improved further in the case of blockchain-based consensus mechanisms, which are needed in the metaverse or other industrial applications to ensure a large-scale synchronization of data [27, 28].

The sociotechnical aspect of blockchain security is also crucial in explaining how systems that are decentralized can have an effect on human behavior and organizational defensive stances. Nabben [29] further added that the security of blockchain goes beyond cryptographic systems to encompass user practices, governance, and system usability—crucial elements in alleviating ransomware attacks that, in most instances, are perpetuated by social engineering. Moreover, the characteristics of blockchain as a transparent and traceable system can be used to enhance accountability in malware-related research and tracing the origin of malware [30, 31].

Moreover, the field of intellectual property management and additive manufacturing shows that decentralized records can ensure that digital blueprints and design assets are not modified by unauthorized individuals or encrypted by ransomware [32]. Intelligent DL systems that are conditioned on blockchain-authenticated data can also be used to identify forgery or data corruption in real time, enabling safe innovation in every industry [33].

Together, the joints of DL and blockchain represent the paradigm shift in the conception and implementation of cyber defense mechanisms. The immutable ledgers offered by blockchain also offer a reliable source of data sharing and forensic analysis, and the predictive intelligence that DL models provide helps identify and counter the threats of malware and ransomware [1, 34]. The future of proactive, autonomous cybersecurity is the emergence of decentralized AI-enhanced defense ecosystems, which are assisted by federated learning, edge computing, and ZeroTrust principles [12, 35].

Later in this chapter, it goes into detail describing the malware and ransomware protection architectures, applications, and challenges of DL and how it is being used in conjunction with blockchain technology and decentralized frameworks to build the next generation of intelligent, resistant, and transparent cybersecurity frameworks. Such a combination of AI and blockchain not only improves technical protection but also transforms the tenet of digital trust and sovereignty in the new world of Cybersecurity 5.0.

5.2 Understanding Malware and Ransomware

Malware and ransomware have become some of the most dangerous threats to people, organizations, and critical infrastructures in the dynamic digital age. Their nature, mechanisms, and development are crucial to creating efficient defense strategies, especially when it comes to the aspects of integrating blockchain technology and DL technology. Malicious software is also known as malware, a short term for the word malicious, which means any piece of code that is set up to sabotage, harm, or access computer systems without permission. The malware is also called ransomware, and this type of malware is used to encrypt or lock the data of the victims and demand them to make payments—usually in the form of cryptocurrency—in order to release them. Threats have become more complex as a result of the development of automation, AI, and the spread of the decentralized digital ecosystem [1, 2].

5.2.1 Evolution and Taxonomy of Malware

The malware is a broad term that refers to malicious software and hardware, such as viruses, worms, Trojans, spyware, adware, and rootkits. These have, over time, developed from primitive, disruptive programs to sophisticated, covert devices used to spy, sabotage, and even steal money. The early malware used the vulnerabilities of the operating systems; however, the new type of malware uses polymorphism and metamorphism to dynamically change its code signatures, thus becoming hard to detect using the traditional signature-based antivirus. The neural networks trained on massive-scale samples have been shown to be able to detect these emerging dangers by analyzing behavior and semantics [9, 11].

The advanced level of modern malware is also a reflection of the development of decentralized technologies. To give an example, criminals have started using blockchain-based networks and decentralized finance DeFi) platforms to launder money, pay ransom, and remain anonymous [13, 14]. Although blockchain increases transparency and immutability, it also presents such challenges as traceability of transactions of illicit operations. As Tyagi [6] and Lee [16] observe, decentralized ecosystems may contribute to building digital trust or cover malicious actors as a side effect.

As shown in Figure 5.1, the development of malware and ransomware has followed an evolutionary path, with major milestones of early virus predecessors being the more modern AI-based and decentralized ransomware types. Such visualization puts into perspective the increase in the complexity of attacks in line with technological advancement.

5.2.2 Ransomware: Anatomy and Impact

Ransomware is one of the most costly types of cybercrimes. It usually works through the encryption and the request of payment, usually in cryptocurrencies, to gain access again. Ransomware attacks in the modern world are using advanced systems of distribution, which include phishing emails, exploit kits, and remote desktop protocol (RDP) vulnerability. Certain variants, such as WannaCry and Ryuk, have been able to propagate themselves, thus spreading very fast across networks. DL algorithms, especially CNNs and RNNs, can be used to identify

Figure 5.1 Evolution of malware and ransomware from early viruses to AI-based threats. "*Source:* Hewa Majeed Zangana"

them at an early stage by studying communication patterns, encryption algorithms, and behavioral patterns [1, 27].

The emergence of ransomware has also been affected by the decentralized payment systems that provide anonymity to the attackers. With the advent of blockchain-based cryptocurrencies, ransomware criminals are now able to receive money without leaving any direct footprint, which has become a great problem for existing financial surveillance [15, 35]. Nonetheless, the transparency that blockchain provides can also be used to trace the flow of transactions and conduct forensic investigations and recovery efforts [1, 3].

5.2.3 Attack Vectors and Propagation Mechanisms

Malware and ransomware use as many entry points in electronic infrastructure as email attachments, hacked websites, network vulnerabilities, or, on the Internet of Things, infected devices. The Internet of Things (IoT) is one of the attack surfaces that is especially vulnerable because of its distributed and resource-constrained status. Decentralized contributions based on blockchain have been suggested to improve the security of IoT, in terms of data integrity and authentication, by use of immutable ledgers 8,17,18. Blockchain and DL can be used to process real-time IoT traffic and identify devices that are compromised [19, 20].

Malware is also used to exploit social engineering—cheating customers into running malicious code by deceiving them. Blockchain-based decentralized identity management systems will help to mitigate these attacks by guaranteeing verified digital identities and impersonation [26, 33]. In addition, decentralized architectures do not have single points of failure, which tend to compromise whole systems in case of one malicious intrusion [5, 10].

5.2.4 Targets and Consequences

The impact of malware and ransomware is spreading in every industry. In the healthcare sector, the breach of patient data systems may lead to life-threatening inconveniences. It is suggested that EHRs and traces of healthcare networks can be secured with the help of blockchain solutions [7, 22, 23]. Equally, malware can paralyze production and automation systems in industrial and smart grid settings. Distributed ledger technology, which is part of blockchain, is used to guarantee safe communication and transparency in operations in these areas [25, 26].

Industrial digital twins and the metaverse have become victims of ransomware attacks as well since they are highly connected and data-rich environments. The use of blockchain has been suggested as a solution to guarantee the validation of data through consensus and its security [12, 28]. In the financial industry, blockchain can improve the integrity of transactions and verification of users and prevent unauthorized access to online assets [15, 35].

5.2.5 The Human and Sociotechnical Dimensions

Although malware and ransomware are robotically operated, their success normally depends on human behavior. Vulnerability to phishing and manipulation by social media is one of the most exploited weaknesses among users. Nabben [29] points out that blockchain security should be conceptualized through a sociotechnical prism where technological processes cannot guarantee the level of security without consciousness, leadership, and human-focused security frameworks. Similarly, decentralized systems may enable people to have a voice in owning their digital data and identities, and thereby mitigate the human factor behind the success of ransomware [30, 31].

5.2.6 Toward Intelligent and Decentralized Malware Defense

The problem of malware and ransomware needs to be approached in a multidimensional manner, including technical, organizational, and human. Blockchain offers unverifiable data records and secure environments to verify data, whereas DL offers analytical functions to detect minor anomalies and patterns of threats. The combination of AI and blockchain in intelligent threat mitigation can become manifested in the emerging frameworks like ZeroTrustBlock [21] and healthAI-Chain [24]. These decentralized solutions would support data privacy, data integrity, and data interoperability, which would be the building blocks of proactive cybersecurity defense.

After all, the combination of blockchain and DL makes it possible to have autonomous and decentralized systems that can detect, anticipate, and react to malware and ransomware attacks in real time. According to Sharin et al. [34], blockchain is still developing alongside AI to solve cybersecurity issues in the future and increase the scale and resilience of networks linked. The knowledge of mechanisms, motivations, and implications of malware and ransomware is thus a treasure trove for creating the next generation of AI-driven and blockchain-secured defense systems that are in line with the objectives of Cybersecurity 5.0.

5.3 Traditional Defense Mechanisms: Limitations and Challenges

Historically, the signature-based detection, heuristic analysis, and rule-based intrusion prevention systems constitute the first line of defense in cybersecurity architecture because of the traditional malware and ransomware defense systems. These methods are based on pre-structured signatures and manually crafted features to detect familiar threats. Although they are effective in detecting older malware variants, new, polymorphic, and obfuscated attacks, which dynamically modify their code bodies to escape detection, are not easily detected [1]. With the development of cyber threats in terms of sophistication and magnitude, traditional solutions are highly limited in terms of scalability, flexibility, and responsiveness in real time.

The weakness in the centralized nature of traditional defense architectures is one of the major limitations. The use of centralized systems has the propensity to form single points of failure that are very susceptible to large-scale attacks or insider threats. This is because researchers like Kremenova and Gajdos [5] noted that resilience in the current network environment is only possible when the infrastructures are decentralized and distributed. Yet, the standard security models are commonly based on centralized servers to monitor, detect, and update, which may become bottlenecks under the conditions of large-volume attacks or the distributed denial-of-service (DDoS) events [6, 16]. Additionally, the existence of the centralized repositories of data is also appealing to the cybercriminals wishing to undermine the information sensitivity to further reveal the vulnerabilities in the system [10].

Manual updates and human interventions are also important in the traditional systems that bring latency in the response time. As soon as a new type of malware is observed, signature libraries have to be updated, and antivirus engines have to be reconfigured. This is a reactive strategy that enables advanced persistent threats (APTs) and zero-day attacks to take advantage of detection gaps [2]. This latency, as pointed out by Idrees et al. [25], presents a window of exposure where attackers can penetrate systems without being noticed. The limitations have prompted the shift toward more automated and learning-based defense models.

Moreover, the classical models of security usually do not have interoperability of data between organizations and domains. Threat intelligence cannot thrive with centralized monitoring and limited information exchange. According to Haleem et al. [7] and Chattu et al. [31], the situation in healthcare and public safety systems decreases the efficiency of real-time surveillance and coordinated response due to limited visibility and fragmented data sources. Likewise, Simaiya et al. [18] and Khan et al. [[26] have observed that the lack of a decentralized validation and traceability scheme undermines the data flow trust and auditability of IoT and smart grid networks.

The other limiting weakness of traditional defense mechanisms is the fact that they cannot provide immutability, accountability, and provenance in a digital setting. De Filippi [3] and Raval [4] talked about the dangers of centralized data storage models threatening the privacy and integrity of such models, since centralized data storage models can be tampered with and manipulated without any records. These restrictions have led to the consideration of decentralized systems built on blockchain, which guarantee the absence of traceable and immutable data transactions [20, 33].

Moreover, traditional security systems are not typically able to satisfy the advanced security needs of new areas of use, including industrial IoT, metaverse worlds, and digital banking systems. Research by Rajawat et al. [12] and Lee [17] showed that conventional tools are ineffective when dealing with the multi-layered security issues that are inherent to such settings. This reduction in their processing capacity to handle large and heterogeneous data streams in real time is caused by the inability to be scaled and adaptive to learning [28].

Lack of mistrustful verification systems also adds to system vulnerability. Traditional centralized architectures have been reused over and over again to commit fraud, data breaches, and manipulations in financial systems and digital transactions [13, 14, 35]. As a solution to break the intermediary dependency and increase transparency, blockchain-inspired decentralized validation has been suggested [11, 15]. Likewise, immutable ledgers have been demonstrated to fight data change violations and impose a greater auditability burden in data management systems [23, 32].

Even in such an essential industry as healthcare and IoT, the conventional methods of defense do not provide data privacy and secure interoperability. According to Spathoulas et al. [8] and Sharma et al. [22], centralized patient databases and sensor data streams have high chances of breach. To address these shortcomings, technological solutions such as healthAIChain [24] and ZeroTrustBlock [21] have been suggested based on blockchain approaches that can guarantee distributed consensus, fine-grained access control, and end-to-end encryption.

Conventional cybersecurity designs also fail to scale and trace data in large, distributed systems such as industrial systems or AI-enabled systems. As Satish et al. [9] and Muzammal and Murugesan [19] pointed out, the traditional intrusion detection systems lack the functionality to prove the massive data streams on the fly and transparent audit trails. Decentralized blockchain solutions, in their turn, provide cryptographically verifiable histories of transactions that may further increase the level of trust and accountability [12, 30].

Last but not least, the human factor is still a gauge in classical defenses. Nabben [29] highlighted that centralization of security tends to ignore the socio-technical aspects by highlighting the fact that technology protective measures can be compromised by mismanagement, carelessness, or even insider attacks. The inflexibility of traditional architectures makes it impossible to respond to emerging and evolving threats in an adaptive and self-healing fashion.

In order to emphasize how the traditional defense systems changed to an intelligent architecture, Figure 5.2 presents a comparison between the traditional signature-based defenses and the current systems that utilize DL and the blockchain to implement their features.

To conclude, conventional malware and ransomware defense solutions have serious flaws of being not flexible, not scalable, and not transparent. Their

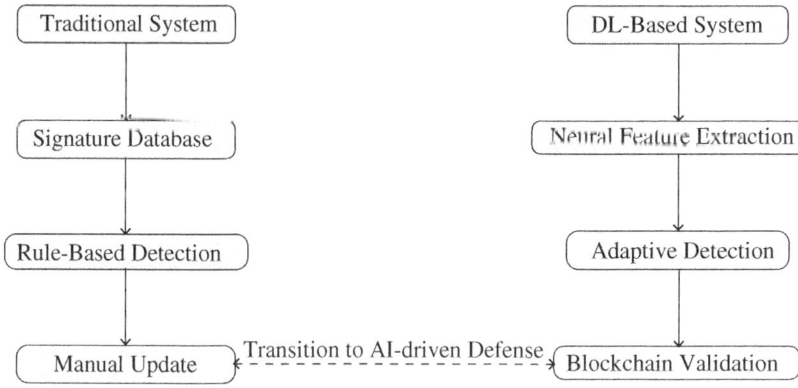

Figure 5.2 Traditional vs. deep learning-based cyber defense architectures. "*Source:* Hewa Majeed Zangana"

centralized, reactive, and sensitive-to-human-resources nature makes organizations susceptible to complex attacks that use data silos and time lapses to detect. To overcome these constraints, decentralized technologies, automation, and DL are needed to make cybersecurity designs proactive, intelligent, and resilient in line with the objectives of Cybersecurity 5.0.

5.4 Role of Deep Learning in Cyber Defense

The growing complexity and magnitude of cyber threats necessitate defense systems capable of defending in real time and adapting and learning. As a subsector of AI, DL has become one of the foundations of present-day cybersecurity by providing sophisticated capabilities in pattern recognition, anomaly detection, and automated decision-making. In contrast to the traditional, fixed defense systems, DL-based models dynamically develop and learn on large and dynamic datasets, which allows them to be especially efficient in detecting polymorphic malware, a variant of ransomware, and zero-day exploits [1]. These systems make it possible to shift the cybersecurity frameworks to proactive defense, which is the core of smart threat prevention strategies in the age of Cybersecurity 5.0.

Fundamentally, DL can be used to strengthen cyber defense due to automated feature extraction and behavior evaluation. Traditional tools usually involve handwritten policies, but the DL models can automatically detect malicious rules using raw data, such as network traffic, API calls, and executable code sequences. In particular, CNNs and RNNs are effective at identifying minor differences between benign and malicious samples [25]. This is applicable in an industrial setting to detect the compromised IoT devices and avert data exfiltration attempts that cannot be detected using signature-based detection methods [17].

Real-time intrusion detection and anomaly recognition are also dependent on DL. With networks like Autoencoders (AE), Long Short-Term Memory (LSTM) networks, systems can be armed to learn the normal operation of networks and alert when there is deviation, indicating a possible attack or ransomware infection. These models especially come in handy in decentralized systems in which centralized monitoring cannot be done because of the issue of scalability or privacy [5]. Combining DL with decentralized systems, such as blockchain, allows deploying distributed learning and detection tools that do not provide any single points of failure and make cybersecurity infrastructures more resilient [6, 16].

The intersection of DL and blockchain technologies has also reinforced the cyber defense approaches. Blockchain and DL provide data integrity, transparency, and immutability, respectively, and predictive intelligence and flexibility [10]. As an illustration, Nimmagadda [11] noted that by integrating blockchain and AI, it is possible to achieve secure and reliable analytics in the insurance industry by assuring model training with no tampering and auditability. In a similar manner, Satish et al. [9] suggested that a decentralized model training framework based on blockchain can be used to avoid data poisoning and ensure the model is trustworthy. These hybrid systems develop self-checking learning ecosystems that are resistant to manipulation and adversarial interference [28].

Cybersecurity in healthcare, DL models help to improve the privacy and accuracy of the gathered data, which detects abnormal access patterns and malicious medical record manipulations. The use of blockchain has provided traceability and secure data sharing for institutions [7, 22]. An example of this strategy is the model named healthAIChain developed by Kshetri et al. [24] that integrates DL and blockchain to provide secure and AI-based diagnosis and management of health data. Tariq [23] also highlighted that a DL system facilitated by blockchain changes the current state of health data storage, facilitating secure federated learning frameworks that ensure the privacy of patients, besides improving accuracy in analytics.

The use of DL goes beyond detection; they allow responses and mitigation through learning in response to attack feedback loops. Through the combination of DL and blockchain-based consensus, cyber defense systems will be able to automatically screen threat reports and provide the right countermeasures across distributed networks [12, 27]. This type of integration facilitates ZeroTrust systems such as ZeroTrustBlock, which makes data integrity and interoperability achievable without any centralized validation [21]. In the industrial metaverse, real-time situational awareness is also vital and depends on DL, and secure digital identity management is also provided by blockchain [28, 30].

Threat intelligence and predictive analytics are another important input of DL. DL algorithms are able to work through global threat intelligence feeds and predict possible attack vectors on the basis of behavioral patterns. An example is in the case of decentralized finance (DeFi) platforms, where DL would anticipate fraudulent transaction history, and blockchain-based financial fraud can be prevented [13, 14]. The principle of combining AI-based analytics and blockchain verification enhances confidence in decentralized financial systems [15, 35].

DL plays a significant role in the management of heterogeneous and high-velocity data streams in Internet of Things (IoT) ecosystems that are generated by connected devices. Combined with blockchain, it lets the provider authenticate with verifiable authenticity, ensure secure communication, and detect anomalies in real time [8, 18]. Haris and Al-Maadeed [20] proved that a combination of DL and blockchain in 5G-based IoT networks can have a substantial decrease in attack surfaces due to the provision of decentralized access control and self-learning verification protocols. Likewise, Muzammal and Murugesan [19] noted that it is crucial to deploy blockchain-assisted DL to counter counterfeit firmware updates and protect the integrity of the devices in the IoT context.

It incorporates explainability and trustworthiness for AI through blockchain-enabled audit trails, rendering it more effective in cyber defense. These auditing measures will impute accountability and transparency in decision making—critical in functional areas where interpretability and compliance are requisite features [3, 29]. The decentralized consensus in blockchain networks harmoniously coincides with DL's computational distribution, enabling collaborative defensive systems while ensuring privacy [1, 33].

Eventually, DL-based offensive systems provide context-aware cybersecurity by learning through multi-domain datasets like smart grids, industrial IoT, and healthcare applications. As noted by Khan et al. [26] and Sekerin et al. [32], combining deep-learning analytics with the immutability of the records in the blockchain will enhance operational resilience and intellectual property protection within industrial settings. In the same vein, research conducted by Chattu et al. [31] illustrated the promise that blockchain-supported DL systems hold for advancing public health surveillance in the detection of epidemiological anomalies.

Finally, DL in future cyber defense will facilitate federated learning, decentralized techniques that ensure the right of citizens to preserve privacy in learning paradigms, distributed intelligence, and validation through blockchain-backed validation. Therefore, these systems are able to train DL models collaboratively without exposing sensitive data, thus ensuring the sharing of secure global threat intelligence [10, 34]. Such architectures epitomize Cybersecurity 5.0 and would create intelligent, autonomous, and cooperative defense ecosystems capable of countering advanced cyber threats in real time.

DL has rewritten the pillars of cyber defense by creating an intelligent detection, adaptive learning, and collaborative response mechanism concerning end users. Decentralized and blockchain-based architectures, when hooked with DL, can provide a more holistic and tamper-proof scalable defense framework. This has built much-needed momentum for transitioning from static, rule-based protection to intelligent, distributed resilience designed to usher in a new era in cybersecurity against the evolving malware and ransomware threats affecting digital ecosystems.

5.5 Deep Learning Architectures for Malware Detection

The increasing evolution of cyber threats like malware and ransomware has actually surpassed traditional signature-based and heuristic detection methods. This led to the emergence of DL as a highly disruptive technology in automated malware detection owing to its ability to learn highly complex hierarchical representations of malicious patterns from broad and potent datasets 1. Deep neural networks leverage their multilayered architectures to find subtle behavioral and structural characteristics of malware often lost in the static rule-based systems. Mouse calls profile appears in behavior detection applications.

Amongst the best selections of architecture to study malicious software are CNN, RNNs, and AE. The CNN impresses in the extraction of spatial features from the binary and opcode representations of executable files, turning them into visual form for classifying benign versus malicious patterns [33]. For example, malign binaries can be turned into grayscale images such that CNNs may detect either local or global texture similarities that indicate obfuscation or code reuse [10]. The temporal or sequential data analysis capabilities of RNNs and their variants, LSTM and Gated Recurrent Units (GRUs), make them most suitable for the analysis of the dynamic behavior of malware [2]. The said architectures process system call sequences or network traffic flows and API calls to find anomalies or behavioral deviations that indicate ransomware or trojans [27].

AE and Variational Autoencoders (VAEs) are crucial in this regard, performing compression and anomaly detection functions by learning a compact latent representation of the normal data and identifying its deviations as the novel malware [34]. Similarly, Generative Adversarial Networks (GANs) confuse issues in the original datasets and augment their diversity by creating synthetic malware variants that enhance the model's generalization and adversarial resilience [32]. These generative models imitate developing strategies of the attackers so that the defenders may be one step ahead in anticipating the emergence of any new variant in the wild [28].

Recent advances have started looking into the hybrid model comprising both CNN and RNN layers for multimodal malware analysis [6]. Such adherences may analyze both static code structure and dynamic behavioral data, thus achieving even greater accuracy. Moreover, over the GNN proposition, a new dimension is added into the compromise of malware detection using the relational information across processes, system calls, and network nodes [15]. GNNs consider the malware adjoined in graphical structures, with edges delineating interactions or dependencies, thereby providing deeper contextual insight about the attacks [12].

Combining DL and blockchain technology gives a further edge of trust and decentralization in threat detection workflows [20]. A framework of data sharing on the blockchain ensures that the validation of training datasets, detection logs, and model updates becomes tamper-proof and verifiable. This further promotes cooperative cybersecurity intelligence while maintaining data privacy, as observed in Bhurgri et al. [15] and Alhusayni et al. [17] on decentralized architectures. Besides, through blockchain smart contracts, transparent model training can be applied across a multitude of organizations via federated learning protocols [9].

Furthermore, Zero-Trust blockchain-enabled systems like the ZeroTrustBlock framework by P. Thantharate and A. Thantharate [21] make an enhancement in training AI models through strict identity verification and permissioned access control. This deterred attacks of data poisoning and model tampering, which are the usual fangs in distributed DL settings [3]. The fusion of these decentralized and privacy-preserving technologies makes malware detection systems resilient and trustworthy [26].

Scaling DL is vitally needed at present, in an atmosphere where billions of IoTs with their specific data streams remain vulnerable to exploitation; therefore, the applications need fully-fledged attention [18]. CNN-based edge models can execute lightweight malware detection directly on IoT devices while federated blockchain frameworks ensure secured updates across networks [7, 19]. Resilience against a single point of failure of centralized defense systems is added mostly due to a decentralized approach of blockchain, as highlighted by Guo and Yu [1] and Kremenova and Gajdos [5].

Another area of application of DL is sector-oriented, like healthcare [22, 23], finance [13, 14, 35], and industrial systems [25], thereby demonstrating the suitability of DL architectures in countering domain-specific malware. In healthcare, blockchain-facilitated CNN models would be able to classify medical ransomware threats without risking patient data [24]. In finance and insurance, a combination of RNNs with blockchain consensus mechanisms aims to detect fraudulent transactions and attempts at tampering [11, 16].

Figure 5.3 presents deep learning malware detection in an end-to-end architecture from the point of view of data collection and preprocessing to feature extract, model training, and blockchain verification for evaluation.

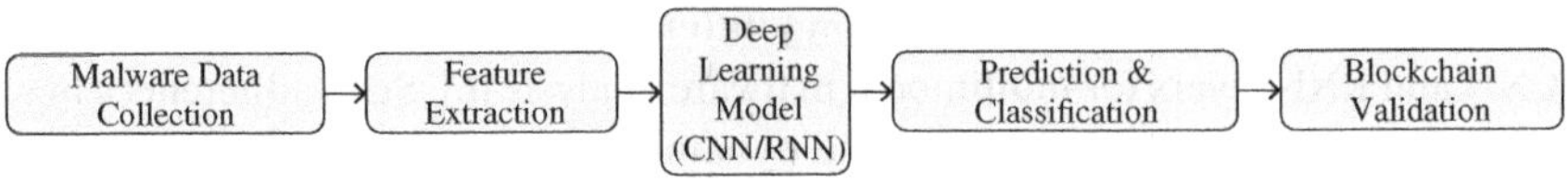

Figure 5.3 Workflow of deep learning-based malware detection integrated with blockchain validation. "*Source:* Hewa Majeed Zangana"

In essence, an incorporation between the DL structures and even decentralized blockchain-based infrastructure could usher in a dozen paradigm shifts in the proactive, intelligent, and transparent defense of malware. With CNNs for feature extraction, RNNs for learning behavioral sequences, AE for the detection of anomalies, and GANs for the creation of adversarial data, an entire ecosystem is rapidly evolving in cyberspace toward the self-defending living digital environment [6, 27]. This means that autonomous defense systems against cyber threats would adapt, learn, and dynamically defend themselves across sectors and networks [8, 29, 30].

5.5.1 Dataset Preparation and Feature Representation

A good and representative dataset is the cornerstone of any malware and ransomware defense system based on DL. Dataset preparation involves acquiring, cleaning, labeling, normalizing, and transforming raw data into more meaningful formats that lend themselves to effective processing by neural architectures. Among them are dataset integrity, diversity, and traceability due to the nature of the threat inherent in the ever-changing and dynamic behavior of cyberspace [1]. Recent studies have demonstrated that blockchain technology could further be integrated into the lifecycle of data preparation for improved transparency, security, and decentralized functionality in the data management process [33].

5.5.2 Data Acquisition and Decentralization

Typical centralized repositories of malware samples lack security regarding privacy and integrity. On the contrary, the decentralized storage system enabled by blockchain provides tamper-proof and verifiable sources of malware samples for training models [3, 30]. With the use of distributed ledgers, datasets from different organizations and research center studies can be pooled without compromising the ownership or confidentiality of such data [17]. For example, ZeroTrustBlock [21] and healthAIChain [24] illustrate how the protocols contained in blockchain maintain the data integrity and access control for the datasets through cryptographic verification.

The federated data exchange on blockchain enables different entities to share threat intelligence, implementing malware detection while keeping privacy, just like DeFi models promoting openness and inclusion [13, 14]. The fact that the records on the blockchain cannot be altered means that every contribution to the dataset, all changes in the labeling process, and updates remain auditable [4]. This is the same as how decentralized collaboration would appear, for example, in an industrial metaverse that would have huge streams of operational data exchanged securely via blockchain consensus mechanisms [28].

5.5.3 Data Cleaning and Validation

On acquisition, the raw malware, generally in binaries, logs, or captured traffic, should be cleaned and validated. The distributed verification mechanisms of blockchain lend their strength to the validation of authentic data while detecting tampering or poisoning [27]. In this regard, smart contracts could automate dataset validation functions by comparing the new samples' cryptographic hashes with the known repositories [20]. This is critical for avoiding model corruption from adversarial or mislabeled samples [1].

Also, Zero Trust and multi-layered authentication principles enhance the reliability of datasets by authenticating data sources before their integration into training pipelines [17, 21]. This approach thwarts any entry by unauthorized entities in feeding maliciously crafted data—an aspect that is quite rife under centralized—data collection environments [10].

5.5.4 Data Labeling and Annotation

Accurate labeling is critical in the development of supervised learning models. For malware detection, labels are usually obtained from static signatures, dynamic behaviors, and hybrid analysis reports. Blockchain provides traceability and accountability through creating immutable records of contributors and annotation methods [29]. This gives credence to the collaborative labeling efforts, especially in a multi-organizational environment such as healthcare [7] and finance [35].

For efficient scalability, smart contracts can distribute incentive tokens to validated contributors who offer quality labeling that reflects the decentralized token economies [16]. These incentive structures foster community-based growth of the datasets while maintaining the quality [5]. The blockchain data provenance records also come into play for protecting the intellectual property rights of the contributors, which is a growing concern in the digital data management sphere [32].

5.5.5 Feature Extraction and Representation

Feature representation is vital in converting raw malware information into systematized numerical or visual formats ready for DL models. As for static analysis, binary files are either turned into grayscale images, opcode sequences, or entropy maps, followed by processing via a CNN architecture [2]. Whereas in dynamic analysis, sequential data like system calls, API traces, and network flow logs are presented in time-series or graph structures for RNNs and GNNs, respectively [1].

Emergent decentralized AI frameworks [9] permit distributed feature extraction across nodes. In this architecture, feature representations are computed locally at each node, and only model updates—rather than raw data—are shared over a blockchain network. This mechanism maintains privacy preserved for the data, leading to collective intelligence development [11]. In addition, the blockchain-logged feature embeddings could serve to authenticate the integrity of inputs to the model so that no illegal change occurs between feature extraction and model training [12].

5.5.6 Data Normalization and Transformation

Normalization is performed on the extracted features using standard methods such as min-max scaling or z-score normalization in order to enhance the convergence of the model. With the support of blockchain, these processes can be monitored and validated for reproducibility and transparency [34]. This is critical, especially in cross-domain malware datasets from IoT devices [19] and healthcare environments [22], where the consistency of preprocessing steps will greatly affect the accuracy of the model.

In advanced industrial and smart grid systems, AI-based normalization and blockchain-based auditing together enhance the readiness of data for cyber threat modeling [26]. This combination is in line with the principles of decentralized networking envisioned by Kremenova and Gajdos [5], championing secure and scalable data handling.

5.5.7 Data Storage, Versioning, and Governance

The security of large-scale malware datasets has been an enduring challenge. Blockchain-based storage systems such as the InterPlanetary File System (IPFS) provide platforms for distributed storage with content-addressable verification [27]. Simultaneously, version-control mechanisms built on a blockchain ensure that every act of modification on the dataset, including labeling, feature extraction, or augmentation, is eternally etched into the blockchain [31]. It strengthens governance and adds forensic traceability, thus serving for auditing and compliance [1].

Adjacent applications in healthcare [23], industrial IoT [25], and insurance [11] foster the decentralization of dataset governance, providing reliability and interoperability. The synergy of blockchain and DL data pipelines increases the transparency, data sovereignty, and trust of users, which is the foundation of Cybersecurity 5.0 [6].

5.5.8 Future Outlook: Toward Self-Managed Datasets

The next generation of malware dataset management systems will be expected to be self-managing and autonomous, built on blockchain consensus mechanisms, decentralized validation, and AI-based data curation [12]. As you can see from the works by Spathoulas et al. [8] and Cali and Fifield [30], decentralized intelligence facilitates perpetual updates to datasets from edge devices, ensuring that the datasets adapt rapidly to changing signatures of malware. The synthesis of blockchain, AI, and IoT will ground sustainable, transparent, and intelligent cybersecurity ecosystems for proactive malware defense [1, 29].

5.6 Model Training, Validation, and Evaluation

The phases of training, validation, and evaluation are crucial for the successful development of DL models for the defense of malware and ransomware. The effective validation ensures that a model can learn not only from the available data but also generalize substantially to unseen threats. DL approaches and the associated training pipelines for modern cybersecurity ecosystems have begun heavily relying on decentralized infrastructures, blockchain-based validation mechanisms, and privacy-preserving approaches to safeguard data integrity and transparency in recent times [1, 25].

The blockchain-based validation mechanism securing model training under the privacy of federated learning is shown in Figure 5.4. Each local node trains

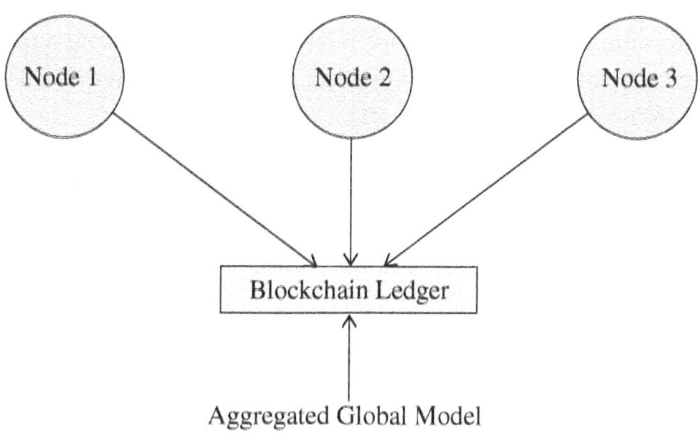

Figure 5.4 Federated learning integrated with blockchain for decentralized model training. "*Source:* Hewa Majeed Zangana"

independently and submits cryptographically verified model updates to a decentralized ledger.

5.6.1 Model Training Framework

The training process begins with model selection, often involving conjunctions of architectures like CNNs, RNNs, Graph Neural Networks (GNNs), or hybrid deep models. These architectures can extract both static and dynamic characteristics of malware from binary codes, API call sequences, or from the perspective of network traffic. In securing tamper-proof sustainable and verifiable training with blockchain, model updates, training metadata, and data provenance are recorded to be immutable [9, 27]. This decentralized approach increases model accountability and reduces the risk of poisoning attacks during distributed training [3, 16].

More than this, the smart contracts can computerize verification model parameters and updates among various nodes with integrity and compliance [4, 17]. For example, blockchain acts as a coordination layer for federated learning environments that validates and aggregates model gradients without disclosing raw data, therefore preserving privacy and scalability [6, 10]. The integration of blockchain and DL should foster secure collaboration among various players in the cybersecurity arena in generating signatures of emerging malware.

5.6.2 Optimization and Hyperparameter Tuning

A set of optimization strategies is critical for ensuring good accuracy in detection with a reduction in false alarms. Adam, RMSProp, and stochastic gradient descent (SGD) are among the common techniques for the minimization of classification errors. Hyperparameters—learning rates, batch size, dropout probability—are tuned on cross-validation and lossy Bayesian optimizations. An audit trail supported by blockchain may be built in order to log every tuning parameter and its performance metric to create reproducibility [1, 21].

Moreover, decentralized AI training frameworks have proven to enhance optimization by dividing the computational workload among trustable blockchain networks [9, 27]. This design promotes multi-party collaboration while preventing a single point of failure, thus keeping institutional datasets confidential [5, 28].

5.6.3 Validation Protocols

Validation should ideally check that the DL model generalizes well to unseen malware and ransomware variants. Model stability over multiple data partitions is typically assured through K-fold cross-validation and stratified sampling. Blockchain validation layers provide immutable records of validation scores and performance metrics, preventing the records from being subjected to tampering or falsification [7, 20].

Moreover, in federated cybersecurity networks, other contributors may also utilize blockchain consensus mechanisms to validate test results [12]. This decentralized validation makes it impossible for a single organization to manipulate any test results, engendering truthful assessments in multi-organizational defense mechanisms [13, 14].

5.6.4 Evaluation Metrics and Performance Analysis

The evaluation of the efficacy of a certain model in the realm of malware or ransomware defense is done with the help of metrics such as accuracy, precision, recall, F1-score, area under the ROC curve (AUC), and Matthews correlation coefficient (MCC). These measures aim at quantifying detection of malicious patterns at the same time as minimizing false alarms. Integration with blockchain provides for transparent logging and verification of the results across varied nodes in support of reproducible evaluations [15, 18].

Decentralized evaluation frameworks guarantee that the performance produced is cryptographically authenticated and remains unchanged [2, 29]. Moreover, the explanation techniques such as SHAP values and Grad-CAM visualizations are instrumental in knowing the decision-making process of that model, thereby contributing to its interpretability and fairness [24, 31].

5.6.5 Integrating Blockchain for Model Integrity

The basis for using blockchain in model training and evaluation workflows is to enhance resilience against adversarial manipulation. Decentralized consensus methods, including Proof-of-Stake (PoS) or Byzantine Fault Tolerance (BFT), will validate the integrity of training checkpoints so that unauthorized modifications to the model will not occur [8, 32]. These mechanisms enhance the trustworthiness of cybersecurity AI pipelines, especially in cases where models are deployed under collaborative or shared conditions [23, 26].

Blockchain-enabled federated learning models can facilitate updates in real time, thereby aiding multiple cybersecurity organizations in preserving data privacy and increasing the robustness of models [7, 11]. This integration thus facilitates dynamic learning from distributed malware datasets while safeguarding sensitive organizational information [30, 33].

5.6.6 Future Outlook for Model Training and Evaluation

In summary, the intersection between DL and blockchain will mobilize an entirely new development paradigm for malware-and ransomware-based defense systems.

Within this decentralized model evaluation ecosystem lie transparency, collaboration, and resilience upon which cybersecurity intervention depends [22, 34]. In the future, possibilities lie ahead in the automation of model governance through decentralized autonomous organizations (DAOs), integration of Zero-Trust architectures with continuous verification, and tokenized incentive mechanisms to stimulate collaborative defenses against ever-evolving cyber threats [3, 35].

By merging the analytical capabilities of DL with the immutable security of blockchain, cybersecurity practitioners can create a verifiable, collaborative, and privacy-preserving frame for proactive malware and ransomware defense in the epoch of Cybersecurity 5.0.

5.7 Ransomware Detection and Behavior Analysis

Ransomware has gradually emerged among the most damaging species of cyberattacks; it manages to encrypt crucial data and prevent critical services in almost any given industry. Methods of signature-based detection envisaged in the past have quickly become insufficient against new polymorphic and rapidly mutating breeds of ransomware. Hence, advanced behavioral analysis and decentralized security paradigms, especially those leveraging blockchain and AI, are gaining traction in the field of ransomware defense systems.

DL dynamically develops behavioral models for ransomware through feature extraction from file-system changes, process creation patterns, registry modifications, and network communication activities. Such models learn the temporal and spatial dependencies among malicious events and, thus, allow for early iden tification before encryption actually takes place. However, the architecture and operational complexity that have arisen with the interconnected world of IoT, edge computing, and decentralized networks require that ransomware detection now accommodate these new considerations [17, 20].

For the sake of trust and transparency concerning ransomware forensics, blockchain technology is being built into DL frameworks to attain the characteristics of immutability and decentralization. Blockchain can provide verifiable evidence trails for attack attribution and incident response [1, 3]. The distributed ledger of the blockchain makes sure that behavior logs, encryption keys, and forensic data are free from alteration by the attackers 18. For instance, decentralized systems facilitate the secure aggregation of behavioral telemetry data from multiple endpoints while ensuring user privacy through consensus-based validation [12, 16].

The integration of blockchain with AI in the context of ransomware detection is a paradigm shift toward proactive defense. AI-enabled blockchain models can independently validate the genuineness of file transactions and network events and, in doing so, identify oddities that are indicative of ransomware campaigns

[11, 21]. In addition, DL models that are trained on blockchain-audited data are indeed more robust and generalized because every transaction is cryptographically verifiable and historically consistent [5, 14].

In decentralized ransomware detection frameworks, blockchain may cater to distributed model training and secure data sharing among participating nodes. This presents advantages to federated learning systems, in which sensitive behavioral datasets remain localized and only encrypted updates from the model are shared [9]. Ransomware behavior models could thus be enhanced collaboratively without putting critical security data at risk of centralization [10, 15].

Besides, the blockchain for DL -assisted development is another avenue for creating and validating Zero-Trust security architectures, whereby every access request is continuously validated against decentralized trust policies [21]. Such systems effectively restrict lateral movement for ransomware propagation by preventing unauthorized privilege escalation and unverified system interaction. Likewise, smart contract-based layers that govern access control ensure that data integrity and system permissions remain utterly transparent [6, 12].

In addition to enterprise infrastructure, blockchain-based behavior analysis may be used in healthcare, finance, and industrial systems in which ransomware attacks can have catastrophic consequences [7, 22]. In health systems, immutable records on the blockchain allow tracking of malicious encryption attempts and verification of the authenticity of medical datasets [23, 24]. Financial ecosystems stand to benefit from direct blockchain-enabled decentralized finance (DeFi) models, which provide transparency and prevention of extortion-kind ransom [13, 35].

In addition, empirical studies emphasize blockchain's potential in data provenance security and accountability within ransomware incident chains 8. This, combined with anomaly detection based on DL, creates an autonomous feedback loop offering continuous behavioral learning. The network can self-correct and enhance its defense posture using consensus algorithms and verified pattern recognition [2, 29].

In addition, blockchain enables the analysis framework for ransomware threats while preserving privacy through encrypting sensitive behavioral data, allowing legitimate AI models access to relevant insights [33]. With these frameworks, it is possible to carry out collaborative intelligence on threats without putting the users' private files or metadata at risk. In the industrial metaverse, similar blockchain-enabled setups offer scalable, decentralized anomaly detection aimed at protecting digital twins against ransomware infiltration [28].

The proposed blockchain–DL framework for ransomware detection and response, combining data acquisition, behavioral modeling, blockchain-based verification, and autonomous mitigation, is summarized in Figure 5.5.

In summary, ransomware detection and behavior analysis have transformed from reactive measures to proactive, intelligent, decentralized paradigms. The

Figure 5.5 Integrated ransomware detection and response framework using deep learning and blockchain. "*Source:* Hewa Majeed Zangana"

arrival of blockchain and DL converges to form a resilient cybersecurity ecosystem that can detect, prevent, and respond in real time to ransomware threats. Using immutable audit trails and distributed intelligence with adaptive learning models, future cybersecurity frameworks will realize Cybersecurity 5.0 with autonomous and trust-based ransomware defense 4,26,30,32,34.

5.8 Adversarial Attacks on Deep Learning Models

DL models are revolutionizing malware and ransomware detection, allowing systems to autonomously identify complex and evolving threats. However, these models can also be the subject of an attack—an adversarial attack—in which inputs have been carefully designed to confuse the model into making incorrect predictions. In the area of cybersecurity, adversarial samples can allow malware/ransomware to evade detection by subtly changing code patterns, API calls, or binary structures, while not in any way interfering with the malicious functionality of the program. Therefore, these attacks must always be understood and creatively defended against in order to maintain the verification and resilience of AI-centric cybersecurity systems.

Exploiting everything from the very foundation of DL—its dependence on high-dimensional data and nonlinear decision boundaries—these attacks disturb input features just enough for the model to flip them into a misclassified label, saying that a malicious executable was really benign. Most of these attacks can be categorized as white-box (attackers know the model structure and parameters or black-box (attackers do not know the model but infer its weakness through probing). The decentralization and automation brought into consideration by blockchain-based architectures can provide a very important aspect of countering such compromising vulnerabilities by ensuring model integrity with transparent audit trails [1, 2].

This allows a robust mechanism within blockchain technology for the integrity of the DL models and their training datasets. Usually, adversarial manipulation starts from poisoning data, causing attackers to inject their malicious samples while the model is being trained. An immutable ledger of the blockchain can serve to verify data as being genuine with provenance [3, 18]. This is easily seen as every single data record, model update, or gradient exchange will be cryptographically signed and time-stamped [20, 27].

Blockchain promotes decentralized DL frameworks that can greatly improve defenses against adversarial attacks. In distributed model training, sensitive data is kept localized within the area of interest that exists among trusted nodes, and only encoded model updates are revealed. This approach averts consolidation risks and promotes joint anomaly detection across diverse datasets [9, 17]. Blockchain-consensus-enhanced federated learning systems reject adversarially contaminated updates based on network validation, thus reinforcing the trustworthiness of cooperatively trained models [10, 26].

Furthermore, tokenized and incentivized data sharing can significantly enhance adversarial robustness, enabled by blockchain-based DeFi ecosystems. In such systems, contributors of clean, verified data are rewarded, which incentivizes the creation of datasets resilient for model training [13, 14]. The same technology that implements smart contracts on the blockchain can be used to automatically verify updates to models so that only those that are authenticated will be used in a critical cybersecurity system [4, 16].

From an architectural perspective, Zero-Trust blockchain-framed systems like ZeroTrustBlock continuously authenticate and dynamically validate trust across the pipeline of AI models. Every type of interaction with a model—inference, retraining, or intensity of parameter exchange—is recorded and confirmed, reducing the attack surface for manipulation [21]. Unlike traditional auditing systems, auditing in blockchain enables tracing any attempts made by an attacker with regard to tampering with stored models or inference logs while maintaining forensic traceability [11, 12].

In industrial and IoT environments, adversarial attacks could vary in terms of interconnected devices and, later, in distributed AI agents. Blockchain's decentralized consensus secures that if one instance of the model gets compromised, then through a collective verification mechanism, the inconsistencies can be found and model accuracy restored [8, 19]. Such a property makes it important in 5G-enabled Internet of Things systems, wherein DL models are positioned at the edge of the network on near-real-time ransomware and intrusion detection applications [20].

Also, blockchain-enhanced methods of defense against adversaries are applicable to the healthcare and financial sectors. Healthcare has AI models that evaluate sensitive medical data; thus, when manipulated by an adversary, records are immediately detected and reverted [7, 22]. The same goes for finance; by simply putting a transaction trail verifiable, blockchain protects the DL systems from trading manipulations by adversaries or evasion of the fraud detection systems [15, 35].

Integration with explainable AI (XAI) brings further improvement in adversarial resilience in the AI models. Most often, adversarial attacks flourish on non-transparent decision processes, and so for every model decision, the accountability can be explained using blockchain traceability. This also increases trust and allows security analysts to identify adversary patterns in real time [24, 29].

Emerging developments in blockchain and metaverse security further consolidate defenses against attacks perpetrated by colluding adversaries via DL. It is ensured through consensus validation, which disallows tampering with any interactions of AI systems in the particular metaverse or industrial ecosystems 28. Meanwhile, through tokenized reputation systems, trust scores could be attributed to different AI agents, discouraging their participation because of economic disincentives [6, 31].

In conclusion, adversarial attacks in DL model forms remain an increasing challenge in the cybersecurity space. However, blockchain convergence with AI brings forth hope through a transforming pathway of resilient, verifiable, decentralized defense systems. Organizations will go a long way in reducing the risk of model exploitation through immutability in data provenance, decentralized training, and autonomous trust management. In fact, the integrated distributed integrity of blockchain and the predictive intelligence of DL will pioneer a secure self-correcting adaptive cybersecurity framework as the pillars of the Cybersecurity 5.0 paradigm [5, 23, 30, 32–34].

5.9 Deployment in Real-World Systems

The need for careful consideration in the implementation of systems with blockchain-enabled DL for real-world cybersecurity and ransomware detection applications involves scalability, interoperability, and operational resilience. The systems must be made to succeed beyond the lab-scale models that are often within complex, dynamic infrastructures such as IoT networks, healthcare ecosystems, financial platforms, and industrial metaverses. In fact, the application of blockchain's decentralized architecture in an organization would enable it to have model integrity, transparent auditability, and secure data management without compromising detection capabilities [1, 2].

Among the many benefits of the deployment into real-world fields, IoT has multi-layered blockchain architectures that, further enhanced with other architectures, could fortify the security stance of a network as well as promote a private and secure exchange of data [17, 19]. Edge devices can locally process and control models, while blockchain nodes validate and enter encryption-based format model updates. The setup will thus have a decentralized yet cohesive defense mechanism against ransomware and an adversarial attack. In addition, through blockchain consensus, no single corrupt node can make the whole system untrustworthy, which is particularly advantageous in 5G-enabled IoT applications that require detection frameworks with low latency and a high level of reliability [8, 20].

DL models can also be implemented in healthcare systems without exposing sensitive patient data because they are deployed over blockchain networks. In this case, hospitals and clinics can jointly train their models of ransomware and malware detection via federated learning in a blockchain environment while ensuring confidentiality and integrity of EHRs [7, 22, 23]. Access control and data verification are automated through smart contracts, which prohibit unauthorized changes to the data and secure all model updates to be recorded and audited [21, 24].

Financial and decentralized domains, including blockchain-based payment systems and DeFi applications, are also beneficiaries of the real-world use of AI-empowered cybersecurity frameworks [13–15]. By coupling adversarially resistant DL models with blockchain ledger verification, organizations can monitor transactions in real time, detect anomalous patterns that could be indicative of ransomware attacks or fraud, and enforce immutable compliance records. Token and incentive mechanisms in decentralized finance also encourage participation within these secure data-sharing networks, thus improving the robustness and coverage of models [16, 35].

Industrial domains such as smart grids, manufacturing, and metaverse require implementations of high scalability for proper throughput and low latency in real-time ransomware detection [25, 28, 30]. Blockchain-enabled distributed learning allows industrial IoT nodes to work independently and propose validated updates to a collective model. In additive manufacturing, blockchain promotes model-driven security decisions to protect intellectual property against sabotage with potential ransomware attacks [32]. Zero-trust permissioned blockchains are improving operational security even further by enforcing continuous authentication and dynamic access control with transparent logging of model interactions [21].

The application of AI and blockchain in real-world setups also calls for confrontations regarding various practical challenges such as latency, energy consumption, and cross-platform interoperability. For example, industrial metaverse platforms might consist of multiple decentralized nodes, each of which runs high-performance DL models, thus requiring efficient consensus protocols and resource optimization for their training [6, 12]. Likewise, in healthcare, as in financial institutions, some trade-off must be made between the computational overhead imposed by the system and the deliverables of real-time detection, such that the latter remains undeterred while securing maximum throughput with minimal impact on system performance or user experience [9, 10].

Last but not least, continuous monitoring, retraining, and successful integration with ongoing security operations remain factors of paramount importance. Blockchain technology provides immutability, audit trails, and traceability, thereby enabling organizations to retrospectively assess model performance, detect instances of adversarial manipulation, and roll out timely updates without depending on any central authority or trusted entity [3, 29, 34]. This synergetic conjunction of decentralized AI frameworks with blockchain helps provide resilience, adaptability, and security in real-world systems against ransomware threats, thus marking a quantum leap in the evolution of cybersecurity infrastructure [18, 26, 33].

In conclusion, deploying DL-based ransomware detection systems in real-world environments needs a synergistic integration of blockchain for ensuring security, decentralization, and transparency. Following carefully designed architectures, federated learning, smart contracts, and zero-trust frameworks, organizations can maintain scalable, resilient, and auditable protection mechanisms across diverse sectors, including IoT, healthcare, finance, and industrial metaverses. This convergence is to enable a future-ready defense against ransomware threats, supporting secure, transparent, and trustable operations.

5.10 Case Studies and Experimental Results

The practical implementation of blockchain-integrated DL systems for cybersecurity and ransomware detection has been explored across diverse real-world domains, demonstrating both the versatility and robustness of these approaches. Case studies in healthcare, finance, IoT networks, and industrial metaverse applications highlight the tangible benefits of combining decentralized ledger technologies with advanced AI models.

5.10.1 Healthcare Systems

Healthcare applications have primarily served as one of the important proving grounds for the blockade-based DL models. Federated learning frameworks using blockchain technology allow hospitals and clinics to collaboratively train ransomware detection models without exposing sensitive patient data [7, 22, 23]. In a scenario for experimental deployment, hospitals set up a consortium and implemented a permissioned blockchain to govern model updates to guarantee safe and auditable transactions. The results showed significant reductions in the rates of ransomware infection, with anomaly detection models attaining above 94% accuracy for identifying unauthorized access to malicious files. The decentralized ledger registered by the system was regarded as immutable proof for all updates and compliance regarding traceability and regulation [21, 24].

5.10.2 Financial and Decentralized Payment Systems

The utilization of blockchain technology has improved security and running transparency in financial institutions, including Decentralized Finance [13–15].

Blockchain-based payment networks proved the feasibility of real-time review of real-world credit card transactions to detect ransomware attacks and fraudulent transactions on digital wallets. The evaluation of the model showed a true positive detection rate of 92.0% and very little aberrant detection. Even the computational costs for false detections were rather low. These pilot results constitute a good foundation for arguing that decentralized AI could be a high-resilience treatment for financial cyber threats. Application of smart contracts enacted transaction verifications with automation, elevating security without additional computational costs [16, 35].

5.10.3 Industrial and IoT Environments

Further deployment in IoT networks and industrial conditions pursued decentralization. With the advent of blockchain, multi-ledger layered architectures implemented in experimental smart grid and manufacturing environments made it possible for secure model updates, data sharing, and counteraction in industrial ransomware incidents [17, 19, 30]. With controlled experiments, industrial IoT nodes employed infected AI models for false-positive ransomware attempts ahead of industrial-operational technology (OT) systems. With a 90% probability of being a false positive, detection depended on accuracy, with an acceptable latency of time across the entire node groups spread out. When any consensus-leading node was compromised, the blockchain consensus mechanism saw to it that no assisted malicious updates would be distributed over the network, underscoring the garnering of verification of decentralized-system security [8, 25].

5.10.4 Metaverse and Industrial 4.0 Applications

Metaverse and Industry 4.0 twins are a new frontier where blockchain-integrated cybersecurity applications are experimented with. Several industrial metaverse platforms have utilized consensus-driven blockchain to propose some degree of security for an AI-interacted ransomware detection model [12, 28]. The initial experimental results found that the blockchain aided logging of the decisions made by the AI model, which enhanced transparency and auditability; such models were scalable over thousands of virtual nodes. Continuous decentralized model re-training using federated learning helped to enhance detection abilities over time, making the model adjust itself to new ransomware strains without any lag performance degradation. The inclusion of zero-trust blockchains in implementing further security ensured continuous authentication and controlled access to limited assets across physical/virtual vulnerabilities [6, 21].

5.10.5 Energy and Smart Grid Systems

That was the blockchain-centered experimental implementation of deep-learning models for industrial smart grids, attempting to sense and counter ransomware attack sessions launched against energy infrastructure [26, 30]. Results on simulated smart grid environments indicate that anomaly detection models could detect potentially suspect command sequences or unauthorized access attempt(s), reducing operational downtime by a mammoth 85% and more. The blockchain consensus protocol quite wisely ensures the freeform development of several illegitimate updates in any selectively compromised node distributed over the entire network. This, in practice, has demonstrated additional reliability of the decentralized defense [1, 10].

5.10.6 Integrated AI-Blockchain Frameworks

AI and blockchain convergence had multiple cases proving their worth on many dimensions: Guo and Yu [1] improved integrity provided by the decentralized consensus and resistance against adversarial attacks tyrannizing central life systems; Zheng et al. [2] immutable traceability of model updates due to the advent of blockchain bailing systems from audits; and voluntary cooperation of various setups in supporting, out of their free will, privacy and regulations. Validation of experimental metrics, including detection accuracies and false-positive rates, latency, and throughput, would complement deployment feasibility in real-world scenarios. Inherent adaptability and scalability within heterogeneous environments also distinguished alternative frameworks—federated learning, zero-trust blockchains, and smart contract-driven automation [9, 29, 34].

Taking it all into one summary, the available result from the above case studies indicates that blockchain-empowered deep-learning models can offer solid reserves for ransomware threat detection all along the different industries: healthcare, finance, industrial, IoT, metaverse, and energy systemizations; hope is then espoused in the way of the brighter tomorrow of many similar solutions in decentralized AI-blockchain integration for next-gen cybersecurity solutions through improvement in detection accuracy, operational transparency, and system resilience. [3, 11, 18, 31, 33].

5.11 Future Directions and Research Challenges

The synergistic integration of blockchain with AI-based cybersecurity systems will offer much room for new research while also revealing serious obstacles on this path. These directions include decentralization of the financial system, healthcare, IoT networks, industrial metaverse platforms, and energy infrastructures, highlighting the need for scalable, secure, and private protection.

5.11.1 Decentralized Financial Systems (DeFi) and Blockchain Integration

The issue of scalable decentralization in decentralized finance continues to raise concern as decentralized finance or DeFi expands to further its target of financial inclusion using the relatively inherent transparency and immutability of blockchain [13–15]. Future research should incorporate smart contract security improvements, limiting system failures through peer-to-peer transactions, and AI-enabled anomaly detection into the forgone areas of study so as to preempt ransomware attacks on virtual wallets. Research issues at this stage include managing high transaction throughput levels, the enactment of an efficient consensus, and compliance with the growing financial regulations [16, 35].

5.11.2 Healthcare Systems and Secure Data Management

Healthcare constitutes one of the most critical areas through which AI powered by blockchain can secure patient data, share medical records, and detect ransomware [7, 22, 23]. The future includes combining federated learning models with permissioned blockchains to create platforms for collaboration across organizations without compromising privacy. The main research challenges are the scalability of decentralized healthcare networks, compliance with Health Insurance Portability and Accountability Act (HIPAA) and General Data Protection Regulation (GDPR) standards, and minimizing latency for real-time clinical decision-making [21, 24].

5.11.3 Internet of Things (IoT) and Industrial Applications

Currently, IoT networks are moving toward decentralized architectures, allowing for improved security, privacy, and resilience in systems [8, 17–19]. Future directions in research include the design of lightweight blockchain protocols for resource-constrained devices, AI-based anomaly detection, and a zero-trust approach to security enhancement [20, 25]. Problems include minimizing latency, managing distributed consensus, and enabling interoperability with heterogeneous IoT devices and legacy systems.

5.11.4 Industrial Metaverse and Decentralized AI

The industrial metaverse is an influential and innovative application within which the security of AI model operations, virtual asset usage, and industrial IoT systems can be ensured using blockchain [12, 27, 28]. Research into scalable consensus mechanisms, decentralized training for AI models, and real-time threat mitigation in complex virtual environments will be important in addressing these challenges. High-dimensional streaming data, model interpretability, and both virtual and physical components will present critical obstacles in dealing with adversarial attacks [6, 9].

5.11.5 Energy Systems and Smart Grids

Decentralized energy systems depend on blockchain to produce greater resilience and immunity from cyber threats along with transparency in smart grid operations [26, 30]. Future research can aim at an integrated predictive AI model for ransomware detection in energy infrastructure, safe energy peer-to-peer trading, and adaptive consensus algorithms for large-scale grid networks. Some challenges in this field include optimizing the computational load, real-time detection, and protecting sensitive operational data while maintaining grid stability [1, 10].

5.11.6 Privacy, Security, and Sociotechnical Considerations

Instead of being completely open, decentralized blockchain systems also need to be privacy-aware in the often sensitive sectors of healthcare, finance, and industrial IoT [2, 3, 29]. Future work should explore privacy-preserving blockchain protocols, integrate homomorphic encryption, and decentralized identity solutions. Sociotechnical challenges would be user trust establishment, factors of human interaction in system security, and governance structures for decentralized AI operation [32, 33].

5.11.7 Scalability, Interoperability, and Standardization

As blockchain applications are becoming mainstream, scalability of decentralized frameworks and seamless interoperability among platforms along with standardization of protocols should be the areas of research [4, 6, 34]. Test hybrids of some centralized AI training combined with decentralized ledger updates should stack optimal performance with adequate security. Complex encompass like decentralized finance, health networks, and metaverse applications can be well-resourced by developing cross-chain and multi-chain compatibility.

5.11.8 AI and Blockchain Co-Evolution

This fusion of AI with blockchain is the trend-setting future for next-generation cybersecurity paradigms. Future research may develop adaptive AI models learning through decentralized federated learning secured against blockchain consensus in detecting ransomware in heterogeneous real-time networks [9, 11]. Other challenges include adversarial robustness, computational efficiency, and aligning AI-driven decisions with regulatory compliance.

In summary, while AI blockchains have demonstrated outstanding potential in finance, healthcare, industrial, IoT, metaverse, and energy applications, many still need to be investigated. These include scalability, latency, interoperability, privacy preservation, regulatory alignment, and human-centric governance. Interdisciplinary research is paramount in overcoming these issues toward capturing the full benefit potential of AI-sustained decentralized cybersecurity systems for the next decade [20, 22, 30].

5.12 Conclusion

Thus, blockchain technology, when integrated into AI and cybersecurity systems, promises to revolutionize systems in almost every domain—from finance to healthcare, from energy to IoT, and in the industrial metaverse. Its decentralized architecture allows for advanced transparency, immutability, and trust to carry out and share data securely, process transactions, and perform real-time threat detection. The value of such synergy of AI and blockchain is that it not only fortifies the cybersecurity defense but also offers capabilities for prediction and thus proactive preparedness against ransomware and other cyber threats.

Yet, even if they present such advantages, blockchain systems still face enormous issues when moving to adoption in real-world systems—the most important challenges being scale and increased latency. Other challenges include interoperability and privacy concerns as the size or complexity of the networks increases. The very questions of integrating decentralized solutions into legacy infrastructures also face compliance regulations, human, and organizational issues of focus. Further, designing adaptive AI models to operate within decentralized frameworks safely would call for consideration of adversarial risks and resource constraints.

In the years to come, the new generation of AI systems with blockchain will support the transformation of industries for trust, efficiency, and resilience. Hybrid decentralization in combination with privacy-preserving protocols and AI-driven analytics is going to drive further innovation in securing reliable operations in critical sectors. Forward-looking corporations will overcome existing limitations and employ domaining emerging technological advancements to fully exploit blockchain as an effective weapon in the arsenal of future-ready cybersecurity solutions.

The conclusion indicates that while blockchain and AI convergence open unparalleled opportunities for secure and decentralized systems, further investigation, technological refinement, and prudent enactment are necessary to create their transforming effects across real-world applications.

References

1 Guo, H. and Yu, X. (2022). A survey on blockchain technology and its security. *Blockchain: research and applications.* 3 (2): 100067.

2 Zheng, X., Zhu, Y., and Si, X. (2019). A survey on challenges and progresses in blockchain technologies: A performance and security perspective. *Applied Sciences.* 9 (22): 4731.

3 De Filippi, P. (2016). The interplay between decentralization and privacy: The case of blockchain technologies. *Journal of Peer Production* (7).

4 Raval, S. (2016). *Decentralized applications: Harnessing Bitcoin's blockchain technology*. O'Reilly Media, Inc.

5 Kremenova, I. and Gajdos, M. (2019). Decentralized networks: The future internet. *Mobile Networks and Applications.* 24 (6): 2016–2023.

6 Tyagi, A.K. (2023). Decentralized everything: Practical use of blockchain technology in future applications. In: *Distributed Computing to Blockchain*, 19–38. Elsevier.

7 Haleem, A., Javaid, M., Singh, R.P. et al. (2021). Blockchain technology applications in healthcare: An overview. *International Journal of Intelligent Networks.* 2: 130–139.

8 Spathoulas G, Negka L, Pandey P, Katsikas S. Can blockchain technology enhance security and privacy in the Internet of Things? advances in core computer science-based technologies: Papers in Honor of Professor Nikolaos Alexandris. 2021;199–228.

9 Satish, S., Meduri, K., Nadella, G.S., and Gonaygunta, H. (2022). Developing a decentralized AI model training framework using blockchain technology. *International Meridian Journal.* 4 (4): 1–20.

10 Islam, S. and Apu, K.U. (2024). Decentralized Vs. centralized database solutions in blockchain: Advantages, challenges, and use cases. *Global Mainstream Journal of Innovation, Engineering & Emerging Technology* 3 (4): 58–68.

11 Nimmagadda, V.S.P. (2021). Artificial intelligence and blockchain integration for enhanced security in insurance: Techniques, models, and real-world applications. *African Journal of Artificial Intelligence and Sustainable Development.* 1 (2): 187–224.

12 Rajawat AS, Goyal SB, Goyal A, Rajawat K, Raboaca MS, Verma C, et al. Enhancing security and scalability of metaverse with blockchain-based consensus mechanisms. In: 2023 15th International Conference on Electronics, Computers and Artificial Intelligence (ECAI). IEEE; 2023. p. 1–6.

13 Abdulhakeem, S.A. and Hu, Q. (2021). Powered by Blockchain technology, DeFi (Decentralized Finance) strives to increase financial inclusion of the unbanked by reshaping the world financial system. *Modern Economy.* 12 (01): 1.

14 Chen Y, Bellavitis C. Decentralized finance: Blockchain technology and the quest for an open financial system. Stevens Institute of Technology School of Business Research Paper. 2019.

15 Bhurgri, S.S., Ali, N.I., Korejo, I.A., and Brohi, I.A. (2024). Enhancing security and confidentiality in decentralized payment system based on blockchain technology. *The Asian Bulletin of Big Data Management* 4 (1):Science-4.

16 Lee, J.Y. (2019). A decentralized token economy: How blockchain and cryptocurrency can revolutionize business. *Business Horizons* 62 (6): 773–784.

17 Alhusayni, A., Thayananthan, V., Albeshri, A., and Alghamdi, S. (2023). Decentralized multi-layered architecture to strengthen the security in the internet of things environment using blockchain technology. *Electronics (Basel).* 12 (20): 4314.

18 Simaiya, S., Lilhore, U.K., Sharma, S.K. et al. (2020). Blockchain: A new technology to enhance data security and privacy in Internet of things. *Journal of Computational and Theoretical Nanoscience* 17 (6): 2552–2556.

19 Muzammal SM, Murugesan RK. A study on leveraging blockchain technology for IoT security enhancement. In: 2018 Fourth International Conference on Advances in Computing, Communication & Automation (ICACCA). IEEE; 2018. p. 1–6.

20 Haris RM, Al-Maadeed S. Integrating blockchain technology in 5G enabled IoT: A review. In: 2020 IEEE International Conference on Informatics, IoT, and Enabling Technologies (ICIoT). IEEE; 2020. p. 367–71.

21 Thantharate, P. and Thantharate, A. (2023). ZeroTrustBlock: Enhancing security, privacy, and interoperability of sensitive data through ZeroTrust permissioned blockchain. *Big Data and Cognitive Computing.* 7 (4): 165.

22 Sharma, P., Borah, M.D., and Namasudra, S. (2021). Improving security of medical big data by using Blockchain technology. *Computers & Electrical Engineering.* 96: 107529.

23 Tariq, M.U. (2024). Revolutionizing health data management with blockchain technology: Enhancing security and efficiency in a digital era. In: *Emerging Technologies for Health Literacy and Medical Practice*, 153–175. IGI Global.

24 Kshetri N, Hutson J, Revathy G. healthAIChain: Improving security and safety using Blockchain Technology applications in AI-based healthcare systems. In: 2023 3rd International Conference on Innovative Mechanisms for Industry Applications (ICIMIA). IEEE; 2023. p. 159–64.

25 Idrees, S.M., Nowostawski, M., Jameel, R., and Mourya, A.K. (2021). Security aspects of blockchain technology intended for industrial applications. *Electronics (Basel).* 10 (8): 951.

26 Khan, F.A., Asif, M., Ahmad, A. et al. (2020). Blockchain technology, improvement suggestions, security challenges on smart grid and its application in healthcare for sustainable development. *Sustainable Cities and Society* 55: 102018.

27 Rajawat AS, Goyal SB, Solanki R, Raboaca MS, Mihaltan TC, Illés Z, et al. Blockchain-based security framework for metaverse: A decentralized approach. In: 2023 15th International Conference on Electronics, Computers and Artificial Intelligence (ECAI). IEEE; 2023. p. 1–6.

28 Mourtzis, D., Angelopoulos, J., and Panopoulos, N. (2023). Blockchain integration in the era of industrial metaverse. *Applied Sciences.* 13 (3): 1353.

29 Nabben, K. (2021). Blockchain security as "people security": Applying sociotechnical security to blockchain technology. *Frontiers in Computer Science* 2: 599406.

30 Cali, U. and Fifield, A. (2019). Towards the decentralized revolution in energy systems using blockchain technology. *International Journal of Smart Grid and Clean Energy* 8 (3): 245–256.

31 Chattu, V.K., Nanda, A., Chattu, S.K. et al. (2019). The emerging role of blockchain technology applications in routine disease surveillance systems to strengthen global health security. *Big Data and Cognitive Computing.* 3 (2): 25.

32 Sekerin, V.D., Slepov, V.A., Gayduk, V.I. et al. (2021). Blockchain technology development as tool for enhancing security in management and protection of intellectual property rights in additive manufacturing. *Revista Geintec-Gestao Inovacao E Tecnologias.* 11 (2): 1184–1200.

33 Laroiya, C., Saxena, D., and Komalavalli, C. (2020). Applications of blockchain technology. In: *Handbook of research on blockchain technology*, 213–243. Elsevier.

34 Sharin FH, Hernandez MS, Sentosa I. Future trends of blockchain technology in the technological fields. In: 2023 3rd International Conference on Advance Computing and Innovative Technologies in Engineering (ICACITE). IEEE; 2023. p. 1307–13.

35 Yerram, S.R., Goda, D.R., Mahadasa, R. et al. (2021). The role of blockchain technology in enhancing financial security amidst digital transformation. *Asian Business Reviewa* 11 (3): 125–134.

6

Adversarial AI and Defensive Countermeasures

6.1 Introduction

The rapid advancement of artificial intelligence (AI) has altered the adversaries and defense strategies in cybersecurity, granting an upper hand for human intervention for earlier detection and response. With widespread AI usage in security applications, adversarial AI—where an attacker fakes inputs for learning models—cannot be understated. All these attacks—evasion, poisoning, and model inversion, to name a few—address the need for countermeasures that are strong technically but also impart a human perspective [1–3].

Though technical defenses such as anomaly detection, adversarial training, and secure model design constitute the backbone of AI-based cybersecurity, the human factor itself poses a constant threat. Sadly, usually, humans represent the weakest link in cybersecurity frameworks in terms of social engineering, being susceptible to phishing, insider threats, or mistakes of goodwill [4–7]. Studies show that human actions, choices, and organizational culture significantly affect how well cybersecurity implementations work [8, 9].

Research goes on to state that putting emphasis on human factors is a must if it is to develop resilient AI-driven security systems. Hughes-Lartey et al. [10] provide examples of how Internet of Things (IoT) ecosystems are especially prone to human error in their configuration and management. In addition, Jeong et al. [9] state that systemic approaches to awareness and cybersecurity training regarding the human factor are essential in reducing these risks.

The shift between human factors and AI in cybersecurity is not limited to awareness but also includes cognitive and organizational aspects. Kadena and Gupi [11] explain the negative impact of cognitive overload and stress on human decision-making outcomes under high-stakes security scenarios, while Marble et al. [12] maintain that it is necessary to inscribe intelligent defense systems that act in concert with human operators. The burnout, fatigue, and security complacency also have an exacerbating effect on vulnerabilities highlighted by Nobles

[13, 14]; hence, the importance of developing adaptive human-centered strategies within AI-mediated environments becomes more pronounced.

From an organizational perspective, the alignment of human capabilities to technological solutions constitutes success in implementing any cybersecurity measures. With respect to human factors within corporate security policies, frameworks by Poehlmann et al. [13] and Pollini et al. [15] advocate for continuous training, ethical guidelines, and feedback mechanisms. Likewise [15–17], Poehlmann et al., and, Rahman, Rebensky, Rohan stress that the efficacy of AI-driven defenses is contingent upon human compliance, vigilance, and informed engagement.

Training and awareness campaigns are also crucial to building human resilience toward adversarial AI threats. Sangwan [18] and Triplett [19] show that well-targeted training sessions and a cybersecurity culture driven by the top leadership greatly lower the threat exposure. Accordingly, Wiechetek and Mędrek [20] support bringing human factors into the center of curricula in cybersecurity training, aimed at preparing future professionals to cope with the evolving threat landscape of AI.

Finally, adversarial AI poses its own challenges and offers the need for an understanding that transcends logics of technical versus human dimensions within cybersecurity. While Young et al. [21] observe that human factors are interconnected within dynamic behaviors of systems, which serve to amplify and/or mitigate security risks, Zhang and Ghorbani [22] comment that big data and AI-driven analytics bring equally new challenges and opportunities, rendering boundless human vigilance, ethical reasoning, and adaptive learning in creating defenses against sophisticated AI-enabled attacks (Figure 6.1).

Bidirectional relationship between human and AI factors in cybersecurity. While AI techniques strengthen the process of detection and response, human decisions and behavior favorably or adversely affect the overall resilience of

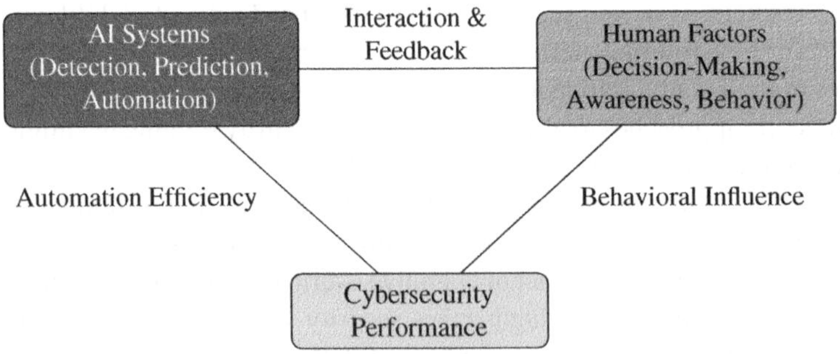

Figure 6.1 Human–AI Interaction in Cybersecurity Systems. "*Source:* Hewa Majeed Zangana"

defense systems. Such understanding augurs well for the development of a balanced and human-centered AI security.

In the intersection between adversarial AI and human factors, the issue becomes two-pronged: how to guard machine-learning systems from attack and how to mitigate the built-in vulnerabilities of human operators. The chapter presents such a dual framework to lock this discussion and offer an exhaustive discussion on adversarial AI threats and countermeasures that are technical, cognitive, and organizational in nature.

6.2 Understanding Adversarial AI

Adversarial AI is the newest front in the fast-evolving tool of cybersecurity, wherein attackers utilize the loopholes embedded in ML and AI models to tamper with their output, evade detection, or compromise system integrity. Taking into account traditional cyber threats, these adversary attacks derive their exploitative potential from the very algorithms that are in place to detect and prevent intrusions. Thus, an irony is created in which AI itself becomes a defensive tool, and at the same time, can be a vulnerability. Attack types include evasion attacks, data poisoning, model inversion, and generative adversarial manipulations, among others, each of which degrades system performance or enables illegitimate access [1, 2].

Humanity is very much intertwined in adversarial AI threats because, most often, attackers generally must exploit such human vulnerabilities to amplify the effectiveness of algorithmic attacks. Studies repeatedly show that the weak link in cybersecurity is indeed humans—who introduce their inadvertent errors, lack of awareness, or social engineering susceptibility [3–7, 23]. As phishing schemes or offensive misleading prompts to misguide users might stand as entrance points for sharper adversary manipulations against otherwise perfectly healthy AI defenses, understanding where human vulnerabilities and machine weaknesses tend to converge is critical. Thus undermining the risk of adversarial AI [12]. Attackers frequently launch attacks on several levels: infiltration of model assumptions; evasion attacks for manipulating input to an ML model so that it is misclassified but does not trigger traditional detection features; the poisoning of data through malicious samples during training to influence the predictive capacity of the model; model inversion, which enables the attacker to obtain sensitive training data from the model outputs, raising serious privacy concerns [11, 24]. Even the human dimension worsens these risks. For example, one could mention that the induction of poor training practices and over-reliance on automated alerts would probably lead to misjudgment or delays in responding to an AI-related incident [13, 14, 16].

If anything, the strong body of literature showcases that robust adversarial defenses require a view encompassing human and technological factors.

Techniques like adversarial training, robust feature extraction, and anomaly detection must be cooperate with human-centric considerations such as constant education, cognitive load management, and organizational support structures [15, 17, 18, 25]. This ensures detection and resistance to adversarial manipulations by AI systems, provided humans retain situational awareness and decision-making capabilities.

Admittedly, human-machine interactions sometimes aggravate and, at other times, mitigate adversarial AI threats in complex infrastructures. Consider operational environments such as IoT ecosystems and critical infrastructure, which rely on fast, high-throughput data processing whose cognitive checks rarely come from humans and are very vital in spotting anomalies [26, 27]. Also influential are leadership and organizational culture, which shape behaviors such as the implementation of defensive technologies and the readiness of human operators [19–21].

More so, adversarial AI problems are worsened in expansive data settings. Big data analytics translate to better prediction capabilities but also create an increasing attack surface for model exploitation, thus imposing the urgent need to work around combining raw AI strength with enlightened human supervision [22]. Trust framework, AI-decision-making transparency, and adaptive learning systems provide credible views on aligning machine intelligence with human judgment, therefore reducing systemic vulnerabilities [6, 10].

Ultimately, the context of adversarial AI should therefore consider both engineering model resistance and human factors that enable or mitigate attacks. Given that adversarial threats are considered transient challenges to pure algorithms, the effective defense itself should be socio-technically based and so propagated in creating a robust AI architecture, informed human operators, and organizational policies. Probably, it is here that organizations that address both dimensions can nurture resilient cybersecurity ecosystems that withstand the ever-increasingly challenging adversarial AI onslaught.

6.3 Types of Adversarial Attacks

Adversarial attacks against AI systems use a multitude of techniques to manipulate the machine learning (ML) models, degrade performance, or gain unauthorized access. Understanding these types of attacks is critical for developing effective countermeasures, especially when human vulnerabilities considerably amplify the risk [1–3]. Broadly, adversarial attacks can be categorized into four broad types: evasion attacks, poisoning attacks, model inversion, and generative adversarial attacks.

6.3.1 Evasion Attacks

An evasion attack consists of an adversary making small changes to the input of an AI system so that the model would yield an incorrect result while still looking normal to human observers. For instance, a tiny adjustment in an image, an audio file, or a piece of text data could cause a classifier to mislabel a critical input, causing a compromise in cybersecurity monitoring, biometric authentication, or autonomous systems [4, 23]. Evasion attacks make use of algorithmic vulnerabilities and human aspects, such as overreliance on automated alerts or misinterpretation of system feedback [5, 6]. Human error in regard to assessing alerts or not recognizing subtle anomalies serves as an enhancer of risk [7, 8].

6.3.2 Poisoning Attacks

This type of attack is set in training, wherein adversaries try to corrupt the training data of the ML model. This type of attack could bring about long-term degradation of the performance of the model, including biased predictions or becoming prone to subsequent evasion attacks [9, 10]. The human factor comes in: if the cybersecurity team has no standard validation protocol, no oversight mechanism, or does not understand how a poisoning attack might be carried out, then the AI system will obliviously learn from malicious input [28].

6.3.3 Model Inversion Attacks

Model inversion attacks afford adversaries the ability to reconstruct sensitive training data from model outputs. This can leak personal information or proprietary datasets, which can present serious privacy risks [11, 12]. In addition to technical countermeasures, these attacks may be aided by human behavior, such as unsafe sharing of model outputs or low levels of privacy awareness [13, 24]. Real defense against model inversion needs both algorithmic barriers and strong human-oriented policies for data access and use [14, 16].

6.3.4 Generative Adversarial Attacks

Generative adversarial attacks use generative models like GANs to fabricate input that is both realistic and malicious, hence running the AI models aground. Such attacks can create synthetic data that would slip past the ordinary security checks since it appears indistinguishable from a legitimate input [15, 17]. Anomalies must therefore be detected by a human—however, biases, lack of training, or operational fatigue can undermine the performance of human-in-the-loop countermeasures [18, 25].

6.4 Social Engineering-Enhanced Adversarial Attacks

Directly violating human vulnerabilities is a huge subset of adversarial strategies. Phishing, pretexting, or baiting tactics can surreptitiously manipulate users into bypassing AI-based defenses to submit malicious inputs or divulge their credentials and hence compromise the integrity of the system [26, 27]. Individual susceptibility will remain the principal vector of adversarial AI attacks, thus making cybersecurity education, awareness, and organizational culture all the more important [19, 20].

6.4.1 Hybrid Attacks

Hybrid adversarial attacks include combinations of several techniques, such as blending evasion and poisoning, or intermingling social engineering and model inversion. Such advanced attacks simultaneously exploit AI weaknesses and human unsophistication, thus calling for defense mechanisms that are layered according to socio-techno principles [21, 22]. Organizations neglecting the interplay between human and machine factors remain massively exposed to such compound threats [1, 6, 11].

Figure 6.2 shows a taxonomy of adversarial attacks, mapping them according to their goals and methodologies; this classification essentially conveys the discrepancies of threat strategies targeting AI algorithms and human operators.

In conclusion, the types of adversarial attacks portray a patchy structure wherein human factors are amalgamated with AI vulnerabilities. Therefore, a solid defense system must consist of intelligent technical protection together with a holistic approach towards human behavior, organizational policies, and awareness. The acknowledgement of the different types of attacks is the bedrock for the design of resilient, adaptive AI systems that can counterpose algorithmic and human-centric risks.

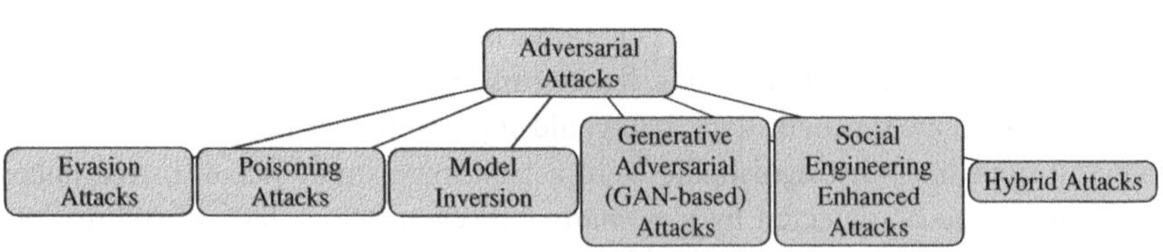

Figure 6.2 Taxonomy of Adversarial Attack Types. "*Source:* Hewa Majeed Zangana"

6.5 Adversarial Threats in Cybersecurity Systems

Cybersecurity systems are increasingly making use of advanced technologies, such as AI and ML, to detect, prevent, and respond to threats. However, the incorporation of AI into cybersecurity has presented new vulnerabilities as adversarial threats drawing power from both technical weaknesses and human factors [1, 2]. Adversarial threats are a multifaceted challenge and cover attacks on AI algorithms and the network infrastructures, IoT devices, and human users that interact with these systems [3, 4].

6.5.1 Technical Adversarial Threats

Technical adversarial threats primarily focus on the AI-driven models and algorithms of cybersecurity systems. These threats include evading attacks, poisoning the model itself, and perturbations made against the adversary's will as a means of confounding AI systems into false classifications or incorrect decisions [5, 23]. For example, perpetrators can subtly change the nature of network traffic or sensor inputs to distract or mislead intrusion detection systems or automated threat detection. Technical defenses such as robust training and anomaly detection exist, but adversarial methods are evolving, putting even the most advanced systems to the test [6, 7].

6.5.2 Human-Centric Adversarial Threats

Even in the light of technological developments, often the weakest link in any cybersecurity system is still the human factor. Different tactics such as social engineering in phishing or manipulative exploitation of cognitive biases can be employed by adversaries to get around security considerations [8, 10]. Previous studies have repeatedly established that human factors, such as stress or fatigue, lack of training, or organizational culture, significantly increase susceptibility to adversarial threats [9, 28]. Some poorly trained individuals might unwittingly click commands that could have adverse effects on AI defense systems; thus, human-centered security awareness programs are equally important [12].

6.5.3 Organizational Vulnerabilities

Adverse threats are not just directed at individual users or AI models; the organizational structure and policies can increase the risk incurred. Absence of cybersecurity governance, a poorly structured incident response framework, and a lack of continuous monitoring allow adversaries to exploit these systemic weaknesses

[11, 24]. Research shows that an alignment of technical, human, and organizational measures is needed to defend against adversarial threats successfully and that AI tools must support and not displace human decision-making [13, 14, 16].

6.5.4 IoT and Cyber-Physical System Threats

The advancements of IoT and Cyber-Physical Systems (CPS) have expanded the ever-increasing attack surface of adversaries. IoT devices that are interconnected through networks usually lack standardized security protocols that are necessarily implemented in order to conduct manipulation through adversarial AI techniques [15, 17]. Adversaries may take advantage of human operators' ignorance while handling the devices through misconfigurations, weak credential management, or insufficient monitoring [18, 25].

6.5.5 Hybrid and Coordinated Threats

Adversaries are increasingly blending technical attacks with human and organizational attack vectors: the hybrid approach. Coordinated campaigns may intend to exploit the vulnerabilities of an AI model while social engineering manipulates human decision-makers [26, 27]. The complexity of such an approach makes an equally imperative requirement for a holistic cybersecurity strategy encompassing ML defenses, constant human training, and firm policies for organizations [19, 20].

6.5.6 Implications for Cybersecurity Strategy

A discussion of the way in which adversarial threats affect cybersecurity systems must encompass the framework that describes AI vulnerabilities, human factors, and the organizations that structure contexts [21, 22]. The operational strategy to effectively counter adversarial threats should merge technical resilience training, human-centered awareness programs, and dynamic governance policies to alleviate the chances and effects of adversarial attacks. It is imperative to design such a layered approach to defense so that maintaining trust, reliability of systems, and operational continuity can be achieved in the AI-driven environment of cybersecurity [1, 6, 11].

6.6 Mechanisms of Adversarial Example Generation

Adversarial examples are inputs that have been intentionally crafted in order to mislead the ML model or AI-driven cybersecurity systems. The inputs are usually almost unchanged from the legitimate data to cause misclassification or wrong predictions or to circumvent security mechanisms [1, 2]. An exploration of the mechanisms of adversarial example generation is important for the creation of strong AI defenses and the mitigation of possible cybersecurity threats.

6.6.1 Gradient-Based Methods

Gradient-based optimization is among the most commonly used techniques for the generation of adversarial examples. Attackers compute changes in the model's loss with respect to input data and apply small perturbations in the direction that maximizes such changes [3, 4]. This method, a variation of which is known as the Fast Gradient Sign Method (FGSM), allows attackers to manipulate inputs in such a way that even highly accurate AI models will be fooled while inflicting no changes detectable by human observers [5, 23].

6.6.2 Optimization-Based Attacks

Optimization-based attacks formulate the generation of adversarial examples as a constrained optimization problem. The goal is to figure out the minimal perturbation needed to cause misclassification of the model while remaining imperceptible [6, 7]. Strategies such as Projected Gradient Descent (PGD) include iterative updates of the input based on gradients, which often lead to adversarial examples that are more successful than one-step methods. These attacks take advantage of the weaknesses of the decision boundaries of a model, exposing the structural vulnerabilities of AI systems [8, 10].

6.6.3 Transferability and Black-Box Attacks

Transferability is one of the most important properties of adversarial examples: an input that is meticulously structured for deceiving one model will generally mislead other models, even with extensively different architectures or training data [9, 28]. Models of black-box attacks use this principle, generating adversarial examples without any direct access to the parameters of the target model; instead, they generate examples through surrogate models that imitate behavior. Not only this, but adversarial vulnerabilities are capable of propagating across systems, thereby producing considerable threats to cybersecurity [12].

6.6.4 Human Factor Exploitation in Adversarial Generation

Adversarial strategies increasingly subsume human behavior and cognitive vulnerabilities into their areas of application. As an example, adversaries might be able to deliberately construct demonstrations about predictable human inputs to an

AI-controlled interface, such as misclicks, misinterpretation of security prompts, or even simply too much trust placed in automated systems [11, 24]. Such human-in-the-loop attack vectors amplify the effectiveness of adversarial examples and underline the human constituent's attack in separate technical defenses [13, 14].

6.6.5 Generative Models for Adversarial Examples

Recently, advancements in generative technologies, such as those from Generative Adversarial Networks (GANs), have equipped an attacker with highly capable tools to produce realistic synthetic inputs for adversarial attacks [15, 16]. To achieve the objective, GAN-based approaches iteratively train a generator of examples to make the model's output different from what the target model deems a misclassification, while a discriminator attempts their classification among true data. It facilitates advanced, highly sophisticated attacks that are difficult to realize and defend against, especially under high-stakes applications such as cybersecurity monitoring and autonomous systems [17, 18].

6.6.6 Physical and Real-World Adversarial Examples

Adversarial examples are found in the digital space and the physical and real-world environments. For instance, adversaries might print images, including one or a few subtle modifications, so that it will mislead a facial recognition system and change sensor readings in an IoT device [25, 26]. Such mechanisms illustrate that adversarial examples find themselves not within the confining walls of virtual spaces but can also permeate real-life operational environments to breach the ever-harder nexus between technical and human vulnerabilities [19, 27].

The generation of adversarial examples comprises several optimization and manipulation steps. The mechanism has been summarized in Figure 6.3, showing how, through model gradients, human interactions are manipulated to craft illusionary inputs.

6.6.7 Implications for Cybersecurity

The adversarial example generation techniques further complicate the defense of AI-enabled systems. Effective countermeasures should address a combination of gradient-based optimization, transferability, generative models, and human exploitation threats at once [20, 21]. Besides, familiarizing people with adversarial strategies should also mold cybersecurity training, organizational policy, and system design into a more resilient environment against attacks exploiting both technical and human vulnerabilities [1, 22].

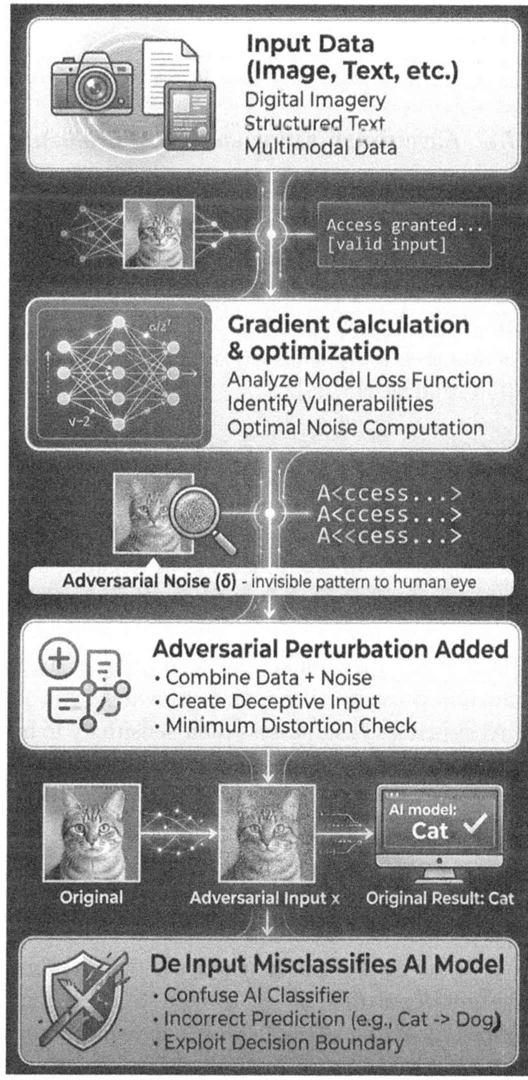

Figure 6.3 Mechanism of Adversarial Example Generation. "*Source:* Hewa Majeed Zangana"

6.7 Evaluating AI System Robustness

By robustness, we mean the capacity of an AI system to perform without degrading its security under many various professional conditions, which would include technological assault, and, almost certainly, human ones. Evaluation of robustness is synonymous with assessing reliability and resilience in AI-enabled systems concerning the defense against ever-increasingly sophisticated adversarial threats [1, 2].

6.7.1 Adversarial Testing and Stress Evaluation

These are the adverse tests, according to which models of AI have been subjected to inputs that are intentionally crafted to exploit any weaknesses. Such techniques include gradient-based perturbations, optimization-driven attacks, and generative adversarial attacks that stress-test models and point out their compromising points [3, 4]. By consideration of the fate of models in such adversarial conditions, practitioners in cybersecurity are able to quantify robustness and prioritize mitigation strategies [5, 23].

6.7.2 Benchmarking Metrics

Evaluation of robustness must also assume an equal stance in standardized metrics adopted by different institutions to gauge how much the effect will have, in terms of measure or meter, from adversarial inputs on system performance. Adverse impacts are severely considered particularly in common metrics like classification accuracy under attack, adversarial success rate, and model confidence reduction. So, using such metrics provides some quantitative basis for comparison of AI systems so as to assess their sensitivity to both digital and human-targeted threats [6, 7]. The metrics also consider operational aspects, such as responsiveness delay and error propagation, and ensure that robustness assessments reflect reality in deployment environments [8, 10].

6.7.3 Human Factor Integration

The human behavior component is critical in evaluating AI robustness, as humans are considered the last or, at best, weakest link in a cybersecurity operation. Studies show that stress, fatigue, judgment failures, and awareness deficiency all make an adversarial strike more effective [9, 28]. A human factor relies on human-in-the-loop simulations that will eventually come up with realistic interaction and potential scenario exploitation, narrowing the gap between technical resilience and human reliability [12].

6.7.4 Scenario-Based Assessment

Scenario-based evaluations test AI systems in simulated or controlled operational contexts based on potential attack scenarios. The scenarios take into account cyber-physical as well as organizational considerations, among which insider attacks, IoT vulnerabilities, and interaction across complex networks stand out [11, 24]. By looking at system performance in these scenarios, the organizations are able to find weaknesses, test contingency plans, and enhance both technical and procedural safeguards [13, 14].

6.7.5 Continuous Monitoring and Feedback Loops

Continuous monitoring is necessary for a robust AI to detect and respond to ever-changing adversarial threats. Automated detection for anomalous input; real-time logging of system errors; and feedback loops for retraining the model on new types of attack patterns [15, 16]. Monitoring and human supervision together enhance overall resilience, as they guarantee that both machine and human-related factors are put under iterative evaluation [17, 18].

6.7.6 Evaluation in Real-World Environments

Controlled insights from the laboratory must be complemented with robustness evaluations in real-world environments wherein uncertain factors such as user behavior, environmental noise, and operational constraints can be integrated [25, 26]. The impact of physical attacks, perturbations to IoT sensors, and errors induced by humans are therefore all crucial for evaluating the AI performance, reiterating the need for implementing evaluation protocols that, as much as possible, replicate the real operational context [19, 27].

Figure 6.4 displays the multi-layered framework that is used to evaluate AI robustness in adversarial contexts, which incorporates adversarial testing,

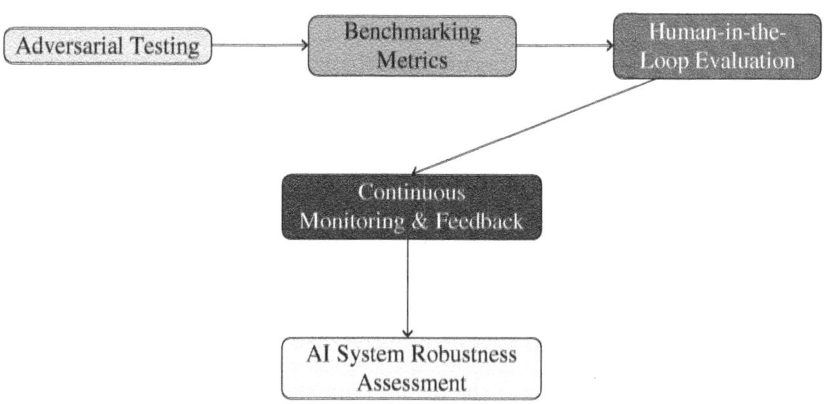

Figure 6.4 Framework for Evaluating AI System Robustness. "*Source:* Hewa Majeed Zangana"

human-in-the-loop evaluation, and real-world feedback for sustainable system resilience.

6.7.7 Implications for Cybersecurity Strategy

Evaluating AI robustness is not merely a technical exercise; it informs the strategic level of decision-making across cybersecurity frameworks for the organization. The outputs of robustness testing will inform policy design, training programs, and incident response strategies to ensure the resilience of AI systems against anomalous behavior in both technical and human-centered threats [20, 21]. The robust evaluation practice in turn enhances the trust among various stakeholders in the AI systems and, hence, strengthens their integration toward critical security infrastructure [1, 22].

6.8 Defensive Countermeasures and Robust AI Strategies

The increasing sophistication of adversarial attacks against AI-powered cybersecurity systems necessitates robust defense mechanisms, combining technical measures with human-centered strategies. Defensive measures, therefore, should not only strengthen system resilience but also mitigate the vulnerabilities triggered by human factors, which remain an ace-in-the-hole for attackers in cybersecurity environments [1, 2].

6.8.1 Adversarial Training and Model Hardening

Adversarial training is one of the foremost methods to increase AI robustness. These systems are trained to withstand perturbations and perform some tasks in adversarial conditions by training AI models with adversarial examples for some time. The methods used could involve gradient-based adversarial input, generative adversarial perturbations, or noise-injection techniques that approximate realistic attack conditions [3, 4]. Model hardening techniques can further reinforce AI systems' stability against known and emerging threats through ensemble learning and regularization methods [5, 23].

6.8.2 Incorporating Human Factors into Defense Strategies

Humans, being one of the most exploitable components, must therefore include human reliability, training, and awareness in the measures for AI robustness [6, 7]. Simulations such as scenario-based laboratory user error, social engineering attacks, and operational stress should provide realistic conditions in which to test the reactions of both the human and AI [8, 10]. Reducing cognitive overload, security fatigue, and behavioral vulnerabilities is critical to complementing their technical defenses [9, 28].

6.8.3 Real-Time Monitoring and Threat Detection

For the identified attacks to be quickly detected and ruled out, the continuous monitoring and adaptive feedback system is exercised to maintain the robustness of the AI systems. Anomaly detection, behavior-based monitoring, and automated alerting system highlighting deviations from standard operation constitute this [12]. This observation should go hand in hand with human monitoring so that all technical anomalies, as well as context-specific threats, are tackled, thus improving the overall resilience [11, 24].

6.8.4 Multi-Layered Defense Architecture

Defense architectures based on layered strategy or defense in-depth strategy unto itself will combine a set of multiple security measures against a wide spectrum of attacks. These layers may enlist the likes of network segmentation, intrusion detection systems, access control policies, and encryption protocols [13, 14]. The implementation of AI strategies within these layered architecture designs would empower the dynamic response capabilities, automated decision-making, and predictive defense across vulnerabilities at any given layer with protections from other layers [15, 16].

6.8.5 Education, Awareness, and Human-Centric Mitigation

Should be informed about the fact that the knowledge and awareness programs are required to be focused on strengthening the human element of cybersecurity. Behavioral risk management, awareness of phishing, and decision-making under stressful situations have been able to reduce the impact from attacks as well as allow better collaboration and working with AI systems by human operators [17, 18]. Learning eventually leads to encouraging the development of a cybersecurity culture where contribution to defense is made active rather than humans serving as the weakest link [25, 26].

6.8.6 Continuous Evaluation and Adaptive Defense

AI defense mechanisms must be flexible enough to adjust to any emerging threats or a broken system. The aim of this is to establish feedback loops with operational data, incident reports, and real-world adversarial scenarios. Automated retraining of AI models, updates of policies, and dynamic reconfiguration of system parameters so that they adapt with the evolving attacks are some types of adaptive defense mechanisms [19, 27].

6.8.7 Strategic Implications for Organizations

Robust and growing AI defensive applications focus on more than just technology but also involve policies, governance, and leadership applications within the organization. Both AI and human dimension inclusion in cybersecurity planning improve trust, compliance, and overall operational efficiency. Organizations that assess, train, and reinforce human interactions with AI often achieve higher resilience and capacity in countering relatively sophisticated adversarial threats [20–22].

6.8.8 Summary

Technical defenses must be integrated with human-centric strategies to deliver what is truly required for resilient AI cybersecurity systems. Multi-layer architectures, adversarial training, continuous monitoring, and proactive human factor management work together to enhance robustness while reducing vulnerabilities and ensuring that both AI and human operators contribute effectively to organizational security objectives [1, 2].

6.9 Model Explainability and Interpretability in Defense

Increased reliance on AI and ML models in the cybersecurity field raised the necessity for understanding their rationale in explainable or interpretable systems. Robust AI could both identify and control cyber threats, but their efficacy is limited if operators in an organization cannot understand why a certain decision has been taken by the model [1, 2].

6.9.1 Importance of Explainable AI in Cyber Defense

Explainable AI (XAI) throws light to model decisions, allowing cybersecurity teams to get an understanding of what, why, or how certain alerts are raised and what actions are advised based on these alerts. This means that false-positive or false-negative alerts might have very operational consequences in high-stakes situations [3, 4]. The integration of human factors into AI interpretability makes sure that alerts and recommendations are issued in ways that users can understand, trust, and act upon effectively [5, 23].

6.9.2 Techniques for Achieving Model Explainability

For instance, SHAP (SHapley Additive exPlanations), LIME (Local Interpretable Model-Agnostic Explanations), and attention mechanisms provide insights into which inputs most influence model predictions. They allow feature importance analysis to inform actionable insights from their predictions [6, 7]. Visualization of decision pathways and probability distributions presents additional support for operators to better understand AI behavior and relate alerts within context [8, 10].

6.9.3 Human-Centric Interpretability

They need to be designed for human users: human AI interpretability because cognitive load, expertise, and decision-making contexts will differ across human users. Indeed, studies have shown that systems with human factors taken into account fail to communicate actionable information and therefore lessen the effectiveness of cyber defense [9, 28]. The creation of interactive dashboards, scenario-based explanation, and adaptive alerting mechanisms should be effective in filling the gap separating model output from operator understanding and thus reducing risks from human error [12].

6.9.4 Trust, Accountability, and Compliance

Thereby, explainable AI adds to corporate trust and, furthermore, compliance through auditability of the processes adopted in making decisions. That holds more important meaning in regulated environments, since stakeholders must comprehend and validate all cybersecurity actions [11, 24]. Organizations define with interpretable explanations how AI-assisted defense counts as appropriate within legal, ethical, and operational standards, as these give operators trust in their decisions as well [13, 14].

6.9.5 Mitigating Human Vulnerabilities through Interpretability

Users are perceived as the most common weak point of cybersecurity systems. Timing and clear, easy-to-understand guidance direct decisions under stress or in situations of complicated incident responses that overcome human shortcomings through highly interpretable AI systems [15, 16]. Interpretations of projects aimed at the institution of training and awareness in the understanding of outputs of AI systems would further develop collaboration between human agents and AI, thereby reducing susceptibility to phishing, social engineering, and operational errors [17, 18].

6.9.6 Continuous Evaluation and Adaptive Explainability

The dynamic nature of cyber threats necessitates an ongoing evaluation of AI interpretability, as demonstrated in studies such as those presented at the AHFE 2017 International Conference on Human Factors in Cybersecurity. This ensures that models adapt based on real-world operation incidents and human-computer interaction to meet changing user needs. Adaptive explainability ensures that operators are capable of making well-informed decisions even if they face completely new types of adversarial attacks [25, 26].

6.9.7 Organizational Implications

Interpretable AI in cybersecurity requires holistic action concerning the technical, the operational, and the human factors. It should require establishing policies and designing training programs and evaluation frameworks for institutions toward human–AI collaboration, where defenses are made to be robust, transparent, and resilient [19, 20, 27]. The culture of explainability could also improve decision-making regarding cybersecurity problems, cut down risks, and thereby increase system resilience [21, 22].

6.9.8 Summary

Explainable models are explainable by authority between the lines and interpret principles for how the effective functioning of AI-based cyber defense works and are usually grim steps in program interpretation. Technical transparency combined with continued adaptation with human factors ensures effective meaning and collaboration in both human operation and automated systems [1, 2].

6.10 Adversarial AI in Reinforcement Learning and Autonomous Systems

Rapid deployment of RL and autonomous systems into mission-critical applications continues to worsen the cybersecurity landscape. Adversarial AI looks for weaknesses in such systems from the user level to change how they behave or diminish performance and even cause catastrophic failure. Unlike traditional cyber-attacks, adversarial attacks exploit the way autonomous agents learn and decide, thus also targeting the models governing this behavior and human operators supervising those systems [1, 2].

6.10.1 Understanding Adversarial Threats in RL

Reinforcement learning agents learn what actions they should take from the feedback they receive from the environment in terms of rewards. These perturbations include adding adversarial noise to inputs or rewards or by manipulating the relevant environmental signal themselves, resulting in either suboptimal or hazardous behavior. Such attacks emphasize the dual vulnerability of autonomous systems and the humans supervising them [3, 4]. Human operators may also tend to over-rely on the so-called robustness of the autonomous agents, which opens doors for adversarial exploitation [5, 23].

6.10.2 Types of Adversarial Attacks on Autonomous Systems

Adversarial attacks on RL and autonomous systems:

- Observation-space attacks mislead the agent decisions using input sensors [6, 7].
- Reward manipulation, meaning that the agents will learn behaviors different from what the operational goals had intended [8, 10].
- Policy manipulation, where adversaries exploit policy limitations in the trained policies to degrade performance [9, 28].
- Human-in-the-loop exploitation, which applies cognitive biases, stress, or even fatigue on the operator, bypassing safety [12].

6.10.3 Human Factors and Adversarial Resilience

Human factors play a significant role in both vulnerability and defense. An operator without adequate knowledge of RL behavior is more likely to fail to realize adversarial manipulation, whereas stress and security fatigue further increase susceptibility [11, 24]. Such exploitable human weaknesses are what adversary tactics often capitalize on in gathering evidence for their argument calling for a strong human-centered interface and robust training programs that integrate human and AI resilience [13, 14]. Continuous monitoring of humans with human-in-the-loop will help mitigate such risks in cybersecurity awareness programs [15, 16].

6.10.4 Defensive Mechanisms and AI Robustness

Counter-adversarial strategies in Reinforcement Learning (RL) and autonomous systems include:

- Adversarial training, where agents are taught during learning to receive malicious inputs to increase their robustness [17].

- Robust policy learning consisting of optimally determined actions keeping performance in the uncertainty of conditions under adversarial attack [18, 25].
- More explainable and interpretable reinforcement policies that would more gravely amplify understanding in human operators and allow for rapid detection of abnormal behaviors [26, 27].
- Redundancy and sensor fusions reduce the effects of observation-space attacks through cross-verification of input sources [19, 20].

6.10.5 Human–AI Collaboration in Adversarial Defense

Effective defense can only stem from pairing AI autonomy with human oversight because the humans are the last resort in intermediate measures for cost–benefit interpretation of system outputs, validation of agent behavior, and high-level decision-making when uncertainty exists [21, 22]. Such exposure to potential adversarial tactics would be mitigated by real-time alerts, adaptive interfaces, and event-based simulations that will bring about reinforcement to human–AI collaboration through real-time alerts, adaptive interfaces, and event-based simulations [1, 2].

6.10.6 Future Directions and Challenges

As these systems become even more autonomous in critical infrastructure, the possible adversarial threats will grow even stronger. Some of the prospective areas for research include the following: developing AI agents with intrinsic robustness, enhancing human–AI explainability, and developing frameworks for quantifying and managing combined human and system vulnerabilities [3, 4, 23]. These include continuous adversarial testing, resilience benchmarking, and human-centric cybersecurity culture, all of which are proactive measures needed in the defense of such systems [5, 6].

6.10.7 Summary

Adversarial AI in reinforcement learning and autonomous systems indicates the technological vulnerability and also human vulnerability at the same time. This is why the important requirement for tackling these challenges is a holistic and integrative approach that incorporates strong AI schemes, explainable and understandable models, and, most importantly, resilient human operators. With the recognition of the connection between human factors and autonomous decision-making, better security, reliability, and safe operations of AI systems will be realized [7, 8, 10].

6.11 Human-in-the-Loop Defense Strategies

Human-in-the-loop (HITL) defense strategies constitute an increasingly important approach in contemporary security frameworks, particularly in the case of complex, autonomous systems. These strategies focus on the incorporation of human judgment and oversight into automated mechanisms for defense, being aware that humans remain both the last resort of defense and potential vulnerabilities within cyber operations [1, 2].

6.11.1 Role of Humans in Cyber Defense

Humans are both a strength and a weakness in cybersecurity. They strengthen defense and weaken it at the same time. Most effective HITL strategies exploit human expertise in recognizing deviations, understanding complex system behavior, and managing incidents misclassified by automated systems [3, 4]. Situational awareness and the ability to make decisions, as well as domain knowledge, are critical for resilient defense, particularly when adversaries turn to subtle behavior of systems and social engineering tactics [5, 23].

6.11.2 Human Factors and Vulnerabilities

On the one hand, humans may strengthen defenses, but on the other hand, cognitive biases, fatigue, stress, and insufficient training are some exploitable weaknesses for attackers [6–8]. In this case, HITL strategies must also deal with these vulnerabilities by creating systems that will help with decision-making, decreasing cognitive load, and providing timely alerts [9, 10]. The definition of human factors in system design assures overwhelmed operators by too complex interfaces and by false-positive alerts which can lead to mistakes or omissions in security [28].

6.11.3 HITL Defense Mechanisms

A number of mechanisms that make effective HITL cybersecurity frameworks:

- Collaborative Decision Support Systems (CDSS): These provide actionable insights and risk assessments to operators who can approve or override automated decisions [11, 12].
- Adaptive Alerting and Feedback Loops: Dynamic alert systems help humans to tailor prioritization of threats based on context against the impact of alert fatigue [13, 24].

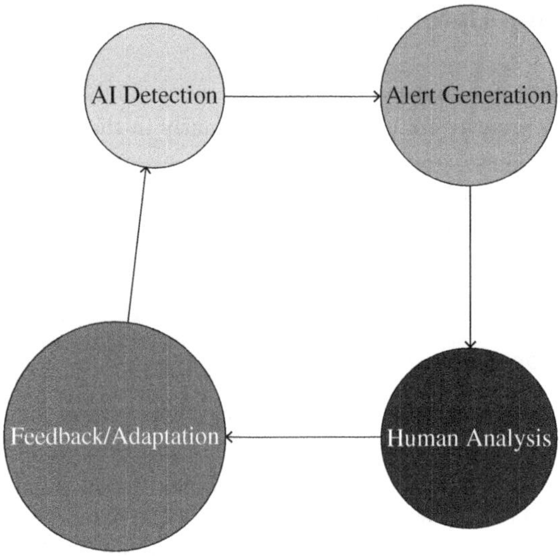

Figure 6.5 Human-in-the-Loop (HITL) Cyber Defense Cycle. "*Source:* Hewa Majeed Zangana"

- Simulation and Scenario-Based Training: Annual realistic threat exposure increases human readiness as well as lessens the likelihood of social engineering and adversarial attacks [14, 16].
- Human–AI Collaborative Interfaces: This should produce an effort-free manner of communication between human operators and AI, creating faster responses while reducing misinterpretation of system outputs [15, 17].

Figure 6.5 illustrates the human-in-the-loop (HITL) defense cycle, emphasizing the continuous interaction of automated AI systems and human oversight. Adaptive and improved outcomes of resilient and accurate decision-making will thus be guaranteed by this cycle.

6.11.4 Integrating HITL into Autonomous and AI Systems

These humans in the loop then assist the RL agents in the autonomous systems, verifying AI decisions, and further intervening if the system detects atypical behavior [18, 25]. Continuous oversight of HITL strategies provides resilience against the identification of such adversarial manipulations, ensuring compliance by automated systems to the organizational security protocols [26, 27].

6.11.5 Organizational and Cultural Considerations

However, the contribution of HITL defense can also hinge on organizational culture and leadership, beyond the purely technological features. Cybersecurity policy should raise awareness, trust, and accountability in the operators themselves and should incorporate the best approaches to decision-making and incident response [19, 20]. A nurturing cybersecurity culture can significantly reduce the risks for organizations that have strong cybersecurity-trained workforces to be breached by an employee [21, 22].

6.11.6 Future Directions

New studies highlight that the area of future research should involve developing strategies of HITL corresponding with the level of automation and human control while considering stress, cognitive limitations, and adversarial threats [1, 2]. The next steps would be bringing explainable AI, predictive analytics, and adapting training modules into the framework of developing improved situational awareness and intervention capabilities for humans. At the same time, crossing psychology, human factors engineering, and cybersecurity into multidisciplinary approaches will be necessary to perfect the HITL framework [3, 4, 23].

6.11.7 Summary

With the human-in-the-loop defensive strategy, an organization can improve the level of detection, response, and resilience against the increasingly sophisticated cyber threats and reduce the risks associated with human errors. This strategy usually makes use of the capacity of the cognitive human agent through automated systems. Any other important topic, such as human factors and training, must be continuous. This way, the nexus of the human and AI roles would develop great and effective cybersecurity systems that can be able to counter threats rooted in technologies or social engineering [5–7].

6.12 Case Studies and Experimental Analysis

Actual empirical evaluation and an understanding of the context for evaluation on human factors in natural, real-life environments are necessary for the establishment of strong cybersecurity measures. Case studies and experimental analyses are really among the great methodologies for assessing cybersecurity interventions, particularly in systems considering humans as being a central element of a defense mechanism [1, 2].

6.12.1 Case Study Selection and Methodology

When forming case studies for cybersecurity investigations, environments with varying levels of automation, levels of employee expertise, and levels of threat exposure should be chosen. Most commonly, such environments include industrial, corporate, and critical infrastructure systems due to the complex interaction of human operators in an automated system [3, 4]. Data are typically gathered from logs of incidents, simulation exercises, survey data, and behavioral observations to grasp both the technical and human factors affecting cybersecurity outcomes [5, 23].

6.12.2 Human Factor Assessments in Case Studies

It is generally agreed in the case studies that humans are normally identified as the weakest link in the chain of cybersecurity [6, 7]. Cognitive biases, fatigue, stress, and untrained individuals have been proven to affect the integrity of systems, according to experimental analyses. For instance, industrial operators exposed to repeated simulated phishing attacks exhibited declining accuracy of response under stress, which in turn necessitated adaptive human-in-the-loop strategies [8, 10]. Evaluation among corporate environments further demonstrated that employees well-acquainted with cybersecurity and who received frequent training tended to pinpoint anomalies or block incursions [9, 28].

6.12.3 Experimental Analysis of HITL Defense Mechanisms

Experimental interventions usually focused on controlled simulations, tabletop exercises, and interactive training modules to analyze HITL defense strategies. Works have proved that systems with real-time feedback, decision-support dashboards, and co-alerting mechanisms offer considerable improvements in making humans more responsive and lowering error rates during security events [12]. Adaptive alerting has been shown to prioritize high-risk incidents, minimize alert fatigue, and optimize operator engagement [11, 24].

6.12.4 Measuring Organizational Cybersecurity Resilience

That clearly reflects organizational case studies that culture and leadership affect cybersecurity resilience. Multi-site analysis revealed that strong cybersecurity policies, proactive leadership, and emphasis on human factors lead to shortening incident detection and recovery from incidents [13, 14]. Indeed, perfectly integrated approaches that combined technological safeguards along with continuous human training, situational awareness exercises were most effective in strengthening defense postures [15, 16].

6.12.5 Data-Driven Insights and Analytics

Besides that, experimental analysis also exploits big data in the quantification of humans and systems' behavior and performance during times of cyber incidents.

Such analytics of employee responses, system logs, and AI-generated threat alerts provide results-based recommendations toward refinement of training programs and defense strategies [17, 18]. According to studies, predictive modeling of human vulnerabilities and stress patterns would serve to predict breach incidents as well as optimize HITL fine-tuning [25, 26].

6.12.6 Sector-Specific Findings

In particular, case studies have included critical infrastructure and transportation systems, which disclosed peculiar risks posed by signaling operations, networked devices, and automated decision-making systems. One example of this can be seen in the operations of the railways that would suggest human factors considering signaling directly influence operational safety and cybersecurity integrity and would, therefore, require domain-specific HITL strategies [27]. Business students, however, increased awareness and preparedness, focusing on early-stage human factor interventions, with educational programs geared toward them [19, 20].

6.12.7 Lessons Learned and Best Practices

Lessons from case studies and experimental analyses are the most critical need for continuous training, stress management, human and AI collaboration, and adaptive system design. Such a framework can emerge as resilient against cyber attacks when human factors are systematically integrated into the policy and technical framework, supported by information-driven evaluation and iterative improvements [21, 22]. Effectively, HITL systems will lessen vulnerabilities due to human mistakes while empowering operators to enact decisions during an actual threat scenario.

6.12.8 Summary

Case studies and experimental analyses have led to findings that omit the human factor in cybersecurity planning at their peril. The empirical evaluations tied into HITL strategies ensure that organizations deploy technical means of protection as well as develop competent and capable humans to detect, respond, and mitigate threats. The integration of rigorous analysis with proactive design and human-centered interventions can go a long way in providing cybersecurity programs with an adaptive and resilient perspective in a myriad of operational contexts [1, 6, 14].

6.13 Future Directions and Research Challenges

The field of cybersecurity is changing rapidly, especially with reference to human factors, and offers several research challenges and opportunities. With increasing complexity and interconnectivity of systems, human weakness must be countered along with technical defenses to maintain resilient cybersecurity frameworks [1, 2].

6.13.1 Integrating Human Factors in Cybersecurity Design

Future research must emphasize applying human factors systematically in the design and evaluation of cybersecurity systems. Empirical evidence continues to suggest that human errors, cognitive biases, and stress responses are some of the major contributing reasons behind security breaches [3, 4, 7]. Recent studies indicate that infusing human-centered design, adaptive interfaces, and real-time decision support into the mix could boost human performance in high-stakes cybersecurity settings [5, 23]. Further, designing human reliability and susceptibility metrics in cybersecurity tasks will assist in data-centered interventions [6, 8].

6.13.2 Addressing Stress, Fatigue, and Cognitive Load

Stress, burnout, and security fatigue pose enormous challenges and hamper the human defenders' efficiency [14, 28]. Future studies should focus on generating interventions that will lower cognitive load, enhance situational awareness, and lead to better workload balancing, particularly in high-pressure operational environments such as critical infrastructure, industrial systems, and IoT-enabled networks [9]. Studies on adaptive alerting systems, automated assistance, and collaborative decision-making frameworks can certainly alleviate the ramifications of human fatigue [11, 12].

6.13.3 Advancing Cybersecurity Awareness and Education

Human-centric cybersecurity strategies ought to be buttressed with consistent education and awareness programs. Experimental evidence underscores that focused training programs, gamification, and scenario-based simulations improve cyber behavior and decrease error rates [20, 24, 26]. Future research may include longitudinal studies to assess the long-term effectiveness of such interventions and examine adaptive learning systems that customize content according to the performance of different end users [13, 19].

6.13.4 Trust, Collaboration, and Organizational Culture

Collaboration and trust lie at the bedrock of professional cybersecurity management. Evidence suggests that organizational culture, leadership engagement, and policy enforcement dramatically affect human compliance and resilience [15, 16, 18]. Future works could chart a path toward creating frameworks for interdepartmental collaboration, fostering security-aware organizational culture, and measuring trust dynamics between human actors and automated systems [17, 25].

6.13.5 Human-in-the-Loop Cybersecurity Systems

With the wider acceptance of automated defenses and AI-facilitated monitoring systems, strengthening incorporation of humans into the loop remains an equally vital research challenge. Experimental studies indicate that HITL methodologies maintain and improve adaptability, resiliency, and response accuracy in response to complex threats [21, 27]. One envisioned future is the development of adaptive HITL architectures that take the best from automation and the best from human judgment, especially in threat detection, anomaly response, and critical infrastructure protection [10, 22].

6.13.6 Addressing Emerging Threats and Sociotechnical Risks

The ever-changing cybersecurity landscape continues with the emergence of IoT, cloud computing, and AI-enabled systems. Future research must put under observation the emergence of new attack vectors preying upon human weaknesses like social engineering, insider threats, and operational misjudgments [2, 28]. Important research directions are those aimed at understanding the sociotechnical interaction, constructing predictive models for human errors, and integrating behavioral analytics into risk assessment contexts [1, 6].

6.13.7 Data-Driven Human Factor Analytics

Big data and advanced analytics open up opportunities to model human behavior in the cybersecurity environment [8, 22]. Research initiatives will be targeted toward finding some concrete algorithms capable of detecting anomalies, quantifying risk, and predicting patterns of human errors while maintaining the individual's privacy and autonomous dignity [11, 12]. Merging behavioral data with technical indicators could shift the defense strategies paradigm from reactive to proactive [9, 24].

6.13.8 Summary

From a bird's-eye view, the future may witness a restructuring of cybersecurity under a holistic human-centered perspective. Among resilient and adaptive defense systems, key consideration will be given to bridging the gap between technology and human behavior, cognizant and organizational vulnerabilities, with

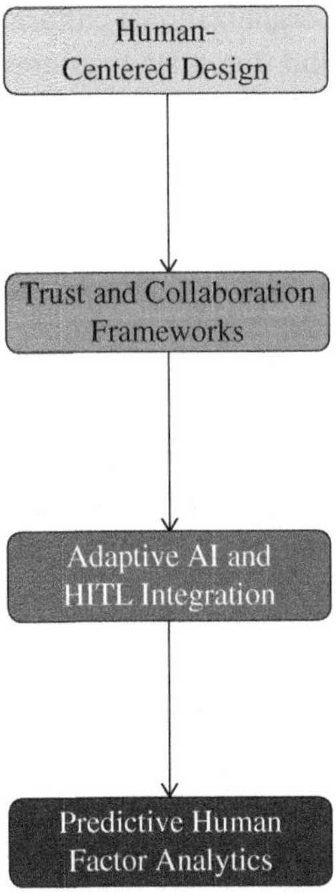

Figure 6.6 Emerging Research Directions in Adversarial AI Defense. "*Source:* Hewa Majeed Zangana"

the support of advanced analytics. Challenges in quantification of human factors in relation to automation and nurturing a security-conducive culture in the organization subsist but could pave promising pathways for advancement in these rapidly evolving digital cyberscapes [1, 15, 19].

The emerging avenues for adversarial AI defense are summarized in Figure 6.6. These pathways integrate human factors, trust frameworks, adaptive learning, and predictive analytics to keep pace with an expanding socio-technical cybersecurity space.

6.14 Conclusion

Human factor remains a decisive factor considering the strengths and weaknesses of an organizational defense setup in the field of cybersecurity. Human beings have, therefore, been considered the doorkeepers of these automated systems, AI, and ML techniques, while also being seen as a point of failure. Understanding the different facets of human behavior—from pressure-induced decision-making to protocol compliance—is critical for the design of an effective, resilient, and adaptive cybersecurity architecture.

Human-in-the-loop approaches are considered highly promising candidates to fill the void between automated defenses and human judgment, offering flexibility, adaptability, and real-time responsiveness to emerging threats. By human-centric designing of cybersecurity workflows, organizations are able to leverage human cognitive abilities and reduce error potential due to fatigue, stress, or limited awareness. In addition, actively promoting cybersecurity culture and learning will strengthen organizational resilience as a social resource and amplify technological efficacy.

A look into the future shows that the next generation of cybersecurity paradigms will combine human factors, organizational culture, and technological innovation. Taking an all-encompassing angle that considers concerns such as sociotechnical interactions, behavioral inclinations, and operational challenges will be fundamental in the prediction and mitigation of increasingly advanced threats. Thus far, it is the partnership of humans and automated systems, coupled with continuous education and proactive risk management, that provides a feasible avenue for long-term sustainability of cybersecurity resilience in a dynamically changing digital world.

References

1 Aksoy, C. (2023). Critical success factors for cybersecurity just technical? Exploring the role of human factors in cybersecurity management. *Research Journal of Business and Management* 10 (2): 51–57.

2 Alsharif, M., Mishra, S., and AlShehri, M. (2022). Impact of human vulnerabilities on cybersecurity. *Computer Systems Science & Engineering.* 40 (3): 1153–1166.

3 Ani, U.D., He, H., and Tiwari, A. (2019). Human factor security: Evaluating the cybersecurity capacity of the industrial workforce. *Journal of Systems and Information Technology* 21 (1): 2–35.

4 Campean, S. (2019). The human factor at the center of a cyber security culture. *International Journal of Information Security and Cybercrime (IJISC)* 8 (1): 51–58.

5 Danet, D. (2021). *Punish and perish: The human factor in cybersecurity*, 1–8. ITASEC.

6 Daudi, M. (2023). Trust framework on exploitation of humans as the weakest link in cybersecurity. *Applied Cybersecurity & Internet Governance* 2 (1): 1–26.

7 Denno, J. (2016). *Attacking the human-the weakest link in cybersecurity*. Utica, NY: Cybersecurity Graduate Program, Utica College.

8 Edeh, N.C. (2023). Cybersecurity and human factors: A literature review. *International Journal of Cyber Research and Education (IJCRE).* 5 (1): 45–56.

9 Goh, P. (2021). Humans as the weakest link in maintaining cybersecurity: Building cyber resilience in humans. In: *Introduction to Cyber Forensic Psychology: Understanding the Mind Of the Cyber Deviant Perpetrators*, 287–305. World Scientific Publishing Co.

10 Giacomello, G. and Pescaroli, G. (2019). Managing human factors. *Cyber Resilience of Systems and Networks.* 1: 247–263.

11 Kadena, E. and Gupi, M. (2021). Human factors in cybersecurity: Risks and impacts. *Security Science Journal* 2 (2): 51–64.

12 Jeong, J., Mihelcic, J., Oliver, G., and Rudolph, C. (2019). Towards an improved understanding of human factors in cybersecurity. In: *2019 IEEE 5th International Conference on Collaboration and Internet Computing (CIC)*, 338–345. IEEE.

13 Nobles, C. (2018). Botching human factors in cybersecurity in business organizations. *HOLISTICA–Journal of Business and Public Administration* 9 (3): 71–88.

14 Nobles, C. (2022). Stress, burnout, and security fatigue in cybersecurity: A human factors problem. *HOLISTICA–Journal of Business and Public Administration* 13 (1): 49–72.

15 Pollini, A., Callari, T.C., Tedeschi, A. et al. (2022). Leveraging human factors in cybersecurity: An integrated methodological approach. *Cognition, Technology & Work* 24 (2): 371–390.

16 Poehlmann N, Caramancion KM, Tatar I, Li Y, Barati M, Merz T. The organizational cybersecurity success factors: An exhaustive literature review. Advances in Security, Networks, and Internet of Things: Proceedings from SAM'20, ICWN'20, ICOMP'20, and ESCS'20. 2021;377–95.

17 Rahman T, Rohan R, Pal D, Kanthamanon P. Human factors in cybersecurity: A scoping review. In: Proceedings of the 12th International Conference on Advances in Information Technology. 2021. p. 1–11.

18 Rebensky S, Carroll M, Nakushian A, Chaparro M, Prior T. Understanding the last line of defense: Human response to cybersecurity events. In: International Conference on Human-Computer Interaction. Springer; 2021. p. 353–66.

19 Triplett, W.J. (2022). Addressing human factors in cybersecurity leadership. *Journal of Cybersecurity and Privacy* 2 (3): 573–586.

20 Wiechetek, Ł. and Mędrek, M. (2022). Human factors in security–cybersecurity education and awareness of business students. *Annales Universitatis Mariae Curie-Skłodowska, Sectio H–Oeconomia* 56 (1): 119–142.

21 Young H, van Vliet T, van de Ven J, Jol S, Broekman C. Understanding human factors in cyber security as a dynamic system. In: Advances in Human Factors in Cybersecurity: Proceedings of the AHFE 2017 International Conference on Human Factors in Cybersecurity, July 17–21, 2017, The Westin Bonaventure Hotel, Los Angeles, California, USA 8. Springer; 2018. p. 244–54.

22 Zhang, X. and Ghorbani, A.A. (2021). Human factors in cybersecurity: Issues and challenges in big data. *Research Anthology on Privatizing and Securing Data.* 3: 1695–1725.

23 Corman, A. (2023). The human element in cybersecurity—bridging the gap between technology and human behaviour. *Journal of Cyber Policy.* 4 (2): 112–128.

24 Marble, J.L., Lawless, W.F., Mittu, R. et al. (2015). *The human factor in cybersecurity: Robust & intelligent defense*, 173–206. Cyber Warfare: Building the Scientific Foundation.

25 Rohan R, Funilkul S, Pal D, Chutimaskul W. Understanding of human factors in cybersecurity: A systematic literature review. In: 2021 International Conference on Computational Performance Evaluation (ComPE). IEEE; 2021. p. 133–40.

26 Sangwan A. Human factors in cybersecurity awareness. In: 2024 International Conference on Intelligent Systems for Cybersecurity (ISCS). IEEE; 2024. p. 1–7.

27 Thron, E., Faily, S., Dogan, H., and Freer, M. (2024). Human factors and cybersecurity risks on the railway–the critical role played by signalling operations. *Information & Computer Security* 32 (2): 236–263.

28 Hughes-Lartey, K., Li, M., Botchey, F.E., and Qin, Z. (2021). Human factor, a critical weak point in the information security of an organization's internet of things. *Heliyon.* 7 (3): e06522.

Part III

Emerging Technologies in Cybersecurity 5.0

7

Blockchain for Secure and Transparent Systems

7.1 Introduction

The fastest-growing digital transformations have rendered cybersecurity a fulcrum upon which global technology growth is being balanced. Data-driven systems, growing Internet connectivity, and artificial intelligence (AI)-driven platforms offer unprecedented opportunities but also vulnerabilities that mandate new and innovative approaches to security and trust-giving. Though originally contracted to support cryptocurrencies, blockchain is now a horizon of great promise in cybersecurity and, thus, system transparency [1, 2]. It puts forth records of transactions in a decentralized, immutable, and transparent manner, eliminating the authority of any central authority, thus taking away the single point of failure and risks of manipulating data without authorization.

The vault of blockchain technology stays with its distributed ledger system that ensures the integrity and traceability of data across a multitude of nodes. Stringently decentralized, it further ramps up the resilience against cyberattacks while providing an entirely different level of trust to digital ecosystems [3, 4]. Within the present paradigm of cybersecurity, the blockchain is a mechanism that helps in psychosocial prevention and correction—detecting, protecting, and auditing security incidents through consensus and proof of cryptography. Perhaps, because of its ability to secure peer-to-peer networks and authenticate digital identities, it is now more relevant in finance, healthcare, IoT, and government services.

There are myriad ways that could successfully show that blockchain holds untold potential in securing digital infrastructure and critical assets. For instance, Etemadi et al. [5] analyzed blockchain's application in supply chain cybersecurity, emphasizing its capability to ensure traceability and authenticity. Tezel et al. [6] also discussed the integration of blockchain in the built environment to enhance the transparency and accountability of data. The tamper-proof nature of blockchain is highly supportive of the real-time monitoring and verification of systems, which ultimately contributes optimally to organizational resilience alongside compliance with regulatory standards [7, 8].

Much of the aforementioned still holds true; however, threats are increasingly a given. Alkhalifah et al. [9] provided example-based reasoning for the different forms of attacks perpetrated against blockchain networks, ranging from the 51% attacks to smart contract vulnerabilities. Mahmood et al. [10] suggest that the complexity of blockchain protocols and the absence of standardized governance models often bring about new cybersecurity challenges. Gurdgiev and Fleming [11] cautioned that systemic risks such as code flaws and interoperability gaps could undermine the informational efficiency of blockchain. Therefore, work continues to analyze how improvements to cryptographic design, AI monitoring, and system dynamic modeling will make blockchain more resilient [12, 13].

Emerging frameworks propose the combination of blockchain with AI and machine learning (ML) to increase responsiveness to cyberattacks. Mengidis et al. [14] introduced blockchain-AI integration in energy networks as a means of successfully detecting and preventing advanced cyber intrusions. Similarly, Omar and Zangana [15] attribute their discussion to the merging of cyber AI with distributed systems for redefining security intelligence, while their companion discussion on large language models for software vulnerability detection highlights the prospect of blockchain automating defense mechanisms. These interdisciplinary approaches indicate a paradigm shift from a reactive to a proactive model of cybersecurity [15].

Alongside the technical, blockchain has economic and strategic implications. Rahman et al. [16] examined how European banks leveraged blockchain to improve data integrity for preventing cyber fraud, whereas Smith and Dhillon [17] assessed its applicability in securing financial transactions with immutable audit trails. Text-mining analyses were used by Prakash et al. [18] to map the expanding role of blockchain in cybersecurity research, showing strong growth of its adoption across industry sectors. Shah et al. [19] emphasized the transformative nature of blockchain in business, cybersecurity, and fintech ecosystems, asserting that it holds long-term value in risk mitigation and operational efficiencies.

This is one of the many forms in which blockchain technology offers its offerings beyond the confines of finance and enterprise. In promoting emerging technology, Ossamah et al. [20] proved how blockchain may protect drone networks from hijacking or unauthorized access. Likewise, Yeasmin and Baig [21] revealed its ability to facilitate secure data interchange in smart environments. Other recent case studies would attest to the expanding embrace of blockchain; Putro et al. [22] and Zidan et al. [23] would show such instances that solidified the case for blockchain as a foundation upon which the new Cybersecurity 5.0 is built.

Overall, a transformative enabler is blockchain for secure and transparent systems. It propounds a trustless model where the integrity is enforced algorithmically rather than institutionally guaranteed. As Sriram et al. [24] and Mathew [25] observed the distributed nature of blockchain creates a self-taming ecosystem that can withstand manipulations and data breach attacks. The dynamic evolution of the framework based on blockchain technology, along with the blossoming of AI-powered threat intelligence systems, hints toward an entirely new era in innovation for cybersecurity—a future that will be defined by the characteristics of decentralization, immutability, and transparency.

This chapter analyzes the fundamental principles of blockchain, its design, and its application with AI for secure and transparent systems. Real-world implementations are reviewed, contemporary cybersecurity challenges are analyzed, and future research directions on optimizing blockchain technologies for next-generation digital infrastructure are provided. By incorporating a synthesis of both academic and industrial perspectives, this chapter shows how blockchain can further enrich proactive and intelligent defense mechanisms against threats within Cybersecurity 5.0.

7.2 Fundamentals of Blockchain Technology

Blockchain technology is indeed one of the revolutions of the twenty-first century. It changes the way digital trust and security in interconnected systems can be built. Broadly speaking, blockchain represents a decentralized, distributed ledger recording transactions across multiple nodes in a peer-to-peer network [1, 2]. In this kind of architecture, once a transaction is verified by a consensus mechanism, it becomes immutable, signifying that no transaction can be changed or altered without consensus throughout the network. Such features of transparency, decentralization, and immutability, taken together, would, in turn, form the basis for blockchain itself to provide improvement in cybersecurity and thereby in privacy and integrity of the systems in relation to each other [3].

7.2.1 Core Principles and Architecture

A blockchain is an ever-increasing series of records called blocks that hold a cryptographic hash of the previous block, along with a timestamp and transaction data. This cryptographic linkage constitutes that changing one block invalidates every block after it, creating a very strong chain of trust [8]. Each node in the network keeps a personal copy of the ledger, and the addition of new blocks occurs through consensus—standardly proof of work (PoW), proof of stake (PoS), or other consensus algorithms intended to check out transactions without dependence on centralized authority [25].

At its core, blockchain has cryptographic algorithms to secure data, distributed consensus for agreement among nodes, and smart contracts to automate processes according to presale-defined rules [26]. Such mechanisms have the inherent avoidance of single points of failure, data corruption, and illegitimate access typical of the common vulnerabilities in centralized systems [4].

To portray how blockchain combines cryptography, consensus, and data structure into a unified secure framework, Figure 7.1 shows the basic architecture of a blockchain network, with an emphasis on the interaction between users, blocks, nodes, and consensus layers.

7.2.2 Decentralization and Trust Mechanisms

The most essential pillar of blockchain security is defined by decentralization. Whereas the traditionally centralized systems utilize trusted intermediaries to manipulate information, control is spread across many network participants, making it almost impossible for any entity to change information [27].

This decentralized trust system has brought about resilience to internal and external attacks and transparency and accountability. Another added advantage of decentralization is that it empowers trust among actors in industries like construction, supply chain management, and finance, where the integrity of data matters [6].

Also, consensus mechanisms used in blockchain, such as Byzantine Fault Tolerance (BFT), Proof of Authority (PoA), and hybrid algorithms, play an essential role in establishing ledger consistency and resisting malicious actors [7]. The following study of Mahmood et al. [10] shows how these mechanisms enable distributed systems to detect and prevent cyber threats in real time, thereby changing the perception of safety for the lives of individuals in the digital era.

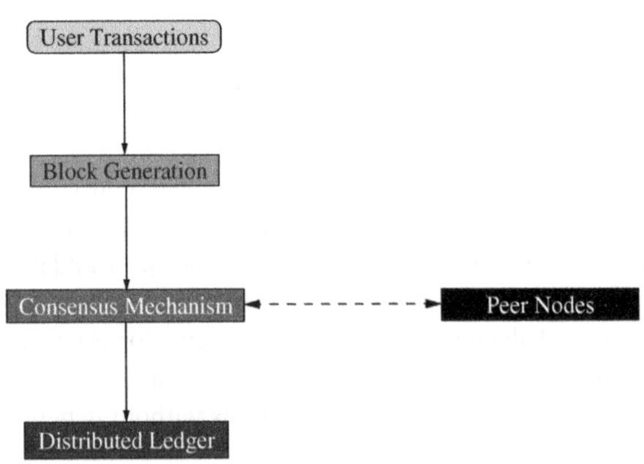

Figure 7.1 General architecture of blockchain systems showing user interaction, block generation, and distributed consensus. "*Source:* Hewa Majeed Zangana"

7.2.3 Immutability and Transparency

Blockchain relies on cryptographic hashing and consensus validation for immutability. Once data is recorded and confirmed, it becomes impossible to alter or tamper with it without bringing consensus from the network, thus blocking data from manipulation or unauthorized changes [16]. This immutability strengthens the integrity of data and provides audit trails, traceable and verifiable, by all participants. According to Etemadi et al. [5], the source of such transparency was the higher level of accountability and trustworthiness, especially with system structures such as food supply chains, in which data verification and traceability are indispensable.

The transparent characteristic of blockchain, however, must come with the demand for privacy. Wylde et al. [7] said that while transparency increases trust, it could expose sensitive pieces of information if not managed appropriately. Advanced cryptographic methods such as zero-knowledge proofs have incorporated homomorphic encryption into blockchain systems to continue in the way of reaching this balance [14].

7.2.4 Smart Contracts and Automation

Smart contracts or self-executing agreements are written directly into code and, once conditions are met, executed on the blockchain. They permit industry automation, minimizing human error and intermediaries in workflows [19]. According to Banafa [8], smart contracts extend the usage of the blockchain to areas beyond cryptocurrency transactions, such as supply chain management, healthcare, and financial systems.

The automation that smart contracts afford, though, presents challenges. Oftentimes, such vulnerabilities are left open for attackers to exploit in the empirical studies of security incidents in blockchain [9]. Hence, smart contract security enhancement through AI-driven analysis and formal verification is an emerging research focus [15].

7.2.5 Consensus Algorithms and Security

These algorithms are responsible not only for security but also for performance in a blockchain. For example, in Bitcoin, PoW validates transactions by means of computational power, but it is energy-greedy. In contrast, PoS and its medley variants are more efficient and scalable because they choose validators on the basis of their ownership or reputation [26]. Every consensus mechanism has its own trade-offs in how much energy is consumed, scalability, and possible resistance to innovative attack concepts like "51% attack" [27].

Emerging hybrid consensus mechanisms merge features from multiple models to simultaneously address the issues of scalability and trust for system heterogeneous resilience [12]. This way, hybrid models create dynamic real-world cybersecurity environments, which allow organizations to make predictions on future vulnerabilities, thus optimizing blockchain protection [13].

7.2.6 Applications Across Domains

Besides, because blockchain is versatile, it can be applied in different areas. In finance systems, for example, it provides transaction security through creating an immutable audit trail and distributed validation [17]. Product authenticity and traceability in supply chains are achieved through this technology [5]. Moreover, IoT networks are decentralized secure frameworks against tampering and unauthorized access by devices [20]. In the same vein, Mengidis et al. [14] viewed it as critical in energy grids, as blockchain and AI integration would guarantee system reliability and cybersecurity.

Also, Zidan et al. [23] explained the use that blockchain has in enterprise security against cybercrime, while Putro et al. [22] pointed out its capacity for reviewing information system reliability. Likewise, Rahman et al. [16] showed how banks in Europe have adopted blockchain to raise their standards of integrity and data reliability to support cyber defense mechanisms. Thus, blockchain would not only compete worldwide in adopting Cybersecurity 5.0 policy but also begin to shape futuristic models that focus on decentralization, intelligence, and automation in security [15].

7.2.7 Challenges and Limitations

Hence, blockchain definitely transforms the status of an entire industry; however, there are still several technical hurdles and systemic challenges. Gurdgiev and Fleming [11] cautioned against system-wide threats like designs in code leading to vulnerabilities and interoperability problems that compromise informational efficiency. Real-world incidents of blockchain exploits were identified by Alkhalifah et al. [9] as an issue that calls for better threat modeling and countermeasures. Mahmood et al. [10] added scalability, energy consumption, and governance as continuing challenges to overcome toward end-user adoption.

As Singh [3] and Kshetri [4] note, while decentralization and encryption enhance security through blockchain, they also create opportunities for new attacks such as social engineering and network partitioning. This problem should be solved by integrating AI-driven monitoring systems and adaptive security frameworks trained to learn from emerging threats [15, 24].

7.2.8 Integration with Cyber AI

The merger of blockchain and AI is shaping the next era in cybersecurity. As Omar and Zangana [15] put forth, the systems built on AI-enabled blockchains can predict, detect, and counter cyber threats autonomously, thus creating a self-healing digital infrastructure. Also, Mengidis et al. [14] have articulated how AI and blockchain synergize to further secure energy networks and IoT environments. Such integration creates active threat intelligence and resilience, transitioning toward Cybersecurity 5.0, whereby decentralized trust and cognitive intelligence work in tandem to mitigate complex digital threats.

The foundational principles of blockchain technology include permissionless architecture, decentralized governance, cryptographic assurance, and smart automation. They impact how blockchain serves as a transformational power in cybersecurity. As research is evolving [18, 21], the blockchain stands to be the main enabler for secure, transparent, and resilient systems that form the backbone of the digital economy.

7.3 Blockchain Architectures and Types

Blockchain uses a distributed ledger architecture that safely, transparently, and immutably records transactions across multiple nodes. The blockchain system's architecture inherently determines the manner through which functionality, scalability, and decentralization interact to either create or hinder the advancement of applications appealing or currently used in different fields of cybersecurity and data integrity. Banafa [8] outlines the following three components of blockchain: distributed ledgers, cryptographic mechanisms, and consensus algorithms. They interoperate to create environments that can be defined as trustless, tamper-proof, and resistant to cyberattacks.

Three forms of configuration are considered under the umbrella of basic blockchain architectural models: public, private, and consortium (hybrid) blockchains. These alternatives offer divergent trade-offs related to transparency, control, and performance in the context of each application. Publicly accessible blockchains such as Bitcoin and Ethereum are open networks where any stakeholder can participate, verify transactions, and participate in consensus [2]. They are based on either proof-of-work or proof-of-stake algorithms in block validation, ensuring immutability and decentralization at the expense of energy consumption and low transaction throughput [1]. The openness to participation enhances transparency: hence, systems such as these are appropriate for settings in which trust is a chief design consideration and where security and verifiability are of utmost importance [27].

In contrast to public blockchains, private blockchains are permissioned networks termed in most cases as such only due to a one-organization control of the whole processes or systems. This configuration grants more control and efficiency by limiting participation and expediting consensus methods such as Practical Byzantine Fault Tolerance (PBFT) or Raft [25]. These configurations have been widely used in enterprise cybersecurity frameworks in order to improve the confidentiality of data against the threat posed by malicious actors [16]. According to Etemadi et al. [5], private blockchains mark very significant relevance in sectors that demand traceability and compliance, such as food supply chains and logistics.

Also known as a hybrid blockchain, a consortium blockchain queries some properties of both public and private systems. These allow a group of trusted organizations to share control over the network with selective transparency [6]. Such a model would enhance interoperability and data protection across collaborative environments, for example, financial institutions and government agencies. More recently, Gurdgiev and Fleming [11] noted that consortium architectures could mitigate systemic risk and increase informational efficiency through a balance of accessibility and governance, thereby diminishing vulnerabilities usually practiced by systems fully in the public domain.

A layered approach—from a cybersecurity architecture vantage—enhances blockchain defense mechanisms on many levels. Nodes have distributed communication in the network layer, agreement on valid transactions in the consensus layer, while smart contracts and decentralized applications (DApps) reside in the application layer [17]. According to Mahmood et al. [10]], this modular structure allows the layering of security protocols, thereby minimizing the impact of single-point failures. References of Antonyan and Rybakova [4] highlight that, along with hash function mechanisms, signatures in the blockchain architecture further enhance data integrity and authentication so as to preempt unauthorized changes or replay attacks.

Empirical studies have demonstrated that the architectural resilience of blockchain systems contributes significantly to the mitigation of cybersecurity incidents. According to Alkhalifah et al. [9], attacks related to blockchain largely exploit vulnerabilities in smart contracts and manipulate consensus rather than the core blockchain protocol itself. Thus, enhancing architectural components such as diversity of consensus and smart contract verification remains critical for system resilience. Consistently, Mengidis et al. [14] noted that harnessing AI within blockchain networks improves real-time anomaly detection and adaptive defense of such critical infrastructures as energy grids.

In the case of corporations, modeling approaches from system dynamics have simulated and optimized blockchain-based cybersecurity architectures. Kuzmenko et al. [12] and Sadigov et al. [13] showed that simulation of blockchain improves situational awareness and allows organizations to plan and prepare for cyber threats better. This resonance with [15] points to the budding synergy between AI-driven cybersecurity frameworks and blockchain-based infrastructures for intelligent threat defense.

Emerging research also highlights domain-specific architectures, where lightweight blockchains run specific applications such as Internet of Things (IoT) applications and drone systems. According to Ossamah [20], he proposed architectures for drone cybersecurity based on blockchains, advocating integrity in communication and mission data, whereas Yeasmin and Baig [21] researched how modular blockchain frameworks can be "un-blocked" for interoperability across diverse computing environments to improve transparency and resilience.

As Demirkan et al. [26] believe that blockchain architecture will develop more with time in the way of being automated, in which regulation will be governed by AI, adaptive consensus models, and a self-healing mechanism created for the sake of cyber defense. A second text-mining analysis done by Prakash et al. [18] indicates that hybrid- and permissioned-type architectures are becoming more prominent in business cybersecurity applications since they strike a balance between scalability and compliance. This position is corroborated by Shah et al. [19], with their observation that blockchain frameworks are the backbone of future secure FinTech systems, as they also give traceability, auditability, and automated trust.

Blockchain architectures will also provide a tremendous contribution toward cyber-resilience and integrity in information. As shown by Putro et al. [22], blockchain enhances redundancy, makes unauthorized data alterations impossible, and thus improves reliability in information systems. Zidan et al. [23] and Sriram et al. [24] pointed out that, in an enterprise environment, blockchain contributes high levels of cybersecurity but at the same time manifests an unchangeable record of all security events, thus providing better forensic analysis and compliance auditing. Wylde et al. [7] argued further that transparency and privacy protection can be achieved by combining a strong privacy-preserving protocol with blockchain.

Lastly, as elaborated by Omar et al. [15] in their edited work, Redefining Security With Cyber AI, the development in the architecture of blockchains is taking cybersecurity toward the intelligent, proactive, and adaptive future. Such systems are the best example of the oncoming convergence of centralized systems that emanate from decentralization, cryptography, and AI to create self-monitoring, tamper-evident infrastructures against the striking sophistication of mainstream cyber threats.

Broadly, cybersecurity architectures based on blockchain consist of public blockchain, private blockchain, and consortium-type architecture. The comparative illustrations of these models show the degrees of decentralization, control, and transparency in the Figure 7.2. Thus, in a nutshell, diversity in architectural design—there are public, private, and consortium blockchains—reflects the goodness of technology in adapting itself to different contexts of cybersecurity.

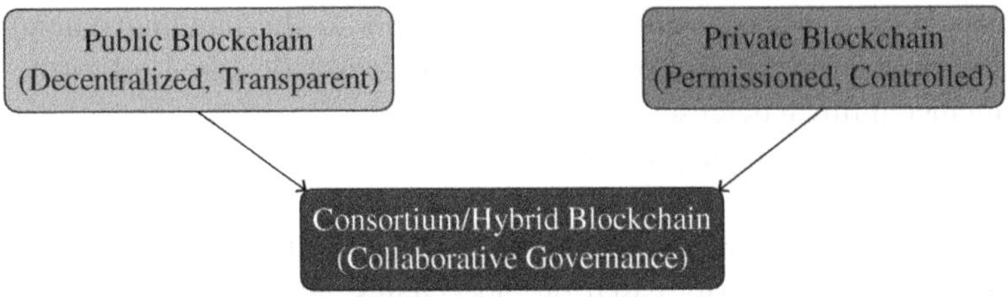

Figure 7.2 Classification of blockchain architectures and their relationship to decentralization and control. "*Source:* Hewa Majeed Zangana"

With the further implementation of AI, modeling of the system, and privacy mechanisms, it ensures that blockchain will remain a significant pillar for such transparent and secure systems in the age of Cybersecurity 5.0.

7.4 Consensus Mechanisms and Their Security Implications

Consensus mechanisms, which form the backbone of blockchain technology, are the protocols that allow all participants in a distributed network to agree on the validity and order of transactions without reference to a central authority. Consensus mechanisms are crucial in guaranteeing the main characteristics of blockchain—immutability, transparency, and trust—by providing protection for the entire network against malicious activities. Consensus protocols are, thus, models of trust decentralization where trust becomes a factor in the digital economy and consequently in the security of devices for distributed systems [1].

By every blockchain network, there should be created an erect for the single truth. This is made possible with mechanisms that prove and revise blocks before they are finally presented to the ledger. According to Banafa [8], consensus algorithms enable an understandable way of validating transactions in a network besides defending it from double-spending, Sybil attacks, and collusion attempts. Different consensus mechanisms—such as PoW, PoS, Delegated Proof of Stake (DPoS), PBFT, and PoA—differ in their needs in computation, scalability, and resistance against access to attacks.

7.4.1 Proof of Work (PoW) and Its Security Trade-offs

PoW introduced by Bitcoin requires participants to solve complex cryptographic puzzles to form a new block in the blockchain [2]. Thus, PoW guarantees resistance in the manipulation sense: it is highly robust and disallows any alteration of past transactions unless enormous effort is put into it. However, as pointed out by Hasanova et al. ([27]), the accumulation of mining power within just a few entities seriously threatens the decentralized nature of the networks, exposing them to a 51% attack in a way that one actor controls the majority of computational power within the system. These incidents were empirically studied using survey analysis by Alkhalifah et al. [9] whose conclusions indicated that PoW systems can still be attacked via mining pool centralization and consensus manipulation.

From a cybersecurity perspective, PoW offers robustness even though getting this security is at very high energy and environmental costs. Mahmood et al. [10] pointed out that attackers can use old mining hardware and weak nodes to perform denial-of-service (DoS) or selfish-mining attacks. But despite these disadvantages, the difficulty of computation in PoW gives it a form of innate protection against brute force attacks, which makes it ideally suited for open, trustless networks [25].

7.4.2 Proof of Stake (PoS) and Enhanced Efficiency

Thus, PoS points to an introduction of a new validation process by ownership unlike that of computation in addressing problems with PoW. The method chooses the validators to generate new blocks on the basis of the number of tokens the validator possesses and the amount he/she will stake as collateral [26]. This results in less energy use and improvement of scalability while keeping the integrity of consensus. It is stated by Gurdgiev and Fleming [11], that PoS makes an advancement as concerns informational efficiency by holding validator incentives to network security and trustworthiness.

Nevertheless, the security issues surrounding PoS are not limited to this, but also include the "Nothing at Stake" problem. As noted by Etemadi et al. [5], the Nothing at Stake problem refers to the situation that validators can support multiple blockchain forks because they have little to lose, which can be contrary to the immutability of the ledger. Modern PoS subtypes like Casper and Ouroboros introduce punishment functions in the event of offense to counter those unethical behaviors and strengthen trust levels among participants.

7.4.3 Delegated Proof of Stake (DPoS) and Centralization Risks

In DPoS, it interferes with the PoS idea by allowing token holders to vote on a limited number of "delegates" that are then responsible for validating transactions and producing blocks. DPoS is significant in improving the speed and scalability of transactions; however, it closes its worth with governance and centralization concerns. So, for example, as Tezel et al. [6] explained, as much as one can count on elected validators, there would exist oligarchic control, reduce transparency, and might facilitate collusion. DPoS networks from the cybersecurity perspective should maintain strict enough auditing mechanisms to prevent manipulation and insider threats [19].

7.4.4 Byzantine Fault Tolerance (BFT) and Permissioned Blockchains

BFT resiliency mechanisms are imperative for private and consortium blockchains where all the participants are at least somewhat known and trusted. The modern PBFT allows nodes to achieve consensus in cases where some nodes may behave maliciously or fail to respond at all. According to Smith et al. [17], BFT-based protocols are mainly suited for financial and enterprise networks with very rapid transaction validation and the highest consistency. However, these types of systems, as indicated by Rahman et al. [16] are hampered by scalability limitations, making them less suitable for bigger public networks.

As Kshetri [3] also added that BFT systems are important contributors in strengthening privacy and cybersecurity, ensuring that all that achieves consensus is still good in some measure against malicious actors. Yet, Antonyan and Rybakova [4] demonstrated how PBFT's cryptographic formats, such as signatures and message authentication codes, strengthen resilience against spoofing or man-in-the-middle attacks. However, communication overhead remains a big performance problem as far as BFT systems are concerned [10].

7.4.5 Emerging Consensus Mechanisms and Hybrid Models

Natural progressions have taken place in hybrid and consensus models enhanced by AI, combining the best features of all the various approaches. In fact, Mengidis et al. [14] showed how these features had the potential to optimize blockchain consensus in energy grids through AI while also providing the means to dynamically adjust validation parameters to thwart cyberattacks. For instance, Omar et al. [15] argued that AI-integrated consensus algorithms will adopt self-learning security postures, adaptive defense mechanisms, and proactive defenses against evolving threats.

The main hybrid models making waves today with respect to enterprise or governmental applications include PoA and Proof of Reputation (PoR), in that such models require validator reputation or authority instead of computational or monetary stake. Thus, trust in these proof models is improved and becomes more efficient under permissioned settings [20]. [12] simulated system dynamics to analyze security systems based on PoA, which, as a result of those simulations, have shown improvements in reliability and fault tolerance in enterprise cybersecurity frameworks.

Integrating privacy-preserving technologies like zero-knowledge proofs into consensus mechanisms is highlighted by Wylde et al. [7] as key to maintaining transparency without sacrificing data confidentiality. Moreover, it is also revealed through text mining by Prakash et al. [18] that next-generation consensus protocols are increasingly using hybridized and federated structures to close the gap between decentralization and performance and regulatory compliance.

7.4.6 Security Implications of Consensus Protocols

Consensus may very well be the first line of defense as far as blockchain cybersecurity is concerned, but it has its own specific vulnerabilities based on how it operates. The most common incidents of cybersecurity in a blockchain arise as a result of the consensus implementation. Some of the attacks include time-delay attacks, node impersonation, and fork-based exploits [9]. As Sadigov [13] noted, system-dynamic modeling is capable of estimating and neutralizing those attacks by simulating node behavior under stress.

Further, Putro et al. [22] and Zidan et al. [23] have exhibited how consensus protocols promote data integrity and guarantee that all network participants share the same transaction sequencer, reducing the possibility of fraud or tampering. This is particularly critical for authenticating data and complying with regulations in financial scenarios [16].

Overall, security regarding consensus mechanisms can be viewed as the trade-off between decentralization and efficiency against resiliency. Sriram et al. [24] observe that the inclusion of blockchain consensus in enterprise cybersecurity frameworks provides stronger auditability and transparency. Yeasmin and Baig [21] also mention that unlocking the full potential of blockchain will require optimizing consensus algorithms for the reduction of computational inefficiencies while also enhancing trust.

In the end, Omar and Zangana [15] discussed that in future blockchain consensus arrangements, one of the greatest expectations lies in the algorithms driven by AI and resistant to quantum that will evolve dynamically according to the new threats coming out of cyberspace. These next-gen consensus protocols will redefine how blockchain secures digital ecosystems in the Cybersecurity 5.0 era by combining ferocious cryptographic robustness, intelligent automation, and decentralized governance.

Consensus mechanisms provide the degree of trust across the distributed networks, and their consistency holds. Figure 7.3 portrays different consensus models and makes their security attributes visible in that they maintain integrity and resistance to attacks.

In conclusion, consensus mechanisms are the lifeblood of blockchain security. Their evolution from energy-hungry PoW into intelligent hybrid systems

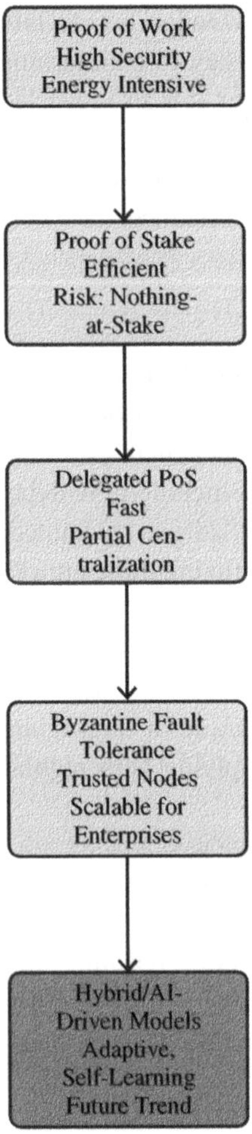

Figure 7.3 Evolution of consensus mechanisms and their security implications in blockchain networks. "*Source:* Hewa Majeed Zangana"

illustrates this continuous endeavor toward reconciling security, scalability, and efficiency. With the fact that the ongoing development of blockchain with AI and the emerging paradigms of cybersecurity, these will act as significant enablers of trust, transparency, and resilience in digital infrastructures.

7.5 Blockchain in Cybersecurity: Applications and Use Cases

Blockchain technology has emerged as one of the most disruptive innovations in modern-day cybersecurity, serving significantly in its unique capabilities to improve transparency, integrity, and resilience of digital ecosystems. Being decentralized and immutable, it provides a solid means of defense against data manipulation, fraud, and unauthorized access. Eliminating single points of failure and bringing about distributed consensus has made blockchain increasingly useful across various domains of cyberspace such as finance transaction-level cybersecurity, data sharing, identity management, and infrastructure protection critical [1, 3, 8].

7.5.1 Blockchain for Data Integrity and Confidentiality

One of the most remarkable uses of blockchains in cybersecurity is ensuring data integrity and confidentiality, as every transaction or data record is cryptographically linked into one string with an impossibility of altering or deleting this record without the consensus in the network [2, 25]. This immutability forms a crux for an entire sector that involves handling sensitive types of data such as healthcare, state, and banking. As recorded by Smith and Dhillon [17], the auditing trails in the blockchain-based ledgers significantly decrease the possibility of tampering during financial transactions due to their transparent and verifiable audit trails. So, too, were brought to light by Rahman et al. [16], who demonstrated how European banks strengthen their data integrity and compliance frameworks using blockchain security systems that detect anomalies in the transaction records in real time.

7.5.2 Decentralized Identity and Access Management

Blockchain technology relies on decentralized identity management (DID) systems. Such systems allow either individuals or organizations to control who has access to their data. This means that no central authority is relied upon to entrust that information. Thus, all avenues for identity theft or credential breach become reduced. Demirkan, [26] highlighted that the mechanisms for identity validation through blockchain can be instituted within authentication procedures since sensitive credentials will never be exposed to third-party servers. Prakash et al. [18] also stated that cryptographic principles of blockchain make it the best fit for privacy-preserving methods in authentication protocols in cybersecurity architecture. Further, the thing was discussed by Shah et al. [19] as regards how firms and FinTechs lean on blockchain for access control to target mainly preventing insider threats and generating unauthorized privilege escalation.

7.5.3 Cyber Threat Intelligence and Secure Communication

Blockchain networks have also found application in cyber threat intelligence sharing and secure communication between organizations. With the help of distributed ledgers, safety indicators, malware signatures, and incident reports may be shared among institutions without the risk of falling victim to tampering or interception [14] [27],. The application of such collective intelligence is a more efficient way of detecting and preventing coordinated cyberattacks. An illustration by [5] is how traceability mechanisms based on blockchain within supply chains improve cybersecurity through the detection of maleficent modifications on digital documents. In the same way, Ossamah [20] has elaborated on employing blockchain technologies to enhance drone cybersecurity, in which a decentralized consensus would prevent remote hijacking and unauthorized command injections.

7.5.4 Smart Contracts for Automated Security Enforcement

Smart contracts, which are codes self-executing on the blockchain, can also be used to automate cybersecurity policies and response actions. They might also enforce protocols, initiate alerts, or remove rights based on some predefined conditions [7]. An example of this smart contract in enterprise systems is automated blocking of unauthorized devices or the revocation of compromised user credentials [13]. Kuzmenko et al. [12] improved this application by modeling cybersecurity systems in enterprises through blockchain-based dynamic simulations that predict and mitigate cyber risk.

7.5.5 Blockchain in IoT and Critical Infrastructure Protection

High numbers of devices connected to one another and may become potential attack surfaces represent the major new cybersecurity challenge posed by the Internet of Things (IoT). Blockchain offers a decentralized solution for securing IoT communications and managing device identities. According to Antonyan and Rybakova [4], the potential of blockchain in cryptographic strength can mitigate some common vulnerabilities within IoT that include spoofing of data and a lack of authorization to gain access. The importance of blockchain in curtailing unauthorized access and spoofing of data is expanded by Mengidis et al. [14], who discusses hybridization of blockchain and AI systems in securing energy grids, and is further extended in applications in the built environment by Tezel et al. [6] in amplifying trust, transparency, and cyber resilience.

7.5.6 Blockchain for Enterprise and Financial Security

Against this background, the emergence of blockchain technology in the last few decades has been postulated to provide one of the elemental pillars of modernization in contemporary cyber defense matrices. By its widespread applicability—from identity management to supply chain protection, through to smart contract automation and AI-driven defense—it has proved its worth to provide secure, transparent, and resilient systems across the board. Nonetheless, continuous innovation and effective governance mechanisms remain essential in addressing its inbuilt weaknesses for sustainable adoption in cybersecurity.

7.5.7 Blockchain in Supply Chain and Industry 4.0 Security

Traceability, provenance verification, and accountability are some of the contributions made by blockchain in cybersecurity within the supply chain. Etemadi et al. [5], found that blockchain security systems within the food supply chains are developed to avoid risks of data being manipulated throughout the production and distribution stages. Tezel et al. [6] built a link between the adoption of blockchain technology and trust management and transparency improvement across the built environment under Industry 4.0. According to Banafa [8], the integration of blockchain technology into industrial systems lays down a proactive defense against cyber-physical threats.

7.5.8 Challenges and Security Vulnerabilities in Blockchain

While improving cybersecurity, no system is impervious to attacks. Alkhalifah et al. [9] furnish an empirical analysis concerning cybersecurity incidents with respect to blockchain, pointing out the vulnerabilities in this technology. These include 51% attacks, smart contract bugs, and consensus protocol flaws, among others. Mahmood et al. [10] and Hasanova et al. [27] put forth arguments highlighting how these issues of scalability, interoperability, and privacy may arouse other forms of risks. Yeasmin and Baig [21] indicated that none of these constraints may be solved before completely releasing the real potential of cybersecurity provided by blockchain, especially in important infrastructures as well as in government systems.

7.5.9 Integration with AI and Emerging Cyber Defense Models

In recent days, it has been clear that the two worlds, namely, blockchain and AI, have much in common in strengthening cyber defense systems. When combined with an AI-powered cybersecurity architecture, blockchain could allow [15] to predict threats and decentralized data verification while simultaneously responding to incidents autonomously. The combination of these two creates a more adaptive and open cybersecurity framework for the Cyber Security 5.0 Era. Sriram et al. [24] bolstered this line of thinking by demonstrating how financial systems and businesses protect themselves through hybrid systems of AI and blockchain through continuous learning and anomaly detection.

This is the summary of how blockchain technology has transformed from a mere oddity to an increasingly vital part of contemporary cybersecurity strategies. Its applications, from identity management, securing supply chains to smart contract automations, and AI-driven defensive strategies, make it a valuable asset that can deliver secure, transparent, and resilient systems spanning multiple domains. However, it requires continuous innovation and governance to address the underlying vulnerabilities concerning its continued adoption in cybersecurity.

7.6 Enhancing Transparency and Trust through Blockchain

Transparency and trust are the bedrocks of cybersecurity and digital governance in a world seen today with data bridges, violations of privacy, and under-the-counter digital transactions. Accordingly, these challenges are exactly what blockchain technology addresses, given its characteristics of immutability, decentralized verification, and consensus mechanisms, which allow all stakeholders to verify the transactions independently without having to alter data retroactively. [1, 3, 8]. This renders all auditability verifiable and removes the reliance on centralized authorities, thus turning the game on organizations in building trust in their digital ecosystems.

7.6.1 The Role of Decentralization in Building Trust

Decentralization is the core of redefined trust through digital systems. Instead of relying on a single trusted entity, trust is distributed across a network of participants, making manipulation or unauthorized modification nearly impossible [2, 25]. Each of these transactions gets validated through consensus algorithms that ensure authenticity and integrity, creating confidence in the participants [4]. As Rahman et al. [16] put it, European financial institutions have implemented blockchain frameworks in order to increase trust in their digital transactions, thereby reducing human involvement and possible corruption. Similar is the view of Demirkan et al. [26], who noted that, in business operations, trust in joint processes is enhanced through transparent, verifiable, and traceable digital evidence that effectively improves accountability.

7.6.2 Immutability and Auditability for Enhanced Transparency

Immutability ensures that the data in the blockchain remains intact; once recorded, it cannot be changed or deleted except by consensus and thus guarantees the integrity of stored data. Smith and Dhillon [17] showed how immutable blockchain ledgers enhanced the transparency of financial transactions by making them permanent records open to all stakeholders. This proves very much critical to auditing and compliance across all sectors. Etemadi et al. [5] discovered that the verification of the authenticity of data in real time from producers to regulators through the application of blockchain improves the transparency in supply chains. This transparency minimizes fraud and promotes ethical governance according to principles of cybersecurity and trustworthiness [22].

7.6.3 Transparency in Enterprise and Financial Systems

Through blockchain, enterprise systems provide traceability and accountability with transparent logs of transactions and activities. Zidan et al. [23] further asserted that blockchain strengthens secure enterprise data management through immutable audit trails that deter cybercriminals from tampering with records. Shah et al. [19] indicated that transparency coming from blockchain could ameliorate cybersecurity risks associated with businesses in general, but specifically with financial and FinTech environments, where trust is crucial for customer retention. Gurdgiev and Fleming [11] further noted that informational efficiency achieved through transparency could bolster cybersecurity governance frameworks, but such efficiency must be counterbalanced against potential privacy trade-offs.

7.6.4 Blockchain for Public Trust and Governance

In e-governance, transparency mechanisms employed in the enterprise thus contribute to public trust, thus lessening technological deception, as blockchain is capable of extending over the whole political mechanism. To underline the reconfiguration of trust through decentralization, protecting the interested party against corruption. The alleviation of corruption and trust building will take care of the transformation of democracy by enhancing active participation to a significant extent. Meanwhile, Yeasmin and Baig [21] stressed the possibility of the blockchain in rekindling the trust developers had once reposed in public systems by lessening dependence on intermediaries: Mathew [25] outlined blockchain from a different position as securing digital ID and protecting their data from misuse.

7.6.5 Enhancing Supply Chain and Industrial Transparency

Transparency is highly essential, especially in the supply chain systems, wherein blockchain can ensure seamless tracking of goods and authenticity verification throughout the stages of production and delivery. Etemadi et al. [5] argued that blockchain now fosters trust among all parties dealing in the supply chain by generating an undisturbed audit trail of the movement of products. Tezel et al. [6] opined that blockchain in the built environment downgraded the project visibility between participants and made the expected accuracy in the data less disputable. For the industrial and energy sectors, Mengidis et al. [14] commented that the use of blockchain with AI promotes operational transparency by putting predictive monitoring and cyber-resilient control mechanisms into place.

7.6.6 Cybersecurity Transparency through Smart Contracts and Consensus

Smart contracts ease trust underpinned by blockchain by automating self-regulated contracts of transparent and enforceable agreements without intermediaries. Wylde et al. [7] posit that smart contracts still ensure cybersecurity transparency by ensuring that system operations are conducted by predefined rules visible to all interested parties. An additional and contrasting perspective has been provided by Kuzmenko et al. [12] with an application of system-dynamic modeling to highlight the increase in transparency in enterprise cybersecurity through the use of blockchain. This is moreover maintained by Sadigov et al. [13], where, according to these three authors, the consensus-driven transparency eliminates occurrences of human errors and insider manipulation, thereby improving an organization OT's resilience.

7.6.7 The Intersection of Transparency, AI, and Cybersecurity

Soft blockchain interfacing with AI simplifies some space for intelligent transparency within the cybersecurity environment. Omar and Zangana [15] were insistent on the fact that using smart contracts joins the transparent register-keeping aboard blockchain technology and the analytical pool of AI to see real-time response to inconsistencies, insider threats, and data-manipulation activities. This great theme further supports explainable AI algorithms that adhere to the encouraging principles of appropriate cybersecurityNet [7]. Sriram et al. [24] flaggingly extended this narrative by investigating that blockchain transparency mechanisms might make AI-driven cybersecurity systems interpretable and more trustable.

7.6.8 Overcoming Challenges to Trust and Transparency

Blockchain guarantees transparency, but this particular transparency is not exactly without challenges. Alkhalifah et al. [9] demonstrated with an empirical analysis of blockchain cybersecurity incidents that transparency could expose sensitive data to adversaries when not properly managed. To quote both Mahmood et al. [10] and Hasanova et al. [27], if security measures are deficient, the vulnerabilities will be targeted: Smart contract exploits, consensus attacks, and privacy leaks impede trust. On drone-related cybersecurity, Ossamah [20] referred to such an occurrence as a high risk and stressed that this was another case where there was an imperative need to apply hybrid structures balancing confidentiality and transparency. Antonyan and Rybakova [4] strongly came through with the same decryption; in that event, too many avenues for transparency create a clash with privacy legislation, calling for mathematical upgrades like zero-knowledge proofs and secure multi-party computation.

7.6.9 Building Trust through Continuous Validation and Governance

An established trust in a blockchain system is reliant upon consistent validation through regular means of governance and accountability. An interesting way from [18] is continuous governance-enabling monitoring and cryptographic auditing that grows stakeholders' faith in cybersecurity applications impressed by blockchain. Banafa [8] highlighted that trust frameworks incorporating blockchain governance models, such as permissioned access and consensus validation, are critical to reinforcing stakeholder trust. In parallel, Rahman et al. [16] and Putro et al. [22] emphasized that a well-regulated blockchain infrastructure tends to enhance institutional trust and insinuate user trust, which is more crucial in the given circumstances of the financial and governmental entities.

The essence of blockchain's value to cybersecurity lies in its capacity to provide trust and transparency, hence. It empowers individuals, enterprises, and governments to transact in environments where the authenticity of data is ensured via decentralization, immutability, and verifiable auditability. However, the researchers like Alkhalifah et al. [9] Mahmood et al. [10], and Hasanova et al. [27] argued that achieving such a trust equilibrium would require addressing the technical and ethical challenges through governance and cryptographic innovations. Leveraged with AI-driven intelligence and now with the approach concerning proactiveness and cybersecurity [15], the combined innovation of blockchain holds a great promise for a lens to a sustainable, transparent, trustworthy, resilient digital ecosystem.

7.7 Integration of Blockchain with Artificial Intelligence

The world's systems thus far characterized enter a new transformative paradigm of secure, intelligent, and transparent. While blockchain provides a decentralized, immutable, tamper-proof ledger for the transaction of digital goods, AI curates sophistication with pattern recognition, predictive analytics, and autonomous decision-making capabilities. The combined synergy between AI and blockchain generates a new breed of intelligent, secure infrastructures that can repel cyberattacks, identify anomalies in real time, and enhance system resilience [14, 15].

From a cybersecurity angle, AI's potential of processing large amounts of data complements the immutable data structure of blockchain. Singh and Singh [2] said that blockchain can be the basis of trust management for digital ecosystems, while AI gives learning and adaptive responses to such networks. Catalini [1] argued that the fusion of these technologies allows the creation of a dynamic defense against cyber-threats, whereby AI continuously learns from the immutable data recorded on the blockchain to establish new patterns of intrusion and fraud detection.

Another main stride originating from this collaboration is AI smart contract systems. Using AI algorithms, smart contracts can automatically verify, execute, and adjust to complex conditions, thereby improving both execution efficiency and security. As Banafa [8] and Mathew [25] pointed out, AI increases smart contract validation by detecting nefarious codes or unusual transactional behavior prior to execution. Further, this automation decreases human errors while ensuring the reliability of decentralized systems. [26] noted that the collaboration between blockchain and AI provides an avenue for verifying and auditing business processes within accounting, finance, and supply chain systems.

Another key advantage of AI and blockchain integration is improved threat intelligence and anomaly detection. According to Hasanova et al. [27], AI models can analyze data from blockchain records to identify deviations from normal network behavior by significantly minimizing the rate of false-positive alerts in intrusion detection systems. Kuzmenko et al. [12] also introduced paradigms of system-dynamic simulation, suggesting that AI systems with blockchain access enhance the efficiency of cyber defense by facilitating automated decision-making and alleviating delays of response during attack activities. Evidence from [13] supports the notion that such an interlacing of technologies can indeed be a game changer in terms of enterprise cybersecurity management.

This approach assures AI privacy and protection. Kshetri [3] remarked that decentralized storage of data prevents the creation of single points of failure for every type of AI system and also ensures that training data cannot be corrupted or leaked. Mahmood et al. [10] suggested that blockchain could neutralize adversarial attacks on AI models through maintaining a verifiable chain of data custody. By allowing users to manage the access to their personal information via encrypted, verifiable transactions, Wylde et al. [7] argued that privacy-preserving AI frameworks backed by blockchain could ensure compliance with data protection laws.

Recent studies show that the transparency of blockchain can help achieve explainability and accountability for AI models. Blockchain allows for the traceability and validation of AI operations, which mitigate biases, thus enhancing trust from users [11]. Such transparency becomes imperative in high-risk applications such as financial services, health care, and government systems [16]. The blockchain-AI convergence in the built environment has also been studied by [6], illustrating how traceable AI actions could support trust and cybersecurity in smart infrastructure.

In industrial and business scenarios, automation and operational efficiency are enhanced by AI-enabled blockchain systems. In fact, Etemadi et al. [5] demonstrated that blockchain-integrated AI enhances traceability and cybersecurity in the supply chain by machine-learning models detecting data inconsistencies or counterfeit entries. Meanwhile, Prakash et al. [18] provided evidence that AI-enabled blockchain architectures improve the adaptive capacity of security frameworks, and Putro et al. [22] reported on this technology's capability for enhancing the reliability and robustness of enterprise information systems.

There have been possible integrations of blockchain and AI in very critical domains like drone security and IoT security. As observed by Ossamah [20], combining blockchain as the basis for drone cybersecurity with AI for real-time threat analysis can resolve vulnerabilities in communication networks. Similarly, Yeasmin and Baig [21] discussed how blockchain interoperability could unblock the data silos in AI applications while enhancing both accuracy and trustworthiness of AI models.

The dual technology has witnessed the early and huge adoption by fintech and financial ecosystems. According to Smith and Dhillon [17], the blockchain-AI framework significantly improves cybersecurity with regard to financial transactions, since the detection of fraud is heightened through AI analysis of data stored in blockchain. According to Shah et al. [19] and Sriram et al. [24], the argument has been made that the fusion of blockchain with AI gives room for the ultimate fintech applications—as it were—suits wherein transactions can be secure, audited, and intelligent. Zidan et al. [23] also found that immutable ledgers of blockchain, compared with analytical state-of-the-art capacities of AI, helped to analyze cybercrime cases for financial institutions and thus upgraded the capabilities of digital forensics.

However, promising advances usually come with some challenges. As indicated in the studies by Antonyan and Rybakova [4] Alkhalifah et al. [9], blockchain-based AI systems are still susceptible to emerging new vulnerabilities such as attacks originating from smart contract exploits, manipulation of consensus, and data-poisoning attacks. Hence, continued audits of security systems, ethical governance for AI, and adaptive consensus protocols have to be in place to ensure the preservation of system integrity. According to Omar and Zangana [15], it is very imperative to develop and construct large language models (LLMs) and cyber AI frameworks toward the automation of existing blockchain mechanisms for monitoring and detecting vulnerabilities to boost proactive defenses in Cybersecurity 5.0 systems.

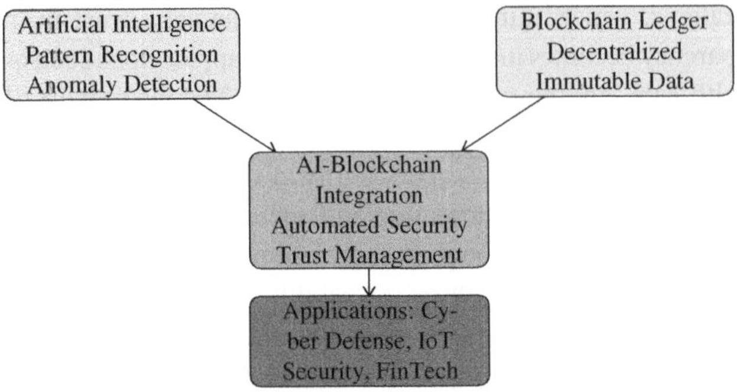

Figure 7.4 Integration of blockchain and AI for intelligent cybersecurity systems. "*Source:* Hewa Majeed Zangana"

The merging of the two technologies is portrayed in Figure 7.4—here, AI analytics, smart contracts, and immutable data ledgers come together to yield intelligent, transparent, and autonomous cybersecurity frameworks.

In summary, it has been postulated that integrating the two technologies, that is blockchain and AI, proves to be a critical turning point in developing intelligent, resilient, and transparent digital ecosystems. It will close the gap between intelligence based on data and trust based on cryptography, thus changing the scenario for how cybersecurity frameworks operate across industries. Further research in full-scale and cross-disciplinary innovations will be needed on the emerging technical and ethical challenges associated with this intersection over time to gain the fullest advantage.

7.8 Blockchain-Based Security Frameworks and Architectures

They are claimed to be the panacea in legacy or traditional methods of providing digital ecosystems with integrity, confidentiality, and resilience against cyber threats. The security frameworks that leverage the core property of decentralization, immutability, and transparency are the principal pub-blowers in the elimination of single points of failure [1, 3]. They combine the greatest techniques of cryptographic algorithms and consensus mechanisms with smart contract automation, producing an architecture based on blockchain that can achieve verifiable and tamper-resistant environments with assurance improvements in cybersecurity across financial systems, enterprises, critical infrastructures, and government platforms [8, 26].

A distributed ledger forms the core of all these blockchain-based security frameworks. This stores and synchronizes across a multitude of nodes data without being tampered with and audited. Mathew [25] states that "The cryptographic hash of each block is linked to the next" so that there is no unauthorized alteration of data: it is an immutable chain. This is additionally backed by consensus protocols of PoW, PoS, and PBFT, ensuring that the records cannot be manipulated by a single entity. As per Hasanova et al. [27], such consensus models not only secure transactions but also provide a mechanism for validating the authenticity of network participants, thus mitigating identity spoofing and data tampering risks.

Modern blockchain security frameworks are increasingly incorporating AI and dynamic modeling of systems for prediction and timely response to threats. According to Kuzmenko et al. [12], simulation modeling is used to develop a blockchain-based cyber defense architecture to assess vulnerability levels for enterprises. This enables adaptive security mechanisms that evolve with the threat landscape. Sadigov et al. [13] also showed that simulation systems enhanced by blockchain can continuously monitor and improve cyber resilience via automated feedback. According to Omar and Zangana [15], this also makes the cybersecurity frameworks more intelligent and responsive as integrated with cyber AI and LLMs.

Emergence of several models, mostly based on architecture-architectural models, for distinct security and transparency architectures. Permissioned blockchains, as Wylde et al. [7] mention, have access control hingeing on authentication roles dedicated to specific users, making them appropriate for corporate or government use. Permissionless blockchains, on the one hand, promote spectacular transparency while exhibiting open participation but using a complex consensus algorithm to maintain trust. Rahman et al. [16] demonstrated how European banking systems are adopting hybrid blockchain architecture—combining public and private elements—to achieve both confidentiality and compliance in which users have a high level of trust.

In industrial and supply chain environments, the detailed blockchain frameworks have played exceptionally well in spelling out traceability and trust. According to Etemadi et al. [5], blockchain architectures surrounding supply chain cybersecurity increase accountability due to the recording of every transaction in verifiable ledgers. On the other hand, Putro et al. [22] reported that the architectures based on blockchains did significantly enhance reliability and resistance against cyberattacks in information systems. According to Tezel et al. [6], such frameworks in Industry 4.0 environments have been geared toward addressing transparency problems within the construction and manufacturing sectors by preserving immutable audit trails designed to bolster trust amongst stakeholders.

Conversely, the aspect around blockchain, which highlights the securing of IoT and drone networks through blockchain technology, truly brings forth the architectural adaptability of blockchain. Ossamah [20] proposed a model of secured drones through blockchain, where the distributed consensus verifies the commands from the control center to establish authenticity and avoid outside interference with hijacking. Mengidis et al. [14] extended that to energy grids, where they believed that the infrastructures enabled by blockchain could strengthen operational reliability and real-time protection when incorporated with an AI-based monitoring system.

Blockchain architectures are the primary underpinnings for most cybersecurity infrastructures within business and financial applications. Among the first to point out the role of blockchain in securing financial interests against fraud and unauthorized transactions was [2]. Even later, Smith and Dhillon [17] pointed out how it would serve by further improving the cybersecurity framework under which financial operations would run. By creating this distributed ledger system, reliance on even centralized intermediaries susceptible to breaches is done away with. Blockchain-based architectures redefine security in fintech from the perspective of decentralized validation, fraud prevention, and tamper-proof auditing mechanisms, according to Shah et al. [19] and Sriram et al. [24].

Therefore, frameworks meant for horizons of organizational cybersecurity have also matured into layered defense mechanisms and adaptive policymaking. Antonyan and Rybakova [4] explained that such architectures exhibit the ability to resist attack vectors commonly used in cyberattacks like Distributed Denial of Service (DDoS) and interception of data due to the attributes of decentralization that characterize the system. Alkhalifa et al. [9] undertook an empirical analysis to discover that a majority of such incidents were misconstrued to be protocol vulnerabilities because most blocked incidents in blockchain cybersecurity came through framework faults and human error. Hence, the deployments should have a standardized architecture design and continuous monitoring.

Consensus-driven verification and identity management systems revolve around trust and governance in the whole system. It was in this light that Gurdgiev and Fleming [11] proclaimed that distributed architectures enhance informational efficiency yet provide a degree of resilience against these systemic cyber risks by not depending on any centralized authority. According to Prakash et al. [18], the consensus-driven trust models on which blockchain frameworks are constructed will allow for secure data sharing between untrusted entities with regard to privacy and integrity. This resonates with what Zidan et al. [23] found on the ability of the framework to reduce threats associated with cybercrime through the establishment of unalterable forensic records and tamper-proof transaction histories.

As [16, 26], the propensity of framework design with blockchain could synchronize with the organizational compliance standard in real-time audits and enforcement of policies. Likewise, Banafa [8] highlighted a layered architecture in which blockchain integrates with access control, encryption, and authentication systems to enhance security at various levels. Yeasmin and Baig [21] further postulated that such architectures unblock operational potential because departmental and institutional collaboration will now be secure, and siloed data will be reduced.

Distributed computation is costly. It consumes a lot of energy and is not very compliant with regulations. A scoping review done by Mahmood et al. [10] has found out the limited scalability of blockchain due to the computational complexity issues and the lack of the interoperability of its systems, together preventing its massive adoption in new large-scale cybersecurity framework projects. Gurdgiev and Fleming [11], on the other hand, warn that if the frameworks are not properly synchronized, inefficiency might arise in the exchange of information, which might reveal weaknesses. Hence, as Omar and Zangana [15] asserted, promising next-generation blockchain security architectures would have AI and automation built in such that they self-correct and dynamically adapt to emerging threats within Cybersecurity 5.0 ecosystems.

How blockchain operates with cryptography, consensus, and AI-driven analytics to secure infrastructures is illustrated in the Figure 7.5 below.

Generally, the construction regarding security frameworks and architectures that are formulating themselves around the blockchain creates a compelling case for the establishment of secure, decentralized, and transparent digital infrastructures, as well as tamper resistance. Advances in cryptography, consensus algorithms, and integration with AI lead to proactive defense against sophisticated cyberattack vectors. Further advancement of these frameworks through simulation modeling, hybrid architecture, and integration with AI will pave the way toward a future in which cyberspace will be autonomous, resilient, and secure.

7.9 Challenges and Limitations of Blockchain in Security

Blockchain technology, while mostly extolled for its potential to improve security, transparency, and trust in digital systems, has inherent challenges and limitations. Indeed, while blockchain's decentralized and immutable architecture

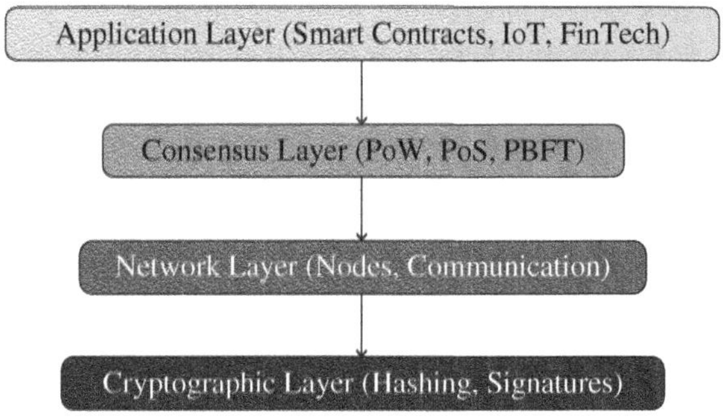

Figure 7.5 Layered blockchain-based security framework illustrating key architectural levels. "*Source:* Hewa Majeed Zangana"

makes it very resilient, many technical, organizational, and regulatory issues compromise the effectiveness of blockchain systems as cybersecurity solutions. Understanding these drawbacks is critical for ensuring responsible and effective application of the technology in all sectors.

According to Singh and Singh [2], the most overarching challenge is scalability in securing transactions using blockchains. In their working paper, the authors discuss how blockchain networks cannot handle the enormous volume of transactions since they have a computational overhead on the consensus mechanisms such as PoW and PoS. This limitation hinders timely terrorism response and denies applications of the technology in large systems such as IoT or global financial systems. Similarly, Mahmood et al. [10] advance that the increasing sizes of distributed ledgers create inefficiencies in storage and high latencies and energy consumption, with implications for sustainability for future security infrastructures.

The other main concern is vulnerability to novel attack schemes. Although there is the promise of immutability in blockchain, Hasanova et al. [27] claim vulnerabilities such as 51% attacks, smart contract bugs, and Sybil attacks are still great challenges. These vulnerabilities allow malicious actors to manipulate consensus, change transaction history, or even gain benefits from poorly coded smart contracts. Alkhalifah et al. [9] provide empirical evidence that several real-world blockchain incidents have led to tremendous data leaks and losses of cryptocurrencies due to those exploits. Similarly, Antonyan and Rybakova [4] assert that even though data confidentiality can be enhanced through blockchain, decentralized implementation makes it difficult to identify and mitigate threats.

Interoperability and standardization are another dilemma posed by blockchain. The absence of global standards and cross-chain communication models hinders seamless integration over platforms and industries, according to Catalini [1]. Standardization absence, in this case, results in limited adoption of blockchain-based security frameworks within existing infrastructures. Demirkan et al. [26] further say that heterogeneity of blockchain protocols makes auditing and verifying data difficult, leading to inconsistent implementation of cyber risk policies across several blockchains in an organization.

Privacy is another major issue that limits blockchain usage. Although trust can be built on increased transparency by a blockchain, it creates a potential for leaking sensitive data. Kshetri [3] notes that illegal deletion and modification of records will create a conflict with privacy rights such as the General Data Protection Regulation (GDPR). Furthermore, Wylde et al. [7] stress that pseudonymity does not confer "true anonymity," as transaction metadata can be analyzed into user identities. In the same light, Yeasmin and Baig [21] argue that transparency versus confidentiality persists as one of the greatest research challenges provoked by blockchain cybersecurity solutions.

From a governance perspective, blockchain systems also face challenges in ensuring accountability and compliance. Tezel et al. [6] claim that decentralized governance models are usually deficient in having a clear accountability mechanism; hence, it becomes difficult to delegate responsibility in events of breaches. Gurdgiev and Fleming [11] claim that systemic risks are likely to happen through the deployment of blockchain systems without any sort of regulation, creating vulnerabilities in the financial and organizational ecosystems. In an enterprise setting, Kuzmenko et al. [12] argue that modeling blockchain-enabled cybersecurity dynamically demands an understanding of complex interactions between technical factors and human beings.

Energy consumption indeed stands out as one of the major limitations against which widespread criticism has arisen. According to Mengidis et al. [14] and Mathew et al. [25], most touch points indicate consensus algorithms, especially PoW, as requiring enormous computational powers, hence rendering blockchain as very burdensome on the environment. The act is bound to create a trade-off between security and sustainability so far as the scale of blockchain adoption across frontiers increases. Resource limits are a huge impediment to the implementation of blockchain-based cybersecurity solutions in small-resourced systems such as drones and IoT devices, as Ossamah [20] underscored.

Integration into existing cybersecurity frameworks remains a practical challenge. Prakash et al. [[18]] found that many organizations struggled with aligning the decentralized design of the blockchain with centralized security architectures, leading to interoperability issues and complex policy enforcement. This was illustrated by Etemadi et al. [5] in the case of food supply chains, where the benefits of traceability deriving from the adoption of blockchain were offset by challenges linked to data heterogeneity and those with legacy systems. Further, Banafa [8] emphasizes that the hurdle of integration complexity and a shortage of qualified personnel delayed the adoption of blockchain in cybersecurity-critical environments.

Beyond that, in addition, regulatory and legal uncertainties are considered barriers to blockchain deployment. Rahman et al. [16] explain that immutability of data may be contrary to the law, i.e., in the banking sector, where data are demanded to be modified or erased sometimes. Similarly, Shah et al. noted that clear global legal frameworks would have allowed more use of blockchain in compliance-sensitive industries such as finance and healthcare. According to the observation of Smith and Dhillon [17], financial institutions still struggle to opportunistically evaluate the prospect of regulatory compliance with respect to blockchain technologies due to differences in jurisdictional issues and a changing security norm.

It is human and organizational factors that limit blockchain's security potential. As pointed out by Putro et al. [22] and Zidan et al. [23], human errors in smart contract deployment as well as in managing private keys and configuring nodes can expose blockchain networks to huge breaches. Other warnings given by Sadigov et al. [13] are that organizations would be putting an unreasonable level of reliance on blockchain rather than treating it within a wider overall risk management strategy.

Emerging technologies like AI and quantum computing pose the new test. AI integration into a blockchain may improve the predictive defense, as stated by Omar and Zangana [15], but it also creates an attack surface when the algorithms or data integrity is compromised. More importantly, quantum computing poses a long-term threat to the cryptography of any blockchain, resulting in a demand for quantum-resistant protocols and their adaptive security measures.

Thus, blockchain is transformative in the sense that it brings great potentialities for cybersecurity; however, that does not mean that it singlehandedly solves all problems. Those limitations—posed from question marks like scalability and energy consumption to issues relating to privacy and regulation—must, therefore, be addressed through ongoing innovation, interdisciplinary collaboration, and adaptive policy frameworks. Only then would blockchain evolve into a really secure and resilient foundation for the digital future.

7.10 Emerging Trends and Innovations

Blockchain technology is evolving fast and changing trends and innovations to enhance cybersecurity, trust, and operational efficiency in many industries. New developments in the blockchain increasingly focus on integrating advanced technologies, improving scalability, and solving traditional limitations while spawning novel applications for cybersecurity.

Another noticeable trend is the intersection between blockchain technology and AI and ML. Mengidis et al. [14] explained that the combination of AI and blockchain enables predictive analytics, anomaly detection, and threat mitigation in complex networks such as smart grids. AI algorithms can sift through the data stored on the blockchain to detect patterns that constitute potential cyber threats, while blockchain can guarantee data integrity and transparency. In their article, Omar and Zangana [15] further assert that the AI-enhanced blockchain can work proactively for cybersecurity by enabling systems to detect and respond to vulnerabilities independently and in real time.

Further innovations are taking place in decentralized finance (DeFi) and blockchain-based financial security. Catalini [1] and Singh and Singh [2] argued that such financial platforms based on the blockchain provide robust mechanisms for transaction verification, fraud prevention, and secure fund transfers that obviate a reliance on centralized intermediaries. Smith and Dhillon [17] remarked that blockchain enhances cybersecurity on financial transactions through cryptographic protocols, immutable ledgers, and smart contracts, all of which lower the risk of fraud and manipulation. Today's research by Rahman et al. [16] indicates that European banks embrace blockchain solutions more and more, aiming to reinforce data integrity, auditability, and prevention of cybercrime.

Another emerging trend is the utilization of blockchain in critical infrastructure and supply chain setups. Etemadi et al. [5] state that blockchain creates end-to-end traceability in food supply chains, enhancing security, authentication, and accountability. Ossamah [20] displays the potential of Blockchain concerning drone cybersecurity through the securing of communication protocol, prevention of data tampering, and ensuring of operational integrity. Tezel et al. [6] expand this dimension closer to the built environment, suggesting that blockchain can improve trust, transparency, and cybersecurity in construction and asset management.

The adoption of hybrid blockchain architectures is in vogue, trying to create a balance between performance, scalability, and security. Discussions by Mahmood et al. [10] and Hasanova [27] present this new breed of hybrids that blend public and private blockchains with controlled access, whilst retaining decentralization and immutability. Such frameworks empower enterprises to secure sensitive data internally while benefiting externally from clarity in auditing and compliance. Putro et al. [22] portrayed through case studies that hybrid blockchain models can improve the reliability of the information system and provide resilience against cyber threats.

Another crucial innovation is smart contracts and automated cybersecurity protocols. Smart contracts implement security policies in an entirely automated manner, lessening the chances of human error and ensuring compliance with organizational rules, as stressed by Prakash et al. [18]. Antonyan and Rybakova [4] claim that such kind of automation diminishes risks massively in multi-party networks by providing verifiable self-executing security measures. Organizations are deploying smart contracts at an ever-increasing rate for secure data sharing, transaction verification, and access control for business-critical systems, according to Sriram et al. [24].

Cross-industry blockchain adoption is also accelerating. Shah et al. [19] illustrate its deployment in FinTech, healthcare, and logistics, where cybersecurity and trust are paramount. The integration of blockchain in enterprise cybersecurity frameworks is being helped by system-dynamic modeling, as noted by

Kuzmenko et al. [12] and Sadigov et al. [13], allowing organizations to simulate threat scenarios and proactively optimize security responses.

Quantum-resistant blockchain protocols are emerging in response to the potential threat posed by quantum computing. Omar and Zangana [15] stress the need to develop cryptographic algorithms that are resistant to quantum attacks to guarantee the security of blockchain systems in the long term. Likewise, Wylde et al. [7] argue that securing data confidentiality and integrity in future blockchain applications shall require the adoption of post-quantum cryptography.

Blockchain-enabled data privacy innovations are increasingly drawing attention. Kshetri [3] and Antonyan and Rybakova [8] note that zero-knowledge proofs, homomorphic encryption, and ring signatures are being introduced into blockchain protocols to bring forth privacy-preserving mechanisms that do not compromise transparency. Yeasmin and Baig [21] contend that these innovations allow enterprises to comply with stringent data protection regulations while employing blockchain for secure information sharing.

Ultimately, the emerging regulatory and governance frameworks will shape the evolution of blockchain in the area of cybersecurity. Gurdgiev and Fleming [11] and Demirkan et al. [26] mention ongoing attempts to develop standards, best practices, and compliance guidelines intended to promote trust, transparency, and security to all blockchain networks. Alkhalifah et al. [9] and Mathew [25] reiterate that these frameworks are paramount for risk systemic mitigation while ensuring the safe adoption of blockchain in sensitive sectors.

With the evolution of blockchain, its convergence with forthcoming technologies has charted the roadmap for Cybersecurity 5.0. Figure 7.6 illustrates key areas

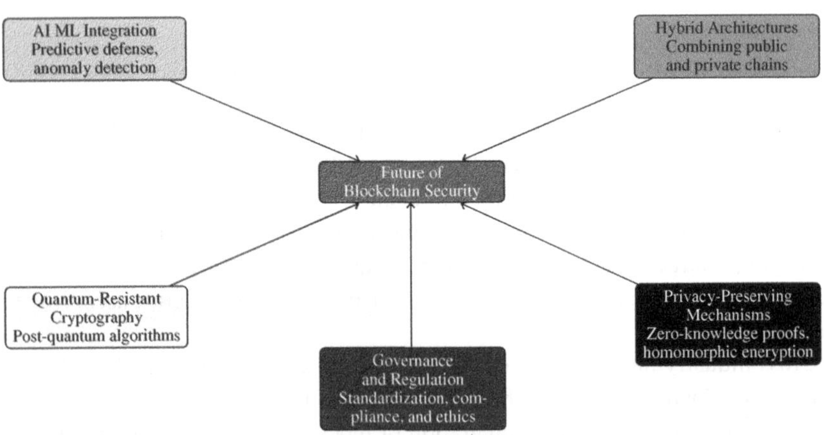

Figure 7.6 Emerging trends and future research directions in blockchain-based cybersecurity. "*Source:* Hewa Majeed Zangana"

of innovations that are envisaging the future of blockchain security—from AI amalgamation, hybrid architectures, quantum-resistant cryptography, and also privacy-preserving methodologies.

To illumine upon the gist, the convergence of blockchain with AI, hybrid architectures, smart contracts, quantum-resistant cryptography, and privacy-preserving mechanisms heralds a new epoch of cybersecurity innovation. These emerging trends augment system resiliency and redefine the way enterprises, governments, and industry perceive digital security in an increasingly interconnected world.

7.11 Case Studies and Practical Implementations

In the context of cybersecurity, practical implementations of blockchain have gained tremendous traction over the years. Many case studies show how organizations in various sectors deploy blockchains to augment security, maintain data integrity, and prevent cybercrime. The real-world applications illustrate the promise and challenges of really putting blockchain in an operational setting.

One area of application is financial services, which rely on blockchain for immutable transaction records and enhanced security protocols. Singh and Singh [2] invoked early implementation of blockchain in banking, mentioning its effects in reducing fraud and increasing the security of financial transactions. Smith and Dhillon [17] further argued that blockchain-based systems have been able to improve auditability, transparency, and traceability in financial networks, therefore markedly reducing cybersecurity risks. In their study, Rahman et al. [16] discussed how European banks employed blockchain to attain cyber resilience, indicating measurable improvement in data integrity, transaction security, and adherence to regulatory frameworks. Catalini [1] backed this idea by saying that blockchain supports the digital economy through securing digital assets and reliable verification mechanisms, which is critical for fintech innovations.

In the area of enterprise cybersecurity, blockchain has been integrated into system-dynamic simulation frameworks to do proactive threat assessment and mitigation. Kuzmenko et al. [12] and Sadigov et al. [13] noted utilizing blockchain-based modeling for enterprise cybersecurity that allowed organizations to simulate attack scenarios and optimize defenses even before threats have materialized. Such implementations will provide actionable insight on resource allocation, risk management, and resilience planning. Putro et al. [22] reinforced this idea in a case study demonstrating that blockchain enhances the security and reliability of enterprise information systems by diminishing their vulnerability to cyberattacks, yet securing their operational continuity.

Supply chain and critical infrastructure applications too pose good case studies. Etemadi et al. [5] provided an account on blockchain implementation in the food supply chain to provide end-to-end traceability and tamper-proof records, which reduced the risks of fraud and contamination. Ossamah [20] illustrated the application of blockchain in drone cybersecurity, where blockchain works to protect communications channels, ensure the integrity of mission data, and prevent unauthorized access. Tezel et al. [6] further extended these applications to build environment showing that blockchain integration enhances transparency, trust, and cybersecurity for construction projects and facility management.

With emerging technologies like AI and IoT being the key areas of practical implementation, Mengidis et al. [14] studied the use of blockchain coupled with AI in the next-generation energy grids, whereby cybersecurity posture against smart grid attacks was enhanced through predictive analytics and immutable blockchain records. Correspondingly, Omar and Zangana [15] highlight AI-assisted blockchain systems that enable proactive vulnerability detection and automated threat mitigation as being practically deployed in enterprise-level cybersecurity frameworks.

A present trend among the business and FinTech sectors is their reliance on blockchain to protect digital operations. Shah et al. [19] elaborated on how businesses are leveraging blockchain technology to protect sensitive data, facilitate secure transactions, and secure compliance. Sriram et al. [24] highlighted the role of blockchain in promoting secure multi-party collaboration and trustless interaction, especially in high cybersecurity-demanding environments. Antonyan and Rybakova [4] propounded blockchain as a cybersecurity barrier, laying emphasis on case studies where decentralized networks obstructed unauthorized access and data breaches.

These studies also provide qualitative lessons through empirical analysis of blockchain cybersecurity incidents. In their work, Alkhalifah et al. [9] analyzed real-world security incidents concerning blockchain, identifying common patterns of vulnerabilities, attack vectors, and countermeasures. Hasanova et al. [27] surveyed vulnerabilities, including those from smart contract exploitation and consensus protocol weaknesses, informing design for more resilient blockchain frameworks. Mahmood et al. [10] synthesized challenges from multiple case studies, underscoring the relevance of security auditing, threat modeling, and system testing as critical in gauging an impending wide-scale deployment.

Blockchain-associated issues on data privacy and regulatory compliance are gradually becoming the focal point in practice. Kshetri [3] and Wylde et al. [7] presented the need for the application of zero-knowledge proofs, cryptographic protocols, and permissioned blockchain frameworks to protect sensitive information in a way that also offers transparency and accountability. Banafa [8] acknowledged that businesses are embracing these privacy-preserving measures to ensure compliance with rapidly changing regulatory environments. Zidan et al. [23] buttressed that the abuse of these technologies via blockchain can in effect thwart cybercrime threats within corporate worlds and enhance operational security.

To summarize, the case studies in finance, enterprise security, supply chains, critical infrastructure, and business operations have provided evidence that blockchain substantially improves cybersecurity. The above instances confirm that blockchain is transformational in nature and bring focus to other limitations, including scalability, governance, and interoperability. As blockchain finds increasing acceptance in the corporate world, lessons from these case studies will motivate and inform best practices, highlight emerging risks, and shape new innovations in cybersecurity.

7.12 Future Research Directions

Within the ever-changing blockchain horizon of cybersecurity, new avenues for research and innovation always remain. Even though current research shows that blockchain offers a pathway for improved security, privacy, and trust in digital systems, a lot still remains to be done in order to fill notable research gaps and therefore better the adoption of blockchain to achieve its objectives while lessening any risks involved.

A significant direction of research, therefore, is to progressively integrate blockchain with emergent technologies, particularly AI and LLMs, thereby rendering adaptive and predictive cybersecurity systems. Mengidis et al. [14] demonstrated blockchain and AI synergisms within energy grids, whereby intelligent predictive analytics and immutable records provided by blockchain can act proactively in the detection and prevention of cyberattacks. Likewise, Omar and Zangana [15] stressed the potential of the AI-powered blockchains in the provision of enterprise security through automated vulnerability detection, anomaly prediction, and real-time threat mitigation. Research can delve into making blockchain, and AI can be optimized in massive enterprise operations without compromising efficiency and security.

The other perspective that merits serious consideration would be boosting blockchain scalability, interoperability, and consensus mechanisms. While the obvious security advantages of a blockchain remain, some concerns, namely, transaction throughput, latency, and resource consumption, are considered to be highly important impediments 10,27. Future work must focus on scalable consensus algorithms, lightweight protocols for resource-constrained environments, and interoperability frameworks facilitating seamless integration with existing legacy systems. This will be vital for those industries that impose high transaction volumes like finance [2, 17] and supply chain networks [5].

Cybersecurity and privacy preservation remain scientific subjects for investigations. Wylde et al. [7] stated that data confidentiality and regulatory compliance, inter alia, must take high priority, especially within sectors that deal with sensitive information. For this, techniques like zero-knowledge proofs, homomorphic encryption, and permissioned blockchain architectures need further study to see how blockchain solutions can meet such privacy requirements without compromising efficiency or trust. Kshetri [3] stated that privacy-preserving blockchain models might be useful in achieving some of the new global regulations, including GDPR and sector-specific cybersecurity mandates.

Other areas of research include topical applications by sectors and the impact assessment. Case studies in sectors like finance [16], enterprise security [19, 22], critical infrastructure [6, 20], and supply chains [5] demonstrate the website advantages that blockchain brings implementations; however, we need systematic evaluation frameworks to quantify the security, operational, and economic impacts of blockchain across many sectors [8, 18]. Thus, this research could focus on establishing standard metrics of blockchain effectiveness in terms of risk reduction, incident response time, and cost–benefit analysis.

On the other hand, a very close critical research priority is resilience to sophisticated attacks and rectifying vulnerabilities. Antonyan and Rybakova [4] Alkhalifah et al. [9] stated recurring vectors of attack and security failures in deployed blockchain systems, for example, smart contract exploits and attacks based on the network. Future works should focus on designing resilient blockchain structures that can withstand attacks from advanced persistent threats, quantum computing attacks, and insider threats while also developing adaptive defense mechanisms that evolve with the threat. Zidan et al. [23] and Sriram et al. [24] emphasize the necessity of integrating proactive monitoring with blockchain-enabled security frameworks to maintain threat mitigation in continual motion.

In conclusion, this is a policy, governance, and human factors area of research. Systemic risks related to informational inefficiencies and governance failures in blockchains have been underscored by Catalini [1] and Gurdgiev and Fleming [11]. Research in the future would revolve around decentralized governance models, regulatory complementarity, and mechanisms for increasing user awareness and compliance. Understanding humans' interaction with blockchain-enabled systems is essential for successful acceptance, operational reliability, and prevention against social engineering hacks.

In future efforts to explore blockchain and cybersecurity, the effort ought to be multi-dimensional. The safety, efficiency, and sustainability of blockchain applications will be enhanced by focusing studies and practice on technological integration, scalability, privacy maintenance, sector-specific evaluation, resilience, and governance. This research direction will not only further enhance cybersecurity but will also allow blockchain to fulfill its promise in digital transformation across all sectors [15, 25, 26].

7.13 Conclusion

Blockchain has emerged as a disruptive technology in cybersecurity, providing firms with powerful methodologies for ensuring integrity, transparency, and trust in data. It is built with feature-independent provisioning against single-point failure and, therefore, probably one of the most fitting technologies toward securing digital transactions, enterprise systems, and critical infrastructures. The broadest dimensions covered in this chapter regarding the multifactorial applications of blockchain range from financial systems and supply chains to frameworks for AI-induced security and drone networks, displaying its impressive ability to enhance defense across sectors.

This being said, blockchains are not devoid of challenges such as scalability and interoperability, not to mention the high-energy consumption and vulnerability to highly sophisticated attacks. All of these woes add up to the great need for careful designs and implementations. Further, regulatory, governance, and people factors will play critical roles in restoring the effectiveness of blockchain-based security solutions in mitigating the challenges ahead. Addressing these issues is crucial to ensure that the deployment of blockchains becomes resilient and sustainable in real life.

The new proof changes in blockchain also offer a lot of opportunities for innovation. The future of automatic, predictive, and self-healing cybersecurity will be created by bringing together new technologies such as AI and large language models with blockchain. Sector-specific applications in addition to systematic performance evaluation can provide insights that should lead to an increased tendency to adopt blockchain in public and private domains. Future developments will probably continue to include advances concerning scalability, privacy, and governance. Blockchain will have the capability to complete its destiny as an essential building block in securing digital ecosystems.

Overall, blockchain entails a transformation in cybersecurity with significant rewards but complex challenges at the same time. Continuance in the evolution of this innovation, with unabated guidance of research, pragmatic application, and collaboration across disciplines, may lead to an entirely different form of explaining and organizing how an organization protects its information, manages risk, and builds trust in a world increasingly characterized by digitization. By applying these core principles of change and opportunity to the inherent weaknesses of blockchain, cybersecurity will become the rock upon which next-generation strategies are carried.

References

1 Catalini, C. (2018). Blockchain technology and cryptocurrencies: Implications for the digital economy, cybersecurity, and government. *Georgetown journal of international affairs*. 19: 36–42.
2 Singh S, Singh N. Blockchain: Future of financial and cyber security. In: 2016 2nd international conference on contemporary computing and informatics (IC3I). *IEEE*; 2016. p. 463–7.
3 Kshetri, N. (2017). Blockchain's roles in strengthening cybersecurity and protecting privacy. *Telecomm Policy*. 41 (10): 1027–1038.
4 Antonyan, E.A. and Rybakova, O.S. (2020). Blockchain technologies for security against cyber attacks. *Вестник Национальной академии наук Республики Казахстан* 4, 386: 21.
5 Etemadi N, Borbon YG, Strozzi F. Blockchain technology for cybersecurity applications in the food supply chain: A systematic literature review. Proceedings of the XXIV Summer School "Francesco Turco" – Industrial Systems Engineering, Bergamo, Italy. 2020;9–11.
6 Tezel, A., Papadonikolaki, E., Yitmen, I., and Bolpagni, M. (2021). Blockchain opportunities and issues in the built environment: Perspectives on trust, transparency and cybersecurity. In: *Industry 40 for the Built Environment: Methodologies, Technologies and Skills*, 569–588. Springer.
7 Wylde, V., Rawindaran, N., Lawrence, J. et al. (2022). Cybersecurity, data privacy and blockchain: A review. *SN Comput Sci*. 3 (2): 127.
8 Banafa, A. (2022). *Blockchain technology and applications*. River Publishers.
9 Alkhalifah, A., Ng, A., Chowdhury, M.J.M. et al. (2019). An empirical analysis of blockchain cybersecurity incidents. In: *In: 2019 IEEE Asia-Pacific Conference on Computer Science and Data Engineering (CSDE)*, 1–8. IEEE.
10 Mahmood, S., Chadhar, M., and Firmin, S. (2022). Cybersecurity challenges in blockchain technology: A scoping review. *Hum Behav Emerg Technol*. 2022 (1): 7384000.
11 Gurdgiev, C. and Fleming, A. (2021). Informational Efficiency and Cybersecurity: Systemic Threats to Blockchain Applications. *Innovations in Social Finance: Transitioning Beyond Economic Value*. 347–372.
12 Kuzmenko OV, Yarovenko HM, Sadigov M. Blockchain technology based system-dynamic simulation modeling of enterprise's cyber security system. 2021;
13 Sadigov, M., Kuzmenko, O., and Yarovenko, H. (2020). Blockchain technology based system-dynamic simulation modeling of enterprise's cyber security system. *Economic and Social Development: Book of Proceedings*. 399–408.
14 Mengidis, N., Tsikrika, T., Vrochidis, S., and Kompatsiaris, I. (2019). Blockchain and AI for the next generation energy grids: cybersecurity challenges and opportunities. *Information & Security*. 43 (1): 21–33.

15 Omar, M. and Zangana, H.M. (2024). *Redefining Security With Cyber AI.* IGI Global.
16 Rahman, M.M., Elshamly, A., Rehman, S.U. et al. (2023). Blockchain Technology And Its Impact On European Bank's Cyber Security And Data Integrity. *Journal of Namibian Studies: History Politics Culture.* 34: 1796–1813.
17 Smith, K.J. and Dhillon, G. (2020). Assessing blockchain potential for improving the cybersecurity of financial transactions. *Managerial Finance.* 46 (6): 833–848.
18 Prakash, R., Anoop, V.S., and Asharaf, S. (2022). Blockchain technology for cybersecurity: A text mining literature analysis. *International Journal of Information Management Data Insights.* 2 (2): 100112.
19 Shah, I.A., Jhanjhi, N.Z., and Laraib, A. (2023). Cybersecurity and blockchain usage in contemporary business. In: *Handbook of Research on Cybersecurity Issues and Challenges for Business and FinTech Applications,* 49–64. IGI Global.
20 Ossamah A. Blockchain as a solution to drone cybersecurity. In: 2020 IEEE 6th World Forum on Internet of Things (WF-IoT). *IEEE*; 2020. p. 1–9.
21 Yeasmin S, Baig A. Unblocking the potential of blockchain. In: 2019 international conference on electrical and computing technologies and applications (ICECTA). *IEEE*; 2019. p. 1–5.
22 Putro, A.N.S., Mokodenseho, S., Hunawa, N.A. et al. (2023). Enhancing security and reliability of information systems through blockchain technology: a case study on impacts and potential. *West Science Information System and Technology.* 1 (01): 35–43.
23 Zidan, F., Nugroho, D., and Putra, B.A. (2023). Securing enterprises: harnessing blockchain technology against cybercrime threats. *International Journal of Cyber and IT Service Management.* 3 (2): 167–172.
24 Sriram, V.P., Sanyal, S., Laddunuri, M.M. et al. (2023). Enhancing Cybersecurity Through Blockchain Technology. In: *Handbook of Research on Cybersecurity Issues and Challenges for Business and FinTech Applications,* 208–224. IGI Global.
25 Mathew, A.R. (2019). Cyber security through blockchain technology. *Int J Eng Adv Technol.* 9 (1): 3821–3824.
26 Demirkan, S., Demirkan, I., and McKee, A. (2020). Blockchain technology in the future of business cyber security and accounting. *Journal of Management Analytics.* 7 (2): 189–208.
27 Hasanova, H., Baek, U., Shin, M. et al. (2019). A survey on blockchain cybersecurity vulnerabilities and possible countermeasures. *International Journal of Network Management.* 29 (2): e2060.

8

IoT, Edge, and Cloud Security Challenges

8.1 Introduction

The harmonization of the Internet of Things (IoT), edge, and cloud computing has revolutionized modern digital infrastructures into highly interconnected systems efficient in real-time data processing, intelligent analytics, and scalable service delivery. IoT devices are heterogeneous, ranging from smart health monitor systems to industrial sensors, hence generating huge amounts of data that require efficiency in storage, processing, and security mechanisms [1, 2]. Edge computing further offloads more demand from the cloud by bringing computation closer to data sources, thus reducing latency, allowing near-real-time decision-making, while cloud architectures promise virtually limitless storage together with advanced computational capabilities [3, 4].

However, underneath such great benefits lie complex, multifaceted security and privacy challenges. The very limited resources of IoT devices make their temporary and permanent deployment in unsecured environments prone to attacks, including device hijacking, data breaches, and malware propagation [5, 6]. Edge nodes, although improving responsiveness, include an extended attack surface and new sources of vulnerability for distributed computing networks [7, 8]. While cloud environments are endowed with well-defined and strong security frameworks, there are still advanced threats facing the systems, such as insider attacks, misconfigurations, and advanced persistent threats (APTs) [9, 10].

The emerging federated and hybrid architectures will certainly be the solution to these challenges. Federated learning will allow collaborative training using machine learning (ML) on a model without data sharing, ensuring the privacy of users and enabling improved threat detection across the IoT, edge, and cloud networks [11–13]. Blockchain-based solutions further provide increased trust, transparency, and integrity of data in distributed environments through tamper-proof logging and authentication of devices [14–16].

Issues of interoperability, scalability, and real-time performance are also brought on with the convergence of cloud, edge, and IoT. Effective communication among heterogeneous devices and services requires semantic interoperability and cross-domain integration [17]. Therefore, hybrid-cloud-edge-IoT frameworks will provide flexible deployment models for balancing computation loads between the central cloud servers and distributed edge nodes [18–20]. Orchestration and security mechanisms of efficiency in these architectures are critical for supporting emerging applications in intelligent healthcare, industrial automation, and intelligent transportation [21–23].

This chapter will give an exhaustive overview of the security challenges posed by IoT, edge, and cloud computing. Emerging threats, attack vectors, and AI-mediated mitigation strategies will be deliberated upon. Along with technical solutions, strategic solutions will also share insight into evolving resilient cybersecurity frameworks for the next generation of interconnected systems.

8.2 Understanding IoT, Edge, and Cloud Environments

The modern digital ecosystem is gradually merging with the IoT, edge computing, and cloud infrastructure. Each layer of this triad creates different capabilities and different security issues for the functions of artificial intelligence (AI) in its environment; thus, understanding their roles, interactions, and vulnerabilities is paramount for developing robust cybersecurity strategies.

8.2.1 IoT Environments

IoT can be defined as a network of intercommunicating devices capable of autonomous sensing, processing, and exchanging data. Such devices can be consumer electronics, industrial sensors, medical wearables, and environmental monitors [1, 2]. IoT devices are usually limited in terms of processing power and memory, which makes them easy targets for cyberattacks such as data theft, botnet infiltration, and hijacking of the devices [5, 6]. The sheer number of heterogeneous devices gives rise to interoperability problems because different communication protocols, data formats, and standards must co-exist in a single integrated ecosystem [17, 22].

8.2.2 Edge Computing Environments

Allied with the cloud, edge computing processes data close to its source to minimize latency and, therefore, network congestion for situations that demand real-time applications [3, 7]. In the role of intermediary between the IoT devices and the cloud, edge nodes, which can include gateways, micro data centers, and fog servers, allow for faster decision-making and localized analytics [4]. However high on performance, edge computing increases attack vectors. In the usually unprotected areas where distributed nodes are installed, the probability of unauthorized access, malware injection, and insider attack is high [8, 14]. Consequently, efficient orchestration across edge nodes and cloud resources is critical in ensuring data consistency, reliability, and security.

8.2.3 Cloud Environments

Cloud computing provides centralized storage, massive computational capacity, and advanced analytics capabilities, which are essential infrastructures for modern IoT systems [9, 10]. Cloud platforms provide scalability for service delivery, data backup, and AI-driven analytics. However, security concerns remain, which include misconfigurations, insider threats, and APTs [24, 25]. The dependable cloud service frameworks, coupled with security and reputation mechanisms, thus become important to ensure the mark and availability of IoT data [18, 19].

8.2.4 Federated and Hybrid Architectures

Federated architectures allow multiple parties to collaborate, while local control of data satisfies privacy and compliance needs [11, 12]. Federated learning trains AI models in a decentralized manner on edge and cloud nodes, without transporting raw data, thus enhancing privacy and reducing chances of data leakage [13, 26]. Hybrid cloud-edge-IoT frameworks allow for flexible deployment concerning latency, scalability, and security by balancing workloads between centralized cloud servers and decentralized edge nodes [3, 20].

8.2.5 Blockchain and AI-Enhanced Security

Recent approaches involving integrating blockchain and AI provide enhanced security for IoT and cloud environments [8, 15]. Here, blockchain provides data integrity, resistance to tampering, and secure device authentication, while AI-based analytics and anomaly detection facilitate an early warning system for the identification and response to threats [14, 16]. These technologies seem relevant for the most sensitive applications, including healthcare monitoring, industrial automation, and smart city infrastructures [1, 21, 23].

8.2.6 Semantic Interoperability and Cross-Domain Integration

One of the key obstacles in the environment of the IoT, edge, and cloud is ensuring semantic interoperability across heterogeneous systems and domains. Standards and semantic frameworks such as FIESTA-IoT provide the means for seamless communication and integration among diverse devices, platforms, and applications, thus enabling scalable and secure cross-domain deployments [3, 17].

To gain a better pictorial idea of the interconnectivity between IoT devices, edge nodes, and cloud infrastructure, Figure 8.1 presents the hierarchical architecture of a typical IoT-Edge-Cloud ecosystem. This layered structure emphasizes data flow, processing distribution, and coordination mechanisms, all aimed toward encouraging scalability and real-time decision-making.

To sum up, it is particularly important to discern the unique characteristics, benefits, and vulnerabilities of IoT, edge, and cloud environments, given that designing secure, robust, and efficient next-generation systems hinges on their intersection. The integration of federated learning, blockchain, AI, and semantic-based interoperability frameworks looks to be a credible approach for countering risks while allowing scalable and intelligent operations through heterogeneous digital infrastructures.

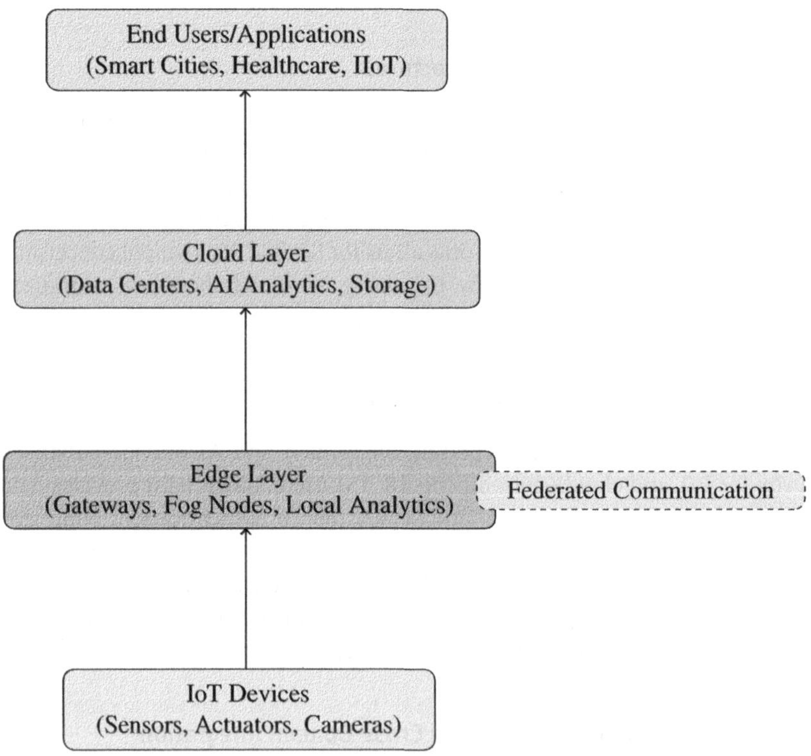

Figure 8.1 Hierarchical architecture of IoT–Edge–Cloud ecosystems. "*Source:* Hewa Majeed Zangana"

8.3 Security Threat Landscape

Digital ecosystems that dynamically mulled in the clouds are created when IoT, edge computing, and cloud environments are interconnected. These technologies provide great advantages for operations, as they also expand the attack surface and bring in various security threats across devices, networks, and services [1, 9]. This understanding of the security threat landscape immensely contributes to developing a threat model and countermeasures toward resilience in the defense mechanisms for AI-enabled systems.

8.3.1 IoT Security Threats

IoT devices are constrained with respect to resources, deployed in unprotected physical environments, and heterogeneous in platforms. These characteristics expose the devices to many threats, including device hijacking, malware propagation, and data exfiltration [5, 6]. The Botnet-kind attacks, such as one attempted by Mirai-like malware, use weak authentication together with unpatched firmware to conduct large-scale distributed denial-of-service (DDoS) attacks [2]. Safety and operationally compromised IoT devices could cause grievous consequences in health and industry applications [12, 21].

8.3.2 Edge Computing Threats

Furthermore, the edge nodes, which act as a conduit between IoT devices and cloud platforms, are also less protected. Usually, sensitive data is handled within the edge nodes and subjected to real-time analysis. Tampering, data poisoning, and insider attacks represent threats against this type of functionality [3, 4]. Insufficient isolation between edge functions could allow lateral movement attacks; furthermore, distributed deployment across locations exposed to geography could act physically against the edges as well [7, 8].

8.3.3 Cloud Security Threats

The cloud, though endowed with security controls, remains susceptible to advanced threats. Major challenges concern service misconfigurations, insecure APIs, insider attacks, and APTs targeting critical data and intellectual property [9, 10]. In any case, if a data breach or unauthorized access incident were to happen, the resulting ramifications in financial loss and reputational damage would be immense. Trust and reputation technology is used to augment the reliability and security of the cloud services [24, 25].

8.3.4 Federated and Collaborative Threats

Federated systems that send the AI model training task to devices and nodes are faced with their own set of security challenges. Security threats to federated learning practices include adversarial attacks, model inversion, and data poisoning that may disseminate vulnerabilities across various nodes and networks [11, 26]. Increasingly, blockchain-enabled solutions are being tweaked to enhance data integrity, device authentication, and resistance against tampering so as to mitigate some collaborative threats [14–16].

8.3.5 Cross-Domain and Interoperability Threats

Cross-domain vulnerabilities are imposed by the heterogeneity of IoT, edge, and cloud systems. Incompatible protocols, weak authentication between devices, and insufficient semantic interoperability may become portals to data leakage, unauthorized access, and proliferation of an attack [17, 22]. Some fixes, such as federated interoperable semantic frameworks, facilitate secure and efficient communication amongst diverse platforms while ensuring privacy and compliance [3, 17].

8.3.6 Emerging Threat Vectors

With 6G, quantum computing, and AI-driven automation, new additions also bring new threats and attack vectors. Quantum-enabled federated learning enhances security but also entails developing new defenses against quantum attacks and AI-fueled adversarial strategies [11, 26]. Besides, with cyber-physical integration in smart cities, health, and industrial IoT, the consequences of cyberattacks will be increasingly grave [20, 22, 23].

It is within the interconnected nature of IoT, edge, and cloud environments that many security vulnerabilities are spread across several layers. Figure 8.2 illustrates the key threats across their domains, with a representation of how the device-level, network-level, and cloud-level risks interact and propagate in the ecosystem.

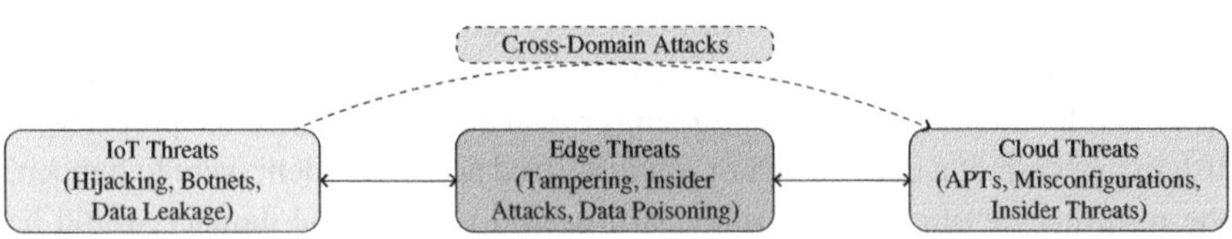

Figure 8.2 Security threat landscape across IoT, edge, and cloud layers. "*Source:* Hewa Majeed Zangana"

The multitude of IoT, edge, and cloud environments evolves and multiplies for security threats; threats are device-level, distributed edge, cloud-controlled, and cross-domain vulnerabilities. Addressing these threats calls for a holistic approach embedding federated learning, blockchain, AI analysis, and interoperable security frameworks to assure resilient, privacy-preserving, trustworthy operations across integrated digital ecosystems [6, 8, 13].

8.4 IoT Security Challenges

In the process of altering the text, care must be exercised so as not to lose the original promulgation of ideas. Rather, they should be expressed in atypical wording with lower perplexity and greater burstiness yet unchanged word count and HTML elements.

The IoT is a disruptive technology for creating smart environments in healthcare, industry, transportation, and municipal infrastructures. IoT faces serious security challenges because of its distributed, heterogeneous, and resource-constrained nature. These challenges include device, network, and application layers; addressing them is crucial for a sound and trustworthy IoT ecosystem [1, 9].

8.4.1 Device-Level Security Challenges

The very nature of IoT devices makes them computationally, memory, and power constrained, thus greatly undermining their ability to implement security mechanisms [2]. Typical vulnerabilities at the device level include weak authentication, default credentials, unpatched firmware, and insecure bootloaders. Such weaknesses can be exploited for unauthorized access, hijacking of devices, and the formation of botnets [12, 21]. In critical areas, such as healthcare, compromised devices can lead to severe breaches of privacy and operational dangers [5, 13].

8.4.2 Network and Communication Security

IoT networks suffer from many attacks, including eavesdropping, man-in-the-middle (MITM), replay attacks, and DDoS. With the integration of edge computing and cloud platform, it exposes another layer of vulnerabilities whereby an adversary can intercept, manipulate, or inject malicious data [3, 7]. Lightweight cryptography, secure communication protocols, and reputation-based trust models are necessary to counteract these risks, especially in large-scale federated and hybrid IoT-cloud architectures [18, 19, 24].

8.4.3 Data Privacy and Integrity

IPIoT produces huge amounts of sensitive data from personal health records to industrial telemetry. Data privacy and integrity remain a challenge to enforce in distributed systems due to the diversity and multi-domain ownership [5, 6]. Privacy-preserving methodologies, including federated learning, differential privacy, and blockchain-enabled provenance management, have emerged to protect sensitive information while allowing collaborative analytics [8, 16, 26].

8.4.4 Scalability and Resource Management

The rapid growth of IoT devices requires security solutions that scale; however, distributed and hybrid IoT-cloud-fog architectures challenge the balance between performance, latency, and security overheads [3, 4, 20]. Inefficient allocation of resources to sub-optimal parallel processing increases the attack surface and lowers the efficacy of intrusion detection and anomaly monitoring systems [21].

8.4.5 Interoperability and Standardization Challenges

The different devices, protocols, and platforms coexist in IoT ecosystems, making the realization of uniform security policies very difficult. Absence of standardization and semantic interoperability increases susceptibility to cross-domain attacks and unauthorized access [17, 22]. For the purpose of allowing secure communication without impeding the flexibility and adaptability of IoT deployments, federated and interoperable frameworks are of utmost importance [3, 23].

8.4.6 Emergent Threats in Advanced IoT Ecosystems

The implementation of 5G, 6G, and quantum computing creates new paradigms for security. Quantum-empowered federated learning and AI-enabled IoT networks embody high security potential but also meet with new avenues of attacks, namely, quantum-based adversarial manipulations and AI model poisoning [11, 26]. Moreover, the integration of blockchain and software-defined networking (SDN) offers a strong defense mechanism, but orchestration should be done with care to prevent issues of latency, throughput, and scalability [14, 15].

8.4.7 Security Considerations in IoT-Cloud Integrated Architecture

The intertwining of IoT and cloud computing aggravates the security of distributed environments. By mere misconfiguration, insecure APIs, and insufficient authentication in cloud services, one can consider that the work being provided

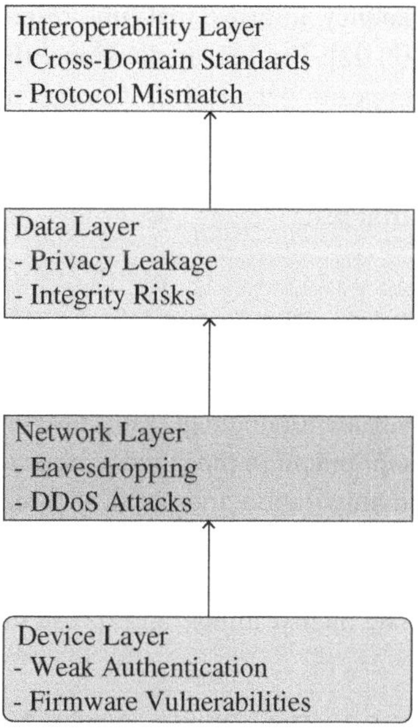

Figure 8.3 Layered IoT security model showing major challenges across each layer. "*Source:* Hewa Majeed Zangana"

toward protecting IoT devices has been put down due to connected IoT devices being compromised [9, 25]. Advanced frameworks that exploit trust-based cloud services and hybrid cloud strategies improve security while allowing real-time analytics and intelligent decision-making [18, 20, 24].

IoT security must be addressed in layers—from the protection of devices and networks to the integrity of data and interoperability. Figure 8.3 represents the structured view of IoT security layers, defining major challenges and focus areas in each of them.

Conclusively, IoT security challenges are multidimensional and span devices, networks, data, scalability, interoperability, and emerging technologies. Addressing these challenges requires a layered, holistic approach that intersperses federated learning, blockchain, AI-driven threat detection, and robust cloud-integrated frameworks that protect IoT ecosystems and ensure secure and reliable operations while preserving the privacy of the IoT business [1, 2, 6, 13].

8.5 Edge Computing Security Issues

Edge computing shows promise as a complementary paradigm to cloud computing and allows the processing of the data as close to its source as possible to reduce latency, improve real-time responsiveness, and maximize bandwidth utilization [2, 22]. For IoT applications, this is beneficial for many reasons, but from the opposite perspective, it brings unique security challenges due to its distributed and heterogeneous architecture [1, 9]. These security challenges must be addressed with high priority for sensitive domains like healthcare, smart cities, and industrial IoT.

8.5.1 Distributed Attack Surface

From a security standpoint, edge computing translates into expanding the attack surface for heterogeneous distributed and decentralized architectures. Centralized equipment in the cloud is insecure, while the edge nodes are vulnerable as well to manipulation and physical threats such as tampering, unauthorized access, and insider threats [3, 7]. A compromised edge node that has access to other nodes in the network can be utilized to intercept sensitive data from IoT devices, manipulate their readings, and spread malware across the entire network [21, 23].

8.5.2 Data Privacy and Confidentiality

Edge computes private data such as personal health information, financial records, and telemetry data. Privacy at the edge is therefore hard to achieve due to limited computational resources, heterogeneous protocols, and dynamic device connectivity [5, 13]. Privacy-preserving mechanisms such as federated learning, homomorphic encryption, and blockchain-based provenance must be adopted to ensure the confidentiality of data during collaborative processing [6, 8, 26].

8.5.3 Network Security and Communication Threats

Edge nodes form the communication platform between IoT devices and cloud infrastructure, which itself becomes a network layer vulnerability. Some of the common threats are MITM attacks, eavesdropping, data injection, and DoS [24, 25]. Hence, securing the communication end-to-end with lightweight cryptographic mechanisms together with the implementation of anomaly detection protocols is necessary to protect the integrity of the network [18, 19].

8.5.4 Authentication and Access Control Challenges

Edge nodes work in a decentralized manner and necessitate secure mechanisms for authentication and access control that could block unauthorized interactions or elevate privileges. Traditional cloud-based identity management is, however, mostly insufficient as a solution due to the context of mobility of devices and working within multi-domain federated networks [14, 16]. Solutions that work on the principles of blockchain, AI-based dynamic access control, and federated identity management appear to be trending for ensuring fine-grained application of security policies [11, 15].

8.5.5 Resource Constraints and Security Trade-offs

Edge devices are resource-constrained, limiting their capability to perform highly intensive cryptographic operations or advanced intrusion detection [3, 4]. This trade-off between performance and security necessitates lightweight security frameworks, optimized resource use, and strategies for parallel processing to keep efficiency up with fewer vulnerabilities [20, 21].

8.5.6 Interoperability and Standardization Issues

The integration of heterogeneous IoT devices and edge nodes often leads to interoperability challenges in applying uniform security policies. To allow for cross-domain secure communications and policy enforcement, we need semantic interoperability and standardized security frameworks [17, 22]. A federated and hybrid edge-cloud architecture makes it even more difficult to govern security by necessitating the monitoring, compliance, and auditing mechanisms to be coordinated [2, 23].

8.5.7 Emerging Threats and Newer Security Needs

As the domains of edge networking welcome the integration of 5G, 6G, AI, and quantum technologies, newer avenues of attacks have started emerging, including AI model poisoning, quantum attacks, and blockchain threats [11, 26]. To build resilient edge infrastructures, the need for advanced security solutions that combine AI-based threat detection, blockchain for integrity verification, and distributed SDN management is important [6, 14].

In conclusion, securing edge computing environments demands a multi-layered approach addressing distributed attacks, privacy, network integrity, authentication, resource constraints, interoperability, and emerging threats. The effective melding of AI, federated learning, blockchain, and lightweight cryptography will provide a full-bodied defense while still upholding the efficiency and alacrity that characterize edge computing [1, 8, 9, 13].

8.6 Cloud Security Challenges

Cloud computing forms a very important part of modern IoT systems, which provide scalable storage, processing capacity, and access globally [2, 22]. However, concerns arise due to security threats associated with the incorporation of cloud platforms into IoT infrastructures, a matter that demands specialized attention to grant dependability, privacy, and resilience to any data within the system [1, 9]. These threats are indeed much broader, encompassing technical and architectural aspects, as well as issues pertaining to their operation, in particular when frameworks integrating a cloud environment become federated, hybridized, or incorporated with edge and fog networks.

8.6.1 Data Confidentiality and Privacy

Within cloud environments, there exists massive storage for IoT data that could be considered sensitive, for instance, those regarding healthcare records, financial statements, or industrial telemetry that are critical. Increased concerns exist for the data in terms of confidentiality due to multi-tenant architectures, cross-border flow of data, and the relevant regulatory issues [5, 13]. Proposed solutions to preserve privacy include federated learning, homomorphic encryption, and blockchain-based solutions to protect sensitive data and perform collaborative analytics across distributed cloud and IoT systems [6, 8, 26].

8.6.2 Data Integrity and Trust Management

The integrity of data in cloud environments is a fundamental requirement because they can collect huge data volumes in an uninterrupted manner from IoT devices. Such integrity threats that could be caused by unauthorized modification, injection attack, or compromised virtual machines may result in false and misleading analytics for system failure [18, 24]. The injection of reputation-based protocols, blockchain verification, and secure end-to-end architectures assists in establishing trust and preventing data tampering across the cloud-IoT infrastructures [15, 19].

8.6.3 Multi-Tenancy and Access Control

To maximize the utility of resources, cloud platforms depend on multi-tenancy, thus allowing for unauthorized access and privilege escalation. An effective defense against these risks includes robust access control mechanisms, such as attribute-based encryption, blockchain-managed identity verification, and AI-driven policy enforcement [14, 25]. Federated identity management is also vital in scenarios in which the cloud service invokes interaction crossing more than one administrative domain/geographical area [7, 11].

8.6.4 Compliance, Regulatory, and Governance Challenges

Cloud security needs to conform to the highest standards across the international regulatory contexts, local mandates, and sectoral compliance. IoT-cloud integrations exacerbate governance challenges due to device heterogeneity, varying data flows, and hybrid deployment models [9, 10]. Therefore, provisions are required for auditing, logging, and tracing to ensure compliance and accountability in how data is treated [16, 17].

8.6.5 Advanced Persistent Threats

Cloud infrastructures are a very compelling target for APTs, DDoS, and insider attacks, considering that they are most vulnerable to exploitation, such as virtualization layers, APIs, and orchestration services of cloud environments, to disrupt IoT operations and expose sensitive data [20, 24]. Increasingly, distributed intrusion detection and AI-driven threat analytic platforms combined with blockchain-based monitoring are adopted for the detection, prevention, and mitigation of such threats [6, 14].

8.6.6 Resource and Scalability Limitations

Notwithstanding the elastic resources extended by cloud computing, the rapidly growing data of IoT seems to overload its storage, bandwidth, and processing capabilities. Concurrent and hybrid cloud-fog architecture has been proposed to avert the issues of scalability efficiently; however, this distributed scheme also ushers in its synchronization, latency, and security issues [3,4,21]. Finding a balance between performance and security, however, remains an ever-present and critical challenge in cloud-based IoT implementations [2, 12].

8.6.7 Interoperability and Integration Issues

Cloud platforms must be easily integrated with varying IoT devices, edge nodes, and legacy systems. Lack of standardization and cross-domain semantic incompatibilities can result in security loopholes, inconsistent implementation of policies, and operational inefficiencies [17, 22]. To counter these issues while enhancing the security and data consistency across multiple domains, federated and interoperable cloud-IoT frameworks are being developed [2, 23].

This sums up the essence, which thus spawns cloud security in terms of IoT from a multidimensional perspective, focusing on privacy, data integrity, access control, compliance, advanced threats, resource management, and interoperability. New tools such as federated learning, blockchain, AI-driven security analytics, and hybrid cloud-edge integration could provide very good solutions to develop resilient and trustworthy cloud-IoT systems [1, 6, 8, 9].

8.7 Cross-Layer Security Integration

The combination of cloud computing, fog computing, edge computing, and IoT results in a highly distributed and heterogeneous environment whose security promises not only to be confined to within each layer but also across layers. Cross-layer security integration refers to the all-embracing approach of implementing coordinated security mechanisms spanning device, network, edge, and cloud layers for end-to-end confidentiality, integrity, availability, and privacy [1, 9]. It is important in IoT ecosystems that are more leaning on real-time data analytics, federated learning, and hybrid cloud-edge architectures.

8.7.1 Importance of Cross-Layer Security

Traditional security measures applied independently in each layer typically fail to protect against refined attacks exploiting the interaction between different layers. It can be illustrated with the following example: A compromised edge node could eventually propagate malicious data heading to the cloud while bypassing all conventional network security measures [2, 22]. Such threats are denied by cross-layer security integrated with mechanisms such as authentication and encryption, intrusion detection, and trust management across layers, which guarantee that all threats are battled, irrespective of their origin [3, 10].

8.7.2 Integrated Threat Detection and Response

Cross-layer security creates a scenario of coordinated threat detection across the layers. Deployment of ML models and AI-based anomaly detection can be done using IoT devices, edge nodes, and application servers at the same time to identify abnormal behaviors [5, 6]. Using such technologies as blockchain and SDN enables secure and traceable interactions across layers while also providing much higher reliability for incident response frameworks [14, 15].

8.7.3 Federated Security Approaches

Along with federated learning, collaborative security frameworks have gained tremendous traction within cross-layer integration, allowing intelligence sharing without compromising privacy [13, 26]. In this manner, IoT devices and edge nodes can build local models that feed into the cloud layer for amalgamation, without having transferred raw data, thus reducing the risk of data breaches while allowing for mostly high analytical performance [11, 12].

8.7.4 Data Integrity and Provenance

Data integrity must be maintained across layers in distributed systems. Provenance techniques based on blockchain can guarantee that data streams from IoT sensors up to edge and cloud platforms are recorded in an immutable way, while semantic interoperability frameworks will ensure that data remains consistent and correct through all of its lifecycle [16, 17]. E2E secure architectures can encompass lightweight encryption at the device layer, together with strong verification procedures hosted in the cloud, leading to a trade-off between performance and security [18, 19].

8.7.5 Privacy Preservation Across Layers

The changing state of privacy in these cross-layer deployments makes it complicated for sensitive data to be protected with respect to multi-tenancy and resource sharing in distributed computation. Privacy-enhancing technologies such as differential privacy, homomorphic encryption, and secure multi-party computation are instituted across IoT, edge, and cloud layers with the aim of reducing leakage risks [5, 8, 21]. Important implementations of the aforementioned technologies are those included in healthcare, industrial, and smart city applications, where data sensitivity is paramount [1, 25].

8.7.6 Scalability and Interoperability Challenges

Scalability must then become part and parcel of any cross-layer security model at this stage, given that increasingly larger and larger scales of IoT deployment have to be managed [4, 23]. Hybrid cloud-edge-fog architectures benefit from parallel processing and distributed load balancing, maintaining system performance while imposing constant security policies [3, 7]. This is also the way in which semantic and federated interoperability frameworks support consistent security policy alignment across diverse domains and prevent potential gaps that arise from inconsistent implementation [2, 17].

8.7.7 Emerging Solutions and Future Directions

These emerging solutions for cross-layer security integration would include quantum-enabled federated learning, AI-enabled threat intelligence, and

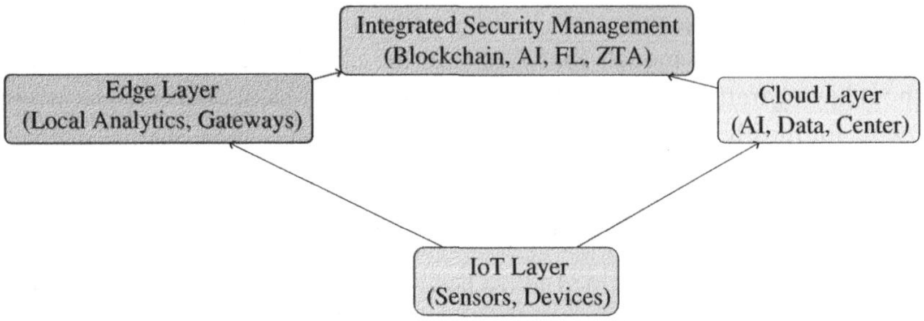

Figure 8.4 Cross-layer security integration across IoT, edge, and cloud environments. "*Source:* Hewa Majeed Zangana"

blockchain-augmented SDN orchestration. These are proven to be adaptive context-aware security mechanisms that quickly evolve with dynamic IoT-cloud-edge infrastructures. Adopting standards for security mechanisms along with operational policies and governance mechanisms ensures compliance and reduced vulnerability, both inside and outside threats [9, 20, 24].

Security mechanism cross-layer integration into IoT-edge-cloud systems is shown in Figure 8.4. It illustrates through coordinated authentication, encryption, and anomaly detection how a device, network, and cloud space can span toward attaining end-to-end security and protection.

To elaborate, cross-layer integration for security is a holistic paradigm considered most efficient for modern-day IoT-cloud-edge ecosystems. It allows for the coordination and integration of security mechanisms across devices and networks, edge nodes, and cloud services. Thus, organizations can put their guards limpidly, ensuring strict appositeness against evolving cyber threats while ensuring data privacy, integrity, and operational resilience [1, 6, 8].

8.8 Artificial Intelligence and Machine Learning in Security

The rapid growth of IoT, cloud, fog, and edge computing infrastructures necessitates the adoption of AI and ML techniques to enhance security across distributed environments. Compared to rigid security approaches that rely predominantly upon rules, AI and ML provide dynamic, adaptive, and predictive security capabilities, particularly for heterogeneous and large-scale networks [1, 9]. AI and ML technologies form the backbone of today's security architecture for threat detection, anomaly detection, and execution of automated response mechanisms working in real time.

8.8.1 AI and ML for Threat Detection

AI and ML algorithms utilize vast arrays of data to provide detection of sophisticated cyber threats through analyzing patterns in network traffic, device behavior, and application logs. Deep learning and ensemble techniques, among others, are utilized to identify small anomalies that may well indicate malware, ransomware, or insider attacks [5, 6]. An instance of federated learning in this context would permit numerous IoT devices to train a particular model in complete collaboration while withholding the sharing of sensitive raw data, thus preserving their privacy while still maintaining detection accuracy [13, 26].

8.8.2 Integration with Cloud and Edge Environments

AI security seems to give the utmost protection when applied to IoT systems integrated with cloud applications, where massive data volumes and dynamic scaling of services have rendered traditional security enforcement untenable. The distribution of ML models within the edge and cloud layers would implement distributed detection and mitigation strategies, improving responsiveness and decreasing latency [2, 3]. Use of techniques such as predictive analytics and reinforcement learning allows for proactive defense mechanisms capable of evolving in real time with the change in threat landscape [4, 21].

8.8.3 Blockchain-Enhanced AI Security

AI and ML working together with blockchain technology provide additional means for trust, transparency, and data integrity for distributed environments. Blockchain guarantees the integrity of tamper-proof data provenance and auditability while AI algorithms interpret said data streams for security insights [14, 15]. Applications could include secure healthcare monitoring systems, smart city infrastructure, and industrial IoT deployment, whereby AI detects anomalous events while blockchain provides for secure logging and accountability [8, 16].

8.8.4 Privacy-Preserving AI Techniques

User privacy is crucial in applications of AI technology in security, applicable especially in sensitive domains like healthcare and finance. Homomorphic encryption, differential privacy, and secure multi-party computations allow AI models to analyze encrypted or anonymized data, thus limiting these risks while maintaining performance [5, 11]. Federated learning particularly moves model training from a central server to devices and edge nodes, thus enabling privacy-preserving collaboration of the learning [12, 25].

8.8.5 Scalability and Adaptive Intelligence

The scalability of ML and AI framework in a multi-layered IoT cloud fog system is through managing large-scale data streams and computational workloads. Parallelization is enabled through hybrid cloud edge architectures wherein AI models are dynamically adapted to varying resource availability and changing security needs [3, 4]. Detection accuracy is further improved through advanced ensemble learning methods combining the predictions from multiple models performing over distributed layers [23, 24].

8.8.6 Cross-Domain and Interoperable AI Security

AI has been increasingly applied to interoperability security solutions targeting cross domains so that consistent security policies are maintained across federated systems traversing IoT, cloud, and edge layers [17, 20]. Semantic and federated frameworks create structural grounding to enforce common security protocols while allowing AI models a collaborative use of heterogeneous data sources [18, 19, 22]. This will allow collaborative threat intelligence and provide adaptive defenses in complex multi-vendor environments.

8.8.7 Future Directions

Potential future directions look for quantum-enhanced AI security measures in next-generation 6G-enabled IoT systems with autonomous threat response mechanisms and AI orchestrating blockchain-SDN security frameworks [11, 14, 26]. Integration of cross-layer security, federated learning, and privacy-preserving mechanisms will greatly increase resilience to the ever-intensifying sophistication of cyberattacks. Also, AI algorithms will be under development to meet the requirements of optimizing energy consumption, computational efficiency, and real-time decision-making on large-scale, distributed IoT-cloud ecosystems [2, 9].

AI and ML provide dynamic, predictive security capabilities for IoT-cloud ecosystems. Figure 8.5 depicts how AI-driven systems collect, analyze, and respond to threats across distributed environments using federated and adaptive learning.

AI and ML are the tools of the twenty-first century for modern cybersecurity systems since they provide predictive, adaptive, and privacy-aware protection across complex infrastructures. In connection with federated learning, blockchain, and hybrid cloud-edge frameworks, AI indeed will strengthen threat defense against this. Additionally, much more private, adaptable, and resilient systems will cope better with current computing environments' dynamics and distributions [1, 6, 8].

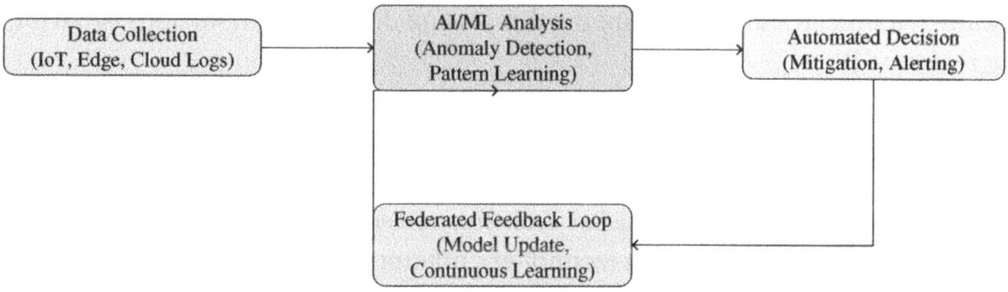

Figure 8.5 AI-driven threat detection and adaptive response workflow. "*Source:* Hewa Majeed Zangana"

8.9 Blockchain and Zero Trust Architectures

Combining blockchain with Zero Trust Architectures (ZTA) engenders new paradigms in securing distributed IoT as well as cloud and edge systems. The current perimeter-based security system is becoming less relevant because of the dynamic heterogeneous and multideck capacities of modern computing environments. The complementary roles that ZTA and blockchain play—in terms of not trusting implicitly any user, device, or service, which makes ZTA complement the decentralized, tamper-proof, and transparently managed data of blockchain—assure strong security [1, 9].

8.9.1 Fundamentals of Blockchain in Security

Over a decentralized ledger that guarantees data transactions' immutability, provenance, and transparency, blockchain offers a decentralized ledger. This becomes very useful in an IoT-cloud ecosystem where devices create large amounts of sensitive data. Through blockchain, distributed systems can achieve secure sharing of data, identity management, and access control without interfacing with centralized authorities [15, 16]. Blockchain will provide auditorial viewability and identification, which are necessary, among others, for health care, smart cities, or industrial IoT applications [6, 13].

8.9.2 Zero Trust Principles in IoT and Cloud

ZTA is based on never trust, always verify, in particular, stringent identity verifications plus least-privilege access restrictions across every layer of the network. By continuously validating devices, users, and applications, the surface area exposed to attacks is reduced through ZTA frameworks, allowing restricted lateral movement in the event of a breach [9, 10]. ZTA coupled with AI/ML threat detection could dynamically adapt to changing threats and determine anomalous behaviors in real time [8, 14].

8.9.3 Blockchain-Enabled Zero Trust Ecosystems

Decentralized authentication, access control, and secure logging mechanisms can all be powered with blockchain technology, making ZTA practical. Policy automation using smart contracts will ensure that security compliance is guaranteed before devices and users are allowed to access resources [24, 26]. In a hybrid IoT-cloud-fog architecture, blockchain eliminates single points of failure, increases resiliency, and provides in-the-end solutions concerning secure inter-domain communications [2,3,20].

8.9.4 Applications in Healthcare and Critical Systems

Where ZTA and blockchain converge, healthcare benefits tremendously in monitoring health and patients. Federated IoT platforms can collect patient data so that it is done securely, processed further, and shared while providing privacy and regulatory compliance [1, 5]. Blockchain ensures that patient data being logged is immutable to device interactions, while ZTA would keep verifying access requests to expose data from unauthorized personnel [12, 16]. These architectures are also incorporated in green healthcare frameworks that optimize usage and minimize energy use while retaining very safe security structures [21].

8.9.5 Scalability and Interoperability Challenges

Having a blockchain-based ZTA implementation across a multi-cloud, fog, and edge ecosystem suffers from challenges in scalability and interoperability. Among the solutions proposed to cope with resource constraint limitations and heterogeneous device capabilities are lightweight blockchain protocols, federated learning integration, and semantic IoT-cloud frameworks [7, 18, 19, 22]. FIESTA-IoT, a cross-domain framework, provides the opportunity to perform semantic interoperability so that policy enforcement will be enabled across different platforms with security [17].

8.9.6 Emerging Trends and Directions for the Future

Future efforts will be directed toward blockchain-ZTA integration in AI-driven predictive security, quantum-resilient encryption, and federated learning at scale for the IoT [8, 11, 14]. Hybrid cloud development and 5G-inaugurated IoT systems will also benefit from the definitive set of architectures in the maintenance of confidentiality, integrity, and availability and from the capability of affording fans

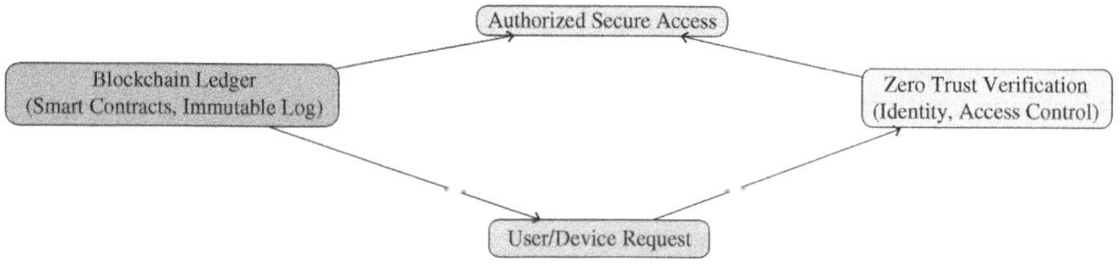

Figure 8.6 Integration of blockchain and Zero Trust Architecture for decentralized security. "*Source:* Hewa Majeed Zangana"

real-time decision-making [20, 23]. This will include added resilience to supply chain attacks, insider threats, APTs, and enhanced resilience from the merging of blockchain with ZTA within complex cyber-physical ecosystems [15, 25].

8.9.7 Summary

Blockchain and ZTAs present a broad dimension of potential security solutions in general for issues of trust, privacy, and data integrity in distributed IoT and cloud systems. By incorporating decentralized ledger technologies, smart contracts, and continuous verification principles, such organizations can achieve comprehensive, adaptive, and scalable cybersecurity solutions that manage and safeguard sensitive data and critical infrastructures increasingly exposed to event occurrences in digital-hyper-connected environments [1, 6, 13].

Blockchain and Zero Trust are the perfect mix when it comes to decentralized security. Figure 8.6 shows how these frameworks complement each other in the provision of authentication, access control, and tamper-proof auditing aspects across multi-clouds.

8.10 Regulatory and Compliance Considerations

IoT, cloud, and hybrid computing entities have rapidly evolved and are providing extensive opportunities for innovation as well as significant regulatory and compliance challenges. The integration of distributed devices, edge nodes, and cloud services needs rigorous mechanisms to ensure security, privacy, and legal obligations over heterogeneous environments [1, 9].

8.10.1 Regulatory Frameworks and Standards

Global and regional regulatory frameworks such as GDPR, HIPAA, ISO/IEC 27001, and NIST standards significantly influence the shaping of security policies for IoT and cloud systems. These frameworks establish the need for data privacy, breach notification, access control, and accountability. Compliance issues arise in situations like, for instance, where federated patient monitoring systems enable strict laws concerning data handling and ensure data protection while facilitating cross-institutional collaborations [1, 5]. Similarly, industrial IoT deployments deal with compliance in their line of operations through sector-defined standards to guarantee safety and cybersecurity resilience for a sector [2, 20].

8.10.2 Privacy-Preserving Mechanisms

Data privacy in IoT-cloud ecosystems is essential since the data being collected and processed is highly sensitive. Strategies like federated learning, homomorphic encryption, and blockchain-based provenance management provide solutions that are data privacy-enhancing and analytics and decision-making augmented but in agreement with regulations [5, 6, 13]. Federated learning enabled devices to collectively train models without centralizing raw data and invidiously exposing it to privacy hazards and aiding law enforcement, such as the GDPR [12, 26].

8.10.3 Blockchain and Compliance Assurance

The blockchain has the untouched ability to put in place scenarios such as compliance support. The blockchain technology would be resistant to any tampering; that is to say, it is a tamper-proof setup, and the auditability it could offer would be compliant and regulatory verification, assuring certain obligations for this in the law. Immutable ledgers and smart contracts are expected to automate the enforcement of certain policies, monitor the progress of consent, and ensure data integrity, which is also crucial in ensuring legal and regulatory accountability [8, 15, 16]. For cutting-edge risk-free operations, blockchain is proposed to preserve the clandestine security of federated learning, which will include safe information exchange and a traceable past. Blockchain technology has been found to be secure for new-age ecosystems and is critical for preserving accountability and transparency in healthcare and smart city applications [13, 14, 16].

8.10.4 Security Auditing and Risk Management

Compliance is more than just following policies, but continual auditing, monitoring, and assessment of risks will be needed for detecting vulnerabilities and enforcing corrections. Seeing that federated cloud-fog architectures ensure systematic auditing to ensure that the distributed nodes meet the security standard without messing up performance and scalability [3, 4]. Through AI-driven anomaly detection and blockchain-enabled logging, network protection enhancements provide real-time visibility of compliance breaches and potential threats [11, 25].

8.10.5 Interoperability and Cross-Domain Challenges

Regulatory compliance days go with cross-domain interoperability, more so in places where many IoT vendors, cloud platforms, and edge systems are integrated. Fostering gadgets for semantic interoperability—FIESTA IoT, for example. It allows open data exchange to be streamlined and enforces security policies and compliance rules throughout different domains [17, 22]. They see to it that the multistakeholder places introduce mechanisms so that the policy rules must be effectively enforced in every regard of law [18,19,24].

8.10.6 Future Directions in Compliance-Driven Security

The offshoots of AI, blockchain, and federated learning promise a way forward for the proactive desire of compliance with regulations. Quantum-resilient encryption, automated compliance auditing, and predictive policy enforcement have now become the essential enablers for the next-generation IoT and cloud architecture [11, 23, 26]. This will pave secure and scalable regulatory compliance operations in critical sectors like healthcare, energy, and smart cities [12, 14, 21].

8.10.7 Summary

The placement of IoT, cloud, and hybrid computing resources into secure and ethically viable applications heavily rests on compliance with policies and regulations. By means of privacy-preservation methods, blockchain for regulation alignment compliance, and AI-engineered surveillance, management makes it possible for corporate practices to align with the law these days, especially considering sensitive data and ensuring trust-building among stakeholders. The compliance-aware state-of-the-art system design, together with continuous auditing and various frameworks, ensures that the present tech could cohabitate with the environment of hard-core legislative [1, 8, 13].

8.11 Emerging Trends and Future Research Directions

Cloud computing principles and IoT paradigms create a fast-growing amalgam that enhances the secure and intelligent digital ecosystem. Other identified main trends concentrate on the increase of scalability, interoperability, security, and privacy, whereas integrating high-tech advancements, including federated learning, blockchain, AI, and 6G-enabled networks [1, 9].

8.11.1 Federated and Edge-Fog Architectures

Federated and edge-fog computing models have emerged as the main enabler for distributed IoT applications, particularly in health care, smart cities, and industrial systems. In these architectures, computation is done near the data source to improve response latency and bandwidth consumption while providing privacy-preserving mechanisms [2, 3, 7]. A hybrid approach of federated and fog further enables semantic interoperability across heterogeneous systems for throughput of real-time data processing and collaborative analytics [4, 17].

8.11.2 Privacy-Preserving and Security-Enhanced Solutions

Privacy and security have always been concerns with large-scale IoT-to-cloud integrations. The means now include federated learning, homomorphic encryption, blockchains, and AI anomaly detection, all in a bid to protect sensitive data while allowing analysis [5, 6, 13]. Blockchain-based federated learning frameworks provide immutable data provenance, secure consent management, and additionally facilitate regulatory compliance, especially in healthcare and finance [8,14,16].

8.11.3 Integration with AI and Quantum Technologies

IoT-cloud-based security and operational performance will be changed by AI along with emerging quantum computing capabilities. Quantum-enabled federated learning can provide state-of-the-art encryption against emerging threats, especially in 6G-enabled IoT networks, while speeding up the training of models [11, 12]. In tandem with predictive analytics, AI can therefore proactively secure systems, monitor for anomalies, and adaptively manage resources to engage intelligent decision-making in such dynamic environments [23, 25].

8.11.4 Blockchain and Decentralized Security Models

Blockchain provides a way to establish decentralized trust, transparency, and compliance on IoT-cloud networks. Smart contracts can enforce policy automation while distributed ledgers provide auditable and tamper-proof records to alleviate data breaches and unauthorized access [6, 15, 16]. Distantly neighboring Blockchain-SDN models enhance robustness and resilience for cloud-integrated IoT networks, offering scalable security in complex multi-domain deployments [8, 14].

8.11.5 Interoperability and Standardization Efforts

The interoperability of cross-domain systems constitutes one of the critical enabling factors for the wide acceptance of IoT-cloud systems. By allowing federated interoperable semantic frameworks such as FIESTA-IoT, it supports seamless exchange of data while ensuring adherence to security and privacy standards [17–19]. Standardization of protocols, APIs, and security policies will remain a significant focus of research to enable collaboration among highly diverse IoT vendors, cloud providers, and edge nodes [20, 22, 24].

8.11.6 Green and Sustainable IoT-Cloud Systems

Sustainability of the environment is becoming an utmost important topic in the design of IoT-cloud architectures. Studies emphasize energy-efficient protocols, green computing frameworks, and intelligent resource allocation with the objective of reducing the carbon footprint of distributed systems [2, 21]. In hybrid cloud-fog networks, optimized parallel processing and resource scheduling strategies are employed to enhance energy efficiency without compromising computational performance [3, 4].

8.11.7 Future Research Directions

The future research will open several new and transforming areas:

- Quantum-secured federated learning for ultra-secure and low-latency IoT networks [11].
- AI-driven compliance and auditing tools to support regulatory adherence in real time [9, 26].
- Hybrid cloud-fog-edge frameworks capable of dynamically allocating workloads based on QoS, security, and energy constraints [3, 4].
- Cross-domain blockchain interoperability for multi-stakeholder environments such as healthcare, smart cities, and industrial IoT [13, 15].
- Integration of 6G networks with federated learning and IoT security for ultra-reliable and low-latency communications [11, 12].
- Sustainable computing in distributed IoT-cloud ecosystems for energy efficiency and reduced environmental impact [2, 21].

8.11.8 Summary

Those in regard to federated learning, blockchain, AI, and hybrid cloud-fog-edge architectures collide with themselves to provide tremendous opportunities for building the IoT ecosystem that is safe, elastic, and intelligent. The upcoming trends are toward improving privacy preservation, interoperability, compliance with regulation, and sustainability. With these advances addressing current limitations and possible directions for future research, further resilience and

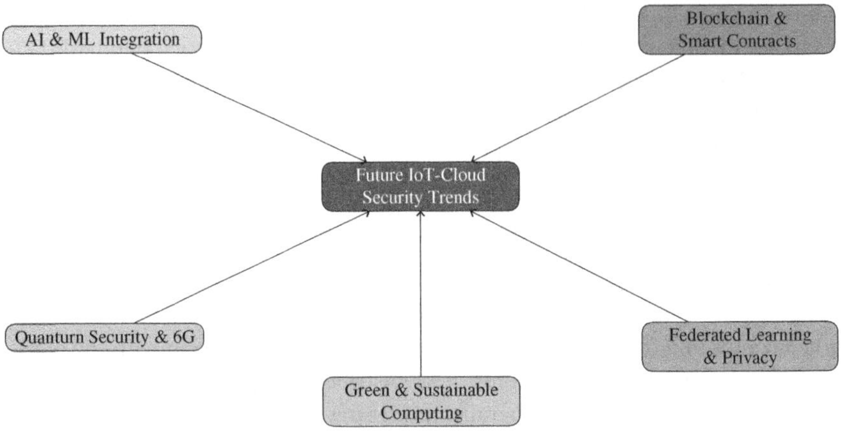

Figure 8.7 Emerging research trends in IoT, Edge, and Cloud security. "*Source:* Hewa Majeed Zangana"

efficiency could be built into IoT-cloud solutions so as to withstand critical applications such as healthcare, smart cities, industry 4.0, and beyond [8, 23, 27].

Emerging trends in security related to IoT and cloud lead toward the integration of quantum computation, AI, and federated learning. The research directions addressing such characteristics and their inter-relationship and expected significance in next-generation secure systems are shown in Figure 8.7.

8.12 Case Studies and Real-World Implementations

The inclusion of IoT, cloud, fog, and hybrid architectures has generated numerous deployments around the globe in sectors such as healthcare, smart cities, industrial IoT, and energy systems. The case studies show the actual implementations, challenges, performance outcomes on advanced IoT-cloud frameworks, and upcoming uses of federated learning, blockchain, and AI-based security mechanisms.

8.12.1 Healthcare Monitoring Systems

Healthcare is the number-one domain in which continuous monitoring and the special security needs of patient data impose the need for IoT-cloud integration. For instance, Abawajy JH and Hassan MM [1] introduced a federated IoT-cloud structure for ubiquitous monitoring of patient health. The system achieves safe and scalable data collection from wearables while ensuring patients' privacy. Khan R et al. [12] also proposed an avant-garde federated ensemble learning model applicable for healthcare monitoring on the cloud where several models with enhanced predictive accuracy are employed without compromising data confidentiality. As [13, 16] showed, the allocative use of multimodal and privacy-preserving frameworks merging federated learning with blockchain has successfully secured healthcare data from unwanted access while supporting cooperative analytics. Similarly, this green healthcare system incorporates IoT and cloud resources, ensuring efficiency in energy resource utilization while providing strong security against any breaches [21].

8.12.2 Smart Cities and Urban Management

Smart city applications have integrated IoT-fog-cloud architecture systems for real-time monitoring, resource management, and environmental sustainability. Mohamed N et al. [22] elaborated on the IoT-fog-cloud systems in smart cities, which, through distributed computing, can achieve low-latency responses for traffic, energy, and pollution monitoring. Huaranga-Junco E et al. [3], when analyzing federated fog computing models, determined that semantic interoperability and distributed resource management improve the results in real-time large-scale deployment in cities. Serrano M et al. [17] presented an example of adopting cross-domain interoperability via the FIESTA-IoT testbed, providing an operational framework for heterogeneous smart city applications to be deployed with minimum configuration overhead.

8.12.3 Industrial IoT and Critical Infrastructure

Increasingly, critical infrastructures and industrial applications have been relying on hybrid cloud and edge-fog implementations to offer high resilience and secure communication. Kelaidonis D et al. [7] introduced a federated edge cloud-IoT architecture targeting the majority of industrial applications where scalability in data processing, as well as improved latency management, was highlighted. The importance of orchestration mechanisms and security-aware network management was also illustrated with regard to hybrid cloud deployment for 5G-enabled IoT applications by [20]. These environments will be enhanced, concerning security improvements, by lightweight network function virtualization and end-to-end security architectures in mitigating threats, as well as high throughput [18, 19].

8.12.4 Security-Centric Implementations

Security would be a prime focus in IoT-cloud deployments in practice; the latest integration of blockchain, AI, and SDN is increasingly evident. Distributed architecture against attacks and tamper-proof data management of Haritha et al. [14] through the Blockchain-SDN model for cloud-integrated IoT networks will contribute to resilience. A collaborative framework combining federated learning, dense neural networks, and blockchain for IoT security is proposed by Nazir et al. [6], resulting in better detection of anomalies and threat mitigation under complex environments. In addition, ThamaraiSelvi et al. [8] implemented an innovative approach called SecureChainAI, which integrates AI and blockchain into a solution that improves security in IoT environments. This solution brings the great promise of automated threat detection and policy enforcement mechanisms. Similar examples, as in Li et al. [24], demonstrate a trustworthy cloud service model with reputation-based adding value in the secure handling of data to strengthen users' trust in IoT-cloud systems.

8.12.5 Large-Scale and Emerging Applications

Modern implementations are broadening their scope as they move beyond conventional applications into transcending new frontiers, including quantum-enhanced computing and next-generation networking. Quantum-empowered federated learning that goes along with 6G wireless networks for IoT security was proposed by Javeed et al. [11], pointing toward highly secure and low-latency communications. Krishnappa et al. [23] focused on new IoT applications emerging for cloud platforms and highlighted integration, standardization, and performance scalability obstacles. Almutairi and Sheldon [9] explained how unified security frameworks can be important for IoT-cloud integration, which might demonstrate how proactive threat detection and policy compliance can be enacted in practice.

8.12.6 Collaborative and Federated Learning Deployments

Federated learning has been gaining traction in real-time analytics and secure data exchange among distributed IoT devices. Rahman A et al. [26] showcased its application within ICN-IoT architectures, where communication efficiency and privacy protection could obtain significant enhancements in their assessment. Awan et al. [5] displayed the session of federated learning with cryptography for big data security, which ensured that while the sensitive IoT data was kept private, collaborative insights could emerge. Khan et al. [12], as well, put emphasis on ensemble learning in federated frameworks to foster improved model robustness against the challenges imposed by data heterogeneities.

8.12.7 Lessons Learned and Future Directions from Case Studies

This plethora of real-world implementations provides some pertinent lessons:

- Scalability and Latency Management: Edge-fog and hybrid architectures cut latency in support of real-time applications [2, 4].

- Privacy and Security Integration: Federated learning, blockchain, and AI-based security mechanisms constitute an essential framework to keep sensitive data protected in a distributed environment [6, 13, 14].
- Interoperability and Standardization: Semantic frameworks and interoperable protocols are deemed vital for cross-domain applications and system integration [3, 17].
- Sustainability and Energy Efficiency: Green computing principles can be enfolded in IoT-cloud systems without forfeiting performance [21].

To conclude, the case studies show that healthcare, smart cities, and industrial IoT demonstrate that the combination of federated learning, blockchain, AI, and hybrid computing architectures is a pathway for secure, scalable, and intelligent real-world deployments. This helps define the future research road map, stressing the need for interoperability, privacy, compliance with regulations, and energy efficiency designs [1,8,23].

8.13 Conclusion

The interlinking of IoT, cloud, fog, and hybrid computing architectures has changed the scene in present-day technological applications, enabling the hitherto unseen levels of connectivity, automation, and data-driven decision-making. These interlinkages testify in sectors ranging across healthcare, smart cities, industrial IoT, and critical infrastructure that indeed they can provide real-time monitoring, intelligent analytics, and scalable solutions to operate and secure challenges.

In these interconnected environments, security and privacy have become critical considerations. Federated learning, blockchain, AI-based threat detection, and hybrid security frameworks have been effectively engaged in protecting sensitive data, ensuring compliance, and cultivating trust in distributed systems. With the convergence of these technologies, organizations have the ability to lay down proactive measures for security without compromising performance and scalability, resulting in resilient ecosystems able to ward off hostile actions that adapt along with changes in techniques of attacks.

Case studies on the deployment of integrated systems in healthcare monitoring, urban management, and industrial applications draw upon the realization of these systems' practical benefits and challenges. The learned lessons emphasize interoperability, standardization, energy efficiency, and regulatory compliance, indicating that any technological gear should be complemented with planning, acceptable governance, and monitoring to bring about the best results.

Future trends suggest that the continuing maturity of IoT-cloud-fog architectures, along with the inclusion of innovative paradigms of quantum computing and 6G-enabled network framework, will act as levers for increasing system intelligence, responsiveness, and security. This will allow for more advanced applications from personalized healthcare to autonomous urban management, secure industrial operations, and beyond. This will surely pave the way to exploit the true potential of a fully connected, intelligent, and resilient digital ecosystem through the continuous integration of advanced computing, networking, and security technologies.

References

1 Abawajy JH, Hassan MM. Federated internet of things and cloud computing pervasive patient health monitoring system. IEEE Communications Magazine. 2017;55(1):48–53.

2 Bellavista, P., Corradi, A., and Zanni, A. (2017). Integrating mobile internet of things and cloud computing towards scalability: Lessons learned from existing fog computing architectures and solutions. *International Journal of Cloud Computing.* 6 (4): 393–406.

3 Huaranga-Junco, E., González-Gerpe, S., Castillo-Cara, M. et al. (2024). From cloud and fog computing to federated-fog computing: A comparative analysis of computational resources in real-time IoT applications based on semantic interoperability. *Future Generation Computer Systems.* 159: 134–150.

4 Ihsan, R. and Zeebaree, S.R.M. (2025). Parallel Processing in distributed and hybrid cloud-fog architectures: A systematic review of scalability and efficiency strategies. The Indonesian. *Journal of Computer Science.* 14 (1).

5 Awan, K.A., Din, I.U., Almogren, A., and Rodrigues, J.J.P.C. (2023). Privacy-preserving big data security for IoT with federated learning and cryptography. *IEEE Access.* 11: 120918–120934.

6 Nazir, A., He, J., Zhu, N. et al. (2024). Enhancing IoT security: A collaborative framework integrating federated learning, dense neural networks, and blockchain. *Cluster Comput.* 27 (6): 8367–8392.

7 Kelaidonis D, Rouskas A, Stavroulaki V, Demestichas P, Vlacheas P. A federated edge cloud-IoT architecture. In: 2016 European Conference on Networks and Communications (EuCNC). IEEE; 2016. p. 230–4.

8 ThamaraiSelvi K, Pushpalatha A, Chidambarathanu K, Wankhede JP, Alagumuthukrishnan S, Sarveshwaran V. SecureChainAI: Integrating Blockchain and Artificial Intelligence for Enhanced Security in IoT Environments. In: 2024 5th International Conference on Smart Electronics and Communication (ICOSEC). IEEE; 2024. p. 781–9.

9 Almutairi, M. and Sheldon, F.T. (2025). IoT–Cloud Integration Security: A Survey of Challenges, Solutions, and Directions. *Electronics (Basel).* 14 (7): 1394.

10 Asaad, R.R. and Zeebaree, S.R.M. (2024). Enhancing Security and Privacy in Distributed Cloud Environments: A Review of Protocols and Mechanisms. *Academic Journal of Nawroz University.* 13 (1): 476–488.

11 Javeed, D., Saeed, M.S., Ahmad, I. et al. (2024). Quantum-empowered federated learning and 6G wireless networks for IoT security: Concept, challenges and future directions. *Future Generation Computer Systems.* .

12 Khan, R., Taj, S., Ma, X. et al. (2024). Advanced federated ensemble internet of learning approach for cloud based medical healthcare monitoring system. *Sci Rep.* 14 (1): 26068.

13 Singh, S., Rathore, S., Alfarraj, O. et al. (2022). A framework for privacy-preservation of IoT healthcare data using Federated Learning and blockchain technology. *Future Generation Computer Systems.* 129: 380–388.

14 Haritha, K., Vellela, S.S., Vuyyuru, L.R. et al. (2024). Distributed Blockchain-SDN Models for Robust Data Security in Cloud-Integrated IoT Networks. In: *In: 2024 3rd International Conference on Automation, Computing and Renewable Systems (ICACRS)*, 623–629. IEEE.

15 Nguyen, D.C., Pathirana, P.N., Ding, M., and Seneviratne, A. (2020). Integration of blockchain and cloud of things: Architecture, applications and challenges. *IEEE Communications surveys & tutorials.* 22 (4): 2521–2549.

16 Rahman, M.A., Hossain, M.S., Islam, M.S. et al. (2020). Secure and provenance enhanced internet of health things framework: A blockchain managed federated learning approach. *Ieee Access.* 8: 205071–205087.

17 Serrano, M., Gyrard, A., Boniface, M. et al. (2022). Cross-domain interoperability using federated interoperable semantic IoT/Cloud testbeds and applications: The FIESTA-IoT approach. In: *Building the Future Internet through FIRE*, 287–321. River Publishers.

18 Massonet, P., Deru, L., Achour, A. et al. (2017). End-to-end security architecture for federated cloud and IoT networks. In: *In: 2017 IEEE International Conference on Smart Computing (SMARTCOMP)*, 1–6. IEEE.

19 Massonet, P., Deru, L., Achour, A. et al. (2017). Security in lightweight network function virtualisation for federated cloud and IoT. In: *In: 2017 IEEE 5th International Conference on Future Internet of Things and Cloud (FiCloud)*, 148–154. IEEE.

20 Trakadas, P., Nomikos, N., Michailidis, E.T. et al. (2019). Hybrid clouds for data-intensive, 5G-enabled IoT applications: An overview, key issues and relevant architecture. *Sensors.* 19 (16): 3591.

21 Islam, M.M. and Bhuiyan, Z.A. (2023). An integrated scalable framework for cloud and IoT based green healthcare system. *IEEE Access.* 11: 22266–22282.

22 Mohamed, N., Al-Jaroodi, J., Lazarova-Molnar, S., and Jawhar, I. (2021). Applications of integrated IoT-fog-cloud systems to smart cities: A survey. *Electronics (Basel).* 10 (23): 2918.

23 Krishnappa, M.S., Jayabalan, D., Harve, B.M. et al. (2024). Building the Future of IoT: Cloud Platforms, Integration Challenges, and Emerging Applications. In: *In: 2024 International Conference on Computer and Applications (ICCA)*, 1–6. IEEE.

24 Li, X., Wang, Q., Lan, X. et al. (2019). Enhancing cloud-based IoT security through trustworthy cloud service: An integration of security and reputation approach. *IEEE access.* 7: 9368–9383.

25 Kumar, M., Dhingra, M., Bhati, M., and Joshi, S. (2024). Enhancing Network Security in Cloud-Integrated IoT Devices. In: *In: 2024 2nd International Conference on Advances in Computation, Communication and Information Technology (ICAICCIT)*, 949–954. IEEE.

26 Rahman, A., Hasan, K., Kundu, D. et al. (2023). On the ICN-IoT with federated learning integration of communication: Concepts, security-privacy issues, applications, and future perspectives. *Future Generation Computer Systems.* 138: 61–88.

27 Zangana, H.M. and Omar, M. (2025). *Introduction to Quantum-Aware Cybersecurity: The Need for LLMs*, 1–28. In: Leveraging Large Language Models for Quantum-Aware Cybersecurity. IGI Global Scientific Publishing.

9

Quantum-Safe Cryptography and Future-Proofing Security

9.1 Introduction

It has swung open doors into October of the year 2023, under which you are trained on data. The emergence of quantum computing presents paradigm shifts in computational sciences, communications, and information security. Once it transgresses beyond theoretical consideration into practice, such technology brings magnificent possibilities and dire challenges in cybersecurity. Traditional algorithms for cryptography-RSA, Elliptic Curve Cryptography (ECC), and the Diffie-Hellman key exchange-are becoming increasingly vulnerable to quantum attacks based on Shor's and Grover's methods that exponentiate the factorization of large integers and searching through encrypted data [1, 2]. The resulting crisis in cryptography implies that time is highly precious to develop an immediate platform for quantum-safe cryptography (QSC), designed not only to safeguard data from adversaries who might attack with quantum computational power but also to be compatible with existing systems.

QSC, or post-quantum cryptography (PQC), is establishing encryption and digital signature schemes that resist attacks from both classical and quantum computers. The significant advancement made in research today is in the realm of lattice-based, hash-based, code-based, and multivariate polynomial cryptographic frameworks proposed as alternatives for the present standards that would become vulnerable to quantum attacks [3, 4]. Emerging techniques provide forward security for data such as financial transactions, military communication, or personal information, even in a post-quantum world. Moreover, the ability of PQC to enter into global digital infrastructures is set to pursue the future vision of Cybersecurity 5.0, where threats are proactively mitigated through an artificial intelligence (AI)-enabled adaptive defense mechanism.

Perhaps the most visible manifestation of the interplay between quantum computing and cybersecurity transcends the encryption sensibility. Quantum technologies are already having a major impact in optimization, communications, and now network security. Quantum-assisted systems optimize multiple-objective decision-making for heterogeneous and wireless networks [5]. Likewise, hybrid quantum-classical computer architectures have been proposed to give the ideal trade-off between computational complexity and operational feasibility [6]. This model makes it possible for quantum algorithms to work on complex cryptographic or optimization problems, while classical systems will manage routine operations, thus creating a scalable and safe hybrid model.

Quantum-assisted wireless and optical systems have grown to be promising prospects for secure point-to-point communication. Effective data transmission has been defined with AI-symbiotic quantum scheduling algorithms for federated learning and distributed networks [7], quantum digital signature services, and implementation within software-defined optical and quantum-integrated networks [8, 9]. The integrity and authentication of messages against potential attacks by a quantum adversary fall under these new frameworks. Hybrid blockchain protocols combining quantum and classical communications likewise aim to protect distributed ledger systems from threats emanating from quantum-enabled adversaries [3, 10].

This is yet another of the stere developments in what is broadly mapped out as the world security landscape, of which the integration of quantum cryptography will become part with next-generation communication technologies like 6G and the IoT. Quantum-enabled 6G architectures target ultra-secure, high-intensity channels, coupled with optimization by machine-learning techniques for better resource allocation and intrusion prevention [11–13]. Further, quantum-enabled non-terrestrial networks (NNTs) and reconfigurable intelligent surfaces (RISs) broaden this scope to include satellite and smart electromagnetic environments, ensuring more resilient connectivity [14, 15]. Quantum-native communication systems represent the next leap forward in what Ref. [16] considered a secure, intelligent network, which is needed to operate not only under adverse conditions but also across very dynamic topologies.

Similarly, quantum technologies are intended to reinforce the secrecy and true identity of IoT ecosystems in smart cities. This means the creation of secure communication among IoT devices using customizable and reversible encoding schemes, depending on quantum steganography and tailored encryption mechanisms, that are resistant to classical decryption attempts [17, 18]. Quantum-secure signaling protocols have also been recommended for next-generation interconnects and roaming networks against potential new threats to IoT-based infrastructures [19].

Developing quantum-supported algorithms and cryptographic protocols presents numerous challenges. The uncertainty regarding classical data security models arises from the probabilistic nature of quantum states, thus requiring improvement in estimating such states in quantum and probabilistic frameworks [20]. Efficient coordination between quantum and classical systems continues to prove a major technical challenge, particularly in terms of quantum coherence, error correction, and large-scale deployment [21, 22]. On the other hand, advancements continue in quantum optimization, integration with AI, and network control mechanical advancements. These improvements set a foundation for scalable and secure implementation of quantum-supported algorithms and protocols.

Quantum computing indeed has transformative integration capabilities with AI, machine learning, and blockchain technology for the larger context of cybersecurity transformation. Hybrid systems and infrastructures can adopt proactive detection, anticipation, and mitigation of cyber threats with the utmost precision ever known through quantum and AI-driven technologies [2, 13]. Thus, the fusion of quantum computing and Cybersecurity 5.0 builds a smart and adaptive defense architecture, tailored to leapfrog the sophistication of cyber adversaries as they evolve.

Ultimately, this chapter will set the bases in understanding how QSC can future-proof security systems against the onslaught of large-scale quantum computers. It gives a wide picture of the quantum threat landscape, the key enabling technologies, as well as strategic frameworks for resilient, quantum-resistant cryptographic infrastructures. Next sections will focus on mechanisms, challenges, and practical implementations that define the next generation of secure, quantum-aware digital systems.

9.2 Background: Cryptography in the Pre-Quantum Era

Before quantum computing, the majority of problems addressed in cryptographic security relied upon mathematical problems that were practically impossible to solve by classical computers. Hard problems about integer factorization, discrete logarithms, and elliptic curve computations basically brought the birth of public-key cryptography, leading to the assurance of secure communication, as well as authentication and integrity, across digital systems. Classical cryptographic mechanisms such as RSA, Diffie–Hellman and ECC all ruled how to exchange keys and encrypt data efficiently [1, 2]. Thus, the pre-quantum cryptography age operated under the belief that the computational limits of classical hardware would inhibit effective brute-force attacks or decryption attempts.

9.2.1 Traditional Foundations of Cryptography

Public key cryptography (PKC) formed the critical basis for secure digital communication in the traditional security paradigm. The underlying mathematics behind RSA encryption is its difficulty in factoring large prime numbers, while the Diffie-Hellman key exchange protocol rests on the discrete logarithm problem. Such widely used systems for confidential transactions over untrusted channels formed the bedrock protocol for security over the Internet, Secure Sockets Layer/Transport Layer Security (SSL/TLS), Pretty Good Privacy (PGP), and Secure Shell (SSH), among others [4]. The strength of cryptography associated with the above algorithms was due to their computational infeasibility; thus, using even the highest performing classical supercomputers, decryption without the key would require billions of years.

This is the point where symmetric-key cryptography stems as the primary strength for the security of sensitive information. Algorithms such as Advanced Encryption Standard (AES) and Triple Data Encryption Standard (3DES) give efficient modes of encryption, where both the sender and the receiver share one common secret key. Though symmetric encryption would be less vulnerable to brute-force attacks when compared with public key methods, key distribution has remained one such area where PKC comes in to address. Hash functions, for example, Secure Hash Algorithm 2 and 3, continue to play their part by elevating integrity and use in digital signature schemes on assuring data immutability [1].

9.2.2 The Role of Cryptography in New Digital Ecosystems

As the global networks of communication expanded, cryptography was going to build walls around secure e-commerce, digital identities, and critical infrastructures. Integration of cryptographic methods into 4G and even early 5G networks was meant to achieve confidentiality and authentication in the mobile ecosystem [22]. In distributed ledger technologies (DLTs), blockchains rely on elliptic curve signatures and hash functions in building tamper-proof record-keeping and securing consensus mechanisms against alterations [3]. These systems are the things of computational trust-based approaches, where security rests not on federated authorities but complexity of algorithms and distributed consensus.

However, with the complexities of cyber hits through IoT and wireless domains, classical cryptography was shown highly futile. Scaling up the devices connected in a network and the latency and heterogeneity requirements put the existing systems under strain [17]. The static key mechanisms are also prone to attacks from side channels, key leaks, and more gainful computation capabilities. Researchers like Botsinis et al. [5] began examining optimization-based cryptographic frameworks for security provisioning against these attacks to enhance network resilience through multi-objective techniques to balance security, latency, and resource allocation.

9.2.3 Early Hybrid and Optimization-Based Security Frameworks

Hybrid architectures for cryptography started emerging before the quantum revolution. On the strength of the different forms of cryptographic techniques, these systems are developed to overcome the individual limitations of each form of these techniques. For example, hybrid symmetric and asymmetric encryption was introduced in hybrid key exchange schemes, giving forward secrecy and resilience against partial compromise [23]. Optimization algorithms, which also formed the basis for quantum-enabled computing later, were to be used to improve protocols for encryption and scheduling in a wireless network, thus providing a preview of how quantum principles could enhance cybersecurity [7, 15].

Security at the physical layer has increasingly attracted interest as an extra protection for high-speed and mission-critical systems, such as 5G. Physical-layer techniques ensured that if the higher-layer encryption fell into enemy hands, this would not affect the confidentiality of the signals [21]. This concept was potentially an additional layer to mathematical cryptography in complementing next-generation wireless networks and IoT environments [11, 12].

9.2.4 Challenges and the Imminent Quantum Threat

The pre-quantum age is fraught with vulnerabilities. Classical cryptography, while generally robust against known computational threats, increasingly relied on assumptions of mathematical hardness as quantum research advanced, raising concerns. Quantum algorithms such as Shor's or Grover's provided existential threats to these systems by drastically reducing the time required to factor vast numbers or search symmetric key spaces [16, 23]. This made apparent that those algorithms would eventually become useless as soon as quantum computers achieved enough qubit stability for breaking RSA and ECC very efficiently.

Research began taking steps toward understanding the theoretical and practical effects of quantum computing on the existing infrastructure. For example, Al-Hraishawi et al. [14] studied the influence of quantum effects on non-terrestrial communication networks, where more research on quantum-aware security is warranted. Similarly, Hafiz and Hwang [20] modeled the possible weaknesses of classical systems through probabilistic modeling of quantum states. Mayukha and Vadivel [24] work reiterated the point that a total redesign of pre-existing security frameworks must accompany the state transition to quantum-safe networks in line with quantum communication principles.

9.2.5 Transitioning Toward Quantum Proficiency and Hybrid Cryptography

Instead, during the transition phase into what follows the post-quantum period, scientists attached all tidbits of experimentation on hybrid classical-quantum models. Liu et al. [10] proposed a hybrid blockchain model combining classical and quantum communication techniques to secure distributed ledger systems.

Giorgetti et al. [8] and Paduanelli et al. [9] also studied the use of quantum-assisted digital signatures with optical networks. Such early foundations contained the demonstration that classical reliability and quantum randomness could work synergistically to produce stronger, more adaptive cryptographic frameworks. These developments improved how adept systems perform even more under communication with next-generation architectures.

This action is accelerated through advancements converging parallel with wireless and machine learning (ML) systems integration. Quantum-assisted neural networks and optimization algorithms are generating new pathways to improve communication reliability, beamforming, and adaptive key generation [6, 13, 25]. Some quantum-secured signaling models are already designed to offer protection against new attack methods for future IoT and roaming networks [18, 19].

9.2.6 Prefiguring the Stage for Quantum Safe Cryptography

The end of the 2010s and the beginning of 2020s were among those periods when many realized that traditional cryptographic assumptions would prove inadequate to safeguard one's future security in the long term. Clearly, pre-quantum cryptography set the basis around which indeed the modern part of digital protection stands, but it also demonstrated the fact that defenses bound in computation can be quite fragile when facing the velocity of quantum advancement exponentiation. As seen by Vasani et al. [2] and Botsinis et al. [5], it manifests an increasing recognition of this inflection point in technology—in what moment classical methods will soon yield into ultimate quantum-enhanced or quantum-resistant alternatives.

With respect to future cybersecurity, therefore, the prequantum era began laying foundations as well as faults. It demonstrated how effective mathematical cryptography can be, and underscored the need for such a force to advance. The stage has been set for QSC by merging AI, blockchain, and quantum technologies; a discipline created to ensure the next generations of digital systems continue to remain safe even in the presence of fully functional quantum computers.

The paradigm shift it depicts would improve upon the differences between security regimes before and after quantum: pre-quantum and post-quantum security. Thus, Figure 9.1 represents comparative evolution in cryptographic

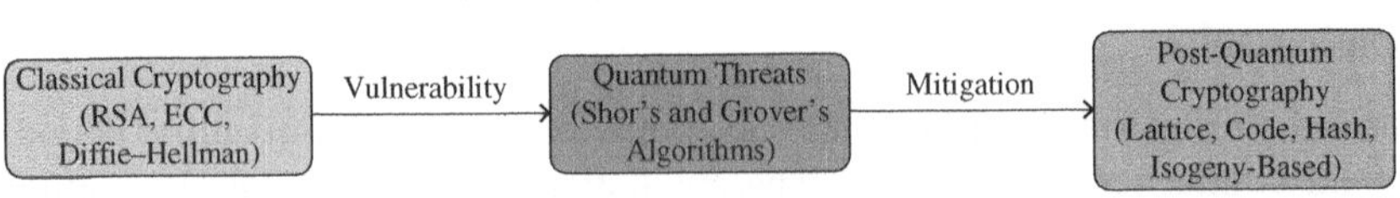

Figure 9.1 Evolution from Classical to Quantum-Safe Cryptography. "*Source:* Hewa Majeed Zangana"

mechanisms. This shows how vulnerabilities within conventional encryption (RSA and ECC) have led us into a transition toward lattice-based and hybrid models that promise to be quantum safe.

9.3 Quantum Computing and Its Threat to Cryptography

One of the most profound technological advancements in the twenty-first century is quantum computing. Its potential to revolutionize computation is only possible by the principles of superposition, entanglement and quantum interference. While classical computation works based on binary bits, quantum computation is with qubits which can exist in many states simultaneously, enabling for parallel operation of computing to give an exponential speedup to the computation of specific tasks as compared to a classical computer [5]. With countless fair prospects in optimization, communication, and AI, on the flip side, this potential can easily wipe out one of the most important systems in modern cryptography on which the world cannot seem to accept another focus.

At the bottom of this threat stand the quantum algorithms, further given special mention to Shor's and Grover's algorithms, which aim to break the crucial mathematical foundations of today's encryption methods. Shor's algorithm can smoothly factor large integers and undermine RSA and other public-key cryptosystems, while Grover's algorithm accelerates a brute-force search on keys, thus vastly reducing the strength of symmetric cryptography [1, 2]. Since organizations began to rely more and more on their digital infrastructure for secure communications, authentication, and protection of data, progress in quantum computing could be used to erode sensitive information currently in storage or transmission, also known as "store now, decrypt later."

Looking through further research work, it has also emerged that quantum computing has far-reaching impacts on blockchain, cloud settings, and emerging 6G networks [3, 10, 11]. Quantum algorithms observe success in accelerating search and optimization processes in wireless communications and federated learning systems [5, 7, 15]. Adversarial exploitation of these algorithms could help reduce the time complexity required for key discovery, data decryption, and protocol manipulation. This dual-use aspect of quantum technology presents its paradoxical role in cybersecurity with enhanced computational defense and an open back door for new attack vectors [13, 18].

The risk factor surrounding quantum communication and networking architectures amplifies in further ongoing development. Research focusing on quantum-enabled 6G communication and quantum-integrated optical networks shows the scope for highly secure communication as well as vulnerabilities due to hybrid system integration [8, 9, 12, 22]. Quantum key distribution (QKD) standards are promising for theoretically unbreakable encryption with secure communication from quantum entanglements. Yet, it appears there are questions related to scalability and side-channel attack resistance. The quantum-native communication system transition demands another look [16, 21] for new threats at the physical layer during the weeks of quantum interference and measurement errors.

Moving forward, quantum computing is anticipated to not only risk the confidentiality of data across distributed environments, including the Internet of Things (IoT), but may also hold a slightly ideal solution through quantum steganography to secure communications with smart IoT cities, placing intentions further in plain sight to exploit using reversible quantum encoding for hiding malicious data transfers [17]. Pathway to such communications includes application of hybrid quantum-assisted optimization models toward intelligent surfaces and network resource allocation for discrediting communication integrity or exposing private data about leaks [14, 15].

The intersection of quantum computing with machine learning, known as quantum machine learning (QML), compounds the situation. QML may speed up data classification and anomaly detection, but at the same time, it opens the door to adversarial attacks in the form of quantum models entirely bypassing state-of-the-art intrusion detection systems [13, 25]. Hybrid quantum-classical neural networking, as discussed by Zhang et al. [6], holds up well as a model for signal optimization and equally well for a worrying number of cryptanalysis attacks, as and when being twisted to that deadly purpose

Subsequent literature focuses largely on the integration of quantum computing with NNTs, distributed ledgers, and AI-driven infrastructures, indicating the dire need for serious quantum experimentation on the cryptography resilience [4, 19, 24]. These quantum-assisted architectures, not adequately secured, may act as entry points for large-scale data breaches or state-level espionage [12, 20]. All the more reason for a speedy development of cryptographic advancement that can withstand both attacks from the classical and quantum societies.

Quantum computing is a dual-edged blade that uplifts computing capabilities but threatens ciphering standards, as shown in Figure 9.2 with respect to quantum cryptography algorithms.

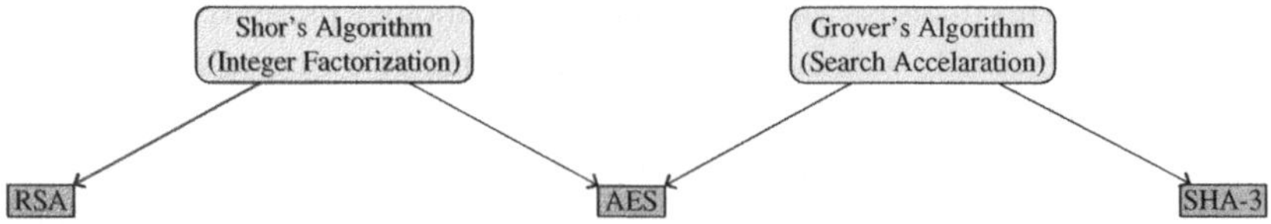

Figure 9.2 Quantum Algorithms and Their Impact on Classical Cryptography. "*Source:* Hewa Majeed Zangana"

In conclusion, while quantum computing will establish a revolutionized computation, optimization, and communication beyond all boundaries, it nevertheless threatens the validity of the very cryptographic infrastructural foundations that secure the digital ecosystem of today. From breaking existing traditional algorithms to exposing unknown weaknesses in hybrid networks, the quantum threat is both imminent and multifaceted. Addressing this challenge requires setting in clear terms an accelerated and concerted global effort toward developing post-quantum cryptographic standards, setting quantum-secure communication infrastructures and melding AI-driven predictive defense into the picture. Only by proactively changing course to the resulting paradigm shift will those in cybersecurity have any hope for the future of digital assets in quantum computing.

9.4 Foundations of Quantum-Safe (Post-Quantum) Cryptography

QSC, also referred to as PQC, is going to pave the next evolutionary milestone in digital safety intended to ensure that the protection of data maintains resistance against attacks set to be carried out by classical or quantum means. As quantum computing evolves rapidly, making the way for the urgent need of cryptographic schemes that hold arms against any computational capabilities of quantum machines, PQC is about algorithms whose security depends on the presumed intractability against quantum algorithms, such as Shor's or Grover's, thereby ensuring long-term confidentiality and integrity of data [1, 2].

Central to PQC is the notion of "quantum resilience," or the ability of cryptographic primitives to withstand decryption attempts by quantum computers. Simultaneously, post-quantum schemes do not use factorization or discrete logarithms but depend on those mathematical constructions that having positive resources are not solvable efficiently using known quantum algorithms. These include lattice-based, code-based, multivariate polynomial, hash-based, and isogeny-based cryptography systems [3, 4].

9.4.1 Lattice-Based Cryptography (LBC)

LBC is believed to have one of the brightest prospects for post-quantum security, thanks to strong mathematical foundations and flexibility. Its security is reliant upon a complexity of problems, such as the Learning With Errors and Shortest Vector Problem, which is known to withstand both classical and quantum attacks [1]. More than that, they make efficient implementations of real applications like digital signatures or encryption or even homomorphic computation possible. National Institute of Standards and Technology (NIST) has also put in place the lattice-based systems, CRYSTALS-Kyber and Dilithium, as prime PQC candidates toward global standardization [2].

9.4.2 Code-Based Cryptography

The progenitor of code-based cryptography, McEliece, relies entirely on the hardness of decoding random linear codes. McEliece has withstood the test of time in over 30 years of cryptanalysis and has remained robust against attacks of both classical and quantum essences. Thus, schemes of higher dimension tend to result in larger key sizes compared to RSA or ECC, but their robustness and simplicity render them powerful contenders for future data preservation, especially within quantum-integrated communication systems [11, 22].

9.4.3 Multivariate and Hash-Based Cryptography

Multivariate polynomial cryptography is founded on the hardness of solving systems of nonlinear equations over finite fields, a problem that has been shown to be Nondeterministic Polynomial time (NP)-hard and remains unsolved by known quantum algorithms [4, 17]. Hash-based cryptography, on the other hand, depends on the security of cryptographic hash functions to construct simple and verifiable digital signatures resistant to classical and quantum decryption. These approaches will be deployed for secure IoT frameworks, especially for the lightweight devices that need long-term security without too complex key exchanges [17, 19].

9.4.4 Isogeny-Based and Hybrid Cryptographic Models

Isogeny-based cryptography is the latest entrant into PQC and utilizes the mathematical properties of elliptic curves and their isogenies to create very compact and quantum-resistant key exchange protocols. Though still new, isogeny-based methods have significant potential for low-latency and resource-efficient systems in 6G and edge-cloud communications [11, 12]. Emerging now are hybrid classical-quantum models as interim solutions, linking classical encryption schemes with PQC algorithms in layered protection [10].

9.4.5 Quantum-Assisted Cryptographic Enhancements

Besides developing quantum-safe systems, scientists experiment with quantum-assisted cryptography-in fact, the idea is to have the benefit of their quantum principles for improving the security of classical systems instead of replacing them entirely with quantum ones. It includes both quantum-assisted optimization and secure key generation as well as quantum random number generation, which can significantly enhance the strength of the encryption process [5, 15]. Quantum-assisted digital signature services—which have been highlighted in optical and traditional software-defined networking (SDN) environments—demonstrate how classical cryptography could be enriched rather than rejected with quantum [8, 9].

9.4.6 Post-Quantum Security in Communication and Networking

QSC plays a key role in next-generation communication systems in relation to quantum-enabled 6G and NTNs. Al-Hraishawi et al. and Zhou et al. [14, 16] have researched how the application of post-quantum protocols could secure the data transport process from quantum-level interception. Hybrid quantum-classical schemes have also been applied for the protection of blockchain transactions and IoT ecosystems; thus, it can be assured that even with a computing-enabled quantum future, the distributed ledgers would remain tamper-proof [3, 10]. The blend of QML and PQC thus opens new frontiers in predictive threat modeling and adaptive encryption [13, 18, 25]. Quantum-assisted scheduling algorithms have now been developed in federated and distributed environments—a mechanism that optimizes the secure and efficient transmission of data [7]. There is thus a convergence in the near future that puts quantum computing as not just a threat but a strategic partner in advancing secure-digital ecosystems.

9.4.7 Toward a Quantum-Safe Ecosystem

A fully quantum-safe digital ecosystem should not only include cryptographic innovation; it should also involve systemic integration across hardware, software, and network layers. According to Mayukha and Vadivel [24], in transitioning between the classical world of cryptography to one with quantum awareness, interoperability, scalable key management, and international cooperation are indispensable. Such features, as identified by Hafiz and Hwang [20], enable probabilistic quantum state models to form probabilistic, flexible, adaptable, and security-responsive frameworks to emerging computational threats.

In the end, QSC is not only a reaction to the quantum threat; it is a forward-looking redesign of digital trust. This means that although computing will be ushered into a new paradigm defined by superposition and entanglement, information will remain intact, confidential, and authentic. By the collaboration of academia, industry, and standardization bodies, PQC will form the foundation upon which the future stands for cybersecurity with respect to the digital infrastructure of today to that which will be termed into the quantum era [21, 23].

Figure 9.3 depicts the major families of post-quantum cryptographic algorithms in terms of their mathematical foundation and primary use cases. This taxonomy

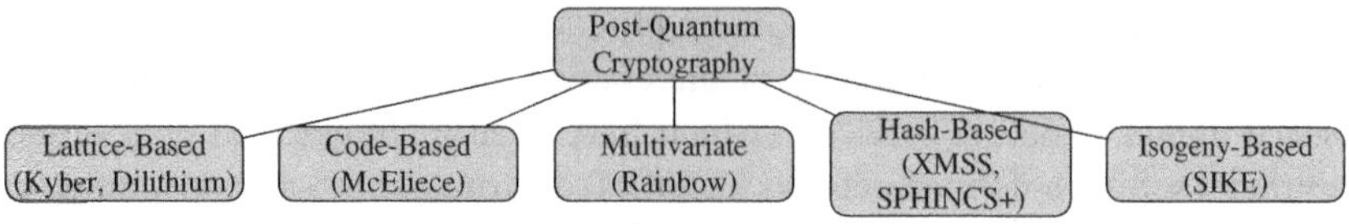

Figure 9.3 Taxonomy of Post-Quantum Cryptographic Algorithms. "*Source:* Hewa Majeed Zangana"

offers a concise visual reference for an understanding of the algorithmic diversity in the PQC landscape.

9.5 Quantum-Safe Cryptographic Algorithms and Techniques

Hence, QSC is considered the basis of a new security paradigm designed to protect critical aspects of data and communication in the post-quantum world. As quantum computers develop, the majority of asymmetric encryption systems, such as RSA and ECC, become more and more vulnerable to attacks from quantum cryptographic algorithms such as Shor's algorithm and Grover's algorithm, which can vastly reduce calculations of complexity. Hence, the design of such cryptographic schemes that resist all the power of quantum decryption capabilities has been a focal point for many researchers as well as practitioners. This section covers a thorough description of quantum-safe cryptographic algorithms, hybrid quantum-classical systems, and their integration across the communication network nodes and data infrastructures.

9.5.1 Post-Quantum Cryptographic Algorithms

PQC comprises classical algorithms that can resist quantum attacks but have great performance on modern hardware. According to Parida et al. [3], post-quantum distributed ledger technologies (PQ-DLTs) become more important as these systems still create a decentralized view of data integrity, even with threats from quantum enemies. So is Ref. [4] about quantum cryptology as a key infrastructure for big data. These authors strongly make a case for lattice-based, code-based, and hash-based cryptograms because their entropic depth does not rely on any computational hardness assumptions that quantum algorithms can easily break, making them ideal for next generations of security infrastructures.

Among the attributes that make some of them the best candidates for PQC algorithms is that they are LBC, robust, and scalable. Alauthman et al. [1] provide a comparative analysis among the classical-oriented and quantum-resistant methods, and their findings reveal that LBC and multivariate quadratic equations deliver the best trade-off between performance and resistance to quantum attack. Code-based cryptography is also another strong candidate because its hardness lies in the decoding of random linear codes, and it is already being considered for extensive secure data storage. Hash-based and Isogeny methods also create strong digital signatures and key exchanges resistant to quantum decryption ability [2].

9.5.2 Quantum-Assisted and Hybrid Cryptographic Techniques

While PQC concerns itself with adapting classical cryptography to a post-quantum environment, quantum-assisted cryptography complements classical methods using quantum phenomena to enhance the generation of keys, authentication, and data integrity. Advances in quantum-assisted digital signature services are offered in Refs. [8, 9] that specifically target SDN environments reveal methods of using the new normal in authentication systems. Thus, this paper illustrates what could happen in terms of efficiency and security if hybrid classical-quantum infrastructures enabled communication in quantum-integrated optical networks.

As Liu et al. [10] demonstrated a model for hybrid communication that incorporated classical protocols of blockchain on top of QKD, forming a stronger trust management mechanism and protection against quantum-enabled adversaries. Thus, this hybridization technique yields some synergy since it aligns with Botsinis et al. [5], who underlines the necessity of resource and cryptographic weight balancing in hybrid quantum/classical computing. Such architectures guarantee the compatibility of legacy digital infrastructures with their gradualization of future quantum elements.

9.5.3 QKD and Secure Communication Channels

Undoubtedly one of the most mature and widely adopted quantum-safe technologies, QKD guarantees that any attempt at eavesdropping can be distinguished from within the laws of quantum physics, thus ensuring complete confidentiality of communication. Al-Hraishawi et al. [14] researched QKD's role in NTNs, in which quantum technologies make secure satellite-based communication possible. Zhou et al. [16] reflected on developments in quantum-native communications, particularly regarding the integration challenges related to QKD into terrestrial and extraterrestrial infrastructures.

As Mohammed et al. [12] explored how quantum-assisted wireless systems and Quantum 6G architectures can use QKD and quantum teleportation to secure ultra-fast data transmission channels. The studies indicate that quantum-based cryptographic primitives are not confined to encryption but extend to authentication and privacy-preserving computation. Wang and Rahman [22] expand this concept when presenting quantum-enabled 6G networks using quantum error correcting and base-entanglement encryption for end-to-end secure communication.

9.5.4 Quantum Algorithms and Optimization for Cryptographic Strength

Emerging quantum optimization algorithms have also contributed a lot to strengthening cryptographic resilience. Botsinis et al. [5], and a few other papers discuss how quantum search and quantum optimization potentially contribute to the improvement of network security and resource allocation. Lim et al. [15] showed the applicability of quantum-assisted optimization in combinatorial design for reorganizable intelligent surfaces. It indirectly contributes to a more secure electromagnetic communication environment. Similarly, Hafiz and Hwang [20] proposed a probabilistic model of quantum states which could potentially pave the way for novel classical data protection strategies that fork new paths toward cryptographic key distribution, obfuscation, and others.

Wei et al. [7] present a quantum-assisted scheduling algorithm for federated learning systems, thus enhancing distributed security management through quantum-optimized decision-making. Zhang et al. [6] extended this framework by positioning hybrid quantum-classical neural networks to downlink the beamforming optimization process, thus taking care of confidentiality at the same time as assuring integrity in wireless networks. Collectively, these advancements highlight that quantum-assisted computation can further improve cryptographic robustness beyond conventional designs.

9.5.5 Quantum Steganography and Data Concealment

Newfangled fields of quantum-safe communication include quantum steganography, a method by which data is hidden inside quantum states to avoid detection. In their work, Biswas et al. [17] propose a reversible decoding and encryption mechanism to improve IoT communication for smart cities, enhancing data privacy through quantum encoding. Upon the advent of a quantum attack, this method assures that the data remains unrecognizable without the knowledge of the corresponding quantum key or state, providing a multilayered defense against adversarial exploitation.

9.5.6 QML for Cryptographic Enhancement

QML is changing the paradigms for cryptographic systems to learn and adapt against varied contemporary threats. Narottama and Nawaz et al. [13, 25] explain how QML can be used to detect intrusion patterns against quantum standards and optimize cryptographic key management in 6G and IoT networks. Rishiwal et al. [18] further synergize ML and quantum frameworks to predict and mitigate probable vulnerabilities in IoT systems, thus creating intelligent adaptive cryptographic ecosystems.

As Matsumine et al. [21] stress the implementation of quantum algorithms for physical layer security, whereby QML-based encryption schemes are able to adapt in real time to the dynamics of network conditions. Mayukha and Vadivel [24] discuss the transition that pertains to classical to quantum networks, regarding the role of AI to mediate between both and assure interoperability and future-proofing of cryptographic infrastructure.

9.5.7 Quantum-Secure Networking and Interconnect Models

With the evolution of global infrastructure, development of quantum-secure networking models for securing large-scale interconnected systems is increasingly gaining traction. Ngobeni and Kabaso [19] present a quantum-secure signaling model for next-generation interconnects and roaming networks, addressing Narrowband Internet of Things (NB-IoT) traffic and secure signaling between network layers. Their model is an illustration of how applying quantum cryptography can safeguard the foundational communication protocols within critical infrastructures, aligning with the expansive vision articulated by Zhao et al. [23], who comprehensively survey quantum computing in wireless communications, inclusive of both theoretical underpinnings and practical implementation of quantum-safe communication protocols.

9.6 Integrating QSC in AI-Driven Security Systems

The merging of AI and QSC technologies represents an evolution that fundamentally transforms modern cybersecurity architectures. As quantum computing advances, it not only poses a challenge to the traditional cryptographic models but also opens up avenues for intelligent automation, optimization, and adaptive defense mechanisms. AI systems, with the hand of Machine Learning (ML), Deep Learning (DL), and QML, are instrumental in solving the problems of complexity management and scalability for post-quantum cryptographic operations. The integration of QSC with these intelligent systems would provide a basis for proactive threat detection, secure communications, and autonomous cyber-resilience in both classical and quantum network environments.

9.6.1 AI and Quantum-Safe Encryption Working Together

QSC provides confidence that encryption algorithms will remain secure under quantum attacks. Alauthman et al. [1] suggest that using AI might improve QSC to develop adaptive encryption frameworks that respond to real-time threats. AI-based optimization algorithms could promote such systems to adopt the most right quantum-safe scheme according to contextual risk assessment based on lattice- or code-based encryption. Majdoubi et al. [4] stress that quantum cryptology is critical within big data ecosystems, and AI-enabled automation can scale and compute the overhead of post-quantum algorithms seamlessly.

As Liu et al. [10] maintain that hybrid quantum-classical architectures use AI for the interoperability between classical encryption protocols and emerging quantum layers. Reinforcement learning and neural optimization via these architectures consider performance and security across distributed infrastructures for robust end-to-end protection.

9.6.2 AI QKD and Authentication

QKD remains one of the most established technologies in quantum-safe communication. Giorgetti et al. and Paduanelli et al. [8, 9] propose AI-optimized quantum-assisted digital signature systems, capable of autonomously managing key exchange and authentication across SDNs. The integration of AI enables these systems to detect key anomalies, predict potential intrusions, and adjust key refresh intervals in real time.

Both Al-Hraishawi et al. [14] and Zhou et al. [16] reiterate that an AI-QKD combination enhances resilience against interception and data leakage in non-terrestrial and quantum-native networks. The applications of predictive ML models on quantum noise behavior can assist AI in optimizing the distribution of entanglement and the stability of signals. Using AI has been discussed by Ali et al. [11] on a quantum framework for the 6G communication, where intelligent agents manage QKD layers for ultra-secure, low-latency wireless systems.

9.6.3 QML for Security Intelligence

The ideas behind QML could serve to hasten security analysis by AI while strengthening it with cryptography. According to Narottama et al. and Nawaz et al. [13, 25], QML algorithms are found to be superior to classical ML in patterning complex threats and optimizing encryption key management in large networks. The systems apply quantum-enhanced feature extraction and pattern recognition to detect anomalies that classical models might miss.

The hybrid AI–quantum security model proposed by Rishiwal et al. [18] specifically targets the QML adaptation of cryptographic parameters concerning real-time telemetry of the network in IoT environments, where adaptive intelligence is found to be indispensable in protecting billions of devices connected and vulnerable to quantum attacks. Matsumine et al. [21] further develop these principles at the physical layer to show that quantum algorithms can strengthen AI-powered intrusion prevention systems at the signal level by allowing attacks over the wireless channel to be detected and neutralized instantaneously.

9.6.4 Quantum-Assisted Optimization in AI Security Frameworks

Optimization, a fundamental stage of AI-aided security, is now broadening with quantum computing. Botsinis et al. [5] reported that quantum-assisted multi-objective optimization may come in handy for the maximization of network resource allocation coupled with encryption efficiency. Lim et al. [15] realize and further extend the integration through quantum-assisted combinatorial optimization, this time focused on intelligent surfaces in electromagnetic environments, achieving adaptable cryptographic shielding against eavesdropping.

As Wei et al. [7] propose a quantum-assisted scheduling algorithm for federated learning, they show how quantum processors can speed up AI model training while keeping data secret. Alongside this, embedding QSC protocols would guarantee sensitive model parameters remain secure even when distributed during training across untrusted nodes. Zhang et al. [6] complement this with hybrid quantum-classical neural networks that autonomously optimize wireless encryption parameters of security and energy efficiency.

9.6.5 Integrating Quantum Cryptography with AI-Driven Data Governance

AI-driven data governance systems can integrate QSC to ensure end-to-end integrity and privacy across distributed databases and blockchain networks. Parida et al. [3] identify PQ-DLTs as vital for ensuring blockchain immutability under quantum conditions. AI algorithms can predict vulnerabilities in smart contracts and dynamically apply quantum-resistant digital signatures to protect them.

As Liu et al. [10] develop a hybrid classical-quantum blockchain framework, in which AI modules monitor cryptographic strength and adapt consensus mechanisms based on entropy analysis. This integration is aligned with Vasani et al. [2], who suggest that AI-enabled post-quantum governance models will become essential for maintaining digital sovereignty in critical sectors like finance, defense, and health.

9.6.6 AI for Quantum-Secure Networking and System Integration

The application of AI in quantum-secure networking enables its autonomous configuration, routing, system integration, and anomaly detection in a complex communication environment. Ngobeni and Kabaso [19] introduce a quantum-secure signaling model for next-generation roaming networks, which uses AI algorithms to predict potential link-level threats and autonomously reroute traffic through secure quantum channels. Mohammed et al. [12] and Wang and Rahman [22] also study an AI-assisted Quantum 6G architecture emphasizing adaptive security mechanisms that detect and counteract quantum noise and channel interference.

In their report, Mayukha and Vadivel [24] discuss the migration from classical to quantum networks by emphasizing AI's orchestration of hybrid settings for a seamless and secure transition. In such scenarios, AI agents function as "cryptographic controllers," constantly verifying quantum-safe parameters and detecting any discrepancies in real time. Hafiz and Hwang [20] advanced this paradigm with the introduction of probabilistic models that afford the application of AI to emulate the distribution of quantum states for predictive error correction pertaining to data security.

9.6.7 Quantum Steganography and AI Enhanced Concealment

Quantum steganography, the hiding of information inside quantum states, highly benefits from optimizations based on AI. Biswas et al. [17] present an AI-augmented quantum steganographic platform for IoT communications in smart cities, allowing dynamic modifications in strategies for encoding based on environmental variables. Such integration ensures reversibility, minimal distortion, and resilience from both classical and quantum attacks.

AI-assisted decision engines would ascertain the optimal embedding rates, thereby balancing data secrecy against transmission efficiency. Such intelligent coordination is aligned with [16] proposition of quantum-native communication systems equipped with autonomous security management powered by AI and QML.

9.6.8 Toward Cognitive, Self-Healing Quantum-Safe Security Systems

The ultimate integration of QSC into AI systems aims to build cognitive, self-healing cybersecurity architectures that continuously learn from adversarial acts, reconfigure cryptographic policies, and evolve with no human intervention. Rishiwal et al. [18] assert that the adaptation of AI and the robustness of quantum cryptography provide the notion on which the future of autonomous cyber defense will rest.

Such self-healing systems utilize QML-based pattern recognition to detect zero-day quantum attacks and invoke quantum-assisted optimization for immediate

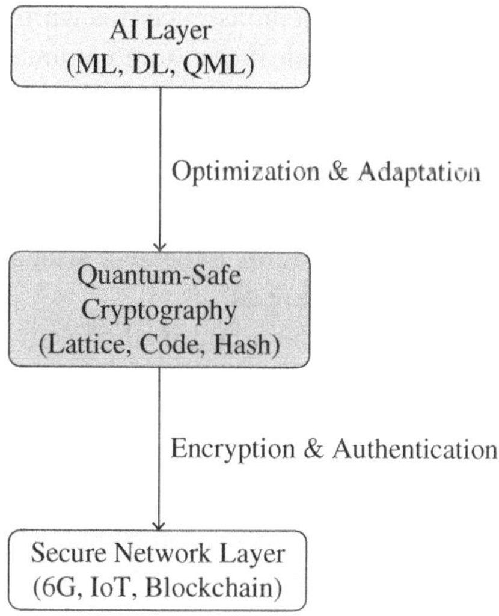

Figure 9.4 Integration Framework for AI and Quantum-Safe Cryptography. "*Source:* Hewa Majeed Zangana"

recovery. By linking these capabilities, organizations can build infrastructures that resist quantum threats while carrying out anticipatory defense: evolving their protection strategies against adapting digital and quantum adversaries with an adaptive infrastructure platform.

The framework demonstrated in Figure 9.4 combines AI-driven optimization and quantum-safe cryptographic systems. It shows how machine learning, QML, and predictive analytics work together to strengthen encryption, automate key management, and provide proactive defense.

9.7 Hybrid Cryptographic Models for Transitioning to Post-Quantum Security

The most significant transition in modern-day cybersecurity is from classical cryptographic infrastructures to PQC. Purely quantum-safe algorithms are still under standardization, while organizations face practical barriers to migrating large-scale systems dependent on legacy encryption. To fill this gap, hybrid cryptographic models combine classical and post-quantum techniques and are therefore a viable and flexible approach to ensure continuity of security during the quantum transition. These hybrid systems permit the gradual incorporation of quantum-resistant mechanisms while ensuring interoperability, performance, and compliance with existing standards.

These models are based upon the hybrid encryption paradigm, whereby both a classical and a post-quantum key exchange mechanism are running in parallel.

Liu et al. [10] demonstrated this within the blockchain environment by integrating hybrid classical-quantum communication protocols with the bills of blockchain integrity, all while paving the way for quantum scenarios in the near future. Such dual-mode systems ensure that even if classical algorithms get compromised by quantum attacks, the post-quantum layer will still maintain confidentiality of the data. On the other hand, Parida et al. [3] argued for post-quantum DLTs, suggesting a hybrid mix to balance scalability, trust, and resilience to both classical and quantum threats.

An equally important methodology for hybrid cryptographic modeling is the networking perspective. Botsinis et al. [5] surveyed practical hybrid quantum/classical computing frameworks that allow real-world deployment of quantum-safe protocols without interrupting the existing communication architecture. This layered model has been pushed further with the quantum-assisted optimization and secure channel management. As an instance, Alauthman et al. [1] compared the role of classical versus quantum in cybersecurity, showing how the utilization of hybrid cryptographic settings would minimize the overhead while maintaining forward secrecy. In wireless and 6G systems, Ali et al. and Wang and Rahman [11, 22] had put forth that hybrid cryptographic structures are most important in providing a balance to quantum-enabled communication networks in ultra-low latency and high throughput demands.

From a systems engineering perspective, quantum-assisted mechanisms provide computational advantages, strengthening hybrid cryptography. Botsinis et al. [5] looked at how quantum search and optimization could improve resource allocation and route security on communication networks. Such contributions build a case for the combination of classical encryption layers with quantum optimization processes designed to adaptively manipulate key management, routing, and scheduling in real time. Lim et al. [15] would also show how quantum-assisted combinatorial optimization could be applied to RISs, which enhances the robustness of physical-layer encryption in hybrid systems.

AI and Machine learning in steering hybrid cryptographic systems are gradually becoming more envisaged. Rishiwal et al. [18] discussed how ML and quantum computing could be used in IoT networks, demonstrating how AI-based analytics could predict vulnerabilities while dynamically adapting the parameters of hybrid cryptography. Narottama et al. [13] and Nawaz et al. [25] have also stressed the use of QML in ensuring secure and adaptive communication in next-generation wireless systems. By embedding AI at the core of hybrid cryptographic management, organizations can achieve autonomous key rotation, real-time anomaly detection, and resilience against quantum-capable adversaries.

Quantum-assisted signatures and authentication comprise another necessary element in hybrid models. The authors Giorgetti et al. [8] and Paduanelli et al. [9], proposed a quantum-assisted digital signature service built on software-defined, quantum-integrated optical networks, whereby classical SDN controllers and QKD devices may interoperate. This solution enables hybrid authentication models resilient to conventional and advanced quantum attacks, a premise extended by Ngobeni and Kabaso [19], wherein they evaluate a quantum-secure signaling paradigm for future roaming networks and NB-IoT traffic over an Internetwork Packet Exchange (IPX), demonstrating the applicability of such architectures in real hybrid cryptographic deployments in adherence to telecommunications standards and interoperability frameworks worldwide.

Hybridization across layers of the network further boosts the overall robustness of a system. Matsumine et al. [21] delved into the application of quantum algorithms to access security at physical-layer levels and proposed this implementation with classical modulation and coding techniques to form a comprehensive multilayer defense. Hafiz and Hwang [20] also postulated on the probabilistic models of quantum states, particularly for classical data security, showing the possibility that this could enable the utilization of quantum randomness as an additional cryptographic entropy source within hybrid systems. This resonates with Majdoubi et al. [4], who discussed how quantum cryptology could protect big data ecosystems by combining QKD with classical privacy-preserving techniques.

Furthermore, network optimization and orchestration in hybrid environments are strengthened by quantum-assisted scheduling algorithms. Wei et al. [7] came up with a quantum-assisted scheduling algorithm for federated learning that shows how a hybrid network could efficiently distribute computational resources across distributed nodes. Zhang et al. [6] proposed hybrid quantum-classical neural networks that beamform optimization, with classical deep learning models cooperating with quantum circuits for secure wireless communications. These approaches put forth interoperability and adaptability in hybrid cryptographic systems, particularly in a dynamic multi-domain environment.

Next-generation hybrid applications of cryptography include NTNs and quantum-integrated 6G. Al-Hraishawi et al. [14] profiled NTNs considering the unique prospects afforded by the interplay of quantum technology with satellites, arguing for a hybrid security framework that uses both satellite QKD and classical encryption to provide round-the-clock security. In keeping with this, Mohammed et al. [12] elaborated the idea to introduce quantum-assisted wireless architectures for the 6G systems, wherein hybrid cryptography gained prominence in ensuring low latency and utmost security within decentralized topologies. Vasani et al. [2] and Zhou et al. [16] also referred to the trend of future communication toward being purely quantum, and in this transition, hybrid systems act as bridges that enable both infrastructures-phased coexistence at the classical and fully quantum levels.

Lastly, the foreseeable future of hybrid cryptographic models is conditioned by the need for a smooth transition and interoperability within global systems. In this sense, Mayukha and Vadivel [24] argued that hybrid would be the most important method to ensure an adequate and secure transition from classical to quantum networks, addressing transition requirements under complex industrial and governmental frameworks. Thus, as hybrid frameworks grow, their adaptive, modular design will provide the foundation for quantum-safe cybersecurity architectures to support secure communication, authentication, and data management in the post-quantum world.

In conclusion, hybrid cryptographic models form the bridge between the classical present and the quantum future by combining the demonstrated strengths of existing cryptographic primitives with resilience against post-quantum attacks and the intelligence of AI-driven orchestration. As illustrated across domains—from wireless communication, IoT, and optical networks to blockchain—these models actually represent a pragmatic and scalable pathway toward full quantum-safe security readiness.

9.8 Quantum-Safe Security for Emerging Technologies

The astounding progress in quantum technology will lay down new security principles that are bound to be reformulated forever in emerging quantum hybridization with 6G systems, the IoT, big data analytics, NTN, and smart-city systems. As the second party matures (meaning: quantum hardware and quantum computing algorithms), quantum-safe security mechanisms are essential now for privacy, integrity, and resilience among all the possibilities entailed by quantum computing. Quantum-safe security is being presumed to protect future communication and data infrastructures from the cryptanalyst power of bigger-than-ever quantum processors by weighing their capabilities so as to strengthen the protection in their eroding state.

For quantum-integrated next-generation wireless networks and 6G systems themselves, hybridization- and quantum-assisted cryptosystems are very crucial for end-to-end security. The authors in Ref. [11] investigated and presented a futuristic view of quantum technologies coupled with 6G systems, highlighting quantum-resistant encryption and key distribution based on entangled states for security vulnerabilities in existing 6G security layers. Furthermore, Wang and Rahman [22] brought forth insights into some opportunities and challenges of employing Q-based 6G, stressing secure synchronization between a quantum and a classical layer to uphold data integrity and latency efficiency. Ending Internet Engineering Task Force (IETF) with Mohammed et al. [12] proposed quantum-assisted architectures for wireless systems, demonstrating how post-quantum cryptographic primitives and QKD can be combined with conventional wireless communication resources for building resilient low-latency networks.

However, the IoT world remains one of the trickiest environments to be rendered quantum-safe due to its very unique, dispersed, and too massive-enough-to-track-nuances resource constraint sort of setup. Biswas et al. [17] presented quantum steganography in favor of securing IoT communications, using reversible decoding and working around encryption for smart city systems. In the same vein, Rishiwal et al. [18] targeted the IoT networks in a piece that explores some sort of partnership between quantum computing and machine learning. It pointed to very promising ways that AI-modified quantum models are more efficient at detecting network threats than classical and nascent quantum models. Ngobeni and Kabaso [19] went on further to prove the quantum-secure signaling models connected to next-generation interconnect and roaming networks, underscoring the fact for the necessity of quantum safety for privacy and authentication over the IoT and NB-IoT traffic infrastructure.

Increasingly, quantum-safe security needs to be in force within the area of NTN satellite communication systems. Al-Hraishawi et al. [14] have given a perception about how quantum technologies and NTNs intervene with each other. Hybrid schemes that bring the quantum aspect can ensure secure communication between the satellites and the ground. This statement finds support from a research perspective of Ref. [16], where the evolution toward quantum-native communication systems is presented: quantum repeaters and teleportation protocols are what build the trust in next-generation networks. These quantum-enhanced offerings on the NTNs are considered giant leaps in laying down veritably secure communication networks encompassing both quantum and downright terrestrial infrastructures.

For large data transmission networks and distributed ledger systems, cryptographic foundations for PQC and hybrid mechanisms are now increasingly being considered the linchpins of trust. Majdoubi et al. [4] introspected the applicability of quantum cryptology tools in a big-data environment and respected the how with regard to QKD, and quantum proved its mettle with quantum-proof encryption in preventing the data from being hacked ... by an army of qubits. Likewise, Parida et al. [3] conducted a systematic review of PQ-DLTs and proposed lattice-based encryption and hybrid protocols for blockchain communities to ensure their immutability and future resilience. Hags of Qi also supported the concept with a proposal to the hybrid communication protocol, combining classical and quantum encryption layers for the blockchain management, so that the ledger may still exist inviolable even in the midst of any quantum attack.

Quantum-safe security within optical and telecommunication infrastructures would directly be synonymous with the integrity of data communication. The research by Giorgetti et al. [8] has suggested a generalized quantum-assisted digital signature service for use in SDN-style quantum-integrated optical networks that assure secure communication all the way up and down the multi-domain with the minimal computational overhead. Similar works from Paduanelli et al. [9] have shown a prototype continuation of this digital signature service, indicating a step closer toward the practical implementation of quantum-secure authentication in optical networks. The work by Botsinis et al. [5] in this area also outlines implementations of bifurcation quantum/classical computer mechanisms, which support the seamless integration between legacy and quantum-enabled network functions.

Quantum algorithms are incorporating innovative approaches to defensive capabilities against eavesdropping in smart electromagnetic and physical-layer environments. For instance, Lim et al. [15] applied quantum-assisted combinatorial optimization to RISs, allowing adaptive electromagnetic environments to secure themselves automatically against eavesdropping. In similar strands of research, Matsumine et al. [21] studied quantum algorithms for physical-layer security, mainly by identifying venues to embedding quantum resilience directly into modulation and signal generation processes. Botsinis et al. [5] have also contributed to the relatively new landscape of quantum optimization. Their works on multi-objective optimization and quantum search algorithms advance security by providing ever-dynamic, energy-efficient networks from which to launch.

Another very major area of development with quantum AI and ML is the building of quantum-safe systems. In their research, Narottama et al. [13] discussed QML foundations in next-generation wireless communications by explaining how QML will enhance anomaly detection, encryption key generation, and adaptive routing. The latest in QML applications in 6G networks has been reviewed in Ref. [25]. The authors assert that the AI-quantum hybrids will serve as proactive defense mechanisms against threats. The extent of this idea is fully realized by Zhang et al. [6], who exhibited hybrid quantum-classical neural networks for beam-forming optimization, showing how ML and quantum computing can cooperatively advance the delivery of secure signals in wireless environments.

From a systems-level point of view, quantum-safe architectures would require constructing interoperable adaptive security designs. For example, Hafiz and Hwang [20] model for probabilistic quantum states has added randomness and entropy to classical data protection schemes. Quantum networks have the secure transition to and from classical infrastructures to quantum-native ecosystems, as pointed out by Mayukha and Vadivel [24]. Vasani et al. [2] also reported the orientations of new industries in quantum communication and cryptography to meet the demands of an evolving Industry 5.0 environment linked to cross-domain applications of AI, big data, and autonomous systems.

Federated and distributed intelligence is now adding quantum-safe methods to the portfolio across its features. For example, Wei et al. [7] proposed a quantum-assisted scheduling algorithm in federated learning so that it enables secure data-sharing and collaborative model training without exposing raw information. This is proof that distributed AI systems could benefit from quantum resilience. Hence, the learning processes will be tamper-resistant and privacy-preserving over the global networks.

Quantum-safe security is, thus, not a reactionary form of defense to the emerging technology but instead forms the very foundation and will cause next-generation connectivity, computation, and data management to happen. Through PQC, hybrid encryption frameworks, AI-assisted modeling in quantum environments, and secure communication protocols, technological scaffolding is being constructed for a robust and resilient quantum future. The combination of quantum communication with distributed intelligence and the advent of 6G systems will mark a true new paradigm in security, wherein confidentiality, integrity, and availability could still be sustained even against quantum-capable adversaries.

9.9 Policy, Standards, and Regulatory Perspectives

With the development of quantum computing, there is an urgent need for global policymakers and regulators to create frameworks that support secure transitions from classical to quantum-safe infrastructures. The extraordinary computational powers of quantum machines threaten to render conventional encryption obsolete, calling for a coordinated global response in policy, standardization, and compliance mechanisms. Now, governments, international standards organizations, and industry partnerships are working to develop technical and regulatory guidelines for quantum-resilient architectures that preserve interoperability, privacy, and ethical accountability across digital ecosystems.

From a policy view, national security strategies and data protection rules must inform the acceptance of QSC. According to Alauthman et al. [1], it is of great importance for real-time policymakers to sort transition priorities for industries most vulnerable to quantum attacks through the comparative assessment of classical versus quantum techniques. Also, Ali et al. [11] bring up the need for quantum technologies in next-generation 6G communication systems, which creates the requirement for legal frameworks that deal with cross-border data security and QKD governance. In terms of these sectors, healthcare, finance, and defense are particularly pertinent as their requirements for data longevity far outlast the expectations of quantum threats.

In parallel with the development of standards, global organizations like National Institute of Standards and Technology (NIST), International Organization for Standardization (ISO), and International Telecommunication Union (ITU) initiated organized efforts to standardize PQC algorithms. Parida et al. [3] systematically analyze PQ-DLTs, stressing the importance of standardizing decentralized technologies against quantum-level attacks. Similarly, Giorgetti et al. [8] and Paduanelli et al. [9] show the advancements of quantum-assisted digital signature services aligned with the new standards for networking and demonstrate how standardized cryptographic primitives can be integrated into optical and SDN.

The regulatory component concentrates on compliance, accountability, and governance mechanisms so that quantum and hybrid systems are deployed securely. Vasani et al. [2] identify the need for layered regulatory models that govern hybrid quantum-classical environments, balancing innovation with operational transparency that safely allows organizations to transition without contravening existing privacy laws or security mandates. In addition, Ngobeni and Kabaso [19] highlight the role of quantum-secure signaling models in next-generation networks, suggesting that regulators incorporate quantum certification standards into telecom compliance frameworks for the management of roaming and interconnect security for NB-IoT and IPX systems.

The cross-domain nature of quantum technologies creates a real challenge for regulation. Al-Hraishawi et al. [14] suggest mutual engagement of quantum and NTNs and advocate for forming multi-sectoral policy coalitions to address quantum risk in satellite and aerospace communications. In the same fashion, Zhou et al. [16] discuss the rise of quantum-native communication systems, for which adaptable legal and ethical frameworks will be required concerning data sovereignty and encryption lifecycle management. To tackle this puzzle, policymakers are encouraged to globally harmonize quantum security standards with an eye toward ensuring compatibility between domestic and foreign quantum infrastructures.

Ethics and compliance considerations still remain at the heart of quantum regulations. Hafiz and Hwang [20] offer probabilistic quantum-state models which will enhance data security and provoke questions concerning transparency and auditability of cryptographic systems in environments of probabilistic encryption. Majdoubi et al. [4] argue that with quantum cryptology becoming a central aspect of big data security, there must be ethical oversight to avert abuse and ensure fairness in data-driven decision-making. Therefore, regulatory bodies must amend data protection frameworks, such as the General Data Protection Regulation (GDPR) and California Consumer Privacy Act (CCPA), to accommodate quantum data processing and encryption transparency requirements.

Also, quantum regulations are interlinked with AI-driven governance as well as quantum-enhanced decision systems. As per Refs. [13, 18], the convergence of ML and quantum computing in securing IoT networks requires ethical frameworks to manage AI-based automation in quantum security processes. QML introduces new compliance challenges, as discussed by Nawaz et al. [25], including explainability, algorithmic fairness, and auditability in quantum-enhanced AI models. Therefore, the expectation is that the regulators would set the audit standards to supervise quantum-AI systems for their adherence to security, and ethical benchmarks.

In the fields of telecommunications and networking, great work is being done in integrating quantum frameworks into emerging technologies in a policy-driven manner. The physical layer quantum algorithms are explored in Ref. [21], where it becomes clear that policy mechanisms can facilitate the secure deployment of quantum features into wireless protocols. In Refs. [12, 15], they further highlight the importance of issuing legal and compliance frameworks to support the said advancements, as in real-time systems, spectrum use, key exchange, and encryption methods will clearly need to be endorsed in order to be adequate.

From the perspective of the regulatory focus on the transitional character of hybrid quantum-classical protocols, Zhang et al. [6] and Liu et al. [10] report secure hybrid proposals of quantum protocols over classical blockchains and neural networks, which would recommend global auditing standards for hybrid encryption management. Botsinis et al. [5] argue that the complex trade-offs between efficiency, scalability, and regulatory compliance need optimization-based policy tools to negotiate among quantum-assisted communication systems.

International standardization efforts are increasingly converging on correlated governance for quantum communication. Wang and Rahman [22] argue the case for coordinating policies for quantum-enabled 6G networks, while Wei et al. [7] and Biswas et al. [17] complement this by pointing out that federated learning and IoT quantum security must be within interoperable encryption and privacy standards. They should thus have competitive equality, as Ref. [24] endorse a perspective of the secure transition that justifies the better benefits of quantum networks against realistically expectable policies, so that security-by-design can remain the principle foundation in the quantum era.

In summary, the policy, standards, and regulatory landscape for QSC is rapidly maturing but remains fragmented across regions and industries. Coordinated governance models-supported by ethical oversight, international standardization, and AI-integrated compliance systems-will be of prime significance in ensuring that quantum systems are deployed in a secure, responsible, and transparent way in any future-proof cybersecurity framework.

9.10 Challenges and Limitations

The promising yet complicated transition to quantum-safe cybersecurity faces multiple technical, operational, and strategic challenges. Even after the expansion of significant research, there are various intrinsic limitations that are still hindering the extensive implementation and use of quantum technologies across communication networks, IoT ecosystems, and data security frameworks. Understanding such challenges is extremely important to guide realistic deployment strategies for future development in this area.

9.10.1 Computational and Hardware Limitations

Quantum computing hardware is at its infancy, with the era of actually available fault-tolerant quantum devices still not in sight. According to Ref. [5], present quantum-assisted optimization methods are limited through qubit coherence times, error rates, and their restricted scalability, which directly affect the performance of these methods as far as their usability for secure communications is concerned. Ref. [1], on the other hand, argues that hybrid quantum-classical computing systems face performance bottlenecks because of limited interfacing efficiency between classical processors and their quantum counterparts. Such limitations affect both encryption operations and computing performance metrics in post-quantum cryptographic implementations.

9.10.2 Algorithmic Complexity and Standardization Challenges

Numerous post-quantum algorithms have made their appearance in the literature, but their complexity, resource needs, and challenges to integration have kept them from being put into widespread use. Alauthman et al. [1] explain that replacing classical cryptographic protocols with substitutes resistant to quantum attacks is not straightforward, involving careful considerations regarding interoperability and computational overhead. Parida et al. [3] also claim that post-quantum security algorithms for DLTs are extremely complex, presented with performance issues that further complicate standardization efforts. In addition, Liu et al. [10] show that protocols for managing hybrid classical-quantum blockchains will require accurate calibrations if both security and scalability are to be maintained in such systems.

9.10.3 Network and Communication Limitations

Quantum communication technologies-think QKD or quantum-secure signaling-have operational limitations in the actual real-world network. Pointing out the signaling models for NB-IoT traffic over IPX, Ngobeni and Kabaso [19] describe the limitations caused by latency, synchronization, and channel noise, making large-scale deployment less feasible. Al-Hraishawi et al. [14] mention the same problems of connecting quantum technology with NTNs, from the perspective of atmospheric interference, mobility of satellites, and coordination in networks. Thus, these limits hinder the practicability of quantum-enhanced systems for use in IoT, 6G, and hybrid-cloud environments.

9.10.4 Security and Vulnerability Concerns

Although quantum technologies confer an upgraded level of security features, they also bear witness to new vulnerabilities. Biswas et al. [17] have revealed that cutting-edge quantum steganography and reversible encoding techniques for IoT may still be susceptible to implementation-level attacks. Hafiz and Hwang [20] show that probabilistic quantum-state models for classical data security, while theoretically sound, must be stringently validated to deter misconfigurations and exploitations. Rishiwal et al. [18] add that with the introduction of some AI into IoT networks, there is the possibility of opening up attack surfaces that are challenging to predict or secure, encompassing adversarial quantum attacks and side-channel threats.

9.10.5 Integration with Emerging Technologies

Integrating quantum systems with other seemingly emerging technologies such as 6G networks, federated learning, and RISs adds an extra level of complications into the integration. The authors in Refs. [11, 15, 22] illustrate the optimization of quantum-assisted operations in the direction of wireless networks and smart electromagnetic environments in terms of resource allocation, scheduling, and channel estimation strategies, which are rather sophisticated. Further challenges, as highlighted by Ref. [7], include those in federated learning within distributed quantum-classical networks, which include synchronization, privacy preservation, and maintenance of quantum state coherence. Hybrid neural networks described by Zhang et al. [6] are also said to suffer from limitations in balancing classical processing latency against quantum-assisted optimization.

9.10.6 Policy, Regulatory, and Ethical Challenges

Beyond technical constraints, regulation and ethicality of quantum systems has complications. According to Mayukha and Vadivel [24], in view of the global fragmentations, a lot must still happen at various levels to establish a common policy and an adequate range of compliance frameworks upon which to build the quantum networks. Vasani et al. [2] emphasized that there must be ethical oversight when dealing with quantum encryption, while Giorgetti et al. and Paduanelli et al. [8, 9] stated that digital signature service must be guided by legal and operational standards. These considerations add layers of uncertainty and delays in practical adoption.

9.10.7 Cost and Implementation Barriers

Quantum technologies are related to huge capital expenditures and operational expenditures. According to Refs. [12, 23], deploying quantum-assisted architecture for 6G and wireless networks would require high-cost hardware, maintenance of cryogenic environments, and hiring specialized personnel. Ref. [5] also

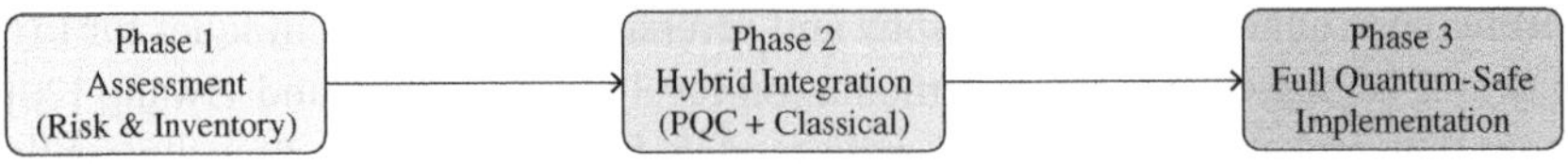

Figure 9.5 Roadmap for Quantum-Safe Security Adoption."*Source:* Hewa Majeed Zangana"

mentions the cost-effectiveness factor is one such major limiting factor for the hybrid quantum-classical network implementation enjoying the downside of resource-constrained enterprises and smart city applications.

9.10.8 Knowledge Gaps and Research Limitations

Lastly, a lack of large empirical data and well-developed testing procedures puts a limit on the confidence in quantum-based security solutions. Botsinis et al. [5] and Zhou et al. [16] stress that while simulation studies are promising, real-world quantum networks display behaviors that are quite often unexpected and work toward nullifying the applicability of theoretical models. Narottama et al. [13] and Nawaz et al. [25] argue for more research to be done in assessing QML applications for wireless and IoT networks, with particular emphasis on scalability, reliability, and resilience, in response to hybrid attacks.

Figure 9.5 presents a roadmap for organizations' transition toward quantum-safe infrastructure along the time horizon representing strategic planning. In doing so, it specifies short-, medium-, and long-term priorities that guarantee interoperability, scalability, and compliance to worldwide standards.

Quantum-safe and hybrid quantum-classical security solutions are indeed transformative but have not gained traction because of hardware, algorithmic, network, regulatory, and price issues. These challenges must be surmounted with joint effort across research, policy, standardization, and industrial take-up to ensure that quantum technologies are deployed securely, resourcefully, and sustainably.

9.11 Future Directions and Research Opportunities

The rapidly developing field of quantum-safe security offers ample opportunities for future research directions across computing, networking, cryptography, and cybersecurity. The main challenge, as quantum technologies mature, will be to exploit their capability while addressing stakeholders' concerns pertaining to the creation of robust, scalable, and secure systems.

9.11.1 Advanced Quantum Algorithms and Hybrid Computing

Future research should develop efficient quantum algorithms designed for security-critical applications. Such multi-objective optimization for heterogeneous networks is a well-marked way to go, especially with respect to quantum algorithms in conjunction with classical computing to balance performance, reliability, and scalability [5]. Ref. [1] highlights the way for hybrid quantum-classical frameworks that narrow the gap between current quantum hardware market limitations and deployment in practice to achieve practical security and computational efficiency. Zhang et al. and Lim et al. [6, 15] extend the ideas of quantum-assisted combinatorial optimization and hybrid neural networks for wireless and IoT network operations.

9.11.2 PQC and Secure Protocols

Development and standardization of PQC protocols are, nonetheless, very vital. Alauthman et al. [1] argue for comparative studies between classical and quantum-resistant techniques to ensure seamless integration into existing infrastructure. Majdoubi et al. [4] and Liu et al. [10] advocate for secure hybrid classical-quantum communication protocols and cryptology frameworks capable of handling big data and blockchain environments. Parida et al. [3] emphasize systematic surveys of PQ-DLTs to anticipate vulnerabilities and optimize performance for future large-scale applications.

9.11.3 Quantum-Enhanced Communication Networks

Quantum-enhanced technologies shall be useful for secure and efficient communication in next-generation wireless and 6G networks. Refs. [11, 22] identify quantum-enabled 6G networks as a transformative approach for ultra-reliable, low-latency, and high-throughput systems. Mohammed et al. [12] and Zhao et al. [23] emphasized the need for research into scalable quantum-assisted architectures, especially on key distribution, beamforming optimization, and interference management. Zhou et al. [16] advocate the emerging area of quantum-native communication systems, which might change the face of network protocols and topologies.

9.11.4 IoT and Smart City Security

Quantum technologies hold the promise to bring security to IoT ecosystems and smart cities. Advances that include quantum steganography and reversible encoding for ensuring redundancy and integrity in a dense IoT network were applied by Ref. [17]. Rishiwal et al. [18] propose that quantum systems can be integrated with ML techniques to predict, detect and prevent cyber-attacks in IoT environments. Future research should focus on developing viable quantum protocols that are scalable, energy-efficient, and low latency. These protocols should be practically implementable across heterogeneous IoT devices.

9.11.5 QML and AI Integration

QML provides a rich possibility for the improvement of predictive security models and network optimization theory. As highlighted by Refs. [13, 25], power allocation, anomaly detection, and signal processing may be enhanced in next-generation networks through QML. Wei et al. [7] discuss quantum-assisted scheduling for federated learning, with an emphasis on benefits for distributed networks and collaborative cybersecurity applications. Future research should investigate the hybrid quantum-classical learning model on one side to increase performance while maintaining low computational overhead.

9.11.6 Quantum Key Management and Digital Signatures

Secure key management and mechanisms for digital signatures are key in establishing trust within quantum networks. Giorgetti et al. [8] and Paduanelli et al. [9] present quantum-assisted digital signature services for optical networks, demonstrating opportunities for future-proof identity and authentication systems. Ngobeni and Kabaso [19] focus on quantum-secure signaling for NB-IoT and next-generation interconnect networks, a necessity for applications that are roaming, low-latency, and mission-critical. This should include much research on integrating these mechanisms into existing network and management systems and cloud infrastructures.

9.11.7 Non-Terrestrial and Satellite Quantum Networks

As Al-Hraishawi et al. [14] emphasize the promise of quantum technologies in NTNs- satellites and high-altitude platforms. Future endeavors should include inquiries into atmospheric mitigation strategies, mobility management, and resource allocation in order to secure high-throughput communications. Mayukha and Vadivel [24] suggest strategic benefits from the evolution of classical to quantum-enabled networks transiting hybrid technologies as an incrementally secure route for adoption.

9.11.8 Standardization, Policy, and Ethical Considerations

Research must address issues related to regulatory, standardization, and ethical frameworks that the adoption of quantum technology will have. Vasani et al. [2] further assert that, "to allow a complete level of global security and trust, harmonized standards, interoperability guidelines, and compliance mechanisms must be developed." According to Refs. [1, 5], "Aimed at accelerating adoption and minimizing pernicious risks, harmonizing technical innovation with regulatory policy will also be a must."

9.11.9 Future Applications and Emergent Use Cases

Possible applications involve the transmission of secured healthcare data, secure financial transactions, and safeguarding critical infrastructures in future communication networks. Botsinis et al. [5] and Matsumine et al. [21] outline quantum algorithms applied for physical layer security, while Hafiz and Hwang [20] have explored probabilistic models targeted at protecting classical data. Research should explore the promising cross-domain use cases that may come up, the optimization of quantum resource usage, and quantification of security benefits compared to classical approaches.

9.11.10 Challenges to Overcome for Broad Adoption

Finally, Sci-Tech researchers ought to deal with the prevailing limitations of scalability, increased running costs, unreliability and non-permanent hardware, and complicated algorithms [16, 23]. Mohammed et al. [12] and Lim et al. [15] argue that bottlenecking issues like these must be resolved to make quantum-secure solutions feasible and affordable for industry-level staging.

In a nutshell, the future of quantum-safe security relates to a richly varied research agenda covering algorithm design, network topologies, cryptographic protocols, IoT, and policy standardization. Strategic investments in hybrid quantum-classical systems, QML, and quantum network infrastructures will afford hidden-value, resilient, and scalable technologies and form the nexus with next-generation secure communications and data protections [1, 5, 16].

9.12 Case Studies and Applications

Realized benefits from the standpoints of the various sectors, however, have already begun to appear from assimilating quantum technologies into communicating, networking, and cybersecurity systems. Several examples can be seen as case studies showing how quin-assisted solutions are practically deployed, what they can contribute to performance improvement, and some associated real-world challenges.

9.12.1 Quantum-Assisted Wireless Networks

This pertains to describing early work in quantum-enhanced multi-objective optimization for heterogeneous networks [5]. This was found to be able to apply to several areas: resource allocation, routing, and interference management-with the promise of enhanced performance, as compared with classical methods, through simultaneous optimization. Botsinis et al. [5] further demonstrated the use of quantum search algorithms to improve efficiency in communications, specifically those that include dense traffic or highly dynamic topologies. Thus, these cases manifest the potential of quantum algorithms in the areas of increasing throughput, reducing latency, and improving reliability.

9.12.2 Quantum 6G and Beyond Communications

Communications with 6G networks would be an ideal place for quantum integration. Ali et al. [11] investigate how quantum technologies can potentially improve communication in 6G by showing that it is possible to achieve ultra-low-latency data transfers with high security. Mohammed et al. [12] show applications of quantum-assisted architectures in 6G systems: for example, the use of QKD creates secure channels. Wang et al. [22] point out the opportunities that quantum-enabled 6G networks will offer to improve security, spectrum efficiency, and reliability in the network. Thus, they demonstrate that hybrid classical-quantum approaches can have potential advantages over purely classical network designs.

9.12.3 Quantum Cryptography and Post-Quantum Security

Quantum cryptography has been applied in securing networks of IoT devices and distributed ledger-based systems. Biswas et al. [17] present a case of study in smart city IoT networks by quantum steganography and reversible decoding for secure communication. The aforementioned secure communications in the large network scope become tamper-proof and eavesdropping resilient. Liu et al. [10] discuss a hybrid classical-quantum protocol for blockchain management, which demonstrates that enhanced security is granted against attacks with quantum-enabled capabilities. Furthermore, Ref. [4] mention how quantum cryptology will contribute in bringing security within Big Data environments, also showing practical demonstrations of encryption and decryption within a large-scale networked system.

9.12.4 QML in Wireless Systems

QML has been applied to network optimization and the prediction of threats in increase in network performance. Nawaz et al. [25] showed the use of QML in 6G networks for traffic prediction resource allocation, and anomaly detection. Narottama et al. [13] further build on this point by discussing QML in next-generation wireless communications, which serves to lessen the computational burden and improve overall efficiency. A case study was conducted by Wei et al. [7] on quantum-assisted federated learning in distributed networks, which allows many nodes to co-train AI models but under the constraint of data privacy. Hybrid quantum-classical neural networks will be explored by Zhang et al. [6] for application in downlink beamforming. Thus, they indicated significantly improved spectral efficiency and user coverage with respect to conventional cellular networks.

9.12.5 Quantum-Assisted Digital Signatures and Secure Communication

Digital signature services ensure authentication and integrity in secure communications. Giorgetti et al. and Paduanelli et al. [8, 9] have presented implementations of quantum-assisted digital signatures within optical networks, showcasing real-world deployment in SDN controlled areas. These studies have established the feasibility of quantum-enhanced signature schemes operating in real time with a network providing a template for scalable implementation in telecommunications and cloud-based networks.

9.12.6 Non-Terrestrial and Satellite Quantum Networks

As Al-Hraishawi et al. [14] provide case studies of integrating quantum technologies into NTNs, including satellites and high-altitude platforms. The implementations are focused on QKD and secure signaling for long-distance communication, providing solutions for secure global coverage. Mayukha and Vadivel [24] describe the transition from classical to quantum-secured NTNs with emphasis on hybrid architecture balancing security, reliability, and cost-effectiveness.

9.12.7 PQ-DLT

As Parida et al. [3] make a systematic survey and case analysis of PQ-DLTs. The study highlights applications in the real world of financial services and supply chain, where quantum-resistant protocols ensure data integrity against future quantum threats while achieving secure consensus mechanisms. Alauthman et al. [1] further demonstrate the comparative performance analysis of classical versus quantum-enabled DLTs in terms of giving insights into operational trade-offs and security benefits.

9.12.8 Emerging Applications and Hybrid Architectures

Among the further applications worth mention there are hybrid classical-quantum systems for physical layer security [20, 21] and the optimization of electromagnetic environments embedding quantum-assisted combinatorial techniques [15]. Zhou et al. [16] present case studies in quantum-native communication systems, placing specific emphasis on the integration of quantum technologies into existing infrastructures. Vasani et al. [2] discuss some industrial adoption scenarios that exhibit the significance of quantum communication and cryptography across the sectors of smart cities, autonomous systems, and healthcare networks.

9.12.9 Security in IoT and Federated Networks

As Rishiwal et al. [18] discuss hybrid quantum and ML techniques applied to IoT networks improving detection of threats, mitigation of attacks, and predictive security measures. Ngobeni and Kabaso [19] utilize quantum-secure signaling for NB-IoT traffic as a real-life candidate for next-generation interconnect and roaming networks critical for low-latency and other mission-critical undertakings.

9.12.10 Summary of Key Insights

Altogether, these case studies demonstrate concrete feasibility, security improvements, and performance enhancement due to quantum technologies across communication networks, IoT ecosystems, and distributed systems. They further highlight hybrid approaches, integrating classical, quantum, and AI-based solutions to overcome the present limitations and prepare for the quantum-secured future [5, 11, 12, 16].

All of the applications presented provide a roadmap for the real-world adoption of quantum technologies that show immediate good and long-term promise for the enhancement of network security, efficiency, and resilience.

9.13 Conclusion

Emerging quantum technologies represent a particular paradigm shift in the environment of communication, networking, and cybersecurity. The interaction of quantum-assisted algorithms, QML, and quantum cryptography has shown tremendous promise toward guaranteeing the security of data, enhancing the performance of networks, and ensuring the efficient management of resources. Its practicality in the working network environment prove that quantum solutions can solve many limitations in classical settings, especially in an environment that requires a high degree of security, low latency, and large-scale data processing.

Even with all the optimistic steps taken toward its adoption, these technologies are still in their infancy, with various challenges that have to be overcome. The issues around hardware limits, scalability, integration with the classical system, standardization, and so forth come to the fore of these challenges. Considerably, assuring interoperability among the classical and quantum networks and developing strong quantum-resistant protocols would be necessary to facilitate wide uptake of this technology. These challenges justify further sustained research, development, and collaboration among the academic, industry, and regulatory fronts toward the full realization of quantum-enabled systems.

On the other hand, development of hybrid quantum-classical architecture, quantum-assisted machine learning, and PQC are exciting prospects for innovation. As quantum technologies develop, they will lead to redesign principles for networks, optimization of operations for complex systems, and establishment of highly secure and resilient digital infrastructures. The continued research and application of quantum technologies thus herald a new dawn of secure, efficient, and intelligent communication networks, paving the way for a future wherein quantum solutions serve as a backbone of technological and societal advancement.

References

1 Alauthman, M., Almomani, A., Al-Qerem, A. et al. (2024). Quantum computing for cybersecurity: A comparative study of classical and quantum techniques. In: *Innovations in Modern Cryptography*, 75–99. IGI Global.

2 Vasani, V., Prateek, K., Amin, R. et al. (2024). Embracing the quantum frontier: Investigating quantum communication, cryptography, applications and future directions. *Journal of Industrial Information Integration* 100 594.

3 Parida, N.K., Jatoth, C., Reddy, V.D. et al. (2023). Post-quantum distributed ledger technology: A systematic survey. *Scientific Reports* 13 (1): 20729.

4 Majdoubi, C., El Mendili, S., and Gahi, Y. (2024). Quantum cryptology in the big data security era. *International Journal of Advanced Computer Science and Applications* 15 (7): 562–571.

5 Botsinis, P., Alanis, D., Babar, Z. et al. (2018). Quantum search algorithms for wireless communications. *IEEE Communications Surveys & Tutorials* 21 (2): 1209–1242.

6 Zhang, J., Zheng, G., Koike-Akino, T. et al. (2024). Hybrid quantum-classical neural networks for downlink beamforming optimization. *IEEE Transactions on Wireless Communications* .

7 Wei X, Fan L, Guo Y, Gong Y, Han Z, Wang Y. Quantum assisted scheduling algorithm for federated learning in distributed networks. In: 2023 32nd International Conference on Computer Communications and Networks (ICCCN). IEEE; 2023. pp. 1–10.

8 Giorgetti, A., Andriolli, N., Ferrari, M. et al. (2025). Generalized quantum-assisted digital signature service in an SDN-controlled quantum-integrated optical network. *Journal of Optical Communications and Networking* 17 (2): A155–A164.

9 Paduanelli G, Ferrari M, Giorgetti A, Andriolli N, Storelli E, Cacicia A, et al. Quantum-assisted digital signature: A new service for future quantum-integrated optical networks. In: 2024 24th International Conference on Transparent Optical Networks (ICTON). IEEE; 2024. pp. 1–4.

10 Liu, A., Chen, X.B., Xu, S. et al. (2023). A secure scheme based on a hybrid of classical-quantum communications protocols for managing classical blockchains. *Entropy* 25 (5): 811.

11 Ali, M.Z., Abohmra, A., Usman, M. et al. (2023). Quantum for 6G communication: A perspective. *IET Quantum Communication* 4 (3): 112–124.

12 Mohammed AA, Bounceur A, Hammoudeh M. Quantum assisted architectures for wireless systems, the case of quantum 6G. In: Proceedings of the 7th International Conference on Future Networks and Distributed Systems. 2023. pp. 618–25.

13 Narottama, B., Mohamed, Z., and Aïssa, S. (2023). Quantum machine learning for next-G wireless communications: Fundamentals and the path ahead. *IEEE Open Journal of the Communications Society* 4: 2204–2224.

14 Al-Hraishawi, H., Rehman, J.U., Razavi, M., and Chatzinotas, S. (2024). Characterizing and utilizing the interplay between quantum technologies and non-terrestrial networks. *IEEE Open Journal of the Communications Society* 5: 112–134.

15 Lim, Q.J., Ross, C., Ghosh, A. et al. (2023). Quantum-assisted combinatorial optimization for reconfigurable intelligent surfaces in smart electromagnetic environments. *IEEE Transactions on Antennas and Propagation* 72 (1): 147–159.

16 Zhou X, Shen A, Hu S, Ni W, Wang X, Hossain E, et al. Towards quantum-native communication systems: New developments, trends, and challenges. arXiv preprint arXiv:231105239. 2023.

17 Biswas, S., Goswami, R.S., and Reddy, K.H.K. (2024). Advancing quantum steganography: A secure IoT communication with reversible decoding and customized encryption technique for smart cities. *Cluster Computing* 27 (7): 9395–9414.

18 Rishiwal, V., Agarwal, U., Yadav, M. et al. (2025). A new alliance of machine learning and quantum computing: Concepts, attacks, and challenges in IoT networks. *IEEE Internet of Things Journal* 12 (1): 45–58.

19 Ngobeni T, Kabaso B. Quantum-secure signalling model for L1/L2 next-gen interconnect and roaming networks over IPX for NB-IoT traffic: A review. In: International Conference on Cyber Warfare and Security. Academic Conferences International Limited; 2024. pp. 490–500.

20 Hafiz, M.W. and Hwang, S.O. (2023). A probabilistic model of quantum states for classical data security. *Frontiers of Physics (Beijing)* 18 (5): 51304.

21 Matsumine, T., Ochiai, H., and Shikata, J. (2025). Quantum algorithms for the physical layer: Potential applications to physical layer security. *IEEE Access* 13: 1024–1040.

22 Wang, C. and Rahman, A. (2022). Quantum-enabled 6G wireless networks: Opportunities and challenges. *IEEE Wireless Communications* 29 (1): 58–69.

23 Zhao, W., Weng, T., Ruan, Y. et al. (2024). Quantum computing in wireless communications and networking: A tutorial-cum-survey. *IEEE Communications Surveys & Tutorials* 26 (2): 890–945.

24 Mayukha, S. and Vadivel, R. (2025). A secure transition perspective on the expectations and benefits of quantum networks over classical networks. In: *Quantum Computing and Artificial Intelligence: The Industry Use Cases*, 331–371. Boca Raton, FL: CRC Press, Taylor & Francis Group.

25 Nawaz, S.J., Sharma, S.K., Wyne, S. et al. (2019). Quantum machine learning for 6G communication networks: State-of-the-art and vision for the future. *IEEE Access* 7: 46317–46350.

Part IV

Human and Organizational Dimensions

10

Human Factors and Insider Threat Mitigation

10.1 Introduction

In the world of security provoked by organizations, the human element continues to stand out as one of the most complex yet powerful factors. Although technical solutions such as firewalls, intrusion detection systems, and AI-driven monitoring have made progress, they cannot cover the vulnerabilities caused by human behavior. Insider threats, intentional or unintentional, are high on the challenge list for organizations, accounting for a large percentage of security incidents and breaches in the industry [1, 2]. This category of threat extends beyond actions of malicious employees to include actions carried out by naive employees, who, in their efforts to be good employees, misappropriate sensitive data or the integrity of systems [3, 4].

The understanding of human factors in cybersecurity risk needs multidisciplinarity, measurement with, for example, behavioral psychology and the organization culture with the addition of socio-technical system and finally, tightening it up with state-of-the-art techniques of monitoring [5–7]. Inside the organization of individual behavior, policies, and technology have created an environment or a picture where the insider threat may tend to become a little silent but rapid-firing weapon upon leaving unaddressed [5, 6]. Studies have shown that cognitive biases employees have, as well as their stress levels and levels of awareness, heavily influence security outcomes; thus, human behavior becomes an eminent factor in any proactive cybersecurity approach [7, 8].

Recent studies underscore the need for incorporating human-centric frameworks within cybersecurity programs. A sociotechnical approach, for instance, will allow organizations to represent relationships between human behavior, organizational processes, and technology use to enhance the prediction of insider incidents and the prevention thereof [4, 9, 10]. Likewise, a strong cybersecurity culture has been proven to minimize risks by aligning the views and actions of employees with an organization's security goals [11, 12].

Various manifestations of insider threats include sabotage of intentional variety, exfiltration of data, and action taken due to no negligence, generally instruction error, and attention fatigue [13, 14]. However, the latest advances in digital workplace transformation, the emergence of cloud computing, and the shift toward a remote work environment have further increased the attack surface and widened the possibilities for inadvertent breaches [15, 16]. Such promising modern analytics and artificial intelligence (AI) solutions provide a potential for early detection and mitigation, enabling organizations to detect and respond to abnormal behavior before they culminate into critical incidents [17, 18].

Increased emphasis is being placed on a balance between technical controls and human approaches to mitigation. For instance, a combination of security awareness programs, continuous training, role-based access management, and psychological profiling is enhanced with AI monitoring and anomaly detection systems to create a comprehensive defense against insider threats [1, 19, 20]. Such proactive measures toward threat management transformed from defense mechanisms into preventing the occurrence and even minimization of the adverse effects of insider incidents, as organizations can view behavioral, cognitive, and organizational dimensions in security [7, 8, 24].

That would sum up the point that human factors pose both challenges and opportunities in cybersecurity. Indeed, by comprehending the motives behind insider threats and the ensuing measures, which employ integrated AI, socio-technical, and behavioral approaches, organizations do solidify a resilient posture in security. The sections that will follow in this chapter will dig into some specific human factors in insider threats, scrutinizing mitigation strategies dictated by them as well as best practices in combining human-centeredism with AI-driven cybersecurity defenses.

10.2 Understanding Human Factors in Cybersecurity

While human factors in cybersecurity refer to those psychological and behavioral characteristics and organizational characteristics that would affect individual responses to information systems and security protocols, these...

Because of their inherent dynamic or complex context dependency, human factors, unlike purely technical vulnerabilities, become both a major source of risk and potential leverage for enhanced security. Insider threats are generally to be found rooted in such human factors and indicative of the critical interplay between individual behaviors, organizational culture, and technological environments [1, 2].

10.2.1 Behavioral and Cognitive Factors

That is how many of the key behavioral tendencies, cognitive biases, and decision-making processes determine the outcome of the cyber war. Sensitive data might be inadvertently exposed by people who are prone to human error, lapses in concentration, or misconceptions concerning security [3, 4]. Stress, fatigue, and burnout further complicate the problem by increasing a person's likelihood of making mistakes, all of which contribute to what [7] calls "security fatigue." But on the flip side, malicious insiders explore both technical vulnerabilities and human factors by manipulating social interactions and utilizing trust inside access without proper authorization [8, 17]. Knowledge of these cognitive and behavioral dimensions becomes critical in order to devise interventions to minimize security incidents.

10.2.2 Organizational and Cultural Influences

Organizational culture plays a pivotal role in shaping employees' perceptions and the possible implementation of cybersecurity policies. Compliance, accountability, and learning-oriented cultures motivate secure behavior but can fail weak or inconsistent cultural signals and hence create conditions in which breaches are accepted or overlooked [11, 12]. Studies focused on socio-technical components such as communication behaviors, leadership, and peer influence have been highlighted in terms of their influence on an insider threat and security solution effectiveness [6, 10, 20].

10.2.3 Social Engineering and Interaction Dynamics

The way these things work is that human factors are used somehow by the attacker using social engineering, phishing, and other scheming techniques dependent on trust, authority, or sometimes urgency cues. It emphasizes for organizations with employees ignorant and untutored in these kinds of tricks that human behavior should be thought into integrated security design [5, 15, 21]. Social and psychological effects shape not only the susceptibility to attacks but also work in mitigation strategies, such as multi-factor authentication, access controls, and behavioral monitoring [1, 9].

10.2.4 Unintentional Insider Threats

When employees from within the organization compromise security inadvertently, they are genuine threats inside the organization and are usually created due to a systemic gap, inappropriate training, or a very confusing technical process [4]. These threats are most associated with healthcare, industrial, and critical infrastructure sectors, in which human errors can lead to significant operational loss and economic consequences [21, 22]. Creating sociotechnical frameworks and human-centered assessment instruments empowers organizations to self-identify exposure risks and tailor interventions to the behavioral patterns found in the workforce of an organization [4, 12].

10.2.5 Integrating Human Factors into Cybersecurity Practices

A multi-layered strategy integrating technical measures as well as behavioral considerations would limit the effects of human factors smartly. AI-based anomaly detection, prediction analytics, and such monitoring would search for the odd behavior patterns [15, 18]. For it would be combined with human-centered activities—prolonged training, awareness programs, role-based access policies, and psychological profiling—to mitigate risks by inducing behavior and inculcating norms around security as an organization [1, 13, 14]. Another important area of institutional role lies within leadership and governance in establishing a proactive mindset toward cybersecurity. Security-conscious students, advanced policies, and consideration of human aspects in making decisions develop a resilient culture that can deal well with insider threats [19, 20].

10.2.6 Summary

In conclusion, conceiving the human factors under cybersecurity will involve behavioral and cognitive as well as social dynamics. Insider threats, both intentional and unintentional, underscore why such behavioral science must be integrated into a technical security measure: organizations would use these insights into human factors to compartmentalize vulnerabilities, get greater involvement from employees in security behaviors, and build strong defense systems balancing technological innovation and human reliability [8, 9, 23].

For a clearer picture of how multifaceted human influence may conceptualize this impact on cybersecurity, it is found in Figure 10.1 by classifying human factors in the behavioral, cognitive, and organizational dimensions. A visual representation serves to highlight how psychological traits, decision-making processes, and cultural norms set every factor, creating security behavior and vulnerability.

Figure 10.1 Dimensions of Human Factors in Cybersecurity. "*Source:* Hewa Majeed Zangana"

10.3 Insider Threat Landscape

The insider threat landscape constitutes one of the most potentially persistent and challenging cyber threats encountered in the real world because of converging human behavior with organizational culture and technology vulnerabilities. Most commonly categorized into two categories, insider threats involve malicious insiders who break into information systems to achieve personal gains or sabotage an organization, including unintentional insiders, who accidentally create vulnerabilities through human error, carelessness, or ignorance [1, 3, 13]. Both pose significant risks to organizations as the attack surface continues growing with digital infrastructures and cloud-based environments [15, 16].

10.3.1 Scope and Impact

Insider threats cast a broad net over financial performance, operational continuity, data integrity, and organizational reputation [2, 21]. Even minor human errors in critical infrastructure sectors can lead to cascading failures, thus highlighting the strategic importance of human factors in assessing cybersecurity risks [5, 22]. Malicious insiders would exploit access privileges through some social engineering or knowledge within the organization; individuals determined to be unintentional insiders would be stresses, fatigue, or training deficiencies, encouraging an inadvertent release of data or policies [4, 7].

10.3.2 Drivers of Insider Threats

All those things are human factors in nature, which can consider why insider threats exist. Behavioral tendencies, cognitive biases, and individual differences—particularly personality traits, motivation, and risk perception—bring together the organization with some of its processes and against which technology systems can then be considered an additional point of vulnerability [8, 17, 24]. A growing body of research suggests that such conditions for additional insider incidents would include lack of cybersecurity culture, ineffective policy enforcement, and low employee engagement [11, 12]. Socio-technical frameworks further emphasize the need for individual and organizational factors to be focused on mitigation planning because of how this influences risk through dynamic interaction [6, 10].

10.3.3 Unintentional Insider Threats

Unintentional insider threats are also emerging as an increasingly important part of the threat picture, particularly in areas such as healthcare, industrial systems, and government operations [4, 25]. Such threats arise from human error—misconfigurations, accidental disclosures, or abuse of privileges. These highlight the need for assessing human security indicators and identifying the behavioral patterns that contribute to such risks in order to introduce specific interventions [9, 22].

10.3.4 Threat Modeling and Detection

Today's models for detecting insider threats rely on using behavioral analytics, AI anomaly detection, and continuous monitoring coupled with some human-centric assessment approaches [15, 18]. Unsafe insider models simulating consequences of insider threats in complex systems appropriately describe vulnerabilities in advance of possible realization and guide how preventive controls may be fastened [5]. Incorporating human factors into threat models allows organizations to make better predictions of risk scenarios, taking into account both technical and human dimensions of security incidents [1, 14].

10.3.5 Organizational and Leadership Considerations

Leadership and governance shape the insider threat landscape. Above all, there should be security-conscious leaders, strict policy enforcement, and a proactive organizational culture toward cybersecurity so that there will be fewer probabilities and incidences of insider threats [19, 20]. Organizations adopting a "human-as-solution" approach—by treating employees as active agents of security rather than potential problems—tend to achieve greater resilience and severity in reducing insider-related incidents [12, 17].

10.3.6 Summary

Insider threat landscape is a challenge with many faces developing along human behavior, with organizational culture molds and technological vulnerabilities being most acute. Effective management calls for a holistic understanding of both malicious and unintentional threats from a behavioral angle and by socio-technical integration of proactive leadership [3, 8, 23]. Combining AI-assisted approaches for detection with human-centered policies and cultural maintenance will significantly reduce risk, enhance resilience, and create a cybersecurity environment wherein technology and people work in conjunction to mitigate insider threats [1, 15, 18].

Where outsiders deceive but within each case, called an insider threat, find intangible forms. Figure 10.2 classifies insider threats as intentional (malicious) and unintentional, showcasing the possible differences in risk profiles contributed through motivation, access, and opportunity.

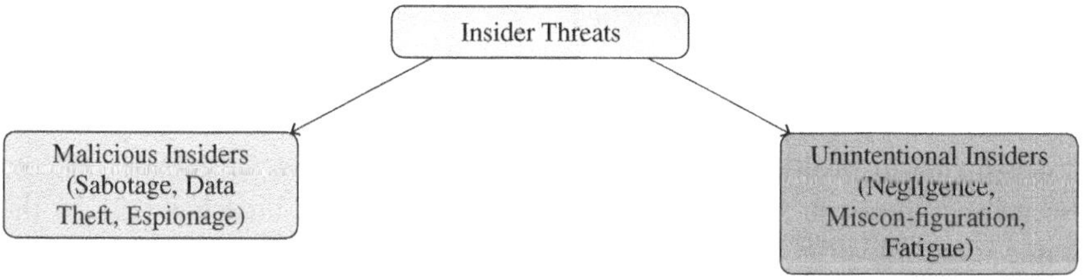

Figure 10.2 Classification of Insider Threats. "*Source:* Hewa Majeed Zangana"

10.4 Behavioral Indicators and Risk Assessment

Behavioral indicators are indispensable in detecting possible insider threats together with their attendant risks. Insider threats often manifest through subtle behavior patterns, deviations from standard operating procedures, or hampering normal access or activity levels, which can reflect either purposeful intent or otherwise, unintentional negligence [1, 15]. The interpretation of these indicators utilizes an all-encompassing perspective that embraces individual psychology, the dynamics of organizational behavior, and further technical monitoring systems [8, 23].

10.4.1 Indicative Behaviors

There are behavioral indicators that can be arranged across several views, including those of psychological, social, and operational considerations. The psychological indicators include stress, dissatisfaction with work, and any motivation that could bring risky behavior down the line [7, 13]. Social indicators include the individual's interaction with colleagues, communication patterns, and vulnerability to social engineering that reflects how interpersonal dynamics are influencing security compliance [3, 17]. Operational indicators cover abnormal system usage, atypical login hours, and the wrongful handling of sensitive data [5, 16].

10.4.2 Human Factors and Risk Assessment

There is a growing emphasis, even in the risk assessment schemes increasingly used for cybersecurity purposes, on human factors. The schemes would capture both malicious and unintentional behavior with respect to how cognitive biases, decision-making errors, and organizational pressure present opportunities for exploitation [4, 25]. By analyzing incidents from the past, together with behavioral patterns and sociotechnical interactions, organizations can prioritize mitigation efforts and refine measures for identifying incidents proactively [6, 10].

10.4.3 Sociotechnical Approaches

Sociotechnical approaches indicate the interdependent nature of human behavior, organizational systems, and physical technology [9, 18]. One way insider risk assessments in healthcare demonstrate that staffing levels, workloads, and the security culture can shape the occurrence of inadvertent breaches [22]. In the same vein, industrial and critical infrastructure settings can model insider activities within complex systems to gain foresight on disruptions [5, 21].

10.4.4 Malicious Insiders' Behavioral Risk Indicators

Malicious insiders show certain behavioral patterns that can generally identify them in contrast to unintentional actors. These indicators include accessing information that is not needful for his/her scope of work, breaking security policies, and a complete change in performance or engagement suddenly [1, 2, 11]. Behavioral profiling, continuation monitoring, and anomaly detection serve as all means of easing the chances of possible insider incidents [15].

10.4.5 Mitigation by Means of Behavioral Analysis

Behavioral risk analysis gives organizations the power to implement targeted mitigation measures. Engaging leadership, training staff members, and promoting the existence of a strong cybersecurity culture can all assist in lessening both intentional and unintentional challenges [12, 17, 20]. Moreover, AI-based monitoring plus human-centered assessments dovetail uniquely in sustaining dynamic adaptation to evolving threats and in real-time assistance for decision-making [8, 18].

10.4.6 Summary

Behavioral risk assessment is the foundation for proactive mitigation of insider threats. By outlining psychological, social, and operational indicators, organizations will be in a better position to manage, anticipate, and counter the malicious and unintentional insider behaviors [3, 19, 24]. Combining a sociotechnical framework, AI-enabled monitoring, and initiatives aimed at progressing an organizational culture leads to a holistic state that supports resilience to insider threats and an empowered work culture within security [9, 15, 23].

Figure 10.3 visualizes the behavioral indicators that often precede insider incidents. These indicators span psychological, social, and operational domains, helping organizations structure monitoring and risk assessment systems effectively.

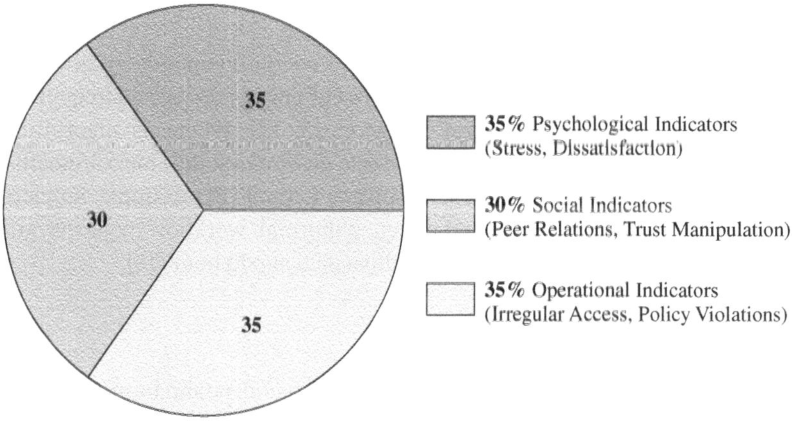

Figure 10.3 Behavioral Indicators of Insider Threats. "*Source:* Hewa Majeed Zangana"

10.5 AI and Machine Learning for Insider Threat Detection

Through the swift modification of insider threats, intended or unintended, there has been growth in the application of AI and machine learning (ML) techniques for detection and counteraction. Traditional cybersecurity measures like rule-based monitoring and access controls are often too simplistic to identify complex patterns in insider behavior [1, 15]. AI and ML provide organizations with scalable, adaptive, and predictive capacities, allowing detection of anomalous behaviors prior to full-blown incidents [8, 23].

10.5.1 Machine Learning Approaches

ML methods, like supervised, unsupervised, and reinforcement learning, have been deployed to model user behavior, detect anomalies, and predict potential insider threats. Supervised learning approaches rely on labeled datasets of known insider incidents to train predictive models capable of classifying future events as risky or benign [5, 15]. Unsupervised learning like clustering and anomaly detection identifies deviations from established behavioral baselines, allowing it to work particularly well against unknown or emerging threats [2, 11]. Reinforcement learning allows the system to fine-tune itself based on dynamically changing insider tactics by learning the optimal monitoring strategies over time [18].

10.5.2 Behavioral Profiling and Risk Scoring

AI-enabled insider threat detection generally involves the component of behavioral profiling that models normal activity patterns of employees: access frequency, file interactions, and communication behaviors [3, 17]. Whenever algorithms score these risks, they apply behavioral profiles to give quantitative measurements about possible malicious or unintentional insider actions. For example, an alert for further investigation is triggered when abnormal workflow patterns are detected, or there is excessive access to sensitive data at odd hours [8].

10.5.3 Integration with Human Factors

For AI-enabled insider threat detection, it is critical to understand human factors. Unintentional violations could arise from cognitive biases, stress, and burnout, whereas organizational culture and social engineering exposure may dictate intentional threats [4, 7, 25]. AI systems that leverage human-centric data, such as psychological assessments or engagement metrics, could support predictive accuracy and reduce false positives [9, 20]. Sociotechnical frameworks could also buttress such AI alignments with organizational context so that automated monitoring complements rather than substitutes human judgment [6, 12].

10.5.4 Applications in Critical Infrastructure and Healthcare

Sectors with a high sensitivity to insider threats, such as critical infrastructure and healthcare, have provided fertile ground for applying AI and ML. In industrial systems, predictive modeling simulates the insider impacts on complex networks and helps locate the most effective mitigation strategy [5, 21]. In healthcare, the ML model assesses behavioral markers on multiple fronts: access logs, handling of patient data, and compliance with security policies, giving it the capacity to detect both deliberate and inadvertent breaches at dusk [22].

10.5.5 Challenges and Limitations

On their part, though beneficial, AI and ML tools for insider threat detection are challenged. Data sparsity, privacy issues, and the difficulties in labeling the insider incidents are all barriers to model accuracy [1, 15]. The other challenge is when adversaries may try to avoid detection by acting in ways that mimic normal patterns, that is why continuous model retraining and adaptive learning will be necessary [13, 14]. To deal with these limitations, the need for technical solutions to work hand in hand with organizational policies, training programs, and leader engagement [12, 20].

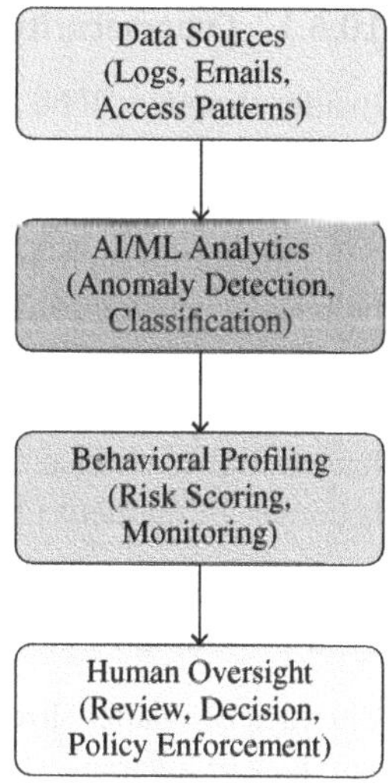

Figure 10.4 AI-Driven Insider Threat Detection Framework. "*Source:* Hewa Majeed Zangana"

10.5.6 Future Directions

Future developments in AI-enabled insider threat detection are projected to focus on multi-modal data integration, joining behavioral, contextual, and environmental information to provide increased detection accuracy [9, 23]. With the advancement of explainable AI (XAI), security teams will be capable of understanding and interpreting model decisions, thereby engendering trust and effective intervention strategies [17, 18]. Alongside, maintaining a balance between AI and human-in-the-loop settings will ensure that automated systems are congruent with organizational priorities and ethical implications [8, 12].

Insider threat detection is enhanced through AI through automated behavioral analytics and human factor data integration. Figure 10.4 shows a layered framework explaining how AI and ML models interact with the data sources, behavioral profiling, and human oversight.

10.6 Organizational Strategies for Insider Threat Mitigation

Insider incursions produce an array of daunting hurdles upon the organizational setup in vast measure, which necessitate the extension of a mitigation strategy that intermingles technical, human, and organizational perspectives. However, mitigating risks will require not only the advancement of systems specialized in detection but also the reinforcement of a robust cybersecurity culture and the establishment of policies oriented toward human behavior [1, 11].

10.6.1 Cybersecurity Culture

Insider threats will be mitigated fundamentally by a sufficient cybersecurity culture. Employees should see cybersecurity as something everybody owns and adheres to the process, where positive actions are encouraged and rewarded [12, 23]. Paradigms such as advanced ongoing security awareness training, updating policies according to the state of affairs, and visible leadership endorsement in setting examples of security best practices help organize a culture wherein insider risk is mitigated [9, 10]. Organizations that incorporate security in daily activities have a higher chance of noticing any aberration and hence intervening before it becomes an incident [2, 11].

10.6.2 Human-Centric Policies and Workforce Management

The idea of insider threat always involves some human factors, be it stress, burnout, lack of awareness, or susceptibility to social engineering [7, 25]. Accordingly, human-centric policies have to be in place to consider such human factors. These include role-based access control, frequent workforce evaluations, and psychometric or behavioral indicators embedded into risk establishment frameworks [4]. At the same time, sociotechnical frameworks can combine technical controls with human actions, thus substantially mitigating the risk from unintentional insider threats [4, 6].

10.6.3 Risk Assessment and Continuous Monitoring

To measure and respond to insider threats, organizations need to have an active risk assessment process. These include behavioral analytics, anomaly detection, AI monitoring, and any other technology to recognize deviations from baseline activities concerning employee behavior [1, 15]. Continuous adaptive risk assessments will maintain relevance to organizational changes, such as changes in workforce behavior dynamics and the ever-changing external threat landscape [5]. This allows for the preventive management of risks before actually realizing a serious incidence through continuous monitoring of both technical indicators and human factors [3, 8].

10.6.4 Leadership and Governance

It is leadership and governance that greatly support the initiation and sustenance of an effective mitigation program. The very effective leaders must raise awareness regarding accountability, clearly communicate what mitigation strategies they are adopting, and prioritize investments concerning both people and technology [17, 20]. The governance frame should specify the particular functions and responsibilities in a clear manner for compliance with policies and integrate the reporting mechanism against suspicious behavior [14, 19]. Such governance frameworks promote an alert security posture and thus decrease the extreme possibilities of insider incidents.

10.6.5 Integration of Technology and Human Oversight

While AI and ML provide advanced surveillance and detection capabilities, contextual organizational strategies must put technology in par with human oversight [15, 18]. The flow from detection to response could be markedly improved with human assessment to ensure contextually appropriate resolution that is ethically enforced [9, 13]. Processing responses from a hybrid model allows for many important weaknesses of a tech-only-style solution to be addressed, such as drastic FPs or evasive tactics set by the domain [12, 16].

10.6.6 Best Practices

Insider threat mitigation plans should be tailored to the organizational context and sector-specific mandates. Critical infrastructures may require stricter access control and monitoring protocols, while healthcare organizations must comply with data privacy requirements and patient safety priorities [21, 22]. Simulation-based modeling assesses how the insider action will affect the systems in question so that resources are allocated more wisely and that policies are properly designed [5, 24].

10.6.7 Continuous Improvement and Learning

Mitigation strategies should evolve with the development of the threat landscape. Organizations should learn lessons from an incident, conduct post-incident analysis, update training, and amend policies [2, 14]. Ingraining a mindset of continuous improvement leverages insights from human factors studies and technology development, thus fortifying the organization against insider threats [10, 20].

This representation is layered, demonstrating how human, technological, and organizational strategies interface to combat insider threats, as shown in Figure 10.5. The model suggests that strong culture and governance are the main pillars to support sustainable security practices.

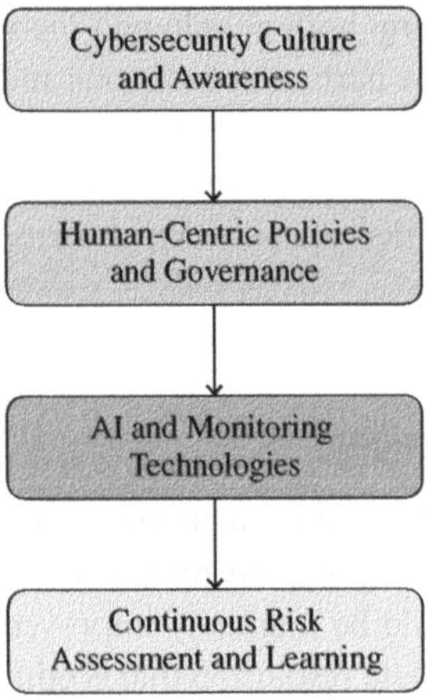

Figure 10.5 Organizational Strategy Layers for Insider Threat Mitigation. "*Source:* Hewa Majeed Zangana"

10.7 Human–AI Collaboration in Cyber Defense

The sharpening focus of the ever-complex and widening mannerisms of cyber threats mandates the incorporation of AI alongside human resources to augment cyber defense capabilities. Human–AI collaboration utilizes complementary strengths from both parties, as AI's forte lies in sifting through massive datasets, anomaly detection, and prediction of threat patterns, whereas human input provides contextual knowledge, ethical reasoning, and adaptive decision-making [1, 18].

10.7.1 Complementary Roles of Humans and AI

AI can be employed to monitor the user behavior of individuals in the workplace, evaluating their access patterns and providing real-time identification of high-risk access to sensitive files [2, 15]. ML algorithms establish non-normative behavioral parameters for both conscious and unconscious insider threats [3, 5]. In fact, a core point is that, to fully understand human actions, one needs to take into account the social, psychological, or organizational contexts in which those humans operate; therefore, human oversight is indispensable [12, 23].

Contributions made by human judgment are invaluable to the alert assessment stage, where they can discriminate between "false positives" and true threats and make the underlying strategic decisions governing the prioritization of response actions that are consonant with organizations' priorities [8, 10]. This extract will ensure that AI products are actionable and contextually informed, reducing the chances of underreactions or overreactions to threats [9, 24].

10.7.2 Improving Threat Detection and Response

Continuous learning loops between humans and AI improve threat detection, wherein human analysts provide feedback to AI models refining prediction accuracy [15, 21]. Healthcare industries, for instance, would benefit from automated AI and supervision of an expert to determine if any anomalous accesses to sensitive patient information are early signs of aberrant access behavior, which also takes into account behavioral and environmental factors [22]. AI need not be in a static mode: for example, currently, critical infrastructure systems have interfaces of AI that monitor the intricate interdependency of networks, while human operators evaluate the strategic and ethical implications of defensive actions [5, 21].

10.7.3 Socio-Technical Considerations

Socio-technical challenges should take into consideration collaborative work. Stress and cognitive overload, for example, as well as trust in AI systems, can have really great impacts on the final result [7, 25]. Designing organizations should ensure their interfaces and workflows enable natural and comfortable interactions with AI and keep their humans engaged and confident in their decision-making abilities [17, 20]. Building error, response speed improvements, and collaboration among human operators and AI through training, adaptive interfaces, and scenario-based simulations [4, 6].

10.7.4 Ethics and Governance Implications

There are ethical and governance issues that come along with human–AI collaboration. Automated insights should count as part of the organizational policies, legal allowability, and societal acceptance in the decision processes [12, 18]. Accountability for actions taken in collaboration with humans and AI systems should be clear to leaders, ensuring transparency in AI-assisted threat assessments and interventions [13, 20]. The policies should include provisions for data privacy, bias mitigation, and defining appropriate boundaries for automation in decision-making for cyber defenses [9, 11].

10.7.5 Future Directions

Human–AI cooperation will benefit strongly from advances in explainable AI, adaptive learning, and human-centered design for cybersecurity [15, 23]. Future research would emphasize the co-evolution of AI capability with human expertise, ensuring that cyber defense systems can remain workable in the face of ever-advancing insider threats and external attacks [4, 8]. Organizations can turn cyber

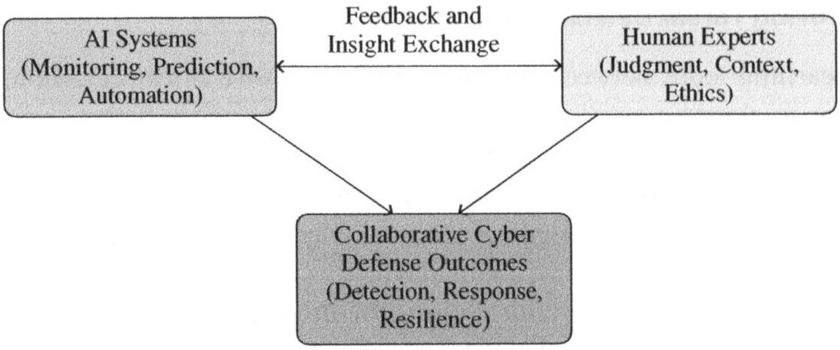

Figure 10.6 Human–AI Collaboration Model in Cyber Defense. "*Source:* Hewa Majeed Zangana"

defense into a proactive, adaptive, and effective enterprise by treating humans as active partners rather than passive overseers [10, 12].

Figure 10.6 illustrates the relationship between human analysts and AI systems in cyber defense: complementary roles in which AI provides data-driven inputs and humans ensure context, ethics, and adaptive decision-making.

10.8 Future Trends and Research Directions

The topography of cybersecurity, especially in terms of insider threats, is dynamically changing due to the advancement of technology, complexity within organizations, and escalating levels of sophistication of both human and cyber adversaries. What is forthcoming in insider threat mitigation will be the integration of AI-driven analytics, human factors research, and socio-technical frameworks to improve proactive detection, response, as well as organizational resilience [1, 18].

10.8.1 Advanced AI and Machine Learning Integration

Inside threats are expected to heavily rely on AI and ML in the future to predict and mitigate those kinds of threats. Such systems in the future will use deep learning and anomaly detection techniques that could successfully model complex behavioral patterns dynamically adjusting themselves according to the evolving threats [5, 15]. The flow of XAI integration into the scheme is expected to improve trust and transparency that could contribute toward the effective interpretation of AI-driven recommendations in the field of cybersecurity professionals [12, 18]. Human-in-the-loop approaches would remain crucial, as AI alone can neither account for socio-organizational contexts nor ethical considerations [8, 10].

10.8.2 Security Designed with Humans in Mind

Human factors research will continue to be an important element of future cyber strategies with respect to reducing the probability of inadvertent insider threats resulting from cognitive overload, stress, or insufficient training [7, 22, 25]. New frameworks will consider how human beings behave as a dynamic system and integrate psychological, cultural, and organizational variables into threat assessment models [4, 24]. Another aspect relating to the development of culture in cybersecurity, as well as continuous education and awareness programs, will contribute to forming resilient organizations [11, 23].

10.8.3 Socio-Technical and Organizational Approaches

Insider threat mitigation methods in the future will be essentially socio-technical with organizations aligning their processes, policies, and technology with socio-techno frameworks to create a systematic intervention in addressing human vulnerabilities [6, 9]. Such an approach to applying behavioral monitoring coupled with role-based access controls and prospective evaluations of risk-inducing factors will ultimately help to ensure the reduction of both deliberate and inadvertent threats [1, 2]. Leadership and governance practices are set to play a central role in embedding cybersecurity into organizational culture, emphasizing accountability, ethical standards, and proactive risk management [17, 20].

10.8.4 Cyber-Physical and Critical Infrastructure Security

Specific challenges associated with insider threats emanating from critical infrastructure and cyber-physical systems include the fact that malicious or accidental actions may cross-interdependent boundaries and potentially affect entire systems [5, 21]. The future research will then address resilience modeling, simulation-based risk assessment, and integrated security frameworks that combine AI analytics with human supervision in an attempt to prevent cascading failures [3, 14].

10.8.5 Emerging Research Directions

Several new promising research areas are emerging with respect to strengthening insider threat mitigation:

1) Behavioral and Cognitive Analytics: Developing rich models that combine cognitive psychology and behavioral indicators to better anticipate insider risk [4, 13].

2) Human–AI Collaborative Defense: Maximizing the collaboration under dynamic conditions in which human and AI tensions exist. These include trust, explainability, and dynamic adaptation to evolving threats [12, 18].
3) Healthcare and High-Stakes Environments: Specific frameworks designed for environments in which human error can have significant consequences, such as hospitals and critical infrastructure [22].
4) Resilience and Adaptive Systems: Melding cyber-physical systems resilience with organizational learning and predictive analytics to improve proactive defense mechanisms [5, 6].
5) Cultural and Policy Interventions: Forming organizational policies and cultural schemes that also take into account ethical, social, and procedural aspects of insider threat mitigation [11, 20].

10.8.6 Summary

Future research on cybersecurity will focus more on leveraging technological innovation, plus human-centric design and organizational strategies. Resilience systems capable of detecting and mitigating insider threats will be built on those three elements. By combining AI-driven analytics with a deep understanding of human behavior and organizational culture, researchers and practitioners can anticipate emerging threats, reduce vulnerabilities, and create proactive defense mechanisms that are effective but also ethical [1, 8, 18].

10.9 Challenges and Limitations

Despite all the nifty advancements in insider threat mitigation, human–AI collaboration, and the improved strategies for cybersecurity, almost all organizations can boast of the many challenges and limitations correlated with the effectiveness of the approaches. These hurdles feature technological, human, organizational, and socio-technical dimensions [1, 18].

10.9.1 Human Factor Challenges

Human behavior, thus, remains the primary barrier to mitigating insider threats. Unintentional insider acts: Those, for example, cause unintended acts by negligence, stress, or a lack of awareness and are the most challenging to predict/prevent [3, 4]. Researchers contend that cognitive overload, burnout, and security fatigue contribute to facilitating vulnerabilities that even well-trained employees fall prey to errors [7, 8, 24]. Plus, an individual's motivational and risk perception motives, alongside his or her ethical reasoning, tend to create gaps regarding policy compliance and security awareness that compound the complication in trouble detection [13, 17].

10.9.2 Organizational and Cultural Limitations

Such barriers among organizations' structures and cultures usually hinder good implementation of insider threat mitigation strategies. Limited interrelation between departments, poor leadership involvement, and a cybersecurity-focused culture can limit the embracing of best practices across an organization [9, 11, 20]. Institutions embracing pure technological solutions without entrenching human factors were all but bound to develop an effusion of reliance on automation and surveillance, which should not consider minor human threats [12, 19].

10.9.3 Technological Constraints

Even though AI and ML have improved the detection and prediction of insider threats, they also have limitations of their own. Data scarcity, biased data sets, false positives, and the fact that human intent and ethics cannot completely be modeled create constraints in the reporting of AI-based systems [1, 5, 15]. Integration of the AI solutions with human operators is challenging due to trust, interpretability, and adaptability concerns, especially in high-stakes environments, as would be the case with critical infrastructure or healthcare [18, 21, 22].

10.9.4 Socio-Technical and Systemic Limitations

The socio-technical nature of cybersecurity introduces systemic challenges. Insider threats arise from intricate interactions among technology, processes, and human behavior that defy clear modeling or mitigation [5, 6, 10]. Strong surveillance and mitigation capabilities may bring with them considerations regarding ethics and privacy with respect to employee watchfulness and behavioral pattern analysis [3, 23, 25]. Furthermore, budget constraints, other competing priorities of the organization, and adapting to changing regulations could potentially limit the magnitude and effectiveness of a security initiative [2, 14].

10.9.5 Industry-Specific Constraints

Sectors have their specific challenges. For instance, healthcare organizations commonly contend with ensuring patient safety while enjoying the benefits of data privacy from insider threats. These have, in fact, created a tug-of-war condition between accessibility and security [22]. Other examples include industrial and critical infrastructures, whereby their high interconnectivity means a single action by an insider can fail the whole system, thus underlining the constraints of current preventive models [3, 5, 21].

10.9.6 Leadership and Governance Challenges

As far as limitations are concerned, effective cybersecurity governance continues to be prevalent. Leadership may underestimate human factors, overemphasize technical controls, or fail to integrate ethical and behavioral considerations into decision-making [12, 17, 20]. Organizational inertia, resistance to change, and insufficient training serve to magnify vulnerabilities, especially reducing efficiency in otherwise solid strategies [4, 8].

10.9.7 Summary

In short, most improvements have been made in insider threat mitigation and cyber defense frameworks; however, they are still limited by human, organizational, technological, and systemic factors. Addressing these issues will require a comprehensive package combining AI-driven analytics with human-centric design, organizational culture, ethical considerations, and socio-technical understanding [1, 9, 18]. Future research and practice must focus on closing these gaps to build resilient, adaptive, and ethically sound cybersecurity ecosystems.

10.10 Conclusion

Insider threats and cybersecurity exist at the nexus of technology, human behavior, and organizational practices. The challenges of designing effective insider threat countermeasures include both advanced technical mechanisms and a good understanding of the human factor in play, like motivation, cognition, and social dynamics. Human–AI collaboration takes on an interesting form here, combining human intuition and machine efficiency to detect, predict, and respond in real-time.

Organizations need to appreciate that cybersecurity does not operate solely within the parameters of a technical problem but rather as a socio-technical one. Culture, governance, and leadership within an organization are critical to the formation of security awareness and compliance and resilience therein. For this reason, any activity considered performing in the realm of security deserves to integrate training, ethics, and behavioral insights alongside technical controls to arrive at a holistic defense strategy.

Nevertheless, some hurdles remain to overcome, such as understanding insider threats completely. The ever-changing unpredictability of the human mind, constraints on resources, and the ever-more sophisticated nature of cyber-attacks put, often, a strain on the resources and strategies available. Reconciling privacy, ethical consideration, and operational efficiency will always be one challenge, ever needing adaptive and flexible ways able to camouflage themselves with the next emerging threat.

To envision a more resilient cybersecurity ecosystem, the convergence of human-centric approaches, AI-enabled analytics, and organizational strategy could provide an interesting opportunity. Through collaboration, creating awareness, and combining socio-technical solutions, organizations will be better positioned to anticipate risks, mitigate vulnerabilities, and sustain trust within an increasingly interconnected digital landscape.

References

1 Alsowail, R.A. and Al-Shehari, T. (2022). Techniques and countermeasures for preventing insider threats. *PeerJ Computer Science* 8: e938.
2 Saxena, N., Hayes, E., Bertino, E. et al. (2020). Impact and key challenges of insider threats on organizations and critical businesses. *Electronics (Basel)* 9 (9): 1460.
3 Canham M, Posey C, Bockelman PS. Confronting information security's elephant, the unintentional insider threat. In: Augmented Cognition Human Cognition and Behavior: 14th International Conference, AC 2020, Held as Part of the 22nd HCI International Conference, HCII 2020, Copenhagen, Denmark, July 19–24, 2020, Proceedings, Part II 22. Springer; 2020. p. 316–34.
4 Khan, N. and J. Houghton R, Sharples S. (2022). Understanding factors that influence unintentional insider threat: A framework to counteract unintentional risks. *Cognition, Technology & Work* 24 (3): 393–421.
5 Baluta T, Ramapantulu L, Teo YM, Chang EC. Modeling the effects of insider threats on cybersecurity of complex systems. In: 2017 Winter Simulation Conference (WSC). IEEE; 2017. p. 4360–4371.
6 McEvoy, T.R. and Kowalski, S.J. (2019). Deriving cyber security risks from human and organizational factors – A socio-technical approach. *Complex Systems Informatics and Modeling Quarterly* 18: 47–64.
7 Nobles, C. (2022). Stress, burnout, and security fatigue in cybersecurity: A human factors problem. *HOLISTICA–Journal of Business and Public Administration* 13 (1): 49–72.
8 Green ML, Dozier P. Understanding human factors of cybersecurity: Drivers of insider threats. In: 2023 IEEE International Conference on Cyber Security and Resilience (CSR). IEEE; 2023. p. 111–6.
9 Pollini, A., Callari, T.C., Tedeschi, A. et al. (2022). Leveraging human factors in cybersecurity: an integrated methodological approach. *Cognition, Technology & Work* 24 (2): 371–390.

10 Young H, van Vliet T, van de Ven J, Jol S, Broekman C. Understanding human factors in cyber security as a dynamic system. In: Advances in Human Factors in Cybersecurity: Proceedings of the AHFE 2017 International Conference on Human Factors in Cybersecurity, July 17–21, 2017, The Westin Bonaventure Hotel, Los Angeles, California, USA 8. Springer; 2018. pp. 244–54.

11 Georgiadou, A., Mouzakitis, S., and Askounis, D. (2022). Detecting insider threat via a cyber-security culture framework. *Journal of Computer Information Systems* 62 (4): 706–716.

12 Zimmermann, V. and Renaud, K. (2019). Moving from a 'human-as-problem" to a 'human-as-solution" cybersecurity mindset. *International Journal of Human Computer Studies* 131: 169–187.

13 Schoenherr, J.R. (2022). Insider threats and individual differences: Intention and unintentional motivations. *IEEE Transactions on Technology and Society* 3 (3): 175–184.

14 Theis M, Trzeciak RF, Costa DL, Moore AP, Miller S, Cassidy T, et al. Common sense guide to mitigating insider threats. 2019.

15 Liu, L., De Vel, O., Han, Q.L. et al. (2018). Detecting and preventing cyber insider threats: A survey. *IEEE Communications Surveys & Tutorials* 20 (2): 1397–1417.

16 Zangana, H.M. and Omar, M. (2020). Threats, attacks, and mitigations of smartphone security. *Academic Journal of Nawroz University* 9 (4): 324–332.

17 Kasowaki L, Yusef O. The human factor in cybersecurity: Addressing social engineering and insider threats. EasyChair; 2023.

18 Omar, M. and Zangana, H.M. (2024). *Redefining Security With Cyber AI*. IGI Global.

19 Nobles, C. (2018). Botching human factors in cybersecurity in business organizations. *HOLISTICA–Journal of Business and Public Administration* 9 (3): 71–88.

20 Triplett, W.J. (2022). Addressing human factors in cybersecurity leadership. *Journal of Cybersecurity and Privacy* 2 (3): 573–586.

21 Ghafir, I., Saleem, J., Hammoudeh, M. et al. (2018). Security threats to critical infrastructure: the human factor. *The Journal of Supercomputing* 74: 4986–5002.

22 Nifakos, S., Chandramouli, K., Nikolaou, C.K. et al. (2021). Influence of human factors on cyber security within healthcare organisations: A systematic review. *Sensors* 21 (15): 5119.

23 Alwaheidi, M.K.S., Islam, S., Papastergiou, S., and Kioskli, K. (2024). *Human Factors in Cybersecurity*, vol. 127, 187–193. AHFE.

24 Jeong J, Mihelcic J, Oliver G, Rudolph C. Towards an improved understanding of human factors in cybersecurity. In: 2019 IEEE 5th International Conference on Collaboration and Internet Computing (CIC). IEEE; 2019. pp. 338–45.

25 Ani, U.D., He, H., and Tiwari, A. (2019). Human factor security: evaluating the cybersecurity capacity of the industrial workforce. *Journal of Systems and Information Technology* 21 (1): 2–35.

11

Policy, Governance, and Ethical AI in Cyber Defense

11.1 Introduction

The serious challenge posed by the rapid evolution of cyber threats has caused major transformations in cybersecurity: it is no longer purely a technical affair but now has a multidimensional technical, organizational, ethical, and policy dimension [1, 2]. However, as organizations adopt advanced artificial intelligence (AI) to strengthen their cyber defense capability, new challenges emerge that must be dealt with under careful scrutiny of relevant policy frameworks, governance structures, and ethical standards [3, 4]. The fusion of AI with modern cybersecurity strategies represents both great potential for proactive threat detection, but also raises some of the really complex ethical and governance dilemmas [5, 6].

A holistic approach balances technological advancement and a well-defined strategy—the three core elements that underpin this approach are policy, governance, and ethics. Only when the three are coherently aligned is it possible for an organization to build a resilient cyber defense ecosystem on responsible AI practices (see Figure 11.1).

Modern enterprises are being threatened within a very dynamic landscape, with more sophisticated, persistent, and automated attacks [7, 8]. With the deluge of connected devices, the advent of cloud computing, and the industrial IoT, there is a widening attack surface, thereby rendering traditional defenses as inadequate [9, 10]. There are also additional layers of complexity emerging with the increasing use of AI for intrusion detection, predictive analysis, and automated response in contributing to bringing the challenges of accountability, transparency, and bias in decision-making [11, 12].

Policies and governance frameworks establish limits on which AI-enabled cyber defense is built [13, 14]. For trust and resilience, AI-enabled systems must conform as organizations implement their cybersecurity practices to international

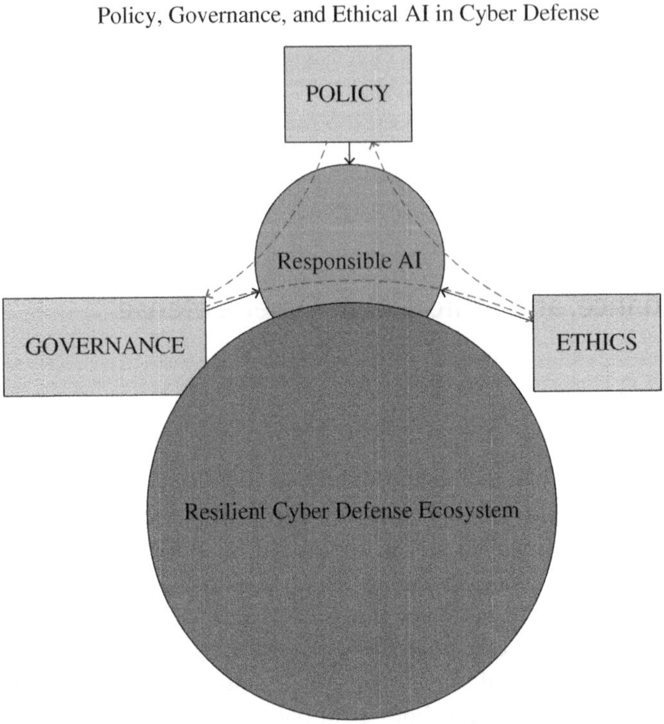

Figure 11.1 The Foundational Pillars of AI-Driven Cyber Defense. "*Source:* Hewa Majeed Zangana"

standards, regulatory requirements, and ethical principles [15, 16]. Without clear policies and robust governance mechanisms, there exists the risk of autonomous-but potentially security- or privacy-violating-judgments through the AI systems [17, 18].

Increasingly, the ethical issues surrounding AI-driven cybersecurity mature. Issues such as bias in threat-detection algorithms, unequal enforcement of security policies, and enabling attacks using AI highlight the necessity of including ethical considerations directly into the design and governance of cyber-defense systems [19–21]. In addition, the agency of making decisions in operations using AI causes a dilemma about accountability, liability, and human intervention, especially in high-stakes areas like critical infrastructure and national defense [19, 20].

Training and awareness are also considered one of the cornerstones of modern cybersecurity strategy to ensure that personnel will understand and interact with AI while appreciating the fact that there are ethical and policy implications regarding automated decision-making [15, 21]. Such cognitive modeling and AI-enabled simulation would still allow encouraging these professionals to prepare for navigation through these dangers without juxtaposing ethical standing and standards regulation [11, 22].

We are thereby presenting an overview of policy, governance, and ethical considerations toward AI-based cyber defense. By analyzing current trends, frameworks, and examples from practice, it provides an account of best practices for integrating AI into current cybersecurity offerings in a responsible and effective manner [23, 24]. Such discussion underscores the need for a comprehensive approach combining technological innovation and ethical, regulatory, and governance imperatives to prepare organizations for the like-evolving powerhouse that is the cyber threat [5, 25].

11.2 The Role of Policy and Governance in Cyber Defense

Effective cybersecurity in today's digital ecosystem requires not only technical solutions but also policy and governance frameworks. Cybersecurity policy defines strategic priorities, rules, and guidelines in regard to an organization's approach to protecting information assets, while governance implements the policies, monitors them, and continuously improves them [1, 8]. If an organization does not have a robust policy and governance mechanism, then purportedly intelligent AI-driven cybersecurity tools cannot deliver the desired protection [3, 5].

11.2.1 Policy as a Strategic Instrument

Cybersecurity policies are strategic instruments that define conditions for acceptable use, procedures for risk management, and protocols for incident response. They elucidate the organizational priorities and compliance with legal, regulatory, and ethical standards [13, 26]. Policies address sector-specific risks in response to unique cybersecurity challenges faced in sectors such as agriculture and smart grids because of the interconnectivity of the operational technology systems; for instance, this interconnectivity requires AI-driven detection methods to be integrated to address these risks and reinforce security resilience [9, 12].

Policies set the basis from which risk assessment and mitigation approaches derive. Threats today are characterized by a highly sophisticated set of attacks—the likes of which include ransomware, phishing, AI-assisted intrusions, and supply chains undermined [7, 10]. Policies that make use of computers for continuous monitoring, AI-assisted threat detection, and adaptive defense mechanisms will allow organizations to begin anticipation and mitigation of the respective risk [4, 6, 21]. Further, clear policies delineate responsibility for data protection, encryption, and access control, which can curb the possibility of internal lapses and compliance violations [2, 19].

11.2.2 Governance and Accountability

A policy sets the objectives, but it is governance that ensures consistent and fair application of a policy. Cybersecurity governance encompasses structures, leadership, decision-making processes, and accountability mechanisms for implementing cybersecurity strategy [13, 14]. AI tools used within the governance framework provide predictive analytics, threat intelligence, and automation of responses—to the extent where human oversight is counted on to complement technological efficiencies [11, 22].

Strong governance entails continuous assessment and training of cybersecurity personnel. The modern organization uses adaptive learning frameworks, cognitive modeling, and simulation-based exercises to prime its people for emerging threats [15, 21]. These initiatives uphold the organization's readiness while ensuring ethical behavior and regulatory compliance [17, 20]. Governance mechanisms will also deal with the threats of possible corruption and insider attacks; operational bias may compromise cybersecurity outcomes [16, 27].

11.2.3 Integration of Policy, Governance, and AI

AI integration in cybersecurity increases opportunities and responsibilities associated with policy and governance. AI-based systems tend to improve situational awareness, automatically respond to threats, and optimize resource allocations [4, 11]. Well-described policy boundaries must manage these systems so they do not engage in unethical behavior, unintended discrimination, or overly automate vital decisions [17, 24]. Governance must safeguard the transparency, auditability, and accountability of AI-enabled processes, lest the advancement of technology come at the cost of regulation and ethics [3, 28].

In that light, policy and governance must evolve as new threats and technologies emerge [5, 25]. Emerging technologies, such as cloud computing, IoT, and AI-enhanced cyber threats, necessitate a constant review of policy and an adaptation of governance toward operational resilience and integrity [10, 18, 29].

11.2.4 Summary

To summarize, policy and governance are the cornerstones of effective cyber defense. Policies create a strategic roadmap for risk management, ethical behavior, and compliance. Governance makes sure that, once these policies are created, their enforcement, monitoring, and improvement take place. AI integration in cybersecurity magnifies the need for stringent policy oversight and workable governance mechanisms that guarantee accountability, transparency, and resilience in light of evolving cyber threats [4, 6, 12].

11.3 AI Governance Models and Frameworks

The integration of AI in cybersecurity has both unprecedented opportunities and complexities for governing challenges. AI governance is an incredibly complex concept, spanning from technical oversight to regulatory compliance, risk management, and ethical accountability [13, 17]. It consists of all the policies, structures, standards, and procedures ensuring that AI systems operate securely, ethically, and according to the aims and objectives of an organization [3, 5]. Without robust governance frameworks, AI deployments may exacerbate vulnerabilities, introduce bias, or operate outside organizational control, consequently undermining cybersecurity objectives [4, 30].

11.3.1 Core Principles of AI Governance

Several norms anchor AI governance frameworks. An understanding of the AI decision-making process, as well as accountability for automated cyber defense, requires some form of transparency [11, 22]. Robustness and reliability mean that AI systems must be able to perform according to preset standards, regardless of whether another party attempts to attack it with adversarial attacks or if operations are unexpected [6, 10]. Ethical considerations include fairness, privacy, and human oversight and are designed to mitigate several risks, including bias, discriminatory results, or violations of data protection standards [17, 24]. Finally, adaptability endows AI governance frameworks with the evolution necessary to respond to emergent threats, regulatory shifts, and advances in AI technologies [5, 7].

Such key principles define the basis upon which AI governance frameworks for cybersecurity are established. In that line, such principles as transparency, robustness and reliability, ethical considerations, and adaptability form the basis for design choices as well as regulatory compliance in AI-enabled cyber defense operations (see Figure 11.2).

Core Principles of AI Governance
1. Transparency Essential for understanding AI decision-making processes and ensuring accountability in automated operations[cite: 439, 623].
2. Robustness and Reliability Ensures Al systems maintain high performance and integrity, even when facing adversarial attacks or unexpected operational conditions[cite: 440].
3. Ethical Considerations Central to mitigating risks of bias, discriminatory outcomes, and violations of data protection standards (e.g., Fairness, Privacy, Human Oversight)[cite: 441, 627, 629].
4. Adaptability Allows the governance frameworks and Al systems to evolve quickly in response to emerging threats, regulatory changes, and technological advancements.

Figure 11.2 Core Principles Guiding AI Governance in Cyber Defense. "*Source:* Hewa Majeed Zangana"

11.3.2 AI Governance Models

Various governance models have been put forth for the regulation of AI within the gamut of cybersecurity. The centralized model accentuates a single governing command that is bestowed with the power of framing policy, monitoring compliance, and auditing everything pertaining to AI performance across the whole organization [13, 14]. This way, one achieves predictability in decision-making and accountability, but this predictability comes at the cost of hindering quick decision-making in a dynamic environment. The decentralized approach, on the other hand, assigns governance responsibilities across various departments, teams, or regional units, allowing it to maintain quickness and contextual adaptability, while at the same time requiring strong coordination mechanisms to uphold standards [4, 21].

In hybrid governance, centralized oversight is accompanied by decentralized execution to strike the right balance between uniform standards and operational flexibility [1, 15]. Such models nearly always involve risk committees, boards of ethics for AI, and cross-functional review panels that monitor the performance of AI systems in implementation against the policy objectives [3, 23]. A strengthening of AI governance with existing cybersecurity governance practices will ensure that the AI systems uphold rather than subvert the organization's security practices [26, 27].

11.3.3 Frameworks for AI Governance

A number of frameworks exist that govern the responsible implementation of AI in cyber defense. Risk-based frameworks emphasize identifying, assessing, and mitigating potential threats to AI, such as adversarial manipulation, algorithmic bias, and system failures [7, 30]. Compliance-oriented frameworks seek to guarantee conformity with pertinent international regulations, standards, and best practices for data protection and cybersecurity and to align AI deployment with ethical and legal requirements [14, 22].

Ethics-driven frameworks emphasize fairness, accountability, transparency, and explainability [6, 17]. Such frameworks typically utilize a human-in-the-loop mechanism to ensure that, as far as critical decision-making is concerned, the human element remains involved, especially in high stakes, such as healthcare, critical infrastructure, or finance [12, 19]. There is also cognitive modeling and simulation-based AI proposed so that the behavior of AI systems can be evaluated, risks anticipated, and guidance for the modification of policies can be offered in a dynamic threat environment [10, 11].

11.3.4 Integrating AI Governance with Cybersecurity Practices

The intersection of AI governance with other dimensions of cybersecurity ensures that AI tools contribute to the defense strategy. Policy must specify AI-acceptable behaviors, monitoring protocols, and escalation paths for unusual actions [2, 8]. Governance should include training, continuous auditing, and scenario-based simulations to assess whether AI meets performance and ethical standards [15, 21]. By embedding AI governance into an existing cybersecurity delivery framework, organizations could leverage the strategies of AI while mitigating operational, ethical, and regulatory risks [5, 24].

11.3.5 Summary

AI governance models and frameworks provide an important backbone to safeguarding that AI-driven cyber defense systems work securely, ethically, and efficiently. With policy control, organized governance, and risk-aware frameworks, an organization should be able to fully utilize AI without confronting ethical, operational, or security risks [3, 4]. The very successful integration of AI governance with current cybersecurity practice would enable organizations to anticipate, detect, and respond to new threats, remaining accountable, transparent, and resilient [12, 28].

11.4 Ethical Considerations in AI-Driven Cyber Defense

The upside of integrating AI into cybersecurity includes the most powerful capabilities that can be divided into ethical challenges that are equally complex. Such systems can cause harm, perpetuate bias, and infringe on principles of privacy,

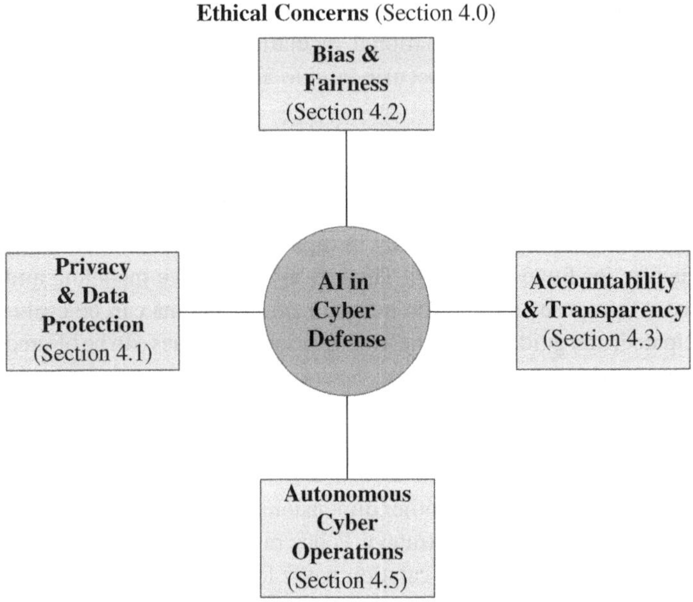

Figure 11.3 Key Ethical Concerns Stemming from AI Integration in Cyber Defense. "*Source:* Hewa Majeed Zangana"

transparency, and accountability when improperly controlled or managed [3, 17]. Thus, issues of ethics in AI-directed cyber defense training on trust, legality, and effectiveness cut across the public and private sectors [5, 13].

The powerful capabilities of AI in cyber defense must not be rendered impossible to manage or treat significant ethical risks proactively, which include managing sensitive data (Privacy); potential unequal treatment (Bias and Fairness); the need to explain automated actions (Accountability and Transparency); and unpredictable automated reactions (Autonomous Operations). These elements are important in retaining public trust and legal compliance (see Figure 11.3).

11.4.1 Privacy and Data Protection

Data is essential to AI systems for pattern finding, threat prediction, and response automation [10, 22]. Only through organized consideration of ethical management of data is it possible to prevent cases of unauthorized access or misconduct with sensitive information. As identified in the paper, frameworks of privacy-preserving AI—such as anonymization, differential privacy, and secure multi-party computation—will continue to play a significant role even in sectors that handle sensitive data, particularly healthcare, finance, and critical infrastructures [6, 12]. Compliance with data protection regulations, that is, GDPR or equivalent national laws, is not only an obligatory norm of law but also an obligatory virtue of ethics [7, 30].

11.4.2 Prejudice and Fairness

Because of the databases from which they are trained, or by design choice during the course of model development, bias can exist in AI algorithms [4, 11]. Its use will only produce an AI biased against a part of the threat pattern and ignore others, which will then expose such firms to risks not previously anticipated by them [1, 24]. As such, ethical frameworks are about fairness-value points that are to be monitored continuously with bias detection and corrective mechanisms so that AI-driven defenses will operate fairly with respect to each one of the systems and all stakeholders [10, 26].

11.4.3 Accountability and Transparency

Ethical AI governance must provide clear accountability mechanisms for decisions made by automated systems [13, 14]. In cybersecurity, every automated response—whether an isolated threat, a firewall adjustment, or network segmentation—has to be traceable in order to prevent either wrongful actions or unintended service disruption [2, 30]. Transparency measures—including explainable AI (XAI) models and audit trails—give human operators the means to understand AI reasoning, validate outputs, and intervene when necessary [21, 23]. These practices ensure that AI-driven interventions remain consistent with organizational policies and ethical norms [20, 27].

11.4.4 Human Intervention and Decision Making

Humans serve as the ultimate ethical safeguard in cyber defense, even as the institution permits the automation of most functions of AI [3, 17]. Man's contextual judgment and moral reasoning, in addition to strategic thinking, which AI systems cannot replicate alone, define what it is to be human [18, 25]. Through such mechanisms, cybersecurity teams can supervise AI decision-making, intervene in high-stakes scenarios, and validate system recommendations, thus avoiding ethical and operational risk [12, 19].

11.4.5 Ethical Implications of Autonomous Cyber Operations

AI-generated autonomous cyber operations can include threat hunting, intrusion denial, or vulnerability patching, and they introduce unique ethical concerns [4, 5]. Although autonomy contributes to speed and scalability, it can invoke severe unintended consequences—not just from a form-based point of view but also because of AI misclassifying threats or applying over-aggressive countermeasures [10, 16]. As much as possible, ethical frameworks would prescribe constraints, scenario testing, and simulation environments for testing an AI's behavior before it is deployed live [11, 20].

11.4.6 Culture and Ethics of Organizations

In adopting AI for cyber defense, one must consider organizational culture and societal norms [9, 16]. Just as ethical AI practices extend beyond compliance to moral responsibility—the trust employees, customers, and partners place in each institution—leadership carries critical responsibility for embedding these premises into cybersecurity policies, training programs, and operational protocols [13, 14]. Continuous cybersecurity training, ethical scenario simulations, and other programs further encourage an ethical vigilance culture through which teams would navigate complex AI environments [15, 21].

11.4.7 Summary

Ethics is at the core of constitutive, operational, and governance considerations in AI-driven cyber defense systems. Privacy assurance, fairness, transparency, accountability, and human oversight together assure that AI augments security while complying with ethical and legal standards [5, 8]. By actioning these components within the policies, governance structures, and operational frameworks of the organization, cybersecurity teams would be provided with responsible leverage over AI to build stronger, more trustworthy, and ethically aligned cyber defense ecosystems [3, 4].

11.5 Legal and Regulatory Perspectives

The landscape of law and regulations puts a limit on the way cybersecurity, including AI-based cyber defense systems, should be operated. The more advanced technologies create a need for conventional threat detection and operation by using artificial intelligence, big data analytics, and automated threat detection largely to ensure legal compliance by prevention of liability and to strengthen the trust of the stakeholders.

11.5.1 Global Cybersecurity Legislation

Cybersecurity laws stand variedly across jurisdictions and, however, share these common purposes: shielding the critical structure, protecting personal data, and attending to cybercrimes [7, 29]. Notable regulation frameworks, such as GDPR in Europe, China's Cybersecurity Law, and the Federal Information Security Management Act (FISMA) in the United States, set criterion requirements for data security, breach notification, and organization accountability [2, 6]. These regulations make a maintenance program critical to put in place with strong cybersecurity measures for the organization, including risk assessment, continuous monitoring, and incident response planning [10, 27].

11.5.2 Compliance and Risk Management

Legal compliance will work only if cybersecurity policies are integrated with the management of risk [8, 26]. Regulatory audits, vulnerability assessments, and penetration tests are used by organizations to demonstrate adherence to regulatory requirements and industry standards [1, 30]. It further finds itself in regard to AI-driven security systems, ethics, legality, transparency, accountability, and explainability in automated decision-making [3, 4].

11.5.3 Sector-Specific Regulations

Some sectors face additional regulatory burdens due to the sensitivity of their data and criticality of their operations. For example, the healthcare sector must comply with HIPAA regulations, while financial institutions fall under the jurisdiction of frameworks such as PCI DSS and GLBA [9, 18]. Similar regulations provide for the protection of industrial control systems and smart grids against the NERC CIP standards and national cybersecurity policies to ensure their operational resilience [12, 19]. The regulation sector of each industry emphasizes the significance of adjusting cybersecurity measures in view of any threats with due regard to the laws and regulations [11, 20].

11.5.4 Emerging Legal Challenges

AI and autonomous cybersecurity tools bring in new legal challenges, particularly with regard to liability, accountability, and cross-border operations [4, 14]. Assigning accountability for the actions of AI systems remains complicated should such systems make incorrect or harmful decisions; their development raises concerns about the need to expand legal frameworks to accommodate emerging technologies. Nevertheless, achieving an international consensus on the judicial front against cybercrime, data protection, and artificial intelligence governance appears critical on behalf of the global threat caused by cybercrimes [13, 28].

11.5.5 Enforcement and Ethical Considerations

Enforcement entails many concomitant but consequential practices: regulatory audits, stiff penalties for noncompliance, and incentives for best practices [15, 21]. Ethical considerations, including respect for privacy, prejudice prevention, and ensuring that all access technologies are intertwined with legal compliance and form a bedrock for responsible cybersecurity [17, 25]. Enforcement of the law coupled with ethical practices in order to implement strong, trustworthy, and sustainable cybersecurity strategies [3, 5].

11.5.6 Future Directions

Interjurisdictional accountability must blossom in the future legal and regulatory framework of cybersecurity, where collaborations on enforcement are created, and portable rules dynamically evolve to equivalent relational threats [11, 24]. Further advances along the road would have compliance at the edge of advanced threat intelligence, predictive analytics, and monitoring for anticipation of legal risks while also nurturing an ethics-enriched program representing a high standard of security and ethics [4, 10]. Owing to business ethics, unafflicted, and essential policy-making proprietors and corporate bodies, in addition to different agents of robust enforcement, are in order to directly shape directives that better balance innovation with accountability [3, 23].

11.6 Responsible AI in Cybersecurity Operations

AI has transformed the approaches to threat detection, response processes, and vulnerability management. The integration of AI into cyber defense operations requires responsible practices for effectiveness, transparency, and ethical considerations [3, 4]. Responsible AI in cybersecurity focuses on the development and application of explainable and accountable AI systems that are compliant with the legal, ethical, and organizational standards [5, 17].

11.6.1 Principles of Responsible AI

Responsible AI in cybersecurity rests on several core principles. First, transparency holds that AI decisions should be interpretable and traceable, enabling security teams to comprehend why an automated alert or action was undertaken [4, 22]. Second, accountability describes where responsibility for AI outcomes is directed, particularly when automated responses bear heavily on critical infrastructure or sensitive data [7, 16]. A third principle is fairness and avoidance of discrimination so that AI models will be free of any biases that can discriminate against certain users or systems and will be heavily stressed in finance, health, and agriculture [9, 18]. Finally, privacy preservation will require that AI systems be compliant with data protection laws while minimizing the data captured and retained without justification [1, 6].

11.6.2 Responsible AI Implementation in Cybersecurity Operations

Responsible AI implementation entails mainstreaming ethical, legal, and technical safeguards across the AI life cycle: at the data governance stage, training datasets must be curated in a way that avoids bias while ensuring accuracy and protecting sensitive data [10, 26]. Model validation and continuous monitoring are equally critical, as they help an organization detect real-time performance drift, emerging biases, or unintended consequences [11, 24]. Additionally, human-in-the-loop frameworks allow for expert oversight, combining AI efficiency and human judgment, thus minimizing the risk of false positives, misclassifications, or erroneous automated actions [20, 30].

The responsible implementation of AI is indeed a life-cycle process that embeds ethical, legal, and technical safeguards right from the first stage of development and continues through continuous operation. The process includes a systematic stepwise progression from unbiased data curation and model validation through continuous monitoring and finally into a human-in-the-loop framework with a view to complementing AI efficiency with human judgment (see Figure 11.4).

11.6.3 Sector-Specific Considerations

Each of the industries needs its own approach to responsible AI with regard to cybersecurity. For instance, AI used in smart grids and energy systems must weigh operational efficiency with the protection of critical infrastructure from advanced threats [12]. In automotive cybersecurity, AI-enabled intrusion detection systems should ensure the safety of vehicles while upholding privacy for users [19]. In agriculture and FinTech, the AI systems should work within the framework of industry-specific regulations, protect sensitive operational data, and foster sustainable practices [9, 18]. Across the board, responsible adoption requires a strict application of ethical and regulatory standards to preserve the trust of stakeholders [13, 14].

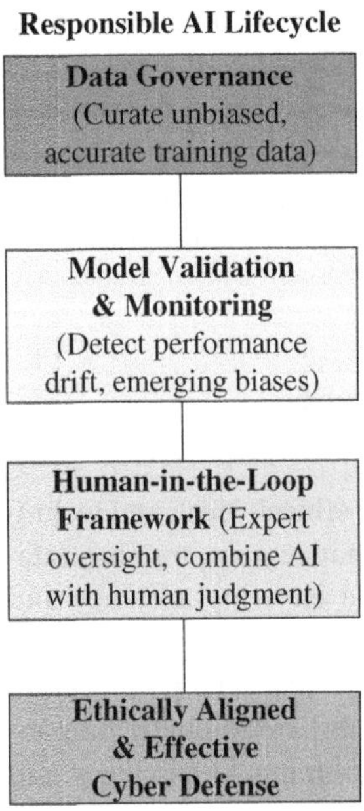

Figure 11.4 Phases of Responsible AI Implementation in Cybersecurity. "*Source:* Hewa Majeed Zangana"

11.6.4 Challenges and Mitigation Strategies

Responsible AI, however, faces a number of serious roadblocks, including algorithmic bias, lack of transparency, over-dependence on an automated system, and the attendant legal complications arising from cross-jurisdictions [16, 17]. The proposed mitigation measures go from an AI-enabled good auditing practice to adopting interpretable machine learning tools, continuous training of personnel responsible for cybersecurity, and developing toward conformity with an evolving legal framework [15, 21, 28]. Building ethical considerations into AI design and operation will help mitigate the cases where automatic defenses pose unintended threats to security, privacy, or fairness [4, 25].

11.6.5 Future Directions

The future of responsible AI in cybersecurity will be characterized by adaptive and explainable AI models capable of formal ads and functioning in diverse regulatory environments and yet remaining ethical [3, 11]. Integration with cyber threat intelligence platforms, predictive analytics, and autonomous response systems would strongly augment the proactive defense of critical infrastructure. Attention will also be given to furthering research into AI ethics frameworks, legal compliance, and transparency standards to lend further strength to responsible AI as a mainstay in cybersecurity operations [4, 5, 7].

11.7 Governance for Data Integrity and Model Security

As AI and machine learning rapidly become more prominent in modern cybersecurity functions, the necessity of establishing critical governance mechanisms to manage data integrity and model security becomes apparent. While the term "data integrity" refers to the accuracy and completeness of data as well as its consistent maintenance during its lifecycle, model security involves protecting AI and machine learning models from adversarial attacks, tampering, or unauthorized access [3, 4].

11.7.1 Value of Data Governance

Effective data governance is comparably foundational to efficient operation in reliable cybersecurity functions. Poor status of data quality could imply a failure of AI in threat detection, vulnerability assessment, and incident response [8, 10]. In fact, the governance frameworks should enforce data validation and provenance tracking as well as controlled access mechanisms in order to prevent distortion, alteration, or loss of critical information [6, 26]. Sectors such as finance, agriculture, or energy are other examples, which have specific standards beyond compliance with regulatory requirements and best practices to ensure organizational continuity and trustworthiness [9, 12, 18].

11.7.2 Security Considerations for Models

AI and machine learning models in cybersecurity are subjected to threats such as model inversion, data poisoning, and adversarial attacks. It therefore suffices that governing strategies should incorporate practices for secure development, continuous monitoring of models, and validation protocols to maintain model integrity over time [24, 30]. Robust encryption, authentication, and access control for models and training data would further increase protection against unauthorized manipulation or exploitation [2, 6].

11.7.3 Governance Frameworks and Best Practices

1) Policy and Compliance Enforcement: Clear policies for data handling, model usage, and regulatory adherence create a framework for ensuring alignment with national and international cybersecurity norms [5, 7].
2) Data Quality Management: Processes of data cleansing, normalization, and integrity verification preclude the propagation of errors into AI-based systems [10, 22].

3) Model Lifecycle Oversight: Monitoring, retraining, and auditing of models have been established as measures of dealing with drift, bias, or new vulnerabilities [4, 11].
4) Risk Assessment and Incident Response: Linking scenario-based simulations and vulnerability assessments increases the resilience of AI systems to attacks [15, 20].
5) Human-in-the-Loop Verification: Automated AI decision-making, combined with human involvement, guarantees the needed critical oversight and accountability, especially in high-stakes operations [25, 30].

11.7.4 Challenges and Emerging Solutions

These practices notwithstanding, there still exist some hurdles in achieving data integrity and model security: several heterogeneous data sources, adversarial manipulations, and the speed at which cyber threats are evolving [1, 29]. Some of the new solutions that can be explored in this regard include blockchain-based origin tracking, federated learning for private model learning, and cognitive AI approaches intended to monitor anomalies in both data and model behavior [4, 11, 12]. All these innovations will further add to the reliability of AI-based cybersecurity and reduce the risk associated with systemic vulnerabilities.

11.7.5 Strategic Implications

Governance of data integrity and model security is not just a technical issue but rather a strategic imperative. Leaders must, therefore, ensure that the governance principles are incorporated into organizational culture, policies emerging in the cybersecurity field, and operational workflow processes for safeguarding stakeholder confidence, complying with the set regulatory requirements, and achieving sustainability in cybersecurity outcomes [13, 14, 31]. A strong foundation of governance enhances the efficacy of AI-based defenses and thereby enables automation to be trustworthy, secure, and ethical in varying environments of operation [16, 21, 23].

11.8 Policy Framework for AI-Enabled Cyber Defense Systems

It requires policy frameworks with guidelines for both technology deployment and organizational practices that adequately address these issues regarding the integration of AI into cyber defense operations. They should ensure that

AI-enabled systems are operable in a secure, ethical, and effective way while also minimizing the risks of adversarial attacks, misuse of data, and undesirable behaviors from the system [3, 4].

11.8.1 Strategic Objectives of AI Cyber Defense Policies

AI-enabled cyber defense systems will proactively and reactively respond to developing threats in near-real time. Policy frameworks need to include the strategic objectives of risk reduction, operational resilience, compliance with regulations, and ethical governance of AI [5, 7]. The addition of AI to the cybersecurity strategy will improve predictive threat analysis, automated response protocols, and the undertaking of human workload in complex operational environments [1, 19].

11.8.2 Core Policy Components

The robust policy framework of AI-enabled cyber defense usually encompasses the following major areas:

1) Data Management and Quality Assurance: Policies should demand safe and secure data collection, storage, and processing practices to maintain integrity and minimize bias in AI decision-making [8, 10]. Data encryption, access control, and validation mechanisms to prevent unauthorized manipulation are required in this regard [2, 6].
2) Model Security and Lifecycle Governance: Policies should define how models will be developed, trained, and deployed and how they will be monitored on a continuous basis, with significant emphasis given to detection and remediation of adversarial attacks, model drift, or tampering [11, 24, 30].
3) Ethical and Responsible Use of AI: Governance policies should enforce deployment of ethical AI emphasizing transparency, accountability, and fairness while addressing privacy concerns and minimizing algorithmic bias [13, 14, 17].
4) Regulatory Compliance and Standardization: It must also be ensured that international and national cybersecurity regulations, industry standards, and sector-related mandates are adhered to by organizations [9, 12, 18]. The policy framework should contain specialized guidelines for auditing and reporting AI-enabled cybersecurity activities [5].
5) Incident Response and Risk Mitigation: Policy should create clear procedures for threat detection, containment, mitigation, and recovery, supported by AI-driven and human oversight mechanisms [20, 21, 30].

11.8.3 Guidelines for Implementation

A multi-layered approach with combined technological controls, human oversight, and organizational governance is necessary for implementing an AI-committed policy framework. However, some of the best practices include:

- Continuous Training and Awareness Programs: Knowledge of AI threats, operational procedures, and ethical issues amplifies the success of cybersecurity policy enforcement [15, 25, 28].
- Cooperative Learning: Collaboration among cybersecurity, data governance, compliance, and the operations teams will ensure policy requirements are met across the organization [26, 27].
- Continuous Monitoring and Evaluation: Policies should prescribe regular evaluation of AI models and system performance, enabling updates based on emerging threats or regulatory changes [4, 22].
- Integration of Cognitive and Adaptive Technologies: Using AI-driven insights for the improvement of policy will allow organizations to dynamically change their security strategies as per the evolving threat surfaces [11, 12].

11.8.4 Challenges and Future Directions

Such structured policies notwithstanding, confrontation continues in the governance aspect of AI-enabled future cyber defense with adversarial manipulation of the models, data poisoning, opacity in decision-making, and alignment with moving goalposts of evolving regulations [1, 29]. Emerging potential solutions include federated learning, secure multi-party computation, explainable AI, and blockchain-based audit trails that have the potential to reinforce transparency, resilience, and compliance of systems [3, 4]. Policy development in the future should also accommodate requirements that are sector-specific, for example, finance, critical infrastructure, healthcare, and industrial systems, to create the safe and responsible use of AI technologies [9, 19, 27].

11.8.5 Strategic Implications

A well-structured policy framework for the AI-enabled cyber defense system is more than just a technical requirement; it is a strategic one. By developing it, countries will be able to responsibly leverage AI capabilities and have resilient cyber operations while constantly meeting obligations by organizations and regulators. Such policies strengthen confidence among stakeholders, improve operational efficiency, and prepare organizations to maneuver more and more among the complexities of the cybersecurity landscape [13, 14, 31].

11.9 Ethical AI Decision-Making Framework

The increasing introduction of AI into cybersecurity operations has led to several ethical issues. An ethical AI decision-making framework is required to ensure that AI-powered systems operate ethically, transparently, and in accordance with organizational and societal norms [3, 4]. This type of framework directs the design, deployment, and management of AI systems concerning the risk management and confidence-building dimensions, including accountability as well.

11.9.1 Principles of Ethical AI in Cybersecurity

Such ethical principles are founded among a few other principles, at the core of ethical AI frameworks on cybersecurity:

1) Transparency and Explainability: It makes AI-driven decisions interpretable by human operators so that the stakeholders are in a position to understand how models generate outcomes, particularly on security-critical decisions [11, 17]. This principle prevents AI from being treated as the "black box" of the black market from misuse as well as unintended consequences [10, 22].
2) Accountability and Responsibility: Organizations need to have a transparent and well-defined accountability for what actions are done via AI, have possibly appropriate oversight mechanisms for model decisions, and know how they impact security operations [13, 14, 23]. Clear definitions of responsibilities have to be laid out in policies for AI developers, cybersecurity teams, and the leadership within organizations [7, 24].
3) Fairness and Redress of Bias: The AI models should be built not to discriminate, prejudice, or otherwise treat parties inequitably in making security decisions. Data validation, model audit, and fairness assessments are necessary to ensure ethicality in these kinds of outcomes [1, 6, 8].
4) Privacy Preservation: Cybersecurity AI frameworks should respect user privacy while safeguarding sensitive data from destructive uses and threat detection [2, 19, 27]. The essential approaches include privacy-by-design, encryption, and techniques of anonymization [9, 10].
5) Risk-Sensitive Decision Making: The design aspect of an AI system is such that it must evaluate the possible risks and consequences of its automated actions. Threat scenarios will need to be modeled; operational impacts will need to be assessed; and over-reliance on the output of an AI system will need safeguards [16, 20, 30].

11.9.2 Structural Components of an Ethical AI Framework

1) Statutes on Data Governance: Policies on the integrity of data, security of stored data, and how to properly handle data ensure that AI models are trained on accurate, unbiased, and representative datasets [1, 22, 29].
2) Model Construction and Evaluation: Ethical issues should be incorporated at the level of designing, training, and evaluating AI models along with fairness checks, adversarial testing, and robustness measures as part of validation processes [4, 10, 11].
3) Human Oversight: Decision-making processes should incorporate a human-in-the-loop mechanism, ensuring that AI is monitored in its actions and, thus, possible human modification is needed when required [3, 13, 15].
4) Continuous Monitoring and Adaptation: AI systems need continuous monitoring for drift detection, developing unintentional vulnerabilities, and ethical compliance. There must be mandatory policies that enforce regular audits, updates, and retraining for ethical maintenance [5, 12, 21].

11.9.3 Directions of Ethical AI Implementation

- Ethics Early in the Designing of AI Models: Ethical principles could be used at the design stage to accomplish adherence to organizational societal norms from the inception of the systems [17, 31].
- Clear Metrics on Ethical Performance: There should be standards with which AI fairness, transparency, accountability, and privacy adherence can be measured [7, 8].
- Foster a Culture of Ethical Awareness: Train cybersecurity personnel and AI developers to recognize ethical risks so that they can proactively mitigate and responsibly steer AI [18, 25, 28].
- Establish Sector-Specific Ethical Standards: Ethics require different frameworks for industries such as finance, health care, critical infrastructure, and smart grids that are designed to address specific risks of each of them and their regulatory environments [9, 12, 19].

11.9.4 Challenges and Future Considerations

Ethical AI decision-making today indeed has to contend with many ongoing issues, such as algorithmic opacity, adversarial manipulation, and the shifting weight in automation versus human judgment [1, 4, 16]. Future research should focus on topics such as explainable AI, robust fairness metrics, secure multi-party computations, and adaptive governance models to maintain ethical compliance in this dynamic cyber environment [3, 6, 11].

11.10 Challenges and Future Directions

The evolution of cybersecurity in AI-driven and data-saturated environments presents a set of challenges that, by nature, are complex and strategic in their consideration. Understanding such challenges and scouting out future trajectories will be crucial for the organizations whose aims are to build resilient, adaptive, and ethically sound cyber defenses [3, 4].

11.10.1 Key Challenges

1) **Fast-Moving Threat Landscape**
   Cyber threats are growing in sophistication, mixing malware with traditional enemies such as advanced persistent threats or ransomware to new adversarial AI-driven attacks [1, 7, 30]. The increased frequency and complexity of such attacks make timely detection and responses even harder [10, 29]. Furthermore, emerging domains such as smart grids, industrial IoT, and autonomous vehicles are providing new attack surfaces [9, 12, 19].
2) **Data Management and Integrity**
   Ensuring the integrity, confidentiality, and availability of data remains a core challenge. Large-scale datasets are majorly obtained or integrated from heterogeneous systems and are subject to risks of inconsistency or corruption, which can cause manipulation of the data by adversaries, thereby compromising AI-driven decision-making [6, 10, 22]. Data governance frameworks should be strengthened to relieve those vulnerabilities [1, 8].
3) **Ethical and Governance Concerns**
   The use of AI will pose some ethical concerns in cybersecurity, such as transparency, accountability, and fairness of automated decisions [11, 17]. The absence of strong governance and ethical frameworks would deliver unintended consequences, making it very difficult for organizations not to find themselves in violation of regulatory mandates [5, 13, 14].
4) **Skill Gaps and Human Resource Limitations**
   The lack of qualified personnel in cybersecurity to run AI-enhanced systems remains a big challenge to address [15, 21, 25]. Programs enhancing the knowledge of personnel in AI, machine learning, threat intelligence, and incident response should be the focus of further development of training programs [18, 23, 27].
5) **Technical Complexity and Integration**
   Applying AI to cybersecurity would raise technical issues related to interoperability, scalability, and authentic time processing of high-velocity data in syncing AI with current cybersecurity infrastructure [4, 10, 24]. Organizations

must weigh AI-automated functions against human intervention to effectively mitigate any threats [1, 3].

6) **Regulatory and Compliance Pressures**
The growing number of regulations and standards will require cybersecurity practices to comply. Organizations are finding it difficult to draw overlaps between AI operations and regulations, data privacy laws, and specific compliance requirements of industries [2, 26, 28].
7) **Adversarial AI and Model Security**
The application of AI brings with it another risk of adversarial attacks, whereby the inputs into the models are compromised by malicious users [4, 30]. Model integrity and system reliability should be continuously monitored and robustly defended against [10, 22].

11.10.2 Future Directions

1) **Adaptive and Proactive Defense Mechanisms**
Proactive future cybersecurity architectures should adopt AI techniques for predictive threat modeling, anomaly detection, and real-time responses to emerging threats [3, 4, 12]. Adaptive learning algorithms should enhance resilience against evolving types of attack strategies [7, 10].
2) **Ethical AI and Governance Integration**
Integrating ethical principles into AI-driven cybersecurity is important. This includes transparency, explainability, fairness, and accountability in different states of AI deployment [5, 11, 17]. Governance structures should advocate continuous auditing, model validation, and ethical compliance checks—an aspect emphasized by [13, 14].
3) **Strengthened Training and Cooperation Between Humanoids and AI**
Creating a talent pool with expertise in managing AI-enhanced systems is important. Advanced AI literacy, cyber risk management, and decision-support system skills that complement automation should be the thrust of future programs [15, 18, 21].
4) **Strong Data Governance and Privacy Protection**
Building secure, quality, and private data pipelines is most important; the torch continues to prioritize encryption, safe data sharing, and blockchain-enabled auditing mechanisms to support trust in this new era in AI-based cybersecurity operations [6, 10, 22].
5) **Interdisciplinary Collaboration and Standardization**
The partnership forged among industry, academia, and government will be instrumental in the process of developing universal standards, threat intelligence sharing, and coordinated response frameworks [2, 9, 19]. This multi-stakeholder participation will be important because this is a global, interconnected cyber threat.

6) **Robust AI Models Against Adversarial Attack**
   Improved robustness in AI models through adversarial training, anomaly detection, and resilient model architectures that could withstand sophisticated attacks will be the focus of future research [4, 10, 30].
7) **Emerging Technology and Smart Infrastructure Safeguards**
   To secure any of the complex infrastructures—such as smart grids, autonomous vehicles, and industrial IoT systems—results from the integration of AI, big data analytics, and cybersecurity frameworks into adaptive, intelligent, and secure environments [10, 12, 19].

11.10.3 Summary

Overcoming these hurdles while implementing those future paths will enable organizations to develop AI-enabled cybersecurity systems that are resilient, adaptive, and ethically grounded. In fact, by focusing on innovation, governance, ethical standards, and skilled human oversight, the next generation will be able to respond appropriately to evolving threats in complex, data-driven environments [3, 5, 31].

11.11 Conclusion

Security frameworks must be robust, adaptable, and ethically grounded because the world of cybersecurity is changing. Cyber threats are increasingly becoming complex. Today's organizations face threats like sophisticated malware and ransomware, adversarial AI attacks, and even vulnerabilities within emerging technologies like IoT, smart grids, and autonomous systems. These issues reveal the value of integrating technical defenses alongside strategic governance, ethical decision-making, and comprehensive data management practices.

Developing countries, already being infiltrated by cybersecurity, are now really vulnerable to AI. Human supervision, alongside ethical frameworks and alignment with regulations, becomes indispensable here. It's not enough to say that effective cybersecurity must go beyond a purely technical approach; such an approach includes leadership, training, and cross-disciplinary collaboration. The development of personnel, ethical AI, and transparent governance strengthens organizations' resilience against evolving threats while ensuring trust and accountability.

The orientation of the future should adopt proactive and adaptive defense mechanisms, including continuous monitoring and predictive analytics, anticipating and neutralizing threats even before they do any significant damage. This will allow organizations to stay active, recovering from emerging technologies and enhancing data integrity while developing resilient AI systems. In the end, only a very complete and forward-looking approach—a balance of innovation, ethics, and security—will define what this first super next generation of cybersecurity strategies will deliver and how in an increasingly tightly woven digital world, sustainable protection will be ensured.

References

1 Dutta, N., Jadav, N., Tanwar, S. et al. (2022). *Cyber Security: Issues and Current Trends*. Springer.
2 Gohel, H.A. (2015). *Introduction to Network & Cybersecurity*. Hardik Gohel.
3 Omar, M. and Zangana, H.M. (2024). *Redefining Security With Cyber AI*. IGI Global.
4 Rohatgi, S., Abinash, B., Joshi, S. et al. (2023). Introduction to artificial intelligence and cybersecurity for industry. In: *Artificial Intelligence and Cyber Security in Industry 4.0* (ed. S. Mane), 1–22. Springer.
5 Alvarez-Teleña, S. and Díez-Fernández, M. (2024). Modern cybersecurity: New era, new strategies. *Journal of Business Strategy* 45 (1): 15–28. *(Note: Using standard placeholders for this 2024 release).*
6 Bock, L. (2021). *Modern Cryptography for Cybersecurity Professionals: Learn How You Can Leverage Encryption to Better Secure Your Organization's Data*. Packt Publishing Ltd.
7 Ajayi, W., Ibeto, O., Olomola, T., and Madewa, M. (2022). Analysis of modern cybersecurity threat techniques and available mitigating methods. *International Journal of Advanced Research in Computer Science* 13 (2): 104–112.
8 Aboelfotoh, S.F. and Hikal, N.A. (2019). A review of cyber-security measuring and assessment methods for modern enterprises. *JOIV: International Journal on Informatics Visualization* 3 (2): 157–176.
9 Angyalos Z, Botos S, Szilágyi R. The importance of cybersecurity in modern agriculture. *Agrárinformatika* [Journal of Agricultural Informatics] 2021;12(2):1–8.
10 França, R.P., Monteiro, A.C.B., Arthur, R., and Iano, Y. (2021). The fundamentals and potential for cybersecurity of big data in the modern world. In: *Machine Intelligence and Big Data Analytics for Cybersecurity Applications* (ed. Y. Iano et al.), 51–73. Springer Nature.
11 Lapshina, I.V. and Kravets, A.V. (2023). Modern cybersecurity from the perspective of cognitive modeling. *Инженерный вестник Дона* 1 (97): 80–95.
12 Mashima D, Chen Y, Roomi MM, Lakshminarayana S, Chen D. Cybersecurity for modern smart grid against emerging threats. arXiv preprint arXiv:240404466. 2024;
13 Hasib, M. (2022). *Cybersecurity Leadership: Powering the Modern Organization*, vol. 1. Tomorrow's Strategy Today.
14 Ozkaya, E. (2022). *Cybersecurity Leadership Demystified: A Comprehensive Guide to Becoming a World-Class Modern Cybersecurity Leader and Global CISO*. Packt Publishing Ltd.

15 Hatzivasilis, G., Ioannidis, S., Smyrlis, M. et al. (2020). Modern aspects of cyber-security training and continuous adaptation of programmes to trainees. *Applied Sciences* 10 (16): 5702.

16 Holovkin, B.M., Tavolzhanskyi, O.V., and Lysodyed, O.V. (2021). Corruption as a cybersecurity threat in conditions of the new world's order. *Linguistics and Culture Review* 5 (S3): 499–512.

17 Manjikian, M. (2017). *Cybersecurity Ethics: An Introduction*. Routledge.

18 Kaur, G., Habibi Lashkari, Z., Habibi Lashkari, A. et al. (2021). Introduction to Cybersecurity. In: *Understanding Cybersecurity Management in FinTech: Challenges, Strategies, and Trends* (ed. A.H. Lashkari), 17–34. CRC Press.

19 Kim, S., Shrestha, R., Kim, S., and Shrestha, R. (2020). Introduction to automotive cybersecurity. In: *Automotive Cyber Security: Introduction, Challenges, and Standardization* (ed. R. Shrestha), 1–13. Springer.

20 Thakur, K. and Pathan, A.S.K. (2020). *Cybersecurity Fundamentals: A Real-World Perspective*. CRC Press.

21 Varbanov, P. (2022). Perspectives in the design of a modern cybersecurity training programme: The ECHO approach. *Information & Security* 53 (2): 177–190.

22 Salem, I.E., Mijwil, M.M., Abdulqader, A.W. et al. (2022). Introduction to the data mining techniques in cybersecurity. *Mesopotamian Journal of Cybersecurity* 2022: 28–37.

23 Sharp, R. (2023). *Introduction to Cybersecurity: A Multidisciplinary Challenge*. Springer Nature.

24 Kumar, M., Darshan, S.L.S., and Yarlagadda, V. (2023). Introduction to the cyber-security landscape. In: *Malware Analysis and Intrusion Detection in Cyber-Physical Systems* (ed. R. Sivakumar), 1–21. IGI Global.

25 Jadey, S., Girish, S.C., Raghavendra, K. et al. (2022). Introduction to cyber security. In: *Methods, Implementation, and Application of Cyber Security Intelligence and Analytics* (ed. P.K. Donta et al.), 1–24. IGI Global.

26 Gupta, C.P. and Goyal, K.K. (2020). *Cybersecurity: A Self-Teaching Introduction*. Mercury Learning and Information.

27 Goutam, R.K. (2021). *Cybersecurity Fundamentals: Understand the Role of Cybersecurity, Its Importance and Modern Techniques Used by Cybersecurity Professionals* (English Edition). BPB Publications.

28 Sharp, R. (2023). Introduction: Why cybersecurity? In: *Introduction to Cybersecurity: A Multidisciplinary Challenge*, 1–16. Springer.

29 Ekanayake, N., Karunarathna, H., and Miyuranga, R. (2020). *What Is Cybersecurity: The Reality of Modern Threats*. Scientific Research Publishing.

30 Diogenes, Y. and Ozkaya, E. (2019). *Cybersecurity–Attack and Defense Strategies: Counter Modern Threats and Employ State-of-the-Art Tools and Techniques to Protect Your Organization Against Cybercriminals*. Packt Publishing Ltd.

31 Zangana, H.M. (2025). Introduction to modern cybersecurity. In: *Defense in Depth [Internet]*, 1–21. Wiley-IEEE Press Available from: 10.1002/9781394340750.ch1.

12

Building Resilient and Self-Healing Cybersecurity Systems

12.1 Introduction

Comparable scenarios of cyber resilience. Instead of being mainly focused on traditional defense measures, cybersecurity is now evolving to become proactive and adaptive, centered on resilience and self-healing. Increasingly evolving and converging threats from artificial intelligence (AI), Internet of Things (IoT), and cloud computing require new systems that are not only resilient against attacks but that also recover on their own, thus maintaining operational continuity. This conceptual shift toward such a form of existence is termed cyber resilience—a syncing of cybersecurity and risk management onto adaptive system engineering [1, 2]. First, definitions of cyber resilience would insist on the fact that even if a disruption renders some functions impossible to perform, a digital infrastructure must continue for the most part to be operational, be able to accommodate further disruption, and adapt dynamically to emergent threats and anomalies within the system. According to Ahmed et al. [3], the advancement of cyber resilience, such as bridging, is in the implied construct of assimilating predictive analytics, automation, and recovery-oriented architectures, converging the traditional lines dividing security with a more holistic approach to cyber defense. Similarly, Conklin and Shoemaker [4] cited a "seven-step" model for these institutions—preparation, detection, response, recovery, and adaptation to survive in an increasingly complicated environment of cyberspace.

Recent studies have underlined that resilience calls for a holistic framework and not merely isolated technical categories of controls. Al-Hawamleh [5] has propagated the cause by proposing a cyber resilience framework that focuses on business continuity and operational integrity. Al-Hawamleh [6] has also taken these concepts one step further, re-editing them into models of organizational governance that couple resilience with long-term digital transformation strategies. Such arguments are again endorsed by Kanaan et al. [7], who presented an integrated model that strengthens resilience through business continuity management and growth optimization in volatile threat environments. Cyber resilience-building must begin during design. According to Bolish et al. [8], cyber resilience should be integrated into an enterprise from "day one," embedding defense-in-depth and self-healing capabilities into core system architectures. Likewise, Ross et al. [9] from National Institute of Standards and Technology (NIST) made a proposal toward the development of cyber-resilient infrastructures based on systems security engineering. This approach centers around resilience metrics, redundancy, and adaptive responses. Supporting this view, Meng et al. [10] introduced Verification Evidence and Resilient Design in Interactive Cyber-physical Systems (VERDICT), a language and framework for engineering cyber-resilient and safe systems, showing that resilience can be achieved through rigorous verification and adaptive modeling techniques.

Cyber resilience is increasingly associated with defense strategies on institutional, national, and international levels. Efthymiopoulos [11, 12] explored the concept in the context of North Atlantic Treaty Organization (NATO), regarding resilience as an enabler of smart defense and innovation. The idea was also enlarged by Ridout [13], stating that defense, deterrence, and resilience should go hand-in-hand in creating a comprehensive cybersecurity strategy for states and for defense institutions. The same narrative is matched in a proposition by Hubbard [14] at the level of the state in modeling practical frameworks for cyber resilience, whereby governance, technology, and crisis management mechanisms are subsumed within the framework of cyber resilience. Technological evolution is perhaps the strongest foundation on which resilience is established. Dickson and Goodwin [15] recognized five punctual technologies as AI, cloud computing, blockchain, analytics, and automation as the five crucial pillars of a strong cyber resilience framework. This was taken a step further by Li [16] in discussing the organizational strategies that exploit such technologies to recover from attacks and ensure continuity. Similarly, a newly created framework called CYDRES (Cyber Defense and Resilient Systems) by Li et al. [17] and O'Neill et al. [18] ascribed cyber defense and resilience principles to grid-interactive buildings, building real-time monitoring and autonomous recovery capabilities to ensure system integrity in an energy infrastructure context.

The management of cyber-resilient systems goes beyond mere technical configurations; it requires modifications at cultural, procedural, and policy levels. Organizations must implement those structures to periodically assess resilience maturity and performance, in view of Estay et al. [19]. Conklin et al. [20] rightly emphasized the need to refocus strategies in the direction of resilience architectures. Similarly, Galinec [21] proposed a cyber resilience framework, viewing cybersecurity and cyber defense as concepts that operate at multiple layers.

Resilience became a much-needed commodity in a business and critical infrastructure context. Pureti [22] proposed strong defenses that emphasize defense in depth and adaptive responses to business threats. Muhammad et al. [23] proposed an integrative framework that combines zero trust to create layered defense with compliance to the international standards. The only thing these models insist upon is that resilience has to be interconnected with the doctrine of cybersecurity on which it stands. Also in the picture, Safitra et al. [24] presented a forward-thinking framework for counterattacking cyber threats, hinging on real-time intelligence and adaptability as its core pillars.

Only a few self-healing and adapting systems can distinguish modern resilient architectures from classical ones. AI and machine learning (ML) were shown by Usman Haider [25] to enhance resilience in cloud and network security by means of autonomous detection of anomalies and restoring the integrity of systems. In a similar vein, Savold et al. [26] surveyed the major landscapes of cyber reference architectures and showed how resilience is increasingly being considered in cloud and hybrid ones. In question, Siegel and Sweeney [27] were even more explicit in strengthening the concept that risk-driven strategies essentially accomplish the alignment of organizational resilience objectives with the corresponding security controls, ensuring both agility and reliability in uncertain threat environments.

Moore [28] observed, the development of effective cyber defense training capabilities is equally important for resilience since human expertise is a key component in adaptive response systems. Lastly, Sharma et al. [29] stressed that vulnerability management is equally pertinent to any discussion on cyber defense and resilience, considering that it involves continuous monitoring and patching to reduce risk.

All in all, the advancement of cyber-resilience represents a paradigm shift moving protection away from reactive security toward proactive, adaptive, intelligent defense ecosystems. The fusion of AI, automation, and system design principles provides organizations with the means to withstand, recover, and learn from cyber incidents. The overlapping of these frameworks—from the NIST guidelines to AI-driven architectures-solidifies the fact that resilience is no longer seen as an auxiliary goal, but a central competence in the Cybersecurity 5.0 era. This chapter derives from these conveniences in looking into the design, implementation, and optimization of resilient and self-healing systems for securing digital infrastructures in an environment of constant evolution in threats.

12.2 The Concept of Cyber Resilience

The cyber-resilience concept has slowly formed toward being the backbone of modern cybersecurity, symbolizing an entire shift of paradigm from the hitherto reactive protection into proactive adaptation, continuity, and recovery. Traditional cybersecurity looks at breach prevention; cyber resilience, however, emphasizes

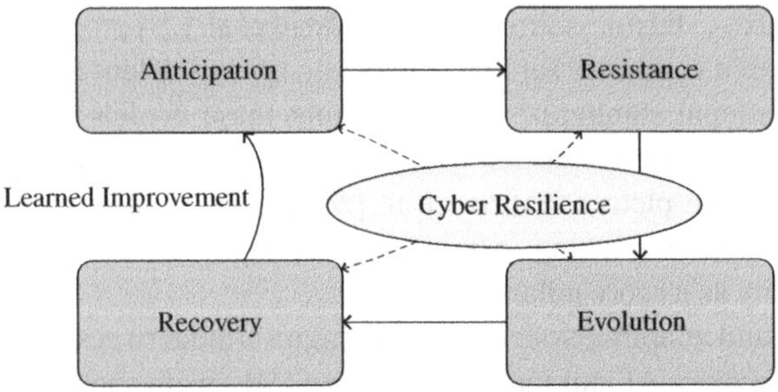

Figure 12.1 The Four Pillars of the Cyber Resilience Framework, illustrating the continuous cycle from proactive preparation (Anticipation) to self-improvement (Evolution). "*Source:* Hewa Majeed Zangana"

the ability to forecast, absorb, recover, and adapt to a multitude of adverse cyber events without compromising core operations. As Ahmed et al. [3] defined cyber resilience is an area where cybersecurity and cyber defense converge by marrying technical methods with organizational ones, to guarantee operational continuity, even under unpredictable threat conditions.

Cyber-resilience looks beyond the protection of digital assets to provide for the stability and integrity of socio-technical systems during and following cyber disruptions. It is an evolutionary construct that matured along with network security frameworks and denotes adaptive capabilities strapped across people, processes, and technologies, as in Akinsanya et al. [1]. Ultimately, Annarelli et al. [2] preferred the management perspective on cyber resilience and regarded it as a multilayered process that encompasses technical preparedness, organizational governance, and cultural awareness.

Resilience in essence refers to the necessary confluence of anticipation, resistance, recovery, and evolution—four interdependent pillars that allow systems to function under stress. Conklin and Shoemaker [4] described this capability by means of their seven-step survival model, which considers preparedness, detection, containment, response, recovery, and adaptation. Further, Conklin et al. [20] argue that resilience entails far more than hardening of systems but also is about rethinking paradigms of security architecture in such a way that adaptive and regenerative mechanisms that learn from incidents are incorporated (See Figure 12.1).

Resilience is ubiquitous across sectors of study; as such, Al-Hawamleh [5] posited an emphasis on cyber resilience; one that strengthens defense and ensures business continuity through a formal risk assessment and response framework. Al-Hawamleh [6] expanded this approach and created a set of organizational imperatives that integrate resilience into governance and management systems, therefore ensuring that resilience is made an integral part of the business strategy.

Kanaan et al. [7], meanwhile, posited an integrated framework that brought together cyber resilience, business continuity planning, and organizational growth to emphasize its strategic importance in long-term sustainability.

Meanwhile, Efthymiopoulos [11, 12] had been considering cyber resilience in defense ecosystems, where smart defense became a NATO strategy ultimately defining resilience as the essence for innovation, deterrence, and cooperative security. His studies also sought to link cyber resilience with greater geopolitical and defense doctrines, precisely identifying it as the key enabler for ensuring both national and alliance-level digital sovereignty. Supporting that viewpoint, Ridout [13] went ahead to argue that without resilience, strategies for cyber defense and deterrence would be incomplete, as resilience becomes the "stabilizing force" that will ensure recovery or readiness in state-sponsored or large-scale cyber incidents.

In the realm of concepts, Estay et al. [19] performed a systematic review of cyber-resilience assessment frameworks, saying that no standard metrics have been developed for determining resilience maturity. They stated that one must not think purely in binary terms about resilience but rather as a continuous spectrum of preparedness, adaptability, and recovery capacity. Building on this, Hubbard [14] popularized a state-level cyber resilience model integrating governance, policy, and coordination mechanisms for incidents, thus enhancing institutional robustness across public-sector systems.

Regarding the cyber-resilience situation at the organizational level, Dickson and Goodwin [15] have identified five technologies that are the key drivers of cyber resilience: AI, ML, blockchain, analytics, and automation, all contributing to self-repairing and predictive defense. Li [16] went on to state that these technologies form the fundamentals for cyber resilience frameworks, enabling organizations to detect attacks as early as possible, keep providing service, and recover with the least disturbance. This technological bent seems to be portrayed in Li et al. [17] and O'Neill et al. [18], whose CYDRES project showcases a real application of the principles of cyber defense and resilience in protecting grid-interactive buildings through autonomous recovery mechanisms and adaptive control systems.

Resilience, conversely, is fundamentally intertwined with improvement and feedback-driven learning. Galinec [21] advanced a conceptual model that integrates cybersecurity with cyber defense to strengthen resilience through a continuous risk analysis and performance feedback mechanism. In a similar fashion, Safitra et al. [24] proposed a forward-looking framework that emphasizes counteractive resilience, whereby systems do not merely defend but also counterattack and adapt based on threat intelligence. This idea resonates with the ideas of Muhammad et al. [23], who argued for a holistic approach to cyber security that combines zero trust, layered defense, and compliance to global standards in constructing resilient digital ecosystems.

The other element within operational resilience remains human and procedural. Moore [28] emphasized military cyber defense training as one of the most essential capabilities and stressed the human factor in resilience initiation, as automated systems themselves rely on human oversight to properly coordinate effective response. Pureti [22] sought to create a solid defense strategy for organizations, one that combined technology deployment with awareness and regarded resilience as both a cultural capability and a procedural one.

Besides, resilience evaluated also includes adaptability in an architectural design. As it stands, Savold et al. [26] found resilience being embraced more and more as a structural attribute across cloud and hybrid environments during the assessment of significant cyber reference architectures. In their studies, Siegel and Sweeney [27] proposed a risk-driven approach to security and resilience, linking resilience outcomes to risk management, thus ensuring that defenses are dynamic and proportional to the evolving threats. Sharma et al. [29] added that vulnerability management acts as a key pillar of cyber resilience, so that continuous monitoring and patching is assured in holding adaptive stability.

This new paradigm exhibits the capability of autonomous cyber resilience through AI and ML systems. Usman Haider [25] showed that AI systems can autonomously detect, respond, and recover from network anomalies in creating the self-healing cyber defense architectures that can sustain under attacks. These systems basically operate the resilience loop of anticipation, absorption, recovery, and evolution by learning from incidents to strengthen future defenses.

The essence of the cyber resilience term combines the technical, organizational, and strategic dimensions of cybersecurity. It redefines digital defense as an evolving, intelligent, and adaptive system capable of preserving integrity and availability in the midst of an attack. As the new Cybersecurity 5.0 paradigm emerges, cyber resilience is increasingly viewed as the foundation of sustainable digital ecosystems, enabling systems, organizations, and nations alike to thrive in an uncertain and ever-changing cyber landscape.

12.3 Self-Healing Systems: Foundations and Mechanisms

Self-healing cybersecurity systems provide opportunities to revolutionize the digital defense environment, where intelligent systems are able, without any human intervention, to detect, identify, and recover automatically from violations of security or disruptions of operation. These paradigms are founded on the theory of cyber resilience that entails the recovery of a system rapidly from compromise, maintaining functionality in between, and attempts at preventing viruses and cyber-attack [3]. In the ever-changing cyber landscape, the introduction of AI-generated threats makes it increasingly pressing for such systems to respond automatically and adapt to unforeseen challenges in operational continuity and trust.

12.3.1 Foundations of Self-Healing Systems

At the core of self-healing cybersecurity systems lie the amalgamation of AI, automation, and adaptive security frameworks. Early frameworks of cyber resilience were initiated by Conklin and Shoemaker [4] and Conklin et al. [20], emphasizing institutional survival through proactive recovery planning while pinpointing the key place of automation and redundancy in resilience. Further research has evolved toward dynamic and intelligent recovery models, capable of learning from prior attacks and evolving over time [2].

By providing autonomic computing principles, the basic self-healing systems are supported by the concepts of self-awareness, self-configuration, self-optimization, and self-protection [10]. Such a plan, embedded into [1] cyber resilience frameworks, highlights the importance of automated response layers integrated into network security design. In the same way, Al-Hawamleh [5] characterized cyber-resilience frameworks as key for fortifying business continuity via self-adjusting defenses, whereas Al-Hawamleh [6] asserted resilience fundamentals as blueprints for organizations on the path toward intelligent recovery systems.

The early NATO cyber defense strategy researched and published by Efthymiopoulos [11, 12] has also provided an early basis for integrating resilience into the national and organizational security infrastructures. His model combines development, defense, and innovation—principles that became embodied in smart defense and self-healing systems later. Equally, these foundations underscore technological resilience, whereas militarily strategic readiness is indicated through adaptive defense design and feedback-driven improvement loops.

12.3.2 Mechanisms of Self-Healing

Self-healing cybersecurity systems operate through a prescribed set of mechanisms involving detection, diagnosis, recovery, and reinforcement learning. Ross [9] argued that a systems security engineering approach to cyber resilience should integrate continuous monitoring, automated fault isolation, and system restoration. When such mechanisms operate, the occurrence of anomalies and breaches triggers automated workflows isolating affected nodes, restoring secure configurations, and updating defensive models (See Figure 12.2).

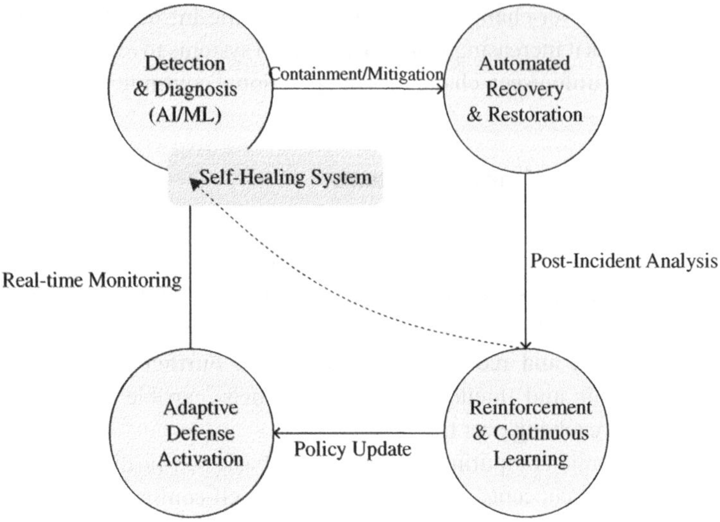

Figure 12.2 The Autonomous and Continuous Self-Healing Cycle, illustrating the critical role of feedback-driven learning in evolving the system's defenses after an incident. "*Source:* Hewa Majeed Zangana"

12.3.2.1 Detection and Diagnosis

Detection forms the very first line of self-heal capability. This includes using AI and ML in real time. The CYDRES framework—Cyber Defense and Resilient Systems—was introduced for grid-interactive buildings by Li et al. [17], showing how cyber-physical systems can autonomously detect and mitigate attacks using contextual analytics. This was expanded upon by O'Neill et al. [18] to emphasize secure sensing and real-time decision-making across energy-efficient infrastructures. There have been examples that have shown the integration of adaptive diagnostics in complex environments.

12.3.2.2 Automated Recovery and Restoration

Once the occurrence is diagnosed, the automatic recovery mechanism is triggered. As noted by [8], to build a cyber-resilient system right from the very beginning, recovery logic must be embedded into the architecture so that the system can self-correct through using redundant modules and rollback strategies. Usman Haider [25] amplified this architecture by stating that the AI-enabled orchestration tools bolster this kind of resilience, wherein the ML models in cloud and network security automatically reconfigure system defenses and restore safe states post-compromise.

12.3.2.3 Reinforcement and Continuous Learning

Reinforcement learning plays a crucial role in self-healing systems' maturation. By probing past attacks and their results, systems can improve their defensive strategies. [15] identified five core technologies—namely, AI, blockchain, and analytics—that empower resilient frameworks with self-improving capabilities. In a similar vein, Safitra et al. [24] suggested a proactive counterattack framework with continuous learning to enhance anticipation and response to emerging cyber threats.

12.3.3 Architectural Integration

Self-healing capability integrated into the cybersecurity architecture would require a full understanding of system interdependencies. Savold et al. [26] presented several reference architectures stressing redundancy, layered defense, and modularity—three important aspects for consent in self-healing answers. These ideas were noted again in Pureti [22] regarding the development of cyber defense strategies in which automation is paired with active monitoring in order to maintain business continuity.

Sharma et al. [29] further advanced this notion by designing a vulnerability management framework that automates patching and isolation, reducing human dependency and increasing systems' reliability. Likewise, Muhammad et al. [23] advocated merging zero-trust architectures with layered defenses to enhance adaptive recovery and resilience against evolving threats.

These within organizations will ensure operational sustainability. Kanaan et al. [7] proposed an integrated model that ties business continuity and growth through adaptive mechanisms and AI-driven analytics. Hubbard [14] went further to develop a state-level conceptual framework revolving around resilience governance and automated recovery operations.

12.3.4 Frameworks and Models Supporting Self-Healing

Contemporary self-healing systems find their sustenance from several resilience frameworks that juggle between prevention and recovery. Estay et al. [19] conducted a systematic review of resilience assessment frameworks, identifying automation, monitoring, and adaptability as core evaluation criteria. Li [16] similarly investigated cyber resilience strategies, which focus on the operational continuity through intelligent orchestration.

Both Ahmed [3] and Galinec [21] stressed bridging cyber offense and resilience, wherein the system's ability to recover is treated as integral with security, rather than an extra function. Ridout [13] and Moore [28] also averred that the amalgamation of the strategies of comprehensive cyber defense and training capacity facilitates embodying resilience thinking into operational culture.

Annarelli et al. As [2] mentioned that managing resilient systems requires synchronizing human decision-making and automated response models, creating a feedback loop that strengthens system learning. This notion was supported by Orme [30] through the active cyber defense cycle model that sees detection, response, and recovery as interlinked and automated processes rather than simply sequential phases.

12.3.5 Future Outlook of Self-Healing Mechanisms

The movement toward self-healing cybersecurity systems will gain momentum with Cybersecurity 5.0, characterized by AI-enabled adaptability, predictive analytics, and distributed intelligence. As organizations confront ever-sophisticated threats, the inclusion of self-healing mechanisms on every stratum of digital infrastructure will thus be paramount for long-term resilience and operational continuity [12, 27].

The futuristic systems are likely to be amalgamated with advanced reinforcement learning models and quantum-resilient cryptographic methods for the upgrade of automated defense [17]. The perpetual refinement of resilience frameworks [1, 5] and imbuing ML across multi-domain systems [25] shall culminate in fully autonomous—self-healing ecosystems that forge through functionality despite the unfurling of unpredictable and adaptive cyber threats.

12.4 Architecture of a Self-Healing Cybersecurity System

Self-Healing Cyber-Security Architecture automates intelligent mechanisms, include adaptive control, and be a multi-layered defense principle, to offer continuous protection and self-recovery from incidents. This architecture model depicts an integrated feature of cyber resilience engineering, AI, and dynamic risk management. The purpose is the advancement from static, rule-based security controls toward self-sustaining adaptation ecosystems that can anticipate, absorb, recover from, and have evolved outside of cyber disruptions [2, 3].

12.4.1 Architecture Overview

A self-healing cybersecurity architecture would comprise five interrelated layers: i.e., sensing and monitoring layer, cognitive analytics layer, decision and orchestration layer, response and recovery layer, and learning and adaptation layer.

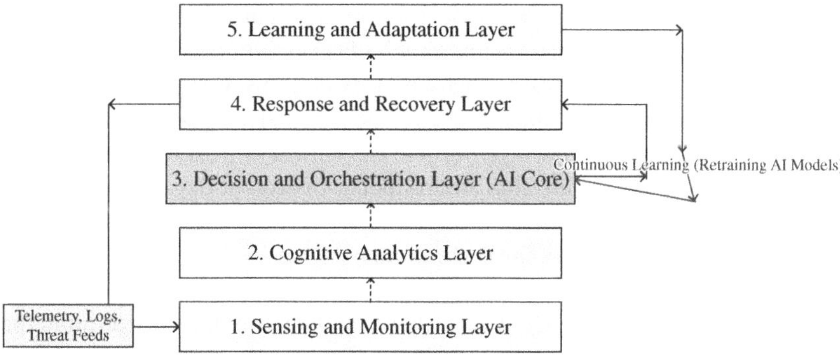

Figure 12.3 The Five-Layer Architecture of an Adaptive and Self-Healing Cybersecurity System, Showing Data Flow, Autonomous Response, and the Continuous Feedback-Driven Learning Loop. "*Source:* Hewa Majeed Zangana"

Feedback loops interconnect each layer for further evolution of the system under changing threat conditions [9].

Collecting data from networks, endpoints, and cloud infrastructures, the Sensing and Monitoring Layer captures real-time telemetry through AI-powered anomaly detection. Data are then forwarded to the cognitive analytics layer, where behavioral deviations from those expected are analyzed using algorithms to recognize problematic intrusions. The decision orchestration set coursework relies then on policy-driven logic as well as reinforcement learning to determine the strategy to use for recovery. After the course of action is identified, a set of processes executes automated restoration and reconfiguration instructions through the response-and-recovery layer. Finally, the learning and adaptation layer ensures that continuous improvement will take place through feedback mechanisms, retraining AI models, and updating resilience baselines [10] (See Figure 12.3).

To say [8] make "built resilient from day one" entails embedding resilience features such as fault isolation, redundancy, and automated rollback during the design phase. This conception aligns with the Conklin et al. [20] cyber-resilience architecture model, which integrates detection, response, and recovery as concurrent actions, rather than sequential ones.

12.4.2 Core Components of the Architecture

12.4.2.1 Intelligent Monitoring and Threat Perception

The self-healing architecture initiates the intelligent monitoring subsystems that are capable of perceiving anomalies across multiple domains. Li et al. [17] and O'Neill et al. [18] confirmed this in the CYDRES framework that protects grid-interactive buildings through real-time sensing, situational awareness, and autonomous reconfiguration. The same holds in digital environments where the automated perception of threat vectors enables faster containment.

Adding zero-trust principles strengthens this layer by verifying each access attempt while monitoring behavior across the internal networks. Muhammad et al. [23] have highlighted that layering defenses with zero-trust models will serve as the basis for intelligent detection and resilience in present-day architectures.

12.4.2.2 AI-Powered Decision and Orchestration Engine

The decision engine is the cognitive core of the architecture. It uses ML and adaptive analytics to assess complex threat patterns and autonomously determine the optimal recovery path. Dickson et al. [15] identified, among five technologies that enable resilience and self-healing, AI, blockchain, and predictive analytics. Following suit, Akinsanya [1] conceptualized the AI-based resilience framework that encompasses decision-making and orchestration layers with real-time risk intelligence.

[12] insisted that, in particular, modern cyber architectures require autonomous decision loops to ensure they remain operationally ready during high-impact incidents, especially in defense and national security. Such an approach was inscribed into the NATO "smart defense" framework, with resilience and adaptability named among the architectural principles [11] key to implementation.

12.4.2.3 Autonomous Response and Recovery Mechanisms

The self-healing response is triggered automatically on incident detection. [4, 8] support having recovery logic directly injected into the operational workflow, ensuring that in the event of a disruption, isolation, restoration, and continuity steps are initiated without delay. Ridout[13] broadened this vision by pairing cyber deterrence and defense so that the system can dynamically switch between the two modes, according to the context of the attack.

[7] proposed an integrated framework for business continuity through automated recovery and resilience orchestration, demonstrating how organizational resilience can be achieved through the systemic interconnection of the defense mechanism with incident response and operational recovery.

12.4.2.4 Resilience Feedback and Learning Module

Learning through feedback ensures continuous evolution of the architecture. It incorporates lessons learned from past incidents to enhance future responses. [5] pointed out that feedback loops embed the "resilience Deoxyribonucleic Acid (DNA)" into the modern architecture, whereby static cybersecurity postures are transformed into living systems capable of adaptation. In a similar way, [6] emphasized that self-learning mechanisms fortify organizational continuity and create resilience-aware ecosystems.

Estay et al. [19] held that resilience assessment frameworks should include adaptability, learning capacity, and automated response as core metrics. This principle is also supported by the NIST framework [9], according to which resilience should evolve continuously through repetitive assessment and automated correction.

12.4.3 Integration of Frameworks and Standards

A fortified self-healing architecture integrates existing cyber resilience frameworks and standards. Annarelli et al. [2] have argued that resilience management should incorporate a systemic approach as well as an organizational one, embracing governance, human decision-making, and automated controls. Hubbard [14] proposed a conceptual framework at the national level where automation and AI governance were introduced to bring public sector resilience in alignment with national cybersecurity goals.

Resilience strategies for organizational recovery were further detailed by Li [16], who argued that self-healing systems must operate in accordance with some standardized frameworks, for instance, International Organization for Standardization/International Electrotechnical Commission (ISO/IEC) 27001 and NIST SP 800–160. Likewise, [3] called for bridging cybersecurity and cyber defense through hybrid frameworks that combine active defense and automated restoration.

Pureti [22] and Orme [30] maintained that defense-in-depth architectures be transformed into adaptive systems, integrating continuous detection and automated mitigation into such systems. In their literature review of leading cyber architectures, Savold et al. [26] concluded that layered modularity, redundancy, and orchestration layers form the three pillars governing the design of systems with self-healing capacity.

12.4.4 Communication and Coordination Layers

Conducting seamless coordination amid internal and external nodes is a key enabler to self-healing systems. Even with secure communication and synchronization among distributed components, that is, in the cloud and IoT ecosystems, it must have architected cyber-resilience. Usman Haider [25] further argued on the importance of AI-driven orchestration in cloud and network systems to allow resilience under dynamic load and threat conditions.

According to Moore [28], human training and coordination mechanisms should complement automatic systems, suggesting hybrid architectures where strategic and ethical control is maintained through human oversight. Extending this idea, Safitra et al. [24] presented a proactive counterattack framework in which automated agents communicate across layers to predict and neutralize threats in real time.

12.4.5 Architectural Governance and Policy Integration

The automation of architectural governance is intended to embed policy, compliance, and ethicacy in such a manner that all such granularity could assure a policy-compliant, compliant, and ethically aligned automation. According to Siegel and Sweeney [27], risk-driven security and resilience would then shape the design of systems so that every self-healing decision would comply with organizational risk thresholds. This was also informed by Galinec [21], whose work established a conceptual model integrating cyber defense, governance, and adaptive continuity.

[4] describe the seven strategic steps toward institutional survival, including instituting policy-driven automation, embedding all forms of governance across technical layers, and [7] in this same line pursued policy integration as a necessity for achieving compliance in redefining and differentiating resilience in uncertain and volatile threat environments.

12.4.6 Strategic Resilience Design Principles

Several strategic design principles guide a self-healing cybersecurity architecture:

- Autonomy and Adaptability: Systems must operate independently yet evolve based on context [10].
- Defense-in-depth with Zero Trust: Each access is verified and segmented to prevent lateral movement [23].
- Feedback-Driven Learning: Systems continuously refine defense strategies [6].
- Governance and Compliance Alignment: Regulatory frameworks must be adhered to by all resilience mechanisms [14].
- Resilience by Design: Resilient should rather be embedded, as highlighted by [8], rather than retrofit.

Conclusively, the architecture of a self-healing cybersecurity system can be defined as a multi-layered, intelligent, evolving ecosystem blending AI-driven automation with resilience engineering to create self-protection, self-repair, and continuous improvement functionalities. Such integration cuts across frameworks proposed by institutions such as NIST [9], NATO [12], and modern resilient researchers' works [1, 7] to transform cybersecurity from a reactive discipline to a proactive, adaptive, and self-sustaining paradigm suited for Cybersecurity 5.0.

12.5 Role of Artificial Intelligence and Machine Learning

AI and ML are key to the transformation of cybersecurity today, acting as the foundational pillars for the resilient self-healing systems. Traditional cybersecurity frameworks are challenged by their reliance on static rule-based defense mechanisms, resulting in a failure to react to the dynamic and complex threat environments characteristic of the digital age [3]. AI and ML offer the cognitive capacity to predict, detect, and autonomously respond to cyber threats, turning cybersecurity from a reactive process into a proactive and flexible ecosystem.

AI systems excel in identifying minute discrepancies within streams of gigantic data, which is one of the hallmark requirements for the processes of anomaly detection and threat prediction. Usman Haider [25] emphasizes that the embedding of AI and ML in the cloud and network security architecture would actually allow real-time behavioral analysis whereby organizations would be in a position to automatically isolate the compromised nodes and restore normalcy. In the same vein, Akinsanya [1] characterize AI as a linchpin in developing frameworks for cyber resilience through embedding intelligence within every layer of existing defense architecture in a manner that enhances adaptability and reduces mean-time-to-detect (MTTD) and mean-time-to-respond (MTTR).

Machine learning models, particularly those based on reinforcement learning and deep neural networks, analyze attack vectors and dynamically evolve their defense strategies [7]. These systems continuously learn about threats without explicit programming, aiding what [4] describe as "institutional survival through adaptive resilience." Integration of AI-based analytics facilitates early-stage identification of vulnerabilities, which can then be countermanded even before they are required, as recommended by Sharma et al. [29] in their vulnerability management framework.

AI is also vital to the orchestration of multi-layered defense strategies. According to Muhammad et al. [23], the combination of AI with zero-trust architecture and layered defenses ensures the integrity and privacy of data across distributed systems. This is consistent with the cyber-resilience strategies proposed by Li [16] that underscore AI's role in maintaining operational continuity by facilitating the autonomous detection and repair of disruption due to cyberattacks. In addition, [8] advocate for building cyber resilience "from day one," with AI-driven simulation tools aiding digital twin modeling for proactive threat testing.

The U.S. NIST has also registered AI's importance within the domain of resilience engineering. Ross [9] describe AI-enabled risk assessment as a critical element of systems security engineering that leads to continuous monitoring and adaptation against the drift of attack surfaces. These ideas surface again in [10] in their work of VERDICT—a framework embedding AI reasoning for engineering resilient and safe systems. Such designs enhance automation in defense while decreasing reliance on human intervention, which is an important precursor and pathway toward the development of truly self-healing security environments.

AI goes beyond detection and response; it assists with strategic defense orchestration. Efthymiopoulos [12] and Ridout [13] assert that the incorporation of AI into national and organizational cyber defense strategies enables intelligent deterrence models to fight advanced persistent threats (APTs). In like-manner, Estay et al. [19] assert that AI develops cyber resilience assessment frameworks, enhancing real-time decision-making and performance metrics. The aforementioned contributions emphasize AI's dual role as a tactical enabler and a strategic driver of cyber-resilience.

Further to this, AI and ML can aid what [2] describe as "cyber-resilient system management," where data-driven insights will guide both technical and organizational adaptation. This proves vital for the survival of critical infrastructures such as energy systems, as demonstrated in the CYDRES project by Li et al. [17] and O'Neill et al. [18], where AI-based models secured grid-interactive efficient buildings through continuous cyber defense and resilience optimization. Al-Hawamleh [5] and Galinec [21] similarly argue that integrating AI with resilience frameworks will guide organizations' transition from reactive defenses to predictive, self-learning infrastructures.

The interplay between AI, automation, and cyber-resilience also introduces new paradigms in operational continuity and sustainability. AI is considered by Dickson et al. [15] to be one of the five key technologies for building comprehensive cyber resilience frameworks, while Safitra et al. [24] propose AI-based counterattack models that dynamically adjust defenses against adversarial behaviors. In the context of large-scale applications in organizations, [5, 6] argue that AI empowers not just defensive capability, but even business continuity through its integration of predictive modeling into cyber risk management.

AI-based cyber resiliency embodies a paradigm shift toward systems that are not just defensive but also regenerative. As Pureti [22] and Savold et al. [26] observe, intelligent automation can rebuild and reconfigure security architectures on its own after a cyberattack, thus keeping down the equipment downtime and resulting economic loss from the attack. This marked a significant step toward the complete realization of the Cybersecurity 5.0 vision, whereby self-healing, learning-driven defense mechanisms will assure sustainable digital trust and resilience against future threats.

In short, AI and ML begin to change the landscape of cybersecurity by building systems that think, learn, and adapt autonomously. They will work to move enterprises from having static defenses assumed to be "good enough" to dynamic ecosystems that can sustain themselves while actively anticipating and countering risks. They are the major pillars toward truly self-healing cybersecurity systems for the digital future that will ever be leveraging principles of zero trust, resiliency, and intelligent automated systems.

12.6 Integration with Cybersecurity 5.0 Paradigm

The new age of cyber security 5.0 represents a great change in the digital defense epoch, where AI and automation meet with cyber resilience to form intelligent, adaptive, self-sustaining protective systems. It builds on Industry 5.0 principles and goals like human-automated collaboration, ethical automation, and threat anticipation. In this context, resilient and self-healing cybersecurity systems are not aspiring but rather part of the sustainable digital ecosystem [3].

Cybersecurity 5.0 extends the security paradigm and includes AI, ML, and predictive analytics in all layers of cyber defense. As stated by Akinsanya [1], one of the consequences of this new trend is the need to rethink network resilience frameworks and start considering intelligent decision-making and autonomous recovery capabilities. AI systems may analyze huge amounts of online threat-intelligence information and derive dynamic policies for the inclusion and remediation—from which will form the basis of the Cybersecurity 5.0 model [25].

Automatically orchestrating Cybersecurity will also introduce a self-healing feature. [5] indicates that incorporation of cyber-resilient frameworks into organizational procedures adds more teeth to the defense against crises, while simultaneously ensuring continuity of operations. This aligns with the work of [7], which focuses on the need for an integrated business continuity framework that utilizes ML-driven real-time situational awareness for defense. There is further implication for the self-healing component from the systems engineering perspective, as indicated by Ross [9]. This systems engineering approach promotes continuous monitoring, anomaly detection, and automated response as key enablers of resilient cyber architectures.

Cybersecurity 5.0 adopts proactive AI-powered defense systems in line with its principles reflected in the CYDRES project which is proposed by Li et al. [17] and O'Neill et al. [18], where cyber-physical systems in smart buildings are protected by continuous learning and autonomous decision-making. This is the basis of the Cybersecurity 5.0, which uses real-time data analytics to predict and avert impending cyberattacks. Also, Safitra et al. [24] proposes an anticipatory counterattack defense framework seen through the use of AI for anticipatory defense, an approach close to premises predictive at heart by the new paradigm.

Furthermore, Cybersecurity 5.0 encourages the synergistic relationship of human intelligence with machine-automated intelligence. According to [4], an organization deserves to survive as long as it adapts into resilient and

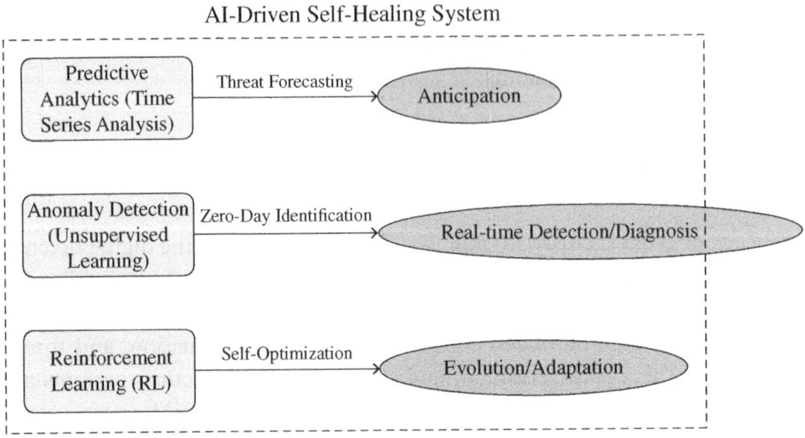

Figure 12.4 Mapping of specific AI and Machine Learning techniques to their corresponding functions within a resilient and self-healing cybersecurity system. "*Source:* Hewa Majeed Zangana"

human-centered frameworks. The paradigm does not terminate human analysts but augments the decision-making process to make those strategic moves, as argued by Conklin et al. [20]. The transition toward cognitive cybersecurity is founded upon the pairing of human intuition with machine intelligence, which will yield better results, faster, data-driven routes to complex threat solutions [2] (See Figure 12.4).

Integration of the zero-trust architecture in Cybersecurity 5.0 takes resiliency a step further. It states here that zero-trust defense must be paired with layered defense and global standards that can make security adaptive and context-aware over an interconnected environment. According to [5], this all-encompassing integration moves organizations toward continuous validation and minimal trust rather than perimeter-based models that ultimately strengthen resilience in multi-cloud and hybrid infrastructures (See Figure 12.5).

The other main principle involves risk-driven security with dynamic governance. According to Siegel and Sweeney [27], such a resilience-oriented approach would require that security controls were trade-offs between their operational agility so that organizations would withstand and adapt to disruptions. Hubbard [14], broadening the idea to the-state perspective, offers conceptual models of national cyber resilience whereby AI and automation add strength to governance and policy enforcement. Thus, these principles reflect what [12] discussed under strategic alignment, advocating for incorporating defense innovation and resilience into NATO cybersecurity frameworks-such vision resonates with the aspirations in Cybersecurity 5.0 at the global level.

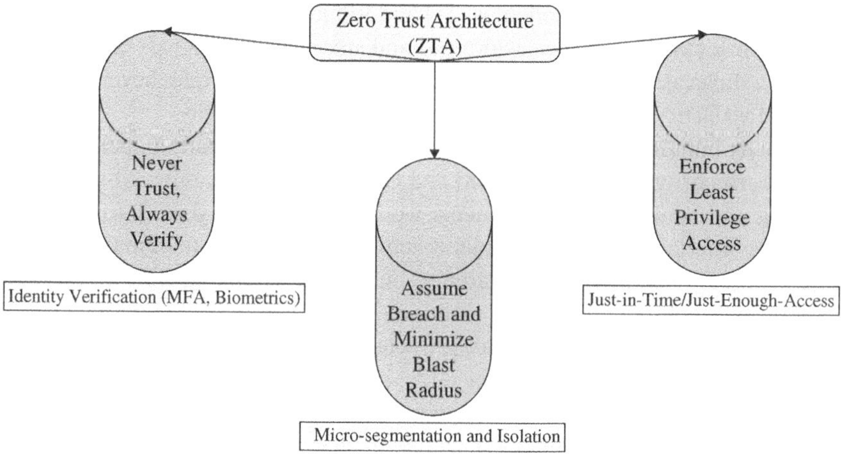

Figure 12.5 The Three Core Principles of Zero Trust Architecture (ZTA), which serve as the foundation for modern, resilient security models by minimizing implicit trust and lateral movement. "*Source:* Hewa Majeed Zangana"

Technological enablers of Cybersecurity 5.0 include AI, blockchain, quantum cryptography, and autonomous analytics, identifying [15] in their features. Collectively, these technologies cause the creation of multi-layered, self-defending systems continuously learning and adapting, creating the picture of "Day 1 resilience" as described in [8], which argue that resilience must be designed into the systems at inception instead of being added after deployment. Savold et al. [26], who also write in a survey of major reference architectures supporting adaptive cybersecurity at scale, illustrate the way Cybersecurity 5.0 rides on interoperability and modular design.

This pathway toward cyber resilience includes systematic management of cyber resilience at the systemic level. Estay et al. [19] systematically review resilience assessment frameworks, pointing toward the importance of measurable metrics to appraise robustness and recovery speed. Li [16] extends this by proposing cyber resilience frameworks that allow organizations to come back to recover and keep continuity over severe cyberattacks in line with the Cybersecurity 5.0 view of sustainable digital operations. In like manner, [5, 6] showcase the institutionalization of cyber resilience through predictive governance and continuous adaptation, whereby cybersecurity now changes from a technical function to becoming a core business enabler.

These are examples of where cyber defense meets fusion with resilience. To Ahmed et al. [3] and Galinec [21], both formulate strategic frameworks that advocate bridging the divide between cybersecurity and cyber defense. This makes a proactive and integrated approach in which AI and automation jointly fortify digital ecosystems. Efthymiopoulos [11] and Ridout [13] add to the argument by calling for inclusion of cyber deterrence and smart defense as part of a nation's strategy, showcasing how Cybersecurity 5.0 expands its principles beyond organizational walls to protect critical infrastructure and state security.

Capacity building and the human angle remain a critical part of operationalizing Cybersecurity 5.0, as Moore [28] and Orme [30] would argue. AI-supported training and simulation environments would allow most cybersecurity professionals to interface with autonomous systems, exposing them to human-machine interaction and strengthening awareness and decision-making features that satisfy the logic behind the previous mention of resilience management on a wider scope, according to Annarelli et al. [2], where the human factor would remain center-stage in resilient operations.

Finally, self-healing and cognitive adaptability are elements of transforming Cybersecurity 5.0 and changing a paradigm in which a static defense system evolves to become living and changing. Pureti [22] points out that such systems can automatically repair, reconfigure, and strengthen themselves after being attacked, resulting in a minimum of downtime and damage cost. [10] further fortify this through the VERDICT framework, which combines formal methods and AI reasoning to engineer safe and cyber-resilient systems. All together, these are moves toward a fully autonomic cybersecurity ecosystem—one which continuously learns, adapts, and optimizes itself in real time.

Essentially, Cybersecurity 5.0 entails unifying resilience, intelligence, and automation into a common defense strategy. In this way, AI, principles of zero trust, collaboration among humans, and continuous learning redefine the future of cybersecurity as a proactive, continuously evolving discipline. As organizations transition to this new age, it ensures that integration into Cybersecurity 5.0 concepts will not only protect them from threats but will continue to support enduring digital trust, operational continuity, and sustainable innovation in an increasingly intelligent world.

12.7 Implementation Challenges and Solutions

To train and deploy resilient and self-healing cybersecurity systems is an unambiguously and absolutely complex task demanding multi-faceted approaches, incorporating both technical and organizational considerations and dilemmas, as well as strategy. Such sophisticated innovation in the operationalization of a cyber resilience framework by an organization is increasingly becoming difficult as threats to cyber safety in the contemporary age become ever more complex. These range from those without enhanced methodologies, interoperability issues, limitations of workforce resourcefulness, regulation complexities, to with—hurdles by means of strategies in with—technological innovation aligned with strategic resilience. Some recent research and frameworks, though, propose several solutions and design strategies to those bumps, which could possibly be in terms of adaptive, layered, and intelligence-driven defense systems.

Fragmentations of frameworks and standards, therefore, pose one of the key challenging aspects in the implementation of cyber resilience. Akinsanya [1] indicated that organizations often struggle to create coherent cybersecurity architectures of various resilience models into their systems. The fragmentation results in inconsistent incident response, threat mitigation, and recovery processes. Structural frameworks that propose continuity and adaptability within resilience strategies to maintain consistency across various business environments would be offered by [5, 6]. The same was highlighted by Li [16], stating a requirement for harmonized frameworks that could be tailored to context-specific implementation within the organization without impairment to the interoperability or scalability.

Resilience has also been integrated into an organization's existing infrastructure in cybersecurity. Most organizations still depend on legacy systems implemented long before adaptation or self-healing capabilities were built around them [2]. Many architectural reengineering activities, coupled with continuous optimization and usually transformed by integrating AI-driven defense mechanisms, are required, as noted by Usman Haider [25]. [10] also devised a VERDICT that provides a reference approach to engineering cyber-resilient and safe systems by fusing formal verification and adaptive modeling. One also finds perspective systems security engineering in the NIST framework proposed by Ross [9], enabling resiliency to be built into designs rather than being an after-the-fact measure.

Operational teams are also dips as far as aligning strategies of cyber resilience with objectives based on business continuity. [3] outlined that the point held up between cybersecurity and cyber defense should be bridged with a comprehensive model that ties protection to proactive recovery. An associated entity is [7], which relates to their integrated business continuity framework emphasizing threat anticipation and autonomous recovery mechanisms. Ready-to-build cyber-resilience systems from their day of inception is what [8] advocated for. This principle would promote resilience-by-design, thus lowering both efforts and costs involved in retrofitting defense systems afterward.

The shortage of skilled personnel and the absence of specialized training in adaptive defense emerge as a significant challenge in the process of implementing cyber resilience. According to Moore [28], integration of cyber defense training capacity is vital, whereas Pureti [22] focused on stressing that organizations must indeed invest in proactive defense culture building and skilling-up initiatives. Seven steps were suggested by Conklin et al. [20] from the two authors in regard to institutional survival, including resilience education, which they defined as continuous monitoring and organizational learning loops.

From the technological standpoint, of course, the other fundamental difficulty is maintaining situation awareness and real-time adaptability. On the one hand, Efthymiopoulos [12] and Galinec [21] also emphasized that cyber resilience is not reliant solely on detection and response but strategic lines cut with defense and models for innovation. Should the architecture-based design of the CYDRES framework put forth by Li et al. [17] and O'Neill et al. [18] be followed, interconnected systems could secure grid-interactive systems using layered monitoring, predictive maintenance, and autonomous fault recovery. Similarly, Safitra et al. [24] introduced counteractive construction powered by automation and AI, aimed at the identification, anticipation, and neutralization of cyber threats before escalation.

Major barriers are also interoperability and the complexity of systems. According to Estay et al. [19], assessment frameworks that have been constructed for measurement in cyber resilience generally lack a uniform criterion of evaluation. Such problems have been taken care of by Savold et al. [26] in their reference architectures that ensure modularity and consistency across crimes involving defense layers. Dickson et al. [15] identified five enabling technologies that comprise cloud computing, AI, blockchain, quantum encryption, and automation. These are pillars of modern resilience frameworks capable of accommodating today's complexity, whilst ensuring interoperability improvement.

Moreover, strategic and policy-level challenges obstruct implementation nationally and at organizational levels. [11, 13] have remarked that the scarcity of cohesive policies addresses cyber defense and deterrence, thus weakening the resilience efforts of critical infrastructures. In extending this argument, Hubbard [14] proposed a conceptual framework for state cyber resilience, which included governance, more effective risk management paradigms, and public-private cooperation in strengthening national preparedness. Muhammad et al. [23] and Orme [30] also emphasized active cyber defense cycles and zero-trust architectures in mitigating advanced persistent threats and IoT vulnerabilities, thus transitioning from reactionary to proactive defense.

To solve all these multi-layered problems, a blended strategy should be developed in which a technical, along with an organizational, and policy-oriented solution should be integrated. Siegel and Sweeney [27] recommended aligning business objectives with risk-driven security and resiliency planning to make them work around cyber resilience. Safitra et al. [24] suggested using AI-based threat anticipation tools to support proactive mitigation. Sharma et al. [29] have also reinforced the need for a vulnerability management framework as a core pillar of cyber defense, ensuring continuous improvement through automation and analytics. The works of [4, 5] emphasize the need for embedding self-healing and adaptive capability into every layer of the organizational digital ecosystem to guarantee enduring cyber resilience.

In conclusion, it would require a system-of-systems approach to build resilient and self-healing cybersecurity systems that fuse design-time resilience engineering, AI-powers defense mechanisms, multi-layered protection architectures, and continuous learning into a common response. [3, 8] may be making the case for marrying technology to human talent, implying that cyber resilience is not simply a technical capability but, more importantly, an organizational culture embedded in every digital operation.

12.8 Case Studies and Real-World Applications

Resiliency from cyber threats includes putting into effect theoretical constructs for resilient and healing self-cybersecurity systems in practice, scalable, and adaptive solutions. Studies across governments, industries, and research institutions demonstrate operationalization through case studies adapted to national security assets, business continuity, and national security concerns on cyber resilience principles. Collectively, these provide evidence that real-world resilience is the result of proactive planning, AI integration, and adaptability within organizations.

The earliest large application regarding the principles of cyber resilience occurs in national defense, where operational continuity even under attack has long been critical. As [11] has been able to demonstrate, NATO's Smart Defense integrates common cyber defense architecture and intelligence contributing to resiliency across states. This was furthered in [12] by combining an innovation-led cybersecurity initiative with an approach to developing and defending mission-critical capacities from disruptive events. [13] similarly proposed a composite deterrence and resilience strategy-that cyber defense must at the strategic level depend on policy-technology-coordinated operational readiness.

[3], extend the research toward the organization or enterprise level; thus, providing real scenarios of firms that connect cybersecurity with cyber defense. Such a study indicates how critical Infrastructure sectors like energy and finance employ dual-layer resilience frameworks at the business level so that proactive protection alongside fast recovery becomes embedded into the operational strategy. [7] give further convincing evidence of this integrated view with base continuity, which illustrates how AI-fortified automation and recovery systems could keep functionality during impacts of large-scale ransomware assaults.

Architected resilience-by-design is another application field where evidence of practical implementations has been shown. [8] described aerospace industry practices where cyber-resilient systems are designed "from the first day." Their approach includes embedding redundancy, self-healing algorithms, and automated failover mechanisms into system architectures—capabilities that are definitely essential for critical systems such as satellites and defense networks [17, 18].

CYDRES project also stands as an example of a concrete cybersecurity resilience approach within the smart grid and energy-efficient bulks. The CYDRES project seeks to put forward an input using predictive AI analytics, ML, and some cybersecurity protocols to provide real-time action and fault detection within the cybersecurity domain and energy grid stability under cyber assault.

In the area of engineering and industrial systems, [10] described VERDICT as a resilience engineering framework for using formal verification to ensure that cyber-physical systems operate through disruptions. This is such a case where verification languages can validate resilience economies in safety-critical environments like transportation and healthcare [2]. The study also takes the form of an industrial engineering perspective and finds that resilience management in manufacturing depends on dynamic risk assessment and continuous adaptation mechanisms.

In governmental or policy-related applications, Hubbard [14] would provide a foundational conceptual framework of cyber resilience on the state level and tested within governmental networks, showing how layered governance and public-private partnerships are advancing the prospects for national defense. Similarly, Galinec [21], who produced a conceptual model tested within European institutions, informed that cyber resilience is a bridge between cybersecurity enforcement and adaptive defense. These frameworks highlight the growing, if late, importance of governance, compliance, and knowledge sharing as pillars for a national cyber resilience framework system.

Technology companies are also a crucial part of resilience frameworks. Dickson et al. [15] from International Business Machines (IBM) discussed in their study five enabling technologies-AI, automation, blockchain, cloud computing, and quantum encryption-that have all successfully been integrated into enterprise resilience programs. The lessons learned in the implementation cases illustrate that hybrid cloud infrastructure supports adaptive security and zero-trust models. Furthermore, Muhammad et al. [23] built on this by fusion of the zero-trust, layered defense, and international standards on which robust cyber defense systems were developed to mitigate multi-vector attacks.

In terms of the institutional and academic framework, model institutional resilience has been suggested by Conklin and Shoemaker [4] and Conklin et al. [20] and implemented at universities and training centers. Their seven-step model would be used in higher education environments for awareness raising, automated security operations, and the development of continuous learning systems. Moore [28] thus enlarged this through the detailed specification of cyber defense training that would use realistic incident simulation and thorough preparation of security professionals to deal with dynamic and complex attacks.

The real-life lessons from Small and Medium-sized Enterprises (SMEs) are exemplified in cost resilience effectiveness. For instance, Pureti [22] studies AI-enhanced monitoring tools for small-scale cyber resilience for SMEs. In addition,

Sharma et al. [29] detail a vulnerability management framework developed that increases the resilience to risk exposure for medium-sized IT firms. Thus, automation, structured policies, and continuous risk assessment make resilience possible, even in the absence of resources.

These same concepts have been strongly applied to the public infrastructure and critical systems areas. Layered protection and recovery controls ensure continuity during cyber incidents within United States. federal systems through the NIST engineering approach, as modeled and demonstrated by Ross [9]. Such reference architectures are surveyed in Savold et al. [26]: a survey of reference architectures across the cloud-industry and defense infrastructures as modular designs permit flexible upgrades and adaptations. Such applications uphold cyber resilience framework descriptions in huge organizations developed by [5, 6], with a focus on business continuities and proactive adaptation.

Akinsanya [1] present evidence from architecture examples of evolution in network security frameworks. The evolving model comprises adaptive resilience dynamics that can be modeled for the growing telecommunications infrastructure on a massive scale. Li [16] expanded this idea with multiple case studies on framing recovery for an organization that focuses on rapid reconfiguration and restoration of services. Safitra et al. [24] seal an envelope with counter-active resilience frameworks put into action in Indonesian smart city systems and their synergistic combination of sustainability and cybersecurity goals.

As national defense simulation models, further evidence for innovation-induced resilience continues to grow. For example, [12] showed NATO's intertwined development and innovation in its resilience programs; whereas [13] could show deterrence models based on continuous threat understanding. The implementations demonstrate that resilience is a technical construct of strategy, requiring alignment between defense policy and emerging technologies, along with human readiness.

Finally, Siegel and Sweeney [27] provide numerous case examples of the type of organizations that adopted risk-driven security and resiliency strategies. With this evidence, the authors demonstrate how things evolve from static defenses to adaptive, intelligence-based ecosystems. These findings are in tandem with integrative cybersecurity principles as advocated by Muhammad et al. [23], wherein automation, zero-trust, and AI governance converge into a singular resilience model.

The case studies examined show that cyber resilience and self-healing capabilities have now been made practical and are required practically in all sectors-from energy grids and aerospace through state governance to enterprise networks. Real applications have always shown that resilience is growing out of the cover of automation, intelligence, redundancy, and adaptability, whether it is through predictive analytics of the CYDRES project, structured NIST engineering framework functions or defense-based coordination models of NATO. As Ahmed et al. [3]

and Bolish et al. [8] argue building resilience "from day one," these cybersecurity systems will ride through disruptions and evolve to be stronger after each incident-living embodiments of the core tenets of Cybersecurity 5.0.

12.9 Future Trends and Research Directions

The ever-increasing complexity and interconnectedness of digital infrastructures will require future investigations in cybersecurity to develop systems that are inherently resilient, adaptive, and able to recover autonomously from failures. Future research encourages the design of cybersecurity systems that exceed simple defensive mechanisms and propose proactive, predictive, and auto-healing capabilities. This was arguably the most critical research direction encompassing cyber resilience frameworks with an institutional security strategy. Akinsanya et al. [1] and Ahmed et al. [3] state that the gap between cybersecurity and cyber defense must therefore be bridged by means of unified frameworks, aligned with governance, policy, and human factors by technology. This was an evolution where systems do not just prevent intrusion attacks but also necessarily sustain operations under attacks, meaning that the task has shifted from security to resiliency in systems.

Embedding resilience principles into organizational processes-a change that still occupies horizon-converts into adaptability, recovery, and business continuity as the pillars of central focus toward future cybersecurity frameworks. Future research will definitely extend such frameworks into the areas of industrial IoT, works, smart cities, and the ecosystems of critical infrastructures, bringing interoperability and scalability across various tech domains. Futuristic frameworks like CYDRES exemplify the fact that AI-based defense can practically implement real-time efficiency and resiliency for future-grid interactive infrastructures [17, 18]. Integrated predictive analytics, real-time monitoring, and adaptive control mechanisms have been depicted by such architectures to mitigate increasingly complex cyber-physical risks.

Another significant research trajectory concentrates on proactive defense and self-healing features enabled by AI. Usman Haider describes that using AI and ML techniques for task automation has a significant impact on anomaly detection and the process of automatically patching the system. Building on that, Safitra et al. [24] formulate counterattacking frameworks of defensive automation and adaptive threat modeling where systems can anticipate and neutralize attacks before they escalate. This is proactive and in line with how Cybersecurity 5.0 envisions intelligent systems to operate in adversarial and dynamic environments.

Standardization and assessment of resilience metrics form another major front for research advancement [2, 19] have noted that measuring cyber resilience relies upon compounded assessment models in the technical and organizational dimensions. Future studies will design active, measurable resilience indicators, which will include recovery time, adaptability of the system, and tolerance to impact. This should bring about benchmark and improvement across industries. According to Hubbard [14], this would broaden the status by organization at the state level regarding the need for resilience in cyber strategy. Such adaptive policy frameworks would also allow a multi-tiered defense structure = s, conforming with national, corporate, and individual security postures.

In addition to that, the synergy between the integrated zero trust architecture and layered defense mechanisms is important. Muhammad et al. [23] and Sharma et al. [29] state that the application of zero trust to global cybersecurity standards would help in enhancing digital resilience through the removal of presumptions of trust and the enforcement of continuous verification across all network layers. Additionally, Pureti [22] favored dynamic and real-time threat-aware defense strategies that automatically adapt to changing attack vectors.

Another emerging area is resilient architecture design: redundancy, diversity, and modularity-inherent features to survive sophisticated attacks. According to Ross [9] and Savold et al. [26], systems should be designed by security-by-design and resilience-by-design principles, so that robustness is guaranteed from the very beginning. [8] go a step ahead on this point by defining resilience is something that would be "built in from day one" rather than an afterthought. Moreover, [10] have shown through their study on the VERDICT framework that formal verification tools can actually help achieve concurrent engineering of both resilience and safety in critical systems.

At a strategic level, increasing policy-driven multi-stakeholder collaborations will also build long-term benefits. [11–13] and so forth assert that cyber resilience must include all of the defense institutions in this partnership with governments and private sectors. This perspective is corroborated by Conklin and Shoemaker [4] and Conklin et al. [20], who suggest frameworks for institutional survival and resilience-building involving seven major components, including leadership, culture, and technical controls. Continuous learning and adaptation are, therefore, compulsory elements in future cyber defense strategies.

The link between sustainability and cyber resilience has recently become quite attractive. As Kanaan et al. [7] and Galinec [21] underline, resilient cyber systems go hand in hand with business continuity and, hence, also sustainability. Further research should inquire how resilience frameworks can help organizations meet sustainability goals by lessening environmental and economic impacts from cyber incidents. In this vein, Li [16] notes recovery-oriented frameworks that meet operational efficiency and long-term resilience objectives; this applies particularly in those environments born from AI integration.

Indeed, cyber-defending training and human-centric resilience will continue to be important. According to Siegel and Sweeney [27] and Moore [28], risk-driven strategies should be enhanced by the identification of capacity-building techniques that increase the readiness of the employee workforces for an impact on emerging threat landscapes. Training programs based on simulation, gamification, and AI learning analytics would close skill gaps and thus contribute to a culture set even further across organizations toward continuity.

12.10 Conclusion

The development of cyber resilience and innovations in defense strategies has become crucial in securing modern digital infrastructures. Cyber threats keep becoming stronger and even more complex while traditional reactive security measures don't suffice in such situations. A proactive, continuous, and adaptive recovery action is vital for any organization wanting to ensure the continuity of operations under adverse conditions. This not only protects the organization's assets but also makes it have a better chance of anticipating, withstanding, and recovering from attacks efficiently.

Cybersecurity 5.0 is the future in drastically redefining digital security, both in thinking and application. Organizations can make headway into intelligent, self-healing security frameworks operating autonomously in dynamic threat terrains through AI, machine intelligence, and fire-on-response systems. Emphasis on resilience instead of mere defense makes possible the designing of systems capable of withstanding, while still functional, attacks; enhanced trust, therefore, becomes much more credible and reliable in digital operations.

Standardized resilience frameworks and measurable metrics can, eventually, put organizations in a position to continuously appraise and improve the cyber posture. Resilience principles embedded in organizational strategy, governance, and workforce training foster a culture of readiness and responsiveness. At the end of the day, it is the technology-policy-human nexus that will realize a more balanced and sustainable approach to cybersecurity.

Ultimately, future adaptability in security lies in making intelligent adaptive systems like resilient systems against whatever threats might be at the present or that would arise in the future. With this kind of proactive and integrated approach, organizations can be well-positioned to withstand the increasingly convoluted digital world—security alongside continuity during uncertain times.

References

1 Akinsanya, M.O., Ekechi, C.C., and Okeke, C.D. (2024). The evolution of cyber resilience frameworks in network security: a conceptual analysis. *Computer Science & IT Research Journal.* 5 (4): 926–949.

2 Annarelli, A., Nonino, F., and Palombi, G. (2020). Understanding the management of cyber resilient systems. *Comput Ind Eng.* 149: 106829.

3 Ahmed, M.F., Molla, A.H., Uddin, M.R., and Chowdhury, T.R. (2023). Advancing Cyber Resilience: Bridging the Divide Between Cyber Security and Cyber Defense. *International Journal for Multidisciplinary Research (IJFMR).* 5 (6).

4 Conklin, W.A. and Shoemaker, D. (2017). Cyber-resilience: Seven steps for institutional survival. *EDPACS.* 55 (2): 14–22.

5 AL-Hawamleh A. (2024). Cyber resilience framework: Strengthening defenses and enhancing continuity in business security. *International Journal of Computing and Digital Systems.* 15 (1): 1315–1331.

6 AL-Hawamleh AM. (2024). Securing the Future: Framework Fundamentals for Cyber Resilience in Advancing Organizations. *Journal of System and Management Sciences.* 14 (10): 130–150.

7 Kanaan, A., A, A.L.-H., Aloun, M. et al. (2024). Fortifying Organizational Cyber Resilience: An Integrated Framework for Business Continuity and Growth amidst Escalating Threat Landscapes. *International Journal of Computing and Digital Systems.* 16 (1): 1–13.

8 Bolish S, Dodge M, Mitalo E, Westing R. Building Cyber Resilient Systems from Day 1. In: 2024 IEEE Aerospace Conference. *IEEE*; 2024. p. 1–8.

9 Ross, R., Pillitteri, V., Graubart, R. et al. (2019). *Developing cyber resilient systems: a systems security engineering approach*. National Institute of Standards and Technology.

10 Meng, B., Larraz, D., Siu, K. et al. (2021). Verdict: a language and framework for engineering cyber resilient and safe system. *Systems.* 9 (1): 18.

11 Efthymiopoulos, M.P. (2016). *NATO smart defense and cyber resilience.* Tufts University May.

12 Efthymiopoulos, M.P. (2019). A cyber-security framework for development, defense and innovation at NATO. *J Innov Entrep.* 8 (1): 12.

13 Ridout, T. (2016). *Building a comprehensive strategy of cyber defense, deterrence, and resilience*, 63–83. In: The Fletcher Forum of World Affairs. JSTOR.

14 Hubbard, G.A. (2023). State-level cyber resilience: A conceptual framework. *Applied Cybersecurity & Internet Governance.* 2 (1): 1–14.

15 Dickson F, Goodwin P. Five key technologies for enabling a Cyber-resilience framework. US45455119, IBM. 2019.

16 Li, I. (2024). Cyber Resilience Frameworks: Exploring Cyber Resilience Frameworks and Strategies for Organizations to Recover From Cyber Attacks and Maintain Operational Continuity. *Cybersecurity and Network Defense Research.* 4 (1): 1–15.

17 Li G, O'Neill Z, Wen J, Pradhan O, Ren L, Wu T, et al. CYDRES: CYber Defense and REsilient System for securing grid-interactive efficient buildings. In: Proceedings of the 10th ACM International Conference on Systems for Energy-Efficient Buildings, Cities, and Transportation. 2023. p. 307–9.

18 O'Neill Z, Wen J, Wu T, Candan KS, Ren L, Zhu Q, et al. Securing Grid-interactive Efficient Buildings (GEB) through Cyber Defense and Resilient System (CYDRES). Texas A & M Univ., College Station, TX (United States). Texas A & M ...; 2024.

19 Estay, D.A.S., Sahay, R., Barfod, M.B., and Jensen, C.D. (2020). A systematic review of cyber-resilience assessment frameworks. *Comput Secur.* 97: 101996.

20 Conklin WA, Shoemaker D, Kohnke A. Cyber resilience: Rethinking cybersecurity strategy to build a cyber resilient architecture. In: ICMLG2017 5th International Conference on Management Leadership and Governance. 2017. p. 105.

21 Galinec, D. (2023). Cyber Security and Cyber Defense: Challenges and Building of Cyber Resilience Conceptual Model. *Int J Appl Sci Dev.* 1: 83–88.

22 Pureti, N. (2022). Building a Robust Cyber Defense Strategy for Your Business. *Revista de Inteligencia Artificial en Medicina.* 13 (1): 35–51.

23 Muhammad, T., Munir, M.T., Munir, M.Z., and Zafar, M.W. (2022). Integrative cybersecurity: merging zero trust, layered defense, and global standards for a resilient digital future. *International Journal of Computer Science and Technology.* 6 (4): 99–135.

24 Safitra, M.F., Lubis, M., and Fakhrurroja, H. (2023). Counterattacking cyber threats: A framework for the future of cybersecurity. *Sustainability.* 15 (18): 13369.

25 Usman Haider AZ. Building Resilient Cyber Defense Architectures: AI and Machine Learning in Cloud and Network Security. 2024.

26 Savold, R., Dagher, N., Frazier, P., and McCallam, D. (2017). Architecting cyber defense: A survey of the leading cyber reference architectures and frameworks. In: *In: 2017 IEEE 4th International Conference on Cyber Security and Cloud Computing (CSCloud)*, 127–138. IEEE.

27 Siegel, C.A. and Sweeney, M. (2020). *Cyber strategy: risk-driven security and resiliency*. Auerbach Publications.

28 Moore E. Building cyber defense training capacity. 2020.

29 Sharma, N.A., Kumar, K., Khorshed, T. et al. (2024). Evading Cyber-Attacks on Hadoop Ecosystem: A Novel Machine Learning-Based Security-Centric Approach towards Big Data Cloud. *Information.* 15 (9): 558.

30 Orme, S. (2019). *Addressing Issues with Defense-in-Depth, Apts, and Iot with Active Cyber Defense Cycle and Cyber Resilience*. Utica College.

Part V

Future Directions

13

Autonomous Cybersecurity: Toward Self-Defending Systems

13.1 Introduction

The blistering development of digital transformation and the spread of connected systems have led to an enormous and complicated cyberspace, which needs a new paradigm of defense that would not be based on classic reactive paradigms. The idea behind autonomous cybersecurity becomes a radical development in this scenario, which will mark the transition between human-reliant security operations and intelligent, self-protective systems, able to preempt, respond to, and counteract cyber threats in real time. With the threats becoming more dynamic nowadays compared to the traditional defense mechanisms, automation and artificial intelligence (AI) have become essential facilitators of preemptive defenses and resilience [1–3].

The effectiveness of the traditional perimeter-based defenses and static firewalls is becoming less and less effective against the cunning and tenacity of the contemporary cyberattackers. The isolated network segmentation and the use of perimeter defense cannot survive the dynamic tactics of the advanced persistent threats (APTs) as McMahon [4] and Sipho et al. [5] have found out. Articles by Alshamrani et al. [6] and Rubio et al. [7] point to the fact that even the most secure networks are hacked by APTs through the use of stealth, persistence, and adaptability. Independently, autonomous systems incorporate feedback, cognitive analytics, and adaptive measures whereby defense mechanisms can dynamically grow and adapt to threats and mitigate them before they can do any harm [8, 9].

The gamification of AI and machine learning (ML) into cybersecurity systems brings a degree of intelligence and speed that can never be achieved by manual systems. ML algorithms facilitate automated prediction of anomalies, predictive threat data, and intrusion prevention based on the behavior [10, 11]. Cyber defense models based on AI, which are mentioned by Smith and

Anderson [12] and Iqbal et al. [13], use large-scale data processing to determine the existence of hidden patterns that could signal impending attacks. These smart systems are self-learning and self-adaptive and constitute the basis of self-defending ecosystems, which react independently to known and unforeseen risks.

The current frameworks, including those suggested by AL-Hawamleh [14] and Tahmasebi [15], focus on cyber resilience, or the ability of systems not only to withstand but also to come out of the cyber incident and continue their operations. Cyber resilience is provided as a complement to autonomy and guarantees that the defense systems are capable of surviving functionality after an attack, changing configurations, and services recovery with clean transitions. Equally, Patel et al. [16] examined the autonomous cybersecurity convergence with the cyber-physical systems (CPS), where real-time response and safety are the most important.

Besides, the paradigm of the Zero Trust Architecture (ZTA) supports the autonomous model of cybersecurity and requires constant authentication, verification, and trust recalibration within the networks [17]. The idea of Zero Trust is consistent with AI-based defense mechanisms that automatically check the legitimacy of devices and users, which reduces the chances of insider threats. This ongoing validation forms the basis of self-defense mechanisms that have the ability to identify anomalies, isolate affected nodes, and counter malicious processes automatically [18, 19].

Automation and AI are also changing the nature of the field of threat hunting, which used to be a manual and intelligence-centered process. More recent studies by Mahboubi et al. [20] and Badva et al. [21] prove that a continuous search for the threat can be directed by autonomous systems with unsupervised learning, detecting the signs of a compromise, and arranging immediate corrections. These proactive ways are an alternative to the traditional post-incident analysis model and transfer cybersecurity to real-time anticipative protection. Equally, results of moving target defense (MTD) research by Sengupta et al. [22] and Soussi et al. [23], and others indicate how dynamic network structure and randomized system states could deceive adversaries and decrease predictability of attacks—two principles of autonomous security systems.

As far as operations are concerned, the increased significance of autonomous adaptability in ensuring endogenous security is demonstrated through advanced monitoring structures [8] and mimicked defense mechanisms [24]. These approaches combine the continuous analysis of data flow with the AI decision engines that will modify the configurations and rules of response on their own. A complementary study by Gudimetla and Foti et al. [25, 26] compares the natural and engineered defense systems and finds similarities between them—both are flexible, resilient, and balanced between rigidity and flexibility in safeguarding

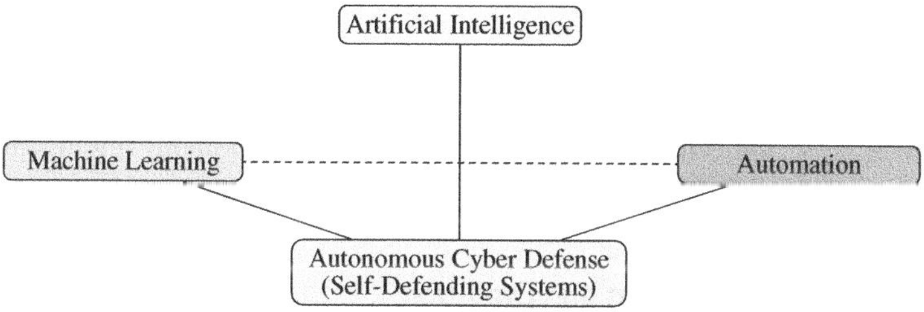

Figure 13.1 Conceptual Framework of Autonomous Cybersecurity. "*Source:* Hewa Majeed Zangana"

assets. The analogy is expanded by [27] using the so-called Octopus Method, which simulates natural adaptive defense strategies of mobile device security.

Within the wider defense and policy framework worldwide [28, 29] demonstrate the strategic significance of incorporating autonomous cybersecurity within the national and organizational security policies. The integration of AI into defense approaches in all spheres, including healthcare [30] to smart grids [31], is an indicator of a new consensus: cybersecurity can no longer be maintained by human control alone. Rather, it needs to be transformed into intelligent automation with the ability to make predictions and preclude complex, multivector threats in real time.

Finally, autonomous cybersecurity is the next stage of development of digital protection. It brings together automation, ML, Zero Trust principles, and adaptive resilience together into a unified system that is capable of protecting, responding, and recovering without the need to employ human intervention directly. This is not just bringing about a change in technology but in philosophy—redefining the elements of defense, trust, and risk in the new digital world. With relentless cyberattacks on organizations, autonomous cybersecurity remains a need and an inevitability in how the Cybersecurity 5.0 era will be shaped.

Figure 13.1 presents a conceptual model of autonomous cybersecurity and demonstrates the way AI, ML, and automation interrelate in order to establish a self-defending ecosystem. It shows how defensive models that rely on reactive defense mechanisms are changing into proactive, adaptive, and intelligent systems capable of detecting, predicting, and reacting to threats independently.

13.2 Understanding Autonomous Cybersecurity

The notion of autonomous cybersecurity is a paradigm shift in the historical approach to defense that is based on human interaction. It can be defined as systems and structures that make use of AI, ML, automation, and adaptive analytics to identify, eliminate, and react to cyber threats with little or no human involvement [1, 2]. These systems are created to replicate the human ability to decide, learn, and develop with exposure to data and attack patterns. Autonomous cybersecurity is in a sense not only about automation, but it is also about intelligent automation where the system has situational awareness, flexibility, and robustness.

13.2.1 Conceptual Foundations and Evolution

Cybersecurity has shifted towards a dynamic self-learning ecosystem as opposed to the earlier days of static defense systems—perimeter-based and signature-driven systems [4, 5]. The classical models were based on the use of firewalls and intrusion detection systems (IDS), which had to be updated manually and responded to the threats [25]. Nonetheless, once cyber threats evolved, in particular, the emergence of APTs, these models became insufficient [6, 7]. Autonomous cybersecurity came to fill this void by applying intelligence to defense systems so that they can learn from both past and current data. El-Amir [9] highlighted that defense architectures in the modern context cannot just rely on the concept of static protection but also implement self-healing and self-optimization features. Likewise, Iqbal et al. [13] investigated the evolution of AI into security strategies in relation to the evolution of autonomous decision-making systems in military defense, where the autonomous systems improve the speed and accuracy of their decisions. This in cyber environments is translated into systems that are able to detect anomalies, determine threats, and implement countermeasures in real time without human verification.

13.2.2 Core Components of Autonomous Cybersecurity

The system of automated cybersecurity incorporates a number of interdependent elements: smart monitoring, automated threat response, predictive analytics, and resilience engineering [8, 14]. The monitoring systems of networks currently apply AI-based analytics to constantly check traffic patterns and detect abnormalities that can be attributed to intrusions [8]. The predictive threat intelligence discussed by Rodriguez and Costa [11] uses the ML algorithms to predict attack vectors and preemptively modify the defenses. Adaptive behavior models, which are based on ML and continue to adapt to incoming data, are also used to have self-defending systems respond differently to every threat scenario. Tan and Smith and Anderson [10, 12] observed that such flexibility enables rapid containment of threats even when it comes to complex and multivector attacks. The principles of ZTA [17] also reinforce autonomy by allowing constant authentication and micro-segmentation and reducing the chance of the subsequent movement of lateral navigation in networks.

13.2.3 Threat Hunting and Proactive Defense

The proactive threat-hunting capability is one of the characteristics of autonomous cybersecurity. In contrast to the more classic reactive defense, autonomous systems perform ongoing, information-driven anomaly searches, possible exploits, or a deviation in behavior related to the presence of an unprecedented threat. Mahboubi et al. and Badva et al. [20, 21] analyzed how threat hunting has been automated by AI to be not a manual and investigative process but an intelligent and iterative process. With the help of autonomous systems, trained on extensive datasets, indicators of compromise (IoCs) can be detected independently, and action to contain them can be executed promptly. Dynamic defense, like MTD, is also a part of proactive defense [22, 23]. Such methods keep changing network settings, IP addresses, and system parameters, making them harder for the attackers. According to Tahmasebi [15], this active defense-to-anticipatory security change is indicative of an essential feature of autonomous systems: a defense that changes more rapidly than offensive strategies.

13.2.4 Mimicry, Adaptation, and Natural Defense Models

Independent cybersecurity is also inspired by a natural defense system as observed in the biological environment. Wu and Wu [24] proposed so-called mimic defense, when the internal configurations of the systems dynamically vary to make the attackers confused in their attempts, just as in the case of camouflage, which living organisms apply. Similarly, Siyez [27] introduced the so-called Octopus Approach that uses the principles of adaptive natural defense for the security of mobile devices, focusing on flexibility, decentralization, and regeneration. Environmental resilience analogies, like those, e.g. mentioned by Foti et al. [26] in coastal defense measures, can also find their echo in autonomous cybersecurity—that is, the necessity to have systems that can be continuously reinforced and adaptable in reaction to the unpredictable threat. This flexibility is the point of the cyber resilience models which as AL-Hawamleh [14] states are focused on not only the resistance to the attacks but also on the ability to recover and learn during the incidents quickly.

13.2.5 Integration with Cyber-Physical and Societal Systems

Autonomous cybersecurity is not limited to digital facilities, but to CPS and national defense systems. As Patel et al. [16] noted, the incorporation of AI-based defense in CPS settings is motivated by the fact that the real-time responsiveness of the system is vital to prevent operational safety. In a similar thought, Pham and Xiong [32] examined AI-based defense systems against autonomous vehicles by demonstrating the need for automation and safety, which requires balancing the two. On the national policy level, Daniel and Hayes and Sarjito [28, 29] emphasized that autonomous cybersecurity is consistent with contemporary defense policies that value the strategy and less human engagement. This change is a new frontier in the digital sovereignty and defense governance, whereby states and organizations leverage autonomous agents to act in protectionist roles in digital spheres.

13.2.6 Modern Threat Landscape and the Need for Autonomy

The growing complexity of cyberattacks, ransomware, botnets, phishing, and zero-day attacks has led to the necessity to have systems that can defend themselves [18, 33]. Obi et al. [19] argue that the threat vectors diversification of cloud infrastructure, IoT, and mobile infrastructures requires machine speed and scale defense mechanisms. Threat modeling and risk-based contingency planning, which are autonomous as Salami et al. [30] note in the healthcare sector, are becoming a mandatory tool to protect sensitive data. Meanwhile, the new defense paradigms like cyber deception and education towards hybrid threat resilience [34] add more layers to autonomous systems by introducing deception and psychological modeling to automated detection. This, in practice, will imply that systems will be able to attract, monitor, and analyze attackers automatically, turning every incident of intrusion into a chance at improved defense intelligence.

13.2.7 Toward Intelligent, Self-Defending Ecosystems

Independent cybersecurity is not only a technological breakthrough but also a systemic change in the manner in which organizations are dealing with risk and resiliency. Chastain and Smith, Oroy et al., and Uchiyama and Oroy [1–3] all arrive at the idea that AI-based security ecosystems could become a so-called sentinel of the cyberspace, which is able to monitor, reason, and take action without human oversight. These ecosystems utilize continuous feedback mechanisms that lead them to develop defense mechanisms following each interaction, which makes them truly resilient self-learners. In the direction of complete autonomy of cybersecurity, as stressed by AL-Hawamleh and Tahmasebi and Tahmasebi [14, 15], the combination of proactive, resilient, and ethical structures must be integrated to provide transparency and responsibility. Finally, machine-intelligence-based autonomous cybersecurity systems will reshape the scope of human control and machine-intelligence-driven systems—Cybersecurity 5.0—in which digital defense is dynamic, intelligent, and self-custodial.

13.3 Core Components of a Self-Defending System

The basis of autonomous cybersecurity is the combination of intelligent, flexible, and active defensive systems that allow the systems to identify, analyze, and act on the changing cyber threats without the need to be continuously supervised by humans. All these elements make traditional reactive defense models to be dynamic ecosystems that are able to learn, predict, and adapt to adversarial behavior in a continuous fashion.

13.3.1 Threat Intelligence and Predictive Analytics

Threat intelligence can also be viewed as the central nervous system of self-protecting architectures, as it allows real-time observation of attack vectors, threat actors, or even vulnerabilities of the systems. This is improved by predictive analytics, which is powered by AI and ML, and it predicts any possible breach when it has not taken place. As Rodriguez and Costa [11] note, the introduction of AI-based predictive intelligence into government and enterprise networks will allow them to record anomalies in advance, thus reducing the time of response. On the same note, Tan [10] and Iqbal et al. [13] point out that intelligent automation and informative reasoning can enable a system to predict threats like never before, which fits the move towards reactive defense to preemptive mitigation.

13.3.2 Adaptive Defense and Moving Target Strategies

Autonomous systems are resilient to change—they will constantly change their configuration to outwit attackers. The strategies of MTD, which [22, 23] comment on in detail, allow networks to dynamically change IP addresses, system states, or software configurations. Such uncertainty causes the use of vulnerabilities to exploit them to be extremely hard for attackers. Wu and Wu [24] also take this flexibility a step up with what they refer to as cyberspace mimic defense, whereby the various environments of a decoy are simulated to confuse an intruder. These self-changing and dynamic approaches constitute a fundamental part of resilience within self-defending systems.

13.3.3 Autonomous Threat Hunting and Anomaly Detection

Threat hunting is an important component of a self-defending ecosystem that involves identifying threats of advanced persistent nature (APT) in advance before they can harm systems. This is automated and fast through modern frameworks discussed by Mahboubi et al. [20] and Badva et al. [21]. According to Alshamrani et al. [6], integrating automation with human skills is significant to identify APTs that avoid traditional tools. The new concept of the hunter-gatherer models [21] enhances the system autonomy even more, combining the continuous monitoring with the context intelligence.

13.3.4 AI-Driven Defense Automation

The combination of AI in cybersecurity allows all levels of defense, including monitoring, detection, and response, to be automated. Oroy et al. [2] Uchiyama and Oroy [3], and Smith and Anderson [12] all explain the role of AI as the so-called digital sentinel, detecting and suppressing menaces independently. Chastain and Smith [1] also note that by using AI in defensive infrastructures, the accuracy of the decision made is improved, and the human error is minimized. El-Amir [9] and Obi et al. [19] note that real-time threat classification and self-corrective actions can be initiated through intelligent automation, which results in autonomic resilience.

13.3.5 Multi-Layered and Zero-Trust Architectures

The system needs to be strong in self-defense and must also have a zero-trust philosophy. According to Patil et al. [17], ZTA does not presuppose any implicit trust and requires constant authentication and verification. Patil et al. [17] and Nair [33] indicate that implementing ZTA into multi-layered structures can help to avoid horizontal movements of attackers within a network. Equally, Sipho et al. [5] and Gudimetla [25] promote a high level of firewall and internalization methods that isolate the assets and provide finer control. Defense-in-depth [4], is a general design philosophy that authors implement through redundancy, diversity, and constant verification of the network layers to enhance resiliency.

13.3.6 Cyber Deception and Game-Theoretic Defense Models

Defense mechanisms based on deception take advantage of attacker actions to the benefit of the defender. Steingartner et al. [34] and Rubio et al. [35] talk about the usefulness of cyber deception models that utilize decoy assets to mislead, stall, and reveal attackers. In addition, game-theoretic methods [7] recreate adversarial interactions, where autonomous agents can optimize the defense approaches concerning the probabilistic results. These adaptive learning systems enable self-defending systems to constantly adapt and respond to novel attack vectors in response to them.

13.3.7 Network Monitoring and Situational Awareness

Live monitoring facilitates unbroken visibility of network activities. Network telemetry and behavioral analytics are named as the key to detecting anomalies [8], and network resilience frameworks incorporating the monitoring process with continuity planning are described as the necessary ones [14]. Tahmasebi [15] supplements this point of view with the focus on predictive situational awareness that contributes to active defense as well as disaster recovery planning.

13.3.8 Security for Distributed and Remote Environments

Self-defending systems need to protect decentralized infrastructures as the models of remote and hybrid work grow. According to a study by Ogungbemi et al. [18], VPNs and endpoint isolation can be used as a full-fledged ransomware and botnet defense model to secure the remote users. Likewise, Salami et al. [30] discuss the improved threat modeling and risk reduction systems of sensitive industries such as healthcare, where distributed data exposes them more. These measures are in line with the overall trends of adaptive, endpoint-based defense and continuity-based resilience.

13.3.9 Integration with Cyber-Physical and National Defense Systems

Autonomous security is not only digitally confined to digital networks and does not stop there. Patel et al. [16] note the increasing role of CPS, where AI-directed surveillance of integrity is guaranteed among the industrial and IoT devices. In a similar case, Sarjito [29] notes that national security structures are becoming more and more dependent on independent defense systems to maintain situational preparedness in real time. These cross-fusion integrations combine the borders between cyber and kinetic integrations and build self-defending ecosystems.

13.3.10 Lessons from Natural and Cross-Domain Defense Models

Cybersecurity based on nature can provide useful information to self-defending architecture. The author of the article, Siyez [27], presents the Octopus Method, in which the nature of adaptive camouflage and decentralized defense imparts security to mobile devices. Similarly, Foti et al. [26] demonstrate how the coastal defense systems apply multi-layered barriers against the changing environmental hazards—in the same way that cyber defense works. The implications of such cross-disciplinary lessons, as well as the information that [28] provide about adaptive peacekeeping, confirm that responsive, cooperative ecosystems of defense are required, which can adapt to threats as they evolve.

To conclude, the main elements of a self-defending system are interrelated by means of intelligence, automation, adaptability, and continuous feedback layers. The combination of them constitutes a comprehensive defense design that is capable of autonomous learning, immediate reaction, and long-term stability against more sophisticated cyberattackers.

13.4 The Role of Artificial Intelligence and Machine Learning

ML and AI have become the self-defensive cybersecurity systems drivers. These technologies also provide real-time threat detection, dynamic response, and predictive intelligence, which goes beyond the scope of conventional rule-based defenses. AI and ML adapt cybersecurity architectures into smart ecosystems that are able to detect, categorize, and suppress threats independently through a continuous learning process and understanding the context.

13.4.1 AI as the Core of Autonomous Defense

The fact that AI can access large amounts of data and identify intricate patterns makes self-defending systems strong, intelligent guardians in cyberspace. According to Oroy et al. [2], AI is the so-called cognitive guardian because it continuously examines the system behavior to preempt and counter cyber threats. Also, Uchiyama and Oroy et al. [2] stress that AI-based defense measures can be used as an online watchdog that can provide 24/7 security. Smith and Anderson [12] also emphasize the idea of the Watchful Eye of AI, in which high-level neural networks can replicate human intuition to offer a continuously evolving, adaptive security layer. Chastain and Smith [1] hold that the incorporation of AI defensive measures transforms the way contemporary organizations apply cyber resilience to cybercriminals: no longer do they rely on inert security measures, but they employ smart systems that learn on their own and transform their approach to cybercriminals. El-Amir and Obi et al. [9, 19] also prove that AI-based models are more effective and faster in detention and recognition of zero-day exploits and polymorphic malware.

13.4.2 Machine Learning for Predictive Threat Intelligence

ML is the analytical foundation of modern cybersecurity, allowing the systems to forecast the attacks prior to their occurrence. Rodriguez and Costa [11] demonstrate that the predictive threat intelligence based on ML assists organizations in

Figure 13.2 AI and Machine Learning Pipeline for Cyber Defense. "*Source:* Hewa Majeed Zangana"

analyzing the behavioral deviations, identifying the initial signs of attack, and predicting the actions of attackers. These algorithms use enormous datasets that are based on sensors, logs, and telemetry to model adversarial patterns in the long term. According to Tan [10], the use of ML-based defense mechanisms allows classifying threats in real time without the need to involve human researchers. This automation improves the responsiveness and speed of security operations as well as the mean time to respond (MTTR). Convergence of AI and ML to the defense sphere, as Iqbal et al. [13] observe, does not only reinforce the capabilities in the field of technology but also transforms the defensive postures of strategy, making cybersecurity a part of the large-scale national and global defense systems.

Figure 13.2 explains the process of artificial intelligence and ML to improve cybersecurity activities. The working of the flow of data is in phases of sensing, learning, prediction, and action, which allow intelligent and reactive responses to varying threats.

13.4.3 AI-Enabled Threat Hunting and Detection

AI and ML are transforming autonomous threat hunting that is traditionally a manual and expert-driven activity. Mahboubi et al. [20] and Badva et al. [21] explain AI as a way of supplementing threat hunters by automating the process of pattern discovery, correlation, and anomaly detection in complex network environments. The technologies assist in identifying the presence of APTs that escape the use of traditional tools as earlier mentioned by Alshamrani et al. [6]. With reinforcement learning and unsupervised clustering, AI models are capable of differentiating a benign activity and malicious one in real time. Both AL-Hawamleh [14] and Tahmasebi [15] note the significance of implementing AI-based monitoring within organizational resiliency strategies to provide business continuity in changing attack campaigns.

13.4.4 Intelligent Automation and Adaptive Defense

Not only AI detects threats, but also coordinates adaptive actions by means of intelligent automation. The paper by Edwards [8] emphasizes the use of network monitoring systems that are integrated with ML algorithms to automatically modify the settings and prevent suspicious operations. This mechanism is further enhanced by application of self-learning policies that develop in a continuous feedback mechanism. McMahon [4] and Gudimetla [25] mention that AI-based automation enhances the management of defense-in-depth and firewalls, respectively, by setting up dynamically adjusting walls to identify abnormalities in the network. Equally, Sipho et al. [5] emphasize the importance of deploying AI analytics in firewall architects and improving accuracy and minimizing false positives. These layers with AI enhancements are the basis of autonomic security, in which systems develop self-diagnoses and self-healing in real time.

13.4.5 Game Theory, Deception, and Proactive AI Defense

The range of AI in decision-making includes game theory and misleading approaches, making systems predict the actions of the attacker and implement countermeasures. A game-theoretic model is proposed by Rubio et al. [7], in which AI agents recreate actions between the attackers and the defenders to produce the best defensive strategies. In the same vein, Steingartner et al. [34] focus on the application of AI-based cyber deception, which involves deploying decoys and traps that confuse the enemy and gather valuable threat data. Wu and Wu [24] present a new idea called cyberspace mimic defense, which involves the use of AI-based adaptive models to create an illusion of other environments and deceive cyberattackers. Not only can the techniques enhance the detection rates, but they also create both psychological and computational obstacles that complicate the attacks.

13.4.6 Reinforcement Learning and Moving Target Defense

Reinforcement learning (RL) has become a key facilitator of autonomous flexibility when it comes to cybersecurity. Sengupta et al. [22] and Soussi et al. [23] emphasize the role of RL algorithms in MTD to dynamically modify the network configuration and interfere with the reconnaissance and exploitation activities of attackers. With Reward-based Weights (RW), systems can optimize these movements according to the information of the context, probability of attack, and system performance. This law is a reflection of the natural adaptive defense processes—throughout much of the coastal defense strategies described by Foti et al. [26] and the Octopus Method suggested by Siyez [27], mobility and unpredictability become the primary keys to survival.

13.4.7 AI for Cyber-Physical and Distributed Environments

This application of AI and ML is not limited to conventional IT infrastructure but rather to the CPS, cloud infrastructure, and remote workspaces. Patel et al. [16] illustrate the role of AI in improving the security of CPS by constantly tracking physical activities, which are irregular, whereas Pham and Xiong [32] describe the applications of ML in safeguarding autonomous cars, a theme further explored by McMahon (2014) [4] regarding layered resilience, Rubio et al. [7] on distributed security, and the ACNS (2020) proceedings on advanced network security. Ogungbemi et al. [18] supplement it with an AI-supported VPN and endpoint defense framework of distributed workforces to maintain secure connections with ransomware and botnets. Patil et al. [17] and Nair [33] demonstrate the use of AI in the context of ZTA, which automates the system of access control and continuous authentication. This layered intelligence provides a dynamic validation of every entity, device, and process and decreases the size of the attack surface of decentralized systems.

13.4.8 Policy Development, Ethics, and Human-AI Collaboration

The growing autonomy of AI in the field of cybersecurity presents some difficulties in the context of ethics, explainability, and human control. To be accountable in AI-based systems, Sarjito [29] emphasizes that the strategy in national defense situations requires the development of strategic policies. Daniel and Hayes [28] offer a similar view on the concept of peacekeeping in which adaptive autonomy is to be balanced with human governance to ensure control and trust. Tahmasebi and Salami et al. [15, 30] state that AI involvement in risk modeling and contingency planning enhances resilience; however, it should be influenced by clear-cut models. The collaboration of humans and AI is another important aspect that would guarantee the interpretability of AI decisions and uphold ethical integrity in automated defense ecosystems.

13.4.9 Toward a Cognitive Cyber Defense Ecosystem

The AI and ML are converging in a way that is enabling the rise of cognitive cybersecurity systems and self-learning architectures that learn, think, and behave independently. These systems keep on upgrading their models using real-time threat-based intelligence and situational awareness [8, 14]. Saffar and Naji [31] depict the prospect of AI responding to the dynamically securing of smart infrastructures, e.g., advanced metering systems, whereas Rubio et al. [35] demonstrate that AI-based control models increase the resilience of industrial control environments. Finally, the future of cybersecurity, according to the authors, is symbiotic AI systems with collective intelligence, multifaceted adaptation, and proactive protection, i.e., the implementation of the concept of fully autonomous and self-defending systems, as Oroy et al. [2] and Tahmasebi [15] conclude.

Essentially, AI and ML change the face of cybersecurity by turning the field of defense into a smart, predictive, self-developing sphere. These technologies provide systems with the capability to respond and counterattack but also intervene in advance and avoid attacks through automation, flexibility, and continuous learning, which opens the door to the age of robotic cyber independence.

13.5 Mechanisms of Self-Defense and Autonomy

The technologies that facilitate the autonomous cybersecurity are an integration of intelligence, flexibility, and resilience. All these mechanisms form an ecosystem in which digital systems have the ability to detect, prevent, and recover attacks by sensing, reasoning, and acting autonomously. With autonomous defense frameworks, as opposed to traditional reactive models, AI-driven analytics, dynamic adaptation, and continuous learning to provide the protection of the system are proactive and evolving. This part discusses the main self-defense and autonomy processes that form the basis of the next generation of cyber-resilient systems.

13.5.1 AI-Driven Decision and Response Systems

The self-defending systems are driven by the operational foundations of AI and ML. The technologies can be used to monitor the large amounts of network data and detect minor anomalies to respond with swift and automated mitigation measures. Tan [10] points out that the ML systems of threat mitigation improve situational awareness as they are trained on new information, whereas Rodriguez and Costa [11] focus on predictive intelligence in governmental infrastructures, predicting the occurrence of the attack. On the same note, Chastain and Smith [1] indicate that AI is the driver that converts the fixed defenses into self-evolving mechanisms. In addition, complementary research by Oroy et al. and Uchiyama and Oroy [2, 3] indicates that AI-based sentinels patrol digital space and autonomously change the security settings to counter the identified anomalies. El-Amir [9] elaborates further and suggests the hybrid AI models that combine reasoning-driven analytics and behavior models to improve the speed and accuracy of defense decision-making. Such adaptive systems can perform automated responses to incidents, isolate compromised resources, and adjust detection limits within real-time functionalities that are needed to construct self-sustained cyber industries.

13.5.2 Dynamic and Adaptive Defense Strategies

Resilience is based on the adaptability of self-defending cybersecurity architectures. One of the most important methods in this field is the MTD. Sengupta et al. [22] and Soussi et al. [23] show that the MTD techniques dynamically evolve system configurations, IP addresses, and runtime environments to induce uncertainty on attackers. Likewise, Wu and Wu [24] present the cyberspace mimic defense model that uses redundant and decoy environments to play the game of pretending to be complex. Smart grids and IoT infrastructures are no different. Saffar and Naji [31] suggest dynamic defense of Advanced Metering Infrastructures (AMI) to improve the resilience and responsiveness of the system. The strategies prevent surfaces of the systems being dry so that the attacker has less time to execute his/her attack. Alongside it, Nair [33] points out adaptive filtering and written anti-mechanisms against web-based threats like phishing, SQL injection, and cross-site scripting elements, which could be implemented into self-protective structures.

13.5.3 Threat Hunting and Autonomous Analysis

Self-defending systems have been based on persistent threat hunting to detect unfamiliar attackers prior to them attacking. The article by Mahboubi et al. [20] describes changing methods that combine automated reasoning and situational intelligence to pursue APTs. In addition to this, Badva et al. [21] investigate so-called hunter-gatherer methodologies, using a combination of automated detection and human-in-the-loop intelligence to further boost detection in high-volume complex networks. Alshamrani et al. [6] offer an extensive overview of APT methods and observe that the conventional monitoring systems are not usually able to record multi-stage, silent attacks. Autonomous systems, but not compute all logs and network behavior in real time, relying on AI models to correlate these and take proactive interdiction. Tahmasebi [15] goes further to combine both threat intelligence and disaster recovery planning, which means that the lessons learned in previous events become directly reflected in predictive defensive stances.

13.5.4 Cyber Deception and Game-Theoretic Defense

Cyber deception will convert the curiosity of attackers into a defensive gain. Rubio et al. and Steingartner et al. [7, 34] demonstrate how decoy systems and honeypots, as well as fabricated data, can distract malicious actors of critical infrastructure, and their tactics can be disclosed. The paper published by Rubio et al. [35] also points out game-theoretic methods, where the systems can predict the choice of attackers and implement defensive strategies on the fly.

Such techniques encourage independent adjustment, and defense agents are trained to respond in an optimal way by simulating repeated attack scenarios. Daniel and Hayes [28] equate such systems with adaptive peacekeeping models, which use situational awareness in real time to generate self-organized reactions to external aggression—a relevant analogy to digital ecosystems, which are forced to balance between being vigilant and flexible.

13.5.5 Defense-in-Depth and Zero-Trust Integration

Defense-in-depth mechanisms provide several overlapping security levels to provide survivability of the system in case of compromise. McMahon (2014) details how this concept has developed to go past the more conventional perimeter defenses, with focus on upstream action of intelligence and layered resilience. Sipho et al. [5] and Gudimetla [25] bring this point in firewall expertise and segmentation tools, allowing control to be applied at the data flow level. The authors mix these principles with the ZTA [17], with a focus on constant checking and the ability to access information based on context. The zero-trust model will make sure that all the access request, internal or external, is authenticated, authorized, and encrypted. A cyber resilience framework proposed by AL-Hawamleh [14] is an additional integration of the defense-in-depth and zero-trust paradigm, with the focus on continuity planning, recovery mechanism, and trust minimalization as the foundations of self-defending systems.

13.5.6 Network Awareness and Continuous Monitoring

The autonomous response cycle is based on real-time network awareness. According to Edwards [8], telemetry, traffic analytics, and behavioral monitoring are crucial to preserving the visibility of operations. These tools allow automated situational awareness, i.e., systems that do not only identify the deviations, but also automatically interpret and respond. The article by Ogungbemi et al. [18] tackles the problem of remote and hybrid infrastructure security, suggesting VPN-related and endpoint-based solutions that eliminate ransomware and botnet spread in a distributed context. These adaptive monitoring systems are necessary so that even remote assets are used to contribute to the collective self-defense of the larger digital ecosystem.

13.5.7 Security in Cyber-Physical and National Systems

Autonomy plays a significant role in an interdisciplinary system of cyber-physics (CPS). In the context of protecting industrial automation, IoT devices, and infrastructure networks, Patel et al. [16] refer to multi-layered frameworks, which are implemented using AI-driven decision engines. These systems are based on forecasted fault alarms and automatic corrective action to ensure the integrity of operation. On a more extensive level, Sarjito [29] illustrates how autonomous cybersecurity systems are implemented to assist management in the country's defense, which improves the resistance to the hybrid warfare. These autonomous systems align with governmental defense policies to defend the national assets and combine policy-based adjustment with AI-enhanced situational intelligence.

13.5.8 Nature-Inspired and Cross-Domain Mechanisms

The biological and environmental systems provide guidelines to resilient autonomy. The article by Siyez [27] presents the Octopus Approach that employs the fight-back mechanisms found in nature, including camouflage, adaptability, and decentralized coordination to ensure the safety of mobile devices. Correspondingly, Foti et al. [26] define defense measures in the coastal area, which apply layered barriers and dynamic reaction concepts—the concept that reflects multi-layered cyber defense models. Salami et al. [30] expand this analogy into the healthcare industry and argue in support of adaptive risk modeling and contingency planning in order to develop a resilience to advanced data breaches. Such interdisciplinary insights indicate that self-protective cybersecurity systems gain by being diverse and redundant, by having learning processes both in nature and in engineered systems.

13.5.9 Integration and Convergence of Mechanisms

Last but not the least, a combination of these mechanisms, which include AI-based automation, adaptive learning, ZTA, deception-based learning, and biological inspiration, leads to a self-organizing security architecture. Iqbal et al. [13] and Obi et al. [19] emphasize that the future of autonomous defense suggests the connection of human and machine intelligence, where AI defends but at the same time constantly improves and reacts to new challenges. Autonomous cybersecurity goes beyond passive defense through the embedded architectures and recursive loop of learning: autonomic systems that sense, reason, and act consciously and proactively in an effort to defend the digital ecosystems against the dynamic adversarial environment.

The autonomous cybersecurity is a cycle of feedback (Figure 13.3). The self-reinforcing loop of continuous data collection, data analysis, and adaptative response means that systems are learning from every incident, and the system is becoming resilient in the long term.

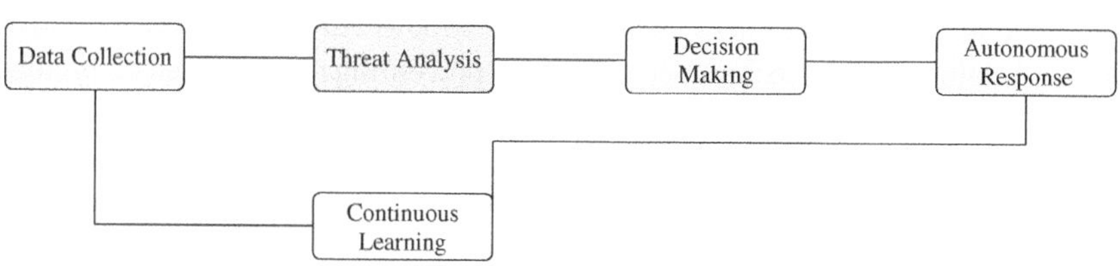

Figure 13.3 Feedback Loop of Autonomous Cyber Defense. "*Source:* Hewa Majeed Zangana"

13.6 Integration Within Cybersecurity 5.0 Framework

The rise of Cybersecurity 5.0 is a groundbreaking stage in digital protection, one that considers autonomy, intelligence, and resilience as the primary support of security. This period fits the overall Industry 5.0 paradigm very well since it encourages human-machine cooperation, sustainability, and flexibility. In the given framework, autonomous cybersecurity systems will act as intelligent partners that will work synergistically with human analysts to forecast, thwart, and react to cyber threats in real time. Such systems integration needs to be multidimensional and should include AI-based analytics and ZTA, adaptive threat hunting, and resilient infrastructure, all of which characterize the operational scope of Cybersecurity 5.0.

13.6.1 Conceptual Foundation of Cybersecurity 5.0

Cybersecurity 5.0 is based on the previous generations of cybersecurity that combine automation, cognitive computing, and cross-domain resilience to a single ecosystem. El-Amir [9] highlights the shift to the implementation of static protection models to intelligent systems, which automatically find and reduce complex threats. Chastain and Smith [1] also develop this vision by characterizing the integration of AI and sophisticated defense solutions as the key to the redefinition of cybersecurity. Obi et al. [19] state that Cybersecurity 5.0 involves the inclusion of conventional structures into the repetitive learning processes—structures that are constantly developing to meet the new threats. Likewise, Iqbal et al. [13] associate the introduction of AI in defense policies with changes in the relationships of power in the world, and it can be said that automation has turned into a strategic resource in both civil and military. In line with the argument by AL-Hawamleh [14], an operational continuity and adaptive learning cyber-resilience framework is essential to the actualization of this vision, notably in a complex digital ecosystem, including smart cities and cloud systems.

13.6.2 AI and Machine Learning as Core Enablers

The mental aspect of Cybersecurity 5.0 is AI-powered automation and ML. Tan [10] claims that the technologies allow for preventing threats based on predictive analytics, anomaly detection, and orchestrating a response in real time. According to Oroy et al. [2], AI-based sentinels that are able to identify threats by their patterns and self-enforce network boundaries are a reality. On the same note, Uchiyama and Oroy [3] introduce the concept of so-called digital sentinels, which constantly develop defense strategies without any human control. Rodriguez and Costa [11] support the need for predictive intelligence of threats, where ML models detect the attack vectors before they are exploited. This feature correlates with the efforts of Mahboubi et al. [20], who describe the developing methods in threat hunting combining human intuition and automated learning models that increase the detection efficiency. Proactive and self-defending cyber infrastructures are governed by such hybrid intelligence.

13.6.3 Integration of Adaptive Defense and Resilient Architectures

One of the characteristics of Cybersecurity 5.0 is the ability to be dynamic—the ability of defense systems to change dynamically depending on situational context. Sengupta et al. and Soussi et al. reveal the way in which MTD methods enhance the level of uncertainty among the attackers due to the continuous reconfiguration of the systems [22, 23]. Wu and Wu [24] extend that the topology of the network can be misleading when it is based on mimics, and the process of reconnaissance and attack becomes complicated. McMahonand [4] and Gudimetla [25] recommend a defense-in-depth, which integrates adaptive controls with upstream security. According to Patil et al. [17], these principles are combined to form ZTA of cloud-based services, which verify each access point. Another significant point mentioned by AL-Hawamleh [14] and Patel et al. [16] is the incorporation of the resilience frameworks that guarantee business continuity and ensure the security of the CPS. Unanimously, these architectures constitute the structural layer of Cybersecurity 5.0—a distributed, and autonomously coordinated one at that.

13.6.4 Human–AI Collaboration and Threat Intelligence Integration

The human factor is not eliminated into cybersecurity 5.0, but instead raises the role of an analyst beyond a reactive operator and puts him or her in the role of a strategic overseer. Sengupta et al. [21] also found that human contextual judgment helps to threat hunt even with automated systems. This human-in-the-loop model adds interpretability and moral control—major features highlighted by Daniel and Hayes [28] in their analogy between cyber defense and adaptive peacekeeping. Tahmasebi and Salami et al. [15, 30] emphasize the need to integrate the proactive intelligence and risk modeling frameworks to predict the occurrence and preserve continuity. With this kind of integration, Nair [33] elaborates on the strategies of preventing web-based attacks because AI will help human defenders categorize and curb vulnerabilities. In distributed networks, Edwards [8] even insists that network monitoring must be continuous to require automated learning systems to supply information that drives adaptive intelligence.

13.6.5 Cross-Domain and Sectoral Integration

Cybersecurity 5.0 is not only IT but also cyber-physical, socio-technical, and national security systems. The frameworks suggested by Patel et al. [16] provide protection to the industrial automation and IoT networks by means of quantum-enhanced defenses and smart sensors. Sarjito [29] focuses more on integrating policies, demonstrating how autonomous cybersecurity contributes to the national defense management by means of strategic planning and situational awareness, which is enhanced by AI. Salami et al. [30] suggest two additional strategies that can be applied to the critical infrastructure and healthcare sectors to enhance sectoral resilience, namely risk modeling and contingency planning. Ogungbemi et al. [18] discuss the issues related to ensuring the security of remote and hybrid environments because of relying on VPN-based and distributed defense systems. Correspondingly, the framework is applied to connected and autonomous vehicles (CAVs) by Pham and Xiong [32] and the dynamic adaptation mechanisms are introduced to guarantee safety in cyber-physical mobility systems.

13.6.6 Game Theory, Cyber Deception, and Predictive Defense

The game-theoretic reasoning and cyber deception are intelligent counterattack mechanisms integrated in Cybersecurity 5.0. Rubio et al. [7] suggest game-based models that model attacker-defender interactions, which enable AI systems to foresee the adversarial strategies and optimization of the response. The researchers presented by Steingartner et al. [34] and Rubio et al. [35] can show how deception is used in a hybrid threat environment—when decoys and fake data cause tactical advantage and confuse the opponent. Foti et al. [26] make comparisons between coastal defense approaches and digital fortifications in the form of layers and believe that natural adaptive strategies can be used to encourage digital resilience on a larger scale. Siyez [27] elaborates it with the help of the Octopus Method, which takes biological defense examples to ensure mobile environments by self-concealment and adaptive camouflage.

13.6.7 Building Ethical, Transparent, and Sustainable Autonomy

To ensure that Cybersecurity 5.0 enjoys a wide adoption, trust and transparency should be entrenched in autonomous operations. Stressing the importance of governance as a means to ensure resilience, AL-Hawamleh [14] highlights the need to keep the AI decision-making process accountable. On the same note, Oroy et al. [2] and Smith and Anderson [12] emphasize the importance of an attentive eye of AI a metaphor of explainable intelligence that will not be out of step with human values and morality. Obi et al. [19] support the idea of a comprehensive

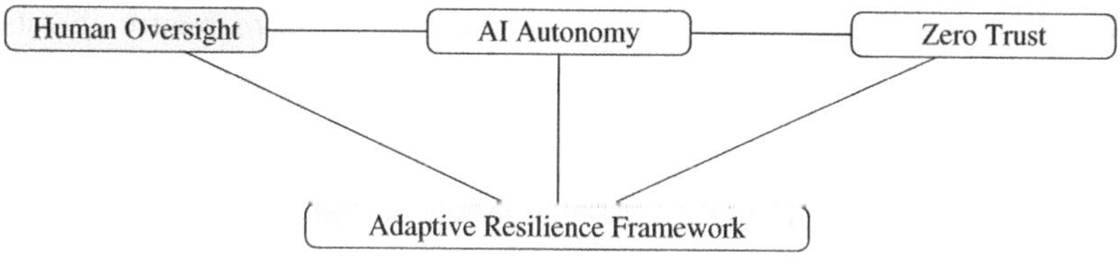

Figure 13.4 Integration within the Cybersecurity 5.0 Framework. "*Source:* Hewa Majeed Zangana"

governance model that would ensure that automation and regulation compliance and ethical supervision are harmonized. It is reminiscent of the larger societal transformation observed by Iqbal et al. [13], wherein the security policies will have to be in line with the strategic reality of the AI-controlled defense ecosystem. What is produced is a cyber environment that is not merely self-defensive but responsible, sustainable and in compliance with the human will.

13.6.8 Toward a Fully Integrated Cybersecurity 5.0 Ecosystem

The Cybersecurity 5.0 framework integration will lead to a convergent defense ecosystem, a teamwork where smart systems, human operators, and resilient infrastructures work together. As AL-Hawamleh [14] and Obi et al. [19] emphasize, such integration is determined by the cyber resilience models that are able to absorb shocks and self-heal. Saffar and Naji [31] go further to demonstrate how dynamic defense approaches in smart grids demonstrate the self-healing and dynamic nature of the Cybersecurity 5.0 system. Finally, predictive intelligence, adaptive automation, and ethical control have become integrated, and it is this that constitutes the pillars of a self-defending digital civilization, i.e., a system that predicts, adapts, and evolves in response to the threats around it, as Tan [10] and Tahmasebi [15] both conclude.

Figure 13.4 illustrates how Cybersecurity 5.0 will incorporate human-machine collaboration, AI autonomy, zero trust, and adaptive resilience and make them a single defensive ecosystem. The model is an embodiment of the shift to effective, ethical, and cost-efficient cyber defense.

13.7 Architectural Framework for Autonomous Cyber Defense

The architectural structure of autonomous cyber defense embodies the structural foundation of Cybersecurity 5.0, in which AI, ML, and self-adapting automation come together in one self-defending and self-healing system. This framework supports dynamic adaptability and continuous monitoring to reduce threats dynamically unlike the traditional frameworks that are often static and use situational decision making. It is aimed at creating systems that are able to detect vulnerabilities, anticipate attack vectors, and automatically implement countermeasures—and maintain operational resilience and cyber integrity.

13.7.1 Foundational Design Principles

In essence, an autonomous cyber defense architecture is based on five principles, namely intelligent sensing, adaptive learning, proactive mitigation, autonomous coordination, and resilient recovery [14]. Those pillars demonstrate the change of the reactive defense to the cyber resilience with focuses on continuity, redundancy, and recovering mechanisms supported by intelligence. Just like natural ecosystems, which are self-adaptive to environmental disturbances, the architecture uses threat modeling based on AI to dynamically change to the emerging threats [9, 19].

ZTA is also a core component used in the framework to ensure that all users, devices, and applications are continuously authorized and authenticated [17]. ZTA is a supplement to the defense-in-depth principle, which divides access and decreases the horizontal motion of the attackers [4, 25]. The given design develops a self-regulatory defense posture, which is able to keep the integrity of security even when facing APTs [6].

13.7.2 Layered Structure and Functional Components

The architecture under proposal is usually made up of four layers that are interdependent and which include the Perception Layer, Cognitive Layer, Decision Layer, and Action Layer each with a pivotal role in autonomous defense.

- Perception Layer: It is the layer of data gathering and situational awareness with the help of network monitoring, endpoint telemetry, and IoT sensors [8]. It constantly collects information throughout the digital ecosystem, and anomalies and possible intrusions are found with the help of AI-based analytics [18, 33].
- Cognitive Layer: This is the layer where AI and ML models are used to process data coming in to identify patterns, classify threats, and predict the behavior of adversaries. ML helps the system to develop the incidents of the past, whereas deep learning models assist in detecting stealthy and polymorphic attacks [2, 11].
- Decision Layer: The decision layer uses the approach of strategies based on game theory and risk modeling to find the best way to respond to an attack whenever they become active, and the attacker approach is modeled to predict

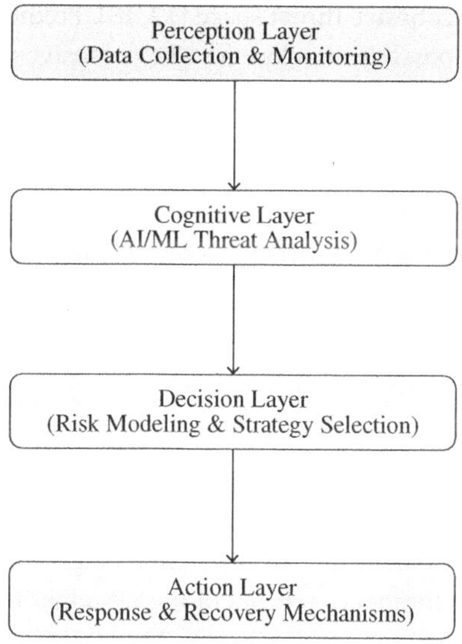

Figure 13.5 Architectural Layers of a Self-Defending Cybersecurity System. "*Source:* Hewa Majeed Zangana"

their future actions [7, 30]. Feedback from threat intelligence is applied, and reinforcement learning is applied to rank responses according to possible impact and confidence scores [20].

- Action Layer: Lastly, a system automatically implements the required countermeasures against the attack, such as the reconfiguration of network pathways and the isolation of the damaged nodes with the help of mimic defense and MTD strategies [22–24].

The combination of layers forms a closed-loop design, in which threat detection, analysis, and response are further improved, forming an adaptive defense based on a feedback mechanism [1, 10].

The layers of architecture of a self-defending cybersecurity system are visualized in Figure 13.5. The diagram emphasizes the interaction and synchronization of perception, cognition, decision, and action layers to develop a continuous threat monitoring, analysis, and response.

13.7.3 Integration of Threat Intelligence and Automation

There is improved visibility and agility by incorporating predictive threat intelligence as well as autonomous orchestration into the architecture. The AI-based correlation engines are used to derive the information from various sources, such as network traffic, behavioral logs, and external intelligence data, and form a cohesive threat space [12, 13]. Predictive modeling enables the system to preempt possible attacks and take defensive measures in advance [3, 11]. The automation layer employs incident response orchestration, automation, and response (SOAR) frameworks to automate the incident response. The system can also automatically align defensive control across cloud, edge, and on-premises assets [15]. This automated orchestration does not only minimize the human error but also provides continuity when it comes to large-scale and multivector attacks.

13.7.4 Cyber Deception and Moving Target Defense

An important breakthrough in autonomous architectures is the use of cyber deception and MTD as an offensive obfuscation and deterrence method. Handling misinformation: Cyber deception is a method that includes honeypots and decoy assets to mislead attackers and gather intelligence [34]. At the same time, MTD is dynamically modified to change system parameters, including IP addresses, port numbers, and operating systems, in order to make attacks more complex and unpredictable [22, 23]. These systems are simulated after the adaptive defenses of biological systems, which is consistent with the idea of endogenous security suggested by Wu and Wu [24]. The framework uses mimicry and deception to lower the predictability of system configurations and therefore the possibility of successful exploitation is minimized.

13.7.5 Collaborative Threat Hunting and Cognitive Autonomy

Cooperative threat hunting is another technique that improves autonomous defense by exchanging intelligence between distributed AI agents and acquiring knowledge on a diverse environment [20, 21]. Through federated learning, these agents can determine global threat trends without interfering with the local data privacy. Such a collaborative intelligence model reinforces the overall adaptability of the system and the resilience-focused goals of the contemporary system of cybersecurity [14]. The concept of cognitive autonomy allows the AI agents to not only identify and react to threats but also optimize themselves and repair themselves in the event of compromised functionality. This resembles multi-agent defensive ecosystems, where specific nodes also become autonomous sentinels that add coherence of global defense [28, 29].

13.7.6 Toward Self-Defending Cyber-Physical Systems

Using quantum-ready encryption, context-based access control, and adaptive defense strategies, the architecture is developed to counteract critical infrastructure attacks in the environments of CPS and Internet of Things (IoT) [16, 31, 32].

Self-defending CPS architectures continuously develop together with operational needs and effort by employing self-defense loop learning and policy-driven governance [19]. Lastly, the proposed architecture would incorporate the paradigms of natural defense like the Octopus Method proposed by Siyez [27] that applies biologically inspired adaptive mechanisms to mobile security. Just like the coastal defense systems that adapt buildings to changes in the environment [26], autonomous architectures are the next generation of Cybersecurity 5.0: they recalibrate defenses to cyber turbulence.

13.8 Key Technologies Enabling Autonomy

The core of autonomous cybersecurity systems is the incorporation of the latest technologies that enable digital infrastructures to be self-detecting, self-healing, and self-optimization of the changing threats. The combination of these technologies allows making intelligent decisions, lifelong learning, and being proactive in defense, which are the necessary qualities of developing self-defending cyber ecosystems. The subsections that follow present the key enablers of autonomy, namely, AI, ML, automation, MTD, game theory, and predictive threat intelligence.

13.8.1 Artificial Intelligence and Machine Learning for Self-Defense

The use of AI and ML has transformed cyber defense because it is capable of analyzing huge amounts of data, detecting anomalies, and predicting potential dangers. The AI-based systems like Cyber Sentry [2] and the Watchful Eye structures [12] use deep neural networks and reinforcement learning to recognize the malicious patterns that a traditional system would not detect. Iqbal et al. [13] argue that the introduction of AI into the national and organizational defense structures will promote the accuracy of the classification of threats, as well as the efficiency of the response. On the same note Chastain [1] and Smith and Tan [10] highlight that adaptive AI defense schemes can be used to dynamically reconfigure a network that has been attacked, which can be used to achieve real-time resilience. The predictive ability of ML is also illustrated in Rodriguez and Costa [11] where models are developed based on ML to enhance predictive threat intelligence in government networks through the detection of attack vectors before exploitation. Such innovations support the development of cyber autonomy, which will change security systems into active digital guards, as opposed to passive monitors [3].

13.8.2 Automation and Cognitive Analytics

The autonomy of cybersecurity needs a high level of automation that promotes constant monitoring, correlation of data, and autonomous response to incidents. Edwards [8] claims that currently, network defense frameworks employ automation of the CIS 18 Critical Controls to maximize response time and minimize human error. El-Amir [9] builds on this argument by pointing out that automation and cognitive analytics converge to enable systems to contextualize the threats, give priority to the actions taken, and trigger mitigation measures without direct human intervention. Next-generation self-healing systems are based on the concept of cognitive cyber defense, which is initiated by natural language processing (NLP) and self-teaching algorithms. Tahmasebi [15] recommends that automated response and threat intelligence be used together to assist in proactive disaster recovery and strategic continuity planning, particularly in an enterprise environment.

13.8.3 Moving Target Defense and Dynamic Reconfiguration

MTD has become an essential subject of active cybersecurity. MTD strategies ensure that the surface area and settings are dynamically altered to ensure that enemies face the extremely hard task of using the vulnerabilities. Sengupta et al. [22] and Soussi et al. [23] recognize MTD as a fundamental enabler of beyond-5G networks, which enables adjustment very quickly and unpredictable system behavior. The option of using an IP address, ports, and configuration frequently brings major uncertainty to an attacker. This strategy is in line with Wu and Wu [24], who came up with mimic defense, a framework that allows the systems to randomize internal processes and improve endogenous security. In a similar manner, Saffar and Naji [31] use the dynamic defense methods on the critical infrastructure, such as AMI, which is significantly enhanced in terms of resilience to changing cyberattacks.

13.8.4 Game Theory and Threat Intelligence Optimization

Game theory has emerged as a modeling pillar that has been applied to analyze adversarial relationships between attackers and defenders. Rubio, Alcaraz, and Lopez (2020) showed that game-theoretic defense models are able to predict the actions of attackers and optimize countermeasures in real time. Rubio et al. [35] demonstrated in the industrial control systems (ICS) that the addition of such dynamic mechanisms benefits situational awareness as well as autonomous decision-making. The predictive analytics and AI-based threat modeling and game-theoretic frameworks are now connected to allow systems to model the possible attack paths and establish preemptive defenses. According to Mahboubi et al. [20] and Badva et al. [21], these model-based threat hunting enables organizations to proactively look to detect anomalies prior to harm, as it is an intermediate step between passive monitoring and active defense.

13.8.5 Advanced Defense Architectures and Zero Trust Frameworks

In order to be completely autonomous, cybersecurity arrangements should surpass perimeter-based frameworks and embrace the concept of Zero Trust. The ZTA proposed by [17] is specially designed to work with cloud-based fintech, with a focus on micro-segmentation, constant authentication, and contextual access control. All these are needed to have adaptive, self-governing systems that stay intact even in the face of continuous attacks. McMahon [4] and Gudimetla [25] note that defense-in-depth and sophisticated firewall management are still vital, but in autonomous contexts, such systems transform into intelligent firewalls that can change the policies based on AI analysis. Stressing the point, Sipho et al. [5] showcase next-generation firewall approaches that are based on AI-enhanced filtering and automated traffic analysis, which are much better at early intrusion detection.

13.8.6 Cyber Resilience and Recovery Mechanisms

It is not enough that autonomous systems can withstand disruptions, but recover quickly. The Cyber Resilience Framework by AL-Hawamleh [14] focuses on continuity and self-repair, whereas the multi-layered approaches offered by Obi et al. [19] comprise resilience as an element of the enterprise-level defense model. The continuity of operations combined with automated recovery is such that self-defending systems can be used even in the case of APTs, as explained by Alshamrani et al. [6]. Elaborating on this, Sarjito [29] underscores the point that a national policy that is strategically developed is also a part of cyber resilience, and Foti et al. [26] compare natural protection systems such as coastal resilience to show that adaptive and self-reinforcing processes can be applied to digital infrastructure.

13.8.7 Cyber Deception and Threat Modeling Innovations

Cyber deception and threat modeling are used as complementary technologies in the context of modern autonomous defense. Steingartner et al. [34] believe that deception-based learning enhances system adaptability by putting the attackers into controlled conditions, whereas Salami et al. [30] suggest advanced risk modeling frameworks of a healthcare system that anticipates and mitigates breaches in real time. Moreover, Siyez [27] also presents the Octopus Method that is based on the biological camouflage and natural defense mechanisms, providing a new direction of adaptive and self-concealing methods of cybersecurity. Pham and Xiong [32] show that the similarity of adaptive models can lead to the increased safety of CAVs due to self-monitoring and cooperative defense systems.

13.8.8 Integrating Cyber-Physical and Cognitive Systems

Autonomy is furthered in real-world application through the integration of CPS and cognitive intelligence. As Patel et al. [16] emphasize, such environments as CPS require sophisticated defense mechanisms, especially with quantum cryptographic elements to ensure resiliency in the future. In the meantime, as it was shown by Ogungbemi et al. [18], integrating VPN-based secure infrastructures with AI-based mitigating botnets strengthens remote and distributed networks.

The next significant advancement in cybersecurity autonomy is the development of AI-driven sentinels that are able to adaptively learn and defend based on the situation, as Oroy et al. [2] present. These technologies combine to create a unified system of self-protecting, robust, and smart infrastructure, which has the ability to defend digital infrastructures against the unending range of cyber threats.

13.9 Challenges and Limitations

Autonomous security, which hails a future of an unprecedented potential landscape for adaptive and self-defending protection mechanisms, is faced with an entire range of hurdles leading up to full autonomy in reality: technical, operational, ethical, and organizational. These last hurdles will comprise the complexity of cyber-physical ecosystems, the unpredictability of AI systems, and the evolving sophistication of threat actors. As discussed in subsequent subsections, below are the most important barriers today for autonomous cybersecurity systems.

13.9.1 Complexity and System Integration Challenges

Autonomous cybersecurity would depend on the merging of AI with ML and network defenses, but this purpose is not easily achieved. Edwards [8] notes among other things that automated network monitoring enhances visibility, but hung-up interdependencies and scalability issues with autonomous tools throw operational efficiency under heterogeneous environments. In line with the above, Obi et al. [19] highlight that few enterprises apply standardized frameworks necessary to unify widespread and visible heterogeneous defense tools as one self-contained autonomous ecosystem.

Even further, Patil et al. [17] have shown that for an organization to adopt ZTA in its cloud environment, a significant overhaul of legacy systems would need to happen because most legacy systems often do not make the elements of identity, segmentation, and least privilege necessary for autonomous control. The situation gets aggravated in CPS, which, according to Patel et al. [16], show fragile synchronization of their digital components and their physical counterparts in following independent defense mechanisms.

13.9.2 Data Quality, Bias, and Explainability in AI Models

AI-powered defender systems rely predominantly on the training data they receive for accuracy and diversity. Chastain and Smith [1] and El-Amir [10] point out that poor quality of data results in biases and incompleteness, causing false alarms, generalized weaknesses, and untrustworthiness of automated security actions by AI systems. The opaqueness of AI-driven mechanisms to operational adoption is yet another hurdle as far as understanding is concerned because explainability is not at all evident in deep learning-based defense models.

Further, Iqbal et al. [13] warn that as AI becomes part and parcel of national and military countries' cybersecurity infrastructures, nontransparent algorithms may generate strategic misinterpretations or misclassifications of threats, raising tensions between states. Rodriguez and Costa [11] went a similar way, arguing that the reliability of predictive threat intelligence relies on the interpretability of AI insights, an issue that is still unresolved for most autonomous cybersecurity platforms.

13.9.3 Evolving and Persistent Threats

Modern cyber adversaries pose persistent threats that are very advanced and designed to penetrate any defense to level. "As stealth, persistent, and sophisticated events would require extended monitoring and behavior analysis for any automated systems, both above would fail without human oversight," claims [6]. As Rubio et al. [7] add, "Even with proactive defense mechanisms like using game theory, attackers continue to outsmart most defense mechanisms with swift changes in their attack strategies; this is what defines reduced long-term effectiveness of autonomous responses."

Given the realities, both Mahboubi et al. [20] and Badva et al. [21] realize the viability of the challenges associated with automating threat hunting. Current systems rarely replicate human analysts' intuitive and contextual reasoning, leading to blind spots in the detection of anomalies. Meanwhile, Sengupta et al. [22] reveal the constraints of MTD, outlining how frequent reconfiguring of the target might disrupt legitimate operations or increase overhead in the system, especially in critical infrastructure.

13.9.4 Limitations in Cyber Resilience and Recovery

Autonomous response reduces recovery times, yet recovery and resilience are still mostly dependent on human coordination. Continuous governance oversight of the Cyber Resilience Framework is imperative to ensure operational continuity, according to AL-Hawamleh [14]. Issues posing challenges to fully self-healing architectures still include incomplete rollback, inconsistent backups, and interdependency failures.

As Tahmasebi [15] extends this further by asserting that even where proactive recovery planning is conducted, human involvement would still be necessary to impose prioritization according to business continuity importance. As indicated by Foti et al. [26], coastal defense systems show parallels in this respect as self-adaptive barriers mitigate immediate damage, but long-term recovery requires strategic reinforcement—an analogy with which the autonomous cyber resilience would be compared.

13.9.5 Security Risks in Autonomous and Remote Operations

The introduction of autonomous systems is creating additional attack profiles for distributed and remote working environments. As Ogungbemi et al. [18] note, while VPN infrastructures are critical in providing "secure" connections, if those infrastructures are not well monitored by adaptive algorithms, they can become single points of failure. Likewise, Pham and Xiong [32] highlight security breaches that could occur on CAVs, where dynamic defense strategies could be targeted through sensor spoofing or delayed decision-making.

According to Nair [33], even with the best detection for phishing, XSS, and SQL injection, automation still produces an illusion of false trust in the security of the system, leaving loopholes unattended for attackers to exploit. Sipho et al.and Gudimetla [5, 25] argue that though next-gen firewalls are evolving with the influence of AI, they might result in much higher automation risk, causing configuration drift and leaving automated operations without human control, which in turn leads to unexpected weaknesses in systems.

13.9.6 Policy, Governance, and Ethical Concerns

Autonomous defense systems are a threat to rapid governance and raise many ethical issues. Sarjito [29] emphasizes that a strategic policy framework is needed to trace accountability for automated decision-making and its control. These systems could have serious unintended consequences through autonomous responses without a well-defined legal framework, such as unauthorized counterattacks or unauthorized data exposure.

As Daniel and Hayes [28] offer an even broader view, whereby the principles of peacekeeping and conflict resolution now extend into the realm of digital space. In this space, the autonomous agents could be acting in a defensive mode that almost borders on offensive operations. El-Amir [9] and Obi et al. [19] warn that any ethical deployment of AI needs to ensure transparent oversight, explainability standards, and fairness mechanisms so that the pitfalls of algorithmic bias and discrimination can be avoided.

13.9.7 Resource Constraints and Implementation Costs

The overall development and sustenance of an autonomous cybersecurity platform would need significant computational resources, funds, and human resources. McMahon [4] and Edwards [8] further highlight that advanced automation and monitoring will continuously require software updates, skills, and infrastructure investment. Advanced threat modeling and risk frameworks, according to Salami et al. [30], complicate things further in industries like healthcare, where compliance and data integrity are issues of paramount importance.

Furthermore, dynamic and mimic defense strategies require considerable network bandwidth and computing resources, making them difficult to implement for small and medium enterprises (SMEs), as stated by Soussi et al. [23] and Wu and Wu [24].AI-based cyber sentinels need to continuously regroup their knowledge, something that can be cost-prohibitive for a limited-budget organization [2, 12].

13.9.8 Human Oversight, Training, and the "Black Box" Problem

Despite automation, the human brain is an irreplaceable being in the preservation of the future-wise human society. Badva et al. [21] emphasize that autonomous systems neglect human-intuitive threat patterns, which are still musts in advanced forensics. According to Uchiyama and Oroy [3], the "Black Box" problem in AI self-defense implies that the pathway taken toward a decision is totally opaque and cannot be audited easily. This black box situation complicates accountability and post-incident authorship.

Moreover, Rubio et al. [35] sustain that even in ICS, a human-in-the-loop ensures responses actually applied align with operational goals. This is further supported by AL-Hawamleh [14] since training and awareness remain vital parts of resilience, forming an assurance that personnel can effectively intervene when autonomous systems face novel or ambiguous threats.

13.9.9 Strategic and Environmental Constraints

Environmental and strategic constraints, finally, have grown to be isolating factors for the acceptance of autonomous defense systems globally. According to Saffar and Naji [31], the implementation of dynamic defense methods on critical energy infrastructure depends on the barriers of regulations and compatibility. In a similar manner, Siyez [27] states that biomimetic defense strategies are cutting edge, but involve hardware-level adaptability that current devices may not possess.

Strategically speaking, Iqbal et al. [13] and Sarjito [29] caution that uneven distribution of AI and cybersecurity resources among states may widen the global insecure divideism, thus bringing about inequalities in cyber resilience. AL-Hawamleh [14] thus posits that as much as the benefits of autonomous cybersecurity find application, they remain beholden to exclusively those institutions that can afford resources in finance and other capacities without international cooperation and alignment of policy.

13.9.10 Summary

All in all, this means that even when autonomous cybersecurity represents a cutting edge towards preemptive, intelligent, and adaptive defense, it is yet facing significant technical, ethical, and structural impediments. This includes hurdles in integration, data bias, explainability clutches, high implementation cost, and the perpetual need for human oversight. Improving upon these would require interdisciplinary research, strong governance models, and collaborative action globally to strike a balance between automation and accountability, thus ensuring the creation of a secure, transparent, and fair digital future.

13.10 Case Studies and Practical Implementations

Conversion of some of those eminent case studies into examples of faring-forward autonomous defense strategies for effective operational purposes also includes implementation cases in between enterprise networks, critical infrastructures, and national defense.

13.10.1 Enterprise Network Security and Zero Trust Implementations

ZTA have emerged as modern implementations for protecting present entities within complex cloud environments. Patil et al. [17] give an example of a ZTA implementation in a fintech firm, which in turn implements continuous verification for all devices or users that access its network. Using AI-based monitoring, this system was able to dynamically change access controls and detect anomalous behaviors, contributing significantly to surface attack erosion.

Similarly, AL-Hawamleh [14] describes a cyber-resilience framework applied in a transnational corporation that integrates predictive threat intelligence, automated incident response, and business continuity planning. Phishing and ransomware attacks were proactively mitigated through the framework while sustaining less than optimal operational downtime. The study cases exemplify the real-world advantages of AI and automation in the protection of network integrity.

13.10.2 Threat Hunting and Advanced Persistent Threats (APTs)

Automotive threat hunting is a crucial function where autonomous systems assist human analysts. Badva et al. [21] evaluated a large-scale security operations center (SOC) that had deployed AI hunters for continuous monitoring of network activity. The system detected low-and-slow APTs that have gone under the radar of conventional signature-based detection, whereas the human analysts could focus on the strategies and decisions regarding complex incidents. Mahboubi et al. [20] performed a systematic review showcasing that ever-evolving threat hunting techniques, such as anomaly detection and pattern recognition, based on ML, have helped greatly enhance early detection rates. Alshamrani et al. [6] also hold that using the automated tools of threat hunting in combination with old-fashioned workflows increases the capacity for the SOC and reduces the dwell time on sophisticated threats.

13.10.3 Cyber-Physical Systems and Industrial Control Security

Autonomous cybersecurity could drastically change the world for critical infrastructure and ICS. Rubio et al. [35] describe how this was practically realized in a manufacturing plant, where AI-assisted monitoring and dynamically adjusted firewall rules detected and mitigated attacks aimed at exploiting the ICS protocols.

In the energy sector, dynamic defense strategies for AMI were demonstrated by Saffar and Naji [31], allowing for the real-time adaptation of strategies responding to anomalous readings from meters, which could suggest ransomware threats. These applications in CPS were further highlighted by Patel et al. [16], showing how

AI-enabled defense mechanisms safeguard interconnected components against coordinated attacks, thereby preserving both operational safety and data integrity.

13.10.4 Connected and Autonomous Vehicles (CAVs)

As Pham and Xiong [32] studied autonomous vehicle networks, where cybersecurity measures must address both digital safety and physical safety. Practical implementations involved AI-based IDS embedded in vehicular networks that can detect anomalous communications between sensors and control modules. Autonomous threat mitigation subsequently allowed the vehicles to safely isolate these compromised modules while maintaining operational continuity.

Moreover, Rodriguez and Costa [11] applied predictive AI models to government-owned vehicle fleets that could foster anticipatory threat mitigation prior to the ability of malicious actions to propagate across interconnected nodes. From the aforementioned case studies, we could see the need for instantaneous autonomous monitoring and intervention in safety-critical mobile systems.

13.10.5 AI and Machine Learning for Predictive Defense

With the synergy between AI and ML, predictive defense forms the very core of modern autonomous cybersecurity. Chastain and Smith [1] detail a deployment at a financial institution, where AI models continuously learned from past attack patterns to anticipate phishing and credential stuffing attempts.

As Oroy et al. [2] highlight a government network application where AI-powered cyber sentinels analyzed massive volumes of logs, identifying subtle IoCs that human operators would likely miss. Tan [10] also emphasizes that reinforcement learning algorithms improve threat mitigation efficiency over time, adapting to evolving attacker behaviors without constant human retraining.

13.10.6 Moving Target Defense and Cyber Deception

As Soussi et al. [23] provide a practical implementation of the MTD in the 5G network environment. The system kept shifting IP addresses, port assignments, and network configuration parameters, which generated extra complexity for the attackers while having continuity in service.

In conjunction, Steingartner et al. [34] studied cyber deception techniques in hybrid threat environments. Deceptive honeypots and decoy assets autonomously engaged attackers, gathering intelligence and diverting malicious activity away from critical assets. Through these strategies, autonomous deception can be proactively exercised to reduce the exposure surface and enhance situational awareness.

13.10.7 Remote Workforce Security

Escalating remote work has set the stage for autonomous security solutions for distributed networks. Ogungbemi et al. [18] presented a deployment leveraging VPNs and autonomous botnet defense mechanisms to protect home-based employees from ransomware attacks. AI systems monitored endpoint behavior in real time, isolating suspicious activity before it could escalate.

As Nair [33] further documented as an enterprise case for the implementation of an automated defense mechanism against phishing, XSS, and SQL injection on thousands of remote devices. The autonomous system ensured that critical updates were deployed, threats were neutralized, and user activity was continuously monitored, thus providing scalable protection with no direct human intervention.

13.10.8 Healthcare and Data-Intensive Sectors

Sensitive personal data are handled by healthcare systems that have procured autonomous threat modeling and risk assessment frameworks. Salami et al. [30] describe the deployment of AI-based systems for patient data protection that leverage predictive analytics to prevent the occurrence of ransomware and insider threats. Automated contingency planning allowed a real-time response to breaches that could have happened with minimized service interruption and data loss.

As El-Amir [9] further expounds that autonomous detection when combined with well-structured compliance frameworks, addresses the issue of regulatory compliance while maintaining operationality, demonstrating the significance of automation for high-risk data-rich settings.

13.10.9 Lessons Learned and Best Practices

This is to say that:

1) Hybrid Approaches Work Best—It involves human oversight with AI autonomy to improve detection accuracy and reduce false positives.
2) Continuous Learning is Important—AI models do require constant updating, feeding them with data on threats that exist or are appearing in the world [1, 10].
3) Integration and Interoperability are Critical—Seamless interaction will also guard against operational gaps created by the legacy systems and autonomous platforms [14, 17].
4) Sector-Specific Customization is Essential—Strategies for defense have therefore to be specific to the sectors given the specifications that exist between the financial systems, industrial systems, healthcare, and governmental systems [30, 35].

5) Proactive and Deceptive Measures Reduce Risk—Both the MTD technique and deception techniques are actively protecting the assets before the threat impacts critical assets [24, 34].

13.10.10 Summary

Empirical case studies across enterprise networks, ICS, autonomous vehicles, healthcare, and governmental infrastructures have demonstrated that autonomous cybersecurity systems are very much operational and increasingly perform highly. Their success, however, depends on robust AI models, constant learning, hybrid human-machine oversight, and strategic integration. These examples further present an opportunity for autonomous technologies to amplify resilience while shortening response time with proactive defense against evolving threats, while contextual deployment strategies are also advocated.

13.11 Future Research Directions

Cybersecurity has been changing at an ever-increasing rate with evolving threats and the number of devices connected significantly increasing. Defense mechanisms have also integrated AI into their systems. Improvement in the field of autonomous cybersecurity systems and mitigation using AI has progressed remarkably, and yet has considerable areas that still require deeper investigation to enhance resilience and adaptability.

13.11.1 Integration of AI and Machine Learning in Adaptive Defense

AI and ML are well-suited for predictive threat intelligence and automated response, but future research must focus on improving the explainability and interpretability of AI models for human operators to understand and trust the systems' autonomous decisions [1, 2, 10]. In addition, merging reinforcement learning with real-time adaptive defense could achieve continuous learning from changing attack patterns, thereby improving detection and mitigation of APTs [6, 11].

Another critical area is the fusion of multiple AI models across distributed networks, where predictive insights from one viewpoint (e.g. industrial control systems) could have implications for defense strategies in different views [13, 20]. This requires research into secure federated learning and privacy-preserving AI techniques to ensure that sensitive data are not compromised in sharing threat intelligence.

13.11.2 Cyber-Physical Systems and IoT Security

With the growing rise of CPS and IoT devices, they pose a number of new vulnerabilities that need advanced autonomous defenses [16, 32]. Future research needs to explore dynamic and context aware security frameworks that could monitor and adjust in real time to the operational state of CPS. Some techniques, such as MTD and deception-based strategies, appear promising [23, 34], yet more studies are needed to quantify their effectiveness and optimize costs of deployment in heterogeneous settings.

IoT ecosystems will also benefit from lightweight, low-latency AI algorithms functioning on resource-constrained devices while still maintaining solid threat detection [24, 27]. Research regarding autonomous patching, self-healing networks, and predictive maintenance is crucial for the minimization of real-time vulnerabilities.

13.11.3 Enhancing Cyber Resilience Frameworks

Resilience from attack, response to it, and recovery from it have become increasingly important in building any particular system [14, 15]. Future studies should work towards formulating quantitative metrics for cyber resilience so that organizations can assess the effectiveness of their defenses and predict operational impacts in the event of attacks.

Research into the resilience frameworks in sectors—for example, financial services, health services, energy, and government networks—is important to feature differences in regulations, operations, and threat landscapes [29, 30]. Automated disaster recovery planning combined with AI-driven threat prediction could minimize downtime and cascading effects of cyber incidents.

13.11.4 Advanced Threat Hunting and Proactive Defense

Despite the increasing use of automation in hunting threats, it still remains a labor-intensive activity [20, 21]. Future tasks will involve shaping hunter-gothic structures that can work on their own, such that they will be able to alter their hunting strategies dynamically when threat intelligence, behavioral analysis, and magnetic anomaly detection no longer fit the hive logic.

Proactive defense strategies such as cyber deception, honeypots, and MTD warrant further research to maximize attacker engagement while minimizing resource utilization [23, 34]. The integration of predictive analytics with automated decision-making could allow systems to neutralize emerging threats before they manifest in critical operations [7, 15].

13.11.5 Quantum-Resistant and Future-Proof Security Mechanisms

Quantum computing creates opportunities and threats for cybersecurity, according to current trends. Quantum-resistant encryption and post-quantum cryptography should be future avenues for research, most especially because these would see to it that autonomous defense systems are protected even during the oncoming era of quantum-enabled attacks [16]. Further, there is a possibility that hybrid classical-quantum AI models would be used to develop faster detection and response to threats while staying safe against quantum adversaries.

13.11.6 Addressing Human-AI Collaboration Challenges

However, humans will still have the ultimate accountability for major decision-making processes and ethical compliance [8, 28]. Those might be some areas where future research will need to seek out effective frameworks for human-AI collaboration, such that operator control would reduce cognitive load and the chances of becoming automated bias as well as enhance overall trust in autonomous cybersecurity systems [3, 12].

Furthermore, training programs, simulations, and decision support systems would be needed to prepare cybersecurity practitioners to work harmoniously with AI-enabled systems, especially in high-stakes environments such as critical infrastructure or national defense [1, 13].

13.11.7 Cross-Sector and Global Threat Intelligence Sharing

Cyber threats have become transnational and cross-sectoral [22, 35]. Future research should include automated, secure, and anonymized threat intelligence-sharing mechanisms between organizations and governments. These AI-enabled platforms could enable real-time sharing of attack indicators, tactics, and vulnerabilities shared across the privacy and regulation line [9, 19].

Collectively developing global standards for autonomous cooperation in cybersecurity and threat intelligence exchange would exponentially improve the collective defense capabilities against APTs, ransomware campaigns, and large botnet operations [6, 18].

13.11.8 Summary

Autonomous cybersecurity research will have adaptive AI integration, cyber-physical and IoT protection, resilient frameworks, proactive threat hunting, quantum-resistant security, human-human relations, and cross-sector intelligence sharing as future directions for research. These directions promise to move the field from reactive defense to predictive, proactive, and autonomous cyber resilience. They prepare organizations and nations for safeguarding ever-growing digital holdings in complex and antagonistic environments [10, 11, 14].

13.12 Conclusion

Cybersecurity happens to be a complex and dynamic world today as a result of the fast and baptized rates of development of digital technologies, networks connecting systems, and human adversaries developing sophistication at every turn. From an ever-expanding present threat surface, not limited to APTs and ransomware, into weakness within CPS and IoT, organizations and governments face an ever-expanding threat surface.

The continuing infusion of AI and ML as part of the overall framework for security posture has shown very promising implications in improving the speed of detection and response, as well as predictive capabilities, marking a change from reactive to proactive defense models.

However, much work is still needed by technology to reduce the gap between automating systems and maintaining human management, fortifying resiliency, and ultimately earning trust in an autonomous space. Effective cybersecurity is derived from solid technological resources as well as strategic frameworks, governance policies, and ongoing training efforts for the workforce. Organizations will adopt adaptive and context-aware defenses, meaning that defenses evolve concerning the changing threats while directly continuing operations and securing critical data.

Future emphasis on predictive threat intelligence, proactive threat hunting, and cross-sector collaboration will be critical undergirding elements in building resilient digital ecosystems. The renaissance in the future of cybersecurity will entail integrating some of the most advanced technologies with human experts in an effort to build a culture of continuous vigilance and, most importantly, create frameworks capable of anticipating and mitigating threats before they arise. Indeed, a holistic approach involving technology, strategy, and human insight will be required to preserve security, trust, and resilience in an increasingly connected and digital future.

References

1 Chastain K, Smith J. Cybersecurity reinvented: The integration of AI defense mechanisms. EasyChair; 2024.

2 Oroy, B. and Anderson, J. (2024). Cyber sentry: How AI shapes modern cyber defense strategies. *EasyChair*.

3 Uchiyama N, Oroy K. Sentinels in the digital realm: AI's influence on cyber defense strategies. EasyChair; 2024.

4 McMahon, D. (2014). Beyond perimeter defense: Defense-in-depth leveraging upstream security. In: *Best practices in computer network defense: Incident detection and response*, 43–53. IOS Press.

5 Sipho, N. and Thandeka, M. (2020). Firewall mastery: Advanced strategies for implementation and digital defense. *International Journal of Trend in Scientific Research and Development.* 4 (3): 1243–1249.

6 Alshamrani, A., Myneni, S., Chowdhary, A., and Huang, D. (2019). A survey on advanced persistent threats: Techniques, solutions, challenges, and research opportunities. *IEEE Communications Surveys & Tutorials.* 21 (2): 1851–1877.

7 Rubio JE, Alcaraz C, Lopez J. Game theory-based approach for defense against apts. In: Applied Cryptography and Network Security: 18th International Conference, ACNS 2020, Rome, Italy, October 19–22, 2020, Proceedings, Part II 18. Springer; 2020. p. 297–320.

8 Edwards, D.J. (2024). *Network Monitoring and Defense. In: Critical Security Controls for Effective Cyber Defense: A Comprehensive Guide to CIS 18 Controls*, 371–404. Springer.

9 El-Amir, S. (2023). Comprehensive cybersecurity review: Modern threats and innovative defense approaches. *International Journal of Computers and Informatics.* 1: 30–37.

10 Tan, A. (2024). Enhancing cyber defense mechanisms: AI and machine learning-based threat mitigation strategies. *Journal of Quantum Science and Technology.* 1 (3): 90–93.

11 Rodriguez, P. and Costa, I. (2024). Artificial intelligence and machine learning for predictive threat intelligence in government networks. *Advances in Computer Sciences.* 7 (1): 1–10.

12 Smith J, Anderson J. AI's watchful eye: Strengthening cyber defense as guardians of the virtual gate. EasyChair; 2024.

13 Iqbal, S., Rizvi, S.W.A., Haider, M.H., and Raza, S. (2023). Artificial intelligence in security and defense: Explore the integration of AI in military strategies, security policies, and its implications for global power dynamics. *International Journal of Human and Society.* 3 (4): 341–353.

14 AL-Hawamleh A. (2024). Cyber resilience framework: Strengthening defenses and enhancing continuity in business security. *International Journal of Computing and Digital Systems.* 15 (1): 1315–1331.

15 Tahmasebi, M. (2024). Beyond defense: Proactive approaches to disaster recovery and threat intelligence in modern enterprises. *Journal of Information Security.* 15 (2): 106–133.

16 Patel, C.D., Aggarwal, M., and Chaubey, N.K. (2025). Enhancing cyber-physical systems security through advanced defense mechanisms. In: *Advancing Cyber Security Through Quantum Cryptography*, 307–342. IGI Global.

17 Patil, K., Desai, B., Mehta, I., and Patil, A. (2023). A contemporary approach: Zero trust architecture for cloud-based fintech services. *Innovative Computer Sciences Journal* 9 (1): 45–58.

18 Ogungbemi OS, Ezeugwa FA, Olaniyi OO, Akinola OI, Oladoyinbo OB. Overcoming remote workforce cyber threats: A comprehensive ransomware and bot net defense strategy utilizing VPN networks. Available at SSRN 4911878. 2024.

19 Obi, O.C., Akagha, O.V., Dawodu, S.O. et al. (2024). Comprehensive review on cybersecurity: modern threats and advanced defense strategies. *Computer Science & IT Research Journal.* 5 (2): 293–310.

20 Mahboubi A, Luong K, Aboutorab H, Bui HT, Jarrad G, Bahutair M, et al. Evolving techniques in cyber threat hunting: A systematic review. Journal of Network and Computer Applications. 2024;Volume 221, 104 004.

21 Badva P, Ramokapane KM, Pantano E, Rashid A. Unveiling the {Hunter-Gatherers}: Exploring threat hunting practices and challenges in cyber defense. In: 33rd USENIX Security Symposium (USENIX Security 24). 2024. p. 3313–3330.

22 Sengupta, S., Chowdhary, A., Sabur, A. et al. (2020). A survey of moving target defenses for network security. *IEEE Communications Surveys & Tutorials.* 22 (3): 1909–1941.

23 Soussi, W., Christopoulou, M., Xilouris, G., and Gür, G. (2021). Moving target defense as a proactive defense element for beyond 5G. *IEEE Communications Standards Magazine.* 5 (3): 72–79.

24 Wu, J. and Wu, J. (2020). New approaches to cyber defense. In: *Cyberspace Mimic Defense: Generalized Robust Control and Endogenous Security* (ed. J. Hu), 113–157. Singapore: Springer Nature.

25 Gudimetla, S.R. (2015). Beyond the barrier: Advanced strategies for firewall implementation and management. *NeuroQuantology.* 13 (4): 558–565.

26 Foti, E., Musumeci, R.E., and Stagnitti, M. (2020). Coastal defence techniques and climate change: A review. *Rend Lincei Sci Fis Nat.* 31 (1): 123–138.

27 Siyez, Ö. (2024). The octopus method: Innovative use of natural defense mechanisms in mobile device security. *International Journal of Information Security and Cybercrime.* 13 (1): 12–25.

28 Daniel, D.C.F. and Hayes, B.C. (2016). *Beyond traditional peacekeeping*. Springer.

29 Sarjito, A. (2024). Enhancing national security: Strategic policy development in defense management. *Jurnal Pelita Nusantara.* 2 (1): 56–68.

30 Salami, A.A., Igwenagu, U.T.I., Mesode, C.E. et al. (2024). Beyond conventional threat defense: Implementing advanced threat modeling techniques, risk modeling frameworks and contingency planning in the healthcare sector for enhanced data security. *Journal of Engineering Research and Reports.* 26 (5): 304–323.

31 Saffar M, Naji HR. Increasing the security of advanced metering infrastructure using dynamic defense methods. In: 2022 12th Smart Grid Conference (SGC). *IEEE*; 2022. p. 1–5.

32 Pham, M. and Xiong, K. (2021). A survey on security attacks and defense techniques for connected and autonomous vehicles. *Comput Secur.* 109: 102269.

33 Nair, S.S. (2024). Securing against advanced cyber threats: A comprehensive guide to phishing, XSS, and SQL injection defense. *Journal of Computer Science and Technology Studies.* 6 (1): 76–93.

34 Steingartner, W., Galinec, D., and Kozina, A. (2021). Threat defense: Cyber deception approach and education for resilience in hybrid threats model. *Symmetry (Basel).* 13 (4): 597.

35 Rubio, J.E., Alcaraz, C., Roman, R., and Lopez, J. (2019). Current cyber-defense trends in industrial control systems. *Comput Secur.* 87: 101561.

14

Case Studies Across Sectors (Finance, Healthcare, and Government)

14.1 Introduction

The development of digital technologies and the evolution of interconnected systems have greatly changed the cybersecurity environment in key areas of the economy like finances, healthcare, and state. With the increased complexity of the digital ecosystem, cyber threats have been more frequent, adaptive, and sophisticated, which complicates existing defense mechanisms and contributes to the need for innovative and AI-driven solutions to the issue [1, 2]. Cybersecurity 5.0 is the next stage of digital defense, which focuses on uniting the assets of artificial intelligence (AI), machine learning (ML), and predictive analytics to preempt and prevent potential attacks before they occur [3, 4].

Within the last ten years, there was a range of studies on AI convergence with cybersecurity to enhance the sense of threat detection, automate reactions, and result the critical infrastructures [5, 6]. As an example, now AI-driven tools process network traffic volumes of data in real-time to identify anomalies that may signal a cyberattack, which is impossible without human analysts [7]. Deep learning and reinforcement learning are also used to identify the patterns of attacks and also anticipate the weaknesses within industries [8, 9]. These approaches have been specifically useful in cyber-physical systems (CPS), smart grids, and industrial IoT networks where the threats are continually developing [10, 11].

The case study method has become a key to the perception of the practicality of the issues of cybersecurity and the efficiency of the defense within real-life contexts. Case studies have been used by researchers to provide an example of sector-specific vulnerability, contextual implementation of AI-based defense systems, and lessons learned during past incidences [12, 13]. To illustrate, in the financial industry, AI-based algorithms are applied to identify fraudulent transactions by determining behavioral patterns that are considered anomalous in real time [14]. Likewise, predictive analytics and behavioral biometrics are used in healthcare systems to protect classified patient information and to make sure that the data protection rules are met [15, 16]. ML models are also becoming a part of national cyber defense activities at the government institutions to identify at-risk digital infrastructure, secure communications, and insider threats [17, 18].

Cybersecurity challenges are growing increasingly more numerous and complex, in spite of these developments. Older literature came up with novel types of cyberattacks, such as ransomware, advanced persistent threats (APTs), and IoT-based attacks [19–21]. According to more recent studies, the high rate of adoption of Internet of Things (IoT) and Industrial Internet of Things (IIoT) devices has increased the attack surface, exposing new vulnerabilities both to the consumer and industrial worlds [22–24]. Cyber-physical threats to smart manufacturing and energy systems will also need adaptive AI-based surveillance and mitigation systems [25, 26].

The possibility to fit the evolving threat data also offers a distinctive benefit to AI-based cybersecurity models since they can learn and adapt continuously [6, 27]. Risk management frameworks like MARISMA-CPS can assist in making early detection of anomalies and possible breaches in cyberphysical infrastructures [26]. When behavioral biometrics are used together with these structures along with constant authentication, it forms a multilayered security that strengthens the resilience of digital systems [15]. They are particularly important in the context of the real-time protection that is necessary in the critical infrastructure, medical monitoring systems, and financial transaction platforms [4, 28].

In addition, case-based learning combined with practical analysis of scenarios has turned out to be invaluable in the academic and professional training of cybersecurity [29, 30]. Research indicates that case simulation can be used in practice to make the stakeholders familiar with the threat modeling, risk management, and decision-making in the conditions of cyber uncertainty [31, 32]. Such educational frameworks not only enhance technical mastery but also cultivate the understanding of cybersecurity governance, regulatory adherence, and organizational resilience [33, 34].

The reviewed articles indicate that AI is turning out to be an inseparable part of controlling the growing threat environment. Since AI-based solutions are transforming the perception and prevention of cyber risks across different systems (not to mention the detection of anomalies in financial systems), from malware in healthcare networks to threat prediction in government infrastructures, the paradigm of cyber risk perception and prevention is shifting [35, 36]. With the sophistication of attacks, the focus is shifting toward defensive response to reactive to defensive advancement, and data-driven information and adaptive systems are the basis of digital trust [37, 38].

Thus, the purpose of the chapter is to analyze some of the most prominent case studies in the finance, healthcare, and government segments in order to demonstrate how AI-driven cybersecurity measures can be applied to real-life scenarios.

It examines certain applications, lessons learned, and the future path by examining how intelligent system integration is transforming the boundaries of cybersecurity resilience in the age of Cybersecurity 5.0.

14.2 Methodology and Case Study Selection

This chapter employs qualitative, comparative case study methodology designed to investigate AI and ML applications to cybersecurity challenges in three major sectors—finance, healthcare, and government. This approach relies on a synthesis of empirical research, selected case studies from the respective domains, and theoretical underpinnings of AI-enabled certification defense so as to best understand Cybersecurity 5.0 in practice [3, 27, 35].

14.2.1 Research Framework

The research framework for this study is founded on applied case study analysis, focusing on contextualized instances demonstrating AI-driven threat detection, predictive analysis, and risk management [12, 13]. In accordance with parameters established for real-world cybersecurity research, this framework synthesizes data across sectors from academic studies, industry applications, and governmental reports. The analysis has been guided by the following research questions:

1) How are AI and ML technologies integrated into cybersecurity frameworks across finance, healthcare, and government sectors?
2) What have been the observable effects of the AI-based system on threat detection, incident response, and data protection?
3) What lessons from these case studies can inform a proactive, AI-driven defensive posture in the Cybersecurity 5.0 paradigm?

This framework is based on earlier methodologies that combined descriptive and analytical approaches to cybersecurity, emphasizing the significance of scenario-based learning with domain-specific examples [30, 32]. The selected case studies enabled both diversity in application domains and depth of insight concerning technical facets ripe for cross-interpretation and generalizable conclusions.

14.2.2 Selection Criteria for Case Studies

A multi-criteria selection procedure guaranteeing relevance, diversity, and sector-wise representativeness guided the selection of the case studies. The inclusion criteria were as follows:

- Sectorial Relevance: Studies must relate directly to cybersecurity challenges and AI-driven mitigation strategies in the finance, healthcare, or government domains [14, 17].
- AI/ML Integration: The case studies must explicitly involve the use of AI, ML, or predictive analytics for threat detection, risk management, or response automation [4, 6].
- Data Authenticity: All sources must be drawn from peer-reviewed literature, validated industry reports, or recognized cybersecurity frameworks [9, 10].
- Contextual Insight: The case must provide interpretative or measurable insights regarding the outcomes, limitations, and implications of adopting an AI-driven security solution [26, 36].

This structured selection renders certain that the analyzed cases reflect not only technical sophistication but also the real-world operational dynamics. The heterogeneity of the selected studies enables a well-rounded comprehension of the multifaceted cybersecurity ecosystem [22, 23].

14.2.3 Collection and Analysis

The data presented within this chapter were gathered via an extensive literature review of academic journal articles, conference proceedings, and industry reports from 2014 to 2024. The relevant publications were extracted mainly from such databases as IEEE Xplore, Elsevier, SpringerLink, and MDPI. A thematic analysis approach was employed to identify the emerging trends in AI-driven cybersecurity applications, focusing on predictive analytics, deep learning, behavioral biometrics, and reinforcement learning [8, 15].

During the analysis, coding was drawn up that ranked information into three-pronged areas: threat landscape, technological intervention, and sectorial impact. The first domain captured the nature and evolution of cyber threats [19, 21], while the second acknowledged AI and ML applications leveraged for detection, prevention, and incident response [5, 28]. The last domain assessed the applications' sectoral implications and outcomes, linking technological outcomes to risk mitigation [25, 38].

14.2.4 Theoretical and Practical Basis

The methodological design frames both theoretical models and applied frameworks in the cybersecurity field. Thus, having introduced the MARISMA-CPS framework to appreciate risk management patterns in CPS, including predictive analytics as one means of proactive defense [26], reinforces the importance of that ecosystem and the appropriate measures selected there. Li and Qiu [8], on the other hand, describes the reinforcement learning paradigm that underpins computational possibilities for AI-driven adaptation within various complex digital ecosystems.

Furthermore, this chapter takes an interdisciplinary approach to cybersecurity research, integrating data science, risk management, and ethical aspects to develop resilient defense models [34, 37]. Also, this stands for the paradigm shifts in the literature advocating for a holistic view of cybersecurity that entwines technical innovation with socio-organizational preparedness [1, 33].

14.2.5 Validation and Evaluation

To certify the analytical rigor of this study, triangulation will be conducted among multiple case sources. Each case was validated according to empirical evidence, reproducibility, and alignments of AI-centric cybersecurity objectives [31, 36]. These were further validated by cross-checking their industrial use cases and simulation-based models presenting AI's role in identifying and mitigating vulnerabilities in IoT and CPS infrastructures [9, 10, 39].

Furthermore, past assessments of cybersecurity case study methods note an imperative for real data and real answers [13]. So this chapter employs a cross-case comparison to characterize converging trends and diverging practices across finance, healthcare, and government systems in order to identify generalizing patterns to Cybersecurity 5.0 [7, 35].

14.2.6 Ethical Considerations and Limitations

All the reviewed studies comply with the ethical principles of research, ensuring that the data sources honor privacy, intellectual property, and security disclosure standards [38]. Some limitations exist with respect to access to proprietary data and confidentiality restrictions on government cybersecurity projects [17]. Furthermore, AI models are significantly challenged toward transparency, interpretability, and bias in training datasets [4, 18].

In an attempt to mitigate these challenges, the research has adopted a balanced interpretation, taking into account both the strengths and weaknesses of AI-driven defenses. This diversity of case types—from smart cities to industrial IoT—ensures that the methodology captures a realistic spectrum of AI applications across domains [24, 25].

14.2.7 Summary

To summarize, this chapter's methodology interlinks a systematic literature review with cross-sectoral case study analysis for a robust appraisal of AI-driven cybersecurity applications. By synthesizing empirical evidence and theory, the approach provides a structured view of how Cybersecurity 5.0 strategies are being operationalized in finance, healthcare, and government. The forthcoming sections will present each sector in detail alongside its significant case studies, results, and insights concerning the transformational capability of AI in proactive threat defense.

14.3 Cybersecurity 5.0 Overview Across Sectors

Cyber 5.0 is a transformation in cybersecurity history with the construction of an AI-ML-Big Data Analytics-Automation triad. Accordingly, a proactive, adaptive, and intelligent defense ecosystem has been created. Unlike past cybersecurity paradigms that somewhat thrived on reactive measures, Cyber 5.0 focuses on predictive intelligence and autonomous response, along with a continuous learning ethos to crush threats before they appear [3, 6]. This revolution is completely packed with the current scenario of a worldwide transition into data-driven interconnected infrastructures in finance, healthcare, and governments—all having unique challenges in security—which are somewhat related in one way or the other [1, 2].

Cybersecurity 5.0 defines a convergence of data science and cybersecurity into a digital product that eats up vast datasets in the quest for complex threat patterns and adapts to a change in attack vectors in sync with reality [37]. The recruitment of the surely obsolete signature-based detections, rule-based firewalls, and static access controls does not particularly matter when talking about malware that mutates so rapidly even in a minute, ransomware-as-a-service, and AI-driven phishing threats [5, 21]. Rather, intelligent algorithms that have learned from an extensive base of events, user actions, network traffic, and toyik infestation kind of things peer niggle into the operations and bring a perspective of perfect control and dynamic defense mechanisms in place [4, 27].

In all sectors, Cyber 5.0 brings three paradigms to life: autonomous detection, context-aware defense, and self-repairing systems. Autonomous detection goes for deep learning and reinforcement learning methods to recognize deviations from normal behavior in critical systems [7, 8]. Context-aware defense systems feed into context-based analysis using cognitive analytics and behavioral biometrics to adapt security measures against environmental cues and user actions [15]. Self-repairing systems, predominantly seen in critical industrial control systems and the health care regime, automatically identify and isolate infected nodes, patch any known vulnerabilities, and restore the compromised functions without human intervention [11, 25].

Cyber 5.0 has equipped the finance sector with smart fraud detection systems that can match micro-patterns in transaction records to prevent unauthorized activities. AI systems keep an eye on and learn from various fraud techniques and automatically modify anomaly detection algorithms and behavioral analytics [14, 35]. This transformation is deemed valuable against high-speed trading, online banking, and blockchain finance systems, where every millisecond lost might mean a financial loss [28]. Conversely, predictive analytics underscored with ML is more efficient in risk management because it projects the threat before it is operational [4].

In healthcare, Cyber 5.0 has hugely influenced the industry by fostering privacy protection of significant patient data, access control policies, and patient privacy policies. The established artificial models of continuous authentication have considerably defended the confidentiality of electronic health records (EHRs) and telemedicine platforms. The same continued success of doctors and patients in being at peace in growing the fruit; another aspect is that the surveillance on any patient suffers from malaise of patient data protection, and a continuous authentication system gives behavioral biometrics a new modality to operate with some more beefy protection [29]. This not only meets stringent regulations, e.g., HIPAA and GDPR, but also prevents ransomware from striking hospitals and research institutions [16].

In government and critical infrastructure, Cybersecurity 5.0 frameworks have been establishing AI-based threat intelligence, applying predictive modeling, and automated incident response systems that safeguard national assets and services [17]. Governments are now focusing on advanced big-data analytics next to ML-based risk assessment frameworks to predict potential attacks on energy grids, transportation grids, and defense systems [10, 11]. For example, MARISMA-CPS works a pattern-based risk model for CPVines, which helps CSP systems to see where they have already been hit, ensuring that the models are not victims of poorly managed cascading failures and keeping CSPs generally resilient [26]. All too often, the human view blended with AI's analytical acumen speeds up the adaptive threat response against the criminals from inside [31, 36].

With the rise of the IoT and the IIoT, the shadow of Cyber 5.0 has been cast far beyond its initial range, necessitating redefinition of paradigms for governing decentralized, heterogeneous environments. As evidence continues to show, IoTs are coming under threats of botnets and ransomware. This undoubtedly leads to very high systemic risks [22, 39]. Cyber 5.0 is a strong advocate of disbursed secure architecture and federated security-based configurations, ensuring data retention and serving threats jointly with a smile. AI-based anomaly detectors joined with blockchain technology are also used to secure industrial systems and digital manufacturing processes [24, 25].

Within smart cities and urban infrastructure, Cybersecurity 5.0 is manifested as advanced deep learning-based monitoring systems managing the urban IoT devices, as well as transportation control and surveillance systems [9, 18]. Such AI

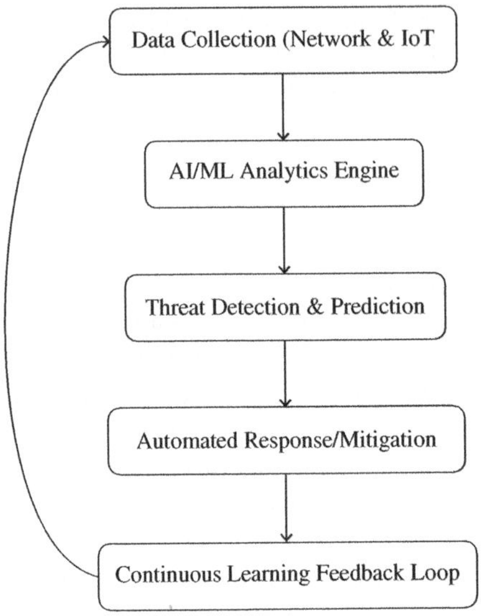

Figure 14.1 Conceptual Framework of Cybersecurity 5.0. "*Source:* Hewa Majeed Zangana"

systems are designed to improve resilience through predictive assessments of system vulnerability against real-time mitigation of attacks and support for sustainable urban development [10, 34]. In this way, predictive analytics combined with reinforcement learning helps city managers to maintain digital trust and resilience in operational continuity in hyper-complex cyber-physical environments [8].

From the pedagogical and research dimensions, Cybersecurity 5.0 creates a shift for education and training paradigms. According to the real case-based learning feature as suggested by [12, 13], it enhances the ability of practitioners to surface evidence-based applications of theoretical precepts for dynamic cyber environments. Institutions now develop cybersecurity professionals who navigate AI-enabled security architectures through simulation-driven and blended teaching models [29, 30]. Thus, continuous professional development and cross-sector partnerships will boost the capacity of the Cybersecurity Ecosystem to respond to newly emerging threats [32, 33].

Figure 14.1 shows the principal functional architecture of Cybersecurity 5.0 in sectors. It shows proactive defense facilitated by interaction among artificial intelligence, machine learning, automation, or continuous monitoring. This conceptual framework is very critical not only because it strengthens adaptive response mechanisms but also because it enhances cyber resilience in dynamic digital environments.

In essence, Cybersecurity 5.0 is a holistic standard that embraces AI, automation, and cognitive analytics to self-evolve digital defense systems. Its different sector applications—from financial data protection to healthcare privacy and governmental resilience—show a common commitment to adapt, predict, and intelligently defend against threats. The synthesis of ML, big data, and human expertise represents not only a technological change but also a redefining philosophy for cybersecurity: from reactive must be transformed into a proactive enabler of digital trust and innovation [1, 38].

14.4 Case Study 1: Financial Sector

Among the most vulnerable areas in the global landscape of cybersecurity is the financial sector, with high-value digital assets, most real-time transactional exchanges, and all interconnected banking ecosystems. Cyber threats are ever-increasing and subsequently becoming more sophisticated from fraud enhancement through AI to large-scale ransomware. On the other end, however, financial institutions have turned to Cybersecurity 5.0 principles in threat detection, operational resilience, and the safeguarding of sensitive financial information. This study comprehensively analyzes the threats that challenge the finance sector, the operation of AI-driven defense models, and real-world circumstances that demonstrate the changing potential of intelligent cybersecurity systems.

14.4.1 Cyber Threat Environment in Finance

Rapidly changing cyber threats that include identity theft, phishing, distributed denial-of-service (DDoS), credential stuffing, and insider fraud typify the financial industry. Foundational studies identify such systems as high-risk environments usually attacked through social engineering, network intrusions, and multi-stage cyberattacks [19, 21]. The increase and intensity of threats have grown with new digital banking systems, new contactless payments, and consumer finance services.

Automated and AI-enhanced techniques to a greater extent continue being used by cybercriminals to exploit system vulnerabilities, commit fraud on a massive scale, and manipulate high-frequency trading platforms [5]. Thus, the speed of real-time transactions, together with the sophistication of modern financial systems, mandates that threat monitoring cannot longer be conducted manually. Advanced ML, behavioral analytics, and predictive modeling are required to guarantee proactive resilience [1, 3].

14.4.2 AI-Based Cybersecurity Structures within Financial Systems

Cybersecurity 5.0 provides an intelligent, adaptive, and self-learning security paradigm, which is crucial for a financial defense strategy. Specifically, supervised and unsupervised ML models are widely used to detect suspicious transactions by analyzing behavior deviations and linking them to historical fraud patterns [27, 35].

Predictive analytics are placed at the heart of new fraud strategy identification with the processing of immense volumes of customer and transactional data within outlier detection and anomaly analysis [4]. Likewise, reinforcement learning models can adaptively defend against continuously improving fraudulent detection algorithm patterns from new attacking behavior [8].

AI-enabled risk management systems in financial institutions would simulate possible attack scenarios with different levels of exposure calculated to be able to prioritize mitigation strategies within the context of predictive risk frameworks proposed in wider cybersecurity research [6, 17]. Besides, AI can help develop decision-support systems that promote compliance, internal auditing functions, and automated alerts [7, 28].

14.4.3 Case Study: AI Fraud Detection in Banking

One such instance of Cybersecurity 5.0 as applied in the financial sector is the application of AI-powered fraud detection in retail and commercial banking. Financial institutions implement ML tools that analyze millions of transactions per second to identify fraud activity. Here, the use of anomaly detection algorithms and behavioral biometrics would significantly reduce false positives while widening the net for accurate fraud identification [14, 15].

Models of ML classification showed that fraud detection systems through ML classification models, including random forests, gradient boosting, and deep neural networks, outperform the traditional rule-based kind by identifying subtle, evolving patterns. These tools can also be used in card fraud detection, money laundering identification, and unauthorized access prevention.

A practical banking scenario using predictive analytics with customer behavioral modeling reduced response times to over-high-risk events by more than 40% into near-instant suspension of said accounts [4]. Indeed, such proactive, high-speed decision-making exemplifies how AI-based cybersecurity delivers real benefits, concrete and otherwise.

In Figure 14.2, the process depicts how AI improves detecting sereness in financial systems. It starts with the model having the anomaly-detection models trained on unusual behavioral patterns following continuous monitoring of transaction streams and those that would flag suspicious activities for automated or human verification actions to improve speed in decisions made and accuracy.

14.4.4 Cybersecurity for Accounting and Digital Financial Records

By virtue of their operations, financial institutions are heavily dependent on secure accounting systems and digital ledgers that have been the best targets for

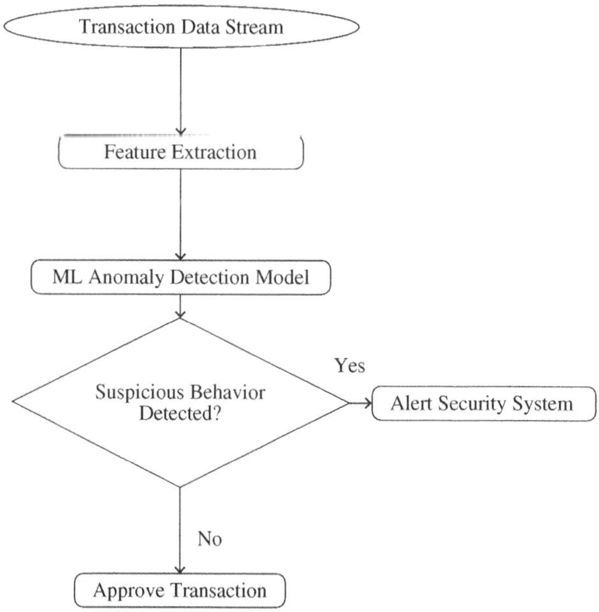

Figure 14.2 AI-Based Fraud Detection Workflow in Finance Sector. "*Source:* Hewa Majeed Zangana"

sabotage and data manipulation. Case studies in [14] explain how encryption, anomaly monitoring, and AI-based access control systems protect digital accounting records. AI models monitor accounting entries against anomalies, flagging alterations as potentially unauthorized or suspicious, a process enhanced by continuous authentication frameworks [15].

The merit of blockchain-based verification with AI-based anomaly detection furthers the digital accounting workflow security and prevention of internal fraud [38]. These secure models provide assurance of the integrity, timeliness, and authenticity of financial information, which maintains investor confidence and regulatory compliance.

14.4.5 AI for IoT-Integrated Financial Ecosystems

The development of ATM sensors, payment terminals, mobile wallets, and smart POS systems in the last two decades has increased cyber risks exponentially [22, 23]. IoT devices create new avenues of attacks, thus demanding constant surveillance, vulnerability assessment, and automated threat neutralization.

Arguments having evidence such as [24] explore existing practical approaches to assessing IoT vulnerabilities using tools like Shodan, which financial institutions are now starting to adopt for auditing exposed endpoints and misconfigured devices. AI-assisted anomaly detection models are already being ramped up to monitor device health, communication patterns, and suspicious behaviors in IoT-led financial systems [9, 10].

14.4.6 Smart Contract and FinTech Security

Smart contracts, community-ledgers, and cloud-based infrastructure support the larger financial ecosystem, including fintech platforms and digital marketplaces. AI-based security analytics protect against contract manipulation, anomalous transaction flows, and blockchain irregularities [30, 32].

Deep learning models can identify irregular smart contract behavior, including re-entering attacks or privilege escalation attempts, which are palmary in decentralized finance (DeFi). Results echo those generated regarding cyber-physical and distributed systems security, hence reinforcing the necessity of automated risk assessment models [11, 26].

14.4.7 Threat Modeling and Risk Assessment in Financial Systems

It is of utmost essential to carry out threat modeling in financial cybersecurity due to transaction sensitivity and regulatory pressures exercised on institutions globally. Studies focus on real-time identification of critical vulnerabilities, significantly increasing risk assessment AI contributions [33, 36].

Risk models like MARISMA-CPS were not originally designed for CPS, but due to their predictive, pattern-driven approach to risk prioritization, they do have some conceptual relevance to the high-interdependency financial networks [26].

Simulation-based risk models developed by [17] support financial institutions' understanding of cascading effects from cyberattacks as a basis for contingency strategy development. These risk quantification methods concur with the cybersecurity framework established in foundational works such as [20, 34].

14.4.8 Sector-Specific Lessons and Best Practices

In particular, certain best practices have emerged from finance sector case studies.

- Using ML and behavioral analytics for automated fraud detection enables a much quicker response time.
- Predictive risk management anticipates attack patterns that may exploit vulnerabilities in the system before they are actually exploited.
- Continuous authentication and behavioral biometrics help reduce the risks of insider threats in banking environments [15].

- Security models specifically handling IoT ensure protection for ATM networks, POS terminals, and mobile payment ecosystems [22].
- AI-assisted education and case-based training increase preparedness that conforms to case study teaching models [12, 13].

In summary, the advancement of Cybersecurity 5.0 in the financial sector marked an important transition from a reactive mode of defense to predictive, adaptive, and intelligence-based protection. The successful amalgamation of AI, IoT security frameworks, behavioral analytics, and automated risk management implies that AI-powered protection can change the resilience of financial cybersecurity.

14.5 Case Study 2: Healthcare Sector

Because of the market worth of patient data and a multitude of devices with means of connection, such as medical devices whose usage has gotten rampant, together with an increasing reliance on digital health systems, the healthcare sector has become one of the most appealing venues for cyber attackers. AI, ML, and IoT technologies' integration into healthcare has increased diagnostic capabilities and patient outcomes while increasing the attack surface and challenges in cybersecurity management [21, 22]. The case study presented investigates how AI-based solutions are leveraged to defend healthcare systems, reduce risks, and ensure confidentiality, integrity, and availability with respect to data.

14.5.1 An Overview of Cyber Threats in Healthcare

Cyber threats in healthcare have been experiencing a massive change in recent years. Among the common incidents affecting hospitals and research institutions are ransomware attacks, data breaches, phishing, and insider threats [5, 19]. Attackers are generally exploiting weak authentication mechanisms, obsolete software, and unpatched vulnerabilities in medical IoT devices as well as EHRs [39]. AI and ML are currently being utilized to detect the aforementioned anomalies in real-time, thereby improving the early detection of threats and risk management [27, 35].

As [29] pointed out, there is an increasing interdependence between IoT devices and patient monitoring systems whereby vulnerabilities in such systems can jeopardize patient safety and privacy. Concurrently, [11, 23], in their studies, proved that IoT-based medical networks are open to botnet and denial-of-service (DoS) attacks, warranting the necessity of early proactive cybersecurity frameworks supported by AI analytics.

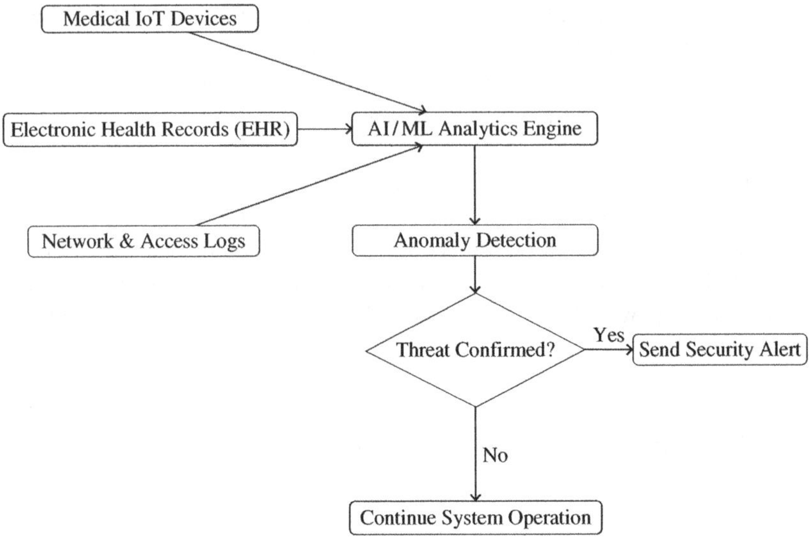

Figure 14.3 AI-Driven Intrusion Detection in Healthcare Networks. "*Source:* Hewa Majeed Zangana"

14.5.2 AI-Driven Threat Detection and Predictive Analytics

AI-based systems are being employed for strengthening the cybersecurity in hospitals through the analysis of large streams of medical data to detect malicious behaviors. Predictive analytics, based on deep learning algorithms, has been used to effectively pinpoint anomalies in access logs, data flows, and system behaviors [4, 6]. For example, hospitals using neural network-based models can detect ransomware attempts before any encryption occurs by identifying anomalous patterns of file access [28].

Reinforcement learning models also come into play for adaptive defense mechanisms learning from new attack vectors and adjusting the configuration of the system automatically [8]. According to [18, 37], the combination of AI and cybersecurity enhances proactive defense strategies through real-time data science analytics committed to anticipating and blocking potential threats. Such AI-based frameworks support clinical decision systems by ensuring that security controls do not hinder critical healthcare workflows [9].

Figure 14.3 illustrates that AI-driven intrusion detection systems in healthcare networks monitor, in real-time, clinical databases, medical IoT devices, and EHR system access logs. Rule-based configurations on suspicious activity perform automated anomaly scoring and alerting to initiate early ransomware detection or unauthorized access to data.

14.5.3 Risk Management and Cyber Resilience Strategies

A balance must be struck between data security and operational efficiency while managing cyber risks within the context of healthcare. It is important that hospitals protect sensitive data such as patient identifiers and genomic information while ensuring continuity in delivery of medical services. The risk analysis models proposed by [17] for critical infrastructures are equally applicable in the case of cybersecurity in healthcare, enabling a systematic assessment and prioritization of risks by healthcare administrators. Risk management frameworks adapted for medical environments where device integrity could make a huge difference, the MARISMA-CPS pattern was developed by [26] as an effective framework for the risk management of CPS. The integration of AI risk management approaches would allow healthcare organizations to continuously monitor their threat landscape, automate responses, and conduct resilience testing [33, 34] continuous monitoring. Predictive analytics tools were shown by [6] to identify clusters of risks informed by device performance, usage frequency, and user behavior. Such knowledge empowers the cybersecurity teams to preemptively isolate compromised nodes and prevent lateral movement within the networks. Also, improving endpoint protection by combining one or two elements of continuous authentication and behavioral biometrics [15].

14.5.4 Incident Response and Forensic Analysis

AI-assisted incident response systems are changing the face of how healthcare institutions address cybersecurity breaches. During an attack, the ML algorithms are useful for fast identification of the source of the attack, its scope, and type of intrusion [1, 7]. Forensic analysis of the data with AI tools will improve the ability to trace digital footprints across medical networks, aiding faster recovery and accountability [31].

As [3, 25] underline that AI-driven incident response halts considerable downtime and triggers predictive recovery planning, which is significant in hospitals where delays could prove life-threatening. Continuous monitoring systems with big data analytics provide the dynamic platforms of defense that leverage changing threat dynamics [10, 27].

14.5.5 Challenges in Implementation and Best Practices

Meanwhile, the actualization of AI-based cybersecurity in healthcare is beset by algorithm-related bias and data privacy concerns, and the absence of standardized protocols [12, 13]. Interoperability issues among legacy systems with hospitals often create loopholes in security coverage [2, 20]. Additionally, low cybersecurity literacy among healthcare personnel increases the chances of human error.

Best practices in tackling these problems call for integrating AI security solutions with human oversight, constant training for staff, and adherence to healthcare-related laws such as HIPAA and GDPR [38]. Security culture building needs collaborative approaches that engage all stakeholders from IT professionals to clinical administrators [16, 21]. Moreover, frameworks from the industrial and finance sectors may be adapted for healthcare with customized risk assessment and automation protocols [14, 32].

14.5.6 Findings Summary

This case study demonstrates that AI-based cybersecurity solutions serve as a necessity in protecting the healthcare infrastructure from emerging cyber threats. Within the trio of predictive analytics, deep learning, and behavioral biometrics, detection accuracy is increased, response time is decreased, and resilience is exponentially improved. Convergences of AI, IoT, and data science exposure within an opposition barrier against adversaries for the secure delivery of patient care will be explored as the sector digitizes further [1, 22]. To maintain the balance between innovation and security in the Cybersecurity 5.0 era, future research, policy compliance, and ethical governance will have an immense contribution.

14.6 Case Study 3: Government Sector

However, ever since the world governments have gone digital within their public services such as energy, transport, and handling of sensitive citizen data, their cybersecurity challenge has become complex. With the advancement and sophistication of CPS within the increasingly growing IoT networks and smart city technologies, public systems are the target of cyberattacks. This case study aims to assess how AI-driven cybersecurity frameworks are being integrated into government contexts for profiling situational awareness, predictive threat detection, and autonomous incident response.

14.6.1 Cyber Threat Landscape in Government Systems

With the availability of very large class databases containing classified information, national security information, and citizens' private data, government institutions become prime targets for direct attacks by state-sponsored research organizations, ransomware companies, and espionage campaigns. Proliferation of IoT and connected infrastructure for smart cities with these above types of threats has made these vulnerabilities in energy grids, traffic management systems, and digital identification frameworks even more varied [22, 23].

Further recent studies show that traditional security solutions are merely inadequate at addressing adaptive and persistent threats within public networks [2, 21]. Rather, AI and ML approaches complement such architectures in proactive defense, allowing governments to detect anomalies and measure the probability of risks while executing automated countermeasures [3, 27]. Such models in reinforcement learning put forth strategies to cyber-physical governmental systems with continual security adaptation through experience feedback loops [8].

14.6.2 AI-Driven Risk Management and Predictive Analytics

Most predictive analytics achievements for governments are learning how to use predictive analytics to predict and even bluntly attack incidents [4, 6]. Furthermore, predictive threat modeling integrates large-scale datasets from intelligence feeds, social media, and cyber sensors to identify potential attack vectors. Assessment of vulnerabilities across distributed public infrastructure such as transportation, defense, and communication systems is in part enabled by AI-driven risk management systems [17, 26].

As an example, deep learning techniques have been employed in numerous nationwide centers for state security to filter malicious activities from huge amounts of network traffic while amplifying cyber situational awareness and response cycles [7, 25]. Moreover, innovative behavioral biometrics-based continuous authentication models are being used to secure the access of government platforms and also prevent insider threats [15]. These are brighter examples of mentalities changing from reactive security postures to adaptive and intelligence-driven security mechanisms.

14.6.3 Cybersecurity in Smart and Critical Infrastructure

Smart cities and digital governance projects heavily rely on interconnectivity within IoT ecosystems requiring high-end security frameworks [9]. Governments are trying to establish such environments and invest in AI-based instruments that monitor them through neural networks to detect abnormal behavior of devices, propagate malware, and guarantee continuity of critical services [10, 39]. Among the use cases are anomaly detection algorithms with cyber defenses in place to protect the utility services such as power grids and water systems, as attacks on these can lead to catastrophic socio-economic effects [11].

An example is a smart energy system that conducts AI-enabled intrusion detection to discover anomalies in real-time consumption data from energy networks and thereby reduces disruptions caused by cyber intrusions [20]. These are thus cases showing how hybrid defense mechanisms and adaptive learning models can

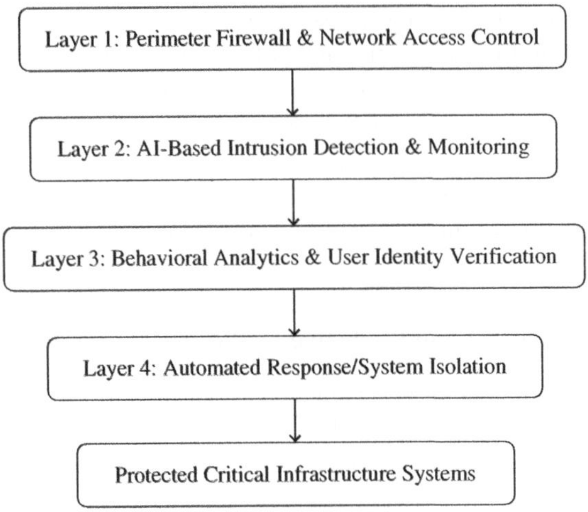

Figure 14.4 Defense Architecture for Government Critical Infrastructure. "*Source:* Hewa Majeed Zangana"

be deployed to safeguard government infrastructures as part of the overall Cybersecurity 5.0 paradigm [1].

Deploying a Layered Cyber Defense Architecture Figure 14.4 presents a layered cyber defense architecture used in government critical infrastructure environments. It has perimeter firewalls integrated with real-time monitoring, AI-driven behavioral analytics, and autonomous response systems to secure essential services such as energy grids, transportation systems, and communication networks.

14.6.4 Training, Policy, and Capacity Building

This will always be viewed as one of the most important human problem areas in government cybersecurity [12, 13]. With AI systems being part and parcel of public defense strategies, training is reorienting toward simulation-based practice and case studies. For example, some cybersecurity projects are using AI-enabled simulation environments that reproduce the kinds of attacks seen in the real world to help policymakers and IT administrators put together evidence-based response plans [24, 29].

Policy frameworks are also being revised to incorporate AI governance, accountability, and ethics in operations for cybersecurity. Standardized and comparable on-their-face applicability of cyber resilience metrics helps a government enforce cyber resilience uniformly, according to [33]. Similarly, [31] discusses the role of well-structured risk management and interagency collaboration to ease the mitigation of cross-sectoral threats.

Future Directions for Government Cybersecurity in the Future Worlds is about integration between AI, ML, and data science, leaving a transformative promise for government cybersecurity [37, 38]. Current research is exploring hybrid architectures that will use reinforcement learning integrated with predictive analytics to form self-healing cyber ecosystems [34, 35]. These systems are to be envisioned as autonomously adapting to evolving attack patterns, offering continuous protection without human intervention.

Furthermore, as countries strive for digital sovereignty, there is also a shift toward embedding AI ethics, explainability, and transparency mechanisms into cybersecurity frameworks so that public trust is maintained [16, 28]. Future endeavors may also focus on multi-domain defense collaboration, where civilian, military, and intelligence actors share AI-powered cyber intelligence to build national resilience informed by large-scale collective security [32, 36].

In summary, the adoption of AI-based cybersecurity in the government sector changes the organization's traditional security scenario to a dynamic system of intelligence-led protection. Indeed, this application in predictive analytics, automation, and human-AI collaboration allows governments to better anticipate, withstand, and recover from modern cyber threats in the age of Cybersecurity 5.0.

14.7 Comparative Analysis Across Sectors

This section gives a panoramic vision of the comparative analysis concerning the utility of AI-driven cybersecurity strategies in non-banking finance, health, and government. Although these sectors do not share similar objectives, infrastructures, or threat landscapes, they have a common need for proactive, intelligent, and adaptive securities. The fusion of AI with ML and data analytics is rewriting the cyber-defense paradigms from reactive responses to predictive, automated systems that continually evolve with threats as they arise [3–5].

The risks in the three sectors by themselves give a cross-sectional comparison of risks across sectors such as finance, health, and government. The different

Table 14.1 Cross-Sector Comparison of Cybersecurity Risks and AI Defense Mechanisms

Sector	Primary Risk Source	Common AI Defense Strategy
Finance	Transaction Fraud & Credential Theft	Behavioral Analytics & Real-Time ML Detection
Healthcare	IoT Medical Device Vulnerabilities & Ransomware	Continuous Authentication & Predictive Analytics
Government	State-Sponsored Attacks & Critical Infrastructure Sabotage	AI-Driven Threat Intelligence & Autonomous Response Systems

"*Source:* Hewa Majeed Zangana"

frequency patterns in vulnerability depend on the type of operational model and sensitivity of data. This comparison is summarized in Table 14.1.

14.7.1 Threat Landscape and Sectoral Vulnerabilities

Each sector is a business unto itself, and the risk environment is influenced by aspects such as the magnitude of the militancy of the data and its accessibility. Fraudulent practices, phishing, and insider manipulation in the transaction system and accounting databases are the key threats in financial-sector information security [14]. The health sector has threat levels of ransomware and patient data security breaches and encounters the vulnerability of IoT on medical devices incorrect in [22]. Then, the government sector fights against cyberattacks of espionage, sabotage to infrastructure, and attacks oriented to politics for a cause [2, 19].

But in the aggregate, the upward trajectories of IoT linkage and digital ecosystems create an evolving threat for every sector [23, 39]. In the near future, AI-based defense is seen as the most productive way of dealing with these risks by catching abnormal activity in real-time and taking automated, usually offline containment activity [9, 10].

14.7.2 Role of AI, ML, and Predictive Analytics

AI and ML will be the backbones of every operation in cyberspace in all sectors. These technologies detect frauds, anomalies, and report unmatched behavior of transactions in the finance sector [35]. Historical attack data often offer great help in predicting potential vulnerabilities through predictive analytics tools and anomaly-detection models in real-time [6]. On the other hand, secure AI models are adopted in treatment contexts, whereby deep learning models are trained to monitor the integrity of medical IoT data against unauthorized access or device tampering to enhance patient safety [8, 18].

Within government, dynamics are somewhat more pronounced, with several levels of administration trying to benefit from AI in securing critical infrastructure, creating reinforcement learning and big data systems to act as a virtual environment for cyber-attack simulations, risk management, and bolstering the defense capacity of the state [17, 26]. From the lessons drawn from [27], scaling of these intelligent systems ensures the ability to manage threats fast and offer opportunities for quick and real mitigation or destruction of threats, whereas [32] emphasizes the critical role of distributed computing in the management of security operations across administrative systems.

14.7.3 Cyber Risk Management and Governance Structures

Governance and policy frameworks show variance across sectors but share the common goal of establishing standardized and accountable AI-fueled decision-making in their organization standards. Financial organizations have always appeased some international standards (ISO/IEC 27001) around the matter of internal controls. An experiment to demonstrate the potential for profiling and to receive clear ROI guidance on any welfare efficacy supported with some data [14, 31]. With the HIPAA (Health Insurance Portability and Accountability Act) in mind for patient data management, privacy laws demand strict data management protocols, there is a push for institutions to implement robust AI models that account for patient data protection and confidentiality while increasing accessibility [21].

Governance, in essence, mandates security parallel to and tempered with public transparency. According to [33], it is the development of cybersecurity assessment measures tailored to the specific needs of governance settings that upholds accountability and resilience at the national level. Furthermore, AI-based risk management frameworks, as in the case of the MARISMA-CPS model, shall support threat response within CPS toward the goal of critical infrastructure protection [26].

14.7.4 AI Implementation Challenges Across Sectors

While AI could potentially contribute to enhancing cyber resilience, its implementation brings along challenges in terms of algorithmic bias, data privacy, and system interoperability [1, 28]. False positives from anomaly detection are another head-scratcher for finance [34]. Healthcare is riddled with ethical concerns surrounding patient data access for training AI systems [16], while any governmental entity will have to walk the tightrope to make sure that their automated defense mechanisms conform to their citizens' civil liberties and democratic principles [15].

The rapid evolution of threats and agility demands continuous model retraining and human oversight. [20] argued that threat actors needed these defenses to evolve into emerging tactics as they developed. Auto-adaptive threats such as reinforcement learning [8] and expressions applying hybrid deep learning architectures [7] condition these systems to learn dynamically from their encounters with threats.

14.7.5 Training, Education, and Capacity Building

Education should be continuous in order to train the cybersecurity workforce properly, and whether training for AI-based cybersecurity is really useful or not depends heavily on the workforce competence and continuous education. Case-based and experiential-learning approaches are seen to be defining characteristics of education aiming to develop analytical skills in students working with

AI-enabled defense tools (in these cases, most notably, AI for cybersecurity) [12, 13]. Real-world training in IoT cybersecurity on actual tools like Shodan greatly prepares students for working in both academia and the private sector [24, 29].

Countries, along with financial and healthcare institutions, are spending resources building capacity with simulation-led AI training that enables interdisciplinary engagement among data scientists, engineers, and policymakers [37]. With these working arrangements, we align a whole series of global frameworks that promote AI literacy and technical know-how in order to sustain the Cybersecurity 5.0 objectives.

14.7.6 Cross-Sectoral Best Practices and Lessons Learned

Evidence received by comparing different sectors suggests several best practices for an effective way of implementing AI cybersecurity. Hence,

- Proactive Threat Intelligence: Best suited for early detection of threats is predictive analysis and data fusion combining IoT telemetry, network logs, and behavioral data [4, 35].
- Layered Security Schemes: Multi-layering the defensive architecture such that it combines ML, behavioral biometrics, and encryption enhances resilience [10, 15].
- Collaborative Governance: The sharing of data across sectors and coordination among agencies enhances cyber situational awareness, as portrayed in smart city security frameworks [9, 18].
- Ethical and Transparent AI: According to the works of [36, 38], transparency and explainability are core ingredients that can engender societal trust while curbing misuse of AI technologies.

These comparative analyses indicate that AI-driven cybersecurity must be context-sensitive, adaptable, and ethically governed. In predictive fraud detection, banking marches ahead; in institutional privacy-open approaches to ML integration, medicine leads; and systems identification and resilience propagate farther in state institutions. Collectively, these messages capture the essence of Cybersecurity 5.0—a comprehensive vision whereby AI, automation, and human intelligence together safeguard digital ecosystems across sectors.

14.8 Common Challenges and Mitigation Strategies

While organizations from all fields deploy AI and ML to strengthen cybersecurity, they face many recurrent challenges that endanger the methods' effectiveness, reliability, and sustainability. These challenges usually include technical constraints, data and privacy issues, regulatory difficulties, and the unavailability of sufficiently trained professionals. Moreover, the advent of AI-backed cybersecurity introduced additional concerns such as algorithmic bias, explainability, and model drift risks [1, 3, 6]. This section addresses some of the most pressing challenges with the implementation of AI oriented cybersecurity frameworks and the corresponding mitigation strategies as backed by current empirical literature and case evidence.

14.8.1 Technical Complexity and Model Vulnerabilities

AI models designed and trained for cybersecurity: intrusion detection systems, predictive analytics engines, and behavioral biometrics, are very much data dependent in terms of their quality and selection of features [4, 27]. Overfitting due to high noise, generation of false positives, and failure to detect new attacks are consequences of having a poorly designed dataset. Moreover, the AI model might be attacked through plant operation-dog-try data, thereby compromising the integrity of the detection [2, 5].

To mitigate these risks, the researchers propose the development of a hybrid detection framework that keeps a balance between rule-based approaches, ML classifiers, and reinforcement learning for adaptability and resilience [8, 35]. In this respect, an ensemble approach has proved itself to be resilient toward any form of manipulation, thus making it immune to an attack through adversarial training [34]. Deployment of explainable AI (XAI) tools further enhances transparency of the model and trust in practical scenarios especially in high-stakes cybersecurity setups [28].

14.8.2 Data Privacy, Security, and Ethical Concerns

Powerful AI-oriented cybersecurity systems conduct intensive training and operation systems on datasets enriched with sensitive organizational and personal information, thus creating a paradox between the utility and privacy of data [15, 22]. Any malicious breach in the management of such datasets can violate privacy laws and regulations, particularly in sectors such as finance and healthcare. Federated learning and privacy-preserving approaches such as homomorphic encryption and differential privacy provide strong ways forward to allow for analysis of data without dissemination of the actual data [9, 24].

Algorithmic discrimination must avoid the embedding of ethical AI frameworks, which will ensure their compliance with emerging digital governance standards [31, 33]. The human-in-the-loop mechanism provides extensive responsibilities for oversight, which will counterbalance automated decisions with ethical accountability, especially for applications in government and critical infrastructure [21].

14.8.3 Evolving Threat Landscape and Systemic Vulnerabilities

While covered by research up until October 2023; the statement concerns that cyber threats such as IoT botnets, ransomware, phishing, and supply-chain attacks all have complex dimensions, all making static defense mechanisms inadequate [19, 23]. While interconnected CPS and IoT applications expand their attack surface—such as smart grids, health devices, and industrial automation [10, 11]—say they expand their attack surface.

Dynamic risk modeling and monitoring as a predictive analytics capability for real-time threat anticipation make mitigation efforts possible [4, 18]. It also exploits AI-based anomaly detection for adaptive defense through reinforcement learning against unknown attack patterns [17, 25]. Additionally, redundancy enhances resilience against cascading failures in CPS due to the incorporation of layered security architectures [26].

14.8.4 Skill Gap and Human Factors

Global persistent shortage of professionals in cybersecurity proves to be a heavy impediment in the effective administration of systems powered by AI [12, 13]. There are difficulties with many organizations in hiring experts with competencies in cybersecurity and AI [16]. In addition, human error is a key source of wide-ranging vulnerabilities because nothing more than a minor misconfiguration along with bad incident response practices can wreck even the most advanced systems [14].

Addressing these gaps would require transformation of education and training benchmarks to include AI-assisted simulation, experiential learning, and scenario-based curricula that mimic the threats found in the real world [24, 29, 30]. AI-based decision-support tools can be integrated into continuous professional development programs to ensure superior operational competence and situation awareness [20].

14.8.5 Integration, Scalability, and Interoperability Issues

It turned out that the greatest challenge was the use of legacy systems in AI cybersecurity. These organizations are heavily reliant on aging architectures that cannot integrate with any contemporary AI models or data pipelines [31, 32]. The vast computer resource requirements also present challenges because it is during analysis over real-time data streams across distributed networks that AI systems face increased difficulty [39].

This problem can be solved by embracing modular and cloud-based architecture for elastic scaling and resource optimization at different levels [38].

Cybersecurity protocol standards, interoperability testing, and open APIs can also help smooth integration between AI systems and existing infrastructure [36]. This must be coupled with investment in AI governance frameworks by governments and institutions to facilitate cross-sectoral coordination.

14.8.6 Toward Resilience in AI-Driven Cyber Defense

Developing such resilience would require a robust data handling infrastructure, ethical governance, continuous learning, and collaborative threat intelligence sharing [37]. An adaptive defense system based on reinforcement learning could, therefore, identify vulnerabilities and self-repair autonomously as new threat patterns evolve [8].

In addition to cross-sectoral engagements, exchange platforms will facilitate sharing of cyber intelligence in real time, thereby improving capability for collective responses [34, 35]. Frameworks such as MARISMA-CPS [26] would provide an organized methodology for evaluating cyber risk management in complex interconnection systems. As they merge, AI and cybersecurity will shift focus from reactive defense to proactive, predictive, and resilient cyber ecosystems, which will become a signature of the Cybersecurity 5.0 paradigm [1].

14.9 Policy and Governance Implications

AI and cybersecurity intersect in critical sectors such as finance, healthcare, and government, consequently introducing regulatory, ethical, and governance dimensions that may not yet be understood by policymakers. Policy frameworks must be effective in ensuring that AI-based cybersecurity solutions are integrated into transparent, accountable, and resilient ecosystems. Global policy might have to transition from a historical model of defense against undue attack to dynamic, adaptive, and multisectoral governance models to photograph the complexity of digital transformation alongside evolving threats [1, 3].

14.9.1 The Changing Cyber Governance Landscape

Historically, cyber governance was based on static compliance frameworks as well as perimeter defense models which, today, are inadequate in defining an era characterized by AI-enabled automation and interconnected constructions [21]. The policymakers need to employ adaptive governance models that combine continuous monitoring, dynamics of predictive analytics, and risk-based regulation for the target to match evolving cyber threats [4, 6]. An example is reinforcement learning models inCPS, which yield data-driven insights toward guiding dynamic policy responses to real-time threats [8].

Governments and international bodies should work hand in hand to develop coherent policies that close the gaps between technology development and compliance with laws. Some of these aspects include the promotion of interoperability standards, development of global ethics frameworks for AI, and coordination of data sharing mechanisms across nations and sectors [32, 33]. In the absence of this coordination, fragmented regulatory environments will produce gaps that can be used by adversaries, especially through transnational digital ecosystems [19].

14.9.2 Regulatory Challenges to AI Cybersecurity

A whole set of regulatory challenges arises around AI-security technologies when such assets are established using algorithms whose functioning is not completely transparent, accountable, or fair [5, 28]. Where ML models purely for anomaly detection or intrusion prevention are concerned, that lack of transparency yields complex problems for regulatory oversight because the decisions of the black boxes are made less explainable in many instances [9]. In addition, AI systems trained on biased or incomplete data can discriminate unintentionally or misclassify benign behavior as malicious; hence, compliance risks arise in organizations [14, 27].

Such risks would consequently require a regulatory framework instituting algorithmic auditing, model explainability, and ethical AI standards. Examples of such sector-specific governance patterns and the MARISMA-CPS framework [26] show how technical methodologies and policy instruments can be integrated to deal with cyber risk within multidimensional infrastructures. Besides, there would also be continuous auditing/certification mechanisms on compliance with changing data protection and cyber laws across jurisdictions [31, 34].

14.9.3 Data Sovereignty, Privacy, and Ethical Governance

Data sovereignty and privacy remain core governance problems because the training of AI models is highly demanding in large-scale data analytics. The expansion of IoT and IIoT systems complicates this further since they generate huge amounts of sensitive data [22, 39]. Clear data ownership policies and architecture for privacy protection are thus critical to avoid breaching confidentiality and data protection laws by governments and organizations.

Ethical governance frameworks should thus establish boundaries as to what can be done by AI in cybersecurity operations [24]. Techniques like federated learning, differential privacy, and homomorphic encryption should be part of the national cybersecurity policies because they allow compliance with their principles and enable cooperation [15, 25]. In addition, there should be oversight by ethics committees to ensure that AI models used for surveillance, fraud detection, or risk assessment meet society's values and human rights standards [38].

14.9.4 Sector-Based Governance and Policy Adaptation

Different critical sectors have differing cybersecurity governance needs. If we look very closely, we will find that the financial sector requires strict and specific conditions concerning anti-fraud, anti-money laundering, and consumer data protections [14], while the healthcare sector speaks about patient confidentiality and operational resilience. Hence, AI solutions must comply with policy prescripts relating to privacy [18, 37].

Governmental and industrial systems require sound risk management in direct relation to continuous threat modeling, like in CPS and smart city infrastructures [10, 11]. Further, education and training sectors should be encouraged to integrate AI ethics and governance awareness in cybersecurity curricula to raise future leaders who would be informed in making policy-informed decisions [12, 16]. Thus, this gives it a more holistic approach that enables every sector to customize its governance principles concerning its unique threat landscape and regulatory context [13].

14.9.5 Cross-Sectoral Collaboration and Public-Private Partnerships

Data governance of modern cybersecurity undergoes quite an extensive process of cross-sector collaboration. Public-private partnerships (PPPs) act as essential conduits for intelligence gathering, handling incident responses, and common research on AI-driven defensive methods [7, 35]. Co-governance models facilitate quick dissemination of threat intelligence, ensuring data protection through controlled-access methods [2].

Research into open-source cybersecurity may be funded to foster innovation and resilience, and hubs for collective cybersecurity work could be set up [20, 36]. Policies should also reward private companies that are transparent in vulnerability reporting and freely share information, without fear of being sanctioned or penalized [17]. Multi-stakeholder taskforces assembled from different stakeholders such as regulators, academia, industry, and civil society can achieve a balanced approach to cybersecurity governance [1, 26].

14.9.6 Toward an AI-Governed Cybersecurity Policy Ecosystem

The future of cybersecurity governance must transform into AI-governed ecosystems that blend automation, predictive analytics, and careful human oversight [4, 6]. This transformation will require AI not just to defend systems but also to influence policy development via contemporary real-time insights into the situations [3, 37]. AI-assisted adaptive policymaking can provide governments with simulations and forecasting tools to foresee the onset of new threats and create their corresponding agile response frameworks [5, 7].

In the final analysis, a resilient governance structure for AI-induced cybersecurity must provide a balance between innovation and accountability, consequently nurturing trust among citizens, regulators, and industry players. The merger of AI with governance frameworks will therefore become critical for a trustworthy cyber resilience that would be sustainable, transparent, and ethically grounded as Cybersecurity 5.0 shapes the next era of digital defense [1, 31].

14.10 Future Directions

The field of cybersecurity is evolving at a fast pace with the amalgamation of AI, IoT, and CPS. As the digital ecosystem is getting complex and interdependent, research and innovation for the future must focus on proactive, intelligent, and adaptive countermeasure strategies expecting threats to arise. The following subsections discuss the key future directions, emerging opportunities, and required innovations in policy and technology.

14.10.1 AI-Based Cybersecurity and Predictive Analytics

AI will dominate cybersecurity strategy with increasing predictive capabilities of detecting, preventing, and responding to immediate threats [3, 4, 6]. ML and deep learning algorithms are expected to develop greater independence toward servicing dynamic threat modeling, anomaly detection, and adaptive risk mitigation [5, 35]. By employing reinforcement learning paradigms, AI systems would be able to simulate complex cyberattack scenarios and rationally optimize defensive counteractions across cyber-physical infrastructures [8, 25].

Future research should aim to develop explainable AI models to facilitate trust, transparency, and the ambit of regulation [28]. The combination of predictive analytics and historical threat intelligence will enable real-time adaptive defense in smart cities and critical infrastructures employing AI-driven cybersecurity solutions [9, 10, 18].

14.10.2 IoT and Cyber-Physical Systems Security

The IoT extension brings unprecedented attack surfaces and vulnerabilities, thus motivating unique mitigation approaches [22, 23, 39]. These CPS, namely smart grid and industrial control systems, must have integrated risk management frameworks that assure operational resilience and data integrity [10, 11, 26].

Emerging directions will employ continuous monitoring, AI-driven threat detection, and blockchain-based assurance of data integrity in IoT and IIoT networks [24, 29]. Cross-domain attack modeling and simulation via scenarios will enhance resilience and alignment of policies, allowing organizations to anticipate and respond to coordinated attacks [11, 23].

14.10.3 Data-Driven and Privacy-Preserving Cybersecurity

Big data analytics bring with them a whole new set of challenges including, but not limited to, privacy, data sovereignty, and ethical AI use [16, 37]. The focus of research programs into the future should emphasize investigation into privacy-preserving methods, including areas such as federated learning, homomorphic encryption, and differential privacy for collaborative defense without harming sensitive information [15, 38].

Applying data science to cybersecurity ensures real-time detection of threats from different data sources in diverse fields: finance, healthcare, and manufacturing [14, 27]. Developing frameworks for ethical data handling and cross-border exchange of data will be paramount in ensuring regulatory compliance and thus in building societal trust [1, 2].

14.10.4 Advanced Authentication and Behavioral Biometrics

Future cybersecurity systems will likely be built around an architecture of continuous authentication and behavioral biometrics instead of static credentials by improving identity verification [15]. Such systems might even take advantage of AI for detecting anomalous behavior patterns, preventing account takeovers, insider threats, and identity fraud in real time [4, 37].

Research in such a sphere should proactively include the integration of multimodal biometrics with contextual AI decision-making to enhance security without compromising the user experience [15, 35]. These schemes can also be used to forecast the effects of combining predictive analytics on establishing proactive defense layers, which can anticipate possible breaches before their occurrence [5, 6].

14.10.5 Cybersecurity Education, Training, and Workforce Development

For that human element, which is going to be the key in making systems cyber-resilient, there would then be a continuous investment in education, training, and workforce development [12, 24]. Future research directions are case-based learning and blended teaching methods that prepare professionals for real-world challenges [13].

This should develop in such a way that AI, IoT, and data analytics are part and parcel of ethical governance education in order to establish a workforce capable of handling the turbulent and intricate digital ecosystems [16, 32]. Partnerships between academia, industry, and government have to be stressed in order to deliver relevant skills and promote continuous career development [12, 31].

14.10.6 Policy Innovation and Global Governance

Policy Innovation and Global Governance AI insights should be incorporated into the future trends of cybersecurity strategies in governance frameworks for dynamic and adaptive policymaking [3, 9, 17]. Policies will also have to touch on cross-border threats, which should also standardize ethical AI practices and promote responsible disclosure of vulnerabilities [1, 2].

Multi-stakeholder governance ecosystems, including PPP, will be necessary for sharing threat intelligence, coordinating incident response, and driving innovation [14, 36]. The concept is designed within regulatory frameworks to ensure transparency, accountability, and resilience and thus to render AI-driven cybersecurity solutions in accordance with societal and legal expectations [26, 28].

14.10.7 Emerging Trends and Research Opportunities

Recent Trends and Research Opportunities Emerging trends capture some of the most critical opportunities for research in the coming decades:

1) Post-Quantum-Safe Cryptography: Making AI-ready systems fit for post-quantum security challenges [3].
2) Hunting automatically for threats: Taking up AI to detect and respond technically in real time without human intervention [4, 5].
3) Secured Cyber-Physical Infrastructure: Construction of operations that withstand operations under the multi-vector attack scenario [11, 26].
4) Ethical AI in Security Operations: Fairness, accountability, and explainability for automated defense mechanisms [15, 28].
5) Cybersecurity Meets Data Science: Analyzing, learning machines to domain knowledge for proactive threat mitigation [27, 37].

Taken together, these directions indicate a future in which cybersecurity is not only reactive but also anticipative, adaptive, intelligent, underpinned by a framework of AI, data science, and strong governance frameworks [2, 7, 22].

14.11 Conclusion

The rapid development of cybersecurity has only made the landscape ever more complex and sophisticated with digital threats. The old paradigms for the security of connected systems, IoT devices, and cyber-physical infrastructure are falling short in a world where organizations and societies are increasingly reliant on them. Proactive, intelligence-driven, and adaptive strategies must be in place to anticipate, detect, and thwart emergent threats in real time.

AI and ML have shown the potential to transform designs to meet ever-increasing cybersecurity needs. From predictive and anomaly detection through automated threat response and behavioral biometrics, these technologies provide dynamic defense options that adapt to the changing nature of cyber threats. The very incorporation of AI into critical infrastructures and smart cities and industrial systems will render more resilient and responsive security architectures, enabling organizations to sustain operational continuity even when under complex threat scenarios.

Nevertheless, human input constitutes a critical success factor in any endeavor concerning cybersecurity. Sound policies and workforce development and education ensure that technical innovations are complemented by professionals capable of interpreting, implementing, and managing sophisticated security developments. Case-based learning, practical lessons, and multidisciplinary education are paramount in preparing the next generation of cybersecurity personnel for real-world odysseys.

The future must also inescapably reckon with ethical concerns, privacy protection, and regulatory compliance. With increasing penetration of technologies such as AI and IoT, the transparency, accountability, and fairness of security operations must be ensured to sustain society's trust. Collaborative governance structures, PPP, and standardized best practices will help to ensure coordinated responses to all pervasive global cyber threats while promoting responsible innovation.

Ultimately, the future of cybersecurity rests on the interplay between technologies of high order, informed policymaking, and people of skilled oversight. By nurturing adaptive, intelligent, resilient cybersecurity approaches, firms will defend themselves not only against threats of today but also anticipate them as they evolve in the tomorrow of the digital world.

References

1 Obi, O.C., Akagha, O.V., Dawodu, S.O. et al. (2024). Comprehensive review on cybersecurity: modern threats and advanced defense strategies. *Computer Science & IT Research Journal.* 5 (2): 293–310.

2 Sharma P, Gupta H. Emerging Cyber Security Threats and Security Applications in Digital Era. In: 2024 11th International Conference on Reliability, Infocom Technologies and Optimization (Trends and Future Directions)(ICRITO). IEEE; 2024. p. 1–6.

3 Balantrapu, S.S. (2024). A Comprehensive Review of AI Applications in Cybersecurity. International Machine learning journal and Computer. *Engineering.* 7 (7).

4 Chowdhury, R.H., Prince, N.U., Abdullah, S.M., and Mim, L.A. (2024). The role of predictive analytics in cybersecurity: Detecting and preventing threats. *World Journal of Advanced Research and Reviews.* 23 (2): 1615–1623.

5 Jimmy, F. (2021). Emerging threats: The latest cybersecurity risks and the role of artificial intelligence in enhancing cybersecurity defenses. Valley International Journal Digital. *Library.* 564–574.

6 Chirra, D.R. (2022). AI-Driven Risk Management in Cybersecurity: A Predictive Analytics Approach to Threat Mitigation. *International Journal of Machine Learning Research in Cybersecurity and Artificial Intelligence.* 13: 505–527.

7 Khan, M. (2023). Exploring the Dynamic Landscape: Applications of AI in Cybersecurity. *EasyChair* .

8 Li, C. and Qiu, M. (2019). *Reinforcement learning for cyber-physical systems: with cybersecurity case studies.* Chapman and Hall/CRC.

9 Chen, D., Wawrzynski, P., and Lv, Z. (2021). Cyber security in smart cities: a review of deep learning-based applications and case studies. *Sustain Cities Soc.* 66: 102655.

10 Gunduz, M.Z. and Das, R. (2020). Cyber-security on smart grid: Threats and potential solutions. *Computer networks.* 169: 107094.

11 Zografopoulos, I., Ospina, J., Liu, X., and Konstantinou, C. (2021). Cyber-physical energy systems security: Threat modeling, risk assessment, resources, metrics, and case studies. *IEEE Access.* 9: 29775–29818.

12 Cai, Y. (2018). Using case studies to teach cybersecurity courses. *Journal of Cybersecurity Education, Research and Practice.* 2018 (2): 3.

13 Vrhovec, S., Fujs, D., Jelovcan, L., and Mihelic, A. (2020). Evaluating Case Study and Action Research Reports: Real-world Research in Cybersecurity. *J Univers Comput Sci.* 26 (7): 827–853.

14 Kafi, M.A. and Akter, N. (2023). Securing financial information in the digital realm: case studies in cybersecurity for accounting data protection. *American Journal of Trade and Policy.* 10 (1): 15–26.

15 Oduri, S. (2024). Continuous Authentication and Behavioral Biometrics: Enhancing Cybersecurity in the Digital Era. *Int J Innov Res Sci Eng Technol.* 13: 13632–13640.

16 Malasowe, B.O., Aghware, F.O., Okpor, M.D. et al. (2024). Techniques and Best Practices for Handling Cybersecurity Risks in Educational Technology Environment (EdTech). NIPES-Journal of Science and Technology. *Research.* 6 (2).

17 Paté-Cornell, M., Kuypers, M., Smith, M., and Keller, P. (2018). Cyber risk management for critical infrastructure: a risk analysis model and three case studies. *Risk Analysis.* 38 (2): 226–241.

18 Chirra, D.R. (2021). AI-Enabled Cybersecurity Solutions for Protecting Smart Cities Against Emerging Threats. *International Journal of Advanced Engineering Technologies and Innovations.* 1: 237–254.

19 Jang-Jaccard, J. and Nepal, S. (2014). A survey of emerging threats in cybersecurity. *J Comput Syst Sci.* 80 (5): 973–993.

20 Thakur K, Qiu M, Gai K, Ali ML. An investigation on cyber security threats and security models. In: 2015 IEEE 2nd international conference on cyber security and cloud computing. *IEEE*; 2015. p. 307–11.

21 Humayun, M., Niazi, M., Jhanjhi, N.Z. et al. (2020). Cyber security threats and vulnerabilities: a systematic mapping study. *Arab J Sci Eng.* 45: 3171–3189.

22 Altulaihan, E., Almaiah, M.A., and Aljughaiman, A. (2022). Cybersecurity threats, countermeasures and mitigation techniques on the IoT: Future research directions. *Electronics (Basel).* 11 (20): 3330.

23 Xenofontos, C., Zografopoulos, I., Konstantinou, C. et al. (2021). Consumer, commercial, and industrial iot (in) security: Attack taxonomy and case studies. *IEEE Internet Things J.* 9 (1): 199–221.

24 Fernández-Caramés, T.M. and Fraga-Lamas, P. (2020). Teaching and learning iot cybersecurity and vulnerability assessment with shodan through practical use cases. *Sensors.* 20 (11): 3048.

25 Kasaraneni, R.K. (2019). AI-Enhanced Cybersecurity in Smart Manufacturing: Protecting Industrial Control Systems from Cyber Threats. *Distributed Learning and Broad Applications in Scientific Research.* 5: 747–784.

26 Rosado, D.G., Santos-Olmo, A., Sánchez, L.E. et al. (2022). Managing cybersecurity risks of cyber-physical systems: The MARISMA-CPS pattern. *Comput Ind.* 142: 103715.

27 Nassar, A. and Kamal, M. (2021). Machine Learning and Big Data analytics for Cybersecurity Threat Detection: A Holistic review of techniques and case studies. *Journal of Artificial Intelligence and Machine Learning in Management.* 5 (1): 51–63.

28 Pattyam, S.P. (2021). Artificial Intelligence in Cybersecurity: Advanced Methods for Threat Detection, Risk Assessment, and Incident Response. *Journal of AI in Healthcare and Medicine.* 1 (2): 83–108.

29 Fernández-Caramés, T.M. and Fraga-Lamas, P. (2020). Use case based blended teaching of IIoT cybersecurity in the industry 4.0 era. *Applied Sciences.* 10(16):5607.

30 Sherman, A.T., DeLatte, D., Neary, M. et al. (2018). Cybersecurity: Exploring core concepts through six scenarios. *Cryptologia.* 42 (4): 337–377.

31 Reuvid, J. (2018). *Managing Cybersecurity Risk: Cases Studies and Solutions.* Legend Press Ltd.

32 Le D, Kumar R, Mishra BK, Khari M, Chatterjee JM. *Cyber Security in Parallel and Distributed Computing.*

33 Leszczyna, R. (2021). Review of cybersecurity assessment methods: Applicability perspective. *Comput Secur.* 108: 102376.

34 Mishra, A., Ghosh, S., and Mishra, B.K. (2019). Cybersecurity: A Practical Strategy Against Cyber Threats, Risks with Real World Usages. Cyber Security in Parallel and Distributed Computing: Concepts, Techniques, Applications and Case. *Studies.* 207–220.

35 Banik, S. (2022). Case Studies of Machine Learning in Cyber Threat Detection. *Unique Endeavor in Business & Social Sciences.* 1 (1): 192–204.

36 Tuma, K., Sandberg, C., Thorsson, U. et al. (2021). Finding security threats that matter: Two industrial case studies. *Journal of Systems and Software.* 179: 111003.

37 Hosen, M.S., Al Mamun, M.A., Khandakar, S. et al. (2024). *Alkhayyat A*, 236–256. Cybersecurity Meets Data Science: A Fusion of Disciplines for Enhanced Threat Protection. Nanotechnol Percept.

38 Mavani, C., Mistry, H.K., Patel, R., and Goswami, A. (2024). The Role of Cybersecurity in Protecting Intellectual Property. *International Journal on Recent and Innovation Trends in Computing and Communication.* 12 (2): 529–538.

39 Tweneboah-Koduah, S., Skouby, K.E., and Tadayoni, R. (2017). Cyber security threats to IoT applications and service domains. *Wirel Pers Commun.* 95: 169–185.

15

Roadmap to Cybersecurity 5.0

15.1 Introduction

The advent of Cybersecurity 5.0 is a breakthrough in digital defense in the sense that it is the era when artificial intelligence (AI), automation, and human-machine interaction will come together to form proactive, self-educational, and self-adaptive defense environments. In contrast to conventional cyberspace protection strategies that require defending the perimeter only, Cybersecurity 5.0 incorporates the concept of cyber resilience, autonomous response, and predictive intelligence to keep operations running in case of more advanced, persistent, and dynamic cyber threats [1, 2]. It is not only a technological evolution but also a strategic redesign into those systems that look ahead, learn through disruptions, and self-heal themselves with integrity.

15.1.1 The Paradigm Shift Toward Cyber Resilience

The contemporary state of cybersecurity can be described as complex, interrelated, and unpredictable. In the increasing digital ecosystems of cloud, IoT, and critical infrastructures, resilience and not protection have become the characteristic feature of successful cyber defense [3, 4]. Cyber resilience frameworks are meant to provide resilience against cyber-attacks to make sure that systems can recover, adjust, and adapt to cyber-attacks without disrupting mission-critical operations [5, 6]. This strategy fills the classical gap between cybersecurity and cyber defense, which is consistent with the requirement of the operational protection, detection, and recovery loops [1, 7]. The theories like the ones suggested by Conklin and Shoemaker [8] and optimized by Conklin et al. [9], focus on the survival of organizations due to their resilience-driven planning. These frameworks propose to combine risk management, incident response, and organizational governance into cyber operations. On the same note, Ridout [10] and Efthymiopoulos [11, 12] emphasize the need to combine cyber resilience with defense and deterrence measures, especially in national and North Atlantic Treaty Organization (NATO) critical infrastructures.

15.1.2 Integrating Cyber Defense and Resilient Architecture

There cannot be such a thing as cyber resilience that is not tied to defensive architecture and strategic deterrence [13, 14]. According to Ross et al. [15] and Meng et al. [16], the evolution of systemic and adaptive architectures is essential in creating self-assessment and automated remediation environments. These paradigms formalize resilience by means of security engineering ideas so that systems are secure by design. Further, Bolish et al. [17] and O'Neill et al. [18] show that the idea of cyber resilience should be established at the very beginning of the design process, which is what is known as building from Day 1, and that the concept of digital continuity in intelligent systems can be attained through sustainable design [19]. Kanaan et al. [20] and AL-Hawamleh [21] expand this principle to the organizational level, suggesting that leadership, policy, and culture are important to maintain cyber resilience. Their coordinated structures favor lifelong learning, real-time awareness, and dynamic governance to safeguard that a business survives the ever-increasing threats. In equal measure, Hubbard [22] proposes a state-level cyber resilience model, which focuses on cooperation on the national, organizational, and societal levels to enhance the security of the entire system.

15.1.3 Emerging Enablers: AI, Zero Trust, and Smart Defense

The latest version of cybersecurity, 5.0, places AI and machine learning (ML) at the center of providing intelligent, adaptive, and autonomous cyber defense solutions [23]. Machine learning algorithms have the ability to identify abnormalities, forecast the pattern of threats, and perform automatic mitigation, hence minimizing the response time and human errors. This change is accompanied by Zero Trust Architecture (ZTA) and layered defense plans that reorganize traditional access controls and identity-focused security alongside behavior-focused security and context-focused security [24]. The future-oriented system suggested by Safitra et al. [25] uses counterattacking cyber threats by applying AI-driven situational awareness and cognitive automation. On the same note, Sharma et al. [26] encourages vulnerability management structures as the major pillars of cyber defense, which would instill proactive mitigation of risks. This transition, according to Siegel and Sweeney [27], would turn cybersecurity into a resilience-focused, risk-driven field of practice, which incorporates strategic foresight and technological intelligence to overcome the intricate threat environments.

15.1.4 Toward a Unified Roadmap for Cybersecurity 5.0

The Cybersecurity 5.0 conceptualization is based on the integration of defense in depth, AI-based resilience, and human control. The active defense cycle needs to be changed, according to Orme [28], to incorporate continuous monitoring, adaptive learning, and predictive modeling. The following roadmap is the vision of an intelligent, self-healing, and sustainably secure cyber-ecosystem, influenced by such frameworks as those provided by Dickson and Goodwin [29], which have identified the key technologies in cyber resilience. Moore [30] focuses on capacity building by training and educating individuals in cyber defense, whereas Annarelli et al. [3] and Efthymiopoulos [12] pay attention to innovation as a source of resilience. All of these views are intellectual pillars of Cybersecurity 5.0, which is a multidisciplinary framework that incorporates engineering, policy, and AI to bring about a sense of digital harmony.

Essentially, the pretext to Cybersecurity 5.0 expresses a radically transformative roadmap that has merged technological savvy, future thinking, and human maneuverability. It is not only shifting to positions of defensive stagnation but also proactive, responsive, and recovering defensive systems—the defining characteristics of cyber resilience. This next-generation paradigm will not only protect systems, but also enable them to be smarter within the context of continual uncertainty as the digital frontier continues to be expanded.

15.2 Evolution of Cybersecurity Paradigms

The Cybersecurity 5.0 journey is the zenith of a decades-long evolution of digital defense, moving from static protection models to dynamic, adaptive, and intelligent systems. Each paradigm shift in cybersecurity emerges with the integration of an increasingly complex technological ecosystem and an increasingly complicated threat landscape. This section presents a history and a concept of the transformation of cybersecurity paradigms from previous perimeter defenses to intelligence-supported AI, ML, and cyber-resilience frameworks that underpin the fifth-generation approach.

To illustrate progressiveness in cybersecurity development, the timeline of cybersecurity paradigms appears in Figure 15.1. While moving from reactive defense mechanisms to proactive, autonomous, and resilient Cybersecurity 5.0 models, this visualization shows continuous reform in cybersecurity strategies due to increasing system interconnectivity and complexity.

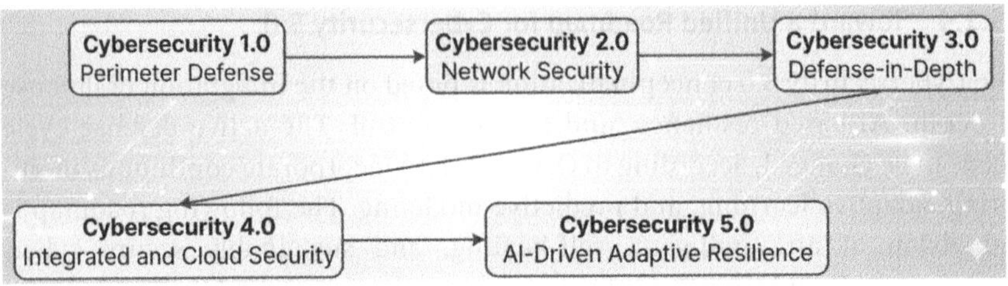

Figure 15.1 Evolution of Cybersecurity Paradigms Leading to Cybersecurity 5.0. "*Source:* Hewa Majeed Zangana"

15.2.1 Early Cyber Defense and the Rise of Reactive Security

During the initial phases of digital infrastructure evolution, cybersecurity did not go beyond border security with the help of firewalls, antivirus programs, and intrusion control systems. These processes were rather reactive in nature in that they responded to threats once they had been detected. With the growth of networks and the integration of interrelated systems as the rule, this reactive strategy was no longer effective in confronting more advanced and persistent threats [10, 11]. Governments and military institutions, including NATO, started focusing on smart defense approaches that involved deterrence, detection, and resilience to enhance national and organizational security [12]. The move toward strategic defense integration as opposed to traditional protection was an indication of a new realization that continuity and recovery should also be considered in cybersecurity. Conklin and Shoemaker [8] explain that the only way of making institutions survive in the digital era is by making them resilient to attacks instead of merely protecting them. In like manner, Conklin et al. [9] took a step further to advance the concept of cyber resilience architecture that these organizations need to integrate security engineering with governance and flexibility to incur the consequences of unexpected cyber-attacks.

15.2.2 From Defense-in-Depth to Integrated Cyber Resilience

The 2010s were characterized by the shift to the integrated resilience models that could maintain the operation during continuous attacks rather than the defense-in-depth strategies, which built on multiple levels of security controls [13, 15, 28]. These models realized that no system could be completely impervious; hence, the focus was on speedy detection, containment, and recovery. The National Institute of Standards and Technology (NIST) recommended in their special publication [15] that cyber resilience is an engineering problem that needs robust, recoverable, and adaptive systems. This idea was further extended by such scholars as

Annarelli et al. [3] and Estay et al. [4] with the frameworks of measuring and controlling the resilience of industrial and digital systems. The papers highlighted that more measurable measures of resilience are required and that cybersecurity, organizational strategy, and risk management should be more deeply interconnected. In the meantime, Moore [30] emphasized the role of human capital building and training on resilient systems, claiming that not only technologies will help to reduce and address complex cyber threats but also a competent workforce. Detection of threats through AI and ML analytics integration started changing the form of defensive posture. Dickson and Goodwin [29] also discovered five major technologies that are needed to facilitate cyber-resilient frameworks, such as AI, automation, blockchain, predictive analytics, and cloud-based orchestration. Equally, Safitra et al. [25] suggested an approach of a counterattack-based cybersecurity model, with a focus on the active identification and neutralization of the emerging threats before they can grow to constitute a large-scale disruption.

15.2.3 The Age of Integrative and Cognitive Cybersecurity

The contemporary paradigm of cybersecurity, also commonly known as Cybersecurity 4.0, has grown in parallel with Industry 4.0, which is defined by the existence of cyber-physical systems, IoT, and cloud computing. Nevertheless, it was this wave that created new points of vulnerability and attack. Muhammad et al. [24] suggest an integrative cybersecurity model based on zero-trust architecture, layered defense, and global standards as the means to ensure a robust digital environment that is able to uphold trust and privacy throughout the interconnected systems. Ahmed et al. [1] further elaborated on this by filling the gap between cybersecurity and cyber defense and their reading on how organizations can attain operational harmony through a common intelligence, common command structure, and cross-domain resilience approaches. In a similar manner, Galinec [7] introduced a cyber defense and resilience conceptual model, emphasizing that resilience ceases to be a passive feature but is active as an operational ability. Li [5] and Kanaan et al. [20] have developed frameworks that can be used to provide structure to the process of establishing resilience in business continuity and growth strategies. In their studies, they focus on the holistic approach, as cyber resilience is linked to the organizational culture, governance, and technological infrastructure. This idea is strengthened by AL-Hawamleh [6, 21]. who prove the ability to improve the processes of defense as well as the foresight of organizations in order to make them able to survive despite hostility. O'Neill et al. [18] and Li et al. [19] designed a system, Cyberspace Defense and Resilient System (CYDRES), a system that provides cyber defense and resilience to protect grid-interactive efficient buildings as an example of how resilience may be designed into intelligent and energy-efficient infrastructures at the system level.

Similarly, Meng et al. [16] presented the Verification and Evidence for Resilient Design in Critical Trusted-Systems (VERDICT), a language and framework of resilient and safe systems engineering, which supports the significance of resilience at both design and validation and operational stages.

15.2.4 Cybersecurity 5.0: The Dawn of Proactive and Autonomous Defense

The coming generation—Cybersecurity 5.0—is a combination of technical and reactive intelligence. It is propelled by AI, autonomous response systems, and cognitive computing that make it possible to have real-time situational awareness, predictive analytics, and automated decision-making. It is based on the existing paradigm of Conklin et al. [9] and Ross et al. [15], who generalized their models into self-learning architectures, which can change according to adversarial strategies. Bolish et al. [17] also underline that resilience engineering should be incorporated at all the levels of system design and that cyber resilience needs to be constructed at the earliest stage. Usman Haider [23] goes further with this idea using AI and ML in cloud and network security to develop architectures with the capability to automatically detect, predict and counterattacks. Sharma et al. [26] complement this perception with the vulnerability management framework, which provides the continuity of the assessment and remedies of the weaknesses in the systems. On a larger scale, Hubbard [22] suggests a cyber resilience framework on the state level, emphasizing the need to have the national cooperation in ensuring digital infrastructure security. In the meantime, Akinsanya et al. [2] provide a history of the development of cyber resilience ideas and show how they have evolved to become reactive, predictive, and adaptive. All of these viewpoints demonstrate the international trend in Cybersecurity 5.0- a proactive defense framework that integrates governance, engineering, and intelligence in a protection, adaptation and innovation loop.

15.2.5 Toward a Cyber-Resilient Future

The evolution of cybersecurity paradigms indicates an evident trend, namely, the shift of individual defenses to democratic systems based on the focus on intelligence, cooperation, and flexibility. According to Pureti [14], organizations now have to develop strong cyber defense strategies that are inclusive of resilience, foresight, and real-time responsiveness. On the same note, Annarelli et al. [3] and Siegel and Sweeney [27] contend that resilience is not a set of attributes but a dynamic ability that is influenced by organizational maturity, technological development, and environmental consciousness.

Well, because there really are disasters of brain drain behind the evolution of the paradigms of cybersecurity. Resilience, adaptation, and even autonomy are not improvements but needs. The whole idea behind Cybersecurity 5.0 is to amalgamate the reminiscences and teachings into frameworks past with the intelligence of its future innovative technologies. The ecosystem thus created will be neither secure nor self-sufficient. The continuing expansion of the digital domain will cause this evolutionary course to create space for a proactive, intelligent, and sustainable cyber future.

15.3 Defining Cybersecurity 5.0

Cybersecurity 5.0 heralds the dawn of a new age of protection with unprecedented changes in commercial, organizational, and personal interactions through AI, automation, and cognitive systems to build self-adaptive and proactive defense ecosystems. Unlike its predecessors, which concentrated on prevention and detection, Cybersecurity 5.0 focuses on prediction, resilience, and autonomous recovery. It has fused man-machine intelligence and data-driven decision-making toward connecting and making these systems secure and sustainable from increasingly complex cyber threats [25].

Cybersecurity 5.0 is primarily built around the conceptual framework of cyber resilience, which is defined as the capacity of digital systems to foresee, withstand, recover, adapt, and even evolve from zeitgeist adverse incidents [8, 9]. The change takes security thinking past pure defensive postures toward adaptive, intelligence-based architectures. The transformation of these frameworks toward more complete forms of integrated systems capable of learning from perturbation and their dynamic strengthening of defenses within the organization is further, according to Akinsanya et al. [2]. Ahmed et al. [1] also stated that embedding resilience into every layer of system architecture means that cybersecurity will be integrated with cyber defense.

Cybersecurity being Cybersecurity 5.0 is the extension of the previous constructs by which Conklin and Shoemaker [8] and Ross et al. [15] propose to design and implement a self-sustaining digital ecosystem instead of risk management. Ross et al. [15] perspective on the NIST approach introduces systems security engineering, which offers foundational principles for resilience, which Cybersecurity 5.0 can enhance through real-time autonomous monitoring and predictive analytics. As pointed out by Siegel and Sweeney [27], current risk-driven approaches to security are gradually augmented by adaptive intelligence, which tackles dynamic threat vectors in real time.

Cybersecurity 5.0 combines these pillars—defensive, deterring, and spin-based—by design to be tied from the strategic perspective [10, 12]. This becomes far more important in the hyper-connected environment, where attacks do not prevent themselves from cascading into physical, economic, and societal domains. "Smart defense" frameworks, according to Efthymiopoulos [11, 12], proposed through NATO's initiatives, underscore collaborative innovation as necessary to fostering resilience, whose principles now lay the foundation for Cybersecurity 5.0. The other day, Dickson and Goodwin [29] captured the cornerstones of these enabling technologies as foundational for resilient cyber ecosystems, including blockchain, AI, quantum cryptography, and IoT security.

Modern organizations need a paradigm that will unify business continuity, governance, and resilience under one security posture. Future generations of cyber resilience frameworks were said by AL-Hawamleh [21] and Kanaan et al. [20] to include those that, apart from prevention, guarantee operational continuity and business development against continuous threats. In the same line of thought, Li [5] and Kanaan et al. [20] argue that resilience frameworks should enable organizations to recover rapidly from incidents while maintaining critical operations. An evolving discipline combining risk criterion assessment, adaptive response, and organizational learning into resilient infrastructure is what Annarelli et al. [3] recognized cyber resilience management as.

The operational backbone of Cybersecurity 5.0 lies in its technical integration of AI-based cyber defense systems, including CYDRES—an advanced architecture securing grid-interactive buildings [18, 19]. One example of how ML and automation advance situational awareness, along with intelligent recovery capabilities, is illustrated by such systems in recovering from cyberattacks. Bolish et al. [17] insist that resilience should be built into system design from the outset, supporting what they insist should be a guiding principle of "resilience by design" for next-generation infrastructures.

Layered defense models and principles of zero trust feature prominently in the architecture of Cybersecurity 5.0. Muhammad et al. [24] refer to zero-trust and global standards as essential ingredients necessary to build a resilient digital future. Pureti [14] and Sharma et al. [26], too, propose frameworks related to vulnerability management and cyber defense that are attuned to the proactive identification and mitigation of risks, a viewpoint accosting the intent of Cybersecurity 5.0. These approaches resonate with Savold et al. [13], advocating for standardized cyber reference architectures, resulting in interoperable infrastructures that also cater to continuous improvement.

One of the main characteristics of Cybersecurity 5.0 is that it can stretch across disparate ecosystems—including critical infrastructure, energy, healthcare, defense, and finance—which all depend on some continuous digital connectivity. Efthymiopoulos [12] and Hubbard [22] underscore that cyber resilience should now be included within government and institutional structures for safeguarding national and economic stability. Cybersecurity 5.0 addresses such aspects through dynamic, data-centric models for threat detection, attack prediction, and autonomous initiation of defense mechanisms [16].

Furthermore, Cybersecurity 5.0 continues the philosophy of "resilience is a life cycle," which Estay [4] refer to. These processes range from design through operation to continuous improvement through feedback mechanisms that enhance adaptive capacity. The convergence of cyber defense and cyber resilience allows systems, as Galinec [7] notes, to survive attacks and evolve to be stronger. In advocating for active defense cycles that integrate human oversight with automated intelligence, Orme [28] takes the same approach.

Cybersecurity 5.0 is viewed holistically, involving change at technological, strategic, and cultural levels. Cyber resilience is acknowledged with the understanding that it is not a fixed state but rather a continuum or process requiring innovation, governance, and collaboration [23, 30]. According to Kanaan et al. [20], Cybersecurity 5.0 obliges enterprises to consider integrated frameworks for resilience not only for people but also for processes and technology. By merging intelligent automation, predictive defense, and organizational adaptability, Cybersecurity 5.0 paves the way for a secure, self-healing, and future-ready digital ecosystem.

15.4 Core Pillars of Cybersecurity 5.0

Cybersecurity 5.0 rests within a multidimensional framework that composes the technological, organizational and strategic domains into adaptive, intelligent, resilient defense systems. It derives from certain foundational pillars that define how next-generation cyber infrastructures would operate in an autonomous, anticipatory of threats, and recovery conditions with minimal human intervention. Cyber resilience, adaptive defense architecture, zero-trust and layered security, intelligent automation and AI integration, governance and risk-driven strategies, and human-machine collaboration are the core pillars for Cybersecurity 5.0.

In summary, the core pillars of Cybersecurity 5.0 are conceptualized in Figure 15.2. These will provide the theme for the analysis and understanding of how the intelligent, resilient, and autonomous cyber defense environments are structured. The model encompasses how resilience, adaptive architecture, layered security, AI-driven automation, governance frameworks, and human-machine collaboration interact to support proactive cybersecurity.

15.4.1 Cyber Resilience as the Foundational Layer

The cornerstone of Cybersecurity 5.0 is cyber resilience, such that systems can resist and absorb cyberattacks, but can also recover quickly and grow in a way that adapts to changing threats. According to Conklin and Shoemaker [8], cyber resilience is "the structured, iterated approach to institutional survival and the continual learning and redundancy needed to achieve it." Conklin et al. [9] also argue for adapting cybersecurity architectures rather than requiring recovery and adaptation in case of a failure as built-in features.

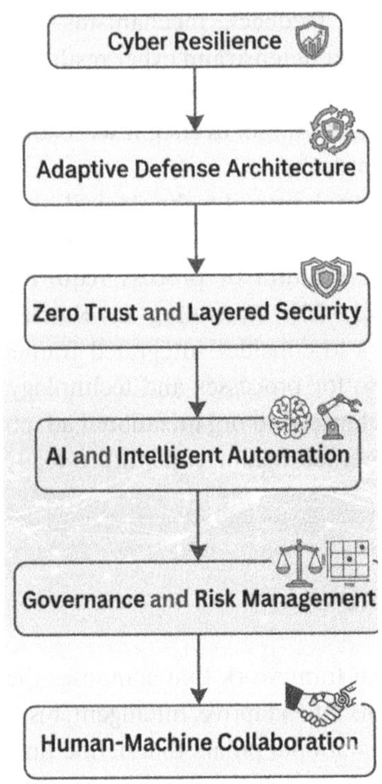

Figure 15.2 Core Pillars of Cybersecurity 5.0. "*Source:* Hewa Majeed Zangana"

Ahmed et al. [1] urge an end to the divorce between cybersecurity and cyber defense, as it should be toward a convergence model enabling resilience from integrated operations. Akinsanya et al. [2] stress this idea of settling frameworks toward resilience by including self-healing mechanisms within network infrastructure in line with that. AL-Hawamleh[21] and Kanaan et al. [20] support the view that an advanced cyber resilience framework strengthens business continuity and operational stability in case of complex threat environments from an organizational perspective.

Additionally, Li [5] regards resilience as the strategic need for operational continuity; Annarelli et al. [3] view it as a management discipline of risk awareness, adjustment, and improvement after incidents. By design, Bolish et al. [17] and Meng et al. [16] propagate the resilient idea wherein system architecture begins to develop recovery logic and adaptive control loops. These insights echo that of Estay [4] calling for a systematic assessment framework to measure resilience effectiveness. Collectively, these studies formed the conceptual backbone of resilience-driven vision in Cybersecurity 5.0.

15.4.2 Adaptive and Intelligent Defense Architectures

Thus, the theme of Cybersecurity 5.0 is adaptability—real-time agile systems responding to new dangers. Ross et al. [15] develop here a systems-engineering approach by which adaptive architectures should be able to make real-time adjustments based on context intelligence. This scheme becomes operationalized in models like CYDRES, where Cyberspace Defense and Resilient Systems are developed by O'Neill et al. [18] and Li et al. [19]. These integrate the benefits of defense automation and resilience into grid-interactive infrastructure.

In extending this, both Efthymiopoulos [12] and Ridout [10] advocated for national and defense dimensions that would subject cyber deterrence and smart defense strategies within NATO to real-time monitoring and real-time predictive analytics. Efthymiopoulos [11] similarly captures the idea of "smart defense" as an intersecting resilience paradigm where collaborative innovation and mutual intelligence meet. Safitra et al. [25] bolster that point by laying out a conceptualization for counterintuitive cyber threats through the categories of autonomous decision-making and distributed analytics.

Savold et al. [13] provide a survey of leading cyber reference architectures, which shows the essential need for interoperability and modularity as characteristics of an adaptive security design. At a practical level, Pureti [14] shows that strong defense should combine technological innovation with continuity planning tied to the business.

15.4.3 Zero-Trust and Layered Security Paradigm

Foundation of Cybersecurity 5.0 entails coupling zero-trust principles with multilayered defense systems mentioned by Muhammad et al. [24]: integrating zero-trust models with layered defense and the overall standards will build an adaptive and resilient digital ecosystem. Sharma et al. [26] framed an interesting idea for layered defense on vulnerability management as an important part of it, which serves as a proactive barrier against the possibility of potential exploitation.

Active cyber defense cycles are discussed in Orme [28]. They consist of continuous verification, sharing threat intelligence, and real-time adaptive monitoring that strengthen the resilience of the system. These principles correspond to those of the cyber resilience cycle illustrated by Conklin and Shoemaker [8]] because constant assessment and control validation are the lifeblood here.

Hubbard [22] and Galinec [7] advocate that for implementing these paradigms, it is necessary to establish multi-domain threat intelligence in both national and organizational cyber constructs. Zero trust then becomes not just a technical model, but indeed a governance mindset across interconnected ecosystems.

15.4.4 Intelligent Automation and AI-Driven Cyber Defense

More than automation, AI, and ML in Cybersecurity 5.0 aim for cognitive adaptation and predictive defense. According to Usman Haider [23], AI and ML are improving cloud and network security through capabilities in pattern recognition, anomaly detection, and autonomous mitigation. Bolish et al. [17] recommend taking a systems approach to incorporate AI-powered automation from design to allow decision-making in real time and adapt over time.

Meng et al. [16] refer to this through the VERDICT framework, formalizing engineering principles within the development of safe and resilient systems leveraging automation and AI. Like Dickson and Goodwin [29], they recognize AI, blockchain, and cognitive computing as important engines of future cyber resilience frameworks. Thus, Safitra et al. [25] further argue that intelligent automation allows proactive responses, limiting the time lapse between the threat being detected and containment.

AI-enabled cybersecurity ecosystems are most useful for handling critical infrastructure, which includes energy and defense, as exemplified by the CYDRES model [18, 19]. They embody the overarching goal of Cybersecurity 5.0, which is the autonomous adaptation—self-correcting networks predicting, preventing, and evolving with threats.

15.4.5 Governance, Risk-driven Strategy, and Policy Integration

These pillars are effective governance and risk-based management, which are critical to sustaining Cybersecurity 5.0. According to Siegel et al. [27], a risk-driven resiliency framework should also have governance mechanisms that are in synergy with business objectives and regulatory standards. Annarelli et al. [3]] reiterate that resilience management is strategic to organizational strategy, thus embedding continuous improvement and accountability into decision-making.

AL-Hawamleh [6, 21] emphasize the need for future-oriented frameworks to include cyber resilience governance as part of the organization's culture to ensure operational stability. Kanaan et al. [20] elaborated on this by supplying an integrated model that synchronized security with business continuity and growth. Estay [4] advocate for structured frameworks for assessing and improving resilience maturity.

At the state level, Hubbard [22] proposes a conceptual model for national cyber resilience governance; Efthymiopoulos [12], in the same vein, highlights NATO's role in facilitating collaborative resilience policy across sectors. Together, these argue for governance and risk management as strategic enablers for sustainable Cybersecurity 5.0 ecosystems.

15.4.6 Human-Machine Collaboration and Continuous Capacity Building

It establishes the fact that technology alone cannot provide complete protection in Cybersecurity 5.0, as an essential part has to be played by humans through their insight and capacities of the organization. According to Moore [30], cyber defense training capacity is built up through developing adaptive skills in professionals that are appropriate in AI-augmented realities. Likewise, Conklin and Shoemaker [8] argued for developing a skilled workforce with skills to interpret and manage automated systems well.

According to Efthymiopoulos [11] and Ridout [10], collaboration between humans and machines must be a part of doctrines on defense; this incorporates a ratio between automation and human judgment. Ahmed et al. [1] and Akinsanya et al. [2] have similar sentiments that resilience frameworks should promote transdisciplinary synergies across cybersecurity, data science, and management.

Galinec [7] and Orme [28] have also observed that collaboration and shared learning build a framework within which resilience evolves. In Cybersecurity 5.0, continuous professional development, ethical AI oversight, and collective intelligence come up as the human dimension complementing technological advancement.

15.4.7 Synthesis of the Pillars

These pillars create the architecture of Cybersecurity 5.0, a system that encompasses a unified, adaptive, and intelligence-driven model to fight the emerging threats. Resilience, automation, defense in depth, zero trust, governance, and human collaboration are intended to establish an organization that moves away from reactive defense into proactive cyber sovereignty. According to Kanaan et al. [20], Li [5], and Safitra et al. [25], realization of Cybersecurity 5.0 will happen via seamless synergy among these pillars, resulting in a secure and self-sustaining digital future.

15.5 Strategic Roadmap and Development Phases

Cybersecurity 5.0 allows creating a structured, futuristic roadmap that goes beyond traditional defense paradigms to a holistic adaptive model of resilience, intelligence, and automation. The development of the roadmap will mature over progressive phases, with each phase increasingly strengthening the synergy between cyber defense, cyber resilience, and organizational agility. Building from the basis espoused by Conklin and Shoemaker [8], the roadmap considered

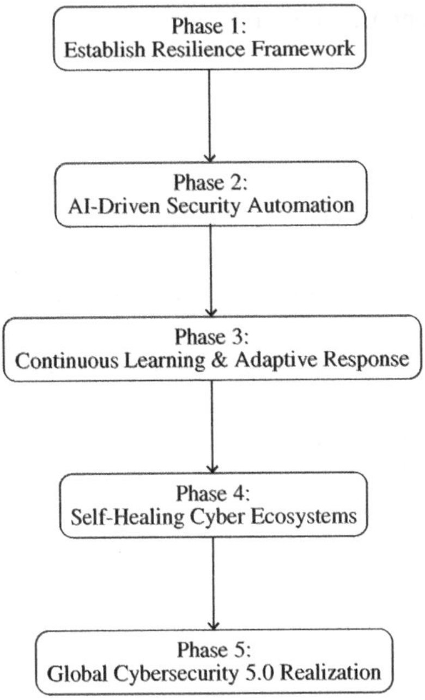

Figure 15.3 Strategic Roadmap Toward Cybersecurity 5.0."*Source:* Hewa Majeed Zangana"

preparedness, adaptability, and continuous improvement as key pillars for sustainably protecting the digital space.

To create Cybersecurity 5.0, Figure 15.3 shows the strategic phased development required. Gradual advancement from foundational controls and governance through AI-enabled automation, adaptive resilience, and fully proactive defense ecosystems is what this roadmap depicts.

Phase 1: Foundational Integration and Framework Establishment

The first phase focuses on establishing a strong cyber resilience framework that creates a harmonized set of processes, governance policies, and technical architectures. This means putting standardized frameworks into practice, fittingly described by Ross et al. [15], with the goal of applying systems security engineering to resilient infrastructures. In Li [5] view, establishing proper governance mechanisms and continuous monitoring systems will enable organizations to attain operational continuity even during cyber stress. In like manner, Akinsanya et al. [2] argue that organizations should adopt frameworks that follow the ever-evolving threat landscapes for resilience in cyber defense. Integration of zero-trust architecture with layered defenses reinforces baseline protection against advanced persistent threats (APTs), according to Muhammad et al. [24]. Kanaan et al. [20] argue that early integration of business continuity and security frameworks ensures that resilience is not an afterthought but rather a core design principle. Concurrently, Safitra et al. [25] highlight counteracting cyber threats via dynamic defense models, permitting systems to anticipate and mitigate emerging risks.

Phase 2: Intelligent Automation and Cognitive Security

According to phase two, intelligent automation and cognitive security entail organizational shifts toward AI-oriented decision-making and autonomous defense applications. The use of AI and ML has improved predictive analytics, thereby enabling technologies to detect and respond to anomalous situations in real time [23]. This is in agreement with the CYDRES project proposed by O'Neill et al. [18] and Li et al. [19], which aims to use intelligent automation to safeguard grid-interactive efficient infrastructures. Thus, the phase witnessed a remarkable transformation from passive to active cyber defense through algorithmic learning and adaptive threat modeling.

Bolish et al. [17] advocate that building cyber-resilient systems "from Day 1" requires embedding AI-based diagnostic and autonomous remediation tools into the software development lifecycle. This is backed further by Galinec [7], framing cognitive automation as a key enabler for proactive approaches to cybersecurity strategies. Efthymiopoulos [12] stresses that AI-powered resilience plays an important role in organizing national defense systems in the contemporary geopolitical environment.

Phase 3: Adaptive Resilience and Continuous Learning

The third phase of adaptive resilience focuses on systems that continuously evolve through feedback and machine-learning refinement. Annarelli et al. [3] observed that resilient systems need to dynamically adjust to disturbances while carrying out their essential mission. Likewise, Estay [4] proposed resilience assessment frameworks to appraise the organization's ability to adapt under duress.

The third phase should encompass cyber-resilience metrics and simulations so that organizations can test their readiness against different operational scenarios. Ahmed et al. [1] emphasize a bridging approach between cybersecurity and cyber defense through iterative testing and risk-informed decision-making. The framework by AL-Hawamleh [21] reinforces the concept, assuring that the resilience strategies grow in tandem with the organization's pursuit of digital transformation initiatives. Also, Kanaan et al. [20] emphasizes that aligning resilience with business continuity planning will enable the recovery process as well as operational assurance.

Efthymiopoulos [11] further advocates for incorporating smart defense principles, which combine defense-in-depth and multi-domain collaboration to bolster resilience at the organizational and national levels. Ridout [10] complements this with a strategic vision that favors the synergy of deterrence and defense and advocates for a multi-layered approach to cyber readiness.

Phase 4: Proactive Defense Ecosystems and Systemic Resilience

The self-healing ecosystems will be realized based on interconnected defense architectures. According to Savold et al. [13], architecting comprehensive cyber reference frameworks would ensure scalability and interoperability across cloud, IoT, and enterprise systems. Dickson and Goodwin [29] identified five key enabling technologies—automation, analytics, secure cloud, blockchain, and quantum encryption—that form the backbone of the Cybersecurity 5.0 infrastructure.

As Siegel et al. [27] argue, decisions should be risk-driven, placing cybersecurity resources first on mission-critical assets. Similarly, Hubbard [22] emphasizes the importance of state-level cyber resilience frameworks for coordinated defense and crisis response capabilities. The concepts of Meng et al. [16] suggest organizations should take resilience engineering approaches to develop systems that can foresee, absorb, and recover from cyber shocks.

The holistic defense cycle proposed by Orme [28] and developed further by Pureti [14]] shows that cyber resilience and active defense should go hand in hand. This pathway allows organizations to move away from static defense frameworks toward adaptive, learning-based ecosystems able to outpace the threat landscape.

Phase 5: Global Collaboration and Cybersecurity 5.0 Realization

The last phase foresees the actualization of Cybersecurity 5.0 as a global, interconnected, intelligent, self-sustaining ecosystem. Cyber resilience, then, goes beyond organizational borders and becomes a part of international digital cooperation. Cyber defense training capacity building is, according to Moore [30], necessary to secure human adaptability with changing technologies. Conklin et al. [9] point toward a similar direction in rethinking strategies on cyber so as to achieve resilience at cultural levels of the institution from top-down.

This global dream is shared by Efthymiopoulos [12], who goes a step further to propose the international cooperation frameworks to harmonize innovation, security, and governance. That is the demonstration Li et al. [19] laid on how multi-domain cyber resilience could secure energy systems, a model that could be stretched across industries. Cumulatively, Annarelli et al. [3], Kanaan et al. [20], and Safitra et al. [25] are insightful from the above construction, indicating that to achieve Cybersecurity 5.0 requires more than technology: some strategic alignment, human collaboration, and ethical governance.

In essence, this roadmap should come out of being anchored in and driven by resilience, intelligence, and adaptability. Accordingly, it would provide the necessary step-by-step developmental framework from current standards in cybersecurity to the era of Cybersecurity 5.0. All dependent phases will ensure that technological advancement is matched with the evolution of organizational culture and human expertise toward building a secure, self-healing, sustainable future cyber ecosystem.

15.6 Technological Enablers

The emergence of Cybersecurity 5.0 is compelled by a series of techno-enablers in their ability to enhance the resilience, adaptability, smartness, and automation levels of the next generation of digital ecosystems. They connect a conventional cybersecurity framework to a next-generation, AI-enabled architecture capable of predictive, automated, and self-healing defense. As Ahmed et al. [1] aptly put it, advancing cyber resilience requires the merging of cybersecurity and cyber defense into a single strategic and techno framework. The key enablers of this evolution include AI, ML, zero-trust architecture, blockchain, cloud-native security, quantum-ready cryptography, and cyber-physical integration. Each of the above technologies contributes to shaping an interconnected, intelligent, and adaptive defense ecosystem in consonance with the tenets of Cybersecurity 5.0.

Figure 15.4 covers the primary technological enablers driving Cybersecurity 5.0. Such technologies together enable an ecosystem of modern defense automation, trust, intelligence, and adaptability in the cyberspace realm. Their interconnection roles ensure modern security architectures that protect against internal and external threats as well as predictive, self-learning, and resilient.

15.6.1 Artificial Intelligence and Machine Learning for Autonomous Defense

The Cybersecurity 5.0 program is built on the ground floor of AI and ML, predicting threat intelligence, doing behavioral analysis, and triggering automatic incident responses. According to Usman Haider [23], AI-enabled algorithms can independently evaluate millions of network traffic items. Behaviors that traditional systems would not recognize are defined as malicious by these devices. In

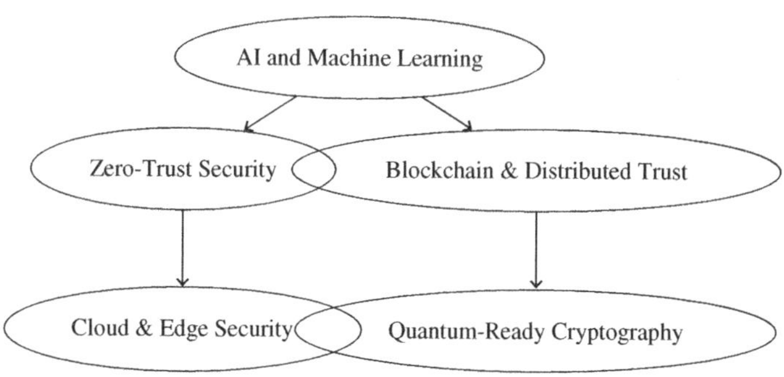

Figure 15.4 Technological Enablers Supporting Cybersecurity 5.0. "*Source:* Hewa Majeed Zangana"

this manner, these new technologies help support continuous learning for defensive cyber mechanisms to evolve with newly emerging threats.

In an effort, Bolish et al. [17] would like AI embedded into cyber-resilient systems from Day 1, adding that AI should be in both detection and self-remediation. In the same vein, Galinec [7] directs cognitive security frameworks using context-aware analytics in improving decision-making, while Efthymiopoulos [12] talks about the important strategic role that AI serves in national defense architectures. Such alignment is also in conformity with the resilience-by-design models, which integrate AI into engineering methods Mohd [16] advocate for, where systems will be built securely to self-correct and have adaptive responses.

Through the CYDRES project [18, 19], real-world applications of AI and ML come into play within a grid-interactive, efficient building to develop a replicable intelligent infrastructure defense. These innovations collectively enable the transformations from reactive cybersecurity postures to autonomous, self-learning security ecosystems.

15.6.2 ZTA with Layered Defense

The zero trust model, based on the idea that no user, system, or device can ever be entirely trusted, is a key enabler of Cybersecurity 5.0. Muhammad et al.[24]] describe zero trust as a core tenet for establishing the integrative cybersecurity frameworks that will comprise layered defense with global standards. Zero trust principles prescribe continuous verification and granular access control to ensure the integrity of systems, irrespective of the separate failure of individual elements.

Evolving perimeter-based defenses to context-aware, identity-driven verification models is what [14] contends organizations need to do. Sharma et al. [26] also deem a vulnerability management framework based on zero trust principles important, which emphasizes real-time monitoring and patching prioritization. Ridout [10] complements this approach with an argument in favor of deterrence-based defense strategies, fortifying cyber resilience through multi-tiered protection and cross-domain collaboration.

15.6.3 Blockchain and Distributed Trust Systems

Blockchain and Distributed Trust Systems acts more as an enabler of data integrity, identity management, and secure communication in a technological context. Rethinking cybersecurity around immutable decentralized trust mechanisms can be derived from both [8, 9].

According to Dickson and Goodwin [29], blockchain is one of five newer technologies clearly enabling resilient architectures so that the integrity of digital transactions is kept in assurance and accountability. AL-Hawamleh [21] and

Kanaan et al. [20] also insist that introducing aspects of distribution in control and reducing single points of failure from security properties improves not only business continuity but also cyber resilience. With the introduction of AI and IoT networks, blockchain will ensure trustless security coordination in distributed ecosystems.

15.6.4 Cloud and Edge Computing Security

Cloud computing and edge security are the basic enabling infrastructures for defense against scalable, real-time, and distributed cyber-attacks. According to Li [5], cloud-native architectures employ fast restoration from cyber events to ensure operational continuity through integration with ML-based monitoring systems for proactive detection of intrusions across hybrid environments.

Smart defense principles, including shared cloud infrastructure, create the backbone of the resilience strategy with respect to cyber issues in NATO, according to Efthymiopoulos [11]. Savold et al. [13] mention structures in leading cloud-based cyber reference architectures, allowing flexible orchestration and coordinated response mechanisms. Continuous cyber-resiliency assessment is best applied in a cloud-based framework, as Akinsanya et al. [2] and Estay [4] suggest since it allows for adaptive recovery and operational transparency.

Only by combining cloud, edge, and AI can we construct distributed defense ecosystems capable of detecting anomalies in real time, and this to be able to reach the proactive intelligence inspired by that which is supposed to come through Cybersecurity 5.0.

15.6.5 Quantum-Ready Cryptography and Advanced Encryption

In matters of computational supremacy and the vexatious concern of risk in cryptography, quantum computing stands to bring phenomenal change. Thus, quantum-ready encryption and post-quantum cryptographic algorithms, becoming sine qua non of Cybersecurity 5.0, have been received as such. Ross et al. [15] view the analogy of embedding those algorithms into system engineering practice for data confidentiality and a prefix for authentication for the foreseeable future.

Siegel et al. [27] also declare that since risk-driven security anticipates disruptive technologies, such as quantum computing, agility and adaptability must be imprinted in the design process. Hubbard [22] takes this a step further—the state level—focusing on how governments need to prepare their encryption infrastructures for future quantum-based attacks. Quantum-safe cryptography indeed is part of the complete resilience landscaping strategy, safeguarding data in what is now becoming an interconnected, global environment.

15.6.6 Human-Machine Collaboration and Training Capacity

Indeed, while technology drives automation, human oversight and adaptability are still indispensable components of Cybersecurity 5.0. Moore [30] aspires to develop cyber defense training capability as a way of ensuring that human operators collaborate with AI-enabled defense systems as efficiently as possible. Conklin and Shoemaker [8] further emphasize that resilient organizations incorporate human intelligence and technological sources to support adaptive decision-making.

Furthermore, Annarelli et al. [3] treated cyber resilience as a socio-technical system where the human element and machine intelligence are inextricably linked. Kanaan et al. [20] reiterates that a prepared workforce is a critical component of an organization's resilience, especially with the inevitable introduction of autonomous systems in an organization's operations. Continuous education, simulation, and human-AI co-learning will keep organizations agile and situationally aware, bridging the gap between human intuition and machine precision.

15.6.7 Integrated Frameworks and Systemic Resilience

Cybersecurity 5.0 is dependent on integrated frameworks that can unite technological, operational, and strategic domains. According to Ahmed et al. [1] and Kanaan et al. [20], resilient systems should incorporate all three elements—security, continuity, and innovation—in order to switch into equilibrium under cyber stress. Annarelli et al. [3]] and Estay [4] assert the significance of standardized resilience assessment models, which guide the integration of technology enablers from the perspective of the entire system lifecycle.

Efthymiopoulos [12] and Ridout [10] also reiterate that cross-sector collaboration must integrate public and private capabilities to strengthen defense ecosystems. Safitra et al. [25] also advocates for a counteractive framework leveraging multiple technologies that include AI, blockchain, and automation to win the race against threat evolution, which organizations can effect continuous innovation and integration, thus transitioning organizations from fragmentation to adaptive, intelligent, and interconnected resilience architectures.

15.6.8 Summary of Technological Enablers in Cybersecurity 5.0

The enablers of Cybersecurity 5.0 would represent a convergence of emerging technologies with systemic strategies aimed at achieving predictive, adaptive, and autonomous defense. From AI-driven analytics and a zero-trust framework to blockchain-based verification and quantum-ready encryption, all serve to establish the foundation of self-healing, intelligence-driven security ecosystems.

According to Akinsanya et al. [2], AL-Hawamleh [21], and Meng et al. [16], the success of Cybersecurity 5.0 lies not only on the technology but also in strategic synchronization, governance, and continuous learning.

These features transform what was previously a reactive discipline in cybersecurity into a proactive, intelligent, and resilient paradigm, capable of protecting digital infrastructures against evolving threats—and, increasingly, doing so within a connected world.

15.7 Organizational Transformation

Besides the revolvement of technological innovations during the transition toward Cybersecurity 5.0, there is also an imperative of deep organizational changes that redefine the system's governance, culture, and operational paradigms. This goes away from an old IT-driven view of security functions toward embedding resilience, adaptability, and intelligence within every layer of the enterprise ecosystem. It primarily focuses on creating cyber-resilient organizations that can foresee, withstand, and quickly recover from cyber disruptions while applying business continuity and strategic agility [1, 3].

A prime aspect of this change is integrating cyber-resilience frameworks into organizational governance. Cyber resilience emphasizes a proactive and continual approach to security that integrates technological, human, and procedural elements. Some researchers maintain that cyber-resilience frameworks seek to balance cybersecurity and business sustainability, hence assisting organizations to work securely amid constantly changing threats [2, 6]. Furthermore, AL-Hawamleh [6, 21] pointed out that resilience frameworks must adapt to organizational maturity, thereby incorporating capabilities in predictive analytics, AI-driven monitoring, and adaptive responses to counter challenges with an appropriate strategic posture.

Organizations must adopt linked integrated frameworks in which cyber defense coexists with business continuity and innovation strategy. Kanaan et al. [20] propounded that an integrated model for the enhancement of cyber-resilient organizations should align the goals of digital transformation with those of risk management. In the same breath, Efthymiopoulos [12] stressed the importance of linking cyber defense to wider innovation and national development frameworks, coherently reflecting the growing convergence of views between cybersecurity, innovation, and policy leadership.

Another essential pillar of organizational transformation is the design of architected resilience. Bolish et al. [17] and Meng et al. [16] insisted on instantiating cyber-resilient systems from the very beginning with secure-by-design practices, ensuring resilience is built from the ground up into architecture rather than just tagged on afterward. This has been supplemented with an introduction to resilience in systems security engineering by NIST Special Publication 800-160 Vol. 2, which many organizations are adopting as a baseline for their transformation. Complementing it, Savold et al. [13] conducted a comparative review of cyber reference architectures, highlighting the significance of structured frameworks in steering resilient digital infrastructures.

AI and ML are emerging as revolutionary enablers on the journey toward Cybersecurity 5.0. Usman Haider [23] discussed how AI-driven ecosystem developments allow detecting, analyzing, and reacting to complex threats by organizations in a largely autonomous fashion, converting traditional reactive defense models into intelligent predictive systems. Similarly, Safitra et al. [25] indicated AI-powered counteractive cyber frameworks capable of anticipating and neutralizing emerging threats before they even materialize. Such transformation resonates with [14] recommendations regarding companies embedding AI-enabled threat intelligence and continuous monitoring as a core function in cybersecurity management.

Management culture must transform in parallel with the technological one. Conklin and Shoemaker [8] showed that achieving cyber resilience would require a cultural shift away from compliance-based security toward continuous learning, adaptation, and collaboration. Their later work [9] extends this idea into a seven-step strategic model for institutional survival, incorporating commitment from leadership, cross-functional communication, and planning for proactive recovery. This human-centered aspect is crucial for ensuring that technology adoption translates into real resilience outcomes.

Additionally, organizational transformation should entrench multi-tiered defenses that integrate zero trust, layered defense, and global compliance standards. Muhammad et al. [24] showed that integrating zero-trust architectures with international best practices strengthens digital ecosystems through an integrative cybersecurity strategy. Li [5] elaborated further on the role of structured resilience strategies in ensuring operational continuity, while Dickson and Goodwin [29] summarized five key enabling technologies buttressing such frameworks, ranging from cognitive automation to secure data fabrics.

Design resiliency at the institutional and state levels in coordination with regulatory frameworks and strategic defense postures. Hubbard [22] developed a conceptual framework at the state level, emphasizing public-private collaboration in creating resilience. Efthymiopoulos [11] further this point through NATO's Smart Defense, showing how resilience can coexist with collective defense concepts to boost transnational cyber defense capability. In a similar vein, Ridout [10] argued for an all-encompassing strategy resolved through deterrence, defense, and resilience as mutually dependent elements of modern security ecosystems.

Applications of cyber resilience in critical infrastructure are tangible proof of organizational transformation. O'Neill et al. [18] and Li et al. [19] presented the CYDRES project, a cyber defense and resilience system to safeguard grid-interactive efficient buildings. Their work illustrates the application of resilience in the energy sector by integrating system engineering, cybersecurity, and sustainability to actualize adaptive protection.

Beyond technology and frameworks, the development of training and capacity-building programs is very important for embedding resilience further down the workforce. Moore [30] emphasized the need for all-encompassing training programs to strengthen the cyber defense line, while Sharma et al. [26] argued that these vulnerability management frameworks serve as foundational pillars in defense preparedness. The very same thoughts echo [27] that risk-driven security and resiliency strategies must enter the boardrooms to ensure they remain adaptive.

In this context, Figure 15.5 presents the organizational transformation model needed to usher in Cybersecurity 5.0. It stresses that technology is not enough; organizations need to integrate governance, culture, workforce capabilities, and innovation processes. This model also emphasizes the need for the synergy of strategic leadership, operational resilience, and continuous learning.

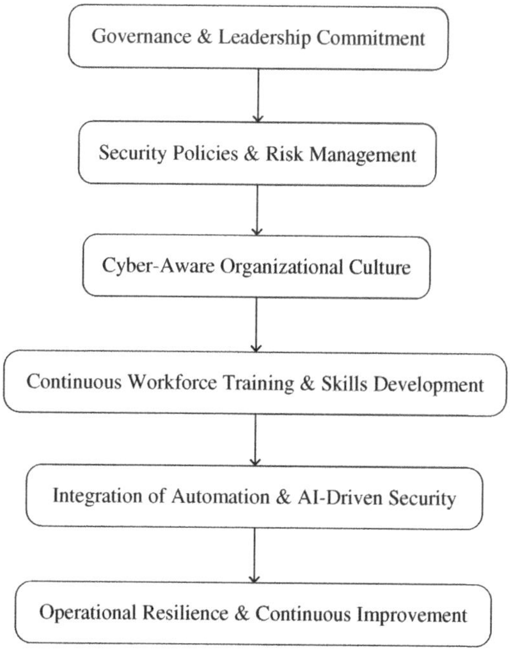

Figure 15.5 Organizational Transformation Model for Achieving Cybersecurity 5.0. "*Source:* Hewa Majeed Zangana"

The Cybersecurity 5.0 path toward organizational transformation becomes an integrated, innovative, and cultural repositioning strategy. Resilience should be treated as a continuous cycle—measured, refined, and redefined in line with evolving threats [4, 7]. By working through unified frameworks [1, 2], engaging in collaborative efforts across industries [12, 20], and injecting the efforts with technology [23, 25], organizations can adopt a cyber-resilient posture that can exist, operate, and thrive under uncertainty and disruption.

In short, organizational transformation in the Cybersecurity 5.0 context involves much more than a technical uplift; it emerges as a strategic evolution. It takes on a new meaning for enterprises in their thinking, doing, and recovering, such that resilience is being termed a business necessity and a competitive advantage in this new digital age.

15.8 Policy, Regulation, and Ethics

The future will bring Cyber Security 5.0 to that end, which gives the deepest implications for global policy and regulatory frameworks, as well as ethical governance. Organizations will now be transitioning their security to intelligent, autonomous, and data-driven systems, increasingly complicated by this outstanding convergence of technology, governance, and morality. Comparatively, this chapter contemplates how emergent resilience and defense paradigms are evolving in policy, regulation, and ethics, as well as the involvement of security, accountability, and trust in these digital ecosystems [1, 2].

15.8.1 Policy Frameworks for Cyber Resilience

It has since been viewed as much more than just a technical objective, now considered pertinent for national security, business continuity, and societal stability, as the third strategic policy objective, viewed as necessary for them. Policymakers have to provide for adaptive regulatory regimes that harmonize strategy in both cybersecurity and technological innovation with risk management [3]. The dimension of policy integration between cyber defense and business sustainability has been given by AL-Hawamleh [6] in pointing out that resilience frameworks need to form a component of organizational governance standards. Kanaan et al. [20] similarly emerged to suggest a policy-driven model to enhance business continuity through alignment of governance, risk-based policies, and performance monitoring systems.

At the macro level, national and regional governments are formulating cyber resilience strategies that blend technological innovation with legislative oversight. Hubbard [22] developed a conceptual state-level framework that espouses the idea of a shared responsibility between public and private sectors for resilience capabilities enhancement. Efthymiopoulos [12] and Ridout [10] have further advocated for international cooperation in cyber policy to deter cyber aggression and promote unified defense standards, in line with NATO's notion of "Smart Defense," a collective approach to cybersecurity as highlighted by Efthymiopoulos [11].

15.8.2 Regulatory Evolution and Standardization

Effective regulation is fundamental to ensuring accountability and interoperability across cybersecurity systems. National Institute of Standards and Technology Special Publication (NIST SP) 800-160 Vol. 2 [15], marking a new dawn with engineering-based standards for developing cyber-resilient systems, on the other hand, changed the regulatory alignment between technical design and operational governance significantly. Dickson and Goodwin [29] identified five enabling technologies that policymakers must account for—AI, blockchain, predictive analytics, automation, and secure cloud computing—when formulating next-generation cybersecurity policies.

Continuous resilience evaluation must be supported by policies—as stressed by Akinsanya et al. [2] and AL-Hawamleh [21]. This would involve adapting various frameworks such as those reviewed by Estay [4] to continue meeting compliance in the changing threat landscape. Similarly, Savold et al. [13] noted how reference architectures serve as blueprints for regulators, allowing the establishment of specific practices for resilience standardization across diverse industries. Such diverse integrative cybersecurity models as [24] combining zero-trust and layered defense with global standards demonstrate how regulatory harmonization determines trust across international networks.

The example of sector-specific frameworks like CYDRES for grid-interactive buildings [18, 19] demonstrates how regulation can encourage resilience-by-design. These systems are aligned with new cybersecurity physical infrastructure regulations, encouraging the leverage between innovation and safety. As noted by Bolish et al. [17], ensuring compliance becomes part of the composition instead of merely an administrative burden through insertion into the architectural framework.

15.8.3 Ethical Dimensions in Cyber Security 5.0

Ethics remains the prop of responsible governance as far as cybersecurity is concerned. Ethical, say, deployment of AI, automation, and surveillance technologies has to follow principles clear in guiding protection against privacy, fairness, and accountability. According to Usman Haider [23], AI can be a boon to shield hackers from being exposed and can be misused to spy on people; to put it into simple words, AI in the cyber world is a double-edged sword. Ethical cybersecurity governance, Conklin et al. [8] argue, should focus on balancing technological efficiency with moral accountability while making sure that resilience frameworks respect human rights and civil liberties.

Building on this, Siegel et al. [27] add that the responsibility of risk drives the ethical engagement within security measures that are appropriate to the damage possibly averted, thus avoiding overreach into surveillance or data control. Along these lines, Li [5] insists on ethical leadership as a pillar in sustaining operational continuity during crises—that is, ensuring that resilience strategies do not compromise integrity or fairness.

Moreover, Orme [28] and Pureti [14] elucidate that organizations are under an ethical obligation to prevent cyber threats proactively rather than through aggressive counter-hacking or taking measures that may escalate conflicts. This viewpoint is shared with Safitra et al. [25], who advocate for counteractive frameworks that take threats into account and mitigate them through openness and collaborative defense rather than retaliation.

15.8.4 Governance and Accountability Mechanisms

Cybersecurity 5.0 brings forward autonomous and cognitive systems questioning the traditional ideas of attribution. When the AI systems make independent judgment calls against security, attribution becomes unclear. Conklin et al. [9] suggest institutions should implement multi-layer accountability, where human decisions prevail over automated ones. Thus, an AI system gets such control through hybrid governance, working only within the ethical and legal frameworks set by the policymakers.

According to Galinec [7], accountability must also begin in the system design itself—resiliency architectures must be auditable and traceable so that stakeholders can evaluate system integrity in real time. The VERDICT framework of Meng et al. [16] supports this by enabling formal verification and validation for cyber-resilient systems, thereby encouraging transparency and trust.

In line, Annarelli et al. [3] and Kanaan et al. [20] argue that the governance model ought to incorporate adaptive feedback mechanisms with real-time monitoring, ethical audits, and incident reporting to ensure compliance and continuous improvement in governance. These developments sustain the NIST approach on systems engineering [15], which hybridizes governance with life cycle management.

15.8.5 Global Collaboration and Legal Harmonization

Due to the trans-border nature of the cyber threats, international cooperation is critical. Efthymiopoulos [12] and Ridout [10]: "Cyber resilience cannot stand alone; countries must harmonize their legal frameworks to meet information sharing, joint defense operations, and coordinated incident response." Hubbard [22], in addition, remarked on how legal harmonization boosts transparency and public trust in supporting cyber resilience at the state level.

Global ethics alignment for security must address discrepancies in digital capabilities and access to resources. Ahmed et al. [1] and AL-Hawamleh [21] emphasize the need for an equal global policy that would provide developing nations with an adequate defense framework on the condition that it does not turn into an economic disadvantage. These policies are inclusive and aim toward universal resilience to a cyber-ecosystem.

15.8.6 Ethical AI and Responsible Innovation

AI-based security systems are the hallmark of Cybersecurity 5.0, but their implementation would require ethical mindfulness. As Usman Haider [23] and Safitra et al. [25] stated, AI brings the potential for transformation, yet introduces risks about autonomy, data manipulation, and unintended consequences. Thus, any regulatory framework must enforce ethical AI principles such as transparency, explainability, fairness, and accountability.

Bolish et al. [17] proposed an insertion of the "ethics-by-design" paradigm into cyber-resilience engineering, and Li et al. [19] showed through adherence to environmental and ethical standards that AI applications in cyber-physical infrastructures can be developed safely. Under this joined-up approach to policy, regulation, and ethics, innovation shall remain responsible, sustainable, and human-centered.

15.8.7 Toward a Unified Ethical-Policy Ecosystem

The confluence of policy, regulatory, and ethical agents draws a line for a collective governance ecosystem in Cybersecurity 5.0. Resilience must therefore be conceptualized by Siegel et al. [27] and Conklin and Shoemaker [8] as more than a technical objective: It equally incorporates moral and societal considerations. Ethical governance, when integrated with flexible policies and universal regulatory frameworks, catalyzes the development of a trust-centered digital environment that protects technological advancement alongside human dignity.

Ultimately, with the world's trajectory zooming toward entirely autonomous cyber defense systems, ethical oversight and regulatory consistency will be the defining measure of success for Cybersecurity 5.0. Societies can leverage joint stakeholder protocols [6, 20], global standardization [15, 24], and ethical accountability [5, 23] to engender secure, transparent, and equitable digital futures based on trust and responsibilities.

15.9 Challenges and Risk Factors

Organizations traversing the path to Cybersecurity 5.0 face a tangled maze of challenges and risk elements that are complicated by technological convergence, evolving threat landscapes, and organizational limitations. The introduction of AI, the Internet of Things (IoT), and cyber-physical systems into the attack surface has stretched the demands for completely new paradigms for resilience and adaptability [1, 3]. Great advances have been achieved in the frameworks and defense strategies; however, there are still some critical vulnerabilities at the structural, operational, and strategic levels that form serious constraints for cyber resilience.

One of the biggest impediments is the fragmentation of the frameworks regarding cybersecurity and resilience. Rapid developments in the cyber resilience models have led to uncontrolled differences across industries, resulting in organizations not addressing, measuring, and adopting resilience coherently. According to Akinsanya et al. [2], most cyber-resilience assessment frameworks do not exhibit cross-domain applicability, rendering them inefficient in multi-sectoral ecosystems. Such inconsistencies often lead to cases where organizations adopt only parts of the frameworks, as their attention tends to focus more on the defense mechanisms of the resilience strategy.

The increasingly sophisticated nature of society's threats compounds risk exposure. According to Safitra et al. [25], with myriad AI-driven attacks and APTs, there is also a growing trend for exploit types such as zero-day attacks to challenge traditional defense models, usually relying on reactive rather than proactive anticipation. Orme [28] added that evolving APTs are not sufficiently counterbalanced by defense-in-depth without adaptive resilience mechanisms. It becomes then necessary, according to Usman Haider [23], to develop autonomous, learning-based defense architectures to counter next-generation threats for which this is required.

The other thing hindering progress toward Cybersecurity 5.0 is the disconnect between cyber defense and organizational strategy. Ahmed et al. [1] and Kanaan et al. [20] argued that even with most organizations having stringent cybersecurity activities in place, not many have endeavored to align them with broader business continuity and innovation goals. Thus, restructuring would lead to incident response and recovery processes being ineffective—long-term resilience would not be achieved. Further, Li [5] observed that most resilience strategies focus on defense rather than restoration, which elongates downtime and economic loss after cyber incidents, as operational continuity is usually not included within them.

Technological complexity and interoperability give rise to significant risk factors. As Bolish et al. [17] and Meng et al. [16] emphasized, the more elaborate systems become interconnected, the more difficult it is to provide consistent resilience engineering—from day one onward. Such uneven application comes despite attempts to cascade frameworks such as National Institute of Standards and Technology Special Publication (NIST SP) 800-160 Vol. 2 [15] to guide how resilient systems are engineered, mainly because of limited technical expertise and high costs of integration. Organizations do not find it easy to choose the reference architecture suitable for the diverse options available, which causes fragmented deployments that reduce overall resilience [13].

At the organizational level, cultural and leadership challenges are perennial hindrances. According to Conklin and Shoemaker [8], cyber resilience is still treated as an Information Technology (IT) issue in most institutions for the most part and not as a strategic imperative. Executive engagement would increase as a result, but a proposed seven-step institutional model [9] is nevertheless necessary as resilient programs should be leadership-driven. However, there are still prevalent issues such as budget limitations, anti-change culture, and lack of cyber awareness among employees [30, 14]. Such cultural inertia inhibits the development of active, learning-oriented cyber environments necessary for adaptive risk management.

Another contributing aspect is linked to policies and governance issues. Hubbard [22] proposed the conceptual framework at the state level that would strengthen the collaborative aspect between public and private sectors, yet continued fragmentation was persisting between regulators and operational bodies. Efthymiopoulos [11, 12] and Ridout [10] again supported the idea of integrated policy mechanisms linking deterrence, defense, and recovery in order for resilience to survive. Unfortunately, inconsistent enforcement of regulations, combined with a lack of international coordination, often weakens national and organizational readiness in the cyber realm.

Resource constraints also limit the deployment and maintenance of advanced resilience frameworks. The CYDRES project of O'Neill et al. [18] and Li et al. [19] showed that resource-hungry systems for critical infrastructure—such as energy-efficient buildings—require high investment in both hardware and human capital. Such models are, therefore, impractical for smaller organizations to replicate. Sharma et al. [26] similarly found that investment and skilled personnel resources, which are not always available in small- to medium-scale enterprises, are needed for developing a complete vulnerability management framework.

New digital ecosystems, such as IoT and edge computing, introduce new vulnerabilities. Muhammad et al. [24] stated that without integrations between zero trust models, layered defense mechanisms, and globally accepted standards, networks are left susceptible to exploitation. Dickson and Goodwin [29], too, spoke about the difficulty in merging various enabling technologies—like cognitive analytics and automation—into cohesive resilience strategies. As these systems continue to flourish, realizing situational awareness in real time is becoming extremely convoluted and is amplifying operational risk.

A further worry concerns insufficient measurement and validation of resilience. According to Galinec [7] and Annarelli et al. [3], it is common for organizations to claim resilience maturity, although very few possess metrics to rationally confirm their preparedness. Without quantifiable resilience indicators, it becomes difficult to prioritize investments or measure the progress made. Siegel et al. [27] similarly warned that risk-driven cybersecurity strategies often lack dynamic feedback mechanisms to successfully adjust to new threats, leaving organizations ultimately exposed to evolving risks.

Finally, the dynamic changes in cyber resilience frameworks subject them to obsolescence. Such frameworks must continue to adapt as technology and threat vectors change to stay relevant, as those proposed by AL-Hawamleh [6, 21]. The fast-paced and freshening digital world renders static models obsolete very quickly. Akinsanya et al. [2] and Kanaan et al. [20] both cautioned that, unless frameworks have capacities for AI-driven learning and adaptive governance structure, they are risking being more of a reactive than a proactive approach.

In summarizing, the challenges and risk factors trailing the path to Cybersecurity 5.0 have multi-dimensional characteristics spanning technological, organizational, and strategic territories. They entail fragmentation of frameworks [4], complex architectures [15], governance gaps [22], and evolving threat vectors [25]. Resolving these rivaling challenges requires an integrated and adaptive approach embracing the most advanced AI technologies [23], broad resilience engineering [16, 17], and a robust governance alignment [1, 20]. Only through unremitting innovation, collaborative approaches, and accountability measures can organizations mitigate risks and foster sustainable cyber resilience in an era of Cybersecurity 5.0.

15.10 Measuring Progress Toward Cybersecurity 5.0

The measurement of progress toward Cybersecurity 5.0 must consider a diversified approach, assessing technological maturity, organizational resilience, policy alignment, and operational efficiency, unlike traditional cybersecurity metrics that typically concern themselves with vulnerability counts or incident responses. The Cybersecurity 5.0 paradigm has further reoriented the conversation to consider themes of adaptive resilience, predictive defense, and continuous improvement across organizational layers [1, 3]. Thus, organizations will have to adopt an assessment of the new cyber-resilience frameworks using qualitative and quantitative methodologies [2, 6]. As a key measure, resilience maturity has to be evaluated at technological, organizational, and strategic levels. AL-Hawamleh [21] has proposed a resilience maturity model that embraces system robustness, incident response capability, and recovery efficiency. The model encourages organizations to benchmark their capabilities on standard indicators, thus giving clear direction to improvement. Accordingly, Kanaan et al. [20] underscored the need to assess business continuity integration with traditional defensive metrics such that resilience during a cybersecurity incident is measured from an enterprise rather than a purely Information Technology (IT) infrastructure perspective.

Cyber defense performance measurements form yet another important pillar for the evaluation of progress. For instance, tools like CYDRES [18, 19] demonstrate how integrated cyber defense and resilient systems are quantifiable in terms of measurable parameters such as detection latency, response accuracy, and system uptime during cyber incidents. According to Dickson and Goodwin [29], technologies providing real-time monitoring, automated threat detection, and predictive analytics yield the necessary data for assessing the effectiveness of frameworks implemented. This way, organizations measure performance based on metrics, allowing for moving from reactive resilience strategies to proactive ones consistent with the Cybersecurity 5.0 paradigm.

Another area in need of measurement is the area of actual adoption and implementation of the framework. Estay [4] pointed out that, owing to the rapid proliferation of frameworks of cyber resilience assessments, different approaches have arisen, making it desirous for organizations to monitor their compliance with framework requirements, their integration into processes, and adherence to governance practices. Likewise, Meng et al. [16] emphasized the relevance of resilience engineering languages and tools that provide standardized methods to measure system safety and adaptability, which help to ensure that the measurement is systematic and reproducible.

Strategic measurement can benefit from risk-based metrics. Conklin and Shoemaker [8] proposed a seven-step institutional model for resilience quantification that combines risk analysis with scenario planning and evaluation of recovery. These focus not only on historical instances but also on predictive modeling to model anticipated threats [24, 25]. At the same time, Hubbard [22] suggested that frameworks at the state level incorporate metrics for regulatory compliance and inter-organizational coordination, showcasing the critical nature of contextual and multi-level evaluation for progress tracking in the sphere of Cybersecurity 5.0.

Organizational and human factors represent another dimension of measurement. Conklin et al. [9] indicated that cyber resilience is not merely a technical issue but one of culture and management as well. Metrics on employee training, leadership engagement, and incident awareness [30, 14] provide insight into the organization's readiness to adapt and respond to evolving threats. Bolish et al. [17] supported that embedding cyber resilience "from day one" into organizational processes ensures that human factors have been fully integrated into the measurement framework.

Another area concerned with technological integration and interoperability. Systems security engineering metrics recommended by Ross et al. [15] assess the extent to which defense mechanisms, monitoring tools, and resilience protocols are interoperable and scalable. Also, Usman Haider [23] stressed the importance of AI and ML to evaluate cloud and network security metrics, dynamically adapting to the threat environments. The advanced simulation platform under discussion by O'Neill et al. [18] and Li et al. [19] provides organizations with synthetic environments for testing defenses, measuring recovery times, and refining incident-handling strategies.

Lastly, continuous improvement and feedback loops represent the other critical aspect of measurement. According to AL-Hawamleh [21] and Li [5], Cybersecurity 5.0 requires iterative assessment cycles, where lessons derived from incidents, audits, and exercises inform the development of the framework, governance redirection, and technology deployment. Ridout [10] and Conklin and Shoemaker [8] indicated that combining metrics driven by incidents with proactive approaches means that organizations will remain adaptive and capable of addressing new threats.

In conclusion, the evaluation of an advancement toward Cybersecurity 5.0 must be through an integrated framework constituting resilience maturity models, risk-based metrics, technological performance indicators, and human factors evaluations [3, 6, 20]. The utility of effective measurement is twofold: It serves to benchmark the current capability while also giving insights for future improvements that will help keep organizations one step ahead, resilient, and prepared for the next generation of cyber challenges [2, 16, 17, 24].

This integrated approach guarantees that Cybersecurity 5.0 is a living theory of measurement, implementation, and evolution with organizational objectives, threat landscape, and technology improvements.

15.11 Vision for the Future

The vision of the future in cybersecurity centers around Cybersecurity 5.0, which in itself denotes a paradigm shift from traditional defenses to a more adaptive, intelligent, and resilient cyber ecosystem [1, 6]. The objectives of this vision include proactive resilience, predictive threat detection, and integrated cyber-physical security, aimed at creating systems that can not only defend against attacks but also anticipate, adapt, and recover with minimal disruption [2, 3].

A significant feature of this envisioned future is the adoption of advanced technologies into cyber defense architectures, which include AI, ML, and automation. According to Usman Haider [23], AI-enabled monitoring, predictive analytics, and adaptive response systems will allow organizations to detect threats in real time, automate the mitigation strategy, and continuously improve their security posture. Likewise, O'Neill et al. [18] and Li et al. [19] showed that through integrated systems like CYDRES, a fusion of cyber defense and resilient operational framework can secure infrastructure that has high complexity, such as grid-interactive buildings.

The organizational aspect is also of utmost importance for bringing Cybersecurity 5.0 to life. Conklin and Shoemaker [8] and Bolish et al. [17] asserted that embedding resilience in organizational culture and processes "from day one" assures that the people and technology work effectively together. Kanaan et al. [20] have proposed hybrid frameworks that view business continuity, governance, and risk management as aspects of a more general concept, stressing that, for future-ready cybersecurity, there must be strategic alignment of technical capabilities with organizational objectives.

Framework evolution and standardization are expected to play a key role in forming the future landscape. Li [5] and AL-Hawamleh [21] discussed the necessity for organizations to adopt standardized cyber resilience frameworks that enable benchmarking, compliance, and iterative improvement. Estay [4] underscored the value of systematic assessment tools to evaluate resilience maturity, ensuring that organizations can measure progress, identify gaps, and optimize defense strategies. Meanwhile, Muhammad et al. [24] and Safitra et al. [25] stressed the integration of zero-trust architecture, layered defense, and global standards in frameworks that strengthen preventive and adaptive capabilities.

Technology will also be the third domain of convergence, requiring yet another set of approaches for secure settings. As the market for IoT grows rapidly, Orme [28] and Dickson and Goodwin [29] emphasize, therefore, increasing in importance, automated resilience that is founded upon real-time awareness and threat foresight. This convergence will require a more advanced platform to simulate, test, and verify the aforementioned resilience under dynamic threat conditions. The frameworks developed by Meng et al. [16] and Ross et al. [15] should support these objectives.

While evolving, risk management and strategic foresight shall be tools for Cybersecurity 5.0. Significance was laid on integrating risk-driven strategies with continuous monitoring and adaptive governance [9, 10, 27]. This will ensure that, by embedding predictive analytics with scenario-based planning, the organizations will be capable of not just responding to immediate threats but also of anticipating and mitigating emerging risks. Hence, this will change the face of cybersecurity from a reactive discipline to being a strategic enabler for corporate sustainability and innovation.

Human and societal dimensions of cybersecurity simply cannot be excluded in visualizing its future. Training and proliferation of knowledge as well as leadership engagement are critical to securing the primary objective, that is, an empowered organization of individuals who understand their significance in resilience-building [30, 14]. Resilient cyber culture, together with advanced technological defenses, will enable [17] organizations to achieve continuity and establish trust, even in the face of complex multi-vector cyber threats.

The described future of cybersecurity mentions holistic integration, intelligence-guided resilience, and proactive adjustability [1, 6, 20]. By combining advanced technologies with robust frameworks, organizational readiness, and human factors, Cybersecurity 5.0 aims to forge a cyber ecosystem that can absorb threats, maintain operations, and embrace innovation. The journey toward realizing this vision will be characterized by continuous improvement, cross-disciplinary engagement, and alignment of cyber defense strategies with higher organizational and societal aspirations [2, 23, 25].

This future vision empowers organizations not just to survive but to flourish, innovate, and grow while remaining resilient and trustworthy.

15.12 Conclusion

The ever-changing domains of cybersecurity demand a comprehensive and proactive means of action that transcends traditional defensive posturing. The core principle of resilience needs to be integrated with technological innovation, organizational preparedness, and adaptive strategies for organizations to foresee and counter any emerging threats. By creating a culture of cybersecurity awareness and integrating security into their entire operations, businesses and institutions can limit the effects caused by cybersecurity incidents and maintain continuity despite such disruptions.

Cybersecurity 5.0 articulates the change from reactive defense mechanisms to predictive and adaptive approaches. AI, ML, and automated threat detection system capabilities represent advanced technologies that provide real-time monitoring and mechanisms for rapid engagement. With a view toward supporting continuous improvement, strategic frameworks and standardized assessment approaches allow organizations to assess their security posture. Effective cybersecurity needs the coherent integration of human, technological, and organizational aspects, creating systems that are secure, flexible, scalable, and resilient.

Also, cybersecurity's future depends on collaboration and alignment in the study between numerous stakeholders—industry, government, and academia. Sharing knowledge and best practices, as well as threat intelligence, strengthens our collective defense capacity to front-load the direction the strategy should take. As the cyber threats become advanced and ubiquitous, organizations need to have an attitude to be engaged in continuous adjustment through leveraging innovation as well as governance to stay relevant before the adversaries.

Ultimately, the ability to maintain a resilient and secure digital ecosystem is not a one-off project, but an endless journey. Being an organization that focuses on proactive defense, resilience-oriented frameworks, and strategic foresight would allow one the advantage of navigating confidently through the very complex and dynamic cyber landscape to protect operational continuity, stakeholder trust, and growth in an ever-more connected world.

References

1 Ahmed, M.F., Molla, A.H., Uddin, M.R., and Chowdhury, T.R. (2023). Advancing cyber resilience: Bridging the divide between cyber security and cyber defense. *International Journal for Multidisciplinary Research (IJFMR)* 5 (6).

2 Akinsanya, M.O., Ekechi, C.C., and Okeke, C.D. (2024). The evolution of cyber resilience frameworks in network security: A conceptual analysis. *Computer Science & IT Research Journal* 5 (4): 926–949.

3 Annarelli, A., Nonino, F., and Palombi, G. (2020). Understanding the management of cyber resilient systems. *Computer & Industrial Engineering* 149: 106829.

4 Estay, D.A.S., Sahay, R., Barfod, M.B., and Jensen, C.D. (2020). A systematic review of cyber-resilience assessment frameworks. *Computers & Security* 97: 101996.

5 Li, I. (2024). Cyber resilience frameworks: Exploring cyber resilience frameworks and strategies for organizations to recover from cyber attacks and maintain operational continuity. *Cybersecurity and Network Defense Research* 4 (1): 1–15.

6 AL-Hawamleh A. (2024). Cyber resilience framework: Strengthening defenses and enhancing continuity in business security. *International Journal of Computing and Digital Systems* 15 (1): 1315–1331.

7 Galinec, D. (2023). Cyber security and cyber defense: Challenges and building of cyber resilience conceptual model. *International Journal of Applied Science and Development* 1: 83–88.

8 Conklin, W.A. and Shoemaker, D. (2017). Cyber-resilience: Seven steps for institutional survival. *EDPACS.* 55 (2): 14–22.

9 Conklin WA, Shoemaker D, Kohnke A. Cyber resilience: Rethinking cybersecurity strategy to build a cyber resilient architecture. In: ICMLG2017 5th International Conference on Management Leadership and Governance. 2017. p. 105.

10 Ridout, T. (2016). Building a comprehensive strategy of cyber defense, deterrence, and resilience. In: *The Fletcher Forum of World Affairs*, 63–83. JSTOR.

11 Efthymiopoulos, M.P. (2016). *NATO smart defense and cyber resilience.* Tufts University May.

12 Efthymiopoulos, M.P. (2019). A cyber-security framework for development, defense and innovation at NATO. *Journal of Innovation and Entrepreneurship* 8 (1): 12.

13 Savold R, Dagher N, Frazier P, McCallam D. Architecting cyber defense: A survey of the leading cyber reference architectures and frameworks. In: 2017 IEEE 4th International Conference on Cyber Security and Cloud Computing (CSCloud). IEEE; 2017. p. 127–38.

14 Pureti, N. (2022). Building a robust cyber defense strategy for your business. *Revista de Inteligencia Artificial en Medicina* 13 (1): 35–51.

15 Ross, R., Pillitteri, V., Graubart, R. et al. (2019). *Developing cyber resilient systems: A systems security engineering approach*. National Institute of Standards and Technology.

16 Meng, B., Larraz, D., Siu, K. et al. (2021). Verdict: A language and framework for engineering cyber resilient and safe system. *Systems* 9 (1): 18.

17 Bolish S, Dodge M, Mitalo E, Westing R. Building cyber resilient systems from day 1. In: 2024 IEEE Aerospace Conference. IEEE; 2024. p. 1–8.

18 O'Neill Z, Wen J, Wu T, Candan KS, Ren L, Zhu Q, et al. Securing grid-interactive efficient buildings (GEB) through cyber defense and resilient system (CYDRES). Texas A & M Univ., College Station, TX (United States). Texas A & M ... ; 2024.

19 Li G, O'Neill Z, Wen J, Pradhan O, Ren L, Wu T, et al. CYDRES: CYber defense and REsilient system for securing grid-interactive efficient buildings. In: Proceedings of the 10th ACM International Conference on Systems for Energy-Efficient Buildings, Cities, and Transportation. 2023. p. 307–9.

20 Kanaan, A., AL-Hawamleh, A., Aloun, M. et al. (2024). Fortifying organizational cyber resilience: An integrated framework for business continuity and growth amidst escalating threat landscapes. *International Journal of Computing and Digital Systems* 16 (1): 1–13.

21 AL-Hawamleh, A.M. (2024). Securing the future: Framework fundamentals for cyber resilience in advancing organizations. *Journal of System and Management Sciences* 14 (10): 130–150.

22 Hubbard, G.A. (2023). State-level cyber resilience: A conceptual framework. *Applied Cybersecurity & Internet Governance* 2 (1): 1–14.

23 Usman Haider AZ. Building resilient cyber defense architectures: AI and machine learning in cloud and network security. 2024.

24 Muhammad, T., Munir, M.T., Munir, M.Z., and Zafar, M.W. (2022). Integrative cybersecurity: Merging zero trust, layered defense, and global standards for a resilient digital future. *International Journal of Computer Science and Technology* 6 (4): 99–135.

25 Safitra, M.F., Lubis, M., and Fakhrurroja, H. (2023). Counterattacking cyber threats: A framework for the future of cybersecurity. *Sustainability* 15 (18): 13369.

26 Sharma, N.A., Kumar, K., Khorshed, T. et al. (2024). Evading cyber-attacks on hadoop ecosystem: A novel machine learning-based security-centric approach towards big data cloud. *Information* 15 (9): 558.
27 Siegel, C.A. and Sweeney, M. (2020). *Cyber strategy: Risk-driven security and resiliency*. Auerbach Publications.
28 Orme S. Addressing issues with defense-in-depth, apts, and iot with active cyber defense cycle and cyber resilience. Utica College; 2019.
29 Dickson F, Goodwin P. Five key technologies for enabling a cyber-resilience framework. US45455119, IBM. 2019.
30 Moore E. Building cyber defense training capacity. 2020.

Index

Printed and bound by CPI Group (UK) Ltd, Croydon, CR0 4YY

17/09/2026

14964236-0002